DATE DUE

OC 30 '01			
FE 5 '02			
DE 17 '04			
MR 22 '07			

DEMCO 38-296

Management

John R. Schermerhorn, Jr.

 John Wiley & Sons, Inc.

New York • **Chichester** • **Weinheim** • **Brisbane** • **Singapore** • **Toronto**

Porter

Think	*Home,*	*Time*	*Hurry home*
of all the fun	*now and forever,*	*has its ways,*	*when you can.*
we have.	*will always be*	*doesn't it?*	*Come laughing, sons.*
Here, there, everywhere,	*wherever*	*Not enough,*	*Tell us*
doing things	*I can be*	*not enough,*	*your*
together.	*with you.*	*I often say.*	*wonderful stories.*
1989	*1992*	*1996*	*1999*

ACQUISITIONS EDITOR	*Ellen Ford/Brent Gordon*
DEVELOPMENT EDITOR	*Marian Provenzano*
MARKETING MANAGER	*Carlise Paulson*
SENIOR PRODUCTION EDITOR	*Patricia McFadden*
SENIOR DESIGNER	*Harold Nolan*
FREELANCE PRODUCTION MANAGER	*Jeanine Furino*
SENIOR PHOTO EDITOR	*Hilary Newman*
ILLUSTRATION COORDINATOR	*Anna Melhorn*
OUTSIDE PRODUCTION SERVICE	*J. Carey Publishing Service*
COVER PHOTOGRAPH	*"Mosaic, Mausoleum of Galla Placida. Ravenna 425–426"/© Art Resource*

This book was set in 10/12 Garamond Book by Progressive Information Technologies and printed and bound by Von Hoffman Press. The cover was printed by Lehigh Press.

This book is printed on acid-free paper.

The paper in this book was manufactured by a mill whose forest management programs include sustained yield harvesting of its timberlands. Sustained yield harvesting principles ensure that the numbers of trees cut each year does not exceed the amount of new growth.

Library of Congress Cataloging-in-Publication Data

Schermerhorn, John R.
    Management / John R. Schermerhorn, Jr._6th ed.
        p.   cm.
    Rev. ed. of: Management for productivity.
    Includes bibliographical references.
    ISBN 0-471-24113-X   (alk. paper)
        1. Management.   I. Schermerhorn, John R.   Management for
productivity.   II. Title.
HD31.S3326   1999
658_dc20   95-11196
                                                                              CIP

Printed in the United States of America
10 9 8 7 6 5 4 3 2

The Management Mosaic

Just like the mosaic featured on the cover of *MANAGEMENT 6/E*, today's workplace offers a rich mix of colors, forms, and impressions. Consistent with these changing times, John Schermerhorn creates a true management mosaic with this latest edition. This mosaic consists of the core text, informative videos, and a comprehensive web site with additional interactive case studies, skills assessments, career tools and teaching resources drawn from the author's own classroom.

As you read through the revised text, you will discover a focus on the dynamics of management in the context of a challenging and new work environment. You will learn about the responsibilities of a manager and what this means for your future career through many practical examples that are interwoven with core concepts and theories. You will appreciate the clear, concise, and engaging writing style that has made this text very successful year after year. And, you will benefit from the solid foundation of research covered, as well as the high quality of examples presented. This Management Mosaic gives you all the tools to attain a better understanding of managing in the new workplace.

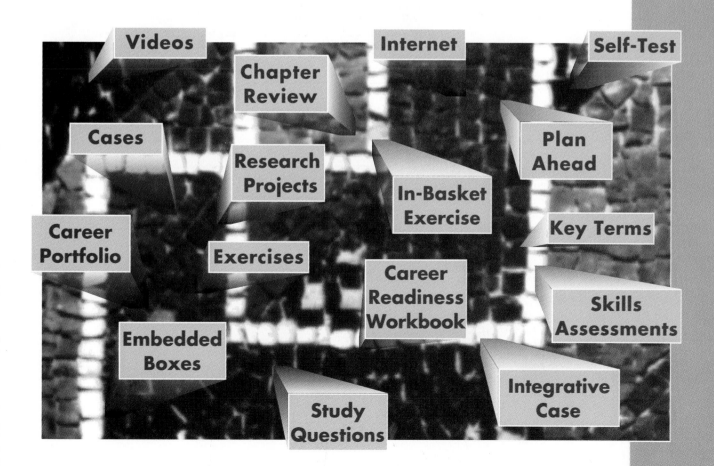

Pedagogical Features

PLANNING AHEAD AND STUDY QUESTIONS

Each chapter opens with two very helpful sections. **Planning Ahead** presents a set of basic **Study Questions** that provide students with the desired learning objectives of the chapter, as well as a framework for a later end-of-chapter review. This is followed by a brief **Opening Headline** which introduces the chapter focus and an opening vignette.

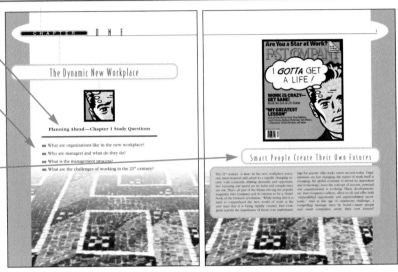

CHAPTER REVIEW

Each chapter concludes with an integrated self-study guide. The **Chapter Summary** offers bullet-list responses to the study questions first posed in the chapter-opening planning ahead section. These lists highlight key issues relating to each major subject heading in the chapter. The summary is followed by a list of **Key Terms** that is keyed to page numbers in the chapter where definitions can be located. Next comes a complete chapter **Self-Test**—consisting of multiple-choice, true-false, short response and application essay questions. This is an excellent way to prepare for examinations, and the author's responses to each question are provided at the end of the book.

EMBEDDED BOXES

To exemplify the importance of the issues managers must face, in-depth examples are embedded in the general text discussion for each chapter. The boxes provide concise and relevant examples without interrupting the flow of the material. The examples range from large, multinational organizations to small, local businesses, and also represent the non-profit sector. The Embedded Boxes are visually illustrated with engaging photographs that bring them to life. Each embedded box is also highlighted by an icon which describes specific applications to issues of

Quality ,

Benchmarking ,

Ethics and
Social Responsibility ,

Globalization .

Diversity ,

MANAGER'S NOTEPADS

To assist in developing practical applications, **Manager's Notepads** are provided in each chapter. These notepads consist of concise lists of helpful hints that describe the "do's" and "don'ts" of managerial behavior. They appear as boxed inserts conveniently placed throughout the text.

MARGIN LIST NOTES AND RUNNING GLOSSARY

The margins of the book offer a built-in study guide and chapter outline. Special **Margin List Notes** call attention to key bulleted or numbered lists of information as they are presented throughout the text. Boldfaced key terms are also called out and defined in the margins. They form a **Running Glossary** of key concepts from the chapter discussion.

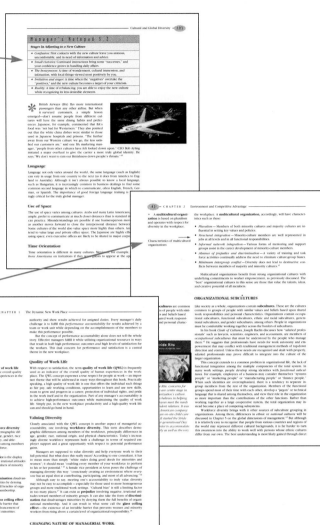

MARGIN PHOTOS

Additional, brief, real-world examples are featured as **Margin Photos** in each chapter. Captions to these photos highlight the ways in which concepts and theories are applied in day-to-day managerial practices in a wide selection of organizations. These dynamic, real-world examples of THE NEW WORKPLACE in action add further applications to the text discussion. Many of these also include web addresses that can be used for further research on the Internet.

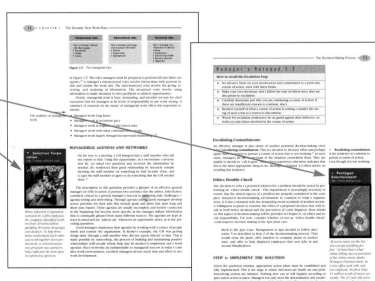

CAREER READINESS WORKBOOK

A key innovative feature unique to this edition of *MANAGEMENT* by Schermerhorn is the Career Readiness Workbook that is built into the text. You will find this a highly useful and distinctive resource that provides an important additional piece of the management mosaic. The Workbook includes the new *Career Advancement Portfolio* available to be created on-line as well as in print copy, *Cases for Critical Thinking, Integrative Learning Activities, Exercises in Teamwork, Management Skills Assessments*, and *Research and Presentation Projects*.

CAREER ADVANCEMENT PORTFOLIO

The Career Advancement Portfolio provides the templates for students to build a career portfolio that documents, in paper or electronic form, one's academic and personal accomplishments. This resource allows the students to frame and summarize their credentials for external review in the quest for internships and full-time employment. It also offers a way for course assignments to be inventoried for purposes of both academic assessment and competency demonstration. The special option for building an electronic career portfolio is especially consistent with the expectations and opportunities of the information age.

The Career Advancement Portfolio can be easily maintained and updated for the purpose of outcome assessment within a course or program of study, as well as for the student's personal and career development.

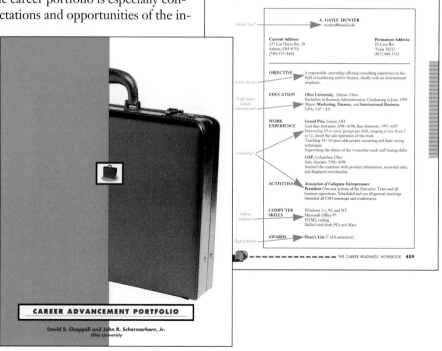

CASES FOR CRITICAL THINKING

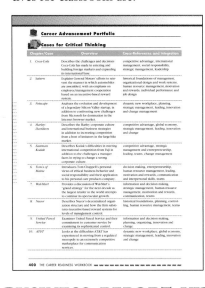

Individual case offerings in Cases for Critical Thinking bring to life the decisions managers must make every day on both a national and global level. The case studies describe both the benefits and consequences of these decisions. Each case concludes with a list of questions for the student to answer concerning the in-depth scenarios they are given. Interactive versions of cases are available on-line through the *MANAGEMENT 6/E* website at http://www.wiley.com/college/scherman6e. These online cases are updated regularly and new cases will be posted to enrich the alternatives for classroom use.

NIGHTLY BUSINESS REPORT VIDEOS

Many of the book's case studies are accompanied by video selections from the highly regarded and respected business news program, Nightly Business Report. These videos are available to instructors for classroom use. In addition, selected videos are included with this book on CD-ROM for student's own viewing.

INTEGRATIVE LEARNING ACTIVITIES

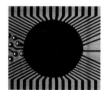

Consistent with the emphasis on integrative thinking and action in the new workplace, the workbook offers two easy-to-use Integrative Learning Activities that can be used to supplement various parts of the course. The In-Basket Exercise places students in decision-making situations that test their leadership and managerial capabilities. The Cross-Functional Integrated Video Case on Outback Steakhouse further allows for various parts of the management process to be examined in the context of a real and highly competitive environment. The case can be used in whole or in parts to best fit the instructor's course design. This case is especially important as an introduction to the importance of functional integration and strategic thinking in management today.

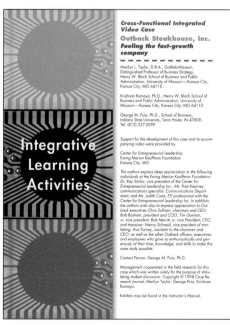

EXERCISES IN TEAMWORK

A rich portfolio of Exercises in Teamwork is available in the workbook. Many options are available, with applications to each chapter so that students can gain a better understanding of the material and actually experience putting this knowledge to practical use. The various exercises present situations that provide the basis for group discussion or individual analysis. Instructions are clear and self-explanatory, and formats for group discussion and class interaction are also provided.

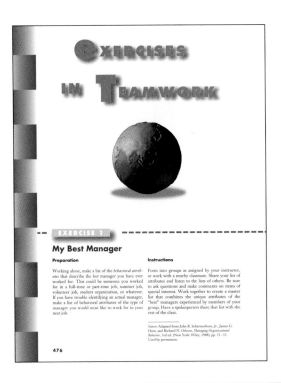

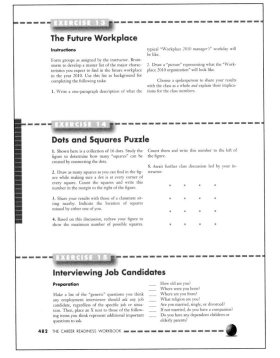

MANAGEMENT SKILLS ASSESSMENTS

Self awareness and insight are critical to one's continued personal and professional development. The workbook appropriately provides a complete set of **Management Skills Assessments** relating to each chapter. By completing the self assessments, students analyze their knowledge of management issues and their possession of the skills necessary to tackle these issues. Each assessment is broken down into instructions on how to complete the assignment, directions for scoring, and an interpretation of the score along with guidelines for understanding its meaning in a larger context. A packet of these assessments is also available on line and in interactive format on the *MANAGEMENT 6/E* website at http://www.wiley.com/college/scherman6e.

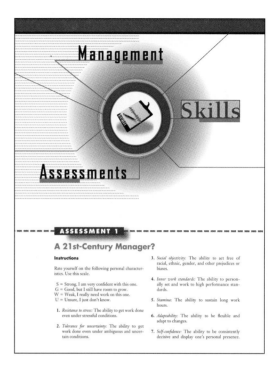

RESEARCH AND PRESENTATION PROJECTS

Management today requires skills at effective communication and in information gathering and analysis. The workbook offers a number of **Research and Presentation Projects** that address these needs by requiring research and formal presentations on timely topics relating to chapter discussions. The projects are designed to enhance a student's research skills, including those involving the Internet and Electronic Databases. The projects also offer important opportunities for students to refine their written and oral presentation skills.

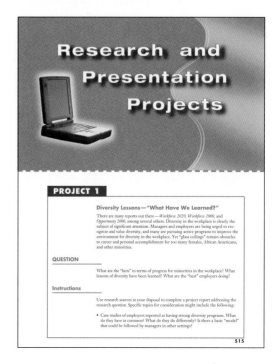

Integrate the Excitement of the Web into Your Course!

MANAGEMENT 6/E WEB SITE

An extensive Web Site has been developed in support of this new edition of *MANAGEMENT*. This site is available at **http://www.wiley.com/college/scherman6e,** and includes the following special resources for instructional enrichment of both instructors and students using the book.

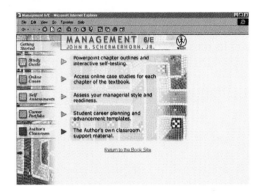

- PowerPoint downloads for text figures and supplementary figures and special class activities and presentations
- Interactive online versions of cases
- Interactive online versions of skills assessments
- Supplementary in-class exercises and activities
- Special "quick-hitters" for use with various chapters, and with special value for large-section class sizes
- Internet links to organizations and information sites relevant to chapter materials
- A full electronic version of the Career Advancement Portfolio
- An online study guide for students

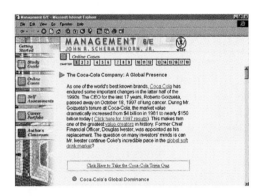

Additionally, the web site features a truly unique and highly valuable resource—The Author's Classroom. This feature takes the instructor inside the author's own classroom to find additional teaching ideas and resources for each chapter. A supplement to the basic Instructor's Manual, this online resource provides teaching tips and class enhancements for treating the core topics of each chapter. By using this resource, the instructor has access to John Schermerhorn's personal PowerPoint presentations, special in-class activities, unique web sites for browsing during class, and more.

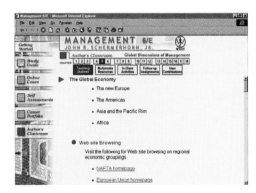

About the Author

John R. Schermerhorn, Jr. is the Charles G. O'Bleness Professor of Management in the College of Business at Ohio University, where he teaches graduate and undergraduate courses in management. Dr. Schermerhorn earned a Ph.D. in organizational behavior from Northwestern University, an MBA (with distinction) in management and international business from New York University, and a BS in business administration from the State University of New York at Buffalo. He has taught at Tulane University, the University of Vermont, and Southern Illinois University at Carbondale, where he also served as Head of the Department of Management and Associate Dean of the College of Business Administration.

At Ohio University Dr. Schermerhorn has been named a University Professor, the university's highest campus-wide honor for excellence in undergraduate teaching. He is committed to instructional excellence and curriculum innovation, and is now working extensively with technology utilization and Internet applications in the classroom. He serves as a guest speaker at colleges and universities, lecturing on developments in higher education for business and management, as well as on instructional approaches and innovations.

Highly dedicated to serving the needs of practicing managers in all types of organizations, Dr. Schermerhorn has written *Management 6/E* to help others bridge the gaps between the theory and practice of management. He has had prior work experience in business and hospital administration, and serves actively as a consultant and management trainer.

Dr. Schermerhorn's extensive international experience adds a unique global dimension to *Management 6/E*. He has worked in China, Egypt, Indonesia, Thailand, Malaysia, Vietnam, the Philippines, Poland, Hungary, Venezuela, and Tanzania. He has also served as a Visiting Professor of Management at the Chinese University of Hong Kong, as on-site Coordinator of the Ohio University MBA and Executive MBA programs in Malaysia, and as Director of the Interdisciplinary Center for Southeast Asia Studies at Ohio University.

A dedicated scholar, Dr. Schermerhorn is a member of the Academy of Management, where he served as chairperson of the Management Education and Development Division. He is known to educators and students alike as senior coauthor of *Managing Organizational Behavior 6/E* (Wiley, 1996) and *Basic Organizational Behavior 2/E* (Wiley, 1997). He has also published numerous articles in the *Academy of Management Journal, Academy of Management Review, Academy of Management Executive, Organizational Dynamics, Asia-Pacific Journal of Management,* and the *Journal of Management Development,* among other scholarly journals.

The Management Mosaic

Management today is like the mosaic featured in the cover art and throughout the design of *MANAGEMENT 6/E*. Now is a time of global diversity and significant change. Just as a mosaic of beautiful tiles offers the beholder a dynamic mix of colors, forms, and impressions, so too does the new workplace. There is no better time than the present to embrace the management mosaic and prepare for an exciting future.

Today's students are tomorrow's leaders and managers. They are the hope of the 21st century. Just as the workplace in this new century will be vastly different from today's, so too must our teaching and learning environments be different from days gone by. Even while continuing to emphasize the relevance of cultural diversity, ethics and social responsibility, the global economy, and the imperatives of quality and high performance, management educators and practitioners must all step confidently forward on paths toward an uncertain future. New values and management approaches are appearing; the nature of work and organizations is changing; the age of information is not only with us, it is transforming our lives.

MANAGEMENT 6/E is part of the same transformation. This mosaic edition has been revised extensively to reflect changing times and with a sincere commitment to continuous improvement and customer service for both students and instructors alike.

Students tell us they liked the self-tests at the end of each chapter in the prior edition. The tests have been continued. Students tell us they want real world examples, but without the confusing mix of boxed materials characteristic of too many textbooks. This text is rich in examples embedded in the normal flow of chapter discussions. Students tell us they want more career support and focus. This edition offers an extensive *Career Readiness Workbook* that offers many and varied personal and professional development opportunities — including the unique *Career Advancement Portfolio* that can be created both in print and online.

Instructors tell us they appreciated the reasonable length of the prior edition and its commitment to straight talk about management theory and practice. The new edition is like one of today's high performance organizations — neat, trim, fast, and highly capable for the task at hand. Instructors tell us they want solid content that covers the major theories and concepts while staying closely tuned to the issues and developments of the day. The new edition still offers the best management foundations while centering them in the real themes, demands, and opportunities of a new and still-developing workplace. Importantly, instructors tell us they want ever-more support for innovative, flexible, and integrative course designs. *MANAGEMENT 6/E* is rich in this respect with great opportunity as a true resource for learning. In many ways this mosaic edition has become a learning instrument, not just a textbook. It is also a very flexible instrument that is responsive to a variety of instructional needs and approaches.

The chapters in *MANAGEMENT 6/E* are presented in one logical order, but they can be used in different sequences according to preference. The running glossary and end-of-chapter review sections offer a built-in study guide to allow independent learning by students. The end-of-book *Career Readiness Workbook* offers an extensive array of options that allow for course enrichment through the use of career portfolios, critical thinking cases, an integrative in-basket and video case, skills assessments, team exercises, and research and presentation projects. Where else can you get such a range of unique and innovative options under one cover to serve the needs of your students?

Proudly and as a colleague, I offer *MANAGEMENT 6/E* as my personal and professional contribution to today's students and tomorrow's managers. It contains my best sense of the issues of the day and the challenges of the future. As management educators, we all face common problems and opportunities when developing courses, working with students, and trying to uphold accreditation standards. This book has been created to support the pursuit of instructional excellence in all such settings. It is based, furthermore, on four constructive balances that I believe remain essential to the agenda of higher education for business and management. They are:

- *The balance of research insights with introductory education.* As educators, we must be willing to make choices when bringing the theories and concepts of our discipline to the attention of the introductory student. The goal should always be to set the best possible foundations for life-long learning. It should not and cannot be to provide, in one course or program of study, everything a student will ever need to know about management or anything else.

- *The balance of management theory with management practice.* As educators, we must understand the compelling needs of students to sense the potential applications of the material they are reading and thinking about. We must continually bring to their attention good, interesting, and recognizable examples. This holds true both for students with very limited work experience and for those already progressing along established career paths.

- *The balance of present understandings with future possibilities.* As educators, we must actively search for the directions in which the real world of management is heading, and we must actively help students explore and address these directions. More importantly, we must select and present materials that can both lead students in the right directions and help them develop the confidence and self-respect needed to deal with them best.

- *The balance of what "can" be done with what is, purely and simply, the "right" thing to do.* As educators, we are role models and we set the examples. We must be willing to take stands on issues like equal employment opportunity, quality of work life, managerial ethics, and corporate social responsibility. We must be careful not to let the concept of "contingency" betray the need for positive "action" in managerial practice. And, we must not allow it to draw students away from understanding the many dimensions of performance "accountability" in a fair and just society.

Today, more than ever before, our students have pressing needs for direction as well as suggestion. They have needs for application as well as information. They have needs for integration as well as presentation. Our instructional approaches and materials must deliver on all of these dimensions and more. My goal is to put into your hands and into those of your students a textbook that can help meet these needs. Whether your classroom is small or large, the opportunities for progress through educational excellence are equally great. *MANAGEMENT 6/E* is my contribution to the future careers of your students and mine.

John R. Schermerhorn, Jr.
Charles G. O'Bleness Professor of Management
Ohio University

Book at a Glance

Like its predecessors, the sixth edition of *MANAGEMENT* introduces the essentials of management as they apply within the contemporary work environment. Its first goal is to cover the appropriate topics in a manner relevant to the dynamic environment of management today and changes taking place in the new workplace. Its second goal is to always do so with sufficient depth so that the introductory student gains a solid foundation in management. The third goal is to do all of this in an interesting, engaging, and applied way — one that holds students' attention and stimulates them to relate actively to both the material at hand and the everyday examples that abound in their experiences.

Positive feedback from faculty and students alike has attested to the success of past editions. Yet, *MANAGEMENT 6/E*, in keeping with the dramatic changes of the decade, has been substantially redeveloped for the instructors and students who must face the challenges of the 21st century. This is not yesterday's management book — it is tomorrow's.

The subject matter of *MANAGEMENT 6/E* remains carefully chosen to meet AACSB accreditation guidelines while allowing extensive flexibility to fit various course designs and class sizes. The book is thorough from a curriculum standpoint but written to meet the needs of the introductory student. Importantly, this is done with special attention to an integrated treatment of the environment, quality operations, cultural diversity, the global economy, and ethics and social responsibility, and the growing influence on new information technologies as paramount concerns and themes of our day.

There are many new things to look for in this edition. Along with updates of core material, the new edition of *MANAGEMENT* offers a number of changes in the organization, content, and design that respond to current themes and developments in the theory and practice of management.

ORGANIZATIONAL CHANGES

- The book is reorganized into five parts with clear application to core themes relevant to today's organizations: Management Today, Context, Mission, Organization, Leadership.

- The fundamentals of the management process are integrated through core chapters on these action themes: Planning — To Set Direction; Organizing — To Create Structures; Leading — To Inspire Effort; Controlling — To Ensure Results.

- Part 1 opens the book with a clear focus on the exciting and dynamic new workplace, the importance of environment and competitive advantage, and the importance of information technology and decision making.

- Part 2 sets the context for management by reviewing the historical foundations, highlighting the importance of the global economy, and offering a strong reminder of the importance of ethics and social responsibility.

- Part 3 integrates both planning and controlling as management functions, and includes an all-new treatment of strategic management and entrepreneurship.
- Part 4 covers the essentials of organizing as a management function, with special attention to new developments in organization designs and work systems.
- Part 5 offers extensive coverage of leadership as a managerial function, including in-depth coverage of motivation and rewards, individual performance and job design, communication and interpersonal skills, teams and teamwork, and innovation and change management.

CONTENT ADDITIONS

Throughout the book every effort is made to bring in the latest thinking and concepts facing managers and organizations today. In addition to core themes of diversity, competitive advantage, quality, globalization, and empowerment, specific coverage has been added in this edition on all of the following topics and more:

multi-cultural organizations . ethnocentrism . cultural relativism .
self management . customer-driven organizations . electronic commerce .
intranets . entrepreneurship . organizational learning . life-long learning .
horizontal organizations . cross-functional teams . virtual teams .
virtual organizations . process value analysis . re-engineering .
informal learning . work-life balance . strategic human resource planning .
performance-based rewards . job stress . alternative work arrangements .
communication barriers . conflict management . negotiation . teamwork .
innovation processes . change leadership . career portfolios

DESIGN FEATURES

The design of *MANAGEMENT 6/E* has been created in specific response to the author's experience as a classroom instructor and with the assistance of helpful feedback from management educators using the prior edition. With a clean and open look in a four-color format, the design is our attempt to provide introductory management students with a book that is consistent in style with the professional literature they can and should be reading.

Taking the benchmark of the professional literature, the new edition introduces each chapter with a "Headlines" feature that provides a variety of anecdotal vignettes to draw the reader into chapter content. The chapters themselves reflect a variety of additional features that visually present the material in an attractive and engaging manner. The design has been selected to help bring the best chapter features to the reader's clear and complete attention.

CHAPTER FEATURES

OPENING HEADLINE

To emphasize the importance of learning as much as we can about the role of managers in this dynamic environment, we open each chapter with a Headline that calls out a key issue or point regarding management today. This is accompanied by a short vignette offering a timely report or example relevant to the chapter and to the new workplace of the 21st century. The vignettes feature real-world people and organizations. They have been carefully chosen to offer a stimulating view of the real challenges facing today's managers.

PLANNING AHEAD

The chapter opening material includes a brief planning ahead section to orient the reader. This includes a set of study questions that are linked to the major subject headings of the chapter. They serve as learning objectives and create a framework for the chapter summary.

EMBEDDED BOXES

Diversity, quality, ethics, social responsibility, benchmarking, the global economy — these are all themes that managers must deal with these issues on a daily basis. To exemplify their importance while still maintaining an integrated presentation of material, we have provided in-depth examples that are embedded by both content and design into the general text discussion. Each provides a concise and relevant example without interrupting the flow of the text. The examples chosen range from large, multinational organizations to small, local businesses, representing both for-profit and nonprofit and manufacturing and service organizations. The embedded boxes are visually illustrated with engaging photographs that bring them to life and each features a visual icon which describes the overall theme of the box. These visual markers are: Diversity (✳), Quality (🏃), Ethics and Social Responsibility (🜲), Benchmarking (☑, and Globalization (🌐).

MANAGER'S NOTEPADS

Manager's notepads are concise lists of helpful hints — the "do's" and "don'ts" of managerial behavior. They are designed as useful theory-into-practice summaries, and to assist readers with understanding the action implications of material being studied. The Manager's Notepads appear as boxed inserts throughout the text and are appropriately designed to resemble the familiar "yellow pads" used by most everyone.

MARGIN PHOTOS

Additional, briefer, real-world examples are called out in the margin photos of the text and illustrated with photos. The captions to these photos highlight the ways in which the concepts and theories presented in the text apply in day-to-day managerial practices in a wide selection of organizations. These dynamic, real-world examples of management in action add further applications to text discussion, without distracting the reader. Where applicable, these margin photos also include the corporate Web addresses that can be used by students to pursue further research on the web.

MARGIN LIST IDENTIFIERS

Margin list notes are provided throughout the text to identify key bulleted or numbered lists of information. The margin notes provide a convenient outline for students to use in studying chapter content and reviewing for examinations.

MARGIN RUNNING GLOSSARY

Boldfaced key terms from the text are called out and defined in the margin, forming a running glossary of the key concepts of the discussion.

CHAPTER SUMMARY

The chapter summary is organized according to the planning ahead study questions and major subject headings of the chapter. The summary repeats each study question and offers in concise bullet-list form an overview of key points from that section of the chapter. It helps put the chapter content into overall perspective, providing answers to the study questions posed at the beginning of the chapter.

CHAPTER LIST OF KEY TERMS

The end-of-chapter list of key terms allows the student to double-check familiarity with basic concepts and definitions. Page numbers are included for easy access to the textual reference.

CHAPTER SELF-TEST

The end-of-chapter self-test has been continued from the last edition. It provides a built-in study guide for the student to prepare for examinations. Multiple-choice, true-false, short-answer, and application essay questions reflect the type of questions the student may be expected to answer on examinations. The author's answers to the self-test questions, including the short-answer and application questions, are found in the back of the book.

 # CAREER READINESS WORKBOOK

An important innovation in *MANAGEMENT 6/E* is the inclusion of the Career Readiness Workbook as part of the hard-bound text. The workbook consists of six components, each of which has been designed to maximize learning opportunities for the student and provide a range of stimulating pedagogical options for the instructor. The complete portfolio of rich learning activities is presented in an easy-to-use format that is geared directly toward career and professional development. They can help students to evaluate their managerial capabilities and are suitable for either in-class or out-of-class assignments and for individual or group use. All materials are well-supported in the Instructor's Manual. The elements in the workbook are: Career Advancement Portfolio, Cases for Critical Thinking, Integrative Learning Activities, Exercises for Teamwork, Management Skills Assessments, and Research and Presentation Projects.

CAREER ADVANCEMENT PORTFOLIO

The unique Career Advancement Portfolio provides the template for students to build a career portfolio that documents, in paper or electronic form, their academic and personal accomplishments for external review. This resource can help them frame and summarize personal credentials for potential internship sources and full-time employers. There is a special option for building an electronic career portfolio and putting it online. In both print and online formats, the Career Advancement Portfolio can be easily maintained and updated for purposes of outcome assessment within a course or program of study, as well as for the student's personal development and career development.

CASES FOR CRITICAL THINKING

The Cases for Critical Thinking bring to life the decisions managers must make every day in these dynamic times, on both a national and global level. Sometimes these choices are wise; other times they have proved to be erroneous. The case studies describe both the benefits and consequences of managers' decisions. Each case concludes with a list of questions for the student to answer concerning the in-depth scenarios they are given. Interactive versions of each case is available online through the *MANAGEMENT 6/E* web site. These online cases will be updated regularly and new cases posted to enrich the alternatives for classroom use.

INTEGRATIVE LEARNING ACTIVITIES

Integration is one of the important thrusts in management education today. Included in the workbook are two easy-to-use and highly involving integrative learning activities that can supplement various aspects of a course. The In-Basket Exercise places students in decision making situations that test their leadership and managerial capabilities, with an opportunity to stress written and oral communication skills. The Cross-Functional Integrated Video Case on Outback Steakhouse further allows for various parts of the management process to be examined in the context of a real situation and a highly competitive environment. The case can be used in whole or in part to best fit the instructor's course design.

EXERCISES IN TEAMWORK

The Exercises in Teamwork offer opportunities to explore, in the team setting, a variety of issues and topics from chapter and class discussions. The team exercises present situations that provide the basis for group discussion or individual analytical exercises. Instructions are clear and self-explanatory; formats for group discussion and class interaction are provided. Additional team exercises are found among the instructional materials available online through the *MANAGEMENT 6/E* web site.

MANAGEMENT SKILLS ASSESSMENTS

A diverse selection of Management Skills Assessments are also included in the workbook. These self-assessment instruments ask the students to analyze their knowledge of management issues and their possession of the skills necessary to tackle these issues in daily life. Each assessment is broken down into instructions on how to complete the assignment, directions for scoring, and an interpretation of the score along with guidelines for its meaning in a larger context. Additional self-assessments are available online through the *MANAGEMENT 6/E* web site.

RESEARCH AND PRESENTATION PROJECTS

The workbook offers a number of Research and Presentation Projects on timely topics relating to the chapter discussions. The projects are designed to enhance students research skills, including those involving the Internet and Electronic Data Bases. Importantly, the projects also offer important opportunities for students to refine their written and oral presentation skills. Each project is introduced with a brief scenario or hypothetical situation. A question is then posed about that situation. The scenario can be used as the basis for a wide variety of course assignments, including individual and group work. Students are pointed toward outside research sources that help them solve the managerial dilemma, including the Internet, library and electronic sources, local case studies of nearby organizations, and comparative field research they can conduct on their own. The responses can be used as the foundation for a professional individual research paper or group project with oral class presentations.

MANAGEMENT 6/E WEB SITE

An extensive web site has been developed in support of *MANAGEMENT 6/E* users. The site is available at *http://www.wiley.com/college/scherman6e,* and offers a range of information which includes the following special resources for instructional enrichment:

- PowerPoint downloads for supplementary figures and class presentations materials
- Interactive online versions of all cases
- Interactive online versions of selected skills assessments
- Supplementary in-class exercises and activities
- Special "quick-hitters" for use with various chapters, and with special value for large-section class sizes
- Internet links to all organizations referenced in the textbook
- An online study guide for students to self-test, study, and review.

Additionally, the web site features a unique resource — The Author's Classroom. This feature takes you inside the author's actual classroom and provides additional teaching ideas and resources for each chapter. An addition to the basic Instructor's Manual, this online resource provides teaching tips and class enhancements for treating the core topics of each chapter, and as they are used in the author's classroom. By using this resource you have access to the author's personal PowerPoint presentations, special in-class activities, unique web-sites for Internet browsing during class, and more.

If you enjoy teaching, you'll enjoy working with The Author's Classroom. And if you stay in touch with this site, you will have access to new materials and resources as they become available to the author's own classes.

INSTRUCTIONAL SUPPORT PACKAGE

MANAGEMENT 6/E is supported by a comprehensive learning package that assists the instructor in creating a motivating and enthusiastic environment. It also provides the student with additional instruments for understanding and reviewing management concepts and with the opportunity to see these concepts in practice.

- The Instructor's Resource Guide is a unique, comprehensive guide to building a system of customized instruction. The manual offers helpful teaching ideas, advice on course development, sample assignments, and chapter-by-chapter text highlights, learning objectives, lecture outlines, class exercises, lecture notes, and answers to all end-of-chapter material. This version of the *Instructor's Resource Guide* also includes a section entitled the "Use of Cases" and the "Case Method." The entire guide is also available on disk.

- A comprehensive Test Bank is available, consisting of 3,000 multiple-choice, true-false, and essay questions categorized by pedagogical element (margin notes, margin terms, or general text knowledge), page number, and type of question (factual or applied). Each question has been subjected to educational testing standards to ensure that the test bank is both valid and reliable and written according to Bloom's taxonomy, which outlines several ways that a good exam can test knowledge. The entire test bank is also available in a computerized version, MICROTEST, for use on IBM PC, XT, or AT computers (or a compatible) running on MS-WINDOWS with two disk drives.

- PowerPoint Slides are available for use in class and in management training programs. Full-color slides highlight key figures from the text as well as many additional lecture outlines, concepts, and diagrams. Together, these provide a versatile opportunity to add high-quality visual support to lectures.

- The comprehensive Video Package offers video selections from the highly respected business news program, *Nightly Business Report (NBR)*. These video clips tie directly to the theme of the management mosaic and bring to life many of the case examples used in the text as well as others from outside sources. Also available is a *Cross-Functional Integrated Video Case on Outback Steakhouse* that corresponds to the integrated case in the text.

- A *Student Video CD-ROM,* included in each copy of the book, offers selected video cases for personal student use and study. Students will have the ability to view the video and instantly link to the interactive online cases on the text web site. A set of viewing questions prompts students to think critically about the issues of the case.

- The Business Extra Program, a partnership between Wiley and the Dow Jones Company, offers an exciting new way to extend your textbook beyond the walls of the classroom. The Business Extra Program is comprised of the *On-Line Business Survival Guide*—which includes a special password for Wiley's *Business Extra web site,* through which your students get instant access to a wealth of current articles, as well as a special offer for the *Wall Street Journal Interactive Edition.* The *On-Line Business Survival Guide* can be packaged with the text by using the set (ISBN 0471-33019-1).

- A web-based course management tool is available for online teaching and learning. Wiley will provide basic content based upon material accompanying the text. Instructors have the option of uploading additional material and customizing existing content to fit their needs.

- A web-based testing, quizzing, and assessment tool is available.

 ## ACKNOWLEDGMENTS

MANAGEMENT 6/E was made possible through the extraordinary efforts of many people. The project was initiated and completed with the support of my editors, Ellen Ford and Brent Gordon, with the assistance of Marian Provenzano, Developmental Editor. As always, a unique team at John Wiley & Sons worked together to build and complete the many facets of this book. Special thanks go to the following superb group of Wiley personnel who worked tirelessly on the project: Joe Heider (publisher), Harold Nolan (designer), Hilary Newman (photo research), Jennifer Carey (of J. Carey Publishing Service), Patricia McFadden, and Jeanine Furino (production), Cindy Rhoads (supplements), and Carlise Paulson (marketing). I also wish to thank Anna Melhorn for overseeing the illustrations and Fred Courtright for his work compiling the permissions.

In this edition, we wanted to offer the best possible selection of cases and to bring them alive on the Internet. To do that, we turned to David Chappell of Ohio University. As Case Editor for the project, he responded with just what we'd hoped for—exceptional quality. His stamp is now indelibly inscribed in the book's learning value. The Cross-Functional Integrated Video Case is a result of the fine work of George Puia of Indiana State University and Marilyn Taylor, University of Missouri, Kansas City.

To Cheryl Wyrick of California State Polytechnic University, Pomona, for PowerPoint presentations and Bonnie Fremgen, University of Notre Dame, for the In-Basket Exercise, goes a special thank you for their original and exceptional contributions.

We also wanted a truly useful instructor's resource guide. For that, we turned to William Gardner of the University of Mississippi, along with the co-authorship of his wife Marilyn Gardner, who also provided a top-quality product. We wanted a substantial test bank. To do that we relied on the skills of Carnella Hardin of Glendale Community College. Finally, we wanted a stimulating and relevant web site. For that, we turned to Ellen Bari of the New Technology Group of John Wiley & Sons and Jim Congdon of InformActive. For the highly substantial and informative NBR Videos, we thank Jack Kahn and Emily Richardson of Nightly Business Report.

Writing and revising a book takes a great toll on one's personal life — a toll that only reveals itself with the passage of time. My wife, Ann, and my sons, Christian and Porter, have made their own special contributions and sacrifices on behalf of this project. As always, I now publicly thank them for making it possible for me to write and endlessly revise the pages that eventually became this book. I again sincerely hope that the results of my efforts meet their expectations.

I offer this final word of thanks to the following colleagues whose willingness to review and critique parts of this book at various stages of its life added immensely to my understanding. Always, I tried to listen and deal constructively with your suggestions. Every point was considered and appreciated. I hope that you, too, feel the final product justifies your fine efforts. Special thanks to

Bonnie Baker, *Siena College*
Santanu Borah, *University of North Alabama*
Mark Butler, *San Diego State University*
Clarence Butz, *Azusa Pacific University*
Kent Carter, *Westminster College*
Bert Connell, *Loma Linda University*
Elizabeth Cooper, *University of Rhode Island*
Kenneth Everard, *The College of New Jersey*
Bonnie Fremgen, *University of Notre Dame*
Terri Friel, *Eastern Kentucky University*
William Gardner, *University of Mississippi*
Gerson M. Goldberg, *Oklahoma Panhandle State University*
Carnella Hardin, *Glendale Community College*
David Hoag, *St. Louis Community College Merimec*
William LaPorte, *Capital Community Technical College*
Lloyd Letcher, *Kansas State University*
Douglas McCabe, *Georgetown University*
Kevin McCarthy, *Baker University*
William Moor, *Arizona State University*
Benjamin Morris, *Saint Leo College*
Ilona Motsiff, *Trinity College*
Chuck Nuckles, *Concordia University*
Vernon A. Quarstein, *St. Leo College*
Michael Raphael, *Central Connecticut University*
James G. Salvucci, *Curry College*
Roy Simerly, *East Carolina University*
Cynthia Singer, *Union County College*
Margaret Sprenz, *David N. Meyers College*
Shanthi Srinivas, *California State University*

Ram Subramanian, *Grand Valley State University*
Burley Walker, *University of Texas*
Bobbie Williams, *Georgia Southern University*
Cheryl Wyrick, *California State Polytechnic University*
Jiaquin Yang, *University of North Dakota*

I would also like to acknowledge those colleagues who contributed to the success of previous editions, helping to establish a foundation for this latest edition. Fifth edition reviewers included:

Robert Allen, *California State Polytechnic University — Pomona*
John Bedient, *Albion College*
Elena Bosch, *Interamerican University of Puerto Rico*
John H. Boyd, *Baylor University*
Kent Carter, *Westminster College*
C.S. Everett, *Des Moines Area Community College*
Janice Feldbauer, *Austin Community College*
Charles Flaherty, *University of Minnesota*
Sharon Green, *California State University — Hayward*
John Hall, *University of Florida*
Carnella Hardin, *Glendale Community College*
Scott Harding, *Normandale Community College*
Raymond G. Hunt, *SUNY Buffalo*
Thomas K. Ingram, *SUNY College at Oswego*
Howard Kingslinger, *Bloomsburg University*
Harry J. Lasher, *Kennesaw State College*
Greg Pierce, *Pennsylvania State University*
Ralph A. Rodriguez, *Temple University*
Douglas Rymph, *Emporia State University*
James Segovis, *Bryant College*
William Smith, *Towson State University*
Nestor St. Charles, *Dutchess Community College*
Dale B. Sullivan, *University of Toledo*
Craig A. Tunwall, *Ithaca College*
Charles E. Tychsen, *Northern Virginia Community College*
Mohamed Wahba, *Hofstra University*
Joseph W. Weiss, *Bentley College*

Earlier editions were reviewed by:

Jack Abraham
Royce Abrahamson
Sonny S. Ariss
Barry Armandi
Larry G. Bailey
Bonnie Baker
Robert M. Ballinger
William Blackerby
Robert Boothe
Gunther S. Boroschek
Steve Brenner
Gil Brookins
Russell V. Brown
Gene E. Burton
John P. Callahan
R. Camehorn

Joseph Cantrell
Kent Carter
Lawrence Carter
James F. Cashman
S. Clark
Jack Cochran
Refik Culpan
Dave Day
James W. Dean
Sylvia De Leon
Gregory G. Dell'Omo
John K. Evans
C.S. Everett
J. Fahrenwald
Ellen Frank
Mary Giovannese

Barbara Gray
Mark Green
Ronald Greenwood
Susan Halfhill
John Hall
Joseph Harder
Timothy Harper
D.E. Harris
Nell Hartley
Paul Hegele
Robert C. Henry
Susan Herman
John A. Hornaday
George S. Huber
Neil J. Humphreys
E. Harvey Jewell

George P. Johnson III
Kathleen P. Jones
Marcia Kassner
Dave Ketchen
Scott King
William L. King
Gus L. Kotoulas
Charles J. Kovarik
Carl J. Kovelowski
Tom Kraven
Patrick Kroll
Marsha J. Kurzynski
Stanley Lau
Jerre G. Lewis
Robert Lindamood
Robert C. Maddox
David Mandeville
Mzamo P. Mangaliso
Ronald J. Marshall
William Mathews

Connie Mayfield
Harriette McCaul
Peggy Miller
Stanley Mithchell
Edward J. Morrison
Abbas Nadim
Wayne E. Nelson
Harvey Nussbaum
Clyde A. Painter
Dennis D. Pappas
John H. Parker
P. Peterson
Jane Pettinger
Michael A. Raphael
Margaret A. Rechter
Paul R. Reed
Gerald R. Rosenfelder
Nick Sarantakes
Richard C. Scamehorn
Allen Shub

William R. Smith
M. Sprence
James M. Stack
Paul L. Starkey
Bob Stock
Lee Wm. Sutherland
Johnny Thomas
Linda K. Travino
Ann Van Gigch
John J. Vilton
J. Wallace
Fred A. Ware
Warren C. Weber
Nathan Weiner
James Welch
Robert R. Wiggins
Robert Wright
Richard Zahn
Alan Zeiber

Brief Contents

Contents

PART 2 • CONTEXT

CHAPTER 4
HISTORICAL FOUNDATIONS OF MANAGEMENT   70

CHAPTER 5
GLOBAL DIMENSIONS OF MANAGEMENT   90

CHAPTER 6
ETHICAL BEHAVIOR AND SOCIAL RESPONSIBILITY   114

PART 3 • MISSION

PART 4 · ORGANIZATION

CHAPTER 10
ORGANIZING—TO CREATE STRUCTURES   200

CHAPTER 11
ORGANIZATIONAL DESIGN AND WORK PROCESSES   220

CHAPTER 12
HUMAN RESOURCE MANAGEMENT   238

PART 5 • LEADERSHIP

CAREER READINESS WORKBOOK

CHAPTER ONE

The Dynamic New Workplace

Planning Ahead—Chapter 1 Study Questions

- What are organizations like in the new workplace?
- Who are managers and what do they do?
- What is the management process?
- What are the challenges of working in the 21st century?

Smart People Create Their Own Futures

The 21st century is here. In the new workplace everyone must respond and adapt to a rapidly changing society with constantly shifting demands and opportunities. Learning and speed are in; habit and complacency are out. That's all part of the theme driving the popular magazine *Fast Company* and its mission to be a "handbook of the business revolution." While noting that it is hard to comprehend the new world of work at the very time that it is being rapidly created, *Fast Company* reports the importance of these core understandings for anyone who seeks career success today. Organizations are fast changing; the nature of work itself is changing; the global economy is driven by innovation and technology; even the concept of success, personal and organizational, is evolving. These developments, say *Fast Company's* editors, affect us all and offer both "unparalleled opportunity and unprecedented uncertainty." And in this age of continuous challenge, a compelling message must be heard—smart people and smart companies create their own futures![1]

Yes, we live and work in a challenging environment of great opportunity and dramatic uncertainty.[2] Personal and organizational success must be forged in workplaces that are being reinvented with the themes of "participation," "empowerment," "involvement," "teamwork," "flexibility," "self-management," and more. Careers must be redefined in terms of "flexibility," "free agency," "skill portfolios," "entrepreneurship," and others. And importantly, all of this is accompanied by continuing calls for higher productivity from organizations and the people who make them run. Society today demands nothing less than the best from all its institutions.

These and many other issues are on the minds of organizational leaders everywhere. They know that success in challenging times requires extraordinary commitments to operating efficiency, technology utilization, product quality, and customer satisfaction. They understand that organizations must build credibility by excelling continuously on performance criteria that include concerns for innovativeness, employee development, and social responsibility as well as measures of profitability and investment value. As Johnson & Johnson CEO Ralph S. Larsen says, "Reputations reflect behavior you exhibit day in and day out through a hundred small things. The way you manage your reputation is by always thinking and trying to do the right thing every day."[3]

ORGANIZATIONS AND THE NEW WORKPLACE

• Whole Foods Market
http://www.wholefoods.com

Mission counts at Whole Foods Market, a natural foods grocery store chain. With a commitment to "improving human health," the firm attracts a highly motivated workforce. Says one: "I just hang on to the fact that my job is good in the larger sense. If people buy the sprouts, they're eating healthier foods . . . it's good for the planet because they're grown organically."

Society in this century has become a society of organizations. Social tasks—from providing goods and services to education and care of the sick and the elderly . . . are now increasingly performed in and through large organizations. . . . Careers in organizations—that is, careers as managers and other professionals—are the principal career opportunities for educated people.[4]

With these words, the noted management theorist and consultant Peter Drucker reminds us of an historical fact. Not only does our society depend upon organizations to provide essential goods and services, we depend individually upon them to provide gainful employment. Everyone has a stake in making sure that organizations perform up to expectations. Good organizations make real and positive contributions to society.

Against this historical baseline, the dynamic pathways to the future can be considered through new benchmarks being set in and by progressive organizations everywhere. Many will be introduced throughout this book. At General Electric, for example, CEO Jack Welch is viewed by some as one of the great corporate leaders of our time. He heads a multinational enterprise with 276,000 employees operating in over 100 countries. He does so using the analogy of the local grocery store. According to Welch: "If the customer isn't satisfied, if the stuff is getting stale, if the shelf isn't right, or if the offerings aren't right, it's the same thing. You manage it like a small organization. You don't get hung up on zeros." And in this context, Welch further highlights an essential dimension of organizations today—success builds from the talents of people. "We have to get everybody in the organization involved" Welch says. "If you do that right, the best ideas rise to the top."[5]

In his leadership style and practices, Jack Welch demonstrates an important point regarding organizations today. People—what they know, what they learn, and what they do with it—are the ultimate foundations of organizational performance. They represent an "intellectual capital" that is indispensable in creating long-term success. The ultimate elegance of the new workplace may well be its ability to combine the talents of many people, sometimes thousands of them, to achieve unique and significant results in what Drucker calls our society of organizations.

At Herman Miller, a manufacturer of designer furniture, respect for employees is a rule of thumb. The innovative and productive firm's greatest strength may be respect for the talents and rights of its employees. The firm's core values include the statement, "Our greatest assets as a corporation are the gifts, talents and abilities of our employee-owners. . . . When we as a corporation invest in developing people, we are investing in our future." Managers report regularly to workers on the firm's profits and productivity. A special incentive plan gives workers a share in financial gains from the productivity improvements they suggest. Former CEO Max DePree says, "At Herman Miller, we talk about the difference between being successful and being exceptional. Being successful is meeting goals in a good way—being exceptional is reaching your potential."[6]

WHAT IS AN ORGANIZATION?

An **organization** is a collection of people working together to achieve a common purpose. In so doing, the members are able to accomplish tasks that are far beyond the reach of anyone acting alone. Furthermore, the *purpose* of any organization is to produce goods and/or services that satisfy the needs of customers. Something useful for society should ideally be produced in order for any organization to be able to justify its existence. Indeed, having a clear sense of purpose that is tied to "quality products" and "customer satisfaction" is increasingly viewed as a source of strength and performance advantage. It is also cited in a recent *Fortune* magazine article as among the most important reasons why employees love their employers.[7] At Medtronics, the large Minnesota-based medical products company, for example, employees are noted for innovation and commitment to a mission with a clear and singular mission—helping sick people get well.[8] The sense of corporate purpose clearly centers attention on a goal that is easily shared: improving the health and well-being of those who use the company's products.

- An **organization** is a collection of people working together in a division of labor to achieve a common purpose.

ORGANIZATIONS AS SYSTEMS

A *system* is a collection of interrelated parts that function together to achieve a common purpose.[9] It is helpful to view organizations as **open systems** that interact with their environments in the continual process of transforming resource inputs into product outputs in the form of finished goods and/or services.

As shown in *Figure 1.1,* the external environment is a critical element in the open-systems view of organizations. It is a source of both resources and customer feedback, and it can have a significant impact on operations and outcomes. Feedback from the environment tells an organization how well it is meeting the needs of customers and society at large. Without customer willingness to use the organization's products, it is difficult to operate or stay in business over the long run. In this open-systems view of organizations, therefore, the customer truly reigns supreme. Consider Medtronic and its corporate purpose again. The ultimate test for the firm rests with the marketplace: Once someone uses a Medtronic product,

- An **open system** transforms resource inputs from the environment into product outputs.

Figure 1.1   Organizations as open systems.

the question becomes "Will they do so again . . . and will they recommend that others do the same?"

PRODUCTIVITY AND ORGANIZATIONAL PERFORMANCE

In the open-systems view of organizations, resources and customers are two critical elements. For an organization to perform well, resources must be well utilized and customers well served. The notion of *value-added* is very important in this context. If operations add value to the original cost of resource inputs, then (1) a business organization can earn a profit—that is, sell a product for more than the cost of making it (e.g., fast-food restaurant meals), or (2) a nonprofit organization can add wealth to society—that is, provide a public service that is worth more than its cost (e.g., fire protection in a community). To achieve such ends, all of an organization's human and material resources must be well utilized in the right way and at the right time to create high-quality products at minimum cost.

Formally defined, **productivity** is a summary measure of the quantity and quality of work performance, with resource utilization taken into account. It can be measured at the individual, group, or organization level. As shown in *Figure 1.2*, productivity may be expressed as success in two dimensions of organizational performance—effectiveness and efficiency.

Performance effectiveness is a measure of task output or goal accomplishment. This is a direct line to ultimate customer service and satisfaction. If you are working in the manufacturing area of a computer firm, for example, performance effectiveness may mean that you meet a daily production target in terms of the quantity and quality of keyboards assembled. By so doing, you allow the company as a whole to maintain its production schedule and meet customer demands for timely delivery and high-quality products.

Performance efficiency is a measure of the resource cost associated with goal accomplishment. It is a measure of outputs realized compared to inputs consumed. Cost of labor is a common efficiency measure. Others include equipment utilization, facilities maintenance, and returns on capital investment. Returning to the example of computer assembly, the most efficient production is that accom-

● **Productivity** is the quantity and quality of work performance, with resource utilization taken into account.

● **Performance effectiveness** is an output measure of task or goal accomplishment.

● **Performance efficiency** is a measure of the resource cost associated with goal accomplishment.

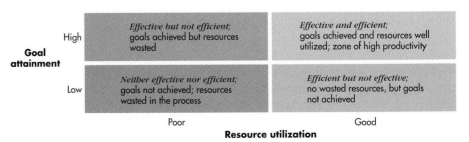

Figure 1.2   Productivity and organizational performance.

plished at a minimum cost in materials and labor. If you were producing fewer computer keyboards in a day than you were capable of this would contribute to inefficiency in organizational performance; likewise, if you made a lot of mistakes or wasted materials in the assembly process this is also inefficient work that raises costs for the organization.

CHANGING NATURE OF ORGANIZATIONS

Perhaps no productivity theme is stronger today than the issue of quality. Indeed, there has been a revolution of sorts among modern-day consumers. They are unrelenting in their demand for quality products and services. Organizations that fail to deliver them and/or do not listen to the needs of customers will be left struggling in our highly competitive environment. References will be made throughout this book to the concept of **total quality management (TQM)** — managing with an organizationwide commitment to continuous improvement and meeting customer needs completely. For the moment, the quality commitment can be recognized as a hallmark of enlightened productivity management in any organization.

> • **Total quality management (TQM)** is managing with an organization-wide commitment to continuous work improvement, product quality, and meeting customer needs completely.

Change will be another continuing theme of this book, and among the many changes affecting organizations, technology must be given special attention. Blending the best of technology with the full potential of people is a cornerstone of any progressive design. We are now seeing more *virtual organizations* that operate with the support of extensive computer networks and, in so doing, are able to work across large geographical distances with a minimum number of full-time employees. We are also experiencing a growth in the use of *cross-functional task forces* that bring together people from different parts of an organization to share problem-solving expertise and coordinate operations. The continuing emphasis on employee participation is further evidenced by *job enrichment* programs for individual workers and *self-managing teams* for groups of workers.

Daimler-Benz employs more than 199,000 people worldwide in its vehicle section. The global maker of luxury Mercedes Benz autos has more than 50 production and assembly plants. Like other world-class manufacturers, the firm actively pursues continuous improvement and strategic operations management. One of its quality experiments centered on the use of self-directed teams to increase worker involvement. After being implemented at the firm's Stuttgart facility, this approach resulted in a 50 percent reduction in defects. All ideas were generated by line workers active in the new work teams.[10]

 ## MANAGERS AND THE NEW WORKPLACE

This book is about managers and the people who work in our new, exciting, and highly demanding workplace. A **manager** is someone in an organization who is responsible for the work performance of one or more other persons. Serving in positions with a wide variety of titles (such as supervisor, team leader, division head, administrator, vice president, and so on), they mobilize people and resources to accomplish the work of organizations and their subunits. Those per-

> • A **manager** is a person who is responsible for the work performance of one or more other persons.

- **Human resources** are individuals and groups that help organizations perform.

sons reporting to managers, whether they are called direct reports, team members, or subordinates, are the essential **human resources** upon which the performance of organizations ultimately depends. They use such material resources as information, technology, raw materials, facilities, and money to help produce goods and services for an organization's customers or clients.

Every manager's job entails a key responsibility: to help an organization achieve high performance by well utilizing *all* its resources, both human and material. This is accomplished through **management** — the process of planning, organizing, leading, and controlling the use of resources to accomplish performance goals. As pointed out in the following comments by management theorist Henry Mintzberg, being a manager in this sense is a most important job:

- **Management** is the process of planning, organizing, leading, and controlling the use of resources to accomplish performance goals.

> No job is more vital to our society than that of the manager. It is the manager who determines whether our social institutions serve us well or whether they squander our talents and resources. It is time to strip away the folklore about managerial work, and time to study it realistically so that we can begin the difficult task of making significant improvement in its performance.[11]

TYPES OF MANAGERS

When we talk about managers, whether at the level of team leader or senior executive, the focus will always be on a shared managerial responsibility — to ensure the accomplishment of high performance results through the efforts of many people. We will also be recognizing that the nature of managerial work is evolving as organizations change and develop with time. A *Wall Street Journal* report describes the transition for managers as: "Not so long ago they may have supervised 10 people sitting outside their offices. Today they must win the support of scores more — employees of different backgrounds, job titles, and even cultures." The report goes on to say that "these new managers are expected to be skilled at organizing complex subjects, solving problems, communicating ideas, and making swift decisions."[12]

- **Top managers** are responsible for the performance of the organization as a whole or of one of its major parts.

Top managers, such as CEO Larsen of Johnson & Johnson, ensure that major performance objectives are established and accomplished in accordance with the organization's purpose. Common job titles at this level are chief executive officer, chief operating officer, president, and vice president. These *senior managers* or *executives* are responsible for the performance of an organization as a whole or for one of its significant parts. They should pay special attention to the external environment, be alert to potential long-run problems and opportunities, and develop appropriate ways of dealing with them. The best top managers are future-oriented strategic thinkers who make many decisions under highly competitive and uncertain conditions.

- **Middle managers** report to top managers and oversee the work of large departments or divisions.

Middle managers report to top managers while they themselves are in charge of relatively large departments or divisions consisting of several smaller work units. Examples are clinic directors in hospitals; deans in universities; and division managers, plant managers, and branch sales managers in businesses. Middle managers should be able to develop and implement action plans consistent with higher level objectives. They should also be team oriented and able to work well with peers to help coordinate activities across the organization. Especially today, middle managers are assuming new responsibilities for implementing complex projects that require the participation of persons from different parts of organizations. At General Electric, for example, corporate troubleshooters or "black belts" have been organized to manage groups that solve problems and create change across divisions and geographic boundaries within the company. One of them, Wendell Barr, recruited a cross-functional team from marketing, human resources, and field operations staff to design a new compensation system.[13]

Manager's Notepad 1.1

Nine Responsibilities of Team Leaders and Supervisors

1. Plan meetings and work schedules.
2. Clarify goals and tasks and gather ideas for improvement.
3. Appraise performance and counsel team members.
4. Recommend pay increases and new assignments.
5. Recruit, train, and develop team members to meet performance standards.
6. Encourage high performance and teamwork.
7. Inform team members about organizational goals and expectations.
8. Inform higher levels of team needs and accomplishments.
9. Coordinate with other teams and support their work efforts.

A first job in management typically occurs as an assignment as **team leader** or **supervisor** — someone in charge of a smaller work unit composed of non-managerial workers. Even though most people enter the workforce as technical specialists, sooner or later they advance to positions of initial managerial responsibility. Job titles for these *first-line managers* vary greatly but include such designations as department head, group leader, and unit manager. For example, the leader of an auditing team is considered a first-line manager, as is the head of an academic department in a university. Managers at this level of responsibility ensure that their work teams or units meet performance objectives that are consistent with the plans of middle and top management. Research confirms their critical importance and suggests that improving supervisory competencies is a good way to raise organizational productivity. *Manager's Notepad 1.1* offers advice on the performance responsibilities of team leaders and supervisors.[14]

In addition to serving at different levels of authority, managers work in different capacities within organizations. **Line managers** are responsible for work activities that make a direct contribution to the organization's outputs. For example, the president, retail manager, and department supervisors of a local department store all have line responsibilities since their jobs in one way or another are directly related to the sales operations of the store. **Staff managers,** by contrast, use special technical expertise to advise and support the efforts of line workers. In a department store, the director of human resources and the chief financial officer would have staff responsibilities.

In business, **functional managers** have responsibility for a single area of activity, such as finance, marketing, production, personnel, accounting, or sales. **General managers** are responsible for more complex units that include many functional areas. An example is a plant manager who oversees many separate functions, including purchasing, manufacturing, warehousing, sales, personnel, and accounting. It is common for managers working in public or nonprofit organizations to be called **administrators.** Examples include hospital administrator, public administrator, city administrator, and human-service administrator.

- **Team leaders or supervisors** report to middle managers and directly supervise nonmanagerial workers.

- **Line managers** directly contribute to the production of the organization's basic goods or services.

- **Staff managers** use special technical expertise to advise and support line workers.

- **Functional managers** are responsible for one area of activity, such as finance, marketing, production, personnel, accounting, or sales.

- **General managers** are responsible for complex organizational units that include many areas of functional activity.

- An **administrator** is a manager who works in a public or nonprofit organization.

ACCOUNTABILITY AND MANAGERIAL PERFORMANCE

Managers everywhere face a common problem. Regardless of the specific work setting in question, every manager must set the conditions through which individuals and groups contribute to organizational productivity. Furthermore, they must do so while being held "accountable" for results achieved. Formally defined, **accountability** is the requirement of one person to answer back to higher

- **Accountability** is the requirement to show performance results to a supervisor.

authority and show results achieved for assigned duties. Every manager's daily challenge is to fulfill this *performance accountability* for results achieved by a team or work unit while depending on the accomplishments of the members to make this performance possible.

But the concept of performance accountability alone does not tell the whole story. Effective managers fulfill it while utilizing organizational resources in ways that result in *both* high performance outcomes *and* high levels of satisfaction for the workers. This dual concern for performance and satisfaction is a central theme in the new workplace.

Quality of Work Life

● **Quality of work life (QWL)** is the overall quality of human experiences in the workplace.

With respect to satisfaction, the term **quality of work life (QWL)** is frequently used as an indicator of the overall quality of human experiences in the workplace. The QWL concept expresses a true respect for people at work — an important theme that will be addressed in many ways throughout this book. Practically speaking, a high quality of work life is one that offers the individual such things as fair pay, safe working conditions, opportunities to learn and use new skills, room to grow and progress in a career, protection of individual rights, and pride in the work itself and in the organization. Part of any manager's accountability is to achieve high-performance outcomes while maintaining the quality of work life. Simply put, in the new workplace productivity and a high-quality work life can and should go hand in hand.

Valuing Diversity

● **Workforce diversity** describes demographic differences (age, gender, race and ethnicity, and able-bodiedness) among members of the workforce.

Closely associated with the QWL concept is another aspect of managerial accountability, one involving **workforce diversity.** This term describes demographic differences among members of the workforce, principally differences in age, gender, race, national origin, and physical characteristics. Today's increasingly diverse workforce represents both a challenge in terms of required employer support and a great opportunity with respect to potential performance gains.

Managers are supposed to value diversity and help everyone work to their full potential. But what does this really mean? According to one consultant, it has to mean more than simply "white males doing good deeds for minorities and women"; it should mean "enabling every member of your workforce to perform to his or her potential."[15] A female vice president at Avon poses the challenge of managing diversity this way: "consciously creating an environment where *everyone* has an equal shot at contributing, participating, and most of all advancing."[16]

● **Prejudice** is the display of negative, irrational attitudes toward members of minority groups.

● **Discrimination** disadvantages minorities by denying them the full benefits of organizational membership.

● The **glass ceiling effect** is an invisible barrier that limits the advancement of women and minorities.

Although easy to say, meeting one's accountability to truly value diversity may not be easy to accomplish — especially for those used to more homogeneous groups and more traditional work settings. "Cultural bias" is still a limiting factor in too many places.[17] It can exist as **prejudice** involving negative, irrational attitudes toward members of minority groups. It can also take the form of **discrimination** that disadvantages minorities by denying them the full benefits of organizational membership. And it can result in what some call the **glass ceiling effect** — the existence of an invisible barrier that prevents women and minority workers from rising above a certain level of organizational responsibility.[18]

CHANGING NATURE OF MANAGERIAL WORK

Among the many changes affecting managerial work today, the concept of the "upside-down pyramid" is one of the most symbolic. As described in *Figure 1.3*, this view offers a new way of looking at organizations and the people in them.

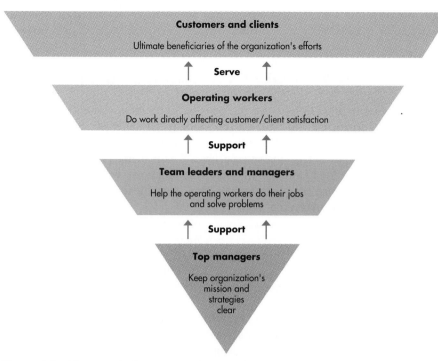

Figure 1.3 The "upside-down-pyramid" view of organizations.

The operating workers are at the top of the pyramid; they are supported in their work efforts by managers located at the bottom. These managers aren't just or-der-givers, they are there to help other people serve customer needs. The impli-cations of *Figure 1.3* are dramatic for day-to-day work in all settings. From this perspective, each individual is a value-added worker—someone who must do something that creates eventual value for the organization's customers or clients. The whole organization is devoted to serving the customer, and this is made pos-sible with the support of managers.

Many trends and emerging approaches to organizations, such as the upside-down pyramid, require new thinking from the people who staff them. We are entering a time when the best managers are known more for "helping" and "sup-porting" than for "directing" and "order-giving." Even in this age of high technol-ogy and "smart" machines, the human resource is indispensable. Worker involve-ment and empowerment are critical building blocks of organizational success. Full human resource utilization increasingly means changing the way work gets done in organizations by pushing decision-making authority to the point where the best information exists—with the operating workers. Jobs in the new work-place are less clearly defined, there is more emphasis on teamwork, and people move from project to project as their skills and expertise are applicable.[19] In-creasingly, even the title of "manager" is being replaced in the organization charts by "coordinator," "coach," or "team leader."

THE MANAGEMENT PROCESS

If productivity in the form of performance effectiveness and performance effi-ciency is a measure of organizational success, "management" is what managers do to achieve it. Success in management requires a capacity to recognize prob-lems and opportunities in daily events, make good decisions, and take appropriate action. This is a process of mobilizing resources to accomplish important tasks.

FUNCTIONS OF MANAGEMENT

The management process involves the four basic functions depicted in *Figure 1.4:* planning, organizing, leading, and controlling. All managers are responsible for the four functions, although research suggests that the relative emphasis on each can vary somewhat by managerial level.[20] Top managers may spend relatively more time on the planning and organizing functions, while first-level supervisors may spend more time on control. Time spent leading appears relatively consistent across all management levels.

Planning

● **Planning** is the process of setting objectives and determining what should be done to accomplish them.

Planning is the process of setting performance objectives and determining what actions should be taken to accomplish them. Through planning, a manager identifies desired work results and identifies the means to achieve them. Take, for example, an Ernst & Young initiative to better meet the needs of its female professionals.[21] Top management grew concerned about the firm's retention rates and a critical report by Catalyst, a research group focusing on corporate women. Chairman Philip A. Laskaway responded by setting a planning objective to reduce turnover rates that were running some 22 percent per year and costing the firm $150,000 per job to hire and train new staff.

Organizing

● **Organizing** is the process of assigning tasks, allocating resources, and arranging activities to implement plans.

Organizing is the process of assigning tasks, allocating resources, and arranging the coordinated activities of individuals and groups to implement plans. Through organizing, managers turn plans into actions by defining jobs, assigning personnel, and supporting them with technology and other resources. Continuing with the Ernst & Young example, Laskaway created a new Office of Retention for the company and hired Deborah K. Holmes as director to head it. As problems were identified in various locations, Holmes convened special task forces to tackle them and recommend location-specific solutions.

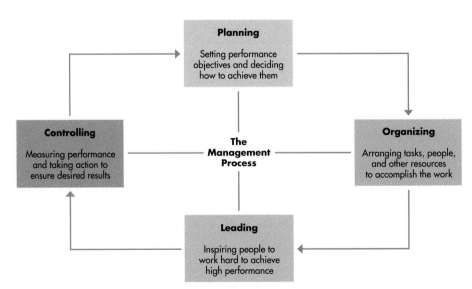

Figure 1.4   Four functions of management.

Leading

Leading is the process of arousing people's enthusiasm to work hard and direct their efforts to fulfill plans and accomplish objectives. Through leading, managers build commitments, encourage activities that support goals, and influence others to do their best work in the organization's behalf. At Ernst & Young, Holmes identified a core issue — work at the firm was extremely intense and women often felt strain because their spouses also worked. She became a champion for improved work-life balance and pursued it through the special task forces. Although she admits that "there's no silver bullet" in the form of a universal solution, new initiatives included "call-free holidays" where professionals do not check voice mail or Email on weekends and holidays and "travel sanity" that limits staffers' travel to four days a week so they can get home for weekends.

- **Leading** is the process of arousing enthusiasm and directing efforts toward organizational goals.

Controlling

Controlling is the process of measuring work performance, comparing results to objectives, and taking corrective action as needed. Through controlling, managers maintain active contact with people in the course of their work, gather and interpret reports on performance, and use this information to plan constructive action and change. At Ernst & Young, Chairman Laskaway and Director Holmes knew what the retention rates were when they started this program, and they have been able to note improvements as the program's work progresses. In one location the retention rates improved from 70 percent to 81 percent in just two years. Although the results vary from place to place, Holmes believes that small positive steps will lead to lasting and significant change. Under the new Office of Retention, the goal of improved work-life balance will continue to be pursued, and retention rates will be used as indicators of performance.

- **Controlling** is the process of measuring performance and taking action to ensure desired results.

MANAGERIAL ACTIVITIES AND ROLES

Although the management process may seem straightforward, things are more complicated than they appear at first glance. In his classic book, *The Nature of Managerial Work,* Henry Mintzberg offers this observation on the daily activities of corporate chief executives:

> There was no break in the pace of activity during office hours. The mail, . . . telephone calls, . . . and meetings . . . accounted for almost every minute from the moment these executives entered their offices in the morning until they departed in the evenings.[22]

Today we would have to add ever-present Email to Mintzberg's list of executive preoccupations.[23] Mintzberg is also careful to note that the manager's day is unforgiving in intensity and pace. The managers he observed had little free time because unexpected problems and continuing requests for meetings consumed almost all the time that became available. And importantly, he points out that the responsibility of executive work was all-encompassing in the continual pressure it placed on improving performance results. Says Mintzberg,

> The manager can never be free to forget the job, and never has the pleasure of knowing, even temporarily, that there is nothing else to do. . . . Managers always carry the nagging suspicion that they might be able to contribute just a little bit more. Hence they assume an unrelenting pace in their work.[24]

In trying to systematically describe the nature of managerial work and the demands it places on those who do it, Mintzberg offers the set of 10 roles depicted

Interpersonal roles	Informational roles	Decisional roles
How a manager interacts with other people • Figurehead • Leader • Liaison	How a manager exchanges and processes information • Monitor • Disseminator • Spokesperson	How a manager uses information in decision making • Entrepreneur • Disturbance handler • Resource allocator • Negotiator

Figure 1.5   Ten managerial roles.

in *Figure 1.5*. The roles managers must be prepared to perform fall into three categories.[25] A manager's *interpersonal roles* involve interactions with persons inside and outside the work unit. The *informational roles* involve the giving, receiving, and analyzing of information. The *decisional roles* involve using information to make decisions to solve problems or address opportunities.

Clearly, managerial work is busy, demanding, and stressful not just for chief executives but for managers at all levels of responsibility in any work setting. A summary of research on the nature of managerial work offers this important reminder:

→ The realities of managerial work

- Managers work long hours.
- Managers work at an intense pace.
- Managers work at fragmented and varied tasks.
- Managers work with many communication media.
- Managers work largely through interpersonal relationships.[26]

MANAGERIAL AGENDAS AND NETWORKS

> On his way to a meeting, a GM bumped into a staff member who did not report to him. Using this opportunity, in a two-minute conversation he: (a) asked two questions and received the information he needed; (b) reinforced their good relationship by sincerely complimenting the staff member on something he had recently done; and (c) got the staff member to agree to do something that the GM needed done.[27]

The description in this quotation provides a glimpse of an effective general manager (or GM) in action. It portrays two activities that the author, John Kotter, considers critical to a general manager's success in mastering daily challenges—agenda setting and networking. Through *agenda setting*, good managers develop action priorities for their jobs that include goals and plans that span long and short time frames. These agendas are usually incomplete and loosely connected in the beginning but become more specific as the manager utilizes information that is continually gleaned from many different sources. The agendas are kept always in mind and are "played out" whenever an opportunity arises, as in the preceding quotation.

Good managers implement their agendas by working with a variety of people inside and outside the organization. In Kotter's example, the GM was getting things done through a staff member who did not report directly to him. This is made possible by *networking*, the process of building and maintaining positive relationships with people whose help may be needed to implement one's work agendas. Since networks are indispensable to managerial success in today's complex work environments, excellent managers devote much time and effort to network development.

● **Solectron Corporation**
http://www.solectron.com

When Solectron Corporation surveyed its 3,200 employees, the company identified workers from 30 nationalities, speaking 40 native languages and dialects. To help them better understand each other and work together more productively, a cultural awareness program was started to help employees be more open in expressing opinions.

MANAGERIAL SKILLS AND COMPETENCIES

A **skill** is an ability to translate knowledge into action that results in desired performance. Obviously, many skills are required to master the challenging nature of managerial work as described in the previous section. The most important ones are those that allow managers to help others become more productive in their work. Robert L. Katz classified the essential skills of managers into three categories: technical, human, and conceptual.[28] Although all three skills are essential for managers, their relative importance tends to vary by level of managerial responsibility.

A **technical skill** is the ability to use a special proficiency or expertise to perform particular tasks. Accountants, engineers, market researchers, and computer scientists, for example, possess technical skills. These are initially acquired through formal education and are further developed by training and job experience. *Figure 1.6* shows that technical skills are most important at lower levels of management.

The ability to work well in cooperation with other persons is a **human skill.** It emerges in the workplace as a spirit of trust, enthusiasm, and genuine involvement in interpersonal relationships. A manager with good human skills will have a high degree of self-awareness and a capacity to understand or empathize with the feelings of others. Given the highly interpersonal nature of managerial work, such skills are critical for all managers. *Figure 1.6* shows them to be consistently important across the managerial levels.

All good managers ultimately have the ability to view situations broadly and to solve problems to the benefit of everyone concerned. This ability to think analytically is a **conceptual skill.** It involves the ability to break down problems into smaller parts, to see the relations between the parts, and to recognize the implications of any one problem for others. As managers assume ever-higher responsibilities in organizations, they must deal with more ambiguous problems having longer term consequences. *Figure 1.6* shows that conceptual skills gain in relative importance for top managers.

Business and management educators are increasingly interested in helping people acquire these skills and develop specific competencies that can help them achieve managerial success. A *managerial competency* is a skill or personal characteristic that contributes to high performance in a management job.[29] A number of these competencies have been implied in the previous discussion of the management process, including those related to planning, organizing, leading, and controlling. Competencies are also implicit in the demands of information-gathering, interpersonal, and decision-making roles. *Manager's Notepad 1.2* reviews some of the skills and personal characteristics that the AACSB, the American Assembly of Collegiate Schools of Business, is urging business schools to help their students develop.[30] Use this notepad as a checklist, noting specific personal

- A **skill** is the ability to translate knowledge into action that results in desired performance.

- A **technical skill** is the ability to use a special proficiency or expertise in one's work.

- A **human skill** is the ability to work well in cooperation with other people.

- A **conceptual skill** is the ability to think analytically and solve complex problems.

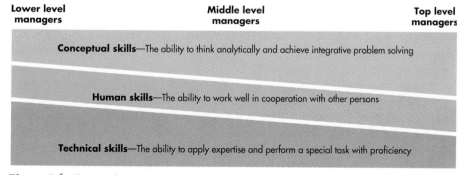

Figure 1.6 Essential managerial skills.

> ### M a n a g e r ' s   N o t e p a d   1 . 2
>
> **Personal Competencies for Managerial Success**
>
> - *Leadership:* Ability to influence others to perform tasks.
> - *Self-objectivity:* Ability to evaluate oneself realistically.
> - *Analytic thinking:* Ability to interpret and explain patterns in information.
> - *Behavioral flexibility:* Ability to modify personal behavior to reach a goal.
> - *Oral communication:* Ability to express ideas clearly in oral presentations.
> - *Written communication:* Ability to express one's ideas clearly in writing.
> - *Personal impact:* Ability to create a good impression and instill confidence.
> - *Resistance to stress:* Ability to perform under stressful conditions.
> - *Tolerance for uncertainty:* Ability to perform in ambiguous situations.

strengths and weaknesses; it offers a good starting point for considering your readiness to pursue a 21st-century career.

THE CHALLENGES AHEAD: WORKING IN THE 21ST CENTURY

British educator and consultant Charles Handy calls today's turbulent times "the age of unreason."[31] Above all, it is an era of high performance expectations. Change is a way of life, and it demands new organizational and individual responses. And along with all this, the quest for high performance is relentless. Everywhere *new* workers are expected to use *new* ways to achieve high productivity under *new* and dynamic conditions. They are expected to become involved, participate fully, demonstrate creativity, and find self-fulfillment in their work. They are expected to be team players who understand the needs and goals of the total organization and who use new technologies to their full advantage.

These conditions are among the many reasons that *Management 6/E* and an introductory course in management are so relevant to your studies. The facts are clear, but they deserve to be pointed out again and again. Those who want to succeed in the 21st-century workplace must reach for the heights of personal competency and accomplishment. They must be self-starters and leaders who find continuing ways to add value to employers even as the environment continues to change. They must be willing, as J&J CEO Larson said, to "do the right things" everyday. Importantly, they must be willing to continuously learn from their experiences so they will be as capable in the future as they are in the present.

Just what are the challenges ahead?

A GLOBAL ECONOMY

Japanese management consultant Kenichi Ohmae suggests that the national boundaries of world business have largely disappeared.[32] At the very least we can say that they are fast disappearing. Who can state with confidence where their favorite athletic shoes or the parts for their personal computer were manufactured? More and more products are designed in one country while their component parts are made in others and the assembly of the final product takes place in still another. Honda's top managers, for example, have no real need for the word *overseas* in everyday business vocabulary. The firm operates as a "global business" that views itself as equidistant from all customers, wherever in the world they may be located.

Government leaders in our global economy worry about the competitiveness of nations just as corporate leaders worry about business competitiveness.[33] The world is increasingly arranged in regional economic blocs, with Asia, North and Latin America, and Europe as the key anchors. But the reach of the global economy and world events keep changing even that. Africa is fast emerging to claim its economic potential, with the advent of nonracial democracy in South Africa attracting more attention and investors to the continent as a whole.

China is a compelling economic power in the Pacific Rim, a region once dominated by Japan. And even with the effects of the Asian economic crisis still being settled, countries like South Korea, Taiwan, Singapore, Malaysia, and Thailand are now well recognized as global players of economic significance. The reach of the already important European Union (EU) is broadening, and it will become larger as the economies of the new republics of Central Europe gain strength. NAFTA, the North American Free Trade Agreement between Canada, the United States, and Mexico, seems to be working, and economic collaboration within Latin America is growing more generally.

 "Going global" as a business enterprise often means adapting products to fit local needs around the world. When Whirlpool Corporation set out to develop a "world washer," market research convinced the product development team that uniformity wouldn't work. Differences between countries in customs, costs, and available materials made it impractical. The team therefore chose a *flexible design* for a lightweight, low-cost washer that could be easily modified to suit local conditions and preferences. It is manufactured in the country where it is to be sold by companies that are Whirlpool affiliates or joint venture partners.[34]

ETHICS AND SOCIAL RESPONSIBILITY

When a well-known business executive goes to jail for some misdeed, we notice; when a major environmental catastrophe occurs because of a business misdeed, we notice. Increasingly, too, we notice the "moral" aspects of everyday managerial and business behavior.[35] Society is becoming strict in its expectation that social institutions conduct their affairs according to high moral standards.

The pressure for ethical and socially responsible conduct is on, and organizations and their managers are responding. You may remember buying compact discs in plastic "longbox" packaging used originally to protect stores against shoplifters. But the bulky containers were not biodegradable. When consumers and environmental groups complained, music companies changed to package designs that satisfied both retailers and their environmentally concerned customers. In addition to such concerns for the natural environment, ethical and social responsibility issues extend into all aspects of organizations, the behavior of their employees, and the changing needs of an increasingly global economy. Consider, for example, this statement from the credo of Johnson & Johnson:[36]

> We are responsible to the communities in which we live and work and to the world community as well. We must be good citizens — support good works and charities and bear our fair share of taxes. We must encourage civic improvements and better health and education. We must maintain in good order the property we are privileged to use, protecting the environment and natural resources.

The Hudson Institute is a public policy research organization based in Indianapolis, Indiana. Members of its Workforce 2020 team view their report as a "wake-up call for American workers, corporations, educators, parents, and government officials."

WORKFORCE DIVERSITY

When published in 1987 by the Hudson Institute, *Workforce 2000: Work and Workers for the 21st Century* created an immediate stir in business circles, among government policymakers, and in the public eye.[37] It called attention to demographic trends that have already made their presence felt in the American workplace: the slow growth of the workforce, fewer younger workers entering the labor pool, the higher average age of the workforce, more women entering the workforce, and the increase in the proportions of minorities and immigrants in the workforce.

A recent report from the Hudson Institute, *Workforce 2020,* further examines diversity themes and trends in the context of new technological and global challenges of the 21st century.[38] Billed by coeditor Carol D'Amico as "a wake-up call for American workers, corporations, educators, parents, and government officials," the book predicts that we will have to learn how to deal with the tight labor pool and a diverse and aging workforce. It warns about a continuing loss of low-skill high-wage jobs and a shortage of workers for high-skill jobs.[39]

The management and social policy implications of these trends are complex and challenging. Many organizations are rapidly embracing the efficiencies of computers and capital-intensive technologies. As technological change accelerates, the demand for workers with the skills to utilize technology to its full advantage also increases. Low-skill workers displaced from declining manufacturing industries will find it increasingly difficult to find new jobs offering adequate pay. The fastest-growing source of future jobs in the United States will be in the service industries and in professional, technical, and sales fields.

The recommendations of *Workforce 2020* call for major changes in public education systems, employer human resource systems, and government policies to address such challenges.[40] Valuing workforce diversity lies at the heart of the challenge. As Bank Boston CEO Charles Gifford says, "Diversity is a strategic opportunity. If we understand how the work force is changing and its impact on the labor pool, new markets, and a growing global economy, we will be better able to capitalize on opportunities."[41]

EMPLOYMENT VALUES AND HUMAN RIGHTS

The new century brings with it new social values and expectations for the protection of human rights in all aspects of society, including employment. Organizations and their members must deal with many new pressures in working relationships as the trends predicted in *Workforce 2020* evolve.[42] Among these many pressures, equal employment opportunity, equity of compensation and benefits, participation and employee involvement, privacy and due process, freedom from sexual harassment, job security, and occupational health and safety are easily found in the daily news.

With growing workforce diversity comes continuing pressures for equal employment opportunities. Even though progress continues to be made, lingering inequalities remain. A study by the research organization Catalyst, for example, shows the following pay differences in the American workplace: minority male managers earn 73 cents for each dollar earned by white male managers, while minority women earned 57 cents and white women earned 59 cents.[43] Catalyst also reports that women held just over 10 percent of corporate officer appointments at 500 large companies.[44] African-American men hold a disproportionately low percentage of technical and professional jobs, even though their unemployment rates can be double those of whites. A Catalyst survey also found 66 percent of minority women in management reporting dissatisfaction with their career advancement opportunities; some 25 percent indicate they plan to leave their companies. Interestingly, the number of African-American-owned businesses is rising faster than U.S. business ownership overall. Even as women and minorities make new inroads to the executive suites, they still hold only a small percentage of senior management jobs.[45] Equity of earnings remains a potent issue in many settings, especially as it relates to the "comparable worth" of work performed by men and women.

Employees are demanding more self-determination on the job — they want to be part of everyday decisions on how and when to do their jobs, and they expect real opportunities to participate in job-related decisions. Concerns abound for employee rights to privacy, due process, protection against job discrimination, and freedom from sexual harassment. Controversies over computerized work monitoring and employee testing for substance abuse, AIDS, and honesty also appear in the news. And job security is a concern at a time when many organizations are cutting back their full-time workers and hiring more part-time or "contingency" workers. "We want more full-time jobs and less part-time jobs" is a common cry of labor unions today.

Reebok was one of only four companies identified as having an office staff of more than 40 percent women in a national survey by the reseach group Catalyst. On the average nationwide, women officers are found mostly in staff roles. They hold just 5.3 percent of top-line jobs.

INFORMATION AND TECHNOLOGICAL CHANGE

Who hasn't been affected by the Internet and the World Wide Web? We live in the new and still exploding world of the information superhighway. Just take a look at the pages of this book — the "URLs" (universal resource locators) that accompany many of the company profiles throughout the text are Internet resources that will enrich your study and help you with assignments. Just join in and follow the links . . . the paths are endless, ever changing, and exciting to explore. If you aren't willing to join in and become a participant, you'll be left behind. It's not an option anymore; it's an entry requirement in the new workplace.

"With computers and high technology," someone once said, "work will never be the same." It's already changed. Notebook computers, supercomputers, computer-assisted design (CAD) and production methods, expert systems, group-decision software, and related developments are all part of our information-intensive workplace and work lives. For better or worse, we now live in a world increasingly dominated by bar codes, automatic tellers, computerized telemarketing campaigns, electronic mail, Internet resources, electronic commerce, and the like.

At one level, new technology is a business resource. It helped Boston Chicken executives, for example, establish their company on the national and international scenes. Linked together through computer networking, senior executives and store managers held team-planning and problem-solving meetings, analyzed weekly performance, and even adjusted store menus in response to customer feedback.[46] When it comes to communication, within the many parts of a business or just person to person, geographical distances hardly matter anymore. Computer networking can bring together almost anyone from anywhere in the world at the mere touch of a keyboard.

Futurist Alvin Toffler makes all this an issue of broad social concern. He considers the speed of business transactions and decision making to be a major power source that should be harnessed by individuals, organizations, and countries. In his book *Powershift* he describes a world complicated by power differences based on access to information technology that have substantial implications for economic development.[47] Toffler states, "the new system for making wealth consists of an expanding, global network of markets, banks, production centers, and laboratories in instant communication with one another, constantly exchanging huge and ever increasing flows of data, information, and knowledge."[48] In a world where change is occurring at an accelerating rate, the impact of emerging information and computer technology must be appreciated. This is

● Ritz-Carlton Hotels
http://www.ritzcarlton.com

A willingness to tackle and solve problems is one of the skills sought by employers today. At Ritz-Carlton Hotels, employees are expected to do whatever is necessary for the well-being of guests. When a front-desk worker gets a complaint about something being broken in a guest room, they are not only expected to call engineering to get it fixed, they follow up with the guest to make sure the repairs were made satisfactorily.

Visit our Career Advancement Portfolio website at www.wiley.com/college/scherman6e

the new age of the "knowledge worker" — someone whose mind is a critical asset to employers. Computer literacy is a knowledge component that must be mastered as a foundation for career success.

CAREERS AND CAREER PORTFOLIOS

The nature of work has changed in more than its technological foundations. British scholar Charles Handy uses the shamrock to describe the career implications of changing employment patterns by organizations. The organizational shamrock has three leaves, and each leaf has a different career implication. In one leaf are the core workers.[49] These *full-time employees* pursue career paths with a traditional character. With success and the maintenance of critical skills, core employees can advance within the organization and may remain employed for a long time. In the second leaf of the shamrock organization are *contract workers.* They perform specific tasks as needed by the organization and are compensated on a contract or fee-for-services basis rather than by a continuing wage or salary. Contract workers sell a skill or service to employers; they will likely service many different employers over time. In the third leaf are the *part-time workers* who are hired only as needed and for only the number of hours needed. Employers expand and reduce their part-time staffs as business needs rise and fall. Part-time work can be a training ground for full-time work in the first leaf, when openings are available.

Today's college graduates must be prepared to prosper in any of the shamrock's three leaves. The typical career of the 21st century won't be uniformly full-time and limited to a single large employer. It is more likely to unfold opportunistically and involve several employment options over time. Skills must be portable and of value to more than one possible employer; these skills must be carefully maintained and upgraded over time. One career consultant describes this scenario with the analogy of a surfer: "You're always moving. You can expect to fall into the water any number of times, and you have to get back up to catch the next wave."[50]

Handy's advice is to maintain a "portfolio of skills" that are always up-to-date and valuable to potential employers. To help prepare you to do just that, the *Career Readiness Workbook* built into this book includes a *Career Advancement Portfolio* that directly responds to Handy's challenge. By following the instructions and templates provided you can build either a paper or electronic portfolio that includes not only a professional resume but also samples of your skills and competencies as demonstrated by actual course work. A well constructed student portfolio can be an important source of advantage in competitive markets for both internships and jobs. Consider what a *Career Advancement Portfolio* can do for you!

While a student at Ohio University, Ronald Larimer has developed a very professional *Career Advancement Portfolio.* It includes his resume documenting leadership activities in student affairs, student work providing computer support for an instructor and his summer work experience. The portfolio also gives examples of Ron's skills at computer programming, use of spreadsheet and data base software, writing skills in the form of a one-page executive memorandum and a research report, as well as a sample PowerPoint presentation. Using his electronic portfolio as the lead, Ron was able to obtain a summer internship between his junior and senior years and compete for his first choice of jobs after graduation.[51]

MANAGEMENT/6E: A FRAMEWORK FOR LEARNING

Management/6E has been designed to facilitate your learning about management, organizations, and the new workplace.

Part 1, Management Today, focuses on the new workplace, environment and competitive advantage, as well as information and decision making. These chapters introduce important developments and forces that impact the emergence of the new management in this age of global competition and high technology.

Part 2, Context, opens with a chapter devoted to the historical foundations of management. This is followed by chapters on the global economy, ethics, and social responsibility. With this background, the study of management can be pursued with a full understanding of the demands and complexities of modern management.

Part 3, Mission, addresses the purpose and goals of organizations and the action foundations for their accomplishment. The core issues are developed in respect to the management functions of planning and controlling. Consistent again with the pressures and demands of the day, this part emphasizes strategic management and entrepreneurship.

Part 4, Organization, focuses on the management function of organizing. The core issues involve structuring organizations for high performance, the alternative approaches to organizational design that are popular today, and the all-important need for human resource management.

Part 5, Leadership, pursues the great opportunities of leadership in organizations. The management function of leading is explored with an emphasis on understanding the personal skills and competencies requisite to leadership success. Topics examined include motivation, individual performance, communication, teamwork and group performance, and the processes of organizational change.

Finally, a unique and exciting *Career Readiness Workbook* is provided to allow you opportunities to extend your learning in directions relevant to a long and successful career. The workbook offers a template for you to build the *Career Advancement Portfolio* referenced in the prior section. It also contains Cases linked to chapters, Integrative Learning Activities to help consolidate your learning, Exercises in Teamwork to provide essential experience with this aspect of the new workplace, Managerial Skills Assessments to help you better understand personal capabilities and developmental needs, and Research and Presentation Projects to practice your research, writing, and presentation skills.

In a word, *learning* is what *Management/6E* is all about. Read, enjoy, and benefit with great career success!

CHAPTER REVIEW

This section should be used as an end-of-chapter "study guide." The *Summary* helps to put the chapter's content into overall perspective. The list of *Key Terms* allows you to double-check your familiarity with basic concepts and definitions. *Self-Test 1* gives you the opportunity to test your basic comprehension of chapter content using sample test questions.

SUMMARY

What are organizations like in the new workplace?

- Organizations are collections of people working together to achieve a common purpose.

- As open systems, organizations interact with their environments in the process of transforming resource inputs into product outputs.

- Productivity is a measure of the quantity and quality of work performance, with resource utilization taken into account.

- Organizations should achieve both performance effectiveness, in terms of goal accomplishment, and performance efficiency, in terms of resource utilization.

- The best organizations today include a focus on total quality management among their productivity and performance objectives.

- In today's dynamic environment, organizations are adopting new forms and practices to meet the challenges of new technology, intense competition, and demanding customers.

Who are managers and what do they do?

- Managers facilitate work accomplishments by people in organizations.

- Top managers concentrate on long-term concerns; middle managers help coordinate activities across the organization; team leaders and supervisors focus on group or work-unit objectives.

- Functional managers work in one business area, such as marketing or finance; general managers are responsible for multiple functions; administrators are managers in nonprofit organizations.

- The manager's challenge is to fulfill a performance accountability while being dependent upon team members or subordinates to do the required work.

- Managers must respect the quality of work life and value diversity in supporting the work efforts and experiences of others.

- The focus of managerial work is increasingly on "coaching" and "supporting" others rather than simply "directing" and "order-giving."

What is the management process?

- The management process consists of the four functions of planning, organizing, leading, and controlling.

- Managerial work is intense and stressful and places a great emphasis on the ability to perform well in interpersonal, informational, and decision-making roles.

- Effective managers create and maintain interpersonal networks that facilitate the accomplishment of task agendas.

- Managers must develop and maintain essential technical, human, and conceptual skills to succeed in a dynamic environment.

What are the challenges ahead?

- Today's turbulent environment challenges managers and organizations in complex and demanding ways.

- Competition and the global economy are changing business, industry, and national economic strategies.

- Strong values demand ethical behavior and social responsibility within and by organizations.

- Demographics are making the workforce increasingly diverse with respect to differences among people in gender, age, race and ethnicity, and able-bodiedness.

- Pressures on employment relationships call for the protection of individual rights to privacy, due process, and freedom from sexual harassment, among other rights.

- Information and technological change are modifying organizations as computers and related information technologies exert their influence on the workplace.

- Careers today require "portfolios" of skills that are continually developed and well communicated to potential employers.

KEY TERMS

Accountability (p. 9)

Administrators (p. 9)

Conceptual skill (p. 15)

Controlling (p. 13)

Discrimination (p. 10)

Functional managers (p. 9)

General managers (p. 9)

Glass ceiling effect (p. 10)

Human resources (p. 8)

Human skill (p. 15)

Leading (p. 13)

Line managers (p. 9)

Management (p. 8)

Manager (p. 7)

Middle managers (p. 8)

Open system (p. 5)

Organization (p. 5)

Organizing (p. 12)

Performance effectiveness (p. 6)

Performance efficiency (p. 6)

Planning (p. 12)

Prejudice (p. 10)

Productivity (p. 6)

Quality of work life (QWL) (p. 10)

Skill (p. 15)

Staff managers (p. 9)

Supervisor (p. 9)

Team leader (p. 9)

Technical skill (p. 15)

Top managers (p. 8)

Total quality management (TQM) (p. 7)

Workforce diversity (p. 10)

SELF-TEST 1

Take this test much as you would in a normal classroom situation. It is a good way to check your basic comprehension of chapter material. Answers may be found at the end of the book.

MULTIPLE-CHOICE QUESTIONS:

1. The process of management involves the functions of planning, _____, leading, and controlling. (a) accounting (b) creating (c) innovating (d) organizing

2. An effective manager achieves both high performance outcomes and high _____ among people doing the required work. (a) turnover (b) effectiveness (c) satisfaction (d) stress

3. Performance efficiency is a measure of the _____ associated with task accomplishment. (a) resource cost (b) goal specificity (c) product quality (d) product quantity

4. The requirement that a manager answer to his or her boss for results achieved by the manager's work group is called _____. (a) dependency (b) accountability (c) authority (d) empowerment

5. Productivity is a measure of the quantity and _____ of work produced, with resource utilization taken into account. (a) quality (b) cost (c) timeliness (d) duration

6. _____ managers in organizations should pay special attention to the environment, looking for problems and opportunities, and finding ways to deal with them. (a) Top (b) Middle (c) Lower (d) First-line

7. The accounting manager for a local newspaper would be considered a _____ manager, whereas the production manager would be considered a _____ manager. (a) general, functional (b) middle, top (c) staff, line (d) senior, junior

8. When a supervisor clarifies desired work targets and deadlines for her work team, she is fulfilling the management function of _____. (a) planning (b) delegating (c) controlling (d) supervising

9. The process of building and maintaining good working relationships with others who may help implement a manager's agendas is called _____. (a) interaction (b) networking (c) politicking (d) entrepreneurship

10. Top managers tend to rely more on their _____ skills than do first-line managers. (a) human (b) conceptual (c) decision making (d) technical

TRUE-FALSE QUESTIONS:

11. Managers usually work at a slow and leisurely pace. T F

12. Continuous improvement is important in total quality management. T F

13. A clear organizational purpose can be a source of performance advantage. T F

14. "Team leader" is an example of a first-line manager. T F

15. Prejudice involves negative attitudes toward minority groups. T F

16. Managers in nonprofit organizations may be called administrators. T F

17. The new workplace is demanding more managerial attention to "directing" and "order giving." T F

18. Human skills are not important for middle managers. T F

19. Managers are at the top of the organization viewed as an upside-down pyramid. T F

20. Demographic trends show an increasing average age in the American workforce. T F

SHORT-RESPONSE QUESTIONS:

21. Explain how "accountability" operates in the relationships between (a) a manager and her subordinates and (b) the same manager and her boss.

22. Explain how the "glass ceiling effect" may work to the disadvantage of African-American middle managers in a large corporation.

23. What does Kenichi Ohmae mean when he uses the term *borderless world?*

24. List and explain the importance of three pressures in the areas of employment values and human rights that managers must be prepared to face in the future.

APPLICATION QUESTION:

25. You have just been hired as the new supervisor of an audit team for a national accounting firm. With 8 years of experience, you feel technically well prepared for the assignment. However, this is your first formal appointment as a "manager." Things are complicated at the moment since the team should have 12 members, but there are 5 vacancies to be filled. Your boss wants the new team to be as "diverse" as possible. How will this situation challenge you to use and develop managerial skills and related competencies so that you can successfully manage diversity on the audit team?

Environment and Competitive Advantage

Planning Ahead—Chapter 2 Study Questions

- What is the environment of organizations?
- What is a customer-driven organization?
- What is the quality commitment in operations?
- Why is organizational culture important?
- What are current directions in organizational cultures?

Make Technology Work for You

Purchasing a pair of shoes at one of Custom Foot's east-coast stores is a high tech experience. Using the latest in computer support and mass customization technology, the firm is able to offer its customers shoes ready made to individual sizes and tastes. The shoes arrive within three weeks of order at a price competitive with premium brands sold off the shelf in other stores. An electronic scanner measures the customer's foot size, leather is chosen from samples, and the order is transmitted by computer to factories in Italy and the United States for manufacturing. There is no inventory kept in the stores, other than display model shoes. CEO Jim Metscher says his store can serve up to 10,000 variations in women's shoes and 7,800 in men's. Currently backed by venture capital, Custom Foot is projecting expansion to 20 stores soon and will add custom-made handbags to its product line. CEO Metscher is also considering mass customization to offer ready-made gloves.[1]

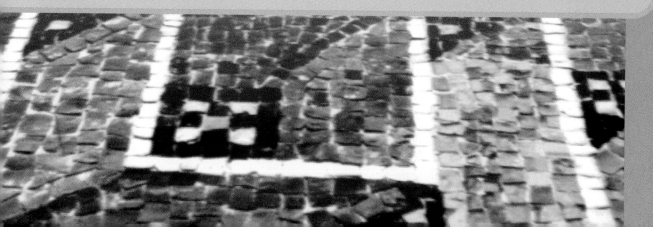

Organizations and managers today are learning to operate and compete in a world that places a premium on information, technology utilization, quality, customer service and speed. This chapter introduces the external environment and the internal culture of organizations as two important considerations in the quest for success in demanding and dynamic times. Custom Foot offers an interesting example of the types of opportunities and approaches available. But the forward-thinking CEO of this small entrepreneurial business isn't alone in the pursuit of innovation and new practices. And importantly, he isn't alone in recognizing that among the many forces in today's environment, information technology is changing the workplace in dramatic and beneficial ways. IBM's CEO Louis V. Gerstner, Jr., puts the challenge this way: "We believe very strongly that the age-old levers of competition — labor, capital, and land, are being supplemented by knowledge, and that most successful companies in the future will be those that learn how to exploit knowledge — knowledge about customer behavior, markets, economies, technology — faster than their competitors."[2]

EXTERNAL ENVIRONMENTS OF ORGANIZATIONS

Once a benchmark for science fiction writers, the dawning of the 21st century presents new demands on organizations and their managers. Success in the environment of tomorrow will be achieved in a world of intense competition, continued globalization of markets and business activities, and even more rapid technological change. Jim Metscher at Custom Foot and Louis Gerstner at IBM seem to be leading their organizations toward a high performance edge, but no organization can hesitate or rest on past laurels in our uncertain world. Consider the problems of Apple Computer, Kmart, and General Motors, all once market leaders who have struggled in recent years to come to terms with competitive industries, demanding customers, and other implications of a changing society.

WHAT IS COMPETITIVE ADVANTAGE?

The open-systems view of organizations, introduced in Chapter 1, highlights the external environment as a supplier of resources and consumer of product outputs. The degree to which this environment, and the many elements and forces within it, is supportive of the organization will have a significant impact on its operations and performance outcomes. Good relationships with suppliers help ensure a smooth flow of needed resources. And, of course, satisfied customers help maintain demand for the goods and/or services produced.

Effective managers understand the environments of organizations, deal successfully with them, and remain alert to spotting changes that require adjustments in operations. Importantly, management attention in dealing with the complex and ever-changing environment is focused increasingly on the concept of **competitive advantage.**[3] This is the utilization of a *core competency* that clearly sets an organization apart from its competitors and gives it an advantage over them in the marketplace. An organization may achieve competitive advantage in many ways, including through products, pricing, customer service, cost efficiency, and quality, among other aspects of operating excellence. But regardless of how the advantage is achieved, the key result is the same — an ability to consistently do something of high value that one's competitors cannot replicate or do as well.

● **A competitive advantage** allows an organization to deal with market and environmental forces better than its competitiors.

This advice has been heard by John Sortino. He started the Vermont Teddy Bear Company by selling teddy bears from his car in Burlington. Since then the firm has grown into a substantial local employer and winner of the prestigious Heritage of New England Award. Past winners include L.L. Bean, Ben & Jerry's Homemade, Inc., and Samuel Adams Beer. Vermont Teddy Bear's products are backed with lifetime and no-questions-asked guarantees, and the Heritage award recognizes those who promote their products truthfully and operate with a commitment to exceptional quality. Sortino credits the award to the workers who fulfill the firm's commitments in their daily work. Says he: "It is everyone working together which creates a successful customer service program."[4]

Competitive advantage is especially important in the demanding global economy.[5] Nowhere in the world can managers rest on past successes and ignore what others are doing, at home or in other countries. Some years ago, at a time when American industry was first coming to grips with fierce competition from Japanese products, American quality pioneer J. M. Juran challenged an audience of Japanese executives with a prediction. He warned them against complacency, suggesting that America would bounce back in business competitiveness and that the words "Made in America" would once again symbolize world-class quality.[6] There seems little doubt today that Juran's prediction was accurate.

Managing organizations for competitive advantage in challenging environments may well be the critical theme of the early 21st century. Corporate leaders and senior executives in all organizations must understand that competitive advantage can only be achieved by continuously scanning the environment and then adapting operations based upon what is learned. The ability to do this begins with the answer to a basic question: What is in the external environment of organizations?

THE GENERAL ENVIRONMENT

The **general environment** consists of all the background conditions in the external environment of an organization. This portion of the environment forms a general context for managerial decision making. The major external environmental issues of our day include factors such as the following:

- *Economic conditions* — general state of the economy in terms of inflation, income levels, gross domestic product, unemployment, and related indicators of economic health.

- *Social-cultural conditions* — general state of prevailing social values on such matters as human rights and the natural environment, trends in education and related social institutions, as well as demographic patterns.

- *Legal-political conditions* — general state of the prevailing philosophy and objectives of the political party or parties running the government, as well as laws and government regulations.

- *Technological conditions* — general state of the development and availability of technology in the environment, including scientific advancements.

- *Natural environment conditions* — general state of nature and conditions of the natural or physical environment, including levels of public concern expressed through environmentalism.

• The **general environment** is comprised of cultural, economic, legal-political, and educational conditions.

What is in the general environment?

Differences in these and related general environment factors are especially noticeable when organizations operate internationally. External conditions vary significantly from one country and culture to the next. Managers of successful international operations understand these differences and help their organizations make the operating adjustments needed to perform within them. The pharmaceutical giant Merck, for example, derives half or more of its business from overseas operations. In a drive to further increase its market share, the firm has entered into cooperative agreements with European companies, conducted research with European partners, and worked with European governments on legal matters.

THE SPECIFIC ENVIRONMENT

● A **specific environment** is comprised of the actual organizations and persons with whom an organization interacts.

● **Stakeholders** are the persons, groups, and institutions directly affected by an organization's performance.

The **specific environment** consists of the actual organizations, groups, and persons with whom an organization must interact in order to survive and prosper. These are environmental elements of direct consequence to the organization as it operates on a day-to-day basis. The specific environment is often described in terms of **stakeholders**—the persons, groups, and institutions who are affected in one way or another by the organization's performance. *Figure 2.1* shows multiple stakeholders as they may exist in the external environment of a typical business firm.

Sometimes called the *task environment,* the specific environment and the stakeholders are distinct for each organization. They can also change over time according to the company's unique customer base, operating needs, and circumstances. Important stakeholders common to the specific environment of most organizations include:

→ What is in the specific environment?

- *Customers*—specific consumer or client groups, individuals, and organizations that purchase the organization's goods and/or use its services.

- *Suppliers*—specific providers of the human, information, and financial resources and raw materials needed by the organization to operate.

- *Competitors*—specific organizations that offer the same or similar goods and services to the same consumer or client groups.

- *Regulators*—specific government agencies and representatives, at the local, state, and national levels, that enforce laws and regulations affecting the organization's operations.

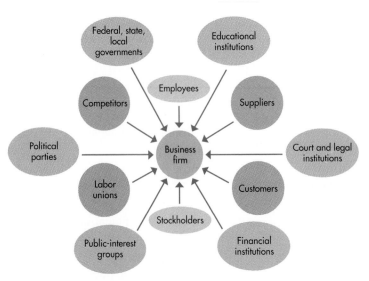

Figure 2.1   Multiple stakeholders in the environment of organizations.

ENVIRONMENTAL UNCERTAINTY

The fact is that many organizations today face great uncertainty in their external environments. In this sense, *environmental uncertainty* means that there is a lack of complete information regarding what developments will occur in the external environment. This makes it difficult to predict future states of affairs and to understand their potential implications for the organization. *Figure 2.2* describes environmental uncertainty along two dimensions: (1) complexity, or the number of different factors in the environment and (2) the rate of change in these factors.[7]

When the affairs of a global firm like the telecommunications giant World-Com are considered in respect to the figure, it is easily viewed as operating in an environment of high uncertainty. As a multinational firm it faces a great number of diverse environmental factors. Many of them, including the nature of the telecommunications industry and its core technologies, are also changing very rapidly. This situation contrasts, for example, with the one faced by your favorite local pizza parlor. Although it may face intense competition, the number of environmental factors to contend with is relatively small and their rates of change are low. It is to be expected that WorldCom executives will have a more challenging and difficult time of adapting to the forces in their environment than the owner of the pizza parlor. The management and organizational implications of uncertainties in the external environment are quite different in each case.

In general, the greater the environmental uncertainty the more attention that management in an organization must direct toward the external environment. It has to be continually studied and monitored to spot emerging trends so that information can be used for decision making. Also, the greater the environmental uncertainty the more need there is for flexibility and adaptability in organizational designs and work practices. Because of the inevitable limits on being able to successfully anticipate developments in uncertain environments, organizations must be able to respond quickly as new circumstances arise and good information becomes available. Throughout this book you will find many examples of how organizations are becoming more flexible in the attempt to better deal with the high amounts of environmental uncertainty that so often prevail in today's dynamic times. These challenges are especially in evidence when industries, such as telecommunications and airlines in the United States, are deregulated and must meet new competitive pressures. They are also in evidence among the world's economies, as firms that were previously state owned are privatized and forced to compete under open market conditions.

A dynamic environment means opportunity for the automobile racing industry. Racing entrepreneurs like O. Burton Smith of Speedway Motor Sports, NASCAR drivers like Jeff Gordon, and simply thousands of fans are turning the racing business into big business indeed. When the stock cars are running at Smith's $140 million Texas Motor Speedway, some 185,000 fans may be in attendance.

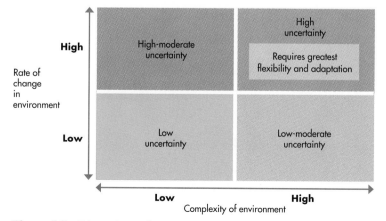

Figure 2.2   Dimensions of uncertainty in organizational environments.

CUSTOMER-DRIVEN ORGANIZATIONS

At Hewlett-Packard, employees work as both customers and suppliers. To someone assembling circuit boards, her supplier is the person making chips and her customer is the person who puts boards into finished components. They are expected to work together to make sure everyone has the quality materials needed to pass a quality product on to the next workstation.

Question: What's your job?
Answer: I run the cash register and sack groceries.
Question: But isn't it your job to serve the customer?
Answer: I guess, but it's not in my job description.[8]

This conversation illustrates what often becomes the missing link in the quest for total quality and competitive advantage: customer service. Contrast this conversation with the following report from a customer of the Vermont Teddy Bear Company, who called to report that her new mailorder teddy bear had a problem. The company responded promptly, she said, and arranged to have the bear picked up and replaced. She wrote the firm to say "thank you for the great service and courtesy you gave me."[9]

WHAT DO CUSTOMERS WANT?

Customers sit at the top when organizations are viewed as the upside-down pyramids described in Chapter 1. And without any doubt, customers put today's organizations to a very stiff test. They demand value-pricing for high-quality goods and services; anything less is unacceptable.

In our increasingly competitive economy, organizations that can't meet quality standards are suffering greatly. Some time ago, Intel Corporation faced a big crisis in customer confidence when a defect was found in its Pentium chip. At first top management of this highly regarded company balked at replacing the chips, suggesting that the defect wasn't really important. But customers were angry and unrelenting in their complaints. Eventually the customers won, as they should. Intel agreed to replace the chips without any questions asked. The company also learned two important lessons of successful businesses today: (1) always protect your reputation for quality products — it is hard to get and easy to lose, and (2) always treat your customers right — they, too, are hard to get and easy to lose.

Customer service can be an important source of competitive advantage. Just imagine the ramifications if every customer or client contact was positive. Not only would they return again as members of a loyal customer base, but they would also tell others and expand the size of that base. Progressive managers understand this concept and work hard to establish and maintain high standards of customer service. They try to provide every customer with goods and services that are high in quality and low in cost, meet their needs, and require only short waiting times.[10]

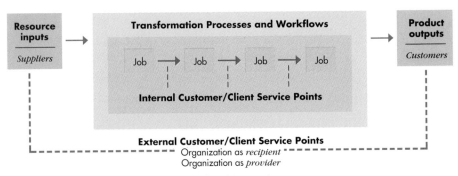

Figure 2.3 The importance of external and internal customers.

The pressure is on all managers to help organizations achieve productivity while meeting customer quality standards. A *Harvard Business Review* survey reports that American business leaders rank customer service and product quality as the first and second most important goals in the success of their organizations, respectively.[11] In a survey by the market research firm Michelson & Associates, poor service and product dissatisfaction were also ranked #1 and #2 as reasons why customers abandon a retail store.[12] But reaching the goals of providing good service and quality products isn't guaranteed, and it isn't always easy. To meet the challenge, organizations must first find out what customers want and then give it to them. This simple prescription is at the heart of any comprehensive approach to productivity development and quality improvement in organizations.

INTERNAL AND EXTERNAL CUSTOMERS

Figure 2.3 expands the open-systems view of organizations introduced in Chapter 1 to now depict the complex internal environment of the organization. In this environment, the various parts of the organization — its different subsystems — are linked to one another in the process of completing the daily work of the organization as a whole. The notion of customer service applies equally well to workflows within the organization as to the relationship between the organization and the ultimate consumer.

External customers are the ones we normally think of in this latter context — they purchase the goods or services produced. They may be industrial customers, that is, other firms that buy a company's products for use in their own operations; or they may be retail customers or clients who purchase or use the goods and services directly. **Internal customers,** by contrast, are found within the organization. They are the individuals and groups who use or otherwise depend on the results of others' work in order to do their own jobs well. According to Edward Fuchs, director of the Quality Excellence Center at AT&T Bell Laboratories, "Whatever your job is, you've got a supplier and a customer." Your supplier has a responsibility to deliver a high-quality product to you; in turn, you have a responsibility to deliver a high-quality product to the next person in the workflow process.[13]

- An **external customer** is the customer or client who buys or uses the organization's goods and/or services.

- An **internal customer** is someone who uses or depends on the work of another person or group within the organization.

CUSTOMERS AND OPERATIONS MANAGEMENT

The branch of management theory specifically concerned with the activities and decisions through which organizations transform resource inputs into product outputs is **operations management.** The product outputs can be either goods or services, and effective operations management is a concern of both manufacturing and service organizations. The resource inputs, or factors of production, include the wide variety of raw materials, technologies, capital, information, and people needed to create finished products. The *transformation process,* in turn, is the actual set of operations or activities through which various resources are utilized to produce finished goods or services of value to customers or clients.

Operations management today is increasingly viewed from a strategic perspective and with close attention to the demands of quality, customer service, and competitive advantage.[14] *Figure 2.4* offers a customer-driven model of operations. The process begins with attention being directed toward the needs of customers: "What do they want? Where do they want it? When do they want it?" Given answers to these questions, resources can be mobilized and actions taken to meet customer expectations. This is the area of "value-added" activity, where people, technology, resources, and structures combine to accomplish the work of the organization. But as noted in *Figure 2.4,* these value-added efforts should

- **Operations management** studies how organizations transform resource inputs into product and service outputs.

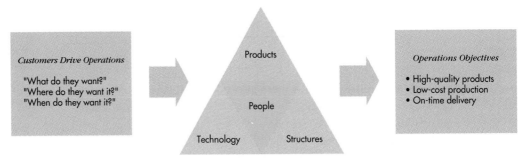

"Value-added" Operations

Figure 2.4 A customer-driven view of organizations.

be guided by very specific operations objectives that reflect customer interests—high-quality, low-cost, and on-time delivery.

COMMITMENT TO QUALITY OPERATIONS

● **ISO 9000 certification** is granted by the International Standards Organization to indicate conformance with a rigorous set of quality standards.

If managing for high performance and competitive advantage is the theme of the day, "quality" is one of its most important watchwords. Customers want quality whether they are buying a consumer product or receiving a service. The achievement of quality objectives in all aspects of operations is a universal criterion of organizational performance in manufacturing and service industries alike. The competitive demands of a global economy are an important force in this race toward total quality operations. Quality standards set by the International Standards Organization (ISO) in Geneva, Switzerland, have been adopted by many countries of the world. Businesses that want to compete as "world-class companies" are increasingly expected to have **ISO 9000 certification** at various levels. To gain certification in this family of quality standards, they must refine and upgrade quality in all operations and then undergo a rigorous assessment by outside auditors to determine whether or not they meet ISO requirements. Increasingly, the ISO "stamp of approval" is viewed as a necessity in international business; the ISO certification provides customers with assurance that a set of solid quality standards and processes are in place. In respect to quality of environmental management systems, for example, the new ISO 14000 series is now setting international standards.

TOTAL QUALITY MANAGEMENT

● **Total quality management** is managing with an organizationwide commitment to continuous improvement, product quality, and customer needs.

The term **total quality management (TQM)** was introduced in Chapter 1. It describes the process of making quality principles part of the organization's strategic objectives, applying them to all aspects of operations, committing to continuous improvement, and striving to meet customers' needs by doing things right the first time. The quality movement around the world has been strongly influenced by the pioneering work of W. Edwards Deming and Joseph M. Juran. Interestingly, their ideas became popular in Japan starting in the early 1950s and only gained prominence in the United States after the Japanese became so successful in world markets by competing with a product quality advantage.[15]

The commitment to total quality operations is now a way of life in world-class firms. In the United States, the Malcolm Baldrige National Quality Awards were established to benchmark excellence in quality achievements. The following list of award criteria indicates the full extent of the day-to-day commitment that is essential to gaining competitive advantage through a commitment to total quality:

- Top executives incorporate quality values into day-to-day management.
- The organization works with suppliers to improve the quality of their goods and/or services.
- The organization trains workers in quality techniques and implements systems that ensure high-quality products.
- The organization's products are as good as or better than those of its competitors.
- The organization meets customers' needs and wants and gets customer satisfaction ratings equal to or better than those of competitors.
- The organization's quality system yields concrete results such as increased market share and lower product-cycle times.[16]

← Quality essentials for the Baldrige National Quality Awards

There are many quality improvement approaches being tested and used around the world. Most begin with an insistence that the total quality commitment applies to everyone in an organization and to all aspects of operations, right from resource acquisition through to the production and distribution of finished goods and services. Consider the following case in point of one American company's quest for quality and competitive advantage.

At the Tennant Company top management realized its survival was threatened. Word arrived that motorized sweepers the firm was shipping to Japan had potentially disastrous defects. They were leaking oil, something the Japanese customers simply wouldn't tolerate. To make things worse, Toyota announced it was coming out with a competing product. A quality consultant pointed out to Tennant's president that the product had to be made right the first time and recommended the elimination of a rework area where 18 top mechanics were assigned. This meant assembly workers had to make fewer errors and catch any they did make. Managers and workers met in small groups to brainstorm on how to improve quality. They changed the shape of the assembly line, rerouted parts deliveries, and revised some production procedures. They were also taught statistical quality control techniques to help monitor defects and establish goals for reducing their frequency.[17]

The consultant in the Tennant Company case was Philip Crosby, who developed what he calls the "four absolutes" of management for total quality control. These are as follows: (1) *quality means conformance to standards* — workers must know exactly what performance standards they are expected to meet; (2) *quality comes from defect prevention, not defect correction* — leadership, training, and discipline must prevent defects in the first place; (3) *quality as a performance standard must mean defect-free work* — the only acceptable quality standard is perfect work; and, (4) *quality saves money* — doing things right the first time saves the cost of correcting poor work.[18]

DEMING'S PATH TO QUALITY

Among the many approaches to quality commitment, the work of W. Edwards Deming is a useful benchmark. The story begins in 1951 when he was invited to Japan to explain quality control techniques that had been developed in the

M a n a g e r ' s   N o t e p a d   2 . 1
Deming's 14 Points to Quality
1. Create a consistency of purpose in the organization to innovate, put resources into research and education, and put resources into maintaining equipment and new production aids.
2. Learn a new philosophy of quality to improve every system.
3. Require statistical evidence of process control and eliminate financial goals and quotas.
4. Require statistical evidence of control in purchasing parts; this will mean dealing with fewer suppliers.
5. Use statistical methods to isolate the sources of trouble.
6. Institute modern on-the-job training.
7. Improve supervision to develop inspired leaders.
8. Drive out fear and instill learning.
9. Break down barriers between departments.
10. Eliminate numerical goals and slogans.
11. Constantly revamp work methods.
12. Institute massive training for employees in statistical methods.
13. Retrain people in new skills.
14. Create a structure that will push, every day, on the above 13 points.

United States. The result was a lifelong relationship epitomized in the "Deming prize" for quality control. This annual award is so important in Japan that it is broadcast on national television. "When Deming spoke," we might say, "the Japanese listened." The principles he taught the Japanese were straightforward . . . and they worked: tally defects, analyze and trace them to the source, make corrections, and keep a record of what happens afterward.[19]

Deming's path to quality follows the basic proposition that the cause of a quality problem may be some component of the production and operations processes, like an employee or a machine, or it may be internal to the system itself. If it is caused by an employee, that person should be retrained or replaced. Likewise, a faulty machine should be adjusted or replaced. If the cause lies within the system, blaming an employee only causes frustration. Instead, the system must be analyzed and constructively changed. A comprehensive, rigorous, and learning-based approach underlies Deming's 14 points to quality as summarized in *Manager's Notepad 2.1.*[20]

QUALITY AND CONTINUOUS IMPROVEMENT

- **Continuous improvement** involves always searching for new ways to improve operations quality and performance.

- A **quality circle** is a group of employees who meet periodically to discuss ways of improving the quality of their products or services.

Employee involvement and participation in the search for quality solutions is an important aspect of the TQM process.[21] It is closely tied to the emphasis on **continuous improvement** — always looking for new ways to improve upon current performance. A basic philosophy of total quality management is that one can never be satisfied; something always can and should be improved upon — continuous improvement must be a way of life.

One way to combine employee involvement and continuous improvement is through the popular **quality circle** concept.[22] A quality circle is a group of workers (usually no more than 10) who meet regularly to discuss ways of improving the quality of their products or services. Their objective is to assume responsibility for quality and apply every member's full creative potential to ensure that it is achieved. Such worker empowerment can result in cost savings from improved quality and greater customer satisfaction. It can also improve morale and commitment, as the following remarks from quality circle members indicate: "This is the best thing the company has done in 15 years." . . . "The program proves that supervisors have no monopoly on brains." . . . "It gives me more pride in my work."[23]

Through quality circles and related quality management techniques, continuous improvement can be made a part of everyday operations. Later in this book, **benchmarking** will be discussed as a useful planning technique (see Chapter 7). It involves identifying other "high performance" organizations, groups, or individuals and then systematically comparing them to one's own ways of doing things. Benchmarking is now a popular way to gain insights for ongoing quality improvements.

Another important aspect of total quality operations is **cycle time** — the elapsed time between receipt of an order and delivery of the finished product. The quality objective here is to find ways to serve customer needs more quickly. The time taken to deliver and develop new products should be based on continuous improvement targets, as should efforts to reduce costs and raise quality. Time, in all respects, is critical to competitive advantage. At Bank Boston, for example, total quality and improved customer service includes a drive to keep cycle times to the minimum in its loan departments — this means speed in processing mortgage loan applications. After all, the quicker the bank can respond to customer requests, the more likely it will keep them from going to competitors.[24]

- **Benchmarking** is a process of comparing operations and performance with other organizations known for excellence.

- **Cycle time** is the elapsed time between the receipt of an order and the delivery of a finished good or service.

QUALITY AND TECHNOLOGY UTILIZATION

This is the age of technology utilization, and technology has a major role to play in the quality aspects of operations. The concept of *lean production* uses new technologies to streamline systems and allow work to be performed with fewer workers and smaller inventories. The use of *flexible manufacturing* allows processes to be changed quickly and efficiently to produce different products or modifications to existing ones. Through such techniques as *agile manufacturing* and *mass customization* organizations are able to make individualized products quickly and with production efficiencies once only associated with the mass production of uniform products.[25]

These and other modern production systems utilize computer-based technologies to better integrate the various aspects of manufacturing as well as allow modifications to be made quickly and in a cost-efficient fashion. At an IBM plant in Charlotte, North Carolina, for example, workers build many different products at any one time, from bar code scanners to fiber optics connectors. Computers at each work station assist in coordinating the work flow and even give advice on assembly operations when asked. In retailing, Levi Strauss & Company has a program called "Personal Pair" which uses flexible manufacturing systems to offer jeans made to someone's personal measurements. And in the building supplies industry, Andersen Windows lets customers design their own windows to specification using the firm's special computer software.[26] In all cases, the utilization of new technology must be supported by involved and skilled employees who utilize them to achieve quality and customer service goals.

Jaguar
http://www.jaguarcars.com

Jaguar's back. The British luxury car maker is experiencing a return to profitability under its new parent, Ford Motor Co. "We're profitable and we've improved," Jacques A. Nasser, Ford's president, has declared. Jaguar suffered previously from quality problems that Ford has successfully corrected. Now the focus is on sales growth.

QUALITY AND PRODUCT DESIGN

Another timely and important contribution to quality management is found in product design. We are all aware of design differences among products, be they cars, stereos, clothes, watches, or whatever. But what may not be recognized is that design makes a difference in how things are produced *and* at what level of cost and quality. A "good" design has eye appeal to the customer *and* is easy to manufacture with productivity. In today's competitive global economy, such designs are strategic weapons. "Design is it," says consultant Tom Peters, arguing that it will be the key to competitive advantage in the future.[27]

One of the masters of product design strategy is Japanese consultant Genichi Taguchi. He has pioneered the concept of *robust design,* meaning that a design is "production proof" and can withstand manufacturing fluctuations that might otherwise cause defects. Taguchi says, "to improve quality, you must look upstream in the design stage. At the customer level it's too late." If, for example, a kiln is producing warped tiles because of humidity or temperature variations, Taguchi would try to adjust ingredients in the clay before spending large amounts to upgrade equipment.[28]

- **Design for manufacturing** is creating a design that lowers production costs and improves quality in all stages of production.

Progressive manufacturers now emphasize **design for manufacturing.** This means that products are styled to lower production costs and smooth the way toward high-quality results in all aspects of the manufacturing processes. Simplicity counts in product design. Manufacturers want products to be safe, readily identifiable, and straightforward to use. Styling is now often developed on the computer and then tested via simulation for its manufacturing implications. Teamwork among engineering, production, marketing, and other functional areas is also improving the design process.

- **Design for disassembly** is the design of products with attention to how their component parts will be used when product life ends.

A manufacturing approach that shows respect for the natural environment is **design for disassembly.** The goal is to design products taking into account how their component parts will be reused at the end of product life. This trend is apparent in automobile manufacturing, where automakers are using more parts that can be recycled. Environmentalism and the rising costs and hazards of waste disposal are stimulating interests in this design approach. For example, computer makers, with Hewlett-Packard an acknowledged leader, are starting to do more in terms of taking back obsolete machines, disassembling them, and then recycling the parts.[29]

THE NATURE OF ORGANIZATIONAL CULTURE

- **Organizational culture** is the system of shared beliefs and values that develops within an organization and guides the behavior of its members.

Culture is a popular word in management these days. Important differences in national cultures will be discussed in Chapter 5 on the global dimensions of management. Now it is time to talk about cultural differences in the internal environments of organizations. **Organizational culture** is defined by noted scholar and consultant Edgar Schein as the system of shared beliefs and values that develops within an organization and guides the behavior of its members.[30] Sometimes called the *corporate culture,* it is a key aspect of any organization and work setting. Whenever someone, for example, speaks of "the way we do things here," they are talking about the culture.

WHAT STRONG CULTURES CAN DO

Although it is clear that culture is not the sole determinant of what happens in organizations, it is an important influence on what they accomplish . . . and how. The internal culture has the potential to shape attitudes, reinforce common beliefs, direct behavior, and establish performance expectations and the motivation to fulfill them. A widely-discussed study of successful businesses concluded that organizational culture made a major contribution to their long-term performance records.[31] Importantly, the cultures in these organizations provided for a clear vision of what the organization was attempting to accomplish, allowing individuals to rally around the vision and work hard to support and accomplish it. In these and related ways organizational culture is a bond that further mobilizes resources for action.[32] *Strong cultures,* ones that are clear and well defined and widely shared among members, discourage dysfunctional work behaviors and encourage positive ones. They commit members to do things for and with one another that are in the best interests of the organization, and then they reinforce these habits. The best organizations have strong cultures that show respect for members and encourage adaptability and continuous improvement in all areas of operations. They are likely, for example, to have cultures that are performance oriented, emphasize teamwork, allow for risk taking, encourage innovation, and make the well-being of people a top management priority.[33]

LEVELS OF ORGANIZATIONAL CULTURE

Figure 2.5 shows two levels of culture in organizations—the "observable" culture and the "core" culture.[34] The *observable culture* is what one sees and hears when walking around an organization as a visitor, a customer, or an employee. In strong culture organizations the observable culture will be readily apparent. It can be seen in the way people dress at work, how they arrange their offices, how they speak to and behave toward one another, the nature of their conversations, and how they talk about and treat their customers.

More formally stated, the observable culture includes the following elements of daily organizational life—through them, new members learn the organization's culture and all members share and reinforce its special aspects over time:

- *Stories*—Oral histories and tales, told and retold among members, about dramatic sagas and incidents in the life of the organization.

- *Heroes*—The people singled out for special attention and whose accomplishments are recognized with praise and admiration among members; they include founders and role models.

- *Rites and rituals*—The ceremonies and meetings, planned and spontaneous, that celebrate important occasions and performance accomplishments.

• **Nordstrom**
http://www.nordstrom-pta.com

Core values at Nordstrom, the highly regarded department store chain, emphasize service to the customer, hard work and individual productivity, never being satisfied, and reputational excellence.

Observable elements of organizational cultures

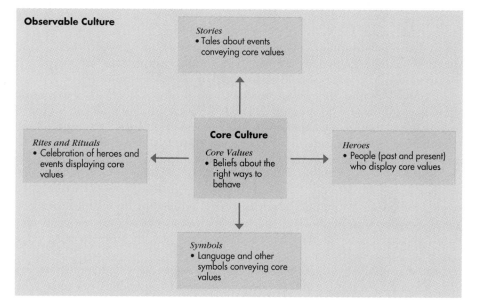

Figure 2.5 Levels of organizational culture—observable culture and core culture.

• *Symbols*—The special use of language and other nonverbal expressions to communicate important themes of organizational life.[35]

Standing at the foundation of what one directly observes in the daily life of an organization is a second and deeper level of culture. This is the *core culture,* and it determines why things are this way. It consists of **core values** or underlying beliefs that influence behavior and actually give rise to the aspects of observable culture just described. Values are essential to strong culture organizations and are often widely publicized in formal statements of corporate mission and purpose. Strong culture organizations operate with a small but enduring set of core values. Successful companies, for example, typically emphasize the values of performance excellence, innovation, social responsibility, integrity, worker involvement, customer service, and teamwork.[36]

> • **Core values** are underlying beliefs shared by members of the organization and that influence their behavior.

In Bell Atlantic's effort to meet the challenges of an increasingly competitive industry, the company has implemented a business strategy of utilizing team-based organizations—known as TBOs. The teams meet regularly to solve problems and improve processes, with the result that those closest to the work have an impact on the way it is done. Through employee involvement and by utilizing the expertise of each member of the team, TBOs achieve the common goal of serving Bell Atlantic customers. Members of a TBO in metropolitan Washington increased revenues by nearly 6% and customer service levels by 14% in just one year.[37]

LEADERSHIP AND ORGANIZATIONAL CULTURE

Leadership of the organizational culture involves establishing and maintaining appropriate core values. Whereas this is most often considered a top management job, the same definition holds for any manager or team leader at any level of responsibility. Just like the organization as a whole, any work team or group will have a culture. How well this culture operates to support the group and its performance objectives will depend in part on the strength of the core values. At any level, these values should meet the test of these three criteria: (1) *relevance*—core values should support key performance objectives; (2) *pervasiveness*—core values should be known by all members of the organization or group; and (3) *strength*—core values should be accepted by everyone involved.[38]

> • **A symbolic manager** uses symbols to establish and maintain a desired organizational culture.

Attention is now being increasingly given to the concept of a **symbolic manager,** someone who uses symbols well to establish and maintain a desired organizational culture. Symbolic managers and leaders talk the "language" of the organization. They are careful always to use spoken and written words to describe people, events, and even the competition in ways that reinforce and communicate core values. *Language metaphors*—the use of positive examples from another context—are very powerful in this regard. For example, newly hired workers at Disney World and Disneyland are counseled to always think of themselves as more than employees; they are key "members of the cast," and they work "on stage." After all, they are told, Disney isn't just any business, it is an "entertainment" business.

Good symbolic managers highlight the observable culture. They tell key *stories* over and over again, and they encourage others to tell them. They often refer to the "founding story" about the entrepreneur whose personal values set a key tone for the enterprise. They often tell about organizational *heroes,* past and present, whose performances exemplify core values. They often use symbolic *rites and rituals* that glorify the performance of the organization and its members. Such ceremonies may be as simple as a spontaneous public congratulation of a work group that exceeded its quality goals or as formal as mass meetings called to announce major organizational accomplishments. For example, the use of rites, rituals, and ceremonies has become almost a corporate symbol at Mary Kay Cosmetics. Gala events, at which top sales performers share their tales of success, are legendary, as are the lavish incentive awards presented at these ceremonies, especially the pink luxury cars given to the most successful salespeople.[39]

 ## DIRECTIONS IN ORGANIZATIONAL CULTURES

Worker empowerment is an important theme today as organizations seek to gain competitive advantages and build cultures to meet the challenges of the new workplace. These cultures should also value diversity in the workforce and ensure that high ethical standards are maintained in individual and organizational performance.

CULTURE AND EMPOWERMENT

Managers at all levels of responsibility are finding that the best way to benefit from a strong culture is through an underlying commitment to employee participation, involvement, and empowerment. The "best" organizational cultures are those that value the talents, ideas, and creative potential of all members. They allow all the human resources of an organization to be utilized to their fullest potential, *and* they allow the people involved to feel good about it. The old-fashioned top-down or "paternalistic" approach just doesn't work well anymore. Progressive managers know this and are trying to create and rebuild organizational cultures on the foundations of empowerment.

There is no doubt that the diversity of today's workforce is valued and supported by Patagonia, Inc. Patagonia sets an interesting standard for employers that want best to meet the needs of workers from Generation X, the 45+ million people born between 1965–1977. Casual is in; formal is out. Gone are the days of "organization man." If you look at the Patagonia's website you might find depicted there a casually dressed employee with feet on the desk. Today, especially for the Gen-xers, jobs should be fun, self-fulfilling, and rewarding. And, that's quite a test for empowerment and corporate culture.[40]

MULTICULTURAL ORGANIZATIONS

The concept of organizational culture brings us back again to issues of workforce diversity. There is no reason why organizational cultures cannot set core values and encourage common work directions that respect the diversity that is now characteristic of our workforces. When supported properly within the corporate culture, workforce diversity can be the source of significant competitive advantage. The term *multiculturalism* refers to pluralism and respect for diversity in

● A **multicultural organization** is based on pluralism and operates with respect for diversity in the workplace.

——————➝

Characteristics of multicultural organizations

the workplace. A **multicultural organization,** accordingly, will have characteristics such as these:

- *Pluralism* — Members of both minority cultures and majority cultures are influential in setting key values and policies.
- *Structural integration* — Minority-culture members are well represented in jobs at all levels and in all functional responsibilities.
- *Informal network integration* — Various forms of mentoring and support groups assist in the career development of minority-culture members.
- *Absence of prejudice and discrimination* — A variety of training and task force activities continually address the need to eliminate culture-group biases.
- *Minimum intergroup conflict* — Diversity does not lead to destructive conflicts between members of majority and minority cultures.[41]

Multicultural organizations benefit from strong organizational cultures with underlying commitments to worker empowerment, as previously discussed. The "best" organizational cultures in this sense are those that value the talents, ideas, and creative potential of all members.

ORGANIZATIONAL SUBCULTURES

● **Subcultures** are common to groups of people with similar values and beliefs based upon shared work responsibilities and personal characteristics.

Like society as a whole, organizations contain **subcultures.** These are the cultures common to groups of people with similar values and beliefs based upon shared work responsibilities and personal characteristics. Organizations contain occupational subcultures, functional subcultures, ethnic and racial subcultures, generational subcultures, and gender subcultures, among others. People in organizations must be comfortable working together across the borders of subcultures.

In his book *Clash of Cultures,* Joseph Raelin discusses how "salaried professionals" such as lawyers, scientists, engineers, and accountants, are members of *occupational subcultures* that must be understood by the people who manage them.[42] He suggests that professionals have needs for work autonomy and empowerment that may conflict with traditional management methods of top-down direction and control. Unless these needs are recognized and dealt with properly, salaried professionals may prove difficult to integrate into the culture of the larger organization.

This concept extends to a common problem in organizational life, the lack of functional integration among the multiple components of the total system. In many work settings, people develop strong identities with *functional subcultures.* For example, employees of a business may consider themselves "systems people" or "marketing people" or "manufacturing people" or "finance people." When such identities are overemphasized, there is a tendency to separate in-group members from the rest of the organization. Members of the functional groups spend most of their time with each other, develop a "jargon" or technical language that is shared among themselves, and view their role in the organization as more important than the contributions of the other functions. Rather than working together as a large cooperative system, the total organization may instead become a place of competing subsystems.

Workforce diversity brings with it other sources of subculture grouping in organizations. Among them, differences in *ethnic* or *national cultures* will be discussed in Chapter 5 on the global dimensions of management.[43] But although it is relatively easy to recognize that people from various countries and regions of the world may represent different cultural backgrounds, it is far harder to turn this awareness into the ability to work well with persons whose ethnic cultures differ from our own. The best understanding is most likely gained through direct

● **Stride Rite**
http://www.striderite.com

At Stride Rite, concerns for children are center stage in the organization's culture. The firm believes in helping its employees meet the needs of dependent relatives. It was the first American company to have an on-site child care facility. It started the Stride Rite Inter-generational Day Care Center to accommodate the elderly as well as the very young.

contact and a personal commitment to remain open-minded when working with persons from different ethnic backgrounds.

As imprecise as our understanding of ethnic subcultures may be, things seem even less clear on matters of race. Although we often speak in everyday conversations about "African American," "Asian American," and "Anglo" or "Latino" cultures, one has to wonder what we really know about these *racial subcultures*.[44] What we do know for sure are the controversies that can develop among and divide persons of different racial backgrounds. Just consider the debates in America over "Afro-centric schools" and the role of English as a national language. Importantly, a key question remains largely unanswered: Where can we find frameworks for understanding alternative racial cultures? If improved cross-cultural understandings can help people work better across national boundaries, why can't improved cross-cultural understandings help people from different racial subcultures work better together?

We live at a time when the general population in many countries is aging and the "graying" of the workforce is a recognized phenomenon. The influence of *generational subcultures* at work is of growing importance given these trends. But the issues are more subtle than young-old issues alone. Raelin, for example, describes "generational gaps" among people who grew up during different periods of history and whose values have thus evolved under very different influences. He notes that the "defiant 60s kids," those who were teens in the 1960s, have a strong need to participate in decision making. They may have difficulty working today with higher level managers whose values were set in the 1950s and who may be more inclined toward top-down operations. You might ask, furthermore, how will the "90s kids" do in the future when working with managers of the "70s" and "80s" subcultures?[45]

Issues of gender relationships and gender discrimination also continue to complicate the workplace. Some research shows that when men work together, a male group culture forms. It typically has a competitive atmosphere, in which the games and stories deal with winning and losing in various situations. It also often involves the use of sports metaphors.[46] When women work together, a rather different female group culture may form. It typically involves more personal relationships with an emphasis on collaboration. One can reasonably ask: What happens when *gender subcultures* mix in the organization? What happens when a representative of one gender subculture is placed in charge of persons from the other? We know that women are still underrepresented in many management capacities, especially in top management ranks. If men primarily control higher levels of organizations, isn't it likely that resulting practices, even corporate cultures, will tend to reflect the values and ways of the majority male subculture? Answers to these and related questions are still needed as progressive managers address gender issues in the workplace.[47]

Service Performance Corporation was rated "outstanding" in the Enterprise Awards for Best Business Practices conducted by Arthur Andersen. The privately held San Francisco company makes the ultimate commitment to customer service in a policy called "The Difficult Yes." CEO David Pasek says, "Our company policy is to find a way to say 'yes' to customer requests . . . Employees don't need approval to satisfy the customer's request, although we do expect them to use good judgment."

ETHICAL CULTURES

There is an important ethical aspect to any organizational culture, and depending on the nature of the culture different ethical standards may guide the behavior of organization members. Top management has an important role to play in creating and maintaining high ethical standards, but managers at every level set the ethical tone in their areas of immediate work responsibility. This can be accomplished in part by ensuring that the guiding corporate culture communicates a desired *ethical climate* — a shared set of understandings about what is considered ethically correct behavior in an organization.[48]

Organizations with strong and positive ethical climates establish clear expectations for their members. They leave little doubt as to what should be done when the inevitable ethical dilemmas occur. They also remind everyone that top management and organizational policies stand behind these expectations. With all the complications of modern society and the new workplace, a positive ethical climate can greatly expand the impact of organizational culture on performance. This important issue will be considered again in Chapter 6 on ethics and social responsibility.

CHAPTER REVIEW

This section should be used as an end-of-chapter "study guide." The *Summary* helps to put the chapter's content into overall perspective. The list of *Key Terms* allows you to double-check your familiarity with basic concepts and definitions. *Self-Test 2* gives you the opportunity to test your basic comprehension of the chapter using sample test questions.

SUMMARY

What is the external environment of organizations?

- Competitive advantage and distinctive competency can only be achieved by organizations that deal successfully with dynamic and complex environments.

- The external environment of organizations consists of both general and specific components.

- The general environment includes background conditions that influence the organization, including economic, socio-cultural, legal-political, technological, and natural environment conditions.

- The specific environment consists of the actual organizations, groups, and persons an organization deals with; these include suppliers, customers, competitors, regulators, and pressure groups.

- Environmental uncertainty challenges organizations and their management to be flexible and responsive to new and changing conditions.

What is a customer-driven organization?

- Any organization must develop and maintain a base of loyal customers or clients, and a customer-driven organization recognizes customer service and product quality as foundations of competitive advantage.

- Customer service is a core ingredient of total quality operations, and it includes concerns for both internal customers and external customers.

- The "upside-down pyramid" is a symbol of how organizations of today are refocusing on customers and on the role of managers to support work efforts to continually improve quality and customer service.

- Operations management is specifically concerned with activities and decisions through which organizations transform resource inputs into product outputs.

- Today, operations management is increasingly viewed in a strategic perspective and with close attention to the demands of productivity, quality, and competitive advantage.

What is the quality commitment in operations?

- To compete in the global economy organizations are increasingly expected to meet ISO 9000 certification standards of quality.

- Total quality management involves making quality a strategic objective of the organization and supporting it by continuous improvement efforts.

- The commitment to total quality operations requires meeting customers needs — on time, the first time, and all the time.

- The use of quality circles — groups of employees working to solve quality problems — is a form of employee involvement in quality management.

Why is organizational culture important?

- The internal environment of organizations includes organizational culture, which establishes a personality for the organization as a whole and has a strong influence on the behavior of its members.

- The observable culture is found in the rites, rituals, stories, heroes, and symbols of the organization.

- The core culture consists of the core values and fundamental beliefs upon which the organization is based.

- In organizations with strong cultures, members behave with shared understandings that support the accomplishment of key organizational objectives.

- Symbolic managers are good at building shared values and using stories, ceremonies, heroes, and language to reinforce these values in daily affairs.

What are the current directions in organizational cultures?

- Organizational cultures typically include the existence of many subcultures, including those based on occupational, functional, ethnic, racial, age, and gender differences in a diverse workforce.

- People in organizations must learn to work together comfortably across subculture borders; they must avoid negative stereotyping and dysfunctional cross-cultural clashes.

- Multicultural organizations operate through a culture that values pluralism and respects diversity.

- The organizational culture should display a positive ethical climate, or shared set of understandings about what is considered ethically correct behavior.

KEY TERMS

SELF-TEST 2

Take this test much as you would in a normal classroom situation. It should offer you a good way to check your basic comprehension of chapter material. Answers may be found at the end of the book.

MULTIPLE-CHOICE QUESTIONS:

1. The general environment of an organization would include _____ . (a) socio-cultural conditions (b) resource suppliers (c) competitors (d) customers

2. Persons and groups affected by an organization's performance are considered as _____ . (a) core beneficiaries (b) heroes (c) monitors (d) stakeholders

3. The two dimensions important in determining the level of perceived environmental uncertainty are the number of factors in the external environment and the _____ of these factors. (a) location (b) rate of change (c) independence (d) interconnectiveness

4. Techniques typically associated with total quality management include: (a) use of benchmarking (b) emphasis on continuous improvement (c) reduced cycle times (d) all of these

5. The field of operations management is primarily concerned with an organization's _____ processes. (a) feedback (b) transformation (c) control (d) performance appraisal

6. Manufacturing for the "three Rs" (reduce the number of parts, reuse parts, and recycle parts) shows concern for _____ . (a) government regulation (b) a global economy (c) mass customization (d) natural environment

7. _____ is when individualized products are made quickly and with production efficiencies similar to those achieved by mass production of uniform products. (a) Lean production (b) Flexible production (c) Mass customization (d) Mass manufacturing

8. Planned and spontaneous ceremonies and celebrations are examples of how _____ can be used help to build strong corporate cultures. (a) stories (b) heroes (c) rites and rituals (d) values

9. A _____ manager uses language metaphors, rites, and rituals to reinforce and build upon a desired organizational culture. (a) symbolic (b) bureaucratic (c) mechanistic (d) adaptive

10. Pluralism and the absence of discrimination and prejudice are two important foundations of the _____ organization. (a) organic (b) multicultural (c) mechanistic (d) symbolic

TRUE-FALSE QUESTIONS:

11. Laws and government regulations are part of the sociocultural conditions in the general environment. T F

12. An organization's regulators are part of its specific environment. T F

13. The most challenging environmental condition is one of moderate-high uncertainty. T F

14. A benchmark is something that gives an organization an advantage over its competitors. T F

15. The importance of *customer service* applies in organizations to both external customers and internal customers. T F

16. ISO 100 certification has become a standard of quality for world-class companies. T F

17. Robust product designs are ones that minimize the risk of errors in production; that is, they are relatively "production proof." T F

18. Age and gender are two possible foundations for subcultures within organizations. T F

19. Strong cultures can help organizations by encouraging positive work behaviors. T F

20. The ethical climate of a business firm is not an important part of its corporate culture. T F

SHORT-RESPONSE QUESTIONS:

21. What operating objectives are appropriate for an organization seeking competitive advantage through improved customer service?

22. What is the difference between an organization's external customers and its internal customers?

23. What is the difference between the observable and core cultures of an organization?

24. Why is it important for managers to understand subcultures in organizations?

APPLICATION QUESTION:

25. Two businesswomen, former college roommates, are discussing their jobs and careers over lunch. You overhear one saying to the other, "I work for a large corporation, while you own a small retail business. In my company there is strong corporate culture and everyone feels its influence. In fact, we are always expected to act in ways that support the culture and serve as role models for others to do so as well. Because of the small size of your firm, corporate culture is not such an important thing to worry about." Do you agree or disagree with this statement? Why?

CHAPTER THREE

Information Technology and Decision Making

Planning Ahead—Chapter 3 Study Questions

- How is information technology changing the workplace?

- What are the current directions in information systems?

- How is information used for problem solving?

- How do managers make decisions?

- How do learning and knowledge management create value?

Welcome to the World of Virtual Learning

Technology empowers people. It is also changing the nature of college education and corporate training. Distance learning is gaining a strategic foothold as new computer technologies become mainstays of instructional support. At Duke's Fuqua School of Business, executives from 19 different countries recently completed an executive MBA program while studying via computer-mediated distance learning programs that also involved several intensive residency periods. At the University of Tennessee, Knoxville, physicians from 11 states are enrolled in a similar distance-learning MBA program that is tailored to their needs. The new Western Governors University is a university without walls; the new Florida Gulf Coast University expects to serve 25 percent of its students through distance learning; and technology-driven distance learning is a core strategy of the University of Phoenix and the Instituto Technologío y de Estudios Superiores de Monterrey, Mexico. And in the corporate sector, companies like AT&T are offering more and more of their training programs through the Internet.[1] Other examples of new directions in virtual education abound.

● **Intellectual capital** is the collective brainpower or shared knowledge of a workforce.

Just as computers and information technologies have changed education and learning processes, they are also dramatically and continually changing the nature of work and organizations themselves. The key is information and the way it flows and is utilized by people in organizations. *More* information about *more* things is being made available to *more* people in organizations *more* quickly than ever before. One of the most important concepts to understand in this regard is **intellectual capital,** which is defined as the collective brainpower or shared knowledge of a workforce that can be used to create wealth.[2]

In this era of information, intellectual capital is a major source of competitive advantage. Knowledge is an irreplaceable resource, and the goal should always be to grow and create it. This is especially true in the global economy, which has been described by Peter Drucker as one in which "the productivity of knowledge and knowledge workers" will become the decisive competitive factor.[3] The information from which knowledge is created, moreover, increasingly moves at high speed through electronic networks that link each of us to the world at large with an access and intensity never before possible. It is time to turn on your computer, open an Internet browser, and search for information. Start with the special *Management 6/E* web site featured in the accompanying margin photo and then go exploring. Welcome to the new and exciting world of information, decision making, and knowledge management!

 INFORMATION TECHNOLOGY AND THE NEW WORKPLACE

The future is now when it comes to the rapidly evolving state of computer and information technologies. Organizations are changing as the new technologies exert their influence. Information departments or centers are appearing on organization charts. The number and variety of information career fields is rapidly expanding. Job titles such as Chief Information Officer and Chief Knowledge Officer are appearing in the senior ranks of organizations. All of this, and more, is characteristic of the great opportunities of our new age of information. At the software firm PeopleSoft, for example, vice president Phil Cullen faced the challenge of trying to achieve an early release for a sophisticated software package. A team used web-based tools and a database on Lotus Notes to facilitate a process that Cullen said "could take months at most companies." The PeopleSoft team consolidated information from employees around the world and provided the feedback needed within two weeks. "It was really amazing," said Cullen, who added, "Then again, it's how we do things around here."[4]

WORK AND THE ELECTRONIC OFFICE

A good example of the everyday impact of information technology, or IT, on work is the *electronic office.* This term refers to the use of computers and related technologies to electronically facilitate operations in an office environment. The electronic office that you may soon enter could be similar to the following.

People work at "smart" stations supported by computers that allow sophisticated voice, image, text, and other data-handling operations. Voice messaging utilizes the voice recognition capabilities of computers to take dictation, answer the telephone, and relay messages. Databases are easily accessed to prepare and analyze reports. Once finished, documents drafted via word processing are stored for later retrieval and/or sent via electronic mail or facsimile transmission to other persons. Standard filing cabinets are few, and little paper is found. Meeting notes are written on electronic pads or jotted in palm-held electronic diaries. All are easily up-loaded into computer files. Mail arrives and is routed to its destination via computer, and it gets posted on electronic bulletin boards to be prioritized and accessed according to its importance. Computer conferencing and videoconferencing are commonplace, and people work with one another every day over great distances — even around the world — without meeting personally face to face.

This is not fantasy. It's real. Progressive organizations are doing all they can to utilize computers and information technology to streamline work, improve operating efficiencies, and make overall performance improvements. Organizations like PeopleSoft are investing in technology in the quest for competitive advantage through lower costs, better quality, and improved customer services. Those that fail to do so will be ill prepared to act quickly enough to succeed in highly competitive situations. Indeed, futurist Alvin Toffler considers the speed of decision making to be a major asset in today's dynamic environments where "speed to market," "quick response," "fast cycle time," and "time-based competition" are the topics of discussion in many executive suites.[5]

ELECTRONIC COMMERCE

If you want to buy a book today, it may be easier to purchase it off the Internet than from your local bookstore. That's not good news for the local retailer, but it accounts for the success of Amazon.com, the virtual bookstore. Amazon.com is a great example of one of the hottest new business developments of our time — **electronic commerce.** Called *e-business* by many, this is a business form in which commercial transactions take place through the use of advanced IT, including special telecommunications and computer mediation.[6] Simply put, e-business is done online rather than face to face. One of the companies most interested in supporting such developments, of course, is IBM. It describes the steps in developing e-business as follows:[7]

> • **Electronic commerce** or *e-business* uses information technology to support on-line commercial transactions.

Steps in developing e-business

Step 1 in E-business — establishing a web site and then using the site to publish information electronically.

Step 2 in E-business — advancing the web site to "self-service" status, where customers can do things like check their account status or trace the location of a package for delivery.

Step 3 in E-business — further advancing the web site to allow "transactions," including the buying and selling of merchandise and managing resource supply and product distribution chains.

"Discover books you'll love at Amazon.com" reads the brochure that arrives with the gift book from your friend. The book comes by priority mail, was ordered online, paid for by credit card, and shipped immediately. The package is even gift wrapped and carries a personal note from the gift giver — entered via computer of course. Amazon advertises the availability of over 400,000 titles and savings of 20 to 40 percent. The firm invites you to shop in their bookstore anytime you want day or night, 365 days a year. After all, the bookstore is online. It is e-business with a capital "E." And it is establishing a new level and form of competition in the bookstore industry. Traditional booksellers are finding it tough to compete against a company that refers to itself as "earth's biggest bookstore" and advertises "Your next book is only a click away."[8]

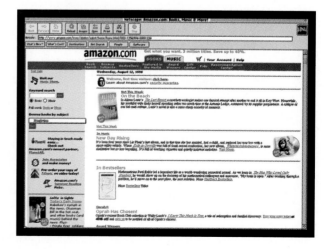

INFORMATION NEEDS OF ORGANIZATIONS

The foundations of e-commerce and the electronic office rest with **information,** or data made useful for decision making. The availability of advanced computer technology has made information more readily available and useful than ever before. At AT&T, for example, technology allowed the firm to analyze over 250 billion call records originating on college campuses and connecting to households. A pattern was found in the data that showed many short calls followed by longer ones from homes back to campuses—an easy way for parents to pick up the bill. In response, AT&T started a successful program called True Ties 800 that offered 1-800 service for families.[9] The 250 billion call records were simply data in the form of raw facts. When analyzed with computer assistance, they became useful as information that influenced the firm's marketing strategy.

The information needs of organizations are described in *Figure 3.1.* Information in the external environment must be accessed and used to successfully manage the organization/environment relationship. Managers need this *intelligence information* to deal effectively with such outside parties as competitors, government agencies, creditors, suppliers, and stockholders. As Peter Drucker says about the information age, "a winning strategy will require information about events and conditions outside the institution." He goes on to add that organizations must have "rigorous methods for gathering and analyzing outside information."[10] In addition to the gathering of intelligence information, organizations also provide to the external environment many types of *public information.* This serves a variety of purposes ranging from image building to product advertising to financial reporting for taxes.

Within organizations, people need vast amounts of information to make decisions and solve problems in their daily work. These vertical and horizontal information flows are shown also in *Figure 3.1.* Higher level managers tend to emphasize information utilization in strategic planning, whereas middle and lower managers focus more on operational considerations involving the implementation of these plans. The information needs of workers center on accomplishing tasks. This involves gathering, storing, sharing, and utilizing information to solve operating problems in order to best meet the needs of internal and external customers. Organizations that are best able to facilitate the fast and easy sharing of information internally are well positioned for competitive advantage.

The Internet becomes a learning resource for students using textbooks published by John Wiley & Sons, Inc. Its web site offers a variety of support and learning enhancements for a full array of products. Tap into the Wiley web site for this book at http://www.wiley.com/college/scherman6e.

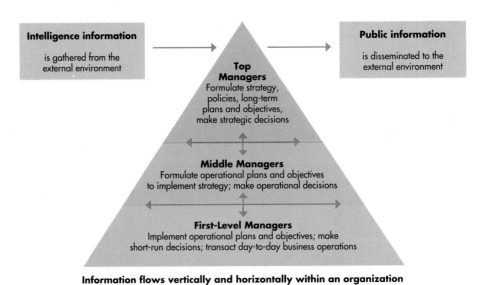

Information flows vertically and horizontally within an organization to facilitate problem solving and decision making.

Figure 3.1 External and internal information needs of organizations.

Fidelity Investments, one of the world's largest mutual fund companies, receives more than 300,000 telephone calls per day. A large percentage are calls handled through an automated response system. When callers speak with a service representative, they have high-tech computer support. The complexities of 401(k) retirement accounts, for example, are programmed in a computer server linked to the workstations. By using the system a representative can easily check to make sure that a customer's transactions meet all legal requirements. The workstations provide instant access to individual accounts as well as specifics on the firm's retirement plans and the various financial products offered by it. Fidelity chairman and CEO Edward C. Johnson III says, "Computers serve two purposes that are absolutely essential: They allow us to serve our customers better and they allow us to keep our expenses within reasonable limits." The firm's former CIO says: "Information technology has moved from a support function to a strategic function." [11]

DEVELOPMENTS IN INFORMATION SYSTEMS

People in any work setting, large or small, must have available to them the *right* information at the *right* time and in the *right* place if they are to perform effectively. This is made possible by **information systems** that use the latest in information technology to collect, organize, and distribute data in such a way that they become meaningful as information. Such systems have the potential to make major contributions to performance in organizations. However, the following factors are considered essential to their success: (1) technical quality of the system, (2) participation and involvement of users in the system design, and (3) management support.

- **Information systems** use IT to collect, organize, and distribute data for use in decision making.

Increasingly, a position entitled **chief information officer** or "CIO" is prominent in the senior ranks of organizational executives. The CIO typically oversees all aspects of computer, information, and telecommunications systems and their utilization. The role of the corporate CIO is central in the making of strategic decisions and in managing competitiveness in a challenging environment. The CIO's job, simply stated, is to ensure that the organization always uses information and computer technology as resources for constructive change and competitive advantage.[12]

- **A CIO** is a senior executive responsible for IT and its utilization throughout an organization.

You will encounter many types of information systems in your career. At times you may be the designer of a new system and you may serve on an information steering committee, but you will always be an end user. In this sense, your task will be to utilize information systems well to make good decisions, to master the performance requirements of complex projects, and more generally to contribute regularly to enhanced organizational productivity. As you look ahead, keep in mind the advice in *Manager's Notepad 3.1*.

MANAGEMENT INFORMATION SYSTEMS

A **management information system,** or MIS, is specifically designed to use IT to meet the information needs of managers as they make a variety of decisions on a day-to-day basis. For example, at C.R. England, a long-haul refrigerated trucking company in Salt Lake City, a computerized MIS monitors over 500 aspects of or-

- **A management information system** uses IT to meet the information needs of managers as they make decisions.

Manager's Notepad 3.1

Avoiding Common Information Systems Mistakes

- Don't assume more information is always better.
- Don't assume that computers eliminate the need for human judgment.
- Don't assume the newest technology is always best.
- Don't assume nothing will ever go wrong with your computer.
- Don't assume that everyone understands how the system works.

---

ganizational performance. The system tracks everything from billing accuracy to arrival times to driver satisfaction with company maintenance on their vehicles. Pay bonuses and extra vacation days are awarded based on driver performance on such goals as safety and fuel consumption. Says CEO Dan England: "Our view was, if we could measure it, we could manage it." [13]

Decision Support Systems

A **decision support system,** or DSS, uses special software to allow users to interact directly with a computer to help make decisions for solving complex and sometimes unstructured problems. Decision support systems are now available to assist in such business decisions as mergers and acquisitions, plant expansions, new product developments, and stock portfolio management, among many others. The capability to interact with a user to address problems makes the DSS a special and more advanced type of management information system.

A fast-growing technology involves **group decision-support systems,** or GDSS, which are interactive computer-based information systems that facilitate group efforts to solve complex and unstructured problems. GDSS software, called **groupware,** allows several people to simultaneously work on a file or database and work together on computer networks. It facilitates information exchange, group decision making, work scheduling, and other forms of group activity without the requirement of face-to-face meetings. Groupware is especially useful in facilitating work by team members who work different shifts or are spread over large geographic distances, even globally. Continuing developments in groupware are expanding the presence and opportunities of *virtual teams* in organizations. As discussed in Chapter 17, on teams and teamwork, the willingness and skills needed to participate effectively in these computer-mediated work groups are increasingly essential to one's personal career portfolio.

Another developing area of information technology is *artificial intelligence,* or AI, a field of study that is concerned with building computer systems with the capacity to reason the way people do, even to the point of dealing with ambiguities and difficult issues of judgment. The managerial applications of this attempt to give computers humanlike capabilities lie in the realm of **expert systems** that mimic the thinking of human experts and, in so doing, offer consistent and "expert" decision-making advice to the user. Some expert systems are rule-based and use a complicated set of "if . . . then" rules to analyze problems. These rules are determined by specialists who work with actual human experts in a certain problem area and then build their problem-solving rules into a computer program. This program then can be applied through direct interaction between the expert system and a database or between the system and inputs provided by the human user. One complaint about the technology is that the use of expert systems "deskills" work by requiring the employee to know less because the computer does more. [14] Advocates, however, point out that expert systems make it easier to concentrate one's attention and problem-solving skills on the most complex matters.

INTRAORGANIZATIONAL SYSTEMS AND INTRANETS

Central to the electronic office is the integration of computers and software into *networks* that allow users to easily transfer and share information through computer-to-computer linkages. **Intranets** are networks of computers that use special software such as Lotus Notes to allow persons working in various locations for the same organization to share databases and communicate electronically. The goal is to promote more integration across the organization and improve operations efficiency and quality. At Ford, for example, more than 120,000 workstations scattered in company offices around the world are linked by an intranet. Using a technology called the Concentric Network, moreover, Ford integrates voice, data, and video in a single network that allows employees to share information and work together in real time. In terms of competitive edge, the firm reports that the time between the point a new car is ordered and delivery is down to 15 days. The firm soon wants to build and sell most of its vehicles "on demand."[15]

A related trend is the emergence of fully integrated **enterprisewide networks** that move information quickly and accurately from one point to another within an organization. For example, a field salesperson may pass on a customer's suggestion for a product modification via electronic mail. This mail arrives at the computer used by a product designer at company headquarters. After creating a computer-assisted design for the product, the designer passes it on simultaneously to engineering, manufacturing, finance, and marketing experts for their preliminary analysis. Working as a virtual team, everyone including the field salesperson may then further consider the design and agree on its business potential.

- **Intranets** are computer networks that allow persons within an organization to share databases and communicate electronically.

- **Enterprisewide networks** use IT to move information quickly and accurately within an organization.

INTERORGANIZATIONAL SYSTEMS AND EXTRANETS

Extranets are computer networks that use the public Internet to allow communication between the organization and elements in its external environment. Using new IT, **interorganizational information systems** are increasingly used to allow information transfers between two or more organizations.[16] They are the basic foundations for the fast-paced developments occurring in electronic commerce or e-business. They are also major components in the computer-based linkages between an organization's suppliers and/or customers. Through *electronic data interchange,* or EDI, companies communicate electronically with one another to move and share documents such as purchase orders, bills, receipt confirmations, and even payments for services rendered.[17] An example of how extranets and interorganizational networking systems are contributing to the emergence of electronic markets for goods and services is provided in *Figure 3.2.*

- **Extranets** are computer networks that use the public Internet for communication between the organization and its environment.

- **Interorganizational information systems** facilitate information transfers among two or more organizations.

 ## INFORMATION AND PROBLEM SOLVING

Information is a foundation for organizational success and it is essential to solving the myriad of problems experienced daily. A **problem** is any difference between an actual situation and a desired situation. The most obvious problem situation is a *performance deficiency,* that is, when actual performance is less than desired. For example, a manager faces a possible problem when turnover or absenteeism suddenly increases in the work unit, when a subordinate's daily output decreases, or when a higher executive complains about something that has been said or done. However, another problem situation emerges as a *performance opportunity* when an actual situation turns out either better than anticipated or offers the potential to be so. The challenge in dealing with any problem, be it a per-

- A **problem** is a difference between an actual situation and a desired situation.

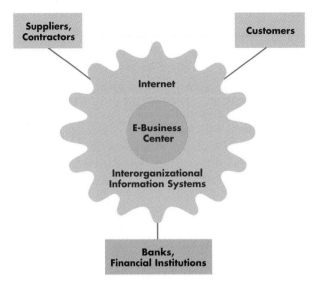

Figure 3.2   How e-businesses work through intranets and interorganizational information systems.

- **Problem solving** is the process of identifying a discrepancy between an actual and desired state of affairs and then taking action to resolve it.

formance deficiency or an opportunity, is to proceed with effective **problem solving**—the process of identifying a discrepancy between an actual and desired state of affairs and then taking action to resolve the deficiency or take advantage of the opportunity. The entire problem-solving process is dependent upon the right information being available to the right people at the right times.

TYPES OF MANAGERIAL PROBLEMS

- A **structured problem** is familiar, straightforward, and clear in its information requirements.

Managers face many problems in their day-to-day work. Some are **structured problems** that are familiar, straightforward, and clear with respect to the information needed to resolve them. Such problems can often be expected to arise in common situations that regularly occur. The manager can therefore plan ahead and develop specific ways to deal with them or even take action to prevent their occurrence. For example, "personnel" problems are common whenever decisions are made on pay raises and promotions, vacation requests, committee assignments, and the like. Knowing this, proactive managers plan ahead so they can handle complaints effectively when they arise.

- A **programmed decision** applies a solution from past experience to the problem at hand.

When problems are structured and routine and tend to arise on a regular basis they can be addressed through standard or prepared responses. Called **programmed decisions,** these are solutions already available from past experience that are appropriate for the problem at hand. A good example is the decision to reorder inventory automatically when on-hand stock falls below a predetermined level. Today, an increasing number of programmed decisions are being assisted or handled by computers using decision-support software.

- An **unstructured problem** involves ambiguities and information deficiencies.

Managers must also deal with **unstructured problems** that involve ambiguities and information deficiencies and often occur as new or unexpected situations. They are most often unanticipated and are addressed reactively as they occur. Unstructured problems require novel solutions. Proactive managers are sometimes able to get a jump on them by realizing that a situation is susceptible to problems and then making contingency plans. For example, at the Vanguard Group executives are tireless in their preparation for a variety of events that could disrupt their mutual fund business. Their biggest fear is an investor panic that overloads their customer service system during a major plunge in the bond or stock markets. In anticipation of this, the firm has trained its accountants, lawyers, and money fund managers to staff the telephones if needed. Contingency plans also exist for more structured problems such as power outages and telephone system failures.[18]

When new and unfamiliar problems arise, **nonprogrammed decisions** are specifically tailored to the situation at hand. The information requirements for defining and resolving nonroutine problems are typically high. Although computer support may assist in information processing, the decision will most likely involve human judgment. Most problems faced by higher-level managers are of this type. This is one reason why the demands on a manager's conceptual skills, as discussed in Chapter 1, increase as one moves toward higher levels of managerial responsibility.

A **crisis problem** is an unexpected problem that can lead to disaster if not resolved quickly and appropriately. No one can avoid crises, and the public is well aware of the immensity of corporate crises in the modern world. The Tylenol poisonings, Chernobyl nuclear plant explosion in the former Soviet Union, and the *Exxon Valdez* oil spill of years past are but a few sensational examples. Managers in more progressive organizations now anticipate that crises, unfortunately, will occur. They are installing "early-warning" crisis information systems and developing crisis management plans to deal with them in the best possible ways.

The ability to handle crises may be the ultimate test of a manager's problem-solving capabilities. The process begins with the identification of the problem. Care must be taken to isolate and identify the real problem(s) underlying the crisis. This is where information and teamwork — the involvement of others — are especially crucial. Unfortunately, research indicates that managers may react to crises by isolating themselves and trying to solve the problem alone or in a small "closed" group.[19] This unfortunate tendency actually denies them access to crucial problem-solving information and assistance at the very time they are most needed. The crisis may even be accentuated if more problems are created because critical decisions are made with poor or inadequate information and from a limited perspective. Intel's initial failure to respond positively to the "crisis" relating to its defective Pentium chip is a now infamous case in point.

* A **nonprogrammed decision** develops a unique and specific solution for the problem at hand.

* A **crisis problem** is an unexpected problem that can lead to disaster if not resolved quickly and appropriately.

PROBLEM ENVIRONMENTS

Figure 3.3 illustrates three different conditions or environments for problem solving in organizations: certainty, risk, and uncertainty. All managers make decisions under each condition, but risk and uncertainty are common to the more complex and unstructured problems faced by top managers. Former Coca-Cola CEO Roberto Goizueta, for example, has been described as having had a "taste for risk" and a "lot of guts." Among his risky moves were introducing Diet Coke to the market, changing the formula of Coca-Cola to create New Coke, and then reversing direction after New Coke flopped.[20]

In a **certain environment,** there is sufficient information for the problem solver to know the possible alternatives and what the results of each would be. This is an ideal condition for problem solving. The challenge is simply to study the

* A **certain environment** offers complete information on possible action alternatives and their consequences.

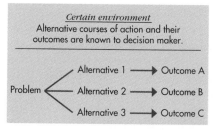
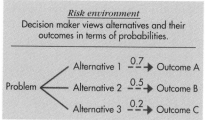
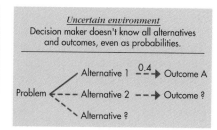

Figure 3.3   Three environments for managerial decision making and problem solving.

- **A risk environment** lacks complete information, but offers "probabilities" of the likely outcomes for possible action alternatives.

alternatives and choose the best solution. Very few managerial problems occur in certain environments, but steps can sometimes be taken to reduce uncertainty.

In a **risk environment,** the problem solver lacks complete information on action alternatives and their consequences but has some sense of the "probabilities" associated with their occurrence. A *probability,* in turn, is the degree of likelihood (e.g., 4 chances out of 10) that an event will occur. Risk is a fairly common decision environment for managers. It is especially typical for entrepreneurs and organizations that depend on ideas and continued innovation for their success.

- **An uncertain environment** is so poor in information that it is difficult even to assign probabilities to the likely outcomes of alternatives.

When information is so poor that managers are unable even to assign probabilities to the likely outcomes of alternatives that are known, an **uncertain environment** exists. This is the most difficult problem environment.[21] Uncertainty forces managers to rely heavily on creativity in solving problems; it requires unique, novel, and often totally innovative alternatives to existing patterns of behavior. Groups are frequently used for problem solving in such situations. In all cases, the responses to uncertainty depend greatly on intuition, educated guessing, and hunches—all of which leave considerable room for error.

HOW MANAGERS DEAL WITH PROBLEMS

In practice, people display three quite different "styles" that are evident in the ways managers and other persons deal with workplace problems. Some are *problem avoiders* who ignore information that would otherwise signal the presence of a problem. Such persons are *inactive* and do not want to deal with problems. *Problem solvers* try to solve problems when they arise. They are *reactive* in responding to information about problems after they occur. *Problem seekers* actively process information and look for problems to solve or opportunities to explore. These persons are *proactive* in anticipating problems before they occur. True problem seekers are forward thinking; they anticipate problems and opportunities and take appropriate action to gain the advantage. Success at problem seeking is one of the ways exceptional managers distinguish themselves from the merely good ones.

- **Systematic thinking** approaches problems in a rational and analytical fashion.

Another distinction in the way managers deal with problems contrasts "systematic" with "intuitive" thinking. In **systematic thinking** a person approaches problems in a rational, step-by-step, and analytical fashion. This type of thinking involves breaking a complex problem into smaller components and then addressing them in a logical and integrated fashion. Managers who are systematic can be expected to make a plan before taking action and then to search for information to facilitate problem solving in a step-by-step fashion.

- **Intuitive thinking** approaches problems in a flexible and spontaneous fashion.

Someone using **intuitive thinking,** by contrast, is more flexible and spontaneous and also may be quite creative.[22] This type of thinking allows us to respond imaginatively to a problem based on a quick and broad evaluation of the situation and the possible alternative courses of action. Managers who are intuitive can be expected to deal with many aspects of a problem at once, jump quickly from one issue to another, and consider "hunches" based on experience or spontaneous ideas. This approach tends to work best in situations of high uncertainty where facts are limited and few precedents exist.[23]

- **Multidimensional thinking** is the capacity to view many problems at once, in relationship to one another, and across long and short time horizons.

Managers should feel confident in applying both systematic and intuitive thinking to problem solving. This is part of the challenge in becoming successful through **multidimensional thinking,** that is, the ability to view many problems at once, in relationship to one another, and across long and short time horizons.[24] Senior managers, in particular, must deal with portfolios of problems and opportunities that consist of multiple and interrelated issues. Good problem solving requires that these problems be "mapped" into a network that can be managed actively over time as priorities, events, and demands continuously change. Effective managers are also able to make decisions and take actions in the short run that benefit longer run objectives. Through all the daily challenges of a complex and shifting mix of problems, there is still a need to retain a sense of direction as each one is resolved. This requires skill at **strategic opportunism** — the ability to remain focused on long-term objectives while being flexible enough to resolve short-term problems and opportunities in a timely manner.[25]

THE DECISION-MAKING PROCESS

Figure 3.4 describes a typical approach to decision making and managerial problem solving. The process begins with identification of the problem and ends with the evaluation of implemented solutions.[26] The five steps in this approach are (1) identifying and defining the problem, (2) generating and evaluating possible solutions, (3) choosing a preferred solution *and* conducting the "ethics double check," (4) implementing the solution, and (5) evaluating results. Importantly, Step 3 in this model includes a built-in "checkpoint" as a way to verify the ethical aspects of a decision before any action is taken.

Working with the following short but true case will help put all five steps into perspective. It reflects how changing times and highly competitive environments can take their toll on organizations, the people that work for them, and the communities in which they operate.

> *The Ajax Case.* On December 31, the Ajax Aluminum Company decided to close down its Murphysboro plant. Market conditions were forcing layoffs, and the company could not find a buyer for the plant. Of 172 employees, some had been with the company as long as 18 years, others as little as 6 months. All were to be terminated. Under company policy, they would be given severance pay equal to one week's pay per year of service. Ajax's top management faced a difficult problem: how to minimize the negative impact of the plant closing on these employees, their families, and the small town of Murphysboro itself.

Think about how you would feel as one of the affected employees. Think about how you would feel as the mayor of this small town. Think how you would feel as a corporate executive having to make the required decisions.

STEP 1: IDENTIFY AND DEFINE THE PROBLEM

The first step of finding and defining the problem is a stage of information gathering, information processing, and deliberation. It often begins with the appearance of **problem symptoms,** which signal the presence of a performance defi-

• **Strategic opportunism** is the ability to remain focused on long-term objectives by being flexible in dealing with short-term problems and opportunities as they occur.

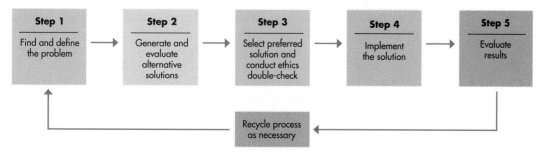

Figure 3.4 Steps in decision making and problem solving.

Ariane Daguin and George Faison know the concept of risk quite well. In their former jobs as sales manager and general manager, respectively, for a New York paté producer, they located a foie gras supplier as good as any in France. When their boss balked at contracting for all the farmer's output, they took a risk. Betting that there was a market, they quit their jobs, invested $15,000 to start D'Artagnan, Inc., and signed the supplier. Their company now grosses some $15 million per year—three times that of their former employer.

ciency or opportunity. The manager's goal at this stage is to assess a situation properly. She or he must look beyond symptoms to find out what is really wrong or how things could be improved. Special care must be taken not just to address a symptom while ignoring the true problem. Merely reprimanding a subordinate for absenteeism, for example, may never solve the underlying problem of dissatisfaction with a new job assignment.

The act of problem finding involves identifying gaps between actual and desired states of affairs and determining their causes. The manager who is good at finding problems is continually searching and scanning the work environment for indicators of potential performance deficiencies or opportunities. In his book *Innovation and Entrepreneurship*, Peter Drucker notes that many managers fail to do this.[27] For example, the success of Japanese firms in the market for "fax" machines may be due in part to the failure of U.S. firms to seize an opportunity. The fax machine was invented in America, and U.S. firms had them ready to sell. But market researchers supposedly—and erroneously—concluded that there was little demand for a product whose cost per message sent was higher than the mail.[28]

The way a problem is originally defined can have a major impact on how it is eventually resolved. Three common mistakes may occur at this critical first step in problem solving. *Mistake number 1* is defining the problem too broadly or too narrowly. To take a classic example, the problem stated as "Build a better mousetrap" might be better defined as "Get rid of the mice." That is, managers should define problems so as to give themselves the best possible range of problem-solving options. *Mistake number 2* is focusing on symptoms instead of causes. Symptoms are indicators that problems may exist, but they shouldn't be mistaken for the problems themselves. Managers should be able to spot problem symptoms (e.g., a drop in performance). But instead of treating symptoms (such as simply encouraging higher performance), managers should address their root causes (such as discovering the worker's need for training in the use of a complex new computer system). *Mistake number 3* is choosing the wrong problem to deal with. Managers should set priorities and deal with the most important problems first. They should also give priority to problems that are truly solvable.

> *Back to the Ajax Case.* Closing the Ajax plant in Murphysboro will put a substantial number of people from this small community out of work. The unemployment created will have a negative impact on individuals, their families, and the community as a whole. The loss of the Ajax tax base will further hurt the community. The local financial implications of the plant closure will be great. The problem for Ajax management is how to minimize the adverse impact of the plant closing on the employees, their families, and the community.

STEP 2: GENERATE AND EVALUATE POSSIBLE SOLUTIONS

Once the problem is defined, it is possible to formulate one or several potential solutions. At this stage, more information is gathered, data are analyzed, and the pros and cons of possible alternative courses of action are identified. This effort to locate, clarify, and evaluate alternative solutions is critical to successful problem solving. The involvement of other persons is very important here in order to maximize information and build commitment. The end result can only be as good as the quality of the alternative solutions generated in this step. The better the pool of alternatives, the more likely a good solution will be achieved.

Common errors in this stage include selecting a particular solution too quickly and choosing an alternative that, although convenient, has damaging side effects or is not as good as others that might be discovered with extra effort. The analysis of alternatives should determine how well each possible course of action deals with the problem while taking into account the environment within which the problem exists — most likely an environment of risk or uncertainty, as previously illustrated in *Figure 3.3*. Typical criteria for evaluating alternatives include the following:

- *Benefits:* What are the "benefits" of using the alternative to solve a performance deficiency or take advantage of an opportunity?

- *Costs:* What are the "costs" of implementing the alternative, including direct resource investments as well as any potential negative side effects?

- *Timeliness:* How fast will the benefits occur and a positive impact be achieved?

- *Acceptability:* To what extent will the alternative be accepted and supported by those who must work with it?

- *Ethical soundness:* How well does the alternative meet acceptable ethical criteria in the eyes of the various stakeholders?

← Criteria for evaluating alternatives

A very basic evaluation involves **cost-benefit analysis,** the comparison of what an alternative will cost in relation to the expected benefits. At a minimum, the benefits of a chosen alternative should be greater than its costs. Various quantitative approaches can help in the analysis of costs and benefits. Many of these are mathematically sophisticated and fall within the realm of management science and operations research, as discussed in the next chapter. In any case, the insights of quantitative analysis must be tempered with human judgment to ensure that an even broader set of criteria are properly considered.

- **Cost-benefit analysis** involves comparing the costs and benefits of each potential course of action.

> *Back to the Ajax Case.* The Ajax plant is going to be closed. Among the possible alternatives that can be considered are (1) close the plant on schedule and be done with it; (2) delay the plant closing until all efforts have been made to sell it to another firm; (3) offer to sell the plant to the employees and/or local interests; (4) close the plant and offer transfers to other Ajax plant locations; or (5) close the plant, offer transfers, and help the employees find new jobs in and around Murphysboro.

STEP 3: CHOOSE A SOLUTION AND CONDUCT THE "ETHICS DOUBLE CHECK"

At this point, a "decision" is made to select a particular course of action. Just how this is done and by whom must be successfully resolved in each problem situation. In some cases, the best alternative may be selected using a cost-benefit criterion; in others, additional criteria may come into play. Once alternatives are generated and evaluated, however, a final choice among them must be made. This is the point of ultimate decision making.

Decision-making Models

Management theory recognizes differences between two major models of decision making, which are shown in *Figure 3.5* — the classical model and the behavioral model. The **classical decision model** views the manager as acting in a certain world. Here, the manager faces a clearly defined problem and knows all possible action alternatives as well as their consequences. As a result, he or she makes an **optimizing decision** that gives the absolute best solution to the problem. The classical approach is a very rational model that assumes perfect information is available for decision making.

Behavioral scientists question the assumptions underlying the classical decision model. Perhaps best represented by the work of Herbert Simon, they recog-

- The **classical decision model** describes how managers should ideally make decisions using complete information.

- An **optimizing decision** results when a manager chooses an alternative that gives the absolute best solution to a problem.

Classical model
Views manager as acting with complete information in a certain environment

- Clearly defined problem
- Knowledge of all possible alternatives and their consequences
- Optimizing decision— choice of the "optimum" alternative

Administrative model
Views manager as having cognitive limitations and acting with incomplete information in risk and uncertain environments

- Problem not clearly defined
- Knowledge is limited on possible alternatives and their consequences
- Satisficing decision— choice of "satisfactory" alternative

Judgmental heuristics approach
Heuristics are adopted to simplify managerial decision making

Decisions are influenced by:
- Information readily available in memory— the available heuristic
- Comparisons with similar circumstances— the representatives heuristic
- Current situation— The anchoring and adjustment heuristic

Figure 3.5 The classical, administrative, and judgmental heuristics approaches to decision making.

nize the existence of *cognitive limitations,* or limits to our human information-processing capabilities.[29] These limitations make it hard for managers to become fully informed and make perfectly rational decisions. They create a *bounded rationality* such that managerial decisions are rational only within the boundaries defined by the available information.

- The **administrative decision model** describes how managers act in situations of limited information and bounded rationality.

The **administrative decision model,** accordingly, assumes that people act only in terms of what they perceive about a given situation. Because such perceptions are frequently imperfect, the decision maker has only partial knowledge about the available action alternatives and their consequences. Consequently, the first alternative that appears to give a satisfactory resolution of the problem is likely to be chosen. Simon, who won a Nobel Prize for his work, calls this tendency **satisficing**—choosing the first satisfactory alternative that comes to your attention. This model seems especially accurate in describing how people make decisions about ambiguous problems in risky and uncertain conditions.

- **Satisficing** involves choosing the first satisfactory alternative that comes to your attention.

Judgmental Heuristics

Faced with complex environments, limited information, and cognitive limitations, people tend to use simplifying strategies for decision making. These strategies are called **heuristics,** and their use can cause decision errors. An awareness of judgmental heuristics and their potential biases can help improve your decision-making capabilities.[30]

- **Heuristics** are strategies for simplifying decision making.

The *availability heuristic* occurs when people use information "readily available" from memory as a basis for assessing a current event or situation. An example is deciding not to invest in a new product based on your recollection of how well a similar new product performed in the recent past. The *potential bias* is that the readily available information may be fallible and represent irrelevant factors. The new product that recently failed may have been a good idea that was released to market at the wrong time of year.

The *representativeness heuristic* occurs when people assess the likelihood of something occurring based on its similarity to a stereotyped set of occurrences. An example is deciding to hire someone for a job vacancy simply because he or she graduated from the same school attended by your last and most successful new hire. The *potential bias* is that the representative stereotype may fail to discriminate important and unique factors relevant to the decision. For instance, the abilities and career expectations of the newly hired person may not fit the job requirements.

The *anchoring and adjustment heuristic* involves making decisions based on adjustments to a previously existing value or starting point. An example is setting a new salary level for an employee by simply raising the prior year's salary by a reasonable percentage. The *potential bias* is that this may inappropriately bias a decision toward only incremental movement from the starting point. For instance, the individual's market value may be substantially higher than the existing salary. A simple adjustment won't keep this person from looking for another job.

Manager's Notepad 3.2

How to Avoid the Escalation Trap

- Set advance limits on your involvement and commitment to a particular course of action; stick with these limits.
- Make your own decisions; don't follow the lead of others since they are also prone to escalation.
- Carefully determine just why you are continuing a course of action; if there are insufficient reasons to continue, don't.
- Remind yourself of what a course of action is costing; consider the saving of such costs as a reason to discontinue.
- Watch for escalation tendencies; be on guard against their influence on both you and others involved in the course of action.

Escalating Commitments

An effective manager is also aware of another potential decision-making error called **escalating commitment.** This is a decision to increase effort and perhaps apply more resources to pursue a course of action that is *not* working.[31] In such cases, managers let the momentum of the situation overwhelm them. They are unable to decide to "call it quits," even when experience otherwise indicates that this is the most appropriate thing to do. *Manager's Notepad 3.2* offers advice on avoiding this tendency.

Ethics Double Check

Any decision to select a potential solution for a problem should be tested by performing an "ethics double check." This requirement is increasingly necessary to ensure that the ethical aspects of a problem are properly considered in the complex, fast-paced decision-making environment so common in today's organizations. It is also consistent with the demanding moral standards of modern society. A willingness to pause to examine the ethics of a proposed decision may well result in both better decisions and the prevention of costly litigation. More details on this aspect of decision making will be provided in Chapter 6, on ethics and social responsibility. For now, consider whether or not an "ethics double check" could improve decision making in the Ajax plant case.

> *Back to the Ajax Case.* Management at Ajax decided to follow alternative 5 as described in Step 2 of the decision-making process. They would close the plant, offer transfers to company plants in another state, and offer to help displaced employees find new jobs in and around Murphysboro.

STEP 4: IMPLEMENT THE SOLUTION

Given the preferred solution, appropriate action plans must be established and fully implemented. This is the stage at which directions are finally set and problem-solving actions are initiated. Nothing new can or will happen according to plan unless action is taken. Managers not only need the determination and creativity to arrive at a decision, they also need the ability and willingness to implement it. One Christmas, for example, a United Parcel Service regional manager learned that the railroad had left a flatcar carrying two UPS trailers on a siding in central

- **Escalating commitment** is the tendency to continue to pursue a course of action, even though it is not working.

• **Pentagon Entertainment**
http://www.pentagon.net

"If you're savvy on the Net, you can get anything for free." At least that's what Adam Lilling says as president of the online music dealer Pentagon Entertainment. In a tiny office and with only one employee, his firm ships $1 million worth of music annually. The 27-year-old entrepreneur is one of a growing number who see the Internet as the path to the future.

• **Motorola**
http://www.mot.com

Motorola uses an intranet to maintain and update complex assembly instructions for use where they are most needed—on the factory floor. When instructions change they are updated on the web server and become immediately available at every terminal on the production floor. Such "cyber instructions" have passed ISO audits without any problems.

Illinois. The manager paid for a high-speed diesel to get the flatcar into Chicago ahead of an Amtrak passenger train. He had two UPS planes diverted to Chicago to get the contents of the trailers to their destinations in Florida and Louisiana in time for Christmas. The manager didn't ask permission but took quick and decisive action to solve the problem. He received high praise from his superiors as a result.[32]

The "ways" in which previous steps have been accomplished can have an additional and powerful impact at this stage of implementation. Difficulties at this stage often trace to the *lack-of-participation error,* or the failure to adequately involve those persons whose support is necessary to ensure a decision's complete implementation. Managers who use participation wisely get the right people involved in decisions and problem solving from the beginning. When they do, implementation typically follows quickly, smoothly, and to everyone's satisfaction. Involvement not only makes everyone better informed, it also builds the commitments needed for implementation.

> *Back to the Ajax Case.* Ajax ran an ad in the local and regional newspapers for several days. The ad called attention to an "Ajax skill bank" composed of "qualified, dedicated, and well-motivated employees with a variety of skills and experiences." Interested employers were urged to contact Ajax for further information.

STEP 5: EVALUATE RESULTS

The decision-making process is not complete until results are evaluated. If the desired results are not achieved, the process must be renewed to allow for corrective actions. In this sense, evaluation is a form of managerial control. It involves a continuing commitment to gathering information on performance results. This can reveal where modifications can be made in the original solution to improve its results over time. It can also set the stage for "go — no go" decisions that avoid the pitfalls of escalating commitment to previously chosen courses of action.

In any evaluation, both the positive and negative consequences of the chosen course of action should be examined. If the original solution appears inadequate, a return to earlier steps in problem-solving may be required to generate a modified or new solution. In this way, problem solving becomes a dynamic and ongoing activity within the management process. Evaluation is also made easier if the solution involves clear objectives that include measurable targets and timetables.

> *Back to the Ajax Case.* The advertisement ran for some 15 days. The plant's industrial relations manager commented, "I've been very pleased with the results." That's all we know. You can look back on the case and problem-solving process just described and judge for yourself how well Ajax management did in dealing with this very difficult problem. Perhaps you would have approached the situation and the five steps in decision making somewhat differently.

LEARNING AND KNOWLEDGE MANAGEMENT

Management theorist Peter Drucker considers knowledge the principal resource of a competitive society and warns that "knowledge constantly makes itself obsolete."[33] This is an age in which intellectual capital counts highly, and knowledge workers — the people who have the knowledge — are critical assets. It is an age of transformation that places increasing value on learning and knowledge management.[34]

ORGANIZATIONAL LEARNING

"Learning," says British Petroleum's (BP) CEO John Browne, "is at the heart of a company's ability to adapt to a rapidly changing environment." He goes on to add, "In order to generate extraordinary value for its shareholders, a company must learn better than its competitors and apply that knowledge throughout its businesses faster and more widely than they do." [35] Like other progressive organizations today, BP is striving to build the foundations of a true **learning organization.** This is an organization that "by virtue of people, values, and systems is able to continuously change and improve its performance based upon the lessons of experience." [36]

There is no doubt that organizations and workers of all types today must continually adapt to new situations if they are to survive and prosper over the long run — this is a reality of work in the 21st century. Consultant Peter Senge, author of the popular book *The Fifth Discipline,* identifies the following core ingredients of learning organizations:[37]

1. *Mental models* — everyone sets aside old ways of thinking.
2. *Personal mastery* — everyone becomes self-aware and open to others.
3. *Systems thinking* — everyone learns how the whole organization works.
4. *Shared vision* — everyone understands and agrees to a plan of action.
5. *Team learning* — everyone works together to accomplish the plan.

← Ingredients of learning organizations

Senge's concept of the learning organization places high value on developing the ability to learn and then make that learning continuously available to all organizational members. BP's CEO Browne says that organizations can learn from many sources. They can learn from their own experience. They can learn from the experiences of their contractors, suppliers, partners, and customers. And they can learn from firms in unrelated businesses.[38] All of this, of course, depends on a willingness to seek out learning opportunities from these sources and to make information sharing an expected and valued work behavior. In addressing the challenges of competing in a global economy, for example, General Electric's CEO Jack Welch says, "The aim in a global business is to get the best ideas from everywhere. . . . Our culture is designed around making a hero out of those who translate ideas from one place to another, who help somebody else." [39]

LIFELONG LEARNING

For each of us individually, this focus on organizational learning highlights the importance of making commitments to personal **lifelong learning.** This process of continuously learning from our daily experiences and opportunities helps us build a portfolio of skills that are always up to date and valuable to an employer. Indeed, learning can be thought of as a skill that can substantially affect your personal and career success. A critical part of job-related learning comes from "learning by doing," and this means that you must always look for good job opportunities that make such learning possible. Consider these comments from workers who recognize the importance of lifelong learning.[40]

> John Waterman, age 30 — "I'm here because I keep learning. Whenever I start to get a little bored, a new project comes along with opportunities for learning."

> Tracy Amabile, age 33 — "The people and the learning are what's primary. I've been provided with a lot of opportunities."

- **Knowledge management** is the processes utilizing organizational knowledge to achieve competitive advantage.

• Ernst & Young
http://www.eycan.com

John Peetz, chief knowledge officer at Ernst & Young, considers knowledge management critical. "It's one of four core processes—sell work, do work, manage people, and manage knowledge." His responsibilities include communicating the importance of sharing knowledge, initiating and supporting projects to distribute knowledge, and managing the firm's technological infrastructure.

KNOWLEDGE MANAGEMENT

A new term is earning a significant place in management theory and practice. The concept of **knowledge management** is used to describe the processes through which organizations develop, organize, and share knowledge to achieve competitive advantage.[41] The significance of knowledge management as a strategic and integrating force in organizations is represented by the emergence of a new executive job title—*Chief Knowledge Officer,* or CKO. This position of CKO is responsible for energizing learning processes and making sure that an organization's portfolio of intellectual assets and pool of knowledge are well managed and continually enhanced.[42] The intellectual assets, furthermore, include such things as patents, intellectual property rights, trade secrets, and special processes and methods, as well as the accumulated knowledge and understanding of the entire workforce.[43]

Knowledge management involves the understanding of and commitment to the information technology described in this chapter. It requires the creation of an organizational culture in which information sharing, learning, and knowledge creation are part of the norm. It requires a special form of organizational leadership that recognizes that intellectual capital is an invaluable asset in this age of transformation. And at the bottom of it all, knowledge management requires managerial and leadership respect for people and their wonderful creative potential in organizations.

> All we are talking about is human dignity and voice—giving people a chance to speak, to have their best idea. That is a global desire of all people who breathe. . . . My job is allocating capital, human and financial, and transferring best practice. That's all. It's transferring ideas, constantly pushing ideas, putting the right people in the right job and giving them the resources to win."[44]
>
> Jack Welch, CEO, General Electric

CHAPTER REVIEW

This section should be used as an end-of-chapter "study guide." The *Summary* helps to put chapter content into overall perspective. The list of *Key Terms* allows you to double-check your familiarity with basic concepts and definitions. *Self-Test 3* gives you the opportunity to test your basic comprehension of the chapter using sample test questions.

SUMMARY

How is information technology changing the workplace?

- Continuing advances in computers and information technology (IT) bring many opportunities for improving the workplace by utilizing information better.

- Today's "electronic" offices with Email, voice messaging, and networked computer systems are changing the nature of office work.

- A major and rapidly growing force in the economy are e-businesses, which engage in electronic commerce through the Internet.

- The many information needs in organizations are served by a variety of information systems using the latest in computer and information technologies.

- An information system collects, organizes, and distributes data so that they become useful information.

- To be effective an information system must be designed to meet the needs of end users.

What are the current directions in information systems?

- A management information system, or MIS, collects, organizes, stores, and distributes data in a way that meets the information needs of managers.

- Decision-support systems (DSSs) provide information and help managers make decisions to solve complex problems.

- Group-decision support systems utilize groupware to allow the computer-mediated exchange of information and decision making by group members.

- Intraorganizational information systems use intranets and networks to allow persons within an organization to share databases and communicate electronically.

- Interorganizational information systems use extranets and the public Internet for communication between the organization and its environment.

How is information used for problem solving?

- Information is data that are made useful for decision making and problem solving.

- A problem is a discrepancy between an actual and a desired state of affairs.

- Managers face structured and unstructured problems in environments of certainty, risk, and uncertainty.

- The most threatening type of problem is the crisis, which occurs unexpectedly and can lead to disaster if it is not handled quickly and properly.

How do managers make decisions?

- The steps in the decision-making process are find and define the problem, generate and evaluate alternatives, choose the preferred solution, implement the solution, and evaluate the results.

- An optimizing decision, following the classical model, chooses the absolute best solution from a known set of alternatives.

- A satisficing decision, following the administrative model, chooses the first satisfactory alternative to come to attention.

- Judgmental heuristics, such as the availability heuristic, the anchoring and adjustment heuristic, and the representativeness heuristic, can bias decision making.

How do learning and knowledge management create value?

- The old ways of management aren't good enough anymore; an age of transformation demands that the best of the past be combined with new thinking so organizations can be competitive in the 21st century.

- A learning organization is one in which people, values, and systems support continuous change and improvement based upon the lessons of experience.

- Lifelong learning involves a personal commitment to continuously seek learning opportunities in one's work.

- Knowledge management is the process of capturing, developing, and utilizing the knowledge of an organization to achieve competitive advantage.

KEY TERMS

Administrative decision
model (p. 62)

Certain environment
(p. 57)

Chief information officer
(p. 53)

Classical decision model
(p. 61)

Cost-benefit analysis
(p. 61)

Crisis problem (p. 57)

Decision making (p. 59)

Electronic commerce
(p. 51)

Enterprisewide networks
(p. 55)

Escalating commitment
(p. 63)

Extranet (p. 55)

Heuristics (p. 62)

Information system (p. 53)

Intellectual capital (p. 50)

Interorganizational
information system
(p. 55)

Intranet (p. 55)

Intuitive thinking (p. 58)

Knowledge management
(p. 66)

Management information
system (p. 53)

Multidimensional thinking
(p. 58)

Nonprogrammed decision
(p. 57)

Optimizing decision (p. 61)

Problem (p. 55)

Problem solving (p. 56)

Problem symptoms
(p. 59)

Programmed decision
(p. 56)

Risk environment
(p. 58)

Satisficing (p. 62)

Strategic opportunism
(p. 59)

Structured problem
(p. 56)

Systematic thinking (p. 58)

Uncertain environment
(p. 58)

Unstructured problem
(p. 56)

SELF-TEST 3

Take this test much as you would in a normal classroom situation. It should offer you a good way to check your basic comprehension of chapter material. Answers may be found at the end of the book.

MULTIPLE-CHOICE QUESTIONS:

1. _____ is the collective brainpower or shared knowledge of an organization and its workforce. (a) Artificial intelligence (b) Groupware (c) Intellectual capital (d) Intelligence information

2. _____ are special computer programs with a series of "if . . . then" rules to help users analyze and solve problems. (a) Expert systems (b) Virtual systems (c) Intranets (d) Extranets

3. The computer software programs that support virtual teamwork in organizations are known as (a) expert systems (b) heuristics (c) groupware (d) virtual systems

4. The third step in the development of an "e-business" is to utilize a web site for _____. (a) publishing information (b) allowing transactions including buying and selling merchandise (c) allowing customers to check their accounts (d) allowing customers to verify their order status

5. A problem is a discrepancy between a/an _____ situation and a desired situation. (a) future (b) past (c) actual (d) planned

6. A/an _____ thinker approaches problems in a rational and analytic fashion. (a) systematic (b) intuitive (c) internal (d) external

7. The first step in the problem-solving process is to _____. (a) identify alternatives (b) evaluate results (c) find and define the problem (d) choose a solution

8. Being asked to develop a plan for increased international sales is an example of the _____ problems that managers must be prepared to deal with. (a) expected (b) unstructured (c) crisis (d) structured

9. Costs, timeliness, and _____ are among the criteria recommended in this chapter for evaluating alternative courses of action. (a) ethical soundness (b) competitiveness (c) self-interest (d) past experience

10. The _____ decision model views managers as making optimizing decisions, whereas the _____ decision model views them as making satisficing decisions. (a) administrative, human relations (b) classical, administrative (c) heuristic, humanistic (d) quantitative, behavioral

TRUE-FALSE QUESTIONS:

11. The Chief Information Officer is typically a middle manager in an organization. T F

12. The "electronic office" described in this chapter is interesting, but it is a long way from reality. T F

13. A field salesperson might interact directly with manufacturing schedulers through an enterprisewide computer network. T F

14. Problems may be either performance deficiencies or performance opportunities. T F

15. The last step in the problem-solving process is to choose a preferred solution. T F

16. Systematic thinking is more flexible and spontaneous than intuitive thinking. T F

17. The least common problem-solving environment faced by managers is risk. T F

18. The escalation trap is an unwillingness to allow the participation of others in the decision-making process. T F

19. Managers should always conduct an "ethics double check" of decisions made during the problem-solving process. T F

20. Lifelong learning is an essential commitment on the part of the individuals who are expected to perform in the learning organizations of the future. T F

SHORT-RESPONSE QUESTIONS:

21. In any organization, what is the purpose of an information system?

22. What three factors are most important to the success of an information system and what are three common information system mistakes that managers should avoid?

23. What is the difference between problem solving and decision making?

24. How would a manager use systematic thinking and intuitive thinking in problem solving.

APPLICATION QUESTION:

25. As a participant in a new "mentoring" program between your university and a local high school, you have volunteered to give a presentation to a class of sophomores on the challenges in the new "electronic workplace." The goal is to sensitize them to developments in office automation and motivate them to take the best advantage of their high school program so as to prepare themselves for the workplace of the future. What will you say to them?

CHAPTER FOUR

Historical Foundations of Management

Planning Ahead—Chapter 4 Study Questions

- What can be learned from classical management thinking?
- What ideas were introduced by the human resource approaches?
- What is the role of quantitative analysis in management?
- What is unique about the systems view and contingency thinking?
- What are the continuing themes as we enter the 21st century?

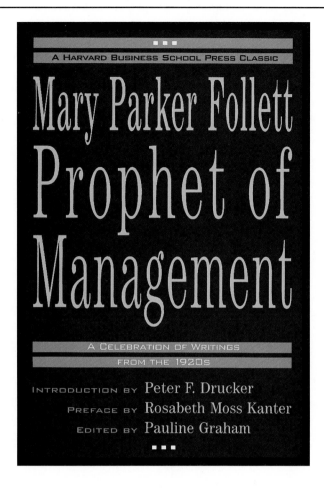

Don't Neglect the Wisdom of History

When Harvard University Press released *Mary Parker Follett—Prophet of Management: A Celebration of Writings from the 1920s,* we were reminded of the wisdom of history.[1] Although writing in a different day and age, her ideas are rich with foresight. She advocated cooperation and better horizontal relationships in organizations, taught respect for the experience and knowledge of workers, warned against the dangers of too much hierarchy, and called for visionary leadership. These ideas remain at the forefront of progressive management today and remind us that Follett was a true *21st*-century thinker. The new workplace is being forged on the themes of empowerment, involvement, flexibility, and self-management. And rather than naively believe that we are now reinventing management practice, it may be better to recognize the historical roots of many modern ideas and admit that we are still trying to perfect them.[2]

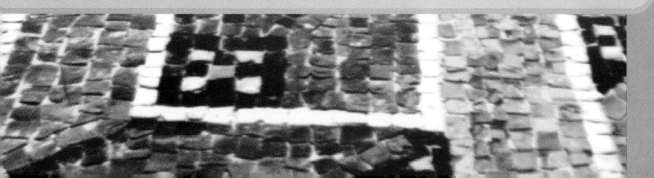

In *The Evolution of Management Thought,* Daniel Wren traces management as far back as 5000 B.C., when ancient Sumerians used written records to assist in governmental and commercial activities.[3] Management was important to the construction of the Egyptian pyramids, the rise of the Roman Empire, and the commercial success of 14th-century Venice. By the time of the Industrial Revolution in the 1700s great social changes helped prompt a great leap forward in the manufacture of basic staples and consumer goods. Industrial change was accelerated by Adam Smith's ideas of mass production through specialized tasks and the division of labor. By the turn of the 20th century, Henry Ford and others were making mass production a mainstay of the modern economy. Since then, the science and practices of management have been on a rapid and continuing path of development.

The legacies of this rich history of management must be understood as we move rapidly into the new conditions and challenges of 21st-century management. The historical context of management thinking can be described in the following framework:

Major schools of management thought

- The *classical approaches* that focus on developing universal principles for use in various management situations.

- The *human resource approaches* that focus on human needs, the work group, and the role of social factors in the workplace.

- The *quantitative or management science approaches* that focus on applying mathematical techniques for management problem solving.

- The *modern approaches* that focus on the systems view of organizations and contingency thinking in a dynamic and complex environment.

- *Continuing directions* that include emphasis on quality and performance excellence, global awareness, and leadership roles for a new management.

CLASSICAL APPROACHES TO MANAGEMENT

The three branches of the classical approach to management are (1) scientific management, (2) administrative principles, and (3) bureaucratic organization. *Figure 4.1* associates each of these branches with a prominent person in the history of management thought and a common assumption about people at work. The classical approaches generally assume that people at work act in a rational manner that is primarily driven by economic concerns. Workers are expected to rationally consider opportunities made available to them and do whatever is necessary to achieve the greatest personal and monetary gain.[4]

SCIENTIFIC MANAGEMENT

In 1911 Frederick W. Taylor published *The Principles of Scientific Management,* in which he makes the following statement: "The principal object of management should be to secure maximum prosperity for the employer, coupled with the maximum prosperity for the employee."[5] Taylor, often called the "father of scientific management," noticed that many workers did their jobs their own way and without clear and uniform specifications. He believed that this caused them to loose efficiency and perform below their true capacities. He also believed that this problem could be corrected if workers were taught and then helped by supervisors to always perform their jobs in the right way.

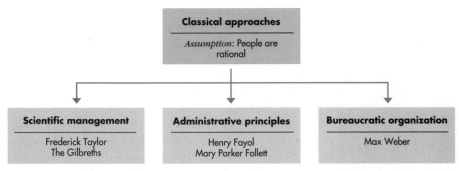

Figure 4.1   Major branches in the classical approach to management.

Taylor used the concept of "time study" to analyze the motions and tasks required in any job and to develop the most efficient ways to perform them.[6] He then linked these job requirements with both training for the worker and a systematic management approach in which supervisors offered proper direction, support, and monetary incentives. Taylor's four principles of **scientific management** are the following: (1) Develop for every job a "science" that includes rules of motion, standardized work implements, and proper working conditions. (2) Carefully select workers with the right abilities for the job. (3) Carefully train workers to do the job and give them the proper incentives to cooperate with the job "science." (4) Support workers by carefully planning their work and by smoothing the way as they go about their jobs.

- **Scientific management** involves a job science that includes careful selection and training of workers, and proper supervisory support.

Taylor tried to use scientific techniques to improve the productivity of people at work. The implications of his efforts, if not his exact scientific management principles, are found in many management settings today. A number of these are summarized in *Manager's Notepad 4.1.* They are also illustrated in the management strategy of Dan Bishop as the CEO of the franchise home-cleaning service Maids International. When faced with the problem of high labor turnover, systematic studies were conducted to show how employees worked. Tasks were defined to eliminate unnecessary and/or inconvenient movements, maids were allowed to rotate jobs while working in four-person teams, and "downtime" was provided for relaxation. Bishop said, "Fatigue and boredom are what burn people out. We tried to eliminate them."[7]

Mentioned in Taylor's first principle, **motion study** is the science of reducing a job or task to its basic physical motions. As contemporaries of Taylor, Frank and Lillian Gilbreth pioneered motion studies as a management tool. In one famous study, they reduced the number of motions used by bricklayers and tripled their productivity.[8] The Gilbreths's work established the foundation for later advances in the areas of job simplification, work standards, and incentive wage plans — all techniques still used in the modern workplace.

- **Motion study** is the science of reducing a task to its basic physical motions.

M a n a g e r ' s   N o t e p a d   4 . 1

Practical Lessons from Scientific Management

- Make results-based compensation a performance incentive.
- Carefully design jobs with efficient work methods.
- Carefully select workers with the abilities to do these jobs.
- Train workers to perform jobs to the best of their abilities.
- Train supervisors to support workers so they can perform jobs to the best of their abilities.

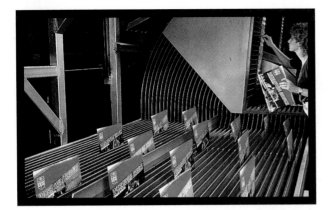

 The ideas of Taylor and the Gilbreth's are evident at United Parcel Service (UPS), where workers are guided by carefully calibrated productivity standards. At regional sorting centers, sorters are timed according to strict task requirements and are expected to load vans at a set number of packages per hour. Delivery stops on regular van routes are studied and carefully timed, and supervisors generally know within a few minutes how long a driver's pickups and deliveries will take. Industrial engineers devise precise routines for drivers, who are trained to knock on customers' doors rather than spend even a few seconds looking for the doorbell. Handheld computers further enhance delivery efficiencies. At UPS, savings of seconds on individual stops add up to significant increases in productivity.[9]

ADMINISTRATIVE PRINCIPLES

A second classical approach to management is based on attempts to document and understand the experiences of successful managers. Two prominent writers in this school of thought are Henri Fayol and Mary Parker Follett.

Henri Fayol

The early work of Henri Fayol, a career executive, scholar, and writer, represents the "administrative principles" school of thought. In 1916, after a career in French industry, Fayol published *Administration Industrielle et Générale*.[10] The book outlines his views on the proper management of organizations and the people within them. It identifies the following five "rules" or "duties" of management, which closely resemble the four functions of management — planning, organizing, leading, and controlling — we talk about today:

Fayol's rules of management

- *Foresight:* To complete a plan of action for the future.
- *Organization:* To provide and mobilize resources to implement the plan.
- *Command:* To lead, select, and evaluate workers to get the best work toward the plan.
- *Coordination:* To fit diverse efforts together and ensure that information is shared and problems solved.
- *Control:* To make sure things happen according to plan and to take necessary corrective action.

Most importantly, Fayol believed that management could be taught. He was very concerned about improving the quality of management and set forth a number of "principles" to guide managerial action. A number of his originals are still part of the management vocabulary. They include Fayol's *scalar chain principle* — there should be a clear and unbroken line of communication from the top to the bottom in the organization; the *unity of command principle* — each person should receive orders from only one boss; and, the *unity of direction principle* — one person should be in charge of all activities that have the same performance objective.

Mary Parker Follett

Another contributor to the administrative principles school was Mary Parker Follett, who was eulogized at her death in 1933 as "one of the most important women America has yet produced in the fields of civics and sociology."[11] In her writings about businesses and other organizations Follett displayed an understanding of groups and a deep commitment to human cooperation — ideas that are highly relevant today. For her, groups were mechanisms through which diverse individuals could combine their talents for a greater good. She viewed organizations as "communities" in which managers and workers should labor in harmony, without one party dominating the other and with the freedom to talk over and truly reconcile conflicts and differences. She believed it was the manager's job to help people in organizations cooperate with one another and achieve an integration of interests.

A review of *Dynamic Administration: The Collected Papers of Mary Parker Follett* helps to illustrate the modern applications of her management insights.[12] Follett believed that making every employee an owner in the business would create feelings of collective responsibility. *Today,* we address the same issues under such labels as "employee ownership," "profit sharing," and "gain-sharing plans." Follet believed that business problems involve a wide variety of factors that must be considered in relationship to one another. *Today,* we talk about "systems" when describing the same phenomenon. Follett believed that businesses were services and that private profits should always be considered vis-à-vis the public good. *Today,* we pursue the same issues under the labels of "managerial ethics" and "corporate social responsibility."

BUREAUCRATIC ORGANIZATION

Max Weber was a late nineteenth century German intellectual whose ideas have had a major impact on the field of management and the sociology of organizations. His ideas developed somewhat in reaction to what he considered to be performance deficiencies in the organizations of his day. Among other things, Weber was concerned that people were in positions of authority, not because of their job-related capabilities, but because of their social standing or "privileged" status in German society. For this and other reasons he believed that organizations largely failed to reach their performance potential.

- **Bureaucracy** is a rational and efficient form of organization founded on logic, order, and legitimate authority.

At the heart of Weber's thinking was a specific form of organization he believed could correct the problems just described—a **bureaucracy.**[13] This is an ideal, intentionally rational, and very efficient form of organization founded on principles of logic, order, and legitimate authority. The defining characteristics of Weber's bureaucratic organization are as follows:

- *Clear division of labor:* Jobs are well defined, and workers become highly skilled at performing them.
- *Clear hierarchy of authority:* Authority and responsibility are well defined for each position, and each position reports to a higher level one.
- *Formal rules and procedures:* Written guidelines direct behavior and decisions in jobs, and written files are kept for historical record.
- *Impersonality:* Rules and procedures are impartially and uniformly applied with no one receiving preferential treatment.
- *Careers based on merit:* Workers are selected and promoted on ability and performance, and managers are career employees of the organization.

Characteristics of Weber's bureaucracy

Weber believed that organizations would perform well as bureaucracies. They would have the advantages of efficiency in utilizing resources and of fairness or equity in the treatment of employees and clients. In his words,

> The purely bureaucratic type of administrative organization . . . is, from a purely technical point of view, capable of attaining the highest degree of efficiency. . . . It is superior to any other form in precision, in stability, in the stringency of its discipline, and in its reliability. It thus makes possible a particularly high degree of calculability of results for the heads of the organization and for those acting in relation to it. It is finally superior both in intensive efficiency and in the

Max Weber

scope of its operations and is formally capable of application to all kinds of administrative tasks.[14]

This is the ideal side of bureaucracy. However, the terms bureaucracy and bureaucrat are now often used with negative connotations. *The possible disadvantages of bureaucracy include:* excessive paperwork or "red tape," slowness in handling problems, rigidity in the face of shifting customer or client needs, resistance to change, and employee apathy. These disadvantages are most likely to cause problems for organizations that must be flexible and quick in adapting to changing circumstances—a characteristic of challenges in today's dynamic organizational environments. As discussed in Chapters 10 and 11 on organizational structures and design, researchers now try to determine when and under what conditions bureaucratic features work best. They also want to identify alternatives to the bureaucratic form. Indeed, current trends in management include many innovative organizational forms that seek the same goals as Weber but with different approaches to how organizations can be structured.

HUMAN RESOURCE APPROACHES TO MANAGEMENT

During the 1920s, an emphasis on the human side of the workplace began to establish its influence on management thinking. Major branches that emerged in this behavioral or human resource approach to management are shown in *Figure 4.2*. They include the famous Hawthorne studies and Maslow's theory of human needs, as well as theories generated from these foundations by Douglas McGregor, Chris Argyris, and others. The human resource approaches maintain that people are social and self-actualizing. People at work are assumed to seek satisfying social relationships, respond to group pressures, and search for personal fulfillment.

THE HAWTHORNE STUDIES

In 1924, the Western Electric Company (predecessor to today's Lucent Technologies) commissioned a research program to study individual productivity at the Hawthorne Works of the firm's Chicago plant.[15] The initial "Hawthorne studies" had a scientific management perspective and sought to determine how economic incentives and the physical conditions of the workplace affected the output of workers. An initial focus was on the level of illumination in the manufacturing facilities; it seemed reasonable to expect that better lighting would improve performance. After failing to find this relationship, however, the researchers concluded that unforeseen "psychological factors" somehow interfered with their illumination experiments. This finding and later Hawthorne studies directed attention toward human interactions in the workplace and ultimately had a major influence on the field of management.

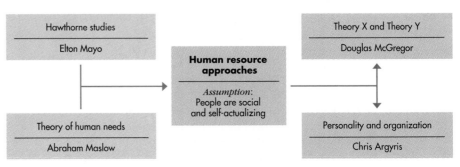

Figure 4.2 Foundations in the human resource approach to management.

Relay Assembly Test-Room Studies

In 1927, a team led by Harvard's Elton Mayo began more research to examine the effect of worker fatigue on output. Care was taken to design a scientific test that would be free of the psychological effects thought to have confounded the earlier illumination studies. Six workers who assembled relays were isolated for intensive study in a special test room. They were given various rest pauses, and workdays and workweeks of various lengths, and production was regularly measured. Once again, researchers failed to find any direct relationship between changes in physical working conditions and output. Productivity increased regardless of the changes made.

Mayo and his colleagues concluded that the new "social setting" created for workers in the test room accounted for the increased productivity. Two factors were singled out as having special importance. One was the *group atmosphere;* the workers shared pleasant social relations with one another and wanted to do a good job. The other was more *participative supervision.* Test-room workers were made to feel important, were given a lot of information, and were frequently asked for their opinions. This was not the case in their, or in the other workers', regular jobs elsewhere in the plant.

Employee Attitudes, Interpersonal Relations, and Group Processes

Mayo's studies continued to examine these factors until the worsening economic conditions of the Depression forced their termination in 1932. Until then, interest focused on employee attitudes, interpersonal relations, and group relations. In one study, over 21,000 employees were interviewed to learn what they liked and disliked about their work environment. "Complex" and "baffling" results led the researchers to conclude that the same things (e.g., work conditions or wages) could be sources of satisfaction for some workers and of dissatisfaction for others. The final Hawthorne study was conducted in the bank wiring room and centered on the role of the work group. A surprise finding here was that people would restrict their output in order to avoid the displeasure of the group, even if it meant sacrificing pay that could otherwise be earned by increasing output. Thus, it was recognized that groups can have strong negative, as well as positive, influences on individual productivity.

Lessons of the Hawthorne Studies

As scholars now look back, the Hawthorne studies are criticized for poor research design, weak empirical support for the conclusions drawn, and the tendency of researchers to overgeneralize their findings.[16] Yet the significance of these studies as a turning point in the evolution of management thought remains intact. The Hawthorne studies helped shift the attention of managers and management researchers away from the technical and structural concerns of the classical approach and toward social and human concerns as keys to productivity. They showed that people's feelings, attitudes, and relationships with coworkers should be important to management, and they recognized the importance of the work group. They also identified the **Hawthorne effect**—the tendency of people who are singled out for special attention to perform as anticipated merely because of expectations created by the situation.

HUMAN RELATIONS MOVEMENT

The Hawthorne studies contributed to the emergence of the **human relations movement** as an important influence on management thought during the 1950s and 1960s. This movement was largely based on the viewpoint that managers

• **Four Seasons Hotels**
http://www.fshr.com

The Toronto-based Four Seasons Hotels takes up to five interviews to find applicants who are sufficiently friendly and capable of teamwork to satisfy job requirements. According to Isidore Sharp, Four Seasons's chairperson, to get a quality workforce, "It's a matter of time, training, patience, and understanding." New employees are assigned to "big brothers" or "big sisters" to learn their jobs; they also receive the necessary tools, including computers, to do their jobs really well.

• **The Hawthorne effect** is the tendency of persons singled out for special attention to perform as expected.

• The **human relations movement** suggests that managers using good human relations will achieve productivity.

- **Organizational behavior** is the study of individuals and groups in organizations.

- A **need** is a physiological or psychological deficiency that a person wants to satisfy.

who used good human relations in the workplace would achieve productivity. Furthermore, the insights of the human relations movement set the stage for what has now evolved as the field of **organizational behavior,** the study of individuals and groups in organizations.

Maslow's Theory of Human Needs

Among the insights of the human relations movement, Abraham Maslow's work in the area of human "needs" is a key foundation. A **need** is a physiological or psychological deficiency a person feels the compulsion to satisfy. This is a significant concept for managers because needs create tensions that can influence a person's work attitudes and behaviors.

Maslow identified the five levels of human needs, shown in *Figure 4.3*: physiological, safety, social, esteem, and self-actualization. His theory is based on two underlying principles.[17] The first is the *deficit principle* — a satisfied need is not a motivator of behavior. People act to satisfy "deprived" needs, those for which a satisfaction "deficit" exists. The second is the *progression principle* — the five needs exist in a hierarchy of "prepotency." A need at any level only becomes activated once the next lower level need has been satisfied.

Maslow suggested that people try to satisfy the five needs in sequence. They progress step by step from the lowest level in the hierarchy to the highest. Along the way, a deprived need dominates individual attention and determines behavior until it is satisfied. Then, the next higher level need is activated and progression up the hierarchy occurs. At the level of self-actualization, the deficit and progression principles cease to operate. The more this need is satisfied, the stronger it grows.

Consistent with the human relations thinking, Maslow's theory implies that managers who can help people satisfy their important needs at work will achieve productivity. Although scholars now recognize that things are more complicated than this, as will be discussed in Chapter 14 on motivation and rewards, Maslow's ideas are still relevant to everyday management. Consider, for example,

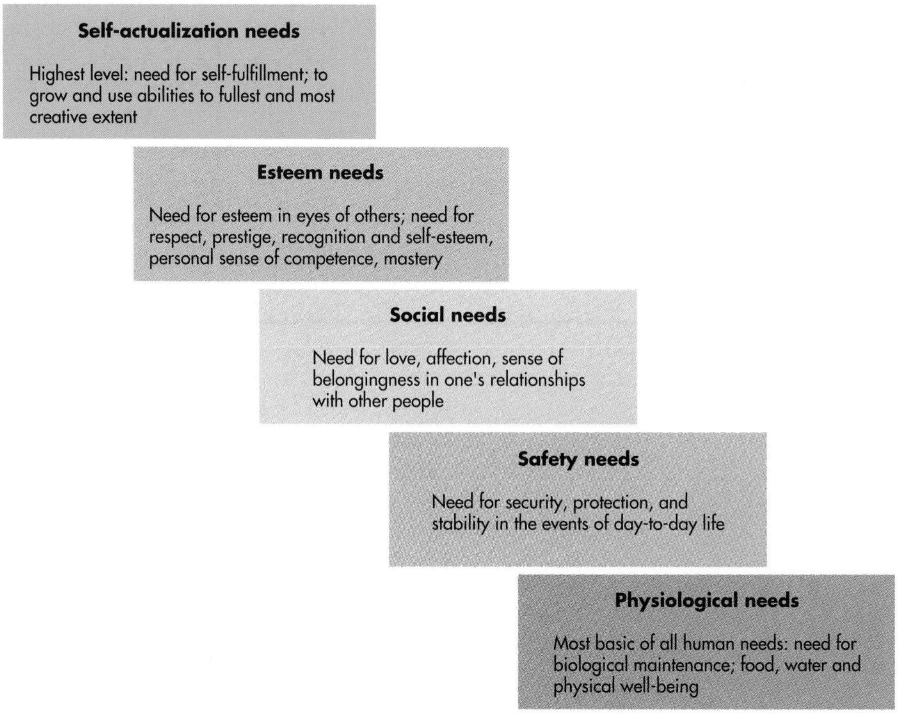

Self-actualization needs

Highest level: need for self-fulfillment; to grow and use abilities to fullest and most creative extent

Esteem needs

Need for esteem in eyes of others; need for respect, prestige, recognition and self-esteem, personal sense of competence, mastery

Social needs

Need for love, affection, sense of belongingness in one's relationships with other people

Safety needs

Need for security, protection, and stability in the events of day-to-day life

Physiological needs

Most basic of all human needs: need for biological maintenance; food, water and physical well-being

Figure 4.3   Maslow's hierarchy of human needs.

the case of dealing with volunteer workers who do not receive any monetary compensation. Susan Forand, the director of training and volunteer services at the Easter Seal Rehabilitation Center in Hartford, Connecticut, has said, "Volunteers have to feel they're fulfilling a need." If volunteer directors in nonprofit organizations do not create jobs that satisfy these needs, she warns that people will simply volunteer to work someplace else.[18]

McGregor's Theory X and Theory Y

Douglas McGregor was heavily influenced by both the Hawthorne studies and Maslow. His classic book *The Human Side of Enterprise* advances the thesis that managers should give more attention to the social and self-actualizing needs of people at work.[19] McGregor called upon managers to shift their view of human nature away from a set of assumptions he called "Theory X" and toward ones he called "Theory Y." If you complete the Managerial Assumptions self-assessment in the text's *Career Readiness Workbook,* it will offer insight into your tendencies with respect to these two sets of assumptions.

According to McGregor, managers holding **Theory X** assumptions approach their jobs believing that those who work for them generally dislike work, lack ambition, are irresponsible, are resistant to change, and prefer to be led rather than to lead. McGregor considers such thinking inappropriate. He argues instead for the value of **Theory Y** assumptions in which the manager believes people are willing to work, are capable of self-control, are willing to accept responsibility, are imaginative and creative, and are capable of self-direction.

An important aspect of McGregor's ideas is his belief that managers who hold either set of assumptions can create **self-fulfilling prophesies** — that is, through their behavior they create situations where subordinates act in ways that confirm the original expectations. Managers with Theory X assumptions act in a very directive "command-and-control" fashion that gives people little personal say over their work. These supervisory behaviors often create passive, dependent, and reluctant subordinates who tend to do only what they are told to or required to do. This reinforces the original Theory X viewpoint. In contrast, managers with Theory Y perspectives behave in "participative" ways that allow subordinates more job involvement, freedom, and responsibility. This creates opportunities to satisfy esteem and self-actualization needs and causes workers to perform as expected with initiative and high performance. This time the self-fulfilling prophesy is a positive one.

Theory Y thinking is very consistent with developments in the new workplace and its emphasis on valuing workforce diversity. It is also central to the popular notions of employee participation, involvement, empowerment, and self-management.

- **Theory X** assumes that people dislike work, lack ambition, are irresponsible and resistant to change, and prefer to be led.

- **Theory Y** assumes that people are willing to work, accept responsibility, and are capable of self-direction and creativity.

- A **self-fulfilling prophecy** occurs when a person acts in ways in order to confirm another's expectations.

Diversity commitments at Digital Equipment Corporation (DEC) are driven by a respect for individual differences and quest for competitive advantage. Digital executives focus on creating work environments within which everyone can achieve his or her true potential. Senior managers participate in diversity business plans that look at representation, management practices and environments. Their jobs are to encourage openness to individual differences, to commit junior managers to diversity goals, and to lead celebrations such as Black History Month, Hispanic Heritage Month, Women's History Month, Native American Week, Asian/Pacific American Heritage Month, Gay Pride Month, AIDS Awareness Month, and Disability Awareness Week.[20]

Argyris's Theory of Personality and Organization

Ideas set forth by the well-regarded scholar and consultant Chris Argyris also reflect a belief in the higher order of human nature advanced by Maslow and McGregor. In his book *Personality and Organization,* Argyris contrasts the management practices found in traditional and hierarchical organizations with the needs and capabilities of mature adults.[21] He concludes that some practices, especially those influenced by the classical management approaches, are inconsistent with the mature adult personality.

Consider these examples. In scientific management, the principle of specialization assumes that people will work more efficiently as tasks become better defined. Argyris believes that this may inhibit self-actualization in the workplace. In Weber's bureaucracy, people work in a clear hierarchy of authority with top-level managers directing and controlling lower levels. Argyris worries that this creates dependent, passive workers who feel they have little control over their work environments. In Fayol's administrative principles, the concept of unity of direction assumes that efficiency will increase when a person's work is planned and directed by a supervisor. Argyris suggests that this may create conditions for psychological failure; psychological success occurs when people define their own goals.

Like McGregor, the belief that managers who treat people positively and as responsible adults will achieve productivity is central to Argyris's thinking. His advice is to expand job responsibilities, allow more task variety, and adjust supervisory styles to allow more participation and promote better human relations. He believes that the common problems of employee absenteeism, turnover, apathy, alienation, and the like may be signs of a mismatch between workers' mature personalities and outdated management practices.

QUANTITATIVE APPROACHES TO MANAGEMENT

About the same time that some scholars were developing human resource approaches to management, others were investigating how quantitative techniques could improve managerial decision making. The foundation of the quantitative approaches to management is the assumption that mathematical techniques can be used to improve managerial decision making and problem solving.

MANAGEMENT SCIENCE FOUNDATIONS

● **Management science** uses mathematical techniques to analyze and solve management problems.

The terms **management science** or **operations research** are often used interchangeably to describe the scientific applications of mathematical techniques to management problems. A typical approach proceeds as follows: A problem is encountered, it is systematically analyzed, appropriate mathematical models and computations are applied, and an optimum solution is identified.

A number of management science applications are commonly used. *Mathematical forecasting* helps make future projections that are useful in the planning process. *Inventory modeling* helps control inventories by mathematically establishing how much to order and when. *Linear programming* is used to calculate how best to allocate scarce resources among competing uses. *Queuing theory* helps allocate service personnel or workstations to minimize customer waiting time and service cost. *Network models* break large tasks into smaller components to allow for better analysis, planning, and control of complex projects. And *simulation* makes models of problems so different solutions under various assumptions can be tested.

Regardless of the specific technique used, the essence of the quantitative management approach includes these characteristics. There is a focus on decision making that has clear implications for management action. The techniques use "economic" decision criteria, such as costs, revenues, and return on investment. They also involve mathematical models that follow sophisticated rules and formulas.

QUANTITATIVE ANALYSIS TODAY

University courses in management science, operations research, and quantitative business analysis provide a good introduction to these quantitative management foundations. Courses in operations management apply them to the physical production of goods and services. Since many of the techniques are highly sophisticated, organizations often employ staff specialists to help managers take advantage of them effectively. But software developments are making these techniques more readily available through easy-to-use applications for desktop and even handheld personal computers. This availability greatly expands their use throughout the workplace and makes it even more important for managers to understand the value of each technique. In all cases, of course, mathematical solutions to problems must be supported by good managerial judgment and an appreciation of the human factor.

• **Xerox**
http://www.xerox.com

Quality helps Xerox retain the high-performance edge in a highly competitive industry. Statistical process controls and better trained employees are part of the formula, as is a dependable network of high-quality suppliers. The best products and manufacturing methods around the world are identified regularly as the benchmarks to be matched.

MODERN APPROACHES TO MANAGEMENT

Modern approaches to management respect the classical, human resource, and quantitative schools. But, they also recognize that no one model or theory applies universally in all situations or to the exclusion of the others. Although remaining sensitive to the insights of history, researchers are now working to extend them in the most appropriate directions for the demands of our dynamic environment.

According to the modern management approaches, people are complex and variable. They have many varied needs that can change over time. They possess a range of talents and capabilities that can be developed. Organizations and managers, therefore, should respond to individual differences with a wide variety of managerial strategies and job opportunities. Key foundations of the modern management approaches include the systems view of organizations and contingency thinking.

SYSTEMS THINKING

Organizations, as introduced in Chapter 1, can be viewed as **open systems** that interact with their environments in the continual process of transforming resource inputs into product outputs (finished goods and/or services). The external environment is a critical element in the open-systems view of organizations. It is a source of both resources and customer feedback, and it can have a significant impact on operations and outcomes. Feedback from the environment tells an organization how well it is meeting the needs of customers and of society at large. Without customer willingness to use the organization's products, it is difficult to operate or stay in business over the long run. The open-systems view of organizations, therefore, helps to keep the spotlight on the all-important customer.

Formally defined, a *system* is a collection of interrelated parts that function together to achieve a common purpose. A *subsystem* is a smaller component of a

• An **open system** interacts with its environment and transforms resource inputs into outputs.

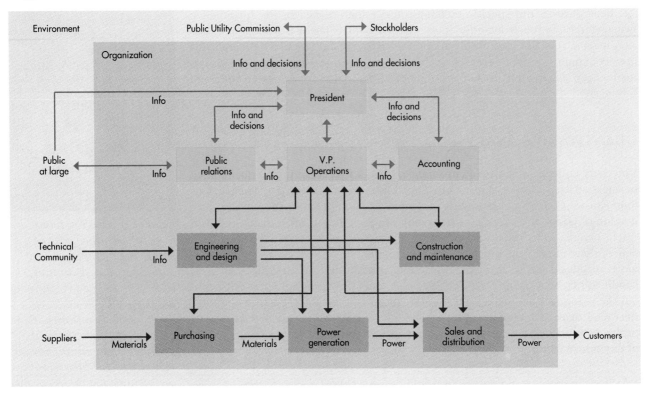

Figure 4.4 Organizations as complex systems: The case of a regional utility. *Source:* Developed from H. Randolph Bobbitt, Jr., Robert H. Breinholdt, Robert H. Doktor, and James P. McNaul, *Organizational Behavior* (Englewood Cliffs, N.J.: Prentice Hall, 1974), p. 219.

larger system.[22] *Figure 4.4* uses the case of a regional electric utility to illustrate the complexity of organizations as interlocking networks of subsystems. The figure shows how the utility's different subsystems must work together so the firm can produce and sell electric power to its customers. It is the job of the president, vice president for operations, and the respective subsystems managers to make this coordinated action possible. They must ensure not only that the necessary subsystem tasks are accomplished (such as purchasing, power generation, distribution, and accounting) but that they get done in an integrated fashion. The ultimate goal is for all subsystems to perform in ways that facilitate high productivity for the entire enterprise.

The figure also shows the president, public relations department, engineering and design group, purchasing unit, and sales and distribution section acting as *boundary spanners*. That is, their jobs include working with outsiders and staying informed about external environmental developments. In today's complex and demanding environment, the need to gather and successfully process information from sources external to the organization is increasingly critical.[23] The open-systems view of organizations helps to keep this responsibility well defined.

CONTINGENCY THINKING

● **Contingency thinking** maintains that there is no one best way to manage; what is best depends on the situation.

Contingency thinking tries to match managerial responses with the problems and opportunities unique to different situations, particularly those posed by individual and environmental differences. In the modern management approach, there is no longer an attempt to find the "one best way" to manage in all circumstances. Rather, the contingency perspective tries to help managers understand situational differences and respond to them in appropriate ways.[24]

Contingency thinking is an important theme in this book, and its implications extend to all of the management functions. For example, consider again the concept of bureaucracy—something Weber offered as an ideal form of organization. From a contingency perspective the strict bureaucratic form is only one possible way of organizing things. What turns out to be the "best" structure in any given situation will depend on many factors, including environmental uncertainty, an organization's primary technology, and the strategy being pursued. Only when the environment is relatively stable and operations are predictable does the bureaucracy work best; in other situations, alternative structures may be needed. Contingency thinking also recognizes that what is a good structure for one organization may not work well for another, and what works well at one time may not work as well in the future as circumstances change.[25]

 ## CONTINUING MANAGEMENT THEMES

These many accumulating insights into management practice have set the foundation for important current trends and directions in management thought. Among the most important is the recognition that we live and work in a dynamic and ever-changing environment that puts unique and never-ending competitive pressures on organizations. Key themes to be considered, as we move into the 21st century include continuing pressures for quality and performance excellence, an expanding global awareness, and the importance of leadership, knowledge workers, and the new management.

QUALITY AND PERFORMANCE EXCELLENCE

The quality theme was first introduced in Chapter 1 and will continue throughout this book.[26] It remains a very important direction in management today. **Quality,** in this sense, is usually defined as the ability to meet customer needs 100 percent of the time. There is no doubt about it—managers in truly progressive organizations are "quality conscious." They understand the basic link between competitive advantage and the ability always to deliver quality goods and services to their customers.

● **Quality** is a degree of excellence, often defined as the ability to meet customer needs 100 percent of the time.

You are already informed about *total quality management* as a comprehensive approach to continuous quality improvement for a total organization. Every effort is made in TQM to build quality into all aspects of the production process from initial acquisition of resources, through the processes and work systems, and all the way to ultimate delivery of the good or service to customers. Importantly, the approach calls for everyone to commit to continuous improvement in all aspects of their work. Not only is TQM focused on customer needs and interests, it emphasizes the importance of employee involvement in all aspects of quality improvement and delivery. There is no doubt that total quality management will remain integral to the success of organizations in the future.

Closely aligned with the pursuit of quality is management commitment to performance excellence, a theme that became prominent when the book *In Search of Excellence: Lessons from America's Best-Run Companies* was published by Tom Peters and Robert Waterman.[27] Based on case investigations of successful companies, they identified the eight attributes of performance excellence shown in *Manager's Notepad 4.2*. These attributes are further representative of many themes and directions common in organizations today.

Manager's Notepad 4.2

Eight Attributes of Performance Excellence

1. *Bias toward action:* making decisions and making sure that things get done.

2. *Closeness to the customers:* knowing their needs and valuing customer satisfaction.

3. *Autonomy and entrepreneurship:* supporting innovation, change, and risk taking.

4. *Productivity through people:* valuing human resources as keys to quality and performance.

5. *Hands-on and value-driven:* having a clear sense of organizational purpose.

6. *Sticking to the knitting:* focusing resources and attention on what the organization does best.

7. *Simple form and lean staff:* minimizing management levels and staff personnel.

8. *Simultaneous loose-tight properties:* allowing flexibility while staying in control.

GLOBAL AWARENESS

We are just emerging from a decade in which the quality and performance excellence themes have been reflected in the rise of "process reengineering," "virtual organizations," "agile factories," "network firms," and other new concepts reviewed in this book. But while the best formulas for success continue to be tested and debated, an important fact remains: Much of the pressure for quality and performance excellence is created by a highly competitive global economy. Nowhere is this challenge more evident than in the continuing efforts of businesses around the globe to transform themselves into truly world-class operations.

When Mercedes Benz set up manufacturing in the United States, the best of its German management practices came too. In fact, evdience of Taylor's scientific management principles are at work now that Mercedes's popular M-class sport utility vehicles are "Made in Alabama." The German automaker expects its American workers to follow precise standards known at SMPs (standard methods and procedures). The SMPs are created by German engineers and specify everything right down to the way a lug nut should be tightened and where a tool should be placed when not in use. Mercedes is hoping that its experience adapting an American workforce to its quality and performance standards will become a guideline as it moves production sites to other parts of the world.[28]

Like the lessons of performance excellence, current trends and directions in global awareness have ties back to the 1980s. That was a time when the success of Japanese industry caught worldwide attention and both scholars and consultants rushed to identify what could be learned from Japanese management practices. *Theory Z,* by William Ouchi, and *The Art of Japanese Management* by Richard Tanner Pascale and Anthony G. Athos, were among the first books calling attention to the possible link between unique Japanese practices and business success.[29]

The term **Theory Z** is still used to describe a management framework that incorporates into North American practices a variety of insights found in the Japanese models.[30] Prominent in the Theory Z approach are such things as long term employment, slower promotions and more lateral job movements, attention to career planning and development, use of consensus decision making, and emphasis on use of groups and employee involvement. And even though Japan's economy and management systems face pressures of their own today, these early lessons of Japanese business experience helped to establish a global awareness that continues to enrich management thinking today. This international dimension of management will be examined thoroughly in the next chapter, with special attention on understanding cultural influences on management practices.

- **Theory Z** describes a management framework used by American firms following Japanese examples.

LEADERSHIP, KNOWLEDGE WORKERS, AND THE NEW MANAGEMENT

Perhaps no other theme is more representative of directions in the new management than leadership, the topic to which Part 5 of this book is devoted in its entirety. And once again, history sets the stage for the future. In his book *No Easy Victories,* John Gardner speaks of leadership as a special challenge and his words are well worth considering today.

> Leaders have a significant role in creating the state of mind that is the society. They can serve as symbols of the moral unity of the society. They can express the values that hold the society together. Most important, they can conceive and articulate goals that lift people out of their petty preoccupations, carry them above the conflicts that tear a society apart, and unite them in the pursuit of objectives worthy of their best efforts.[31]

Leadership and the new management will be singled out again and again in *Management 6/E* as important keys to organizational performance. And the performance of organizations, in turn, is the key to any society's economic development and growth. Managers of the 21st century will have to excel as never before to meet the expectations held of them and of the organizations they lead. Importantly, we must all recognize that new managerial outlooks and new managerial competencies appropriate to the new workplace are requirements for future leadership success.

New managers must accept and positively respond to the complex challenges of a changing world. Some years ago, a series of interviews with executives, management consultants, and business school professors provided *U.S. News & World Report* with a list of requirements for the "21st century executive." The list seems as appropriate now as we enter the new century as it did when we were looking forward to it. The 21st century manager must be a:

The 21st century manager

- *Global strategist*—who recognizes interconnections among nations, cultures, and economies in the world community and is able to plan and act with due consideration of them.

- *Master of technology*—who is comfortable with existing high technology, and who understands technological trends and their implications and is able to use them to the best advantage.

- *Consummate politician* — who understands the growing complexity of government regulations and the legal environment and is able to work comfortably at the interface between them and the interests of the organization.

- *Leader/motivator* — who is able to attract highly motivated workers and inspire their enthusiasm by creating a high-performance climate where individuals and teams can do their best work.[32]

In Chapter 3 on information and decision making we discussed the special challenges of this age of information. It is an age in which Peter Drucker considers knowledge the principle resources of a competitive society. Drucker, however, also cautions that knowledge constantly makes itself obsolete.[33] In a society where knowledge workers are increasingly important, new managers must be well educated . . . and they must continue that education throughout their careers. Success in turbulent times comes only through continuous improvement. The new management requires everyone to be unrelenting in efforts to develop, refine, and maintain job-relevant skills and competencies. It requires leaders with strong people skills, ones attuned to the nature of an information/service society, ones who understand the international dimensions, and ones who establish commitments to life-long learning. And, the new management places a premium on personal leadership qualities. Consider, for example, this comment by former corporate CEO and college president Ralph Sorenson: "It is the *ability to make things happen* that most distinguishes the successful manager from the mediocre or unsuccessful one, . . . The most cherished manager is the one who says 'I can do it,' and then does."[34]

"Do it," advises Sorenson. "Of course," you may quickly answer. But don't forget that the 21st-century manager must also do the "right" things — the things that really count, the things that add value to the organization's goods and/or services, the things that make a real difference in performance results and competitive advantage, and the ethical things. Those are challenging directions for leadership, knowledge workers, and new management.

CHAPTER REVIEW

This section should be used as an end-of-chapter "study guide." The *Summary* helps to put the chapter's content into overall perspective. The list of *Key Terms* allows you to double-check your familiarity with basic concepts and definitions. *Self-Test 4* gives you the opportunity to test your basic comprehension of chapter content using sample test questions.

SUMMARY

What can be learned from classical management thinking?

- Frederick Taylor's four principles of scientific management focused on the need to carefully select, train, and support workers for individual task performance.

- Henri Fayol suggested that managers should learn what are now known as the management functions of planning, organizing, leading, and controlling.

- Max Weber described bureaucracy with its clear hierarchy, formal rules, and well-defined jobs as an ideal form of organization.

What ideas were introduced by the human resource approaches?

- The human resource approaches shifted attention toward the human factor as a key element in organizational performance.

- The historic Hawthorne studies suggested that work behavior is influenced by social and psychological forces and that work performance may be improved by better "human relations."

- Abraham Maslow's hierarchy of human needs introduced the concept of self-actualization and the potential for people to experience self-fulfillment in their work.

- Douglas McGregor urged managers to shift away from Theory X and toward Theory Y thinking, which views people as independent, responsible, and capable of self-direction in their work.

- Chris Argyris pointed out that people in the workplace are adults and may react negatively when constrained by strict management practices and rigid organizational structures.

What is the role of quantitative analysis in management?

- The availability of high-power desktop computing provides new opportunities for mathematical methods to be used for problem solving.

- Many organizations employ staff specialists who apply their expertise in quantitative management science and operations research to solve problems.

- Quantitative techniques in common use include various approaches to forecasting, linear programming, and simulation, among others.

What is unique about the systems view and contingency thinking?

- Organizations are complex open systems that interact with their external environments to transform resource inputs into product outputs.

- Resource acquisition and customer satisfaction are important requirements in the organization environment relationship.

- Organizations are composed of many internal subsystems that must work together in a coordinated way to support the organization's overall success.

- Contingency thinking avoids "one best way" arguments, and recognizes the need to understand situational differences and respond appropriately to them.

What are the continuing themes as we enter the 21st century?

- The commitment to meet customer needs 100 percent of the time guides organizations toward total quality management and continuous improvement of operations.

- The global economy is a dramatic influence on organizations today, and opportunities abound to learn new ways of managing from practices in other countries.

- This is the age of information in which knowledge and knowledge workers are major resources of modern society.

- New managers must accept and excel at leadership responsibilities to perform as global strategists, technology masters, consummate politicians and leader/motivators.

KEY TERMS

Bureaucracy (p. 75)
Contingency thinking
    (p. 82)
Hawthorne effect (p. 77)
Human relations
    movement (p. 77)
Management science
    (p. 80)

Motion study (p. 73)
Need (p. 78)
Open system (p. 81)
Operations research
    (p. 80)
Organizational behavior
    (p. 78)
Quality (p. 83)

Scientific management
    (p. 73)
Self-fulfilling prophesies
    (p. 79)
Theory X (p. 79)
Theory Y (p. 79)
Theory Z (p. 85)

SELF-TEST 4

Take this test much as you would in a normal classroom situation. It should offer you a good way to check your basic comprehension of chapter material. Answers may be found at the end of the book.

MULTIPLE-CHOICE QUESTIONS:

1. The assumption that people are complex with widely varying needs is most associated with the _____ management approaches. (a) classical (b) neoclassical (c) behavioral (d) modern

2. The father of scientific management is _____. (a) Weber (b) Taylor (c) Mintzberg (d) Katz

3. The Hawthorne studies are an important foundation of the _____ approaches to management thinking. (a) classical (b) human resource (c) administrative (d) quantitative

4. Advice to study a job and carefully train workers to do that job with financial incentives tied to job performance would most likely come from _____ in the classical school of management thought. (a) scientific management (b) contingency management (c) Henri Fayol (d) Abraham Maslow

5. The highest level of need in Maslow's hierarchy is the level of _____ needs. (a) safety (b) esteem (c) self-actualization (d) physiological

6. Conflict between the mature adult personality and a rigid organization was a concern of the human relations theorist _____. (a) Argyris (b) Follett (c) Gantt (d) Fuller

7. When people perform in a situation as they are expected to, this may be due to the _____ effect. (a) Hawthorne (b) Mayo (c) contingency (d) open-systems

8. Linear programming and queuing theory are examples of techniques found in the _____ approach to management. (a) classical (b) quantitative (c) bureaucratic organization (d) modern

9. Resource acquisition and customer satisfaction are important when an organization is viewed as a/an _____. (a) bureaucracy (b) closed system (c) open system (d) pyramid

10. Long-term employment, consensus decision making, slow promotions, and lateral job movement are characteristic of the _____ management framework. (a) Theory X (b) Theory Y (c) Theory Z (d) contingency

TRUE-FALSE QUESTIONS:

11. In contingency management thinking there is always one "best way" to manage. T F

12. The bureaucracy was described as an ideal form of organization by Max Weber. T F

13. Maslow's hierarchy of needs is part of contingency thinking. T F

14. Organizations consist of subsystems whose activities must be integrated and coordinated. T F

15. The role of quantitative analysis is not important in management today. T F

16. "Sticking to the knitting" is one of the eight attributes of performance excellence in organizations. T F

17. Theory Z is based on insights from Japanese management practices. T F

18. Modern management theory now rejects all of the insights of the classical approaches. T F

19. The human relations movement is a forerunner to the field of organizational behavior as we know it today. T F

20. Mary Parker Follett was an important contributor to the classical approach to management. T F

SHORT-RESPONSE QUESTIONS:

21. List three of McGregor's Theory Y assumptions that are consistent with the current emphasis on participation and involvement in the workplace.

22. How do the deficit and progression principles operate in Maslow's hierarchy-of-needs theory?

23. Define *contingency thinking* and give an example of how it might apply to management.

24. Explain why the external environment is so important in the open-systems view of organizations.

APPLICATION QUESTION:

25. Enrique Temoltzin has just been appointed the new manager of your local college bookstore. Enrique would like to make sure the store operates according to Weber's bureaucracy. Is this a good management approach for Enrique to follow? Why or why not?

Global Dimensions of Management

Planning Ahead—Chapter 5 Study Questions

- What are the management challenges in a global economy?
- What are the forms and opportunities of international business?
- What complicates the environment for global operations?
- How does culture create global diversity?
- How do management practices and learning transfer across cultures?

Live and Work in a Global Village

There is no doubt about it. We live in an international community. Led by CNN, network television brings on-the-spot news from around the world into our homes, 24 hours a day. Newspapers from around the world can be read from the Internet at the touch of a keyboard on your desktop PC. It is easy to stay informed as reporters tell us the latest on the economies of Asia, strife and conflict in Bosnia and Kosovo, and political developments in the nations of Africa, among many examples. The far corners of the globe are more directly accessible than ever before. It is possible to board a plane in Minneapolis and fly nonstop to Beijing; it is sometimes less expensive to fly from Columbus, Ohio, to London than to Albany, New York. Colleges and universities offer an increasing variety of study abroad programs. Email links us to friends and work partners around the world and at low cost. We live today in a truly global village and you must learn to participate in a global workplace.

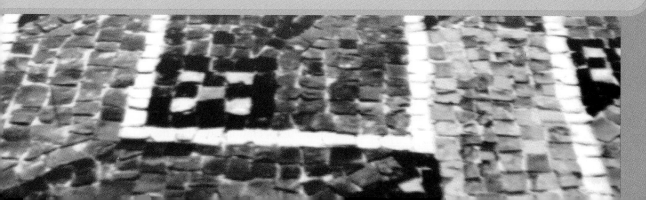

The global village isn't just for tourists and travelers. It is time to recognize the emergence and implications of a global workplace.[1] When Germany's Daimler-Benz announced a merger with America's Chrysler, the world noticed and we wondered about future consolidation of the global automobile industry. But this is just one example of a business world in which national boundaries are increasingly blurred. It is already difficult to buy a car that is really "made in America," since so many components are manufactured in other countries. The gas station with the green-and-white "BP" logo is operated by British Petroleum; the familiar "Shell" station is brought to you courtesy of Royal-Dutch/Shell. And did you know that the majority of McDonald's sales are now coming from outside of the United States, and that some of its most profitable restaurants are located in places like Moscow, Budapest, Beijing, and elsewhere? Astute business investors know all this and more. They buy and sell only with awareness of the latest financial news from Hong Kong, London, Tokyo, New York, Johannesburg, and other of the world's financial centers. In this time of high technology, furthermore, they don't even have to leave home to do it—the latest information is readily available on the Internet.

- **International management** involves the conduct of business or other operations in foreign countries.

As the world shrinks, and as the operations of organizations large and small increasingly span national boundaries, new tests of managerial skills and viewpoints are emerging. The term used to describe management in organizations with business interests in more than one country is **international management.** Today's business leaders must think and act globally in the quest for competitive advantage. And as they do, the challenges and opportunities of international management must be mastered. Procter & Gamble, for example, pursues a global strategy with a presence in more than 70 countries. Coke and Pepsi compete aggressively for the markets of China, India, and other countries. These and other companies actively pursue international business opportunities in search of:

Reasons for engaging in international business

- *Profits:* Global operations offer profit potential.
- *Customers:* Global operations offer new markets to sell products.
- *Suppliers:* Global operations offer access to needed raw materials.
- *Capital:* Global operations offer access to financial resources.
- *Labor:* Global operations offer access to lower labor costs.

THE GLOBAL ECONOMY

- The **global economy** is based on the worldwide interdependence of resource supplies, product markets, and business competition.

This is the age of a **global economy,** one based on worldwide interdependence of resource supplies, product markets, and business competition.[2] The significance of this globalization of business and commerce is described by scholar and consultant Rosabeth Moss Kanter as: "one of the most powerful and pervasive influences on nations, businesses, workplaces, communities, and lives . . ."[3] Success in meeting the challenges of our global economy will be earned by a new breed of manager who is informed about international developments, transnational in outlook, competent in working with people from different cultures, and always aware of regional developments in a changing world.

THE NEW EUROPE

- The **European Union (EU)** is a political and economic alliance of European countries.

The new Europe is a place of dramatic political and economic developments. The **European Union (EU)** is a grouping of 15 countries who agreed to support mutual economic growth by removing barriers that previously limited cross-border trade and business development.[4] Expectations are that the EU will expand to include at least 25 members in the near future. At present only Switzerland and

Norway from Western Europe remain outside the group; at least a dozen countries, including several new republics of the former Soviet Union have applied to join or expressed interest in joining.

As an economic union, the EU is putting the rest of the world on notice that European business is a global force to be reckoned with. Members are linked through favorable trade and customs laws intended to facilitate the free flow of workers, goods and services, and investments across national boundaries. Businesses in each member country have access to a market of over 375 million consumers, compared to 220 million in the United States and 120 million in Japan. Among the important business and economic developments in the EU are agreements to eliminate frontier controls and trade barriers, create uniform minimum technical product standards, open government procurement to businesses from all member countries, unify financial regulations, lift competitive barriers in banking and insurance, and even seek a common currency—the "Euro."

The latter development, European monetary union, is of striking significance and its impact will be on the lead of Europe's march into the 21st century. When 11 EU countries agreed in 1998 to adopt the Euro as a new common currency, they set the stage for what *Business Week* referred to as "an unstoppable market process that will sweep away structures Old Europe held so dear—national corporations and banks, rigid work rules, generous work rules."[5] Although there is still political and economic risk to Europe's economic and monetary union, the expected benefits include higher productivity, lower inflation, and steady growth.

All of this must also be considered in context with another dynamic element in the European scene—continuing legacies of the collapse of communism in the former Soviet Union and in nations formerly dominated by it. The traumas and tragedies of divisive civil and ethnic strife in the region of the former Yugoslavia are still in the news. Changes in political systems and governments add to the risk for foreign investors. Yet Western businesses are responding to opportunities not only in Russia, but in such diverse places as Belarus, Latvia, and the Ukraine. For Eastern and Central Europe as a whole, the themes are social progress and economic growth. Business continues to make strong gains in the Czech Republic, Poland, and Hungary, in particular, and world-class standards are emerging as managers learn the demands of competitive and free markets.

It wasn't too long ago that workers at Petofi Printing & Packaging Co., a formerly state-owned cardboard box and container maker in Kecskemet, Hungary, drank beer at work and didn't worry too much about making containers in the wrong colors and sizes. Today it's a different story in the newly privatized Petofi Printing & Packaging Co. New machinery and worker incentives have replaced communist-era machines and labor practices. Petofi now has a quality assurance lab checking on its suppliers and has won quality awards from the World Packaging Organization. It achieved ISO 9000 certification and is competing well against Western rivals who have difficulty meeting its cost-plus-quality advantages.[6]

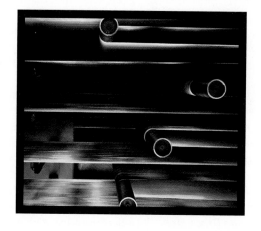

THE AMERICAS

Turning now to the Americas, the United States, Canada, and Mexico have joined together in the **North American Free Trade Agreement,** or **NAFTA.** This agreement largely frees the flow of goods and services, workers, and investments within a region that has more potential consumers than its European rival, the EU. Today, for example, Mexico imports more than $42 billion annually from the

• **NAFTA** is the **North American Free Trade Agreement** linking Canada, the United States, and Mexico in a regional economic alliance.

United States.[7] Getting approval of NAFTA from all three governments was not easy. Whereas Canadian firms worried about domination by U.S. manufacturers, American politicians were concerned about the potential loss of jobs to Mexico. Some calls were made for more *protectionism,* or government legislation and support to protect domestic industries from foreign competition. Whereas Mexicans feared that free trade would bring a further intrusion of U.S. culture and values into their country, Americans complained that Mexican businesses did not operate by the same social standards as they did—particularly with respect to environmental protection and the use of child labor.

• ***Maquiladoras*** are foreign manufacturing plants that operate in Mexico with special privileges.

Often at issue in NAFTA controversies are the operations of ***maquiladoras,*** foreign manufacturing plants allowed to operate in Mexico with special privileges in return for employing Mexican labor.[8] *Maquiladora* firms are allowed to import materials, components, and equipment duty free. They employ lower cost Mexican labor to assemble these materials into finished products, which can be exported with duty paid only on the "value added" in Mexico. Critics of *maquiladoras* accuse them of exploiting the availability of lower cost Mexican labor and giving away jobs that would otherwise go to Americans. They also point to high "social costs" as a continuing influx of workers overburdens services in Mexican border towns and the region becomes increasingly "Americanized."

Advocates argue that *maquiladoras* bring increased employment and prosperity and help develop more highly skilled local workers. Reports indicate that they are flourishing, gaining in productivity, and creating jobs. General Motors, Ford, Philips, and United Technologies are just a few of the multinationals that have increased their *maquiladora* operations.[9] The utilization of Mexican labor force skills and the global reach of these operations are also growing. Gary Cowger, president of General Motors of Mexico, says: "Our Mexican engineers developed a right-hand drive Suburban for Australia and South Africa. We are shipping from Mexico to Central America, Egypt, the Middle East, Ecuador, Peru, and Chile."[10]

• **Quicksilver Enterprises**
http://www.quicksilver-aircraft.com/index.html

Quicksilver Enterprises, a California maker of popular ultra-light airplanes, decided to license a Brazilian distributor to build and sell the planes in that country. But six months after the Brazilians had learned how to build, fly, and fix the planes, royalty payments to Quicksilver stopped. The Brazilian company claimed it had changed the design and created a new plane. Quicksilver took a loss of over $100,000.

Optimism regarding business and economic potential extends throughout Central and South America as well.[11] Many countries of the region are cutting tariffs, updating their economic policies, and welcoming foreign investors. Chile is discussed as the next NAFTA partner, and other countries may soon follow. Some even seek the creation of a Free Trade Area of the Americas (FTAA), a proposed free-trade zone that would stretch from Point Barrow, Alaska, all the way to Tierra del Fuego, Chile. In addition to NAFTA, other pieces of this potential pan-American economic union are already in place.[12] The MERCOSUR agreement links Bolivia, Brazil, Paraguay, Uruguay, and Argentina; the Andean Pact links Venezuela, Colombia, Ecuador, Peru, and Bolivia; and the Caribbean Community, CARICOM, is also growing as an economic linkage. The possibility of a single monetary unit, along the EURO model, is being discussed within Mercosur. Clearly, the great significance of Latin America to world trade is a message being heard by many North American business and government leaders.

ASIA AND THE PACIFIC RIM

Although the region's recent financial problems have taken some of the luster off, Asia must still be respected for what *Fortune* magazine calls a "megamarket."[13] McDonald's, for example, already has some 4,500 outlets in the region and is planning to add 2,000 more.[14] Asia is not only still growing as a power in the world economy, it has already achieved superpower status. And this respect must not be limited to just Japan, China, and what have become known as the "four Tigers" of South Korea, Hong Kong, Taiwan, and Singapore. It must be more broadly accorded in the region as a whole. In Southeast Asia the long-term potential of the economies of Malaysia, Thailand, and Indonesia is already significant, the Philippines is gaining attention, and Vietnam is more frequently in the news. Of course, Japan's economic power is an ever-present theme in Asia and in the global economy as a whole. Japanese companies account for a large majority of *Fortune's* "Pac Rim 150"—an annual listing of the largest Asian firms. But sprinkled among the list can be found a number of emerging world-class competitors from other Asian countries: Samsung (South Korea), Sime-Darby (Malaysia), and Siam Cement (Thailand), to name just three.

Wherever you travel or do business in the Asian region, "opportunity" is the watchword of the day. Even with the recent economic crisis taken into account, the Asia and the Pacific Rim economies are soon expected to be larger than those of the current EU. The forum for **Asia-Pacific Economic Cooperation (APEC)** is gaining prominence as the platform for a regional economic alliance. Member countries already represent a third of the global marketplace, and APEC countries rank as the world's top market for cars and telecommunications equipment. It is not just "low-cost" labor that attracts businesses to Asia; the growing availability of highly skilled "brainpower" is increasingly high on its list of advantages. India, for example, with a growing economy and the second largest population in the world, is gaining a world-class reputation for its software industry.

China is the world's largest single-country marketplace (estimated at 1.2 billion consumers). It is also controversial. The country's relations with the global economy remain complicated by human rights concerns and poor protection of foreign copyrights and intellectual property, among other issues. Still, China is a major export power whose manufacturing plants supply many major foreign retailers. Many outside firms—including RJR Nabisco, Coca-Cola, Procter & Gamble, and H.J. Heinz—are trying hard to penetrate China's vast markets with products manufactured there. To date, foreign investment in China has exceeded U.S.$100 billion. The country's importance in the global economy will surely increase in the future.[15] Executives at Salient Systems, an Ohio manufacturer of railway weighting systems recognize the potential and the complications in this opportunity. They are working with China's Ministry of Railways on a $4 million project, and expect a long-term market for their products. But they've also had to learn how to protect their intellectual capital and manage the financial details. Says Chief Financial Officer, Sharron Harrison, "in China, the language barrier and the great distance are extremely difficult."[16]

- **APEC, Asia-Pacific Economic Cooperation,** is a platform for regional economic alliances among Asian and Pacific Rim countries.

AFRICA

Look at the map in *Figure 5.1*. Africa is a continent increasingly featured in the news. Although often the focus of reports on ethnic turmoil and civil strife in countries struggling along pathways to peace and development, Africa also stands as a region that beckons international business.[17] Whereas foreign businesses tend to avoid the risk of trouble spots, they are giving increased attention to stable countries with growing economies. A *Wall Street Journal* analysis singles out Uganda, the Ivory Coast, Botswana, South Africa, and Ghana for their positive business prospects.[18] The same report also notes that Congo, Nigeria, and Angola are especially rich in natural resources. On the discouraging side, however, the rates of economic growth in sub-Saharan Africa are among the lowest in the world. Many parts of the region suffer from terrible problems of poverty and the ravishment of a continuing AIDS epidemic. Africa's need for sustained assistance from the industrialized countries, including business investments and foreign aid is well established.[19]

Figure 5.1 Africa, continent of opportunity.

There is a turnaround underway in the East African nation of Mozambique. This former Portuguese colony is emerging from years of civil war that began with its independence in 1975. A local entrepreneur now says, "Mozambicans, sick of war, want a working society." And economics plays an important role. The country is now home to billion dollar infrastructure projects financed by development agencies. A railroad corridor from the capital of Maputo to Johannesburg, South Africa, is under construction. McDonald's, as you might expect, is already checking locations for possible restaurant sites.[20]

A report by two Harvard professors recently analyzed the foreign investment environment of Africa and concluded that the region's contextual problems are manageable.[21] "In fact they should be viewed as opportunities," says James A. Austin one of the co-authors. He adds: "If a company has the managerial and organizational capabilities to deal with the region's unique business challenges, then it will be able to enter a promising market."[22] Post-apartheid South Africa, in particular, has benefitted from political revival, is experiencing economic recovery and attracting outside investors. United States investments in the country have increased sharply since Nelson Mandela became president. The American government is promoting trade and investment with Africa, with a special emphasis on facilitating U.S. investments in African businesses and infrastructure projects.[23] Coca-Cola is one firm that is responding to the call, projecting 15% growth rates as part of its regional business plan. CEO M. Douglas Ivester says: "We see an Africa more directly accountable for its own destiny than it has for centuries."[24]

FORMS OF INTERNATIONAL BUSINESS

● An **international business** conducts commercial transactions across national boundaries.

An **international business** conducts for-profit transactions of goods and services across national boundaries. International businesses of all types and sizes are the foundations of world trade. They are the engines for moving raw materials, finished products, and specialized services from one country to another in the global economy.

The common forms of international business are shown in *Figure 5.2.* When a business is just getting started internationally, global sourcing, exporting/importing, and licensing and franchising are the usual ways to begin. These are *market entry strategies* that involve the sale of goods or services to foreign markets but do not require expensive capital investments. Joint ventures and wholly owned subsidiaries are *direct investment strategies.* They require major capital commitments but create rights of ownership and control over operations in the foreign country.

MARKET ENTRY STRATEGIES

● In **global sourcing** materials or components are purchased in various parts of the world for assembly at home into a final product.

A common first step into international business, **global sourcing** is the process of manufacturing and/or purchasing components around the world and then assembling them into a final product. It is an international division of labor in which activities are performed in countries where they can be done well at the lowest cost. Global sourcing for cars assembled in the United States, for example,

Figure 5.2 Five common forms of international business—from market entry to direct investment strategies.

may mean purchasing windshields, instrument panels, seats, and fuel tanks from Mexico as well as electronics for antilock braking systems from Germany.

A second form of international business involves **exporting,** selling locally made products in foreign markets, and/or **importing,** buying foreign-made products and selling them in domestic markets. Because the growth of export industries creates local jobs, governments often offer special advice and assistance to businesses that are trying to develop or expand their export markets. Many U.S. policymakers look to export industries, large and small, as one way to correct trade imbalances. One example is an export initiative that came by chance for Franklin Jacobs, owner of St. Louis-based Falcon Products, Inc., a small manufacturer of restaurant furniture and equipment. While on a tour through Europe he says, "I discovered that my products were a lot better and a lot cheaper" than those on the market there. An opportunist, Jacobs rented exposition space at the United States Embassy in London, shipped a container load of his furniture, received over U.S.$200,000 in orders, and embarked on a new export initiative.[25]

A foreign firm may pay a fee and enter into a **licensing agreement** giving it the rights to make or sell another company's products. This international business approach typically grants access to a unique manufacturing technology, special patent, or trademark rights held by the licensor. It is one way to transfer technology from one country to another. **Franchising** is a form of licensing in which the licensee buys the complete "package" of support needed to open a particular business. As in domestic franchising agreements, firms like McDonald's, Kentucky Fried Chicken, and others sell facility designs, equipment, product ingredients and recipes, and management systems to foreign investors, while retaining certain product and operating controls.

- In **exporting** local products are sold abroad.

- **Importing** is the process of acquiring products abroad and selling them in domestic markets.

- A **licensing agreement** occurs when a firm pays a fee for the rights to make or sell another company's products.

- **Franchising** provides the complete "package" of support needed to open a particular business.

DIRECT INVESTMENT STRATEGIES

To establish a direct investment presence in a foreign country, many firms enter into **joint ventures** or co-ownership arrangements for business operations. This form of international business may be established by equity purchases and/or direct investments by a foreign partner in a local operation; it may also involve the creation of an entirely new business by a foreign and local partner. International joint ventures are "strategic alliances" that help participants to gain things through cooperation that otherwise would be difficult to achieve independently. One study reports that executives expect their companies to experience 50% growth in revenues from alliances by 2000.[26] In return for its investment in a local operation, for example, the outside or foreign partner often gains new markets and the assistance of a local partner who understands them. In return for its investment, the local partner often gains new technology as well as opportunities for its employees to learn new skills by working in joint operations. *Manager's Notepad 5.1* offers a checklist for choosing joint venture partners.[27]

A **wholly owned subsidiary** is a local operation completely owned and controlled by a foreign firm. Like joint ventures, foreign subsidiaries may be formed through direct investment in startup operations or through equity pur-

- A **joint venture** establishes operations in a foreign country through joint ownership with local partners.

- A **wholly owned subsidiary** is a local operation completely owned by a foreign firm.

Manager's Notepad 5.1

Checklist for Joint Ventures

- Choose a partner familiar with your firm's major business.
- Choose a partner with a strong local workforce.
- Choose a partner with future expansion possibilities.
- Choose a partner with a strong local market for its own products.
- Choose a partner with shared interests in meeting customer needs.
- Choose a partner with good profit potential.
- Choose a partner in sound financial standing.

chases in existing ones. When making such investments, foreign firms are clearly taking a business risk. They must be confident that they possess the expertise needed to manage and conduct business affairs successfully in the new environment. This is where prior experience gained through joint ventures can prove very beneficial.

ENVIRONMENT AND GLOBAL OPERATIONS

- A **multinational corporation (MNC)** is a business firm with extensive international operations in more than one foreign country.

Many companies do business abroad, but a true **multinational corporation,** or **MNC** for short, is a business firm with extensive international operations in more than one foreign country. Premier MNCs found in annual *Fortune, Business Week,* and *Wall Street Journal* listings of the world's largest firms include General Electric, Exxon, and AT&T from the United States; Nippon Telegraph & Telephone, Mitsubishi Bank, and Toyota Motor of Japan; and Royal Dutch/Shell of the Netherlands and Great Britain.[28] Also important on the world scene are *multinational organizations* (MNOs)—like the International Red Cross, the United Nations, and the World Bank—whose nonprofit missions and operations span the globe.

TYPES OF MULTINATIONAL CORPORATIONS

A typical MNC operates in many countries but has corporate headquarters in one home or host country. Gillette, Royal Dutch/Shell, and Sony are among the ready examples. Although they are true multinationals and derive substantial sales and profits from international sources, these companies and others like them typically also maintain strong national identifications. Consider, for example, 3M Corporation. Although earning some 46% of its sales in the United States, another 25% come from Europe, 18% from the Asia-Pacific region, and 9% from Latin America, Canada and Africa.[29]

The ways in which MNCs operate globally vary considerably.[30] An *ethnocentric* MNC exerts strict headquarters control over foreign operations, tries to operate abroad largely the way it does at home, and often creates local resentment by failing to respect local needs and customs. A *polycentric* MNC gives its foreign operations more operating freedom, respects market differences among countries, and pursues "multidomestic" strategies that treat each country as a separate competitive domain for such things as product designs and advertising campaigns. Other MNCs are more *geocentric* companies that seek total integration of global operations, try to operate across borders without home-based prejudices, make major decisions from a global perspective, distribute work among worldwide points of excellence, and employ senior executives from many different countries.

Many of the world's MNC's are becoming increasingly polycentric and geocentric in business strategy and practice. As the global economy grows more competitive, multinationals are acting more like **transnational corporations** that operate worldwide without being identified with one national "home."[31] Executives with transnationals view the entire world as the domain for acquiring resources, locating production facilities, marketing goods and services, and for brand image. Nestlé is a good example in foods; Asea Brown Boveri, or ABB, is another in diversified conglomerates. When one buys a Nestlé product in Brazil or has a neighbor working for ABB in Columbus, Ohio, who would know that both are actually registered Swiss companies?

> • A **transnational corporation** is an MNC that operates worldwide on a borderless basis.

✓ Among the American automakers, Ford Motor Company is moving in a transnational direction. The pathway to the future, say Ford executives, is borderless management and a global mindset. Even with its long history of international involvement—Henry Ford had a sales branch in France by 1908 and a manufacturing facility in England by 1911—the company is still learning how to master the challenges of global operations. The company is globalizing product development, purchasing, sales, and manufacturing. Multifunctional teams staffed from around the world develop new cars and trucks as the firm strives to become a true global company.[32]

ENVIRONMENTAL CHALLENGES IN THE GLOBAL ECONOMY

Becoming a transnational corporation is not easy; the environment of global business is complex and dynamic. Global executives must understand and deal successfully with many differences in economic, legal-political, and educational systems. The strength of global operations must always be blended well with realities of the local environment. As ABB Chairman Percy Barnevik says: "Too many peo-ple think you can succeed in the long run just by exporting from America to Europe. But you need to establish yourself locally and become, for example, a Chinese, Indonesian, or Indian citizen."[33]

As noted earlier, regional economic cooperation is increasing. But differences in economic systems around the world must still be recognized. Countries like Russia, Poland, Estonia, and others of the former Soviet Union used to operate with *central-planning economies*. That is, the central government made basic economic decisions for an entire nation. Such decisions largely determined the allocations of raw materials, set product or service output quotas, regulated wages and prices, and even distributed qualified personnel among alternative employers. Now these countries are trying to establish viable *free-market economies* such as those common to Germany, Canada, the United States, and other industrialized nations. Although they may vary in exact form, free-market economies operate under capitalism and the laws of supply and demand. As economies change from central planning to free markets they often face controversies over rising prices, unemployment, business competition, and the challenges of **privatization**—the selling of state-owned enterprises into private ownership. Foreign investment is crucial to the success of these developments.[34]

> • **Privatization** is the selling of state-owned enterprises into private ownership.

- In the **General Agreement on Tariffs and Trade (GATT)** and **World Trade Organization (WTO)** member nations agree to ongoing negotiations and reducing tariffs and trade restrictions.

- **SBC Communications**
http://www.sbc.com
- **Telekom Malaysia**
http://www.telekom.com.my

Democracy, private enterprise, and rural development are contributing to a turnaround in many of Africa's national economies. SBC Communications and Telekom Malaysia have invested heavily in regional telephone systems. The oil and minerals industries have helped the Ivory Coast; Mali is developing fruit as a cash crop. Says a Senegalese aid worker, "Our societies are rich with boundless energy and systems that work."

Among the chief worldwide economic issues, the **General Agreement on Tariffs and Trade (GATT)** and its successor the **World Trade Organization (WTO)** deserve special attention. Both are international accords in which member nations agree to ongoing negotiations and the reduction of tariffs and trade restrictions. The most recent negotiations, called the Uruguay Round, were often complicated. Many nations, like the United States, face internal political dilemmas involving the often conflicting goals of seeking freer international trade while still protecting domestic industries. These dilemmas can make it difficult to reach international agreement on trade matters.

Legal environments also vary widely, and organizations are expected to abide by the laws of the host country in which they are operating. The more home and host-country laws differ, the more difficult and complex it is for international businesses to adapt to local ways. Common legal problems in international business involve incorporation practices and business ownership; negotiating and implementing contracts with foreign parties; protecting patents, trademarks, and copyrights; and handling foreign exchange restrictions. In the United States, executives of foreign-owned companies must worry about antitrust issues that prevent competitors from regularly talking to one another. They also must deal with a variety of special laws dealing with occupational health and safety, equal employment opportunity, sexual harassment, and other matters — all constraints potentially different from those they find at home. Mitsubishi, the Japanese auto manufacturer, came face-to-face with this in the form of sexual harassment and discrimination claims pursued by the federal Equal Employment Opportunity Commission in behalf of female employees at the firm's Normal, Illinois plant.[35]

People are essential resources of organizations, and as educational systems vary from one country to the next so too does the availability of labor. The *Harvard Business Review's* World Leadership Survey reports that business executives in many parts of the world are worried about actual or potential "human resource deficits."[36] They recognize that problems of illiteracy and the absence of appropriate skills in the available workforce can compromise operations. They also increasingly recognize the broader social challenge of becoming more actively involved in education and training to help build supplies of qualified labor in a host country.

PROS AND CONS OF MULTINATIONAL CORPORATIONS

In this complex environment and at a time when consumer demand, resource supplies, product flows, and labor markets increasingly span national boundaries, the actions of MNCs are increasingly influential in the global economy. The United Nations has reported that MNCs hold one-third of the world's productive assets and control 70 percent of world trade. Furthermore, more than 90 percent of these MNCs are based in the northern hemisphere.[37]

Both the global corporations and the countries that "host" their foreign operations should mutually benefit from any business relationship. The potential host-country benefits include larger tax bases, increased employment opportunities, technology transfers, the introduction of new industries, and the development of local resources. *Figure 5.3* shows, however, that things can and do go wrong in MNC-host country relationships. Host countries sometimes complain that MNCs extract excessive profits, dominate the local economy, interfere with the local government, do not respect local customs and laws, fail to help domestic firms develop, hire the most talented of local personnel, and do not transfer their most advanced technologies.[38]

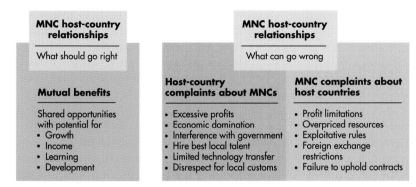

MNC host-country relationships	MNC host-country relationships	
What should go right	What can go wrong	
Mutual benefits	**Host-country complaints about MNCs**	**MNC complaints about host countries**
Shared opportunities with potential for • Growth • Income • Learning • Development	• Excessive profits • Economic domination • Interference with government • Hire best local talent • Limited technology transfer • Disrespect for local customs	• Profit limitations • Overpriced resources • Exploitative rules • Foreign exchange restrictions • Failure to uphold contracts

Figure 5.3 What should go right and what can go wrong in MNC-host country relationships.

Of course executives of MNCs sometimes feel exploited as well in their relations with host countries. Consider China, where major cultural, political, and economic differences confront the outsider.[39] Profits have proved elusive for some foreign investors, some have faced government restrictions making it difficult to take profits out of the country; some have struggled to get needed raw materials, both domestically and from abroad. The protection of intellectual property is an ongoing concern of foreign manufacturers, and managing relationships with government agencies can be very complicated. Even though Motorola runs the largest foreign-owned operations inside China, for example, it must still negotiate business plans with the government. Says the firm's chief country representative K. P. To: "Even if you're wholly owned, you still need strong support from the government."[40]

MNCs may also encounter difficulties in the country where their headquarters are located. Even as many MNCs try to operate more geocentrically, home-country governments and citizens tend to identify them with local and national interests. When an MNC cuts back or closes a domestic operation to shift work to a lower cost international destination, the loss of local jobs is controversial. Corporate decision makers are likely to be engaged by government and community leaders in critical debate about a firm's domestic social responsibilities. Home-country criticisms of MNCs include complaints about transferring jobs out of the country, shifting capital investments abroad, and engaging in corrupt practices in foreign settings.

ETHICAL ISSUES IN MULTINATIONAL OPERATIONS

The ethical aspects of international business deserve special attention. The subject of foreign corrupt practices is a source of continuing controversy in the United States and for the managers of its MNCs. In 1977, the Foreign Corrupt Practices Act made it illegal for firms and their managers to engage in a variety of corrupt practices overseas, including giving bribes and excessive commissions to foreign officials in return for business favors. This law specifically bans payoffs to foreign officials to obtain or keep business, provides punishments for executives who know about or are involved in such activities, and requires detailed accounting records for international business transactions. Critics believe the law fails to recognize the "reality" of business as practiced in many foreign nations. They complain that American companies are at a competitive disadvantage because they can't offer the same "deals" as competitors from other nations — deals that locals may regard as standard business practice.

"Sweatshop" operations, which employ local labor at low wages and often in poor working conditions, are another concern in the global business arena. Net-

• **Kemet Electronics**
http://www.kemet.com

The town of Shelby, North Carolina, knows just how cutthroat the global economy can be. The announcement that Kemet Electronics would lay off some 500 local employees and shift their jobs to Mexico hurt. Says Nancy Blackburn, a Kemet employee: "I worked all this time to get what I've got, and now it's gone. I thought I had found security."

works of outsourcing contracts are now common as manufacturers follow the world's low-cost labor supplies — countries like the Philippines, Sri Lanka, and Vietnam are popular destinations. Yet Nike has learned from problems in Asia that a global company will be held publicly accountable for the work standards and employment practices of its foreign subcontractors. Facing activist criticism, the company revised its labor practices with recommendations from a review by the consulting firm Goodworks International and an audit by the accounting firm Ernst & Young.

Child labor is another controversial issue, made especially visible by activist concerns regarding the manufacture of handmade carpets in countries like Pakistan. Initiatives to eliminate child labor include an effort by "Rugmark" to discourage purchases of carpets that do not carry its label. The Rugmark label is earned by a certification process to guarantee that a carpet manufacturer does not use child labor.[41]

Yet another ethical issue in international business relates to global concerns for environmental protection. Not only is the world's citizenry worried about disasters, such as the pollution aftermath of the Gulf War, but more generally it expects global corporations to always respect the natural environment and pursue safe industrial practices. Industrial pollution of cities, hazardous waste, depletion of natural resources, and related concerns are now worldwide issues. As global corporate citizens, MNCs are expected to uphold high standards in dealing with them — whenever and wherever they operate.

CULTURE AND GLOBAL DIVERSITY

- **Culture** is a shared set of beliefs, values, and patterns of behavior common to a group of people.

Culture is the shared set of beliefs, values, and patterns of behavior common to a group of people. Anyone who has visited another country knows that cultural differences exist. **Culture shock,** the confusion and discomfort a person experiences when in an unfamiliar culture, is a reminder that many of these differences must be mastered just to travel comfortably around the world. But the important business and managerial implications of sociocultural differences must also be understood. An American exporter, for example, once went to see a Saudi Arabian official. He sat in the office with crossed legs and the sole of his shoe exposed — an unintentional sign of disrespect in the local culture. He passed documents to the host using his left hand, which Muslims consider unclean, and he refused to accept coffee when it was offered, suggesting criticism of the Saudi's hospitality. The price for these cultural miscues was the loss of a $10 million contract to a Korean better versed in Arab ways.[42]

- **Culture shock** is the confusion and discomfort a person experiences when in an unfamiliar culture.

- **Ethnocentrism** is the tendency to consider one's culture as superior to all others.

Ethnocentrism, or the tendency to view one's culture as superior to others, must be avoided. Local customs vary in too many ways for most of us to become true experts in the many cultures of our diverse world. Yet there are things we can do to respect differences, successfully conduct business abroad, and minimize culture shock. Self-awareness and reasonable sensitivity are the basic building blocks of cultural awareness, as suggested in *Manager's Notepad 5.2.*[43]

POPULAR DIMENSIONS OF CULTURE

The first impressions of a traveler often include recognition and even "shock" over cultural differences. Among the popular dimensions of culture that should be recognized are those relating to language, use of space, time orientation, religion, and the role of contracts.[44]

> ### Manager's Notepad 5.2
>
> **Stages in Adjusting to a New Culture**
>
> - *Confusion:* First contacts with the new culture leave you anxious, uncomfortable, and in need of information and advice.
> - *Small victories:* Continued interactions bring some "successes," and your confidence grows in handling daily affairs.
> - *The honeymoon:* A time of wonderment, cultural immersion, and infatuation, with local things viewed most positively by you.
> - *Irritation and anger:* A time when the "negatives" overtake the "positives," and the new culture becomes a target of your criticism.
> - *Reality:* A time of rebalancing; you are able to enjoy the new culture while recognizing its less desirable elements.

British Airways (BA) flys more international passengers than any other airline. But when it surveyed customers, a simple lesson emerged—don't assume people from different cultures will have the same dining habits and preferences. Japanese, for example, commented that BA's food was "not bad for Westerners." They also pointed out that the white china dishes were similar to those used in Japanese hospitals and prisons. "The further away from our Western culture we go, the less satisfied our customers are," said one BA marketing manager,  "people from other cultures have felt looked down upon." CEO Bob Ayling initiated a major overhaul to give the carrier a more truly global identity. He says, "We don't want to ram our Britishness down people's throats."[45]

Language

Language not only varies around the world, the same language (such as English) can vary in usage from one country to the next (as it does from America to England to Australia). Although it isn't always possible to know a local language, such as Hungarian, it is increasingly common in business dealings to find some common second language in which to communicate, often English, French, German, or Spanish. The importance of good foreign language training is increasingly critical for the truly global manager.

Use of Space

The use of space varies among cultures. Arabs and many Latin Americans, for example, prefer to communicate at much closer distances than is standard in American practice. Misunderstandings are possible if one businessperson moves back as another moves forward to close the interpersonal distance between them. Some cultures of the world also value space more highly than others. Americans tend to value large *and* private office space. The Japanese are highly efficient in using space; even executive offices are likely to be shared in major corporations.

Time Orientation

Time orientation is different in many cultures. Mexicans, for example, specify *hora Americana* on invitations if they want guests to appear at the appointed

- In a **monochronic culture** people tend to do one thing at a time.

- In a **polychronic culture** time is used to accomplish many different things at once.

time; otherwise, it may be impolite to arrive punctually for a scheduled appointment. The anthropologist Edward T. Hall describes **monochronic cultures** in which people tend to do one thing at a time, such as schedule a meeting and give the visitor one's undivided attention for the allotted time.[46] This is standard American business practice. In **polychronic cultures,** by contrast, time is used to accomplish many different things at once. The American visitor to an Egyptian client may be frustrated by continued interruptions as people flow in and out of the office and various transactions are made.

Religion

Religion is also important as a cultural variable. It is a major influence on many people's lives, and its impact may extend to business practices regarding dress, food, and interpersonal behavior. Religion is a source of ethical and moral teaching, with associated personal and institutional implications. The traveler and businessperson should be sensitive to the rituals, holy days, and other expectations associated with religions in foreign countries. When working with Muslims, for example, it should be remembered that the Islamic holy month of Ramadan is a dawn-to-dusk time of fasting. Similarly, Islamic banks operate within guidelines set forth in the holy *Koran* and therefore charge no interest.

Role of Contracts

Cultures vary in their use of contracts and agreements. In the United States a contract is viewed as a final and binding statement of agreements. In other parts of the world, including the People's Republic of China, it may be viewed as more of a starting point; once in place, it will continue to emerge and be modified as the parties work together over time. McDonald's found this out when the Chinese government ignored the firm's lease on a restaurant site in downtown Beijing and tore down the building to make room for a development project. In the United States, contracts are expected to be in writing; requesting a written agreement from an Indonesian Muslim who has given his "word" may be quite disrespectful.

VALUES AND NATIONAL CULTURES

Geert Hofstede, a Dutch scholar and international management consultant, studied personnel from a U.S.-based MNC operating in 40 countries.[47] His research offers one framework for understanding the management implications of broad differences in national cultures. *Figure 5.4* shows how selected countries rank on the five dimensions Hofstede now uses to describe the values of national cultures:[48]

Hofstede's dimensions of national cultures

- *Power distance:* The degree to which a society accepts the unequal distribution of power in organizations.

- *Uncertainty avoidance:* The degree to which a society tolerates risk and situational uncertainties.

- *Individualism-collectivism:* The degree to which a society emphasizes individual self-interests versus the collective values of groups.

- *Masculinity-femininity:* The degree to which a society emphasizes assertiveness and material concerns versus greater concern for human relationships and feelings.

- *Time orientation:* The degree to which a society emphasizes short term considerations versus greater concern for the future.

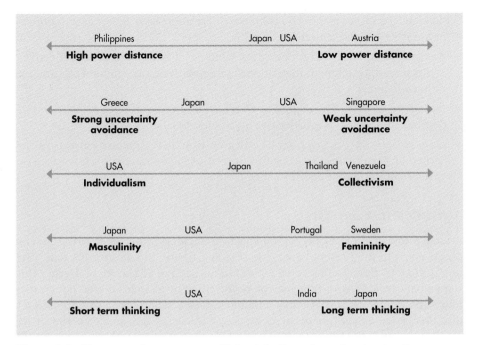

Figure 5.4 How countries compare on Hofstede's dimensions of national culture.

Hofstede's framework helps identify some of the managerial implications of cultural differences. For example, workers from high power-distance cultures, such as Singapore, can be expected to show great respect to people in authority. In high uncertainty-avoidance cultures, employment practices that increase job security are likely to be favored. In highly individualistic societies (the United States ranked as the most individualistic country in Hofstede's sample), workers may be expected to emphasize self-interests more than group loyalty. Outsiders may find that the workplace in more masculine societies, such as Japan, displays more rigid gender stereotypes.[49] And the corporate strategies of businesses in more long-term cultures are likely to be just that—more long-term oriented.

UNDERSTANDING CULTURAL DIFFERENCES

Another framework for understanding cultural differences offers some integration of both the notions of popular and national cultures just discussed. In a research study consisting of some 15,000 respondents from 47 countries, Fons Trompenaars identifies systematic differences in the ways relationships are handled among people, attitudes toward time, and attitudes toward the environment.[50] By better understanding these patterns of difference, he suggests we can improve our cross-cultural work effectiveness.

Relationships with People

According to Trompenaars's framework, there are five ways in which people differ culturally in the way they handle relationships with one another. They include the individualism-collectivism notion just discussed, as well as additional considerations:

- *Universalism vs. particularism:* The degree to which a culture emphasizes rules and consistency in relationships or accepts flexibility and the bending of rules to fit circumstances.

- *Individualism vs. collectivism:* The degree to which a culture emphasizes in-

● **Nike**
http://www.nike.com

Nike ran into problems when a design for one of its training shoes was misinterpreted by Muslims. The mark was supposed to resemble "flames" but in its visual presentation resembled the word Allah *as written in Arabic. Some called for a boycott of Nike products.*

dividual freedoms and responsibilities in relationships or focuses more on group interests and consensus.

- *Neutral vs. affective:* The degree to which a culture emphasizes objectivity and reserved detachment in relationships or allows more emotionality and expressed feelings.

- *Specific vs. diffuse:* The degree to which a culture emphasizes focused and in-depth relationships or broader and more superficial ones.

- *Achievement vs. prescription:* The degree to which a culture emphasizes an earned or performance-based status in relationships or awards status based on social standing and nonperformance factors.

Attitudes toward Time

Attitudes toward time in the Trompenaars framework differ in the relative emphasis given to the present versus the past and future. In cultures that take a *sequential view,* time is considered a continuous and passing series of events. This somewhat casual view of time may be represented by a circle and the notion that time is recycling, in the sense that a moment passed will return again. In cultures that take a *synchronic view,* by contrast, time takes on a greater sense of urgency. It is more linear, with an interrelated past, present, and future. Pressures to resolve problems quickly so that time won't be "lost" are more likely in synchronic than sequential cultures.

Attitudes toward the Environment

Trompenaars also recognizes that cultures vary in their approach to the environment. In cultures that are *inner-directed,* people tend to view themselves as quite separate from nature. They are likely to consider the environment as something to be controlled or used for personal advantage. In cultures that are *outer-directed,* people tend to view themselves as part of nature. They are more likely to try and blend with or go along with the environment than to try to control it.

MANAGEMENT ACROSS CULTURES

● **Comparative management** is the study of how management practices differ systematically from one country and/or culture to the next.

The four management functions—planning, organizing, leading, and controlling—are as relevant to international operations as they are to domestic ones. Yet, as the preceding discussion of culture should suggest, they must be applied appropriately from one country and culture to the next. **Comparative management** is the study of how management systematically differs among countries and/or cultures. Today we recognize the importance of learning about how management is practiced around the world. Competition and the global economy have given rise to the *global manager*—someone comfortable with cultural diversity, quick to find opportunities in unfamiliar settings, and able to marshal economic, social, technological, and other forces for the benefit of the organization.[51] Says Robin Willett, Group Deputy Chairman of Willett Systems, Ltd. of the United Kingdom: "Our aim has always been to be a truly global company, not simply an exporter. We work very hard at developing and maintaining an international mindset that is shared by everyone—from senior management to staff."[52] Global managers, simply put, apply the management functions successfully across national and cultural borders.

PLANNING AND CONTROLLING GLOBAL OPERATIONS

The complexity of the international operating environment makes global planning and controlling especially challenging. Picture a home office somewhere in the United States, say Chicago. Foreign operations are scattered in Asia, Africa, South America, and Europe. Planning must somehow link the home office and foreign affiliates, while taking into account different environments, cultures, and needs. Increasingly, new technology facilitates the planning and control of global operations through vastly improved communications systems. Computer-based global networks allow home and field offices to share databases, electronically transfer documents, and even hold conferences and make group decisions through computer links and video conferencing.

Digital Equipment Corporation (DEC) has established Digital Asean in Singapore to manage its subsidiary and joint venture operations in Southeast Asia. Digital's "Borderless Asean" strategy involves developing business partnerships with software companies, information technology consultants, and marketing agencies. Warehousing for the region is outsourced to a Singaporean firm with operations in neighboring countries. In the dynamic and complex environment of the Asia-Pacific Basin, the company seeks business expansion through integration with the regional economy.[53]

Business firms planning investments in foreign countries must remain cautious about the risks of doing business across political borders. **Political risk** is the potential loss of one's investment in or managerial control over a foreign asset because of political changes in the host country. In general, the major threats of political risk come from social instabilities as a result of ethnic or other differences, armed conflicts and military disruptions, shifting government systems through elections or forced takeovers, and new laws and economic policies.

Political-risk analysis is a planning process that forecasts the probability of these and other political events that can threaten the security of a foreign investment. The stakes can be quite high. It is obvious, for example, that foreign investors suffered in the political turmoil of Iraq's invasion of Kuwait. It may be less obvious that in a single day it was possible for a U.S. firm in Mexico to lose close to one-third of its foreign assets overnight. How? Because the Mexican government decided to allow its currency, the peso, to float in the international money markets. The net result was a loss in the value of Mexican assets valued in U.S. dollars. Not all multinationals were caught totally by surprise. Firms that had done their political-risk analysis well took protective measures ahead of time.

- **Political risk** is the possible loss of investment or control over a foreign asset because of political changes in the host country.

ORGANIZING AND LEADING GLOBAL OPERATIONS

The same factors that challenge the planning and controlling functions in the international arena also affect managerial efforts to organize and lead. Organizing to meet the needs of global operations is a complex challenge. A common approach for organizations just getting started in international business is to appoint a vice president or other senior manager to oversee all foreign operations. This may be fine for limited international activity, but expanded global involvement usually requires a more complex arrangement.

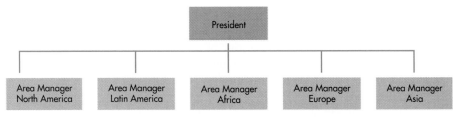

Figure 5.5   A multinational geographical structure for international operations.

A *multinational geographical structure* is shown in *Figure 5.5*. It arranges production and sales functions into separate geographical units, so that activities in major areas of the world are given special executive attention. Another important option is the *multinational product structure* shown in *Figure 5.6*. It gives worldwide responsibilities to product group managers, who are assisted by area specialists on the corporate staff. These specialists provide expert guidance on the unique needs of various countries or regions. Ford, IBM, and Bristol-Myers Squibb are but three of many firms that have reorganized to deemphasize geographical boundaries and focus more on worldwide industry or product groups.[54]

An indispensable rule of thumb for staffing international operations is stated this way by one successful international business owner: "Hire competent locals, use competent locals, and listen to competent locals." But global success also depends on the work of **expatriates,** employees who live and work in foreign countries on short-term or long-term assignments. For progressive firms, assigning home office personnel to foreign operations is increasingly viewed as a strategic opportunity. Not only does this offer the individuals challenging work experiences, it also helps bring into the executive suite culturally aware managers with truly global horizons and interpersonal networks of global contacts. Of course, not everyone performs well in an overseas assignment. Among the foundations for success are such personal attributes as a high degree of cultural awareness and sensitivity, a real desire to live and work abroad, family flexibility and support, as well as technical competence in one's job.[55]

● An **expatriate** lives and works in a foreign country.

ARE MANAGEMENT THEORIES UNIVERSAL?

Management practices in North America and Western Europe frequently have been used as models around the world. Increasingly, however, a significant question is asked—"Are management theories universal?" Geert Hofstede, whose framework for understanding national cultures was introduced earlier, believes they should not be applied universally.[56] He worries that many of these theories are ethnocentric and fail to take into account cultural differences. For example, he argues that the American emphasis on *participation* in leadership reflects the culture's moderate stance on power distance. National cultures with lower

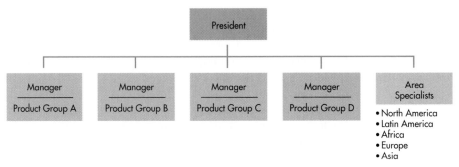

Figure 5.6   A multinational product structure for international operations.

scores, such as Sweden and Israel, are characterized by even more "democratic" leadership initiatives. France and some Asian countries with higher power-distance scores seem less concerned with participative leadership.

Hofstede also points out that the motivation theories of American scholars are value laden, with an emphasis on individual performance. He considers this viewpoint consistent with the high individualism found in Anglo-American countries such as the United States, Canada, and the United Kingdom. Elsewhere, where values are more collectivist, the theories may be less applicable. Even a common value, such as the desire for increased humanization of work, may lead in different management directions. Until recently, practices in the United States largely emphasized broadening jobs to enrich them for *individual* workers. Elsewhere in the world, such as in Sweden, the emphasis has been on broadening jobs for *groups* of workers. As interest in greater "teamwork" grows, a lingering question remains as to how well this practice fits highly individualistic cultures.

Similar cautions are in order for Japanese management practices, which have also attracted great interest over the years. More specifically, researchers have characterized Japanese management along the following lines.[57] The first such factor is *lifetime employment.* Many Japanese intend to work an entire career for one employer. Both the organization and the individual are expected to grow and mature together over time. The second factor is *job rotation and broad career experience.* Japanese managers tend to rotate through many jobs. They emphasize gaining broad experiences, not just specialized skills. They accept gradual career advancement and try to become well informed about the organization as a whole. Third is *shared information.* Japanese firms emphasize information sharing at all levels of responsibility. This includes information on performance objectives and accomplishments as well as on proposed activities and problems. The interpersonal "networks" built through job rotation are helpful in conducting business. The fourth factor is *collective decision making.* Japanese managers like to make group decisions that spread responsibility for results and create a team feeling. In the *ringi* system, agreement is gained from individuals or groups affected by a decision well before any actions are implemented. Fifth is a *quality emphasis.* Japanese firms emphasize product quality and *kaizen,* or quest for continuous improvement. Everyone is expected to produce high-quality work and to work with others to solve quality problems and advance quality objectives.

But as interesting as these concepts are, the lessons of Japanese management practices aren't easy to translate.[58] Any transfers of these lessons must allow for the important cultural differences between Japan and other parts of the world, as are evident in *Figure 5.4.* Moreover, recent observers also note the unique role of **keiretsu** in Japanese business success. These are long-term industry alliances or business groups that link together various businesses—manufacturers, suppliers, and finance companies—to attain common interests. The companies involved often own stock in one another; boards of directors may overlap; and it is common to do business with one another on a preferential basis. This practice is criticized by outsiders as a potential trade barrier that makes it hard for them to do business in Japan. It is also criticized as a source of unfair competition for Japanese firms operating in other countries, such as the antitrust-conscious United States. For example, Tenneco executives were dismayed when Mazda USA stopped buying their products and shifted orders to a *keiretsu* firm that had just set up a plant in Kentucky. On the topic of doing business with suppliers, one unnamed Japanese auto executive said, "First choice is a *keiretsu* company, second is a Japanese supplier, third is a local company."[59]

GLOBAL ORGANIZATIONAL LEARNING

In the dynamic and ever-expanding global economy, cultural awareness is helping to facilitate more informed transfers of management and organizational prac-

● Honda
http://www.honda.com

Honda builds a "world car," but customers in different countries can still expect styling that suits their preferences. The company is using an innovative "platform" that can be bent and stretched to fit styling preferences in different markets. This saves millions in costs and boosts sales. The European Honda Accord is short and narrow, the American larger, the Japanese sportier and compact.

● **Keiretsu** is a Japanese term describing alliances or business groups that link together manufacturers, suppliers, and finance companies with common interests.

tices. We live at a fortunate time when managers around the world are realizing they have much to share with and learn from one another. "Global organizational learning" is a timely and relevant theme. This point is evident in the following words of Kenichi Ohmae, noted Japanese management consultant and author of *The Borderless World:*

> Companies can learn from one another, particularly from other excellent companies, both at home and abroad. The industrialized world is becoming increasingly homogeneous in terms of customer needs and social infrastructure, and only truly excellent companies can compete effectively in the global marketplace.[60]

Yes, we do have a lot to learn from one another. Yet it must be learned with full appreciation of the constraints and opportunities of different national cultures and environments. Like the American management practices before them, Japanese approaches and those from other cultures must be studied and adapted for local use very carefully. This applies to the way management is practiced in Mexico, Korea, Indonesia, Hungary, or any other part of the world. As Hofstede states, "Disregard of other cultures is a luxury only the strong can afford. . . . [The] consequent increase in cultural awareness represents an intellectual and spiritual gain. And as far as management theories go, cultural relativism is an idea whose time has come."[61]

The best approach to comparative management and global management learning is an alert, open, inquiring, and always cautious one. It is important to identify both the potential merits of management practices found in other countries *and* the ways cultural variables may affect their success or failure when applied elsewhere. We can and should be looking for new ideas to stimulate change and innovation. But we should hesitate to accept any practice, no matter how well it appears to work somewhere else, as a universal prescription to action. Indeed, the goal of comparative management studies is not to provide definitive answers but to help develop creative and critical thinking about the way managers around the world do things, and about whether or not they can and should be doing them better.

CHAPTER REVIEW

This section should be used as an end-of-chapter "study guide." The *Summary* helps to put the chapter's content into overall perspective. The list of *Key Terms* allows you to double-check your familiarity with basic concepts and definitions. *Self-Test 5* gives you the opportunity to test your basic comprehension of chapter content using sample test questions.

SUMMARY

What are the management challenges in a global economy?

- International management is practiced in organizations that conduct business in more than one country.

- The global economy is making the diverse countries of the world increasingly interdependent regarding resource supplies, product markets, and business competition.

- The global economy is now strongly influenced by regional developments that involve growing economic integration in Europe, the Americas, and Asia, and the economic emergence of Africa.

What are the forms and opportunities of international business?

- Five forms of international business are global sourcing, exporting and importing, licensing and franchising, joint ventures, and wholly owned subsidiaries.

- The market entry strategies of global sourcing, exporting/importing, and licensing are common for firms wanting to get started internationally.

- Direct investment strategies to establish joint ventures or wholly owned subsidiaries in foreign countries represent substantial commitments to international operations.

What complicates the environment of global operations?

- Global operations are influenced by important environmental differences among the economic, legal-political, and educational systems of countries.

- A multinational corporation, or MNC, is a business with extensive operations in more than one foreign country.

- True MNCs are global firms with worldwide missions and strategies and that earn a substantial part of their revenues abroad.

- MNCs offer potential benefits to host countries in broader tax bases, new technologies, employment opportunities; MNCs can also disadvantage host countries if they interfere in local government, extract excessive profits, and dominate the local economy.

- The Foreign Corrupt Practices Act prohibits American MNCs from engaging in corrupt practices in their global operations.

How does culture create global diversity?

- Management and global operations are affected by the dimensions of popular culture, including language, space perception, time perception, religion, and the nature of contracts.

- Management and global operations are affected by differences in national cultures, including Hofstede's dimensions of power distance, uncertainty avoidance, individualism-collectivism, masculinity-femininity, and time orientation.

- Differences among the world's cultures may be understood in respect to how people handle relationships with one another, their attitudes toward time, and their attitudes toward the environment.

How do management and learning transfer across cultures?

- The management process must be used appropriately and applied with sensitivity to local cultures and situations.

- The field of comparative management studies how management is practiced around the world and how management ideas are transferred from one country or culture to the next.

- Cultural values and management practices should be consistent with one another; practices that are successful in one culture may work less well in others.

- The concept of global management learning has much to offer as the "borderless" world begins to emerge and as the management practices of diverse countries and cultures become more visible.

KEY TERMS

Asian-Pacific Economic
  Cooperation (APEC)
  (p. 95)
Comparative management
  (p. 106)
Culture (p. 102)
Culture shock (p. 102)
Ethnocentrism (p. 102)
European Union (EU)
  (p. 92)
Expatriates (p. 108)
Exporting (p. 97)
Franchising (p. 97)
General Agreement on
  Tariffs and Trade
  (GATT) (p. 100)

Global economy (p. 92)
Global manager (p. 106)
Global sourcing (p. 96)
Importing (p. 97)
International business
  (p. 96)
International management
  (p. 92)
Joint ventures (p. 97)
Keiretsu (p. 109)
Licensing agreement
  (p. 97)
Maquiladora (p. 94)
Monochronic cultures
  (p. 104)

Multinational corporation
  (p. 98)
North American Free Trade
  Agreement (NAFTA)
  (p. 93)
Political risk (p. 107)
Polychronic cultures
  (p. 104)
Privatization (p. 99)
Transnational corporation
  (p. 99)
Wholly owned subsidiary
  (p. 97)
World Trade Organization
  (p. 100)

SELF-TEST 5

Take this test much as you would in a normal classroom situation. It should offer you a good way to check your basic comprehension of chapter material. Answers may be found at the end of the book.

MULTIPLE-CHOICE QUESTIONS:

1. The possible reasons for going international in business include the quest for _____. (a) increased profits (b) new markets (c) lower labor costs (d) all of these

2. A _____ is a foreign firm that operates with special privileges in Mexico in return for agreeing to employ Mexican labor. (a) *keiretsu* (b) *maquiladora* (c) *jacaranda* (d) *zapatista*

3. A common direct investment strategy for going international is _____. (a) exporting (b) joint venture (c) licensing (d) global sourcing

4. When a government makes economic decisions such as the distribution of labor and other resources to businesses, it is operating like a _____ economy. (a) free-market (b) competitive (c) central-planning (d) supply-side

5. If a change in government results in the expropriation of foreign assets, the loss to the foreign firms might be considered a _____ risk of international business. (a) multinational (b) political (c) competitive (d) social

6. In _____ cultures, members tend to do one thing at a time; in _____ cultures, members tend to do many things at once. (a) monochronic, polychronic (b) ethnocentric, geocentric (c) collectivist, individualist (d) totalitarian, democratic

7. _____ involves the sale of government-owned assets into private hands. (a) Privatization (b) Capitalization (c) Incorporation (d) Licensing

8. A firm operating with individual vice presidents for Asia, Africa, and Europe would be using a multinational _____ structure. (a) product (b) function (c) geographic (d) matrix

9. In Hofstede's study of national cultures, America was found to be the most _____ among the 40 countries in his sample. (a) individualist (b) collectivist (c) masculine (d) power distance

10. _____ is the shared set of beliefs, values, and patterns of behavior common to a group of people. (a) Collectivism (b) Confucianism (c) Culture (d) Enthnocentrism

TRUE-FALSE QUESTIONS:

11. International business is something only large, not small, businesses can pursue. T F

12. Businesses from countries within the EU benefit from agreements to remove barriers to cross-border trade among member nations. T F

13. Within Asia, the only countries of economic importance are Japan, South Korea, China, Taiwan, and Singapore. T F

14. Joint ventures are primarily designed to help the local partner gain technology and expertise from the foreign partner. T F

15. A company that seeks total integration of its global operations is referred to as a geo-centric company. T F

16. Religion is one aspect of culture that is not important to cross-cultural business dealings. T F

17. American management theories have been found to be universally applicable around the world. T F

18. The Foreign Corrupt Practices Act is a law regulating the practices of American firms in their foreign business dealings. T F

19. An ethnocentric company would emphasize central control and careful direction by headquarters of all foreign operations. T F

20. *Keiretsu* are long-term alliances that link Japanese businesses to one another. T F

SHORT-RESPONSE QUESTIONS:

21. Why is NAFTA important for American businesses?

22. Why do host countries sometimes complain about the operations of MNCs within their borders?

23. Why is the "power-distance" dimension of national culture important in management?

24. Choose a region of the world (Europe, the Americas, Africa, Asia) and describe its significance in the global economy.

APPLICATION QUESTION:

25. Kim has just returned from her first business trip to Japan. While there, she was impressed with the use of quality circles and work teams. Now back in Iowa, she would like to start the same practices in her canoe manufacturing company of 75 employees. Based on the discussion of culture and management in this chapter, what advice would you offer Kim?

CHAPTER SIX

Ethical Behavior and Social Responsibility

Planning Ahead—Chapter 6 Study Questions

- What is ethical behavior?
- How do ethical dilemmas complicate the workplace?
- How can high ethical standards be maintained?
- What is corporate social responsibility?
- How does government regulation influence business behavior?

Make this World a Better Place

The good news is that more and more organizations are adding a new job title–Vice President of the Environment–to their executive suites. These senior managers work on everything from a company's recycling program to long-term corporate environmental policies. Global warming, global sustainability, and environmental protection are all on the agenda as organizations pursue what some call "the greening of the bottom line."[1] The goal of "Taking Better Care of Our World" has been prominent at Quad/Graphics' since the firm's founding, and reflects a commitment to minimizing the company's environmental impacts.[2] And at DuPont, line managers are evaluated annually on how well they manage their environmental responsibilities. Vice president Paul Tebo says, "Our attitude is corporate environmentalism is a long-term cost saver for the company."[3]

The bad news is that not all reports from the corporate world are always as positive as the prior examples. Consider these actual reports from past news stories. *Item:* Firm admits lowering phone contract bid after receiving confidential information from an insider that an initial bid "was not good enough to win." *Item:* Company admits overcharging consumers and insurers more than $13 million for repairs to damaged rental cars. *Item:* Executives get prison terms for selling adulterated apple juice; the juice labeled "100% fruit juice" was actually a blend of synthetic ingredients.

And that's not all. Consider these words from a commencement address delivered a few years ago at a well-known school of business administration. "Greed is all right," the speaker said. "Greed is healthy. You can be greedy and still feel good about yourself." The students, it is reported, greeted these remarks with laughter and applause. The speaker was none other than Ivan Boesky, once considered the "king of the arbitragers."[4] It wasn't long after his commencement speech that Boesky was arrested, tried, convicted, and sentenced to prison for trading on inside information.

It is time to get serious about the moral aspects and social implications of decision making in organizations. In your career and in the work of any manager the ultimate task must be considered to be more than simply meeting performance expectations. Performance goals must always be achieved through ethical and socially responsible action. The following reminder from Desmond Tutu, archbishop of Capetown, South Africa, is applicable to managers everywhere:

> You are powerful people. You can make this world a better place where business decisions and methods take account of right and wrong as well as profitability. . . . You must take a stand on important issues: the environment and ecology, affirmative action, sexual harassment, racism and sexism, the arms race, poverty, the obligations of the affluent West to its less-well-off sisters and brothers elsewhere.[5]

WHAT IS ETHICAL BEHAVIOR?

- **Ethics** are the code of morals that sets standards as to what is good or bad, or right or wrong in one's conduct.

- **Ethical behavior** is accepted as "right" or "good" in the context of a governing moral code.

For our purposes, **ethics** can be defined as the code of moral principles that sets standards of good or bad, or right or wrong, in one's conduct and thereby guides the behavior of a person or group.[6] In concept, the purpose of ethics is to establish principles of behavior that help people make choices among alternative courses of action. In practice, **ethical behavior** is what is accepted to be "good" and "right" as opposed to "bad" or "wrong" in the context of the governing moral code.

LAW, VALUES, AND ETHICAL BEHAVIOR

There is clearly a legal component to ethical behavior; that is, any behavior considered ethical should also be legal in a just and fair society. This does not mean, however, that simply because an action is not illegal it is necessarily ethical. Just living up to the "letter of the law" is not sufficient to guarantee that one's actions can or should be considered ethical. Is it truly ethical, for example, for an employee to take longer than necessary to do a job? To make personal telephone calls on company time? To call in sick to take a day off for leisure? To fail to report rule violations by a coworker?

None of these acts are strictly illegal, but many people would consider one or more of them to be unethical. Indeed, most ethical problems arise when people are asked to do or find themselves about to do something that violates their personal conscience. For some of them, if the act is legal they proceed with confidence. For others, however, the ethical test goes beyond the legality of the act alone. The issue extends to personal **values** — the underlying beliefs and attitudes that help determine individual behavior. To the extent that values vary among people, we can expect different interpretations of what behavior is ethical or unethical in a given situation.

• **Values** are broad beliefs about what is or is not appropriate behavior.

Consider how a founder's values drive the natural products firm Tom's of Maine. Founded by Tom Chappell and his wife Kate, the company was described by the Council of Economic Priorities as one of the "saints of social responsibility." Tom's products cost more, but for the extra price customers get the satisfaction of knowing they support a company whose products don't pollute the environment. Tom says, "I believe we have been able to expand upon the historical point of view that business is just for making money to a broader view that business is about doing good for others in the process of getting financial gain."[7] At Tom's of Maine the mission statement says — "we do not need to sacrifice our responsibility to society, the environment, our community, or our coworkers to be profitable or successful."[8]

ALTERNATIVE VIEWS OF ETHICAL BEHAVIOR

There are many different interpretations of what constitutes ethical behavior. *Figure 6.1* shows four views of ethical behavior that have been discussed over the years.[9] The first is the **utilitarian view.** Behavior that would be considered ethical from this perspective delivers the greatest good to the greatest number of people. Founded in the work of 19th-century philosopher John Stuart Mill, this is a results-oriented point of view that tries to assess the moral implications of decisions in terms of their consequences. Business decision makers, for example, are inclined to use profits, efficiency, and other performance criteria to judge what is best for the most people. A manager may make a utilitarian decision to cut 30 percent of a plant's workforce in order to keep the plant profitable and save jobs for the remaining 70 percent.

• The **utilitarian view** considers ethical behavior as that which delivers the greatest good to the greatest number of people.

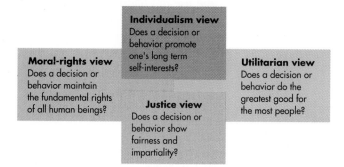

Individualism view
Does a decision or behavior promote one's long term self-interests?

Moral-rights view
Does a decision or behavior maintain the fundamental rights of all human beings?

Utilitarian view
Does a decision or behavior do the greatest good for the most people?

Justice view
Does a decision or behavior show fairness and impartiality?

Figure 6.1 Four views of ethical behavior.

- The **individualism view** considers ethical behavior as that which advances long-term self-interests.

- The **moral-rights view** considers ethical behavior as that which respects and protects fundamental rights.

- The **justice view** considers ethical behavior as that which treats people impartially and fairly according to guiding rules and standards.

- **Procedural justice** concerns the degree to which policies and rules are fairly administered.

- **Distributive justice** concerns the degree to which people are treated the same regardless of individual characteristics.

The **individualism view** of ethical behavior is based on the belief that one's primary commitment is to the advancement of long-term self-interests. If self-interests are pursued from a long-term view, the argument goes, such things as lying and cheating for short-term gain should not be tolerated. If one person does it, everyone will do it, and no one's long-term interests will be served. The individualism view is supposed to promote honesty and integrity. But in business practice it may result in a *pecuniary ethic,* described by one observer as the tendency to "push the law to its outer limits" and "run roughshod over other individuals to achieve one's objectives."[10]

Ethical behavior under a **moral-rights view** is that which respects and protects the fundamental rights of people. From the teachings of John Locke and Thomas Jefferson, for example, the rights of all people to life, liberty, and fair treatment under the law are considered inviolate. In organizations today, this concept extends to ensuring that employee rights such as the following are always protected: right to privacy, due process, free speech, free consent, health and safety, and freedom of conscience.

Finally, the **justice view** of moral behavior is based on the belief that ethical decisions treat people impartially and fairly according to guiding rules and standards. This approach evaluates the ethical aspects of any decision on the basis of whether it is "equitable" for everyone affected. One justice issue in organizations is **procedural justice**—the degree to which policies and rules are fairly administered. For example, does a sexual harassment charge levied against a senior executive receive the same full hearing as one made against a shop-level supervisor? Another issue is **distributive justice**—the degree to which people are treated the same regardless of individual characteristics based on ethnicity, race, gender, age, or other particularistic criteria. For example, does a woman with the same qualifications and experience as a man receive the same consideration for promotion?

CULTURAL ISSUES IN ETHICAL BEHAVIOR

The influence of culture on ethical behavior is increasingly at issue as businesses and individuals travel the world. As businesses seek markets, resources, and opportunities in diverse ends of the Earth, corporate leaders must master difficult challenges when operating across borders that are cultural as well as national. Levi CEO Robert Haas says that addressing ethical dilemmas as a corporate executive ". . . becomes even more difficult when you overlay the complexities of different cultures and values systems that exist throughout the world."[11]

- **Cultural relativism** suggests there is no one right way to behave; ethical behavior is determined by its cultural context.

Those who believe that behavior in foreign settings should be guided by the classic rule of "When in Rome do as the Romans do" reflect the position of **cultural relativism.**[12] This is the notion that there is no one right way to behave and that ethical behavior is always determined by its cultural context. When it comes to international business, for example, an American executive guided by rules of cultural relativism would argue that the use of child labor is okay if it is consistent with local laws and customs. *Figure 6.2,* however, contrasts this posi-

Cultural relativism	Ethical imperialism
←	→
No culture's ethics are superior. The values and practices of the local setting determine what is right or wrong.	Certain absolute truths apply everywhere. Universal values transcend cultures in determining what is right or wrong.
When in Rome, do as the Romans do.	*Don't do anything you wouldn't do at home.*

Figure 6.2 The extremes of cultural relativism and ethical imperialism. *Source:* Developed from Thomas Donaldson, "Values in Tension: Ethics Away from Home," *Harvard Business Review,* Vol. 74 (September–October, 1996), pp. 48–62.

Manager's Notepad 6.1

How Companies Can Respect Core or Universal Values

Respect for human dignity

- Create corporate culture that values employees, customers, and suppliers
- Keep a safe workplace
- Produce safe products and services

Respect for basic rights

- Protect rights of employees, customers, and communities
- Avoid anything that threatens safety, health, education, living standards

Be good citizens

- Support social institutions, including economic and educational systems
- Work with local government and institutions to protect environment.

tion with an alternative that suggests if a behavior or practice is not okay in one's home environment it shouldn't be acceptable practice anywhere else. In other words, ethical standards are more universal in nature and should apply absolutely across cultures and national boundaries. Critics of such a universal approach claim that it is a form of **ethical imperialism,** or the attempt to externally impose one's ethical standards on others.

Business ethicist Thomas Donaldson discusses the debate between cultural relativism and ethical imperialism. Although there is no simple answer, he finds fault with both extremes. He argues instead that certain fundamental rights and ethical standards can be preserved while values and traditions of a given culture are respected.[13] The core values or "hyper-norms" that should transcend cultural boundaries focus on human dignity, basic rights, and good citizenship. With a commitment to core values creating a trans-cultural ethical umbrella, Donaldson believes international business behaviors can be tailored to local and regional cultural contexts. In the case of child labor, for example, the American executive might ensure that any children working in a factory under contract to his or her business would be provided schooling as well as employment. See *Manager's Notepad 6.1* for Donaldson's suggestions on how corporations can respect the core or universal values.

> • The attempt to externally impose one's ethical standards on other cultures is criticized as a form of **ethical imperialism.**

ETHICS IN THE WORKPLACE

A classic quotation states, "Ethical business is good business." The same can be said for all persons and institutions throughout society. But the real test is when a manager or worker encounters a situation that tests his or her ethical beliefs and standards. Often ambiguous and unexpected, these "ethical dilemmas" are part of the challenge of modern society.

WHAT IS AN ETHICAL DILEMMA?

An **ethical dilemma** is a situation that requires a choice regarding a possible course of action that, although offering the potential for personal or organizational benefit or both, may be considered unethical. It is a situation in which action must be taken but for which there is no clear consensus on what is "right"

> • An **ethical dilemma** is a situation with a potential course of action that, although offering potential benefit or gain, is also unethical.

The Council on Economic Priorities is part of an initiative called Social Accountability 8000, or SA8000. It proposes labor standards and a certification system to show that firms do not use child or forced labor, offer safe working conditions, pay sufficient wages for workers' basic needs, respect rights to organize, and don't regularly require more than 48-hour workweeks.

and "wrong." The burden is on the individual to make good choices. An engineering manager speaking from experience sums it up this way: "I define an unethical situation as one in which I have to do something I don't feel good about."[14]

In a survey of *Harvard Business Review* subscribers, most of the ethical dilemmas reported by managers involved conflicts with superiors, customers, and subordinates.[15] The most frequent issues involved dishonesty in advertising and communications with top management, clients, and government agencies. Problems in dealing with special gifts, entertainment, and kickbacks were also reported. Significantly, the managers' bosses were singled out as sometimes pressuring their subordinates to engage in such unethical activities as supporting incorrect viewpoints, signing false documents, overlooking the boss's wrongdoings, and doing business with the boss's friends. While you consider the potential difficulties of these situations, here is a short case to test yourself. It was originally presented to this same sample of managers. What would you do?

> The Case of the Foreign Payment: The minister of a foreign nation asks you to pay a $200,000 consulting fee. In return for the money, the minister promises special assistance in obtaining a $100 million contract that would produce at least a $5 million profit for your company. The contract will probably go to a foreign competitor if not won by you.

Among the *Harvard Business Review* subscribers responding to this case, 42 percent said they would refuse to pay; 22 percent would pay but consider it unethical; 36 percent would pay and consider it ethical in the foreign context.

RATIONALIZATIONS FOR UNETHICAL BEHAVIOR

Why might otherwise reasonable people act unethically? Think back to the earlier examples and to those from your experiences. Consider the possibility of being asked to place a bid for a business contract using insider information, paying bribes to obtain foreign business, falsifying expense account bills, and so on. "Why," you should be asking, "do people do things like this?" In fact, there are at least four common rationalizations that may be used to justify misconduct in these and other ethical dilemmas.[16]

Four ways of thinking about ethical behavior ➤

- Convincing yourself that the behavior is not really illegal.
- Convincing yourself that the behavior is really in everyone's best interests.
- Convincing yourself that nobody will ever find out what you've done.
- Convincing yourself that the organization will "protect" you.

After doing something that might be considered unethical, a rationalizer says, *"It's not really illegal."* This expresses a mistaken belief that one's behavior is acceptable, especially in ambiguous situations. When dealing with "shady" or "borderline" situations in which you are having a hard time precisely defining right from wrong, the advice is quite simple: When in doubt about a decision to be made or an action to be taken, don't do it.

Another common statement by a rationalizer is: *"It's in everyone's best interests."* This response involves the mistaken belief that because someone can be found to benefit from the behavior, the behavior is also in the individual's or the organization's best interests. Overcoming this rationalization depends in part on the ability to look beyond short-run results to address longer term implications and to look beyond results in general to the *ways* in which they are obtained. For example, in response to the question, "How far can I push matters to obtain this performance goal?" the recommended answer is often, "Don't try to find out."

Sometimes rationalizers tell themselves, *"No one will ever know about it."* They mistakenly believe that a questionable behavior is really "safe" and will never be found out or made public. Unless it is discovered, the argument implies, no crime was really committed. Lack of accountability, unrealistic pressures to perform, and a boss who prefers "not to know" can all reinforce such thinking. In this case, the best deterrent is to make sure that everyone knows that wrong-doing will be punished whenever it is discovered.

Finally, rationalizers may proceed with a questionable action because of a mistaken belief that *"the organization will stand behind me."* This is misperceived loyalty. The individual believes that the organization's best interests stand above all others. In return, the individual believes that top managers will condone the behavior and protect the individual from harm. But loyalty to the organization is not an acceptable excuse for misconduct; organizational loyalty should not stand above the law and social morality.

FACTORS INFLUENCING ETHICAL BEHAVIOR

It is almost too easy to confront ethical dilemmas from the safety of a textbook or a college classroom. In practice, people are often challenged to choose ethical courses of action in situations where the pressures may be contradictory and great. Increased awareness of the factors influencing ethical behavior can help you better deal with them in the future. *Figure 6.3* shows these influences emanating from the person, the organization, and the environment.

The Person

Family influences, religious values, personal standards, and personal needs, financial and otherwise, will help determine a person's ethical conduct in any given circumstance. Managers who lack a strong and consistent set of personal ethics will find that their decisions vary from situation to situation as they strive to maximize self-interests. Those who operate with strong *ethical frameworks,* personal rules or strategies for ethical decision making, will be more consistent and confident since choices are made against a stable set of ethical standards.

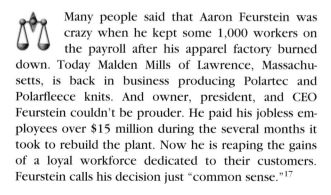

Many people said that Aaron Feurstein was crazy when he kept some 1,000 workers on the payroll after his apparel factory burned down. Today Malden Mills of Lawrence, Massachusetts, is back in business producing Polartec and Polarfleece knits. And owner, president, and CEO Feurstein couldn't be prouder. He paid his jobless employees over $15 million during the several months it took to rebuild the plant. Now he is reaping the gains of a loyal workforce dedicated to their customers. Feurstein calls his decision just "common sense."[17]

The Organization

The organization is another important influence on ethics in the workplace. We noted earlier that a person's immediate supervisor can have an important effect on the employee's behavior. Just exactly what a supervisor requests, and which

Figure 6.3 Factors influencing ethical managerial behavior — the person, organization, and environment.

actions are rewarded or punished, can certainly affect an individual's decisions and actions. The expectations and reinforcement provided by peers and group norms are likely to have a similar impact. Formal policy statements and written rules, although they cannot guarantee results, are also very important in establishing an ethical climate for the organization as a whole. They support and reinforce the organizational culture, which can have a strong influence on members' ethical behavior. At the Body Shop, founder Anita Roddick created an 11-point charter to guide the company's employees: "Honesty, integrity and caring form the foundations of the company and should flow through everything we do — we will demonstrate our care for the world in which we live by respecting fellow human beings, by not harming animals, by preserving our forests." Recent criticisms of Body Shop operations, however, reflect the inadequacy of formal statements alone to influence ethical behavior.[18]

The Environment

Organizations operate in external environments composed of competitors, government laws and regulations, and social norms and values, among other influences. Laws interpret social values to define appropriate behaviors for organizations and their members; regulations help governments monitor these behaviors and keep them within acceptable standards. The Foreign Corrupt Practices Act discussed in the last chapter is one example. It sets standards for American companies that prohibit bribery practices abroad. Although complex, the law guides the firms away from making payments to foreign political parties or candidates and government officials in attempting to induce them to make special decisions favoring the company.

The climate of competition in an industry also sets a standard of behavior for those who hope to prosper within it. Sometimes the pressures of competition contribute further to the ethical dilemmas of managers. Former American Airlines president Robert Crandall once telephoned Howard Putnam, then president of now-defunct Braniff Airlines. Both companies were suffering from money-losing competition on routes from their home base of Dallas. A portion of their conversation follows:[19]

Judy Connelly started Florist Directory Assistance/Florist Search, Inc., under unusual circumstances. She had $25,000 and two years of experience in a similar business that left her with a lot of motivation to open her own business. She didn't like her former boss's business tactics. So Connelly quit to run her own firm as a direct competitor.

Putnam: Do you have a suggestion for me?
Crandall: Yes. . . . Raise your fares 20 percent. I'll raise mine the next morning.
Putnam: Robert, we —
Crandall: You'll make more money and I will, too.
Putnam: We can't talk about pricing.
Crandall: Oh, Howard. We can talk about anything we want to talk about.

The U.S. Justice Department disagreed. It alleged that Crandall's suggestion of a 20 percent fare increase amounted to an illegal attempt to monopolize airline routes. The suit was later settled when Crandall agreed to curtail future discussions with competitors about fares.

MAINTAINING HIGH ETHICAL STANDARDS

Progressive organizations support a variety of methods for maintaining high ethical standards in workplace affairs. Some of the most important efforts in this area involve ethics training, whistleblower protection, top management support, formal codes of ethics, and strong ethical cultures.

ETHICS TRAINING

Ethics training, in the form of structured programs to help participants understand the ethical aspects of decision making, is designed to help people incorporate high ethical standards into their daily behaviors. An increasing number of college curricula now include courses on ethics, and seminars on this topic are popular in the corporate world. But it is important to keep the purpose of ethics training in perspective. An executive at Chemical Bank put it this way: "We aren't teaching people right from wrong—we assume they know that. We aren't giving people moral courage to do what is right—they should be able to do that anyhow. We focus on dilemmas."[20] Many of these dilemmas arise as a result of the time pressures of decisions. Most ethics training is designed to help people deal with ethical issues while under pressure and to avoid the four common rationalizations for unethical behavior that were discussed earlier.

Manager's Notepad 6.2 presents a seven-step checklist for making ethical decisions when confronting an ethical dilemma.[21] It offers a convenient reminder that the decision making process includes responsibility for double-checking a decision *before* taking action. The key issue in the checklist may well be Step 6— the risk of public disclosure of your action and your willingness to bear it. This is perhaps the strongest way of all to test whether a decision is consistent with one's personal ethical standards.

- **Ethics training** helps people better understand the ethical aspects of decision making.

Manager's Notepad 6.2

Checklist for Making Ethical Decisions

Step 1. Recognize the ethical dilemma.

Step 2. Get the facts.

Step 3. Identify your options.

Step 4. Test each option: Is it legal? Is it right? Is it beneficial?

Step 5. Decide which option to follow.

Step 6. Double check your decision by asking two follow-up questions:

   "How would I feel if my family finds out about my decision?"

   "How would I feel about this if my decision is printed in the local newspaper?"

Step 7. Take action.

WHISTLEBLOWER PROTECTION

• A **whistleblower** exposes the misdeeds of others in organizations.

Agnes Connolly pressed her employer to report two toxic chemical accidents, as she believed the law required; Dave Jones reported that his company was using unqualified suppliers in the construction of a nuclear power plant; Margaret Newsham revealed that her firm was allowing workers to do personal business while on government contracts; Herman Cohen charged that the ASPCA in New York was mistreating animals; Barry Adams complained that his hospital followed unsafe practices.[22] They were **whistleblowers,** persons who expose the misdeeds of others in organizations in order to preserve ethical standards and protect against wasteful, harmful, or illegal acts. All were fired from their jobs. Indeed, whistleblowers face the risks of impaired career progress and other forms of organizational retaliation, up to and including termination.[23]

Today, federal and state laws increasingly offer whistleblowers some defense against "retaliatory discharge." But although signs indicate that the courts are growing supportive of whistleblowers, legal protection can still be inadequate. Laws vary from state to state, and federal laws mainly protect government workers.[24] Furthermore, even with legal protection, potential whistleblowers may find it hard to expose unethical behavior in the workplace. Some organizational barriers to whistleblowing include a *strict chain of command* that makes it hard to bypass the boss; *strong work group identities* that encourage loyalty and self-censorship; and *ambiguous priorities* make it hard to distinguish right from wrong.[25]

In the attempt to remove these and other blocks to the exposure of unethical behaviors, some organizations have formally appointed staff members to serve as "ethics advisors." Others have set up formal staff units to process reported infractions. One novel proposal goes so far as to suggest the convening of *moral quality circles* to help create shared commitments for everyone to work at their moral best.[26] Some tentative guidelines on whistleblowing are provided in the the *Manager's Notepad 6.3.*[27]

TOP MANAGEMENT SUPPORT

Top managers have the power to shape an organization's policies and set its moral tone. They also have a major responsibility to use this power well. They can and should serve as models of appropriate ethical behavior for the entire organization. Not only must their day-to-day behavior be the epitome of high ethical con-

---

Manager's Notepad 6.3

"Do" and "Don't" Tips for Whistleblowers

• *Do* make sure you really understand what is happening and that your allegation is absolutely correct.

• *Don't* assume that you are automatically protected by law.

• *Do* talk to an attorney to ensure that your rights will be protected and proper procedures followed.

• *Don't* talk first to the media.

• *Do* keep accurate records to document your case; keep copies outside of your office.

• *Don't* act in anticipation of a big financial windfall if you end up being fired.

duct, but top managers must also communicate similar expectations throughout the organization . . . and reinforce positive results. Unfortunately, communication from the top may subtly suggest that top management does not want to know about deceptive or illegal practices by employees. And if top management is known to use organizational resources for personal pleasure, lower level employees may expect to be able to do likewise.

Even though top managers bear a special responsibility for setting the ethical tone of an organization, every manager is also in a position to influence the ethical behavior of the people who work for and with them. This means that all managers must act as ethical role models and set an ethical tone in their areas of responsibility. Care must be taken to do this in a positive and informed manner. The important supervisory act of setting goals and communicating performance expectations is a good case in point. A surprising 64 percent of 238 executives in one study, for example, reported feeling under pressure to compromise personal standards to achieve company goals. A *Fortune* survey also reports that 34 percent of its respondents felt a company president can create an ethical climate by setting *reasonable* goals "so that subordinates are not pressured into unethical actions."[28] Clearly, a supervisor may unknowingly encourage unethical practices by exerting *too* much pressure for the accomplishment of goals that are *too* difficult.

FORMAL CODES OF ETHICS

Formal **codes of ethics** are official written guidelines on how to behave in situations susceptible to the creation of ethical dilemmas. They are found in organizations and in professions such as engineering, medicine, law, and public accounting. In the professions, ethical codes try to ensure that individual behavior is consistent with the historical and shared norms of the professional group. The National Association of Accountants has a formal code of ethics to guide internal accountants working for corporate employers. Among other things, the code requires an accountant to report to company superiors any improper behavior that may be observed. Association officials feel the code gives management accountants a standard to point to if asked to "cook the books" or overlook accounting abuses.

Most codes of ethical conduct identify expected behaviors in terms of general organizational citizenship, the avoidance of illegal or improper acts in one's work, and good relationships with customers. In a related survey of companies with written codes, the items most frequently addressed included workforce diversity, bribes and kickbacks, political contributions, the honesty of books or records, customer—supplier relationships, and the confidentiality of corporate information.[29] In the increasingly complex world of international business, codes of conduct for manufacturers and contractors are becoming more prevalent. The Walt Disney Company, for example, expects certain commitments of all manufacturers of its merchandise as specified in a formal code of conduct. Among the many areas covered, the document states the following: *child labor*— "Manufacturers will not use child labor"; *involuntary labor*— "Manufacturers will not use any forced or involuntary labor, whether prison, bonded, indentured, or otherwise"; *coercion and harassment*— "Manufacturers will treat each employee with dignity and respect, and will not use corporal punishment, threats of violence or other forms of physical, sexual, psychological or verbal harassment or abuse."[30]

Although interest in codes of ethical conduct is growing, it must be remembered that the codes have limits; they cannot cover all situations, and they are not automatic insurance for universal ethical conduct. The value of any formal code of ethics still rests on the underlying human resource foundations of the or-

- A **code of ethics** is a written document that states values and ethical standards intended to guide the behavior of employees.

- **GE Plastics**
http://www.ge.com/plastics

Annual service projects are part of community relations activities at GE Plastics from Cartagena, Spain, to Bay of St. Louis, Mississippi. In Pittsfield, Massachusetts, 250 GE Plastics employees and family members renovated a wildlife sanctuary by constructing a 24-by-48-foot maintenance building. Community service projects such as this are part of GE Plastics's culture.

ganization—its managers and other employees. There is no replacement for effective hiring practices that staff the organization with honest and moral people. And there is no replacement for the leadership of committed managers who are willing to set the examples and act as positive role models to ensure desired results.

CORPORATE SOCIAL RESPONSIBILITY

• **Corporate social responsibility** is the obligation of an organization to act in ways that serve the interests of its stakeholders.

It is now time to shift our interest in ethical behavior from the level of the individual to that of the organization. To begin, it is important to remember that all organizations exist in complex relationship with elements in their external environment. In Chapter 2, in fact, we described the environment of a business firm as composed of a network of other organizations and institutions with which it must interact. In this context, **corporate social responsibility** is defined as an obligation of the organization to act in ways that serve both its own interests and the interests of its many external *stakeholders*. As defined in Chapter 2 these are individuals and groups who are affected in one way or another by the behavior of an organization. This includes being affected in one way or another by its commitment to social responsibility. The leadership beliefs that guide socially responsible organizational practices are described as follows:[31]

Beliefs guiding socially responsible practices

- The belief that people do their best in healthy work environments that allow for job involvement, respect for contributions, and a good balance of work and family life.

- The belief that organizations function best over the long run when located in healthy communities with high qualities of life.

- The belief that organizations realize performance gains and efficiencies when they treat the natural environment with respect in all of their operations.

- The belief that organizations must be managed and led for long-term success.

- The belief that the reputation of an organization must be protected to ensure consumer and stakeholder support.

SOCIAL RESPONSIBILITY AND CORPORATE PERFORMANCE

In academic and public policy circles, two contrasting views of corporate social responsibility have stimulated debate: the classical view that argues against it and the socioeconomic view that argues for it.[32] The *classical view* holds that management's only responsibility in running a business is to maximize profits. In other words—the business of business is business and the principal concern of management should always be to maximize shareholder value. This narrow "shareholder" and "profit-driven" model is supported by Milton Friedman, a respected free-market economist. He says, "Few trends could so thoroughly undermine the very foundations of our free society as the acceptance by corporate officials of social responsibility other than to make as much money for their stockholders as possible."[33] The arguments *against* corporate social responsibility include fears that the pursuit of this goal will reduce business profits, raise business costs, dilute business purpose, give business too much social power, and do so without business accountability to the public.

The *socioeconomic view* holds that management of any organization must be concerned for the broader social welfare and not just for corporate profits.

This broad-based and stakeholder model is supported by Paul Samuelson, another distinguished economist. He states, "A large corporation these days not only may engage in social responsibility, it had damn well better try to do so."[34] Among the arguments *in favor of* corporate social responsibility are that it will add long-run profits for businesses, improve the public image of businesses, and help them to avoid more government regulation. Also, the point is that businesses have the resources and ethical obligation to act responsibly. Furthermore, the public wants them to do so.

Today, there is little doubt that the public at large expects businesses and other organizations to act with genuine social responsibility. Stakeholder expectations are increasingly well voiced and include demands that organizations integrate social responsibility into their core values and daily activities. Going back to Tom's of Maine once again, founders Tom and Kate Chappell clearly state: "The company remains committed to environmental and social responsibility while developing a product line with the highest quality natural ingredients."[35]

On the research side, there is increasing evidence that high performance in social responsibility can be associated with strong financial performance and, at worst, has no adverse financial impact. The argument that acting with a commitment to social responsibly will negatively affect the "bottom line" is hard to defend. Indeed, recent evidence suggests the existence of a *virtuous circle* in which corporate social responsibility leads to improved financial performance for the firm and this in turn leads to more socially responsible actions in the future.[36] There seems little reason to believe that businesses cannot serve the public good and a broad pool of stakeholders as well as advance the financial interests of their shareholders. Even as the research and debate continues on this important concept, these historical comments by management theorist Keith Davis may still best sum up the corporate social responsibility debate.

> Society wants business as well as all other major institutions to assume significant social responsibility. Social responsibility has become the hallmark of a mature, global organization. . . . The business which vacillates or chooses not to enter the arena of social responsibility may find that it gradually will sink into customer and public disfavor.[37]

The Gap, Inc.
http://www.gap.com

Labor practices and employment conditions in overseas contractors' firms are a problem for a growing number of multinational companies. Human Rights groups praise the monitoring plan set up by The Gap, Inc., at an El Salvador plant. The plan uses church, university, and labor leaders to interview workers away from the plant to find out how they are being treated.

SOCIAL RESPONSIBILITY AUDITS

There are many action domains in which social responsibility can be pursued by business firms and other organizations. These include concerns for ecology and environmental quality, truth in lending and consumer protection, and aid to education as well as service to community needs, employment practices, diversity practices, progressive labor relations and employee assistance, and general corporate philanthropy, among other possibilities. At the organizational level, a **social audit** can be used at regular intervals to report on and systematically assess an organization's resource commitments and action accomplishments in these and other areas. You might think of social audits as attempts to assess the social performance of organizations, much as accounting audits assess their financial performance.

A formal assessment of corporate social performance might include these four criteria: (1) Is the organization's *economic responsibility* met? (2) Is the organization's *legal responsibility* met? (3) Is the organization's *ethical responsibility* met? (4) Is the organization's *discretionary responsibility* met?[38] As you move down the list, the criteria progress toward ever-greater demonstrations of socially responsible activities. An organization is meeting its economic responsibility when it earns a profit through the provision of goods and services desired by customers. Legal responsibility is fulfilled when an organization operates within the

● A **social audit** is a systematic assessment of an organization's accomplishments in areas of social responsibility.

law and according to the requirements of various external regulations. An organization meets its ethical responsibility when its actions voluntarily conform not only to legal expectations but also to the broader values and moral expectations of society. The highest level of social performance comes through the satisfaction of an organization's discretionary responsibility. Here, the organization voluntarily moves beyond basic economic, legal, and ethical expectations to provide leadership in advancing the well-being of individuals, communities, and society as a whole.

 Levi Strauss acts to protect worker rights in its contract plants in Asia. The firm was the first U.S. multinational to establish strict guidlines for the treatment of workers and for the environmental impacts of foreign plants making its products. A team of company inspectors makes routine visits to more than 700 contract factories. They look for health and safety hazards, the use of child labor, and wage standards, among other concerns. The firm halted contracts in Burma over human rights concerns and it paid for the education of a Bangladesh contractor's under-age employees. Although Levi still wants to do more, its guidelines and action-oriented program have been cited by the Council on Economic Priorities as a "good beginning."[39]

SOCIAL RESPONSIBILITY STRATEGIES

- An **obstructionist strategy** avoids social responsibility and reflects mainly economic priorities.

- A **defensive strategy** seeks to protect the organization by doing the minimum legally required to satisfy social expectations.

Figure 6.4 describes different degrees of commitment by organizations to the four social responsibility criteria just described. The continuum of corporate responsibility shows a desirable shift in emphasis from acting obstructionist, at the one extreme, to displaying progressive citizenship, at the other.[40]

An **obstructionist strategy** ("Fight the social demands") reflects mainly economic priorities; social demands lying outside the organization's perceived self-interests are resisted. If the organization is criticized for wrongdoings, it can be expected to deny the claims. A **defensive strategy** ("Do the minimum legally required") seeks to protect the organization by doing the minimum legally neces-

Proactive strategy	"Take leadership in social initiatives" Meet economic, legal, ethical, *and* discretionary responsibilities
Accommodative strategy	"Do minimum ethically required" Meet economic, legal, and ethical responsibilities
Defensive strategy	"Do minimum legally required" Meet economic and legal responsibilities
Obstructionist strategy	"Fight social demands" Meet economic responsibilities

Commitment to corporate social responsibilities

Figure 6.4 Four strategies of corporate social responsibility—from "obstructionist" to "proactive" behavior.

sary to satisfy expectations. Corporate behavior at this level conforms only to legal requirements, competitive market pressure and perhaps activist voices. If criticized, intentional wrongdoing is likely to be denied.

Organizations pursuing an **accommodative strategy** ("Do the minimum ethically required") accept their social responsibilities. They try to satisfy economic, legal, and ethical criteria. Corporate behavior at this level is congruent with society's prevailing norms, values, and expectations, but at times it may only be so because of outside pressures. An oil firm, for example, maybe willing to "accommodate" with clean-up activities when a spill occurs, but remain quite slow in taking preventive measures in the first place. Finally, the **proactive strategy** ("Take leadership in social initiatives") is designed to meet all the criteria of social performance, including discretionary performance. Corporate behavior at this level takes preventive action to avoid adverse social impacts from company activities, and it even anticipates or takes the lead in identifying and responding to emerging social issues. A growing number of progressive organizations like Quad/Graphics pursue proactive social responsibility goals, with concern for the natural environment prominent now among them.

- An **accommodative strategy** accepts social responsibilities and tries to satisfy prevailing economic, legal, and ethical performance criteria.

- A **proactive strategy** meets all the criteria of social responsibility, including discretionary performance.

Quad/Graphics is a Wisconsin-based printing company whose clients include *Time, Newsweek,* and *U.S. News & World Reports,* among many others. Almost everything used in its plants is reused or recycled and the use of toxic chemicals greatly reduced. The firm constantly searches for less-polluting inks, more efficient printers, and ways to minimize solid and liquid wastes. The firm's mission statement says, "Our goal is wise, balanced use of all resources. . . . We are proactive in creating and maintaining an 'environment for excellence' . . . Giving loving care to Mother Earth *is* good business."[41]

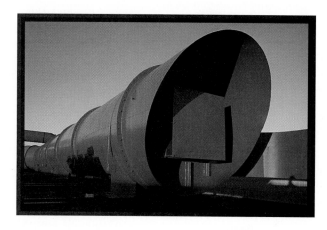

GOVERNMENT REGULATION OF BUSINESS

If organizations do not act responsibly on their own, governments will often pass laws and establish regulating agencies to control their behavior. It may not be too farfetched to say that behind every piece of legislation—national, state, or local—is a government agency charged with the responsibility of monitoring and ensuring compliance with its mandates. You know these agencies best by their acronyms: FAA (Federal Aviation Administration), EPA (Environmental Protection Agency), OSHA (Occupational Safety and Health Administration), and FDA (Food and Drug Administration), among many others.

As is the underlying legislation itself, the activities of government agencies are often subject to criticism. Public outcries to "dismantle the bureaucracy" and/or "deregulate business" reflect concerns that specific agencies and their supportive legislation are not functional. Many times an agency's interpretation of a law and/or way of seeking compliance are criticized, not the law itself.

THE COMPLEX LEGAL ENVIRONMENT

Business executives often complain that many laws and regulations are overly burdensome. Small business owners, in particular, express concerns that regula-

The City of San Francisco is a social activist. Like a growing number of cities, San Francisco now requires companies that do business with it to offer benefits to domestic partners of their employees, the same benefits that spouses would enjoy. Although some critics complain that municipalities are overstepping their authority with such actions, the trend is growing.

tions raise costs by creating the need for increased paperwork and staff to maintain compliance and by diverting managerial attention from important productivity concerns.[42] In reality, the legal environment is both complex and constantly changing. Many themes already discussed as being key areas of social responsibility are backed by major laws. Managers must stay informed about new and pending laws as well as existing ones. As a reminder of the positive side of legislation, consider four areas in which the U.S. government takes an active role in regulating business affairs.

The first area is *occupational safety and health.* The Occupational Safety and Health Act of 1970 firmly established that the federal government was concerned about worker health and safety on the job. Even though some complain that the regulations are still not strong enough, the act continues to influence the concerns of employers and government policymakers for worker safety. Second is the area of *fair labor practices.* Legislation and regulations that prohibit discrimination in labor practices are discussed in Chapter 12 on human resource management. The Equal Employment Opportunity Act of 1972 and related regulations are designed to reduce barriers to employment based on race, gender, age, national origin, and marital status. Third is *consumer protection.* The Consumer Product Safety Act of 1972 gives government authority to examine and force a business to withdraw from sale any product that it feels is hazardous to the consumer. Children's toys and flammable fabrics are within the great range of products affected by such regulation. The fourth area concerns *environmental protection.* Several antipollution acts, beginning with the Air Pollution Control Act of 1962, are designed to eliminate careless pollution of the air, water, and land.

INTEGRATING ETHICS, SOCIAL RESPONSIBILITY, AND PERFORMANCE

Trends in the evolution of social values point to ever-increasing demands from governments and other stakeholders that organizational decisions reflect ethical as well as high-performance standards. Today's workers and managers, as well as tomorrow's, must accept personal responsibility for doing the "right" things. Broad social and moral criteria must be used to examine the interests of multiple stakeholders in a dynamic and complex environment. Decisions must always be made and problems solved with ethical considerations standing side by side with high performance objectives, be they individual, group, or organizational. Indeed, the point that profits and social responsibility can go hand in hand is being confirmed in new and creative ways.

As public demands grow for organizations to be accountable for ethical and social performance as well as economic performance, the manager stands once again in the middle. It is the manager whose decisions affect "quality-of-life" outcomes in the critical boundaries between people and organizations and between organizations and their environments. Everyone must be more willing to increase the weight given to ethical and social responsibility considerations when making these decisions.

CHAPTER REVIEW

This section should be used as an end-of-chapter "study guide." The *Summary* helps to put the chapter's content into overall perspective. The list of *Key Terms* allows you to double-check your familiarity with basic concepts and definitions. *Self-Test 6* gives you the opportunity to test your basic comprehension of chapter content using sample test questions.

SUMMARY

What is ethical behavior?

- Ethical behavior is that which is accepted as "good" or "right" as opposed to "bad" or "wrong."

- Simply because an action is *not illegal* does not necessarily make it ethical in a given situation.

- Because values vary, the question of "What is ethical behavior?" may be answered differently by different people.

- Four ways of thinking about ethical behavior are the utilitarian, individualism, moral-rights, and justice views.

- Cultural relativism argues that no culture is ethically superior to any other.

How do ethical dilemmas complicate the workplace?

- When managers act ethically they can have a positive impact on other people in the workplace *and* on the social good performed by their organizations.

- An ethical dilemma occurs when someone must decide whether or not to pursue a course of action that, although offering the potential for personal or organizational benefit or both, may be considered potentially unethical.

- Managers report that their ethical dilemmas often involve conflicts with superiors, customers, and subordinates over such matters as dishonesty in advertising and communications as well as pressure from their bosses to do unethical things.

- Common rationalizations for unethical behavior include believing the behavior is not illegal, is in everyone's best interests, will never be noticed, or will be supported by the organization.

How can high ethical standards be maintained?

- Ethics training in the form of courses and training programs helps people better deal with ethical dilemmas in the workplace.

- Whistleblowers expose the unethical acts of others in organizations, even while facing career risks for doing so.

- Top management sets an ethical tone for the organization as a whole, and all managers are responsible for acting as positive models of appropriate ethical behavior.

- Written codes of ethical conduct formally state an organization's expectations of its employees regarding ethical conduct in workplace affairs.

What is corporate social responsibility?

- Corporate social responsibility is an obligation of the organization to act in ways that serve both its own interests and the interests of its many external publics, often called stakeholders.

- Criteria for evaluating corporate social performance include economic, legal, ethical, and discretionary responsibilities.

- Corporate strategies in response to social demands include obstruction, defense, accommodation, and proaction, with more progressive organizations taking proactive stances.

How does government influence business?

- Government agencies are charged with monitoring and ensuring compliance with the mandates of law.

- Managers must be well informed about existing and pending legislation in a variety of social responsibity areas, including environmental protection and other quality-of-life concerns.

- All decisions made and actions taken in every workplace should allow performance accountability to be met by high ethical standards and socially responsible means.

KEY TERMS

Accommodative strategy (p. 129)

Codes of ethics (p. 125)

Corporate social responsibility (p. 126)

Cultural relativism (p. 118)

Defensive strategy (p. 128)

Distributive justice (p. 118)

Ethical behavior (p. 116)

Ethical dilemmas (p. 119)

Ethical imperialism (p. 119)

Ethics (p. 116)

Ethics training (p. 123)

Individualism view (p. 118)

Justice view (p. 118)

Moral-rights view (p. 118)

Obstructionist strategy (p. 128)

Proactive strategy (p. 129)

Procedural justice (p. 118)

Social audit (p. 127)

Utilitarian view (p. 117)

Values (p. 117)

Whistleblowers (p. 124)

SELF-TEST 6

Take this test much as you would in a normal classroom situation. It should offer you a good way to check your basic comprehension of chapter material. Answers may be found at the end of the book.

MULTIPLE-CHOICE QUESTIONS:

1. _____ are personal beliefs that help determine whether a behavior will be considered ethical or unethical. (a) Values (b) Attitudes (c) Motives (d) Needs

2. Under the _____ view of ethical behavior, a businesswoman would be considered ethical if she reduced a plant's workforce by 10 percent in order to cut costs and save jobs for the other 90 percent. (a) utilitarian (b) individualism (c) justice (d) moral rights

3. A manager's failure to administer a late-to-work policy the same way for everyone is an ethical violation of _____ justice. (a) ethical (b) moral (c) distributive (d) procedural

4. Influences on a person's ethical behavior at work may come from _____ sources. (a) environmental (b) organizational (c) personal (d) all of these

5. A/an _____ is someone who exposes the ethical misdeeds of others. (a) whistleblower (b) realist (c) ombudsman (d) stakeholder

6. Behavioral guidelines on matters such as _____ are often found in an organization's formal code of ethics. (a) bribes (b) political contributions (c) relationships (d) all of these

7. The U.S. Equal Opportunity Act of 1972 is an example of government regulation of business with respect to _____. (a) fair labor practices (b) consumer protection (c) environmental protection (d) occupational safety and health

8. In the final analysis, high performance goals in organizations should be achieved by _____ means. (a) any possible means (b) cultural relativism (c) ethical imperialism (d) ethical and socially responsible means

9. The most progressive organizational response to its corporate social responsibility is a/an _____ strategy. (a) accommodative (b) defensive (c) proactive (d) defensive

10. Two questions for conducting the ethics double-check of a decision are: (a) "How would I feel if my family found out about this?" and (b) "How would I feel if _____." (a) my boss found out about this (b) my subordinates found out about this (c) this was printed in the local newspaper (d) this went into my personnel file

TRUE-FALSE QUESTIONS:

11. A behavior that is legal will always be considered ethical. T F

12. The moral-rights view of ethical behavior emphasizes respect for fundamental human rights shared by everyone. T F

13. Treating everyone the same regardless of race or gender is an issue of distributive justice. T F

14. Cultural relativism argues for core values that absolutely apply anywhere in the world. T F

15. Convincing yourself that a behavior is not really illegal is one way to rationalize unethical behavior. T F

16. Strong work group identities are among the organizational barriers to whistle-blowing. T F

17. The only managers who serve as ethical role models in an organization are the very top managers. T F

18. The classic view of corporate social responsibility holds that a firm's only responsibility is to maximize profits. T F

19. In a social audit, a firm meeting its legal responsibilities is satisfying the highest level criterion of social responsibility. T F

20. Ethical dilemmas faced by practicing managers sometimes involve excessive pressure from their bosses. T F

SHORT-RESPONSE QUESTIONS:

21. Explain the difference between the individualism and justice views of ethical behavior.

22. List four common rationalizations for unethical managerial behavior.

23. What are the major elements in the socioeconomic view of corporate social responsibility?

24. What role do government agencies play in regulating the socially responsible behavior of businesses?

APPLICATION QUESTION:

25. A small outdoor clothing company has just received an attractive offer from a business in Bangladesh to manufacture its work gloves. The offer would allow for substantial cost savings over the current supplier. The company manager, however, has read reports that some Bangladesh businesses break their own laws and operate with child labor. How would differences in the following corporate responsibility strategies affect the manager's decision whether or not to accept the offer: obstruction, defense, accommodation, and proaction?

CHAPTER SEVEN

Planning – To Set Direction

Planning Ahead—Chapter 7 Study Questions

- Why is planning an essential management function?
- What types of plans are used by managers?
- What are the different approaches to planning?
- What planning tools and techniques are useful?
- How does management by objectives facilitate planning?

Know What You Want to Accomplish

CEO T. J. Rodgers of Cypress Semiconductor Corp. is known for meticulous planning and careful control. Cypress employees work with clear and quantified performance goals, which they typically set by themselves—it's important to Rodgers that the goals are "self-imposed." The goals are entered into an organizationwide computer database. Anyone in the company can review another person's goals, even those of Rodgers. On most days, there are over 10,000 goals on the system, each with expected dates of accomplishment. During weekly progress reviews, goals may be redefined and any needed corrective action taken. A monthly report summarizes accomplishments for everyone in the company. Says Rodgers—"We want people to decide what they are going to do, why it makes sense, how important it is, and when they will complete it."[1]

Management involves looking ahead, making good plans, and then helping people take the actions needed today in order to best meet the challenges of the future. The planning system used by T. J. Rodgers is very high on performance accountability—Cypress employees are expected to achieve results. But importantly, Rogers emphasizes that the system is also designed to find problems before they interfere with performance. He says: "Managers monitor the goals, look for problems, and expect people who fall behind to ask for help before they lose control of or damage a major project."

PLANNING AS A MANAGEMENT FUNCTION

• **Planning** is the process of setting objectives and determining what should be done to accomplish them.

The process of management involves planning, organizing, leading, and controlling. The first of these functions, **planning,** sets the stage for the others. It is a process of deciding exactly what one wants to accomplish and how to best go about it. When planning is done well, it creates a solid platform for further managerial efforts at *organizing*—allocating and arranging resources to accomplish essential tasks; *leading*—guiding the efforts of human resources to ensure high levels of task accomplishment; and *controlling*—monitoring task accomplishments and taking necessary corrective action.

This centrality of planning in the management process is extremely important to understand. In today's demanding organizational and career environments it is essential to always stay one step ahead of the competition. This involves striving always to become better and better at what you are doing, and to be action oriented. An Eaton Corporation annual report, for example, once stated: "Planning at Eaton means taking the hard decisions before events force them upon you, and anticipating the future needs of the market before the demand asserts itself."[2] One way managers in progressive organizations try to get a "jump" on the future is with a total quality approach to planning that involves listening to their customers and then using this information for better planning.

A U.S. Healthcare, planning for satisfied employees results in satisfied customers. Realizing that good customer relations are keys to success of this health maintenance organization (HMO), company executives have made staff development a key planning objective. Training for new employees is divided between classroom instruction and supervised on-the-job experience. After training, another planning objective is activated: to increase efficiency by promoting job satisfaction. To encourage interaction among workers, very few offices have doors, and the workforce is divided into groups of 8 to 10 people. Rewards for speedy processing of customers' claims are distributed quarterly.[3]

• **Objectives** are specific results that one wishes to achieve.

• A **plan** is a statement of intended means for accomplishing objectives.

THE PLANNING PROCESS

In the planning process, **objectives** identify the specific results or desired outcomes; the **plan** is a statement of action steps to be taken in order to accomplish the objectives. The recommended steps in the systematic planning process described in *Figure 7.1* include the following:

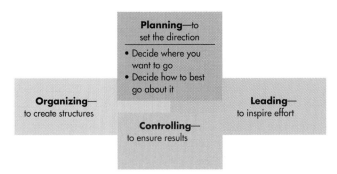

Figure 7.1   The role of planning in the management process.

Step 1. Define your objectives. Identify desired outcomes or results in very specific ways. Know where you want to go; be specific enough that you will know you have arrived when you get there or know how far off the mark you are at various points along the way.

Step 2. Determine where you stand vis-à-vis objectives. Evaluate current accomplishments relative to the desired results. Know where you stand in reaching the objectives; know what strengths work in your favor and what weaknesses may hold you back.

Step 3. Develop premises regarding future conditions. Try to anticipate future events. Generate alternative "scenarios" for what may happen; identify for each scenario things that may help or hinder progress toward your objectives.

Step 4. Analyze possible action alternatives, choose the best among them, and decide how to implement. List and carefully evaluate the possible actions that may be taken. Choose the alternative(s) most likely to accomplish your objectives; describe step by step what must be done to follow the chosen course of action.

Step 5. Implement the plan and evaluate results. Take action and carefully measure your progress toward objectives. Do what the plan requires; evaluate results; take corrective action and revise plans as needed.

Five steps in the planning process

As just described, the planning process is a form of the decision-making and problem-solving processes introduced in Chapter 3. It is a systematic framework for approaching an important task — setting performance objectives and deciding how to achieve them. Furthermore, in the complex setting of the modern workplace planning must not be thought of as something that is done primarily by outside consultants or staff experts. And it must not be considered as something that people always do while working alone in quiet rooms, free from distractions, and at scheduled times. Rather, planning must become a part of everyday work routines. It must be an ongoing activity that is continuously done in an otherwise hectic and demanding work setting.[4] As this chapter will also describe, the best planning is always done with the participation and involvement of the people whose work efforts are required if the objectives are to be achieved.

BENEFITS OF PLANNING

Organizations in today's dynamic times are facing pressures from many sources. Externally, these include greater government regulations, ever more complex technologies, the uncertainties of a global economy, and the sheer cost of investments in labor, capital, and other supporting resources. Internally, they include the quest for operating efficiencies, new structures and work arrangements, greater diversity in the workforce, and related managerial challenges. As you would expect, planning in such circumstances offers a number of benefits and important advantages for the performance of organizations and for the careers of those who work in them.

More Focus and Flexibility

Good planning improves focus and flexibility, both of which are important to the performance success of people and organizations in highly competitive and dynamic environments. An *organization with focus* knows what it does best, knows the needs of its customers, and knows how to serve them well. An *individual with focus* knows where he or she wants to go in a career or situation and is able to retain that objective even in difficult circumstances. An *organization with flexibility* is willing and able to change and adapt to shifting circumstances and operates with an orientation toward the future rather than the past or present.[5] An *individual with flexibility* factors into career plans the problems and opportunities posed by new and developing circumstances—personal and organizational.

Action Orientation

Planning is a way for people and organizations to stay ahead of the competition and always become better at what they are doing. It helps avoid the complacency trap of simply being carried along by the flow of events or being distracted by successes or failures of the moment. It keeps the future visible as a performance target and reminds us that the best decisions are often made before events force them upon us. Management consultant Stephen Covey points out that the most successful executives "zero in on what they do that 'adds value' to an organization." He suggests that instead of working on too many things, it is important to step back and identify the most important things to be doing.[6] Indeed, planning helps to us to stay proactive rather than reactive in our approach to things. It does so because it makes us more: (1) *results oriented*—creating a performance-oriented sense of direction; (2) *priority oriented*—making sure the most important things get first attention; (3) *advantage oriented*—ensuring that all resources are used to best advantage; and, (4) *change oriented*—anticipating problems and opportunities so they can be dealt with best.[7]

Improved Coordination

Planning improves coordination. The many different individuals, groups, and subsystems in organizations are each doing many different things at the same time. But even as they pursue their specific tasks and objectives, their accomplishments must add up to meaningful contributions toward the needs of the organization as a whole. Good planning throughout an organization can create a *hierarchy of objectives* in which objectives at each level of work are linked together in means-ends fashion. That is, higher level objectives as *ends* are directly tied to lower level objectives as the *means* for their accomplishment.

Figure 7.2 uses the example of quality management to show how such a hierarchy of objectives can guide and integrate efforts within a large manufacturing firm. The corporate-level quality objective is "Deliver error-free products that meet customer requirements 100 percent of the time." This translates down the hierarchy in means-ends fashion as a series of supporting objectives at each level. For one of the shift supervisors, it finally becomes a formal commitment to "assess capabilities of machine operators and provide/arrange appropriate training." Good planning helps ensure that the supervisor's hard work in this example will make a positive contribution to the corporate-level quality objective.

• Lucent Technologies
http://www.lucent.com

Lynn Mercer achieved a reputation as an effective plant manager for Lucent Technologies. In her environment of constant change, plans must be made and implemented quickly. Her philosophy is to create a mission from the top and allow workers to develop the methods. She says, "If I give you the end game, you can find your way there."

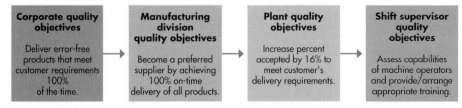

Figure 7.2 A sample hierarchy of objectives for total quality management.

Better Control

When planning is done well, control gets better. The control process will be described in Chapter 9 as measuring performance results and taking corrective action to improve things as necessary. Planning helps make this possible by defining the objectives—desired performance results, and identifying the specific actions through which they are to be pursued. If results are less than expected, either the objectives or the action being taken, or both, can be evaluated and then adjusted in the control process.

Figure 7.3 offers a reminder that planning and controlling work closely together a management functions. Without planning, control lacks a framework for measuring how well things are going and what could be done to make them go better. Without control, planning lacks the follow-through needed to ensure that things work out as intended. Importantly, both the planning and control processes work best if objectives are well stated in the first place. There is simply no substitute for a good performance objective. When executives at Hoechst Celanese, for example, decided they needed to improve the firm's performance in workforce diversity they set very specific objectives: "at least 34% representation of females and minorities at all levels of the company by 2001."[8] The way this objective is stated makes it easy to measure progress toward its accomplishment.

Better Time Management

One of the side benefits that planning offers as a result of improved focus and flexibility, coordination, and control in our personal affairs is better time management. Lewis Platt, chairman of Hewlett-Packard, says that "basically, the whole day is a series of choices."[9] These choices have to be made in ways that allocate your time to the most important priorities. Platt says that he is "ruthless about priorities" and that you "have to continually work to optimize your time."

Most of us have experienced the difficulties of balancing available time with the many commitments and opportunities we would like to fulfill. Each day, we are bombarded by a multitude of tasks and demands in a setting of frequent inter-

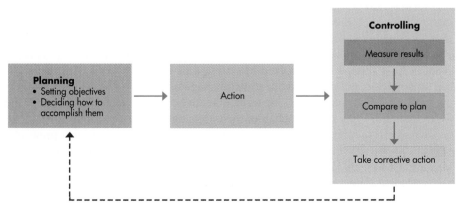

Figure 7.3 The integrated nature of organizational planning and controlling.

Manager's Notepad 7.1

Tips on How to Manage Your Time

- *Do* say "No" to requests that divert you from work you should be doing.
- *Don't* get bogged down in details that should be left to others.
- *Do* establish a system for screening telephone calls and handling Email.
- *Don't* let "drop-in" or unannounced visitors use too much of your time.
- *Do* prioritize work tasks in order of importance and urgency.
- *Don't* become "calendar bound" by losing control of your schedule.
- *Do* work tasks in priority order.

---

ruptions, crises, and unexpected events—the manager's job is especially subject to such complications. In these circumstances it is easy to lose track of time and fall prey to what consultants identify as "time wasters."[10] In the process, too many of us allow our time to be dominated by other people and/or by what can be considered nonessential activities.[11] No one knows this better than the college student who is trying to prepare for final examinations and papers, even as day-to-day life in the dormitories proceeds as normal.

Most of us maintain "to do" lists that are typically packed full of items. One key to time management and performance success is to determine which "to dos" are the priorities, and then address them. You should always attend first to the things that are most urgent and important. But Stephen Covey also reminds us that "you should spend as much time as possible doing important things that *aren't* urgent."[12] That is, don't forget to invest your time wisely by always working on important rather than unimportant things. Some additional tips on how to manage your time are included in the *Manager's Notepad 7.1*.

TYPES OF PLANS IN ORGANIZATIONS

Managers face different planning challenges in the flow of activity in organizations. In some cases the planning environment is stable and quite predictable; in others it is more dynamic and uncertain. In all cases managers must understand the different types of plans and be able to use them effectively.

SHORT-RANGE AND LONG-RANGE PLANS

Organizations require plans that cover different time horizons. A rule of thumb is that *short-range plans* cover 1 year or less, *intermediate-range plans* cover 1 to 2 years, and *long-range plans* look 3 or more years into the future. Top management is most likely to be involved in setting long-range plans and directions for the organization as a whole, while lower management levels focus more on short-run activities that serve the long-term objectives. However, all levels must be aware of and try to work on behalf of the long-range objectives. In the absence of an integrated hierarchy of objectives and a long-range plan, there is a great risk that the pressures of daily events may create confusion and divert attention from important tasks. In other words, we may be working hard but without sustainable and clear long-term results.

The importance of the long term in our planning horizons is of special concern to management researcher Elliot Jaques. His research suggests that people vary in their capability to think out, organize, and work through events of different time horizons.[13] In fact, he believes that most people work comfortably with only 3-month time spans; a smaller group works well with a 1-year span; and only about one person in several million can handle a 20-year time frame. These are provocative ideas, especially since managers working at various levels of authority must plan over quite different time periods. Although a supervisor's planning challenges may rest mainly in the 3-month range, the next higher manager may deal with a 1-year range, while a vice president deals with 3 years, and a chief executive is expected to have a vision extending 5 to 10 years or more. Career progress to higher management levels, therefore, clearly requires the conceptual skills to work well with longer-range time frames.[14]

STRATEGIC AND OPERATIONAL PLANS

Plans differ not only in time horizons but also in scope. **Strategic plans** address long-term needs and set comprehensive action directions for an organization or subunit. Top management planning of this scope involves determining objectives for the entire organization and then deciding on the actions and resource allocations to achieve them. There was a time, for example, when many large businesses sought to diversify into unrelated areas. A successful oil firm might have acquired an office products company or a successful cereal manufacturer might have acquired an apparel company. These decisions represent strategic choices regarding future directions for these companies and their use of scarce resources. Instead of reinvesting in areas of core compentency, they were spending available monies on unrelated and probably unfamiliar areas of business activity. In Chapter 8 we will examine the process through which such strategic choices are made and how they can be analyzed. For now, suffice it to say that diversification strategies haven't always proved successful. Many companies following them have since reversed course and followed the alternative strategy of divesting of unrelated businesses to focus on their core areas of expertise.

> • A **strategic plan** is comprehensive and addresses longer term needs and directions of the organization.

Operational plans define what needs to be done in specific areas to implement strategic plans and achieve strategic objectives. Typical operational plans in a business firm include *production plans*—dealing with the methods and technology needed by people in their work; *financial plans*—dealing with the money required to support various operations; *facilities plans*—dealing with the facilities and work layouts required to support task activities; *marketing plans*—dealing with the requirements of selling and distributing goods or services; and *human resource plans*—dealing with the recruitment, selection, and placement of people into various jobs.

> • An **operational plan** is of limited scope and addresses activities to implement strategic plans.

Figure 7.4 uses the case of a firm undergoing a restructuring to show how a clear hierarchy of strategic and operational plans integrates and directs actions in

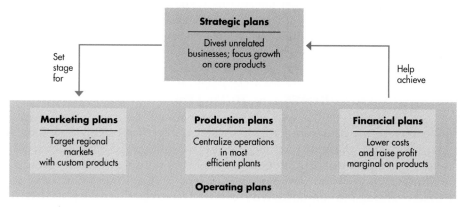

Figure 7.4 How strategic and operational plans should support each other.

organizations. Good strategic plans set the stage for operational plans, which, in turn, serve the strategic plans by identifying the activities and resources needed to accomplish them.

POLICIES AND PROCEDURES

- A **standing plan** is used more than once.

- A **policy** is a standing plan that communicates broad guidelines for decisions and action.

Among the many plans in organizations, **standing plans** in the form of organizational policies and procedures are designed to be used over and over again. They set guidelines that direct behavior in uniform directions for certain types of situations regardless of where or when they occur in an organization. A **policy** communicates *broad guidelines* for making decisions and taking action in specific circumstances. In matters relating to the workforce, for example, typical human resource policies address such matters as employee hiring, termination, performance appraisals, pay increases, and discipline, for example. With the demographic changes now taking place in the workforce and with continuing developments in the legal environment, many organizations are finding it necessary to update their human resource policies and even add new ones.

Policies should focus attention on matters of special organizational consequence and then guide people in how they are supposed to deal with them. Good policies on matters such as AIDS/HIV, alcohol and substance abuse, and sexual harassment, for example, can help ensure that employees' daily actions and decisions are consistent with organizational values, strategies, and objectives.[15] Such policies are important to all types of organizations, large and small alike. Consider the issue of sexual harassment. The law defines it as any "unwelcome sexual conduct" that creates a "hostile work environment."[16] This wording is subject to interpretation, and enlightened employers take great pains to clearly spell out their policies and the methods of implementation. When Judith Nitsch started her own engineering consulting business, for example, she remembered the lessons of her corporate experience. Nitsch defined a sexual harassment policy, took a hard line in its enforcement, and appointed both a male and a female employee for others to talk with about their sexual harassment concerns.[17]

- A **procedure** or **rule** is a standing plan that precisely describes what actions are to be taken in specific situations.

Rules or **procedures** are plans that describe exactly what actions are to be taken in specific situations. They are often found stated in employee handbooks or manuals as "SOPs" — standard operating procedures. Whereas a sexual harassment policy like Judith Nitsch's, for example, sets a broad guideline for action, sexual harassment procedures define precise guidelines to be followed when someone believes they have been subjected to such harassment on the job. Under the policy, Nitsch will want to ensure that everyone receives fair, equal, and nondiscriminatory treatment should an alleged violation occur. One way to do this is to establish clear procedures regarding how a sexual harassment complaint is handled. Of course, once the rules are in place it is important to follow through and make sure that people both understand and follow the rules. When Digital Equipment Corporation updated its sexual harassment policy, the company implemented training programs to communicate corporate procedures to all employees. Actual cases drawn from the company's experience were used as part of the training.[18]

BUDGETS AND PROJECT SCHEDULES

- A **single-use plan** is used only once.
- A **budget** is a plan that commits resources to projects or activities.

In contrast to standing plans, which remain in place for extended periods of time, **single-use plans** are each used once to meet the needs of well-defined situations in a timely manner. **Budgets** are single-use plans that commit resources to activities, projects, or programs. They are powerful tools that allocate scarce resources among multiple and often competing uses. Good managers are able to bargain for and obtain adequate budgets to support the needs of their work units or teams. They are also able to achieve performance objectives while keeping resource expenditures within the allocated budget.

A *fixed budget* allocates resources on the basis of a single estimate of costs. The estimate establishes a fixed pool of resources that can be used, but not exceeded, in support of the specified purpose. For example, a manager may have a $25,000 budget for equipment purchases in a given year. A *flexible budget*, by contrast, allows the allocation of resources to vary in proportion with various levels of activity. Managers operating under flexible budgets can expect additional resource allocations when activity increases from one estimated level to the next. For example, a manager may have a budget allowance for hiring temporary workers if production orders exceeds a certain volume.

In a **zero-based budget,** a project or activity is budgeted as if it were brand new. There is no assumption that resources previously allocated to a project or activity will simply be continued in the future. Instead, all projects compete anew for available funds. The intent is to totally reconsider priorities, objectives, and activities at the start of each new budget cycle. When zero-based budgeting was introduced to executives of a major division of Campbell Soups, for example, managers discovered that 10 percent of the marketing budget was going to sales promotions no longer relevant to current product lines. Zero-based budgeting is used by businesses, government agencies, and other types of organizations to make sure that only the most desirable and timely programs receive funding.

- A **zero-based budget** allocates resources to a project or activity as if it were brand new.

Project schedules are single-use plans that identify the activities required to accomplish a specific major project—for example, the completion of a new student activities building on a campus, the development of a new computer software program, or the implementation of a new advertising campaign for a sports team. In each case, the project schedule would define specific task objectives, activities to be accomplished, due dates and timetables for the activities, and resource requirements. Importantly, a good project schedule sets priorities so that everyone involved knows not only what needs to be done but also in what order so that the entire project gets finished on time. One way of doing this is with a *Gantt chart.* The example in *Figure 7.5* shows how such charts visually display the expected progress of each required activity from start to finish in a large pro-

- A **project schedule** is a single-use plan for accomplishing a specific set of tasks.

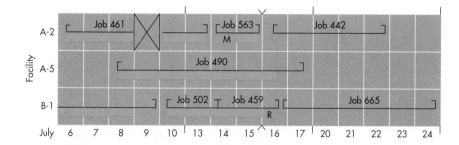

	Gannt chart symbols
⌐	Scheduled start of an operation
⌐	Scheduled completion of an operation
⋈	Time unavailable for scheduling (e.g., preventive maintenance)
—	Scheduled worktime
▬	Actual progress
V	Date of last charted progress
M	Delay caused by materials
R	Delay caused by repairs
T	Delay caused by tool trouble
A	Operator absent

Figure 7.5 A sample GANTT chart for project planning.

Manager's Notepad 7.2

What to Include in a Business Plan

- *Executive summary* — overview of business purpose and highlight of key elements of the plan
- *Industry analysis* — nature of the industry, including economic trends, important legal or regulatory issues, and potential risks
- *Company description* — mission, owners, and legal form
- *Products and services description* — major goods or services, with special focus on uniqueness vis-à-vis competition
- *Market description* — size of market, competitor strengths and weaknesses, five year sales goals
- *Marketing strategy* — product characteristics, distribution, promotion, pricing, and market research
- *Operations description* — manufacturing or service methods, supplies and suppliers, and control procedures
- *Staffing description* — management and staffing skills needed and available, compensation and human resource management systems
- *Financial projection* — cash flow projections 1–5 years
- *Capital needs* — amount of funds needed to run the business, amount available, amount requested from new sources

ject. Computer programs are now available to provide this type of project planning support.

BUSINESS PLANS

- A **business plan** describes the direction for a new business and the financing needed to operate it.

When people start new businesses, either independent ones or as new components of larger organizations, they can benefit greatly from having a good **business plan.** This is a plan that describes all the details necessary to set direction for a new business and to obtain the necessary financing to operate it. When done well, a business plan offers clear direction to an enterprise. Says, Ed Federkeil who founded a small business called California Custom Sport Trucks: "It gives you direction instead of haphazardly sticking your key in the door everyday and saying — 'What are we going to do?'"[19] Banks and other financiers want to see a business plan before they loan money or invest in a new venture; senior managers want to see a business plan before they allocate scarce organizational resources to a new project. Importantly, the detail thinking required to prepare a business plan can contribute to the success of the new initiative.[20]

Although there is no single template for a successful business plan, there is general agreement that a plan should have an executive summary, cover certain business fundamentals, be well-organized with headings, be easy to read, and be no more than about 20 pages in length. Basic items that should be included in a business plan are summarized in *Manager's Notepad 7.2.*[21]

APPROACHES TO PLANNING

Managerial planning in organizations can be approached in different ways. Of particular insight are distinctions between inside-out and outside-in planning, top-down and bottom-up planning, and contingency planning.

INSIDE-OUT VERSUS OUTSIDE-IN PLANNING

The intent of **inside-out planning** is to focus future effort on what you are already doing but always try to find ways of doing it better. Planning from the inside out does not result in dramatic changes in direction, but it can be effective and it can help in making good resource allocation decisions. A planning specialist, Dick Levin, tells of a friend who used this inside-out planning to succeed in a highly competitive industry:

> My good friend Jim is president of a very successful mini-conglomerate in the communications industry. Jim says the measure of an organization's success is its "humpability factor"—his term for sheer work, output, effort, push, drive. Jim says once he established absolute, unflagging humpability in his organization, the firm found that it could do anything better than the competition. Jim's focus is on the inside—keeping up the humpability of the troops. "Whatever comes through the door, we can probably make money at it," he says.[22]

Levin has another friend, Sid, who uses **outside-in planning** in his search for business advantage. That is, he analyzes the external environment and looks for specific niches or opportunities that can be exploited. Sid operates in the highly competitive corrugated box business. He once made boxes used in department stores for dresses, hosiery, and the like. But demand slipped as stores stopped including boxes with material purchases. Sid looked around at his options in the corrugated box industry. He saw large and established firms waging wars with one another for this market. Instead of competing with them, he decided to serve a market niche they were avoiding—the small special-order business.

Planning in most settings should combine the inside-out and outside-in approaches for the best results. In general, inside-out planning is more appropriate when you want to do what you and/or others are already doing but want to do it better. The planning objective in this case is to determine "how" to do it better. Outside-in planning tends to be best when you need to find a unique niche for your activities, that is, do something no one else is doing. The planning objective here is to find the external opportunity that you can pursue to best advantage.

- **Inside-out** planning focuses on internal strengths.

- **Outside-in planning** focuses on external opportunities.

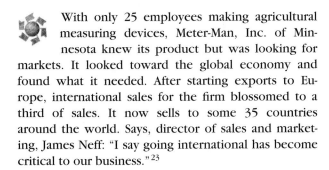

With only 25 employees making agricultural measuring devices, Meter-Man, Inc. of Minnesota knew its product but was looking for markets. It looked toward the global economy and found what it needed. After starting exports to Europe, international sales for the firm blossomed to a third of sales. It now sells to some 35 countries around the world. Says, director of sales and marketing, James Neff: "I say going international has become critical to our business."[23]

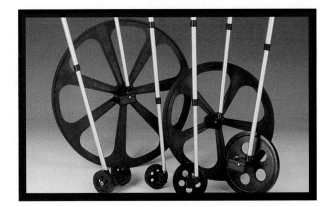

TOP-DOWN VERSUS BOTTOM-UP PLANNING

In **top-down planning**, senior management sets the broad objectives for an organization and then allows lower management levels to make operating plans within these boundaries. The initiative in **bottom-up planning**, by contrast, begins at lower levels. As plans are passed up the hierarchy from level to level they express needs and directions consistent with operating level perspectives. The question obviously becomes: Is one approach better than the other? Should planning start

- **Top-down planning** begins with broad objectives set by top management.

- **Bottom-up planning** begins with ideas developed at lower management levels.

at the top and then filter down, or should it begin at the bottom and build up to the top? Another of Dick Levin's classic examples lends some insight into these questions by using an interesting case in point, planning in a university:

> My university sets a terrible example of bottom-up long-range planning—we're comprised of 14 colleges and schools, enrolling 21,000 students. Periodically, the chancellor puts out a memo to the vice-chancellors and provost calling for a long-range plan, and the vice-chancellors and provost put out a memo to all the schools and colleges calling for a long-range plan, and the deans of the schools and colleges put out a memo to all the department heads calling for a long-range plan, and the department heads put out a memo to their faculties calling for a long-range plan. Then the faculty members send their long-range plan to their department heads, and the department heads edit, condense, and retype the plans, put them into a common binder, and send them to their deans who edit, condense, and retype all the department plans, put them into a common binder, and send them to the vice-chancellors or provost, who edit, condense, and re-type them, put them into a common binder, and send them to the chancellor's planning assistant who edits, retypes, and condenses them and adds a bit of editorial glue before putting them in a common binder and giving them to the chancellor. End of tale. End of plan too.[24]

• Burger King
http://www.burgerking.com

• McDonald's
http://www.mcdonalds.com

Outside-in planning has its place in the "burger wars." Soon after Burger King introduced its version of the McDonald's "BigMac" sandwich, McDonald's offered something quite similar to Burger King's "Whopper." The tendency among fast food makers' is toward an outside-in strategy of "if-you-can't-beat-'em, copy-'em."

Both bottom-up and top-down planning approaches have advantages and disadvantages. When followed to the extreme, bottom-up planning does not define an integrated direction for the organization as a whole. This is part of the problem described in the quotation from Dick Levin. Yet we also know that a major advantage of this approach is its potential to generate high commitment and a sense of ownership among those involved in the planning process. Top-down planning, on the other hand, ensures a common direction but can fail in implementation because of insufficient lower level commitments to action.

The best planning probably begins at the top and then proceeds in a participatory way that allows for substantial lower-level involvement. Whether the focus is on planning for a team or group, a large division, or an entire organization, managers are well advised to begin the planning process by communicating to all concerned the basic planning objectives and assumptions. They should seek inputs from lower levels to clarify the needs and assumptions. They should suggest some action alternatives and be open to others. They should actively invite feedback and incorporate it into modifications of proposed plans. And, always, they should work hard to get the commitments of others whose support will be critical in implementing the eventual plan of action.

CONTINGENCY PLANNING

Planning, by definition, involves thinking ahead. But the more uncertain the planning environment, the more likely that one's original assumptions, predictions, and intentions may prove to be in error. Even the most carefully prepared alternative future scenarios may prove inadequate as experience develops. Unexpected problems and events frequently occur. When they do, plans may have to be changed. It is best to anticipate during the planning process that things might not go as expected. Alternatives to the existing plan can then be developed and readied for use when and if circumstances make them appropriate.

This is the process of **contingency planning,** identifying alternative courses of action that can be implemented if and when an original plan proves inadequate because of changing circumstances.[25] Of course, changes in the planning environment must be detected as early as possible. "Trigger points" that indicate that an existing plan is no longer desirable must be preselected and then monitored. Sometimes this is accomplished simply by good forward thinking on the part of managers and staff planners; at other times, it can be assisted by a "devil's advocate" method, in which planners are formally assigned to develop "worst-case" forecasts of future events.

- **Contingency planning** identifies alternative courses of action that can be taken if and when circumstances change with time.

PLANNING TOOLS AND TECHNIQUES

Planning is clearly essential to the success of the management process. The benefits, however, are most often realized when the planning approaches are comprehensive and the foundations are well established. In the latter regard, the useful planning tools and techniques include forecasting, the use of scenarios, benchmarking, participative planning, and the use of staff planners.

FORECASTING

A **forecast** is a vision of the future. Forecasting is the process of making assumptions about what will happen in the future.[26] All good plans involve forecasts, either implicit or explicit. Periodicals such as *Business Week* and *Fortune* regularly report a variety of forecasts as a service to their readers — forecasts of economic conditions, interest rates, unemployment, and trade deficits, among other issues. Some are based on *qualitative forecasting,* which uses expert opinions to predict the future. In this case, a single person of special expertise or reputation or a panel of experts may be consulted.

- A **forecast** is an attempt to predict future outcomes.

By contrast, *quantitative forecasting* uses mathematical and statistical analysis of data banks to predict future events. Managers often rely on staff experts or outside consultants to prepare and even interpret these forecasts for them. *Time-series analysis* is a popular quantitative forecasting technique. It makes predictions by using statistical routines such as regression analysis to project past trends into the future. Forecasters also use *econometric modeling,* whereby complex computer models simulate future events based on probabilities and multiple assumptions. Predictions are statistically made based on the relationships discovered among variables included in the models. General economic trends are often forecasted via econometric models. *Statistical surveys* use statistical analysis of opinion polls and attitude surveys, such as those reported in newspapers and on television, to forecast events. They are typically used to predict future consumer tastes, employee preferences, and political choices, among other issues. The usefulness of such surveys, of course, varies greatly according to their underlying rigor, the type of research design used, and the nature of the statistics used to analyze results.

In the final analysis, forecasting always relies on human judgment. Even the results of highly sophisticated quantitative approaches still require interpretation. Forecasts should always be viewed as subject to error and therefore treated cautiously. Managers should remember that forecasting is not planning; planning is a more comprehensive activity that involves deciding what to do about the implications of forecasts once they are made. At GE Appliances, for example, no detail is neglected as the firm's planners study new international markets. Investment plans are made only after each country's unique points are studied carefully so that a mix of products and marketing approaches can be tailored to its needs. To generate the types of business returns expected by GE's senior management team, only a rigorous and detailed analysis of any opportunity will suffice.[27]

USE OF SCENARIOS

● **Scenario planning** identifies alternative future "scenarios" and makes plans to deal with each.

A long-term version of contingency planning called **scenario planning** involves identifying several alternative future "scenarios" or states of affairs that may occur. Plans are then made to deal with each should it actually occur.[28] Identifying different possible scenarios ahead of time helps organizations operate more flexibly in dynamic environments.

Royal Dutch/Shell, for example, has been doing scenario planning for many years. The process began some 15 years ago when top managers asked themselves a perplexing question: "What would Shell do after its oil supplies ran out?" The question was approached by creating alternative future scenarios while remaining sensitive to the nature of growing environmental changes. Although recognizing that planning scenarios can never be inclusive of all future possibilities, a Royal Dutch/Shell planning coordinator once said that scenarios help "condition the organization to think" and remain better prepared than its competitors for "future shocks."[29]

BENCHMARKING

● **Benchmarking** uses external comparisons to gain insights for planning.

Another important influence on the success or failure of planning involves the frame of reference used as a starting point. All too often, planners have only a limited awareness of what is happening outside the immediate work setting. Successful planning must challenge the status quo; it cannot simply accept things the way they are. One way to do this is through **benchmarking,** a technique that makes use of external comparisons to better evaluate one's current performance and identify possible actions for the future. The purpose of benchmarking is to find out what other people and organizations are doing very well and plan how to incorporate these ideas into one's own operations. This powerful planning technique is increasingly popular in today's competitive business world. It is a way for progressive companies to learn from other "excellent" companies, not just competitors. It allows them to analyze and thoroughly compare all systems and processes for efficiencies and opportunities for innovation.

PARTICIPATION AND INVOLVEMENT

● **Participative planning** includes the people who will be affected by plans and/or asked to help implement them.

Participation is a very key word in the planning process. The concept of **participative planning** requires that the process include people who will be affected by the resulting plans and/or will be asked to help implement them. Participation can increase the creativity and information available for planning. It can also increase the understanding, acceptance, and commitment of people to final plans.

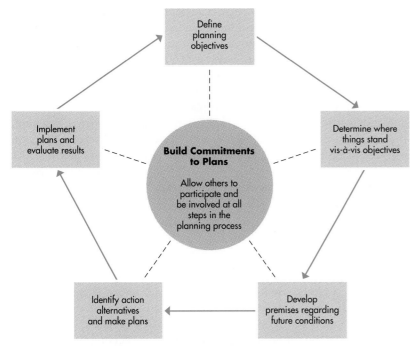

Figure 7.6 How participation and involvement build commitment to the plans.

Indeed, planning in organizations should not be done by individuals. It should be organized and accomplished in a participatory manner that includes the contributions of many people representing diverse responsibilities and vantage points.

The centrality of participation in the planning process is highlighted in *Figure 7.6.* To create and implement the best plans, proper attention must always be given to genuinely involving others during all planning steps. Even though this process may mean that planning takes more time, it can improve results by improving implementation. When 7-Eleven executives planned for a dramatic overhaul of the firm—including a new information system and the introduction of new "upscale" products and services such as selling fancy meals-to-go, they learned a hard lesson on the value of participation in planning. Although their ideas sounded good at the top, franchisees balked at the level of operations. The executives found that they needed to take time to sell the franchise owners before the advantages of their new corporate strategies could be realized.[30]

ROLE OF STAFF PLANNERS

As the planning needs of organizations grow, there is a corresponding need to increase the sophistication of the overall planning system itself. In some cases, staff planners are employed to take responsibility for leading and coordinating planning for the organization as a whole or for one of its major components. These planners should be skilled in all steps of the formal planning process as well as in the use of the participative, benchmarking, and scenario-planning approaches just discussed. They should also understand the staff, or advisory, nature of their roles. In general, this means a staff planner is expected to assist line managers in preparing plans, develop special plans upon request, gather and maintain planning information, assist in communicating plans to others, and monitor plans in progress and suggest changes.

● **Xerox**
http://www.xerox.com

Benchmarking pays off at Xerox, where management uses its Japanese competitors to benchmark production cost comparisons. They also find benchmarks from outside their industry, looking at firms who are known for special expertise. A planning team once visited L.L. Bean, Inc. and prepared a report that helped revamp Xerox's warehouse and distribution systems.

Given clear responsibilities and their special planning expertise, staff planners can bring focus to efforts to accomplish important, often strategic, planning tasks. But one risk is a tendency for a communication "gap" to develop between staff planners and line managers. This can cause a great deal of difficulty. Resulting plans may lack relevance, and line personnel may lack commitment to implement them even if they are relevant. One trend in organizations today is to deemphasize the role of large staff planning groups and to place much greater emphasis on the participation and involvement of line managers in the planning process. Returning again to the example of at General Electric, CEO Jack Welch carefully limits the size of the firm's planning staff. He helped dismantle a large planning group that emphasized voluminous written reports. Now, GE employs only a few planners whose responsibilities are limited to *advising* line managers.[31]

MANAGEMENT BY OBJECTIVES

● **Management by objectives (MBO)** is a process of joint objective setting between a superior and subordinate.

A useful planning technique employed by many organizations is **management by objectives,** or **MBO** for short. Formally defined, MBO is a structured process of regular communication in which a supervisor and subordinate jointly set performance objectives for the subordinate and review results accomplished.[32]

THE CONCEPT OF MBO

In its simplest terms, MBO requires a formal agreement between the supervisor and subordinate concerning (1) the subordinate's performance objectives for a given time period, (2) the plans through which they will be accomplished, (3) standards for measuring whether or not they have been accomplished, and (4) procedures for reviewing performance results. This process is illustrated in *Figure 7.7.* Note that the supervisor and subordinate *jointly* establish plans and *jointly* control results in any good MBO action framework. They agree on the high-priority performance objectives for the subordinate along with a timetable for their accomplishment and the criteria to be used in evaluating results.

A major advantage of MBO is that it clearly focuses the subordinate's work efforts on the most important tasks and objectives; another is that it focuses the supervisor's work efforts on areas of support that can truly help the subordinate meet the agreed-upon objectives. Because the process involves direct face-to-face communication between supervisor and subordinate, MBO contributes to relationship building. It also gives the subordinate a structured opportunity to participate in decisions that affect his or her work. This is consistent with Douglas McGregor's Theory Y approach to management (see Chapter 4) and encourages self-management rather than external control.[33] The motivational value of goal

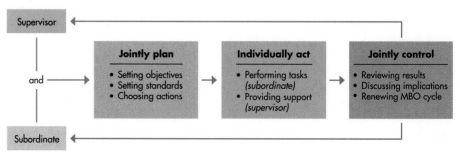

Figure 7.7 A planning framework for management by objectives.

setting, to be discussed in Chapter 14, further suggests that participation in the MBO process can create a powerful enthusiasm to fulfill one's performance obligations.[34]

PERFORMANCE OBJECTIVES IN MBO

Performance objectives are essential parts of the MBO process. How the objectives are specified and the way in which they are established will influence how well MBO works. Three types of objectives may be specified in an MBO contract. *Improvement objectives* document intentions for improving performance in a specific way and with respect to a specific factor. An example is "to reduce quality rejects by 10 percent." *Personal development objectives* pertain to personal growth activities, often those resulting in expanded job knowledge or skills. An example is "to learn the latest version of a computer spreadsheet package." Some MBO contracts also include *maintenance objectives,* which formally express intentions to maintain performance at an existing level. In many organizations, the MBO process emphasizes improvement and personal growth objectives. In all cases, performance objectives are written and formally agreed to by both the superior and subordinate. They also meet the following *criteria of a good performance objective:*

1. specific — targets a key result to be accomplished,
2. time defined — identifies a date for achieving results,
3. challenging — offers a realistic and attainable challenge, and,
4. measureable — is as specific and quantitative as possible.

◄———
Criteria of a good performance objective

One of the more difficult aspects of MBO relates to the last criterion — the need to state performance objectives as specifically and quantitatively as possible. Ideally, this occurs as agreement on a *measurable end product,* for example, "to reduce housekeeping supply costs by 5 percent by the end of the fiscal year." But some jobs, particularly managerial ones, involve performance areas that are hard to quantify. Rather than abandon MBO in such cases, it is often possible to agree on performance objectives that are stated as *verifiable work activities.* The accomplishment of the activities can then serve as an indicator of progress under the performance objective. An example is "to improve communications with my subordinates in the next 3 months by holding weekly group meetings." Whereas it can be difficult to measure "improved communications," it is easy to document whether or not the "weekly group meetings" have been held.

HOW TO MAKE MBO WORK FOR YOU

MBO is one of the most talked about and debated management concepts of the past 25 years, and it has many advocates and critics.[35] As a result, good advice is available on what to do and what not to do if MBO is to be used to maximum advantage. Things to avoid doing in MBO include tying it to pay, focusing too much attention on only those objectives that are easily quantified, requiring excessive paperwork, and having supervisors simply *tell* subordinates their objectives. On the other hand, *Manager's Notepad 7.3* offers six steps for making sure MBO succeeds in practice. The steps convey the key ingredient of "participation" discussed earlier.

None of this advice is lost on many of today's best managers. Although they may describe what they are doing by different names, it has a common thread that is consistent with the MBO concept: If you want high performance from individual contributors, you must hire the best people, work with them to set challenging performance objectives, give them the best possible support, and hold

> ## Manager's Notepad 7.3
>
> **Steps to Successful MBO**
>
> *Step 1.* An individual lists key performance objectives for a time period with target dates for accomplishing them.
>
> *Step 2.* Objectives are reviewed and discussed with the supervisor, and an agreed-upon set of objectives is documented.
>
> *Step 3.* The supervisor and subordinate meet regularly to review progress and make revisions or update objectives as needed.
>
> *Step 4.* At a specified time, such as after 6 months, the individual prepares a "performance report" that lists major accomplishments and comments on discrepancies between expected and actual results.
>
> *Step 5.* This self-appraisal is discussed with the supervisor with an emphasis on its implications for future performance.
>
> *Step 6.* A new set of objectives is established for the next time period, as in Step 1, and the MBO cycle begins anew.

them accountable for results. Look back at the chapter-opening example of Cypress Semiconductor, and you will see all of these elements at work.

The next two chapters explore further the elements and processes of planning and controlling, including the topics of strategic management and entrepreneurship. Before moving on to them, however, consider the following quotations. The response of the second to the first nicely concludes this initial look at the fundamentals of planning.[36]

> I am the master of my fate, I am the captain of my soul.
> —*W. E. Henly*

> Not without a plan, you're not.
> —*Dick Levin*

CHAPTER REVIEW

This section should be used as an end-of-chapter "study guide." The *Summary* helps to put the chapter's content into overall perspective. The list of *Key Terms* allows you to double-check your familiarity with basic concepts and definitions. *Self-Test 7* gives you the opportunity to test your basic comprehension of the chapter using sample test questions.

SUMMARY

Why is planning an essential management function?

- Planning is the process of setting performance objectives and determining what should be done to accomplish them.

- A plan is a set of intended actions for accomplishing important objectives.

- Planning sets the stage for the other management functions—organizing, leading, and controlling.

- The steps in the planning process are (1) define your objectives, (2) determine where you stand vis-à- vis objectives, (3) develop your premises regarding future conditions, (4) identify and choose among alternative ways of accomplishing objectives, and (5) implement action plans and evaluate results.

- Good planning improves performance through better focus and flexibility, action orientation, coordination, control, and time management.

What types of plans are used by managers?

- Short-range plans tend to cover a year or less, while long-range plans extend up to 5 years or more.

- Strategic plans set critical long-range directions; operational plans are designed to implement strategic plans.

- Standing plans, such as policies and procedures, are used over and over again.

- Single-use plans, such as budgets and project schedules, are established for a specific purpose and time frame.

- A business plan sets forth the direction and financial requirements for a new business venture.

What are the different approaches to planning?

- Inside-out planning looks at internal strengths and tries to improve upon what is already being done.

- Outside-in planning looks for opportunities or "niches" in the external environment that can be pursued to advantage.

- Top-down planning helps maintain direction; bottom-up planning builds commitment.

- Contingency planning identifies alternative courses of action that can be implemented if and when circumstances change in certain ways over time.

What planning tools and techniques are useful?

- Forecasting, a prediction of what will happen in the future, is a planning aid but not a planning substitute.

- Scenario planning through the use of alternative versions of the future is a useful form of contingency planning.

- Planning through benchmarking utilizes external comparisons to identify desirable action directions.

- Participation and involvement open the planning process to valuable inputs from people whose efforts are essential to the effective implementation of plans.

- Specialized staff planners can help with the planning of details, although care must be taken to make sure they work well with line personnel.

How does Management by Objectives facilitate planning?

- Management by objectives is a process through which supervisors work with their subordinates to "jointly" set performance objectives and review performance results.

- The MBO process is a highly participative form of integrated planning and controlling.

- MBO should clarify performance objectives for the subordinate and also identify support needed from the supervisor.

• Only when the MBO process is truly mutual and participative can its full benefits be realized.

KEY TERMS

Benchmarking (p. 148)

Bottom-up planning (p. 145)

Budget (p. 142)

Business plan (p. 144)

Contingency planning (p. 147)

Forecast (p. 147)

Inside-out planning (p. 145)

Management by objectives (p. 150)

Objectives (p. 136)

Operational plan (p. 141)

Outside-in planning (p. 145)

Participative planning (p. 148)

Plan (p. 136)

Planning (p. 136)

Policy (p. 142)

Procedures (p. 142)

Project schedule (p. 143)

Rules (p. 142)

Scenario planning (p. 148)

Single-use plan (p. 142)

Standing plan (p. 142)

Strategic plan (p. 141)

Top-down planning (p. 145)

Zero-based budget (p. 143)

SELF-TEST 7

Take this test much as you would in a normal classroom situation. It should offer you a good way to check your basic comprehension of chapter material. Answers may be found at the end of the book.

MULTIPLE-CHOICE QUESTIONS:

1. Planning is defined as the process of _____ and _____. (a) developing premises about the future, evaluating them (b) taking action, evaluating outcomes (c) measuring past performance, targeting future performance, (d) setting objectives, deciding how to accomplish them

2. The benefits of planning include _____. (a) improved organizational focus and flexibility, (b) improved organizational coordination (c) better organizational control (d) all of those

3. A _____ is an example of an operational plan in a business firm. (a) benchmark (b) strategy (c) forecast (d) marketing plan

4. _____ planning by a business looks for market niches or opportunities that can be pursued to advantage. (a) Top-down (b) Bottom-up (c) Inside-out (d) Outside-in

5. Organizational policies establish _____. (a) precise action guidelines (b) broad action guidelines (c) flexible budgets (d) zero-based budgets

6. Supervisors and team leaders spend most of their time working on _____ plans. (a) long-range (b) short-range (c) strategic (d) standing

7. The use of expert opinions by business leaders is an example of _____ forecasting. (a) qualitative (b) quantitative (c) econometric (d) statistical

8. _____ planning identifies alternative courses of action that can be taken if and

when certain situations arise. (a) Benchmarking (b) Participative (c) Tactical (d) Contingency

9. A good performance objective is _____. (a) open ended with no deadline (b) specific (c) really impossible to accomplish (d) hard to measure

10. A/an _____ creates an integrated network of means-end chains throughout an organization. (a) strategic plan (b) Gantt chart (c) hierarchy of objectives (d) flexible budget

TRUE-FALSE QUESTIONS:

11. Good planning helps managers with the controlling process. T F

12. Planning is a form of time management. T F

13. A policy on organizational treatment of employees with the HIV virus is an example of a single-use plan. T F

14. Top-down planning is better than bottom-up planning for building employee commitment to the implementation of plans. T F

15. In any organization it is best to leave all planning to formally appointed staff planners. T F

16. Top managers spend most of their time dealing with strategic plans. T F

17. If forecasting is done well it is not necessary for managers to plan. T F

18. A flexible budget is a single-use plan. T F

19. Planning is one aspect of the management process in which participation and involvement are not important. T F

20. The best objectives in MBO are those set by supervisors for their subordinates. T F

SHORT-RESPONSE QUESTIONS:

21. List the five steps in the planning process.

22. What is the major difference between strategic and operational plans? Give examples to support your answer.

23. What is planning through benchmarking and how might it be used by the owner/manager of a local bookstore?

24. Explain the concept of zero-based budgeting.

APPLICATION QUESTION:

25. Put yourself in the position of a management trainer. You are asked to make a short presentation to the local Small Business Enterprise Association at their biweekly luncheon. The topic you are to speak on is "How Each of You Can Use Management by Objectives with Your Employees." What will you tell them and why?

CHAPTER EIGHT

Strategic Management and Entrepreneurship

Planning Ahead—Chapter 8 Study Questions

- What is strategic management?
- What types of strategies are used by organizations?
- How are strategies formulated?
- What are the issues in strategy implementation?
- What is entrepreneurship?

Get (and Stay) Ahead with Strategy

Wal-Mart's master plan is famous in the world of retail strategy—consistently low prices and high customer service. Now America's largest retailer and located in all 50 states, the firm was started by the late Sam Walton in Bentonville, Arkansas. "Mr. Sam" gave Wal-Mart its start by operating in small southern towns. With success came entry into broader national markets and international expansion. Industry analysts point to Wal-Mart's "productivity loop"—ability to offer lower prices and better service than its rivals—as a major competitive advantage. All this is backed up by the latest in technology. A sophisticated corporate satellite system and computer network keeps the home office in touch with operations at all stores. Inventories are monitored around the clock so that stores are rarely out of the items customers are seeking. Wal-Mart has a strong presence in Mexico, has struggled with its forays into South America and Asia, and is now expanding into Europe with the purchase of the German retailer Wertkauf. Given Wal-Mart's impressive track record and strength, the question is "Can other budget retailers keep up?" Of course, the visionaries at Wal-Mart are probably asking another question: "How can we stay ahead?"[1]

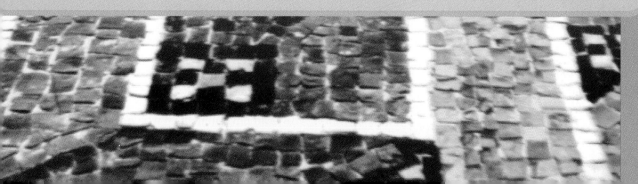

We will surely see many changes in competitive retailing in the years ahead. The industry is being challenged on many fronts, including catalog sales, home shopping by television, and the growth of electronic commerce. Success will come to those with a sense of future opportunities, clear visions about what needs to be done, and the strong management and organizational systems needed to get them accomplished. Similar forces for change confront managers in all organizations. This is the competitive domain of "strategy."

STRATEGY AND STRATEGIC MANAGEMENT

● A **strategy** is a comprehensive plan that sets direction and guides the allocation of resources to achieve long-term objectives.

Formally defined, a **strategy** is a comprehensive action plan that identifies long-term direction and guides resource utilization to accomplish an organization's mission and objectives with sustainable competitive advantage. It is a plan for using resources with consistent *strategic intent*, that is, with all organizational energies focused on a unifying and compelling target.[2] In the case of Coca-Cola, for example, strategic intent has been described as "To put a Coke within 'arm's reach' of every consumer in the world." To gain competitive advantage, an organization must deal with market and environmental forces better than its competitors. The task of crafting strategies with this potential can be daunting. Consider the retailing industry again. Wal-Mart, Kmart, and Target each began operating in 1962. Of the 10 top discounters they faced in that year, none exists today. They were killed by competition.

STRATEGY AND COMPETITIVE ADVANTAGE

● **America West Airline**
http://www.americawest.com

The America West Airlines' corporate mission statement reads, "America West will support and grow its market position as a low-cost, full-service nationwide airline. It will be known for its focus on customer service and its high-performance culture. America West is committed to sustaining financial strength and profitability, thereby providing stability for its employees and shareholder value for its owners."

A strategy is an action focus that links an organization to its environment. It represents top management's "best guess" regarding what must be done to ensure future success. At Wal-Mart, this seems deceptively simple: Find out what customers want, then provide it for them at the lowest prices and with better service. In practice, the choice of strategy is a complex and risky task.[3] Any strategy defines the direction in which an organization intends to move in a competitive environment. At the same time that one organization is trying to create advantage for itself its competitors are doing the same. Importantly, all this takes place in environments where large amounts of uncertainty often complicate the strategic planning process.[4]

The competitive nature of organizational environments varies in the following ways.[5] In a *monopoly environment* there is only one player and no competition. This creates absolute competitive advantage that delivers sustainable and most likely excessive business profits. One of the concerns about Microsoft as a supplier of computer operating systems is that it is or is close to monopoly status in respect to the market on computer operating systems. The *oligopoly environment* contains a few players who do not directly compete against one another. Firms within an oligopoly sustain long-term competitive advantages within defined market segments. In the absence of competition within these segments, they can also reap excessive business profits. This describes conditions in the breakfast cereals market, for example. The industry is dominated by three large players—Kellogg's, Post, and Ralston Purina. They control some 80% of the market and it is difficult for a new player to break in. From the customers standpoint, both monopoly and oligopoly are disadvantageous. The lack of competition may keep prices high and product/service innovations low.

The global economy has helped to create for many businesses today an *environment of hypercompetition*. This is an environment in which there are at least several players who directly compete with one another. An example is the fast-food industry where McDonald's, Burger King, Wendy's, and others are all competing for the same customers. Because the competition is direct and intense any competitive advantage that is realized is temporary. Successful strategies are often copied and firms must continue to find new strategies that deliver new sources of competitive advantage, even while trying to defend existing ones. McDonald's, for example, had to mount an aggressive campaign to defend its french fries — called in its advertising "America's Favorite Fries," from copycat attack by Burger King.[6] In hypercompetition, there are always some winners and losers. Business profits can be attractive but intermittent. The customer generally gains in this environment through lower prices and more product/service innovation.

THE STRATEGIC MANAGEMENT PROCESS

The demands of hypercompetition in the global economy call for strategies that one analyst calls "bold," "aggressive," and "fast-moving." **Strategic management** is the process of formulating and implementing strategies to advance an organization's mission and objectives and secure competitive advantage. The essence of strategic management is to look ahead, understand the environment, and effectively position an organization for competitive success in changing times. Wal-Mart's current CEO, David Glass, must think strategically as he tries to position Wal-Mart in new markets to help meet the retailing challenges of the early 21st century. He is thinking strategically when deciding how to use new technologies to maximum advantage. He is thinking strategically when deciding to invest in the potential of new European markets. And he is thinking strategically by spending time talking to customers and employees and learning what is really happening where it really counts — in the stores.

> • **Strategic management** is the process of formulating and implementing strategies.

When the strategic management process is successful, the resulting strategies for Wal-Mart and any organization should focus attention on clear, consistent, and long-term objectives. They should build from insightful understandings of a competitive environment. They should build from intimate knowledge of the organization. And they should be implemented with commitment and resolution.[7]

Figure 8.1 describes two major responsibilities in the strategic management process. The first is *strategy formulation.* This involves assessing existing strategies, organization, and environment to develop new strategies and strategic plans capable of delivering future competitive advantage. Peter Drucker associates this process with a set of five strategic questions: (1) *What is our business mission?* (2) *Who are our customers?* (3) *What do our customers consider value?* (4) *What have been our results?* (5) *What is our plan?*[8]

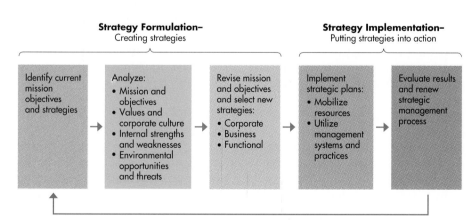

Figure 8.1 The strategic management process — strategy formulation and strategy implementation.

Manager's Notepad 8.1

Five Strategic Management Tasks

1. Identify organizational mission and objectives.
   Ask, "What business are we in? Where do we want to be in the future?"

2. Assess current performance vis-à-vis mission and objectives.
   Ask, "How well are we currently doing?"

3. Create strategic plans to accomplish purpose and objectives.
   Ask, "How can we get where we really want to be?"

4. Implement the strategic plans.
   Ask, "Has everything been done that needs to be done?"

5. Evaluate results; change strategic plans and/or implementation processes as necessary.
   Ask, "Are things working out as planned, and what can be improved upon?"

The second strategic management responsibility is *strategy implementation.* Once strategies are created, they must be acted upon successfully to achieve the desired results. As Drucker says, "The future will not just happen if one wishes hard enough. It requires decision—now. It imposes risk—now. It requires action—now. It demands allocation of resources, and above all, of human resources—now. It requires *work*—now."[9] This is the responsibility for putting strategies and strategic plans into action. Every organizational and management system must be mobilized to support and reinforce the accomplishment of strategies. Scarce resources must be utilized for maximum impact on performance. All of this, in turn, requires a commitment to mastering the full range of strategic management tasks posed in *Manager's Notepad 8.1.*[10]

ANALYSIS OF MISSION, VALUES, AND OBJECTIVES

The strategic management process begins with a careful assessment and clarification of organizational mission, values, and objectives.[11] As first discussed in Chapters 1 and 2, **mission** or *purpose* of any organization may be described as its "reason" for existence. In today's quality-conscious and highly competitive environments, the sense of purpose must be directly centered on serving the needs of customers or clients. After all, their satisfaction and continued support are the ultimate keys to organizational survival. Simply put, the best organizations have a clear purpose in society and direct resources in the direction of its fulfillment. At Mary Kay Cosmetics this is defined as "To give unlimited opportunity to women." At 3M it is "To solve unsolved problems innovatively." At Merck it is "To preserve and improve human life."[12]

- The **mission** of an organization is its reason for existence as a supplier of goods and services to society.

Mission Statements

One way to formalize a sense of organizational purpose is in the form of a written **mission statement.** Once created, such a statement can and should be reviewed regularly during the strategic management process. A good mission statement is precise in identifying the *domain* in which the organization intends to operate—including the *customers* it intends to serve, the *products* and/or *services* it intends to provide, and the *location* in which it intends to operate. The mission statement should also communicate the underlying *philosophy* that will

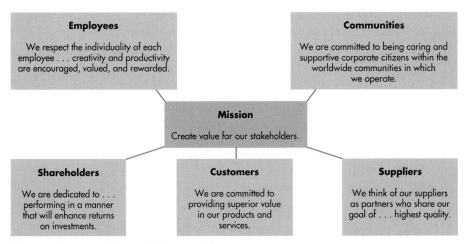

Figure 8.2   External stakeholders and the corporate mission statement.

guide employees in these operations. Baxter International's mission statement seems to meet each of these requirements: "We will be the leading health-care company by providing the best products and services for customers around the world, consistently emphasizing innovation, operational excellence, and the highest quality in everything we do."[13]

An important test of corporate purpose and mission is how well it serves the organization's *stakeholders*. You should recall that these are employees and members of the external environment, customers, shareholders, suppliers, creditors, community groups, and others who are directly involved with the organization and/or affected by its operations. In the strategic management process, the stakeholder test can be done as a *strategic constituencies analysis.* Here, the specific interests of each stakeholder are assessed along with the organization's record in responding to them. *Figure 8.2* gives an example of how stakeholder interests can be reflected in a mission statement.

Core Values

Behavior in and by organizations will always be affected in part by *values,* which are broad beliefs about what is or is not appropriate. **Corporate culture** was earlier defined in Chapter 2 as the predominant value system of the organization as a whole.[14] Through corporate cultures, the values of managers and other members are shaped and pointed in common directions. In strategic management, the presence of strong core values for an organization helps build institutional identity. It gives character to an organization in the eyes of its employees and external stakeholders, and it backs up the mission statement. Shared values also help guide the behavior of organization members in meaningful and consistent ways. For example, core values at Merck include corporate social responsibility, science-based innovation, honesty and integrity, and profit from work that benefits humanity. At Nordstrom, the large department store chain, the core values include service to the customer above all else, hard work and individual productivity, and excellence in reputation.[15]

- **Corporate culture** is the predominant value system for the organization as a whole.

Objectives

Whereas a mission statement sets forth an official purpose for the organization, **operating objectives** direct activities toward key and specific results. These objectives are shorter term targets against which actual performance results can be measured as indicators of progress and continuous improvement. Any and all op-

- **Operating objectives** are specific results that organizations try to accomplish.

erating objectives should have clear means-end linkages to the mission and purpose. Any and all strategies should, in turn, offer clear and demonstrable opportunities to accomplish operating objectives. According to Peter Drucker, the operating objectives of a business might include the following:[16]

Benefits of strategy →

- *Profitability:* Producing at a net profit in business.
- *Market share:* Gaining and holding a specific share of a product market.
- *Human talent:* Recruiting and maintaining a high-quality workforce.
- *Financial health:* Acquiring financial capital and earning positive returns.
- *Cost efficiency:* Using resources well to operate at low cost.
- *Product quality:* Producing high-quality goods or services.
- *Innovation:* Developing new products and/or processes.
- *Social responsibility:* Making a positive contribution to society.

ANALYSIS OF ORGANIZATIONAL RESOURCES AND CAPABILITIES

- A **SWOT analysis** examines organizational strengths and weaknesses and environmental opportunities and threats.

- A **core competency** is a special strength that gives an organization a competitive advantage.

Two critical steps in the strategic management process are analysis of the organization and analysis of its environment. They may be approached by a technique known as **SWOT analysis:** the analysis of organizational Strengths and Weaknesses as well as of environmental Opportunities and Threats.

As shown in *Figure 8.3,* a SWOT analysis begins with a systematic evaluation of the organization's resources and capabilities. A major goal is to identify **core competencies** in the form of special strengths that the organization has or does exceptionally well. They are things that can become sources of competitive advantage.[17] Core competencies may be found in efficient manufacturing technologies, special knowledge or expertise, superior technologies, or unique product distribution systems, among many other possibilities. But always, and as with the notion of strategy itself, they must be viewed relative to the competition. Simply put, organizations need core competencies that do important things better than the competition and that are very difficult for competitors to duplicate.

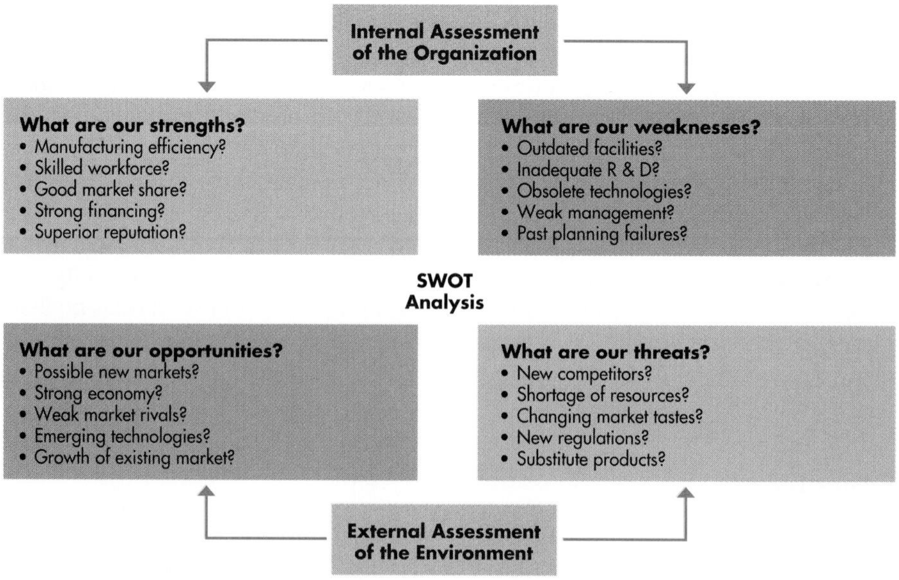

Internal Assessment of the Organization

What are our strengths?
- Manufacturing efficiency?
- Skilled workforce?
- Good market share?
- Strong financing?
- Superior reputation?

What are our weaknesses?
- Outdated facilities?
- Inadequate R & D?
- Obsolete technologies?
- Weak management?
- Past planning failures?

SWOT Analysis

What are our opportunities?
- Possible new markets?
- Strong economy?
- Weak market rivals?
- Emerging technologies?
- Growth of existing market?

What are our threats?
- New competitors?
- Shortage of resources?
- Changing market tastes?
- New regulations?
- Substitute products?

External Assessment of the Environment

Figure 8.3 SWOT analysis of organizational strengths and weaknesses and environmental opportunities and threats.

Figure 8.3 highlights several reference points for the internal analysis of organizational strengths. These include technology, human resources, manufacturing approaches, management talent, and financial strength, among others. Organizational weaknesses, of course, are the other side of the picture. They can also be found in the same or related areas and must be identified to gain a realistic perspective on the formulation of strategies. The goal in strategy formulation is to build on strengths and minimize the impact of weaknesses.

ANALYSIS OF INDUSTRY AND ENVIRONMENT

A SWOT analysis is not complete until opportunities and threats in the external environment are also analyzed. Given a sense of mission, values and objectives, it is necessary to assess how actual and future environmental conditions may affect their fulfillment. Potential influences include *macro environment* factors such as developments in areas like technology, government, social structures and population demographics, the global economy, and the natural environment. They also include the specific influences of the *industry environment* with respect to an organization's resource suppliers, competitors, and customers.

When Howard Schultz joined Starbucks in 1982 the firm was a small coffee retailer in Seattle. But Schultz saw more potential than this in the firm's future. He had a vision that included Starbuck's becoming a national chain of stores offering the finest coffee drinks and with a clear mission: "To educate consumers everywhere about fine coffee." The stores would be staffed by expert brewers who explained coffees as they were served. And, these employees would be given stock options to provide a sense of ownership in the company. Today Starbucks has grown to over 2,300 stores across North America and is expanding internationally. CEO Schulz says: "Moving forward, we will continue to pursue opportunities that increase long-term value for our shareholders and our partners, provide unique experiences for our customers, and bring us ever closer to our goal of becoming the most recognized and respected brand of coffee in the world."[18]

As shown in *Figure 8.3* there are many factors to be considered in the analysis of environment. Opportunities may be found in such areas as possible new markets, a strong economy, weaknesses in competitors, and emerging technologies. Weaknesses, however, may be identified in such things as the emergence of new competitors, resource scarcities, changing customer tastes, and new government regulations, among other possibilities. In respect to the external environmental as a whole, furthermore, the more stable and predictable it is, the more likely that a good strategy can be implemented with success for a longer period of time. But when the environment is composed of many dynamic elements that create many uncertainties, more flexible strategies that change with time are needed. Given the nature of competitive environments today, strategic management must be considered an ongoing process in which strategies are formulated, implemented, revised, and implemented again in a continuous manner.

STRATEGIES USED BY ORGANIZATIONS

Organizations use different levels and types of strategies. As shown in *Figure 8.4,* strategies at the corporate, business, and functional levels should all work together to accomplish objectives and create a long-term sustainable competitive advantage.[19] If we look at the Taiwanese bicycle maker Giant, for example, the firm is pursuing a corporate strategy of global growth and expansion. This is supported in part by an aggressive research and development strategy that invests 2% of annual sales revenues to keep Giant on the leading edge of technological innovation in the industry. Says President Anthony Lo: "We're very conservative and always think about how to be in a safe position to survive 50 or 100 years from now. The only way to do that is to go global and to keep learning and building up our knowledge of the industry."[20]

LEVELS OF STRATEGY

● A **corporate strategy** sets long-term direction for the total enterprise.

The level of **corporate strategy** directs the organization as a whole toward sustainable competitive advantage. For a business it describes the scope of operations by answering the following *strategic question:* "In what industries and markets should we compete?" The purpose of corporate strategy is to set direction and guide resource allocations for the entire enterprise. In diversified conglomerate organizations like General Electric, corporate strategy identifies the different areas of business in which a company intends to compete. The firm presently pursues business interests in aircraft engines, appliances, capital services, lighting, medical systems, broadcasting, plastics, and power systems, for example. Typical strategic decisions at the corporate level relate to the allocation of resources for acquisitions, new business development, divestitures, and the like across this business portfolio. Increasingly, corporate strategies for many businesses include an important role for global operations such as international joint ventures and strategic alliances.

● A **business strategy** identifies how a division or strategic business unit will compete in its product or service domain.

Business strategy is the strategy for a single business unit or product line. It describes strategic intent with respect to a given industry or market, such as GE's appliances division. In large conglomerates like General Electric, the term **strategic business unit (SBU)** is often used to describe such divisions when they operate with separate missions within a larger enterprise. The selection of strategy at this level involves answering the following *strategic question:* "How are we

● A **strategic business unit (SBU)** is a major business area that operates with some autonomy.

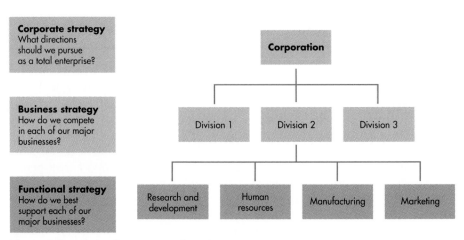

Corporate strategy
What directions should we pursue as a total enterprise?

Business strategy
How do we compete in each of our major businesses?

Functional strategy
How do we best support each of our major businesses?

Corporation — Division 1, Division 2, Division 3 — Research and development, Human resources, Manufacturing, Marketing

Figure 8.4   Levels of strategy in a large business.

going to compete for customers in this industry and market?" Typical business strategy decisions include choices about product/service mix, facilities locations, new technologies, and the like. In single-business enterprises, business strategy is the corporate strategy.

Functional strategy guides the use of resources to implement business strategy. This level of strategy focuses on activities within a specific functional area of operations. Looking again at *Figure 8.4*, the standard business functions of marketing, manufacturing, finance, and research and development illustrate this level of strategy. The *strategic question* to be answered in selecting functional strategies becomes "How can we best utilize resources to implement our business strategy?"

> • A **functional strategy** guides activities within one specific area of operations.

TYPES OF STRATEGIES

Within organizations, it is common to speak of four alternative types of "grand" or "master" strategies. They include (1) *growth strategies* that pursue larger size and expanded operations, (2) *retrenchment strategies* that reduce the size and/or scope of operations, (3) *stability strategies* that try to maintain existing operations, and (4) *combination strategies* that pursue two or more of these strategy types at the same time.[21]

Growth Strategies

Growth strategies seek an increase in size and the expansion of current operations. They are popular in part because growth is necessary for long-run survival in some industries. Coca-Cola, for example, pursues a highly aggressive and global growth strategy; Wal-Mart pursues aggressive growth nationally and is embarked upon an international one. There is a tendency to equate growth with effectiveness, but that is not necessarily true. Any growth must still be well managed to achieve the desired results.

> • A **growth strategy** involves expansion of the organization's current operations.

There are different ways to grow. Organizations can grow through *concentration* — that is, by using existing strengths in new and productive ways and without taking the risks of great shifts in direction. This can be done through market development, product development, and innovation. Organizations can also grow through *diversification,* the acquisition of or investment in new businesses in unrelated areas. Although diversification provides an obvious avenue for growth, it also adds operating complexity. The requirements of managing new and unfamiliar business areas can be complicated. Growth through diversification does not bring guaranteed success.

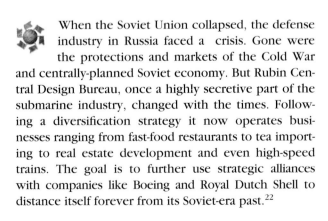 When the Soviet Union collapsed, the defense industry in Russia faced a crisis. Gone were the protections and markets of the Cold War and centrally-planned Soviet economy. But Rubin Central Design Bureau, once a highly secretive part of the submarine industry, changed with the times. Following a diversification strategy it now operates businesses ranging from fast-food restaurants to tea importing to real estate development and even high-speed trains. The goal is to further use strategic alliances with companies like Boeing and Royal Dutch Shell to distance itself forever from its Soviet-era past.[22]

Retrenchment Strategies

- A **retrenchment strategy** involves reducing the scale of current operations.

Retrenchment strategies, sometimes called *defensive strategies,* reduce the scale of operations in order to gain efficiency and improve performance. The decision to retrench can be difficult for managers to make since it, at least on the surface, seems to be an admission of failure. But in today's era of challenging economic conditions and environmental uncertainty, retrenchment strategies are used frequently and with new respect. When many of Asia's economies went into turmoil recently, this strategy gained new prominence among the region's firms. Many firms ended their diversification and acquisition initiatives and refocused on core businesses, while trying to reduce the scale of operations and cut costs.

There are different ways to strategically cut back. Retrenchment by *turnaround* is a strategy of "downsizing" to reduce costs and "restructuring" to improve operating efficiency. Retrenchment by *divestiture* involves selling parts of the organization to refocus on core competencies, cut costs, and improve operating efficiency. Finally, *liquidation* involves closing operations through the complete sale of assets or the declaration of bankruptcy.

Stability Strategies

- A **stability strategy** maintains the present course of action.

A **stability strategy** maintains the present course of action without major operating changes. Stability is sometimes pursued when an organization is doing well and the environment is not perceived to be changing. It is pursued when time is needed to consolidate strengths after a period of growth or retrenchment. It can also be pursued when decision makers are unwilling to take the risks of making strategic changes.

Combination Strategies

- A **combination strategy** involves stability, growth, and retrenchment in one or more combinations.

A **combination strategy** uses the other strategies in combination. The larger and more complex the organization, in fact, the more likely it is that combination strategies will be utilized. Combination strategies are also common in dynamic and highly competitive environments. A large multi-business conglomerate like General Electric, for example, may seek growth overall, but it may do so by growing some of its component businesses, stabilizing others, and retrenching still others.

STRATEGY FORMULATION

When developing strategies of any types it is important to remember the goal—sustainable competitive advantage. Traditionally, the major *opportunities for competitive advantage* have been found in the following areas:[23]

Opportunities for competitive advantage →

- *Cost and quality*—where strategy drives an emphasis on operating efficiency and/or product or service quality.
- *Knowledge and timing*—where strategy drives an emphasis on innovation and speed of delivery to market for new ideas.
- *Barriers to entry*—where strategy drives an emphasis on creating a market stronghold that is protected from entry by others.
- *Financial resources*—where strategy drives an emphasis on investments and/or loss sustainment that competitors can't match.

Furthermore, in today's global economy of intense hypercompetition these advantages must be considered temporary. Sooner or later an advantage of the moment will be eroded as changing environments and the moves of competitors take their toll over time.[24] Thus, the challenge of strategy formulation is not a static one. It is a dynamic challenge that must be continually revisited to keep pace with changing circumstances. Managers, strategic planners, and consultants alike must make good use of the alternative approaches to strategy formulation that are now available.

PORTFOLIO PLANNING

The **portfolio planning** approach is designed to help managers invest scarce organizational resources among competing business opportunities, including the mix of product lines and business units. The approach is similar to an individual choosing among alternative stocks, bonds, and real estate to create a personal investment "portfolio." The goal of a *portfolio strategy* is to identify a mix of investments that best serve organizational objectives.[25] It is most useful for addressing corporate-level strategy in multibusiness or multiproduct situations. The approach can help managers decide how the major grand strategies of growth, retrenchment, and stability should be applied for the organization and its subunits.

Figure 8.5 summarizes a popular portfolio planning approach developed by the Boston Consulting Group and known as the **BCG matrix.** This approach ties strategy formulation to an analysis of business opportunities according to market growth rate and market share.[26] As shown in *Figure 8.6,* this comparison results in the following four possibilities: (1) *stars*—high market share/high-growth businesses; *cash cows*—high market share/low-growth businesses; *question marks*—low market share/high-growth businesses; and *dogs*—low market share/low-growth businesses.

Stars are high market share businesses in high-growth markets. They produce large profits through substantial penetration of expanding markets. The preferred strategy for stars is growth, and further resource investments in them are recommended. *Question marks* are low market share businesses in high-growth markets. They do not produce much profit but compete in rapidly growing markets. They are the source of difficult strategic decisions. The preferred strategy is growth, but the risk exists that further investments will not result in improved market share. Only the most promising question marks should be targeted for growth; others are retrenchment candidates.

- A **portfolio planning** approach seeks the best mix of investments among alternative business opportunities.

- The **BCG matrix** analyzes business opportunities according to market growth rate and market share.

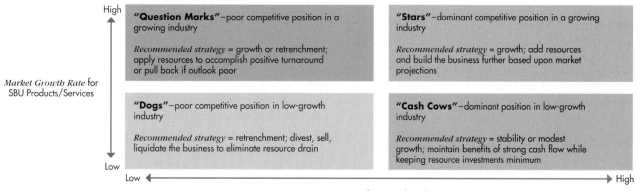

"SBU" = Strategic Business Unit

Figure 8.5 The BCG matrix: a portfolio model for corporate strategy formulation.

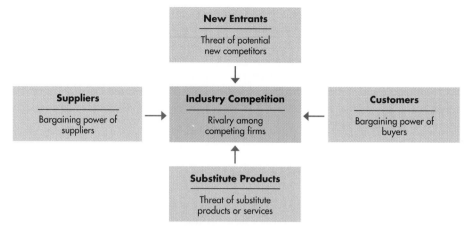

Figure 8.6 Five strategic forces affecting industry competition. *Source:* See Michael E. Porter, *Competitive Strategy* (New York: The Free Press, 1980).

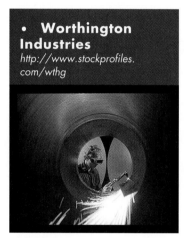

Worthington Industries, a premier supplier of steel and plastic products, pursues a distinct human resource strategy based on trust. There are no time clocks and all full-time employees are on salaries. Almost all absences are fully paid. The firm provides free coffee, in-plant barbershops, and medical-wellness centers. Not surprisingly, Worthington has made Fortune*'s list of "100 Best Companies to Work for in America."*

● A **differentiation strategy** seeks competitive advantage by goods and/or services that are clearly different from the competition.

Cash cows are high market share businesses in low-growth markets. They produce large profits and a strong cash flow. Because the markets offer little growth opportunity, the preferred strategy is stability or modest growth. "Cows" should be "milked" to generate cash that can be used to support needed investments in stars and question marks. *Dogs* are low market share businesses in low-growth markets. They do not produce much profit, and they show little potential for future improvement. The preferred strategy for dogs is retrenchment by divestiture.

Although it can oversimplify a complex decision situation, portfolio planning with the BCG matrix is a useful strategic planning tool. Its major appeal rests largely in helping managers focus attention on the comparative strengths and weaknesses of multiple businesses and/or products. At GE, once again strategies must be well managed to create the right portfolio of some 150 plus businesses at any point in time. GE's senior executives seek to do this by defining the goal as holding only those businesses that are or can be number one or number two in their industries. They concentrate resources on these businesses.

PORTER'S COMPETITIVE STRATEGIES

Michael Porter, management consultant and scholar, criticizes the portfolio approaches for leading corporate strategists into unwarranted diversification.[27] His *competitive strategies model* offers an alternative that gives special attention to the organization's current and potential competitive environment. As described in *Figure 8.6* the relevant forces are the threats of new competitors entering the market, the bargaining power of suppliers, the bargaining power of customers, the threats of substitute products or services, and rivalry or jockeying for position among existing firms in the industry.

From Porter's perspective, a good SWOT analysis begins by examining these competitive forces in an organization's environment. This provides a frame of reference for further assessment of organizational strengths and weaknesses. Then strategies can be chosen that give the organization a strategic advantage relative to its competitors. The three *generic strategies* organizations may pursue are (1) *differentiation* — distinguishing one's products from those of the competition; (2) *cost leadership* — minimizing costs to operate more efficiently than competitors; (3) *focus* — concentrating on serving one special market or customer group.

Organizations pursuing a **differentiation strategy** seek competitive advantage through uniqueness. They try to develop goods and services that are clearly different from those made available by the competition. The objective is to attract customers who become loyal to the organization's products and lose interest in those of competitors. This strategy requires organizational strengths in marketing, research and development, technological leadership, and creativity. It is highly dependent for its success on continuing customer perceptions of product quality and uniqueness.

A family-owned company in New Philadephia, Ohio, Endres Floral Company has found its niche by selling "a better rose." And sell it does, shipping more than 5 million roses per year to wholesalers. With 50 employees and 6 acres of greenhouses, the firm grows 170,000 rose bushes and harvests twice each day. To compete with lower cost producers from South America, the firm differentiates itself on quality; Endres red roses are supposed to last 10 days to 2 weeks without drooping. They are stored in computer-controlled coolers and shipped in special containers. No Endres rose is out of water more than 10 minutes after cutting. A genuine Endres rose can be in a customer's home within 24 hours.[28]

A second generic strategy in Porter's model is the **cost leadership strategy.** Organizations pursuing this strategy try to continuously improve the efficiency of production, distribution, and other organizational systems. The objective is to have lower costs than competitors and therefore achieve higher profits. This requires tight cost and managerial controls as well as products that are easy to manufacture and distribute. Of course, quality must not be sacrificed in the process. Wal-Mart, for example, aims to keep its costs so low that it can always offer customers the lowest prices and still make a reasonable profit. Most discount retailers operate with 18 to 20 percent gross margins. Wal-Mart accepts half of that and still makes the same or higher returns.

- A **cost leadership strategy** seeks to lower costs than competitors by efficiency of organizational systems.

Organizations pursuing a **focus strategy** concentrate attention on a special market segment with the objective of serving its needs better than anyone else. The strategy focuses organizational resources and expertise on a particular customer group, geographical region, or product or service line. This should also help develop strength through differentiation or cost leadership, or both. Importantly, the focus strategy requires a willingness to concentrate and the ability to use resources to special advantage in a single area. Cathay Pacific, long one of Asia's leading airlines, refocused on the tourist trade to bolster lagging revenues during the region's economic crisis. The firm offered dramatic discounts and special travel packages in attempting to lure customers from its rivals.

- A **focus strategy** concentrates attention on a special market segment to serve its needs better than the competition.

ADAPTIVE STRATEGIES

The major premise of the Miles and Snow *adaptive model* is that organizations should pursue product/market strategies that are congruent with the nature of their external environments.[29] A well-chosen strategy, in this sense, allows an organization to adapt successfully to environmental challenges. The **prospector strategy** involves pursuing innovation and new opportunities in the face of risk and with prospects for growth. This is best suited to a dynamic and high-potential environment. A prospector "leads" an industry by using existing technology to new advantage and creating new products to which competitors must respond. Fred Smith's original idea for Federal Express, the company he

- A **prospector strategy** pursues innovation and new opportunities in the face of risk.

- A **defender strategy** emphasizes existing products and current market share without seeking growth.

- An **analyzer strategy** seeks the stability of a core business while selectively responding to opportunities for innovation and change.

- A **reactor strategy** simply responds to competitive pressures in order to survive.

- **Product life cycle** is the series of stages a product or service goes through in the "life" of its marketability.

founded, was based on this strategic approach. In a **defender strategy,** an organization avoids change by emphasizing existing products and current market share without seeking growth. This strategy is suited only for a stable environment and perhaps declining industries. Defenders, as do many small local retailers, try to maintain their operating domains with only slight changes over time. As a result, many suffer long-term decline in the face of competition.

The **analyzer strategy** seeks to maintain the stability of a core business while exploring selective opportunities for innovation and change. This strategy lies between the prospector and reactor strategies. It is a "follow-the-leader-when-things-look-good" approach. Many of the "clone" makers in the personal computer industry are analyzers; that is, they wait to see what the industry leaders do and how well it works out before modifying their own operations. Organizations pursuing a **reactor strategy** are primarily responding to competitive pressures in order to survive. This is a "follow-as-last-resort" approach. Reactors do not have long-term and coherent strategies. Some public utilities and other organizations operating under government regulation may use this strategy to some extent.

PRODUCT LIFE CYCLES

A **product life cycle** is a series of stages a product or service goes through in the "life" of its marketability. In terms of planning, different business strategies are needed to support products in the life cycle stages of *introduction, growth, maturity,* and *decline.*[30] Products in the introduction and growth stages lend themselves to differentiation and prospector strategies. They require investments in advertising and market research to establish a market presence and build a customer base. In the maturity stage, the strategic emphasis shifts toward keeping customers and gaining production efficiencies. They may involve focus and an attempt at cost leadership. These strategies may hold initially as the product moves into decline. But at some point defender or analyzer characteristics may appear, as strategic planners seek ways to extend product life.

Understanding product life cycles and adjusting strategy accordingly is an important business skill. Especially in dynamic times, managers need to recognize when a product life cycle is maturing. They should have contingency plans for dealing with potential decline, and they should be developing alternative products with growth potential. Consider what happened at IBM, a firm that dominated the market for large mainframe computers for years. As customers began to use ever more powerful PCs, the mainframe became less important to their operating systems. When the cellular phone industry was starting to use new digital technologies, Motorola continued to emphasize its successful — but older, analog products. Both IBM's and Motorola's top managers failed to properly address industry trends and their companies suffered losses of momentum to very aggressive competitors.

EMERGENT STRATEGIES

Not all strategies are clearly formulated at one point in time and then implemented step by step. They take shape, change, and develop over time as modest adjustments to past patterns. James Brian Quinn calls this a process of *logical incrementalism,* whereby incremental changes in strategy occur as managers learn from experience.[31] This approach has much in common with Henry Mintzberg's and John Kotter's descriptions of managerial behavior, as described in Chapter 1.[32] They view managers as planning and acting in complex interpersonal networks and in hectic, fast-paced work settings. Given these challenges, effective managers must have the capacity to stay focused on long-term objectives while still remaining flexible enough to master short-run problems and opportunities as they occur.

Such reasoning has led Mintzberg to identify what he calls *emergent strategies.*[33] These are strategies that develop progressively over time as "streams" of decisions made by managers as they learn from and respond to work situations. There is an important element of "craftsmanship" here that Mintzberg worries may be overlooked by managers who choose and discard strategies in rapid succession while using the formal planning models. He also believes that incremental or emergent strategic planning allows managers and organizations to become really good at implementing strategies, not just formulating them.

STRATEGY IMPLEMENTATION

No strategy, no matter how well formulated, can achieve longer term success if it is not properly implemented. This includes the willingness to exercise control and make modifications as required to meet the needs of changing conditions. More specifically, current issues in strategy implementation include re-emphasis on excellence in all management systems and practices, the importance of leadership and top management teams, and the responsibilities of corporate governance.

MANAGEMENT PRACTICES AND SYSTEMS

The rest of this book is all about strategy implementation. In order to successfully put strategies into action the entire organization and all of its resources must be mobilized in support of them. This, in effect, involves the complete management process from planning and controlling through organizing and leading. No matter how well or elegantly selected, a strategy requires supporting structures, a good allocation of tasks and workflow designs, and the right people to staff all aspects of operations. The strategy needs to be enthusiastically supported by leaders who are capable of motivating everyone, building individual performance commitments, and utilizing teams and teamwork to best advantage. And, the strategy needs to be well and continually communicated to all relevant persons and parties. Only with such total systems support can strategies succeed through implementation in today's environments of change and innovation.

Common strategic planning pitfalls that can hinder implementation include both failures of substance and failures of process. *Failures of substance* reflect inadequate attention to the major strategic planning elements—analysis of mission and purpose, core values and corporate culture, organizational strengths and weaknesses, and environmental opportunities and threats. *Failures of process* reflect poor handling of the ways in which the various aspects of strategic planning were accomplished. An important process failure is the lack of participation error discussed in the last chapter. This is failure to include key persons in the strategic planning effort.[34] As a result, their lack of commitment to all-important action follow-through may severely hurt strategy implementation. Process failure also occurs as too much centralization of planning in top management or too much delegation of planning activities to staff planners or separate planning departments. Another process failure is the tendency to get so bogged down in details that the planning process becomes an end in itself instead of a means to an end. This is sometimes called "goal displacement."

The best point of departure for a manager who wants to minimize the risk of these and other implementation problems is to start with a good strategy. *Manager's Notepad 8.2* offers useful guidelines on how to double-check a strategy.[35]

• **McDonald's**
http://www.mcdonalds.com

In a memorandum to the U.S. owner/operators of McDonald's restaurants, Vice Chairman Jack Greenberg called the company's french-fries "the gold standard of the industry." After saying that "Nobody can beat us when we do it right," he went on to issue three "must-dos" to keep the fries ahead of the competition: Staff the fries station all day long, check the temperatures at least three times a day, and salt the fries properly.

Manager's Notepad 8.2

How to Double-check a Strategy

Check 1: Is the strategy consistent with your mission and values?

Check 2: Is the strategy feasible, given your strengths and weaknesses?

Check 3: Is the strategy responsive to opportunities and threats?

Check 4: Does the strategy offer a sustainable competitive advantage?

Check 5: Is the risk in the strategy a "reasonable" risk?

Check 6: Is the strategy flexible enough?

LEADERSHIP AND TOP MANAGEMENT TEAMS

Strategic management is a leadership responsibility. Effective strategy implementation and control depends on the full commitment of all managers to supporting and leading strategic initiatives within their areas of supervisory responsibility. To successfully put strategies into action the entire organization and all of its resources must be mobilized in support of them.

One of the realities of organizations today is that the complexity of environment and operations makes it difficult for one individual to lead a large organization. Increasingly, top management is being viewed as a team leadership situation. A *top management team* is one that is headed by a chief executive officer or president and entails, at a minimum, the senior managers reporting directly to this position. Some organizations have gone so far as to formally define a chief executive committee that is responsible for running day-to-day operations and reports directly to the CEO. Members of these executive committees are supposed to contribute their respective expertise and energies to the shared leadership role. Organizations that have tried such an approach include Nordstrom department stores, with four co-presidents, and Microsoft, with a three-person "Office of the President."[36]

In theory at least, these teams at the top of organizations are supposed to share information and work together to facilitate the strategic management of an enterprise. One of the difficulties encountered, however, is the task of creating true teamwork.[37] As we will discuss in Chapter 17 on teams and teamwork, it takes hard work and special circumstances to create a real team. Teams at the top are no different in this sense than teams at other levels and locations in organizations. Unless top management teams work up to their full potential, the advantages they can bring to the strategic management process will be lost or minimized.

CORPORATE GOVERNANCE

* **Corporate goverance** is the system of control and performance monitoring of top management.

Organizations today are experiencing new pressures at the level of **corporate governance.** This is the system of control and performance monitoring of top management that is maintained by boards of directors and other major stakeholder representatives. In businesses, for example, corporate governance is enacted by boards, institutional investors in a firm's assets, and other ownership interests. Each in its own way is a point of accountability for top management.[38]

Boards of directors are formally charged with ensuring that an organization operates in the best interests of its owners and/or the representative public in the case of nonprofit organizations. Controversies often arise over the role of *inside directors* who are chosen from the senior management of the organization and *outside directors* who are chosen from other organizations and positions external to the organization. Whereas in the past corporate boards may have been viewed as largely endorsing or confirming the strategic initiatives of top management, today they are increasingly expected to take active roles in ensuring that the strategic management of an enterprise is successful. AT&T's board of directors, for example, received considerable criticism for what many outside interests considered its lack of assertiveness in evaluating the performance of former CEO Robert Allen. Under pressure, Allen was eventually replaced.

If anything, the current trend is toward greater emphasis on corporate governance. Top managers probably feel more accountability for performance than ever before to boards of directors and other stakeholder interest groups. Furthermore, this accountability relates not only to financial performance but also to broader social responsibility concerns. There are institutional investors who purposely buy stock in a company to gain a voice in shareholder meetings. They do this to bring pressure on organizations to behave in socially responsible ways. Such pressure was felt by PepsiCo and Texaco for their controversial involvements in Burma, a country whose totalitarian rulers were accused of human rights abuses. Under pressure, both PepsiCo and Texaco terminated their business interests in that country.

 # STRATEGY AND ENTREPRENEURSHIP

Today's dynamic environment demands that organizations and their managers adapt and renew themselves continually to succeed over time. People and organizations not only must change — they must change *frequently* and at a rapidly accelerating pace. Success in the highly competitive business environments, in particular, depends on **entrepreneurship.** This term is used to describe strategic thinking and risk-taking behavior that results in the creation of new opportunities for individuals and/or organizations.[39] These opportunities frequently appear in the form of new business ventures, such as the now familiar Domino's Pizza and Federal Express's overnight package delivery, or as new goods or services, such as the popular 3M Post-It Note.

* **Entrepreneurship** is dynamic, risk taking, creative, and growth oriented behavior.

WHO ARE THE ENTREPRENEURS?

An **entrepreneur** is a risk-taking individual who takes action to pursue opportunities in situations others may fail to recognize as such or may even view as problems or threats.[40] In the business context, an entrepreneur starts new ventures that bring to life new product or service ideas. Typical *characteristics of entrepreneurs* include the following:

* **An entrepreneur** is willing to pursue opportunities in situations others view as problems or threats.

← Characteristics of entrepreneurs

* *Internal locus of control:* Entrepreneurs believe that they are in control of their own destiny; they are self-directing and like autonomy.

* *High energy level:* Entrepreneurs are persistent, hard working, and willing to exert extraordinary efforts to succeed.

* *High need for achievement:* Entrepreneurs are motivated to act individually to accomplish challenging goals.

* *Tolerance for ambiguity:* Entrepreneurs are risk takers; they tolerate situations with high degrees of uncertainty.

* *Self-confidence:* Entrepreneurs feel competent, believe in themselves, and are willing to make decisions.

• *Action oriented:* Entrepreneurs try to act ahead of problems; they want to get things done quickly and do not want to waste valuable time.

A common image of an entrepreneur is as the founder of a new business enterprise that achieves large-scale success. Anita Roddick's Body Shop, Bill Gates's Microsoft, and Sam Walton's Wal-Mart are but a few dramatic examples of this type of entrepreneurship. But entrepreneurs also operate on a smaller scale. Those who take the risk of buying a local McDonald's or Subway Sandwich franchise, opening a small retail shop, or going into a self-employed service business are also entrepreneurs. Similarly, anyone who assumes responsibility for introducing a new product or change in operations within an organization is also demonstrating the qualities of entrepreneurship.

ENTREPRENEURSHIP AND SMALL BUSINESS

• A **small business** has fewer than 500 employees, is independently owned and operated, and does not dominate its industry.

Entrepreneurship plays an important role in the formation of smaller enterprises. A **small business** is commonly defined as one with 500 or fewer employees. The U.S. Small Business Administration, or SBA, also states that a small business is one that is independently owned and operated and that does not dominate its industry.[41] Almost 99 percent of American businesses meet this definition, and the small business sector is very important in most nations of the world. Among other things, small businesses offer major economic advantages in that they create many job opportunities and they are the source of many new goods and services. The most common ways to get involved in a small business are to (1) start one, (2) buy an existing one, or (3) buy and run a franchise. Today, as the following example shows, the global economy and expanding international business are sources of considerable entrepreneurial opportunity.

Small businesses have a high failure rate. As many as 60 to 80 percent fail in their first 5 years of operation. Although many factors affect such outcomes, an important foundation for such success in the business plan discussed in Chapter 7. This is a written document that describes the nature of the business as well as exactly how an entrepreneuer intends to start and operate it. Writing such a business plan helps the entrepreneur "think" through the various details of setting up a business.[42] Typically, this plan will be shared with banks, venture capitalists, and other potential investors in order to attract any additional funds that may be needed to make the startup possible. Small business success will also always be based on the entrepreneur's ability to implement the management process of planning, organizing, leading, and controlling.

Entrepreneur Steven Bernard started his dream company to sell premium potato chips in 1989. He "kettle-cooked" his chips to make them distinctive. After building annual sales to some $7 million he sold Bernard's Cape Cod Potato Chips to Anheuser-Busch. Under its new owners the company floundered and was in danger of being shut down. Bernard bought the company back in 1996, and sales are projected to reach $30 million annually.

SMALL BUSINESS DEVELOPMENT

With small business playing an important role in the economy, a variety of resources are available to promote the development of small and medium scale enterprises. At the level of the federal government, the United States Small Business Administration works with state and local agencies to support a network of over 1,000 Small Business Development Centers nationwide. They offer guidance to entrepreneurs and small business owners — actual and prospective, in how to set up and successfully run a business operation. Often these centers are associated with universities or colleges and offer opportunities for students to learn first-hand the nature of small business and entrepreneurship. At the Silicon Valley Small Business Development Center, for example, Jean Jaffess and her partners in Mambo Design & Consulting were able to find assistance on writing a business plan, understanding financial reports, and tax requirements.[43]

In addition to the SBDC's, state governments typically offer special assistance in helping small businesses get involved in exporting. In Ohio, the International Trade Division maintains a staff of some 40 professionals and offices in several locations abroad, including Hong Kong, Mexico and Brazil. Says Susan Baker, owner of the Ohio River Bear Company: "Maybe I could have started exporting without help from the state, but surely not as quickly or easily."[44]

There is also considerable attention devoted to the notion of *business incubation,* where special facilities offering a variety of shared administrative services and facilities are set up to help small businesses get started. The idea is that by nurturing the new businesses in the incubators they will be able to grow more quickly and become healthy enough to survive on their own. And, of course, with survival the economic benefits of job creation and new members joining the local business community are expected. The National Business Incubation Association is headquartered at Ohio University and serves as the network hub of business incubation professionals around the nation.

ENTREPRENEURSHIP AND LARGE ENTERPRISES

Larger organizations also depend on entrepreneurial workers willing to assume risk and encourage the creativity and innovation so important to continued success in dynamic and competitive environments. Yet this task is especially challenging in very large and complex systems whose natural tendencies may be toward stability, rigidity, and avoidance of risk. The concept of **intrapreneurship** — described as entrepreneurial behavior on the part of people and subunits operating within the confines of large organizations, brings deserved attention to this situation.[45]

- **Intrapreneurship** is entrepreneurial behavior displayed by people or subunits within large organizations.

To enhance their competitive edge through intrapreneurship, however, managers often find that success depends on the ability of large organizations to act like small ones. To do this, some large organizations create small subunits, often called *skunk works,* in which groups of people are allowed to work together in a setting that is highly creative and free of many of the restrictions of large organizations. A classic example occurred at Apple Computer, Inc., where a small group of enthusiastic employees was once sent off to a separate facility in Cupertino, California. Their mandate was straightforward: to create a state-of-the-art, user-friendly personal computer. The group operated free of the firm's normal product development bureaucracy, set its own norms, and worked together without outside interference. The Jolly Roger was even raised over their building as a symbol of independence. It worked. This is the team that brought the now famous Macintosh computer into being. The legendary success of the Macintosh is a fitting reminder of the importance of this chapter's focus on strategic management and entrepreneurship in organizations.

CHAPTER REVIEW

This section should be used as an end-of-chapter "study guide." The *Summary* helps to put the chapter's content into overall perspective. The list of *Key Terms* allows you to double-check your familiarity with basic concepts and definitions. *Self-Test 8* gives you the opportunity to test your basic comprehension of the chapter using sample test questions.

SUMMARY

What is strategic management?

- A strategy is a comprehensive plan that sets long-term direction and guides resource allocation to accomplish an organization's mission.

- Strategic thinking involves the ability to understand the different challenges of monopoly, oligopoly, and hypercompetition environments.

- Strategic management is a responsibility for the formulation and implementation of strategies that support organizational mission and objectives in a competitive environment.

- The strategic management process begins with analysis of mission, clarification of core values, and identification of objectives.

- The strategic management process involves a SWOT analysis of organizational resources and capabilities and industry/environment opportunities and threats.

What types of strategies are used by organizations?

- Corporate strategy sets direction for an entire organization; business strategy sets direction for a business division or product/service line; functional strategy sets direction for the operational support of business and corporate strategies.

- The grand or master strategies used by organizations include growth — pursuing expansion; retrenchment — pursuing ways to scale back operations, stability — pursuing ways to maintain the status quo, and combination — pursuing the strategies in combination.

How are strategies formulated?

- The BCG matrix is a portfolio planning approach that classifies businesses or product lines as "stars," "cash cows," "question marks," or "dogs."

- Porter's model of competitive strategy identifies three major generic strategic options: differentiation — distinguishing one's products from the competition; cost leadership — minimizing costs relative to the competition; and focus — concentrating on a special market segment.

- The adaptive model focuses on the congruence of prospector, defender, analyzer, or reactor strategies with demands of the external environment.

- The product life-cycle model focuses on different strategic needs at the introduction, growth, maturity, and decline stages of a product's life.

- The incremental or emergent model recognizes that many strategies are formulated and implemented incrementally over time.

What are current issues in strategy implementation?

- Management practices and systems — including the functions of planning, organizing, leading, and controlling — must be mobilized to support strategy implementation.

- Among the pitfalls that inhibit strategy implementation are failures of substance, such as poor analysis of the environment, and failures of process, such as lack of participation in the planning process.

- Increasingly, organizations utilize top management teams to energize and direct the strategic management process.

- Corporate governance, involving the role of boards of directors in the performance monitoring of organizations, is being addressed as an important element in strategic management today.

What is entrepreneurship?

- Entrepreneurship is risk-taking behavior that results in the creation of new opportunities for individuals and/or organizations.

- An entrepreneur is someone who takes strategic risks to pursue opportunities in situations others may view as problems or threats.

- Entrepreneurship results in the founding of many small business enterprises that offer job creation and other benefits to economies.

- In the United States, small businesses have access to a variety of forms of support and assistance, including Small Business Development Centers funded by government sources and business incubators.

- Intrapreneurship, or entrepreneurial behavior within larger organizations, is important in today's dynamic and competitive environments.

KEY TERMS

Analyzer strategy (p. 170)

Business strategy (p. 164)

BCG matrix (p. 167)

Combination strategy (p. 166)

Core competencies (p. 162)

Corporate culture (p. 161)

Corporate governance (p. 172)

Corporate strategy (p. 164)

Cost leadership strategy (p. 169)

Defender strategy (p. 170)

Differentiation strategy (p. 168)

Entrepreneur (p. 173)

Entrepreneurship (p. 173)

Focus strategy (p. 169)

Functional strategy (p. 165)

Growth strategy (p. 165)

Intrapreneurship (p. 175)

Mission (p. 160)

Operating objectives (p. 161)

Portfolio planning (p. 167)

Product life cycle (p. 170)

Prospector strategy (p. 169)

Reactor strategy (p. 170)

Retrenchment strategies (p. 166)

Small business (p. 174)

Stability strategy (p. 166)

Strategic business unit (SBU) (p. 164)

Strategic management (p. 159)

Strategy (p. 158)

SWOT analysis (p. 162)

SELF-TEST 8

Take this test much as you would in a normal classroom situation. It should offer you a good way to check your basic comprehension of chapter material. Answers may be found at the end of the book.

MULTIPLE-CHOICE QUESTIONS:

1. The most appropriate first question in the strategic planning process is _____.
   (a) "Where do we want to be in the future?" (b) "How well are we currently doing?"
   (c) "How can we get where we want to be?" (d) "Why aren't we doing better?"

2. An important purpose of strategic planning is to give an organization a _____ in the marketplace. (a) clear structure (b) sustainable competitive advantage (c) cash cow (d) strategic alliance

3   In a complex business such as the conglomerate General Electric, a/an _____-level strategy sets strategic direction for a strategic business unit or product division. (a) institutional (b) corporate (c) business (d) functional

4. An organization that is downsizing to reduce costs is implementing a grand strategy of _____. (a) growth (b) cost differentiation (c) retrenchment (d) stability

5. The _____ is a predominant value system for an organization as a whole. (a) code of ethics (b) organizational climate (c) institutional personality (d) corporate culture

6. A _____ in the BCG matrix would have a high market share in a low-growth market. (a) dog (b) cash cow (c) question mark (d) star

7. In Porter's model of competitive strategy, one of the three generic strategies is _____. (a) divestiture (b) market penetration (c) focus (d) diversity

8. A _____ is a term used to describe a small group of people operating with independence and in the expectation of being highly creative within a large organization. (a) skunk works (b) product team (c) focus group (d) leadership council

9. The _____ objectives of organizations are specific results for the organization to accomplish on a day-to-day basis. (a) official (b) operating (c) informal (d) institutional

10. The customer generally gains through lower prices and greater innovation in _____ environments. (a) monopoly (b) oligopoly (c) hypercompetition (d) central planning

TRUE-FALSE QUESTIONS:

11. Concentration and diversification are common ways for businesses to pursue growth strategies. T F

12. An organization pursuing a stability strategy is always going to lose competitive advantage. T F

13. Core competencies can be identified in the analysis of organizational strengths and weaknesses. T F

14. In the adaptive model of strategy formulation, a prospector strategy responds to events without having an overall guiding strategy. T F

15. The incrementalism view of strategy implementation views strategies as being implemented without any changes. T F

16. Lack of participation is a common failure of process in strategic planning. T F

17. Most entrepreneurs have high needs for achievement and high tolerance of ambiguity. T F

18. The mission statement is an expression of short-term operative objectives for the organization. T F

19. Portfolio planning is considered most useful at the level of functional strategy. T F

20. Entrepreneurial behavior is not possible within large organizations. T F

SHORT-RESPONSE QUESTIONS:

21. What is the difference between corporate strategy and functional strategy?

22. How would a manager perform a SWOT analysis?

23. What is the difference between entrepreneurship and intrapreneurship?

24. What is strategic management?

APPLICATION QUESTION:

25. Kim Harris owns and operates a retail store selling the outdoor clothing of an American manufacturer to a predominately college student market. Lately, a large department store has opened a similar department and is selling similar clothing manufactured in China, Thailand, and Bangladesh at lower prices. Kim believes he is starting to lose business to this store. Assume you are part of a student team assigned to do a management class project for Kim. Kim's question for the team is "How can I apply Porter's generic strategies to better deal with my strategic planning challenges in this situation?" How will you reply?

Controlling – To Ensure Results

Planning Ahead—Chapter 9 Study Questions

- What is the control process?

- What types of controls are used in organizations?

- How do organizational systems assist in control?

- How can operations management improve control?

Facts Can Be Your Best Friends

Volant Inc., a Colorado-based ski maker, was in trouble when consultant Mark Soderberg was hired. A plant tour revealed thousands of half-finished skis stacked here and there, up to 40 percent of a day's production being scrapped, and dissatisfied customers left with unfilled orders. His approach? Admit the facts, stop production, analyze systems, and address quality problems. Doing what he calls "just the basics of manufacturing," Soderberg cut work-in-process inventories, set up control systems to track defects during production, and organized workers into "process analysis" teams to tap their ideas. Within two years the orders were flowing again and production was smooth and efficient. As quality went up, costs went down. And with the ski business under control, management was able to consider other strategic moves to counter the seasonality of skis, such as entering the golf or biking markets.[1]

"Keeping in touch . . . Staying informed . . . Being in control." These are important responsibilities for every manager. But *control* is a word like *power;* if you aren't careful when it is used, it leaves a negative connotation. Yet, as the example from Volant Inc. shows, control plays a positive and necessary role in the management process. To have things "under control" is good; for things to be "out of control" generally is bad. This chapter introduces the fundamentals of controlling as a basic managerial responsibility and as an important key to sustained organizational productivity.

CONTROLLING AS A MANAGEMENT FUNCTION

● **Controlling** is the process of measuring performance and taking action to ensure desired results.

When introduced in Chapter 1 as part of the management process, **controlling** was defined as a process of measuring performance and taking action to ensure desired results. The purpose of controlling is straightforward — to make sure that plans are fulfilled and that actual performance meets or surpasses objectives. The foundation of control is information. Henry Schacht, the former CEO of Cummins Engine Company, once discussed control in terms of what he called "friendly facts." He stated, "Facts that reinforce what you are doing . . . are nice, because they help in terms of psychic reward. Facts that raise alarms are equally friendly, because they give you clues about how to respond, how to change, where to spend the resources."[2]

THE IMPORTANCE OF CONTROLLING

Figure 9.1 shows how controlling fits in with the rest of the management process. *Planning* sets the directions and allocates resources. *Organizing* brings people and material resources together in working combinations. *Leading* inspires people to best utilize these resources. *Controlling* sees to it that the right things happen, in the right way, and at the right time. It helps ensure that the performance contributions of individuals and groups are consistent with organizational plans. It helps ensure that performance accomplishments throughout an organization are consistent with one another in means-ends fashion. And it helps ensure that people comply with organizational policies and procedures.

STEPS IN THE CONTROL PROCESS

The classic example of the control process operating in its purest form is a home thermostat. We set the thermostat to a desired temperature. When the room gets

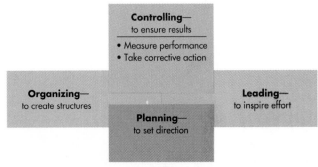

Figure 9.1   The role of controlling in the management process.

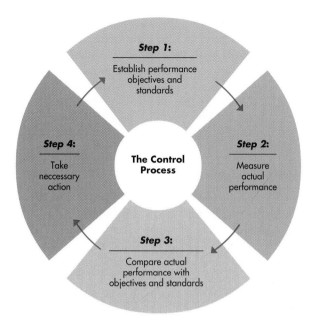

Figure 9.2 Four steps in management control.

too cold or hot, that is, when conditions deviate from the setting, the thermostat senses the difference and takes corrective action by turning on the heater or air conditioner. Once the desired temperature is achieved, the furnace or air conditioner is automatically turned off. This illustrates a **cybernetic control system** — one that is self-contained in its performance monitoring and correction capabilities. The control process as practiced in organizations is not cybernetic, but it does follow similar principles. As shown in *Figure 9.2*, the management control process involves four steps: (1) establish objectives and standards; (2) measure actual performance; (3) compare results with objectives and standards; and (4) take corrective action as needed.

- A **cybernetic control system** is self-contained in its performance-monitoring and correction capabilities.

Step 1: Establishing Objectives and Standards

The control process starts when performance objectives and standards are set through planning. It can't begin without them. In this first step of the process, performance objectives are defined and the standards for measuring them are set. Two types of standards can be used. **Output standards** measure results in terms of performance quantity, quality, cost, or time. Examples include percentage error rate, dollar deviation from budgeted expenditures, and the number of units produced or customers serviced in a time period. **Input standards,** by contrast, measure effort in terms of the amount of work expended in task performance. They are used in situations where outputs are difficult or expensive to measure. Examples include conformance to rules and procedures, efficiency in the use of resources, and work attendance or punctuality.

- An **output standard** measures performance results in terms of quantity, quality, cost, or time.

- An **input standard** measures work efforts that go into a performance task.

Step 2: Measuring Actual Performance

The second step of the control process is to measure actual performance. The goal here is to measure accurately the performance results (output standards) and/or the performance efforts (input standards). In both cases, the measurement must be accurate enough to spot significant differences between what is really taking place and what was originally planned. A common management failure in this regard is an unwillingness or inability to measure the performance of people at work. Yet without measurement, effective control is not possible.

General Electric CEO Jack Welch has found that leaders must make extra effort to push new quality programs. He says, "You have to tell your people quality is critical to survival, you have to demand everybody gets trained, you have to cheerlead, you have to have incentive systems, you have to say 'We must do this.'"

Managers need to get comfortable with the act of measurement. When Linda Sanford was appointed head of IBM's sales force, she came with an admirable performance record during a 22 year career with the company. Notably, Sanford grew up on a family farm where she developed an appreciation for both teamwork and measuring results. "At the end of the day, you saw what you did, knew how many rows of strawberrys you picked." At IBM she was known for walking around the factory just to see "at the end of the day how many machines were going out of the back dock."[3]

Step 3: Comparing Results with Objectives and Standards

Step three in the control process is to compare measured performance with objectives and standards to establish the need for action. This step can be expressed as the following *control equation:*

$$\text{Need for Action} = \text{Desired Performance} - \text{Actual Performance}$$

There are different ways of accomplishing the comparison of desired and actual performance. First, it can be a *historical comparison* that uses past performance as a benchmark for evaluating current performance. Second, it can be a *relative comparison* that uses the performance achievements of other persons, work units, or organizations as the evaluation standard. Third, it can be an *engineering comparison* that uses engineered standards set scientifically through such methods as time and motion studies. The delivery routines of drivers for UPS, for example, are carefully measured in terms of expected minutes per delivery on various routes.

In Chapter 7 the concept of benchmarking was formally introduced as a planning approach. Here, its importance to the control process is also clear. Benchmarking is rapidly gaining popularity as a means of identifying best practices, with the emphasis always on the question: "What can I or we do better?"[4] Without rigorous and regular measurement comparisons — be they historical, relative, or engineering driven, answers to this question are difficult to get. In an Ernst & Young survey of fast-growing small businesses, for example, more than 80% were found to be using benchmarking to improve their performances. The comparisons were most likely to involve industry norms, a primary competitor, the industry leader, and similar world-class firms.[5]

Step 4: Taking Corrective Action

The control equation indicates that the greater the measured difference between desired and actual performance, the greater the need for action. The last step in the control process, accordingly, is taking any action necessary to correct or improve things. This allows for a judicious use of **management by exception** — the practice of giving priority attention to situations that show the greatest need for action. This approach can save valuable time, energy, and other resources, while allowing all efforts to be concentrated on the areas of greatest need.

● **Management by exception** focuses managerial attention on substantial differences between actual and desired performance.

Two types of exceptions may be encountered. The first is a *problem situation* in which actual performance is below the standard. The reasons for this performance deficiency must be understood. Corrective action is required to restore performance to the desired level. The second exception is an *opportunity situation* in which actual performance is above the standard. The reasons for this extraordinary performance must also be understood. Action should then be taken to continue this higher level of accomplishment in the future. The original plans, objectives, and standards can also be reviewed to determine if they should be updated.

Once again, measurement is the key to the control process. Consider, for example, how Allstate Corporation uses a "diversity index" to quantify its performance on diversity issues. Each year the firm surveys employees on how well it is doing in meeting its goals of bias-free customer service and respect for all employees. Managers are then rated by their employees on a diversity index that reflects how well their behaviors match expectations. The diversity index scores help determine annual pay bonuses.[6]

EFFECTIVE CONTROLS

Like other aspects of the management process, controlling must be done well to have a positive impact on behavior in organizations. One of the problems with controls is that many senior managers are too busy and/or unwilling to double-check the progress of their own decisions. Once plans are made, they may tend to assume both that they are correct and that they are working even as situations change with time.

At Bell Atlantic the CEO appoints a senior-level executive to specifically monitor corporate performance on the top 20 to 30 priorities. In this way, objectives are revisited, results analyzed, new conditions taken into account, and plans and activities adjusted to maximize performance. Such an independent review helps to ensure that the control process operates even at the highest levels of the organization.[7]

Sometimes even well-intentioned controls don't work as expected. Some time ago, for example, the Boy Scouts of America had a problem. Membership data reported from the field were being falsified. This happened at the time when the organization was undertaking a national drive to increase membership. Controls were instituted to conduct careful reporting and accounting of all new members. To their chagrin, the leaders of the drive found something that other managers have also discovered — people don't always respond to controls in the intended manner. The membership drive and reporting pressures motivated Boy Scout field workers to increase the number of new members reported, but it had not motivated them to increase the number of Boy Scouts actually enrolled.[8]

This case highlights an important dilemma faced by managers: At the same time that controls are designed to ensure certain performance outcomes, human reactions to the controls can render them ineffective and even dysfunctional. Truly effective controls channel human energies toward improved work performance instead of toward attempts to "beat the system," as was apparent in the Boy Scout case. The best controls in organizations share the following characteristics:

- *Controls should be strategic and results oriented.* They support strategic plans and focus on significant activities that make a real difference to the organization.

Characteristics of effective control systems

- *Controls should be understandable.* They should support decision making by presenting data in understandable terms; they should avoid complex reports and statistics.

- *Controls should encourage self-control.* They should allow for mutual trust, good communication, and participation among everyone involved.

- *Controls should be timely and exception oriented.* They should report deviations quickly, lending insight into why the variance occurs and what might be done to correct it.

- *Controls should be positive in nature.* They should emphasize development, change, and improvement; they should minimize penalty and reprimand.

- *Controls should be fair and objective.* They should be considered impartial and accurate by everyone, and they should be respected for one fundamental purpose — performance enhancement

- *Controls should be flexible.* They should leave room for individual judgment and should be modifiable to fit new circumstances as they arise.[9]

TYPES OF CONTROLS

Three major types of managerial controls — feedforward, concurrent, and feedback, are shown in *Figure 9.3.*[10] Each is relevant to a different phase of the organization's input-throughput-output cycle of activities. And importantly, each is very important to the quest for long-term productivity and high performance.

FEEDFORWARD CONTROLS

• A **feedforward** or **preliminary control** ensures that proper directions are set and that the right resources are available before the work begins.

Feedforward controls, also called **preliminary controls,** are accomplished before a work activity begins. They ensure that objectives are clear, that proper directions are established, and that the right resources are available to accomplish them. By making sure that the stage is properly set for high performance, feedforward controls are preventive in nature. They are designed to eliminate the potential for problems later on in the process by asking an important but often neglected question: "What needs to be done before we begin?" This is a forward-thinking and proactive approach to control rather than a reactive and defensive one. The quality of resources is a key concern of feedback controls. At McDonald's, for example, preliminary control of food ingredients plays an important role in the firm's quality program. The company requires that suppliers of its hamburger buns produce them to exact specifications, covering everything from texture to uniformity of color. Even in overseas markets, the firm works hard to develop local suppliers that can offer dependable quality.[11]

CONCURRENT CONTROLS

• A **concurrent control** focuses on what happens during the work process.

Concurrent controls focus on what happens during the work process. Sometimes called *steering controls,* they monitor ongoing operations and activities to make sure things are being done according to plan. Ideally, concurrent controls allow corrective actions to be taken before a task is completed. The key question

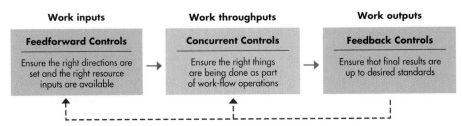

Figure 9.3 Three types of controls: feedforward, concurrent, and feedback controls.

is "What can we do to improve things before we finish?" Here, the focus is on quality of task activities during the work process. This approach to control can reduce waste in the form of unacceptable finished products or services. Taking McDonald's again as an example, ever-present shift leaders provide concurrent control through direct supervision. They constantly observe what is taking place even while helping out with the work. They are trained to intervene immediately when something is not done right and to correct things on the spot. Detailed instruction manuals also "steer" workers in the right directions as their jobs are performed.[12]

FEEDBACK CONTROLS

Feedback controls, also called *postaction controls,* take place after work is completed. They focus on the quality of end results rather than on inputs and activities. They ask the question "Now that we are finished, how well did we do?" Restaurants, for example, ask how you like a meal . . . after it is eaten; a final exam grade tells you how well you performed . . . after the course is over; a budget summary informs managers of any cost overruns . . . after a project is completed. In these and other circumstances the feedback provided by the control process is useful information for improving things in the future. It also provides formal documentation of accomplishments that may be used for allocating performance-based rewards. Employees at a McDonald's restaurant never know when a corporate evaluator may stop in to sample the food and the service. When this happens, however, the evaluator provides feedback with the goal of improving future operations.[13]

● **A feedback control** takes place after an action is completed.

INTERNAL VERSUS EXTERNAL CONTROL

Managers have two broad options with respect to control. They can rely on people to exercise self-control over their own behavior. This strategy of **internal control** allows motivated individuals and groups to exercise self-discipline in fulfilling job expectations. Alternatively, managers can take direct action to control the behavior of others. This is a strategy of **external control** that occurs through personal supervision and the use of formal administrative systems. Organizations with effective control typically use both strategies to good advantage. However, the trend today is to increase the emphasis on internal or self-control. This is consistent with the renewed emphasis on participation, empowerment, and involvement in the workplace.

● **Internal control** occurs through self-discipline and self-control.

● **External control** occurs through direct supervision or administrative systems such as rules and procedures.

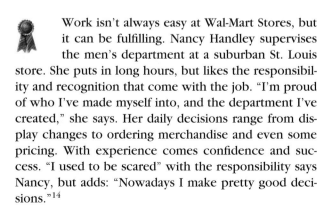

Work isn't always easy at Wal-Mart Stores, but it can be fulfilling. Nancy Handley supervises the men's department at a suburban St. Louis store. She puts in long hours, but likes the responsibility and recognition that come with the job. "I'm proud of who I've made myself into, and the department I've created," she says. Her daily decisions range from display changes to ordering merchandise and even some pricing. With experience comes confidence and success. "I used to be scared" with the responsibility says Nancy, but adds: "Nowadays I make pretty good decisions."[14]

Internal control is self-control. It is exercised by people who are motivated to take charge of their own behavior on the job. Douglas McGregor's Theory Y perspective, introduced in Chapter 4, recognizes the willingness of people to exercise self-control in their work.[15] Of course, McGregor also recognized that people are most likely to exercise self-control this when they participate in setting performance objectives and standards. Reliance on an internal control strategy also requires a high degree of trust. When people are expected to work on their own and exercise self-control, managers must give them a chance to meet these expectations.

The potential for self-control is increased when capable people have a clear sense of organizational mission, know their performance objectives, and have the resources necessary to do their jobs well. It is also enhanced by participative organizational cultures in which people are expected to treat each other with respect and consideration, are allowed to exercise personal initiative, and are given ample opportunities to experience satisfaction through job performance.

ORGANIZATIONAL CONTROL SYSTEMS

Each component in an organization's control systems should contribute to maintaining predictably high levels of performance. Internal control should be encouraged and supported; external control should be appropriate and rigorous. The management process provides for a certain amount of control when planning, organizing, and leading are well done. Additional and comprehensive control is provided by appropriate systems such as those dealing with compensation and benefits, employee discipline, and financial information.

MANAGEMENT PROCESS CONTROLS

The day-to-day operations of the management process can go a long way in helping to control behavior in organizations. In planning, *control via strategy and objectives* occurs when work behaviors are initially directed toward the right end results. When performance goals are clearly set and understood, lack of performance because of poor direction in one's work is less likely to occur. *Control via policies and procedures* operates in similar ways. To the extent that good policies and procedures exist to guide behavior, an organization's members are more likely to act uniformly on important matters. *Control via learning* occurs when past experience is systematically considered and incorporated into future strategies, objectives, policies, and procedures.

Management control is also facilitated by good organizing. *Control by selection and training* occurs when capable people are hired and given the ongoing training needed to perform their jobs at high levels of accomplishment. The closer the match between individual skills and job requirements, the less need there is for external control and the greater the opportunity for internal control to exert its influence. *Control via performance appraisal* occurs when individual performance is assessed and evaluated to ensure high performance results and to identify areas where training and development is needed. *Control via job design and work structures* operates in similar fashion. It involves putting people to work in jobs that are designed to best fit the job holder's talents. When such jobs are properly tied to well-coordinated workflows and operations, this structure adds substantially to the control built into the day-to-day work process.

Leadership contributes to *control through performance modeling*. This means that leadership sets the example and that workers have good models to follow in their job activities. *Control by performance norms* occurs when team

The Society for Human Resource Management
http://www.shrm.org

The Society for Human Resource Management reports that up to 25 percent of job applications and resumes contain errors. It is important to check the references of job applicants to make sure that you get the right person to fill openings. Some employers are now going to paid job tryouts to try to make better selection decisions. Says one small business owner, "You wouldn't buy a car without test driving it."

or group members share commitments to high performance standards and reinforce one another's efforts to meet them. *Control via organization culture* occurs in similar fashion, when an organization's leadership helps build strong values for the organization as a whole.

COMPENSATION AND BENEFITS SYSTEMS

Base compensation plays an important role in attracting a highly qualified workforce to the organization. *If* compensation is attractive and competitive in the prevailing labor markets, it can make the organization highly desirable as a place of employment. And *if* you get the right people into jobs you can reduce costs and boost productivity over the long run. After all, the more capable a person is, the more self-control one can expect that person to exercise. When the wage and salary structure of an organization is unattractive and uncompetitive, however, it will be difficult to attract and retain a staff of highly competent workers. The less capable the workforce, the greater the burden on external controls to ensure desired levels of performance.

The use of incentive compensation systems will be discussed in Chapter 14 on motivation and rewards. When properly implemented, such "pay-for-performance" and "merit pay" plans serve as control systems. They can be strong influences on individual and group behavior. One corporate executive offers the following guideline for making sure that incentive compensation has the desired impact: "Pay very poorly for poor performance; pay poorly for average performance; pay well for above-average performance; pay obscenely well for outstanding performance."[16]

Because of the growing importance of a worker's total compensation package, fringe benefits also have control implications. Their attractiveness can also affect an organization's ability to recruit and retain a qualified workforce. In today's environment of rising costs and workforce diversity, fringe benefits—from health insurance to pension plans to child and elder care and more, can be very expensive. Many employers are now trying to provide individuals with more choice in selecting benefits that suit their needs. At the same time, employers are seeking ways to reduce expenditures by asking employees to pay more of the fringe benefit's cost—an unpopular move with employees and labor unions alike. A substantial proportion of union strikes, for example, now include issues relating to workers' health-care coverage.

● **United States Army**
http://www.army.mit

Continuous improvement is the theme of the U.S. Army's After Action Review program. Exercises are videotaped and monitored by trained observer-controllers. The results are peer reviewed, with participants commenting on one another's performances and the observer-controllers giving immediate feedback. The Army Chief of Staff says, "in high-performance organizations, the parts are supported to talk to one another."

✳ At Steelcase Inc. employees can choose from a smorgasbord of benefits that help to satisfy diverse needs. A growing number of two-career couples as well as intense competition for labor were among the factors that initially contributed to an emphasis on flexibility in employment benefits at Steelcase, the Grand Rapids, Michigan office furniture manufacturer. Now employees can select a mix of the programs that offer both financial and quality-of-life benefits. Employees have options for child-care services, tuition assistance for further education, and other employee-assistance options as well as the more traditional health and retirement benefits.[17]

EMPLOYEE DISCIPLINE SYSTEMS

Absenteeism . . . tardiness . . . sloppy work. . ., the list of misbehaviors can go on to even more extreme actions: falsifying records . . . sexual harassment . . . embezzlement. All are examples of behaviors that can and should be formally

Manager's Notepad 9.1

"Hot Stove Rules" of Employee Discipline

- *A reprimand should be immediate:* A hot stove burns the first time you touch it.

- *A reprimand should be directed toward someone's actions, not their personality:* A hot stove doesn't hold grudges, doesn't try to humiliate people, and doesn't accept excuses.

- *A reprimand should be consistently applied:* A hot stove burns anyone who touches it, and it does so every time.

- *A reprimand should be informative:* A hot stove lets a person know what to do to avoid getting burned in the future — "Don't touch."

- *A reprimand should occur in a supportive setting:* A hot stove conveys warmth but also operates with an inflexible rule — "Don't touch."

- *A reprimand should support realistic rules:* The don't-touch-a-hot-stove rule isn't a power play, a whim, or an emotion of the moment; it is a necessary rule of reason.

- **Discipline** is the act of influencing behavior through reprimand.

- **Progressive discipline** is the process of tying reprimands to the severity and frequency of misbehavior.

C & S Mystery Shoppers of North Brunswick, New Jersey, is in the control business. The firm's workers "shop" at the invitation of store executives who are interested in finding out how well they are doing. Mystery shoppers look for empty shelves, misplaced items, and service inadequacies. For a fee the firm's undercover shoppers give its customers, the store executives, the "shopper's view" of their operations.

addressed in employee discipline systems. **Discipline** can be defined as influencing behavior through reprimand. Ideally, this form of managerial control is handled in a fair, consistent, and systematic way.

Progressive discipline ties reprimands to the severity and frequency of the employee's infractions. Under such a system, penalties vary according to how significant a disruptive behavior is and how often it occurs. For example, the progressive discipline guidelines of one university state: "The level of disciplinary action shall increase with the level of severity of behavior engaged in and based on whether the conduct is of a repetitive nature." In this particular case, the ultimate penalty of "discharge" is reserved for the most severe behaviors (e.g., any felony crime) or for continual infractions of a less severe nature (e.g., being continually late for work and failing to respond to a series of written reprimands and/or suspensions).

The goal of a progressive discipline system is to achieve compliance with organizational expectations through the least extreme reprimand possible. But even this type of control can have unpleasant consequences. Sometimes the relationships between managers and disciplined workers take on an adversarial character. Sometimes managers wait too long and fail to take disciplinary action until a problem is very severe. And sometimes poor attitudes form among persons who can't seem to change and keep receiving ever-harsher punishments.[18]

One way to develop a consistent personal approach to disciplinary situations is to remember the analogy of the "hot stove rules" of discipline. They begin with a simple rule: "When a stove is hot, don't touch it." We also know that when this rule is violated, you get burned — immediately, consistently, but usually not beyond the possibility of repair. Six "hot stove rules" for using reprimands in disciplinary action are described in the accompanying *Manager's Notepad 9.1.*[19]

INFORMATION AND FINANCIAL CONTROLS

Budgets, as noted in Chapter 7 are plans that allocate resources to activities. When the utilization of resources is considered from the standpoint of managerial control, the use of information in financial analysis of firm or organizational performance is critical. The pressure is ever present today for all organizations to use their resources well and to perform with maximum efficiency. New developments include increased accounting attention to *activity-based costing,* which at-

Manager's Notepad 9.2
Popular Financial Ratios [with *preferred directions* ⇧ or ⇩]
Liquidity Ratios:
[⇧] Current ratio = Current assets/Current liabilities
[⇧] Acid test = (Current assets - inventory)/Current liabilities
Leverage Ratios:
[⇩] Debt ratio = Total debts/Total assets
[⇧] Times interest earned = Profits before interest and taxes/Total interest
Asset Management Ratios:
[⇧] Inventory turnover = Sales/Average inventory
[⇧] Total asset turnover = Sales/Total assets
Profitability Ratios:
[⇧] Net margin = Net profit after taxes/Sales
[⇧] Return on investment (ROI) = Net profit after taxes/Total assets

tempts to assign true costs to products and services in respect to resources consumed by all activities associated with their creation and accomplishment. They also include debate over the concept of *economic value added,* which attempts to measure financial performance by examining value added by all activities at the level of each job, work unit or business process.

Along with these directions, managers should also be able to understand and assess for control purposes the following important financial aspects of organizational performance: (1) *Liquidity* — ability to generate cash to pay bills; (2) *Leverage* — ability to earn more in returns than the cost of debt; (3) *Asset management* — ability to use resources efficiently and operate at minimum cost; and, (4) *Profitability* — ability to earn revenues greater than costs. These financial aspects of organizational performance can be assessed using a variety of financial ratios. Importantly, these ratios can be used to set goals and then tracked to provide for historical comparisons within the firm or in external benchmarking relative to industry performance. *Manager's Notepad 9.2* provides a brief summary of the most popular financial ratios used in the control process.

 ## OPERATIONS MANAGEMENT AND CONTROL

Control is an essential part of operations management, where the emphasis is always on utilizing people, resources, and technology to the best advantage. Among the important aspects of operations management, purchasing control, inventory control, project management and control, and statistical quality control all deserve attention.

PURCHASING CONTROL

In today's economy the rising costs of materials seem to be a fact of life. Controlling these costs through efficient purchasing management is an important productivity tool. Like an individual, a thrifty organization must be concerned about how much it pays for what it buys. Regarding the purchasing function, an AT&T vice president says, "Nothing we do is more important."[20] And at Nynex, now a part of

Bell Atlantic, a new head of purchasing attacked purchasing costs with dramatic results: The cost of copiers was cut by 50 percent by reducing the number of different models used from 40 to 7; the cost of printing was slashed 33 percent by contracting with a short list of suppliers; payment agent fees were reduced by 30 percent by revising the fee structure and contracting with just one supplier.[21]

Among the approaches now being tried to control the costs of purchases, the following trends seem evident. To *leverage buying power* more organizations are centralizing purchasing to allow buying in volume. They are committing to a *small number of suppliers* with whom they can negotiate special contracts, gain quality assurances, and get preferred service. They are also finding ways to work together in *supplier-purchaser partnerships* so they can operate in ways that allow each partner to contain its costs. An example is the relationship between Arrow Electronics, a New York-based parts supplier, and Bailey Controls, its Ohio-based customer. Arrow keeps a warehouse in Bailey's factory and stocks it according to Bailey's bimonthly order forecasts. Bailey provides the space; Arrow does the rest. Bailey lowers its purchasing costs and gains preferred service; Arrow gains an exclusive supplier contract and more sales volume.[22]

INVENTORY CONTROL

- **Inventory** consists of materials or products kept in storage.

Inventory is the amount of materials or products kept in storage. Organizations maintain inventories of raw materials, work in process, and/or finished goods. They keep these inventories to maintain flexibility in their production/operations processes, smooth out periods of excess or undercapacity, meet periods of unusual demand, and/or achieve economies from large-scale purchases. Because inventories represent major resource investments, they must be well managed. The basic principle of inventory control is to make sure that it is just the right size for the tasks at hand.

- The **economic order quantity (EOQ)** method orders a fixed number of items every time an inventory level falls to a predetermined point.

The **economic order quantity (EOQ)** is a method of inventory control that involves ordering a fixed number of items every time an inventory level falls to a predetermined point. When this point is reached, a decision is automatically made (more and more often now by computer) to place a standard order. The best example is the supermarket, where hundreds of daily orders are routinely made on this basis. These standard order sizes are mathematically calculated to

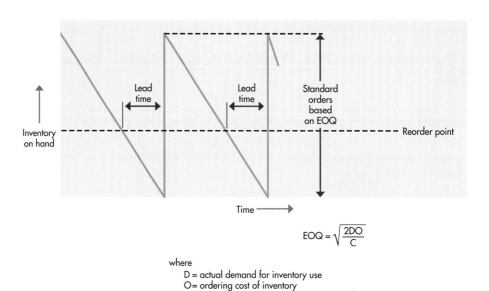

$$EOQ = \sqrt{\frac{2DO}{C}}$$

where
    D = actual demand for inventory use
    O = ordering cost of inventory
    C = carrying cost of inventory

Figure 9.4 Inventory control by economic order quantity (EOQ).

Manager's Notepad 9.3

Success Factors for JIT Systems

- *High quality of supplies:* Users must receive only *good* materials from suppliers. Relationships must be built and maintained with very dependable, high-quality suppliers.

- *Manageable supplier network:* A minimum number of suppliers is best. Most Japanese auto companies use fewer than 250 parts suppliers; General Motors uses many times that number.

- *Geographical concentration:* Relatively short transit times from supplier plants to customer plants — less than 1 day — are necessary. In Japan, most of Toyota's suppliers are located within 60 miles of its plants.

- *Efficient transportation and materials handling:* Transportation between suppliers and users must be reliable. Parts must be delivered as close as possible to points of use.

- *Strong management commitment:* Management must take the actions and make the arrangements needed to ensure that the system works.

---

minimize two costs of inventory. First, the *ordering costs* are the costs of placing an order, including the costs of communication, shipping, and receiving. Second, the *carrying costs,* or holding costs, include the costs of storing and insuring the items in inventory as well as any finance charges. *Figure 9.4* shows the cycle of orders and reorders characteristic of an EOQ-controlled inventory. The objective is always to have new inventory arrive just as old inventory runs out. This minimizes the total cost of the inventory.

Another approach to inventory control is **just-in-time scheduling** or "JIT." Made popular by the productivity of Japanese industry, JIT systems try to reduce costs and improve workflow by scheduling materials to arrive at a work station or facility "just in time" to be used. This minimizes carrying costs since almost no inventories are maintained — materials are ordered or components produced only as needed. *Kanban,* for example, is a Japanese word for the piece of paper that accompanies a bin of parts. When a worker first takes parts from a new bin, the *kanban* is routed back to the supplier and serves as an order for new parts.

> • **Just-in-time scheduling (JIT)** schedules materials to arrive at a work station or facility "just in time" to be used.

JIT systems not only reduce costs in many instances, they can also help to maximize the use of space and improve the quality of results. Richard J. Schonberger, the noted consultant in operations management, says that the just-in-time approach may be the most important productivity-enhancing management innovation since the turn of the century.[23] All this is true, he says, merely because the system allows production and purchasing to be done in small quantities and no earlier than necessary for use. *Manager's Notepad 9.3* points out that the just-in-time approach requires special support if it is to work right.

PROJECT MANAGEMENT AND CONTROL

The term *project* is used to describe a production task that involves a complex set of actions that must be accomplished in a particular sequence. An example would be the production of a nuclear submarine or the construction of an athletic stadium. **Project management,** in these and other settings, is the responsibility for making sure that various activities are completed on time, in the order specified, and with high quality.

> • **Project management** makes sure that all activities in a project are completed on time, in the order specified, and with high quality.

Among the techniques used to facilitate project management is the **program evaluation and review technique, PERT,** which identifies and controls the

> • The **program evaluation and review technique (PERT)** identifies and controls the many separate events in complex projects.

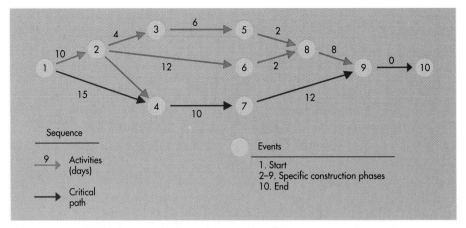

Figure 9.5 A PERT diagram showing the critical path for a construction project.

many separate events required to complete a project. The use of PERT diagrams, such as the one shown in *Figure 9.5,* is common in project management. The diagrams chart the relationships between various phases of a project, with key activities being identified according to anticipated time requirements. The model helps control a project by clearly identifying all required activities, the paths between them, and the due dates for their completion. It ensures that all activities on all paths get done in proper sequence and on time. The path requiring the longest time to accomplish is designated the *critical path* and it gets special attention in the control process. Any delays encountered in this path will lengthen the entire project and, most likely, increase costs. Computer software is now available to help managers utilize PERT schedules for even very complex projects.

STATISTICAL QUALITY CONTROL

The theme of total quality management has been with us since Chapter 1. In the context of control systems, **quality control** involves checking processes, materials, products, and services to ensure that they meet high standards. This responsibility applies to all aspects of production and operations, from the selection of raw materials and supplies right down to the last task performed on the finished good or service.

● **Quality control** involves checking processes, material, products, or services to ensure that they meet high standards.

Sun Microsystems posts plastic laminated instructions by each workstation used by temporary workers who fill in for fulltimers. The instructors help make sure that the work gets done the same way. This type of quality safeguard is typical in organizations that have ISO 9000 certification. Sun's worldwide operations vice president believes in the standard, which has become a requirement in the global marketplace. According to him, "Among ISO's strengths are that it requires you to do what you say you're going to do." One of the things ISO requires is the monitoring of customer complaints. Sun established an online system to track product defects found anywhere by an employee or customer. Sun now recommends that its own suppliers have ISO certification — just another form of quality assurance for this maker of network computer systems.[24]

Statistical quality control is the use of statistical techniques to improve operations quality. As an illustration, consider the case of an engine crankshaft for an automobile. These crankshafts are first molded and then machined to the correct dimensions. Because of variation in the parts, wear on the equipment, and/or differences in the skills of machine operators, not all crankshafts will have exactly the same dimensions after machining. That's not completely bad in itself because the crankshaft will still perform properly so long as its dimensions are within certain limits. For instance, the diameter at a certain point on a crankshaft should be 1.28 inches; the part will still function if the diameter is between 1.26 inches (the lower control limit) and 1.30 inches (the upper control limit).

The quality of these crankshafts might be checked by measuring each one as it is completed. If the diameter of a crankshaft is within the upper and lower control limits, it passes; otherwise, it fails and must be reworked. An occasional crankshaft falling outside the limits would not be cause for managerial concern; it would simply be rejected. However, several rejects might mean that the machining process is out of control and requires correction. This same control concept can be applied through statistical sampling. In such cases, instead of checking every part batches of a product or service are checked by taking a random sample from each. Because of the inherent difficulty of carefully inspecting every raw material input or product/service output, larger and more complex operations accomplish most quality control in this way.

It is often helpful to keep track of trends graphically, such as with the **control chart** in *Figure 9.6*. The basic purpose of a control chart is to display work results on a graph that clearly delineates *upper control limits (UCL)* and *lower control limits (LCL)*. A process is in or out of control depending on how well the results remain within these established limits. For example, the trend shown by the data in *Figure 9.6* indicates that the production process should be halted to reset or repair the machine in question or retrain the operator.

When statistics and quality come together in a systematic quality control program, great things can happen. At General Electric, for example, the firm's quest for competitive advantage in global markets is driven now by a program referred to as "Six Sigma."[25] Developed from benchmarking by GE executives of two firms known for their quality accomplishments — Motorola and Allied Signal, this program commits GE to always delivering quality goods within six standard deviations of a desired result. This means that statistically the firm's quality performance will tolerate no more than 3.4 defects per million — a perfection rate of 99.9997 percent! As tough as it sounds, that's the standard set for quality and control in the new workplace.

• **Statistical quality control** is the use of statistical techniques to assist in quality control.

• A **control chart** displays work results on a graph that shows upper and lower control limits (UCL and LCL).

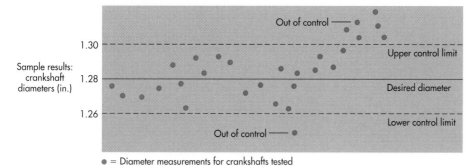

Sample results: crankshaft diameters (in.)

Out of control

1.30 — — — Upper control limit

1.28 — Desired diameter

1.26 — — — Lower control limit

Out of control

● = Diameter measurements for crankshafts tested

Figure 9.6   A sample control chart.

CHAPTER REVIEW

This section should be used as an end-of-chapter "study guide." The *Summary* helps to put the chapter's content into overall perspective. The list of *Key Terms* allows you to double-check your familiarity with basic concepts and definitions. *Self-Test 9* gives you the opportunity to test your basic comprehension of the chapter using sample test questions.

SUMMARY

What is the control process?

- Controlling — the fourth management function, is the process of monitoring performance and taking corrective action as needed.

- The four steps in the control process are (1) establish performance objectives, (2) measure actual performance, (3) compare results with objectives, and (4) take necessary action to resolve problems or explore opportunities.

- Control must be done well in order to have a positive impact on behavior in organizations; unintended consequences sometimes interfere with the control process.

- Effective controls will be results oriented, clear, fair, flexible, and timely and include a substantial opportunity for self-control.

What types of controls are used in organizations?

- Feedforward controls, also called preliminary controls, are accomplished before a work activity begins; they ensure that directions are clear and that the right resources are available to accomplish them.

- Concurrent controls, sometimes called steering controls, monitor ongoing operations and activities to make sure that things are being done correctly; they allow corrective actions to be taken while the work is being done.

- Feedback controls, also called postaction controls, take place after an action is completed and focus on end results; they address the question "Now that we are finished, how well did we do and what did we learn for the future?"

- External control is accomplished through personal supervision and the use of formal administrative systems.

- Internal control occurs through individuals taking personal responsibility for their work; it means that they exercise self-discipline in fulfilling job expectations and is consistent with many progressive developments in the new workplace.

How do organizational systems assist in control?

- Control through the management process is contributed when the management functions of planning, organizing, and leading are well implemented.

- An organization's compensation and benefits system assists in control by helping to attract and retain a high-quality workforce.

- Discipline, the process of influencing behavior through reprimand, is part of an organizational control system.

- Information and financial controls are essential in the control process, with useful financial ratios addressing liquidity leverage, asset management, and profitability.

How can operations management improve control?

- Effective operations management can improve the control of purchasing, inventories, projects, and product quality.

- The economic order quanity (EOQ) method controls inventories by ordering a fixed number of items every time the inventory level falls to a given point.

- Just-in-time scheduling (JIT) attempts to reduce costs and improve workflows by scheduling materials to arrive at a work station "just in time" to be used.

- Statistical quality control uses graphical and statistical methods to ensure that products and processes meet standards.

KEY TERMS

Concurrent control (p. 186)

Control chart (p. 195)

Controlling (p. 182)

Cybernetic control system (p. 183)

Discipline (p. 190)

Economic order quantity (p. 192)

External control (p. 187)

Feedback control (p. 187)

Feedforward control (p. 186)

Input standards (p. 183)

Internal control (p. 187)

Inventory (p. 192)

Just-in-time scheduling (JIT) (p. 193)

Management by exception (p. 184)

Output standards (p. 183)

Preliminary control (p. 186)

Program evaluation and review technique (PERT) (p. 193)

Progressive discipline (p. 190)

Project management (p. 193)

Quality control (p. 194)

Statistical quality control (p. 195)

SELF-TEST 9

Take this test much as you would in a normal classroom situation. It should offer you a good way to check your basic comprehension of chapter material. Answers may be found at the end of the book.

MULTIPLE-CHOICE QUESTIONS:

1. The management function of controlling is defined as the process of measuring performance and _____ to ensure desired results. (a) taking action (b) measuring accomplishments (c) giving directions (d) appraising performance

2. The first step in the control process is to _____. (a) measure actual performance (b) establish objectives and standards (c) compare results with objectives and standards (d) take necessary action

3. The practice of giving attention to situations showing the greatest need for action is called management by _____. (a) objectives (b) results (c) efficiency (d) exception

4. The control equation states that need for action = _____ − _____.
    (a) profits, losses (b) desired performance, actual performance (c) inputs, outputs
    (d) results, resources

5. To be effective, managerial controls should be _____. (a) rigid and inflexible
    (b) as complex as possible (c) strategic and results oriented (d) subjective

6. Good planning facilitates control by _____. (a) creating job designs and work
    structures (b) selecting and training employees (c) establishing policies and proce-
    dures (d) encouraging positive norms

7. The _____ method of inventory control orders a fixed number of items every
    time an inventory level falls to a predetermined point. (a) statistical control (b) carry-
    ing cost (c) ordering cost (d) economic order quantity (EOQ)

8. The Japanese word *kanban* is associated with the _____ method of inventory
    control. (a) PERT technique (b) statistical quality control (c) just-in-time (JIT) sched-
    uling (d) economic order quantity (EOQ)

9. A/an _____ displays work results on a graph that clearly delineates upper con-
    trol limits (UCL) and lower control limits (LCL). (a) economic order quantity (EOQ)
    (b) control chart (c) statistical process record (d) just-in-time (JIT) schedule

10. The financial ratio obtained by dividing current assets by current liabilities is called
    the _____. (a) acid test (b) liquidity ratio (c) current ratio (d) net margin

TRUE-FALSE QUESTIONS:

11. It can be said that the management function of controlling sees to it that the right
    things happen in the right way and at the right time. T F

12. Examples of input standards of control include the percentage error rate and the
    number of customers serviced in a time period. T F

13. The management function of control is concerned about "problems," but not "op-
    portunities." T F

14. At McDonald's, the ever-present shift leaders exercise concurrent control through
    direct supervision of workers as they prepare food and serve customers. T F

15. The internal control strategy that relies on motivated individuals to exercise self-
    discipline is important in today's workplace. T F

16. External controls include compensation and benefits systems as well as discipline
    systems. T F

17. Control can be improved by better organizing. T F

18. Because inventories are an essential requirement of any business, there is very little
    managers can do to control inventory costs. T F

19. Geographical concentration of suppliers is one of the requirements of an effective
    JIT system. T F

20. Statistical quality control can help in a total quality management (TQM) program. T F

SHORT-RESPONSE QUESTIONS:

21. What is the difference between feedforward controls and feedback controls?

22. How does McGregor's Theory Y relate to the concept of internal control?

23. How does a progressive discipline system work?

24. What is statistical quality control?

APPLICATION QUESTION:

25. In a luncheon conversation with a friend, you happen to mention that your organization is committed to just-in-time scheduling, or "JIT," as you refer to it. Your friend, a recent college graduate, isn't familiar with the concept and asks, "What is JIT and why should I be familiar with it?" How will you respond to the question?

Organizing – To Create Structures

Planning Ahead—Chapter 10 Study Questions

- What is organizing as a management function?
- What are the major types of organization structures?
- What are the new developments in organization structures?
- What organizing trends are changing the workplace?

Structures Must Support Strategies

Management scholar and consultant Peter Drucker calls the fast-growing brokerage firm Edward Jones "the Wal-Mart of Wall Street." He describes the firm as having an innovative structure that directly supports its strategy. The firm, like Wal-Mart, established itself in rural America. The structure is unique, with a strong core surrounded by largely independent satellite units. Drucker likens it to a "confederation of highly autonomous entrepreneurial units bound together by a highly centralized core of values and services." A values-driven commitment to the customer is a common bond between the entrepreneurial Edward Jones brokers, as is a focus on long-term investing and a safety-first orientation. Given that, the brokers have the freedom to deal with customers in their own way and in their small-town settings. The firm is now testing its face-to-face and customer-oriented brokerage strategy with expansion into the suburbs of large cities. Of course, it's a competitive business. Brokerage giant Merrill Lynch is starting a new push of its own—to open small brokerage offices in small rural towns.[1]

In the realm of what we might still call the traditional or pyramid form of organization, Edward Jones' approach — management through a strong central core surrounded by autonomous and entrepreneurial units — is a benchmark. By building a well-focused yet market-responsive structure, the firm has established and sustained a niche in the highly competitive financial services industry. A growing number of organizations in all industries are using a variety of new forms or structures in the quest for productivity and competitive advantage. Some are experimenting with non-traditional designs that we will discuss with respect to team, network, or boundaryless organizations. A key word is restructuring, and it is applied to management initiatives that involve downsizing, rightsizing, and delayering organizations in the search for productivity gains. Furthermore, among the vanguard organizations, those that outperform the rest, one also finds an emphasis on support for employees, responsiveness to client or customer needs, flexibility in dealing with a dynamic environment, and continual attention to quality improvements.[2] In these progressive organizations, the best managers are always seeking new ways to organize the workplace to achieve high performance and a high-quality work life.

ORGANIZING AS A MANAGEMENT FUNCTION

- **Organizing** is the process of arranging people and resources to work toward a common purpose.

Formally defined, **organizing** is the process of arranging people and other resources to work together to accomplish a goal. As one of the basic functions of management it involves both creating a division of labor for tasks to be performed and then coordinating results to achieve a common purpose. *Figure 10.1* shows the central role organizing plays in the management process. Once plans are created, the manager's task is to see to it that they are carried out. Given a clear mission, core values, objectives, and strategy, organizing begins the process of implementation by clarifying jobs and relationships. It identifies who is to do what, who is in charge of whom, and how different people and parts of the organization are related to one another. All of this, of course, can be done in different ways. The challenge is to choose the best form to fit the demands of a given situation.

WHAT IS ORGANIZATION STRUCTURE?

- **Organization structure** is a system of tasks, reporting relationships, and communication linkages.

The way in which the various parts of an organization are formally arranged is usually referred to as the **organization structure.** This is the system of tasks, workflows, reporting relationships, and communication channels that link together the work of diverse individuals and groups. Any structure should both al-

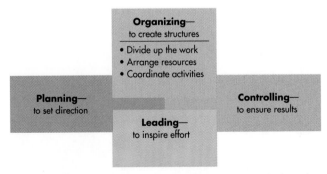

Figure 10.1   Organizing viewed in relationship with the other management functions.

Manager's Notepad 10.1
What You Can Learn from an Organization Chart
• *The division of work:* Positions and titles show work responsibilities.
• *Supervisory relationships:* Lines show who reports to whom.
• *Communication channels:* Lines show formal communication flows.
• *Major subunits:* Positions reporting to a common manager are shown.
• *Levels of management:* Vertical layers of management are shown.

locate task assignments through a division of labor and provide for the coordination of performance results. A good structure that does both of these things well can be an important asset to an organization.[3] Unfortunately, it is easier to talk about good structures than it is to actually create them. This is why you often read and hear about *restructuring.* This term refers to the process of changing an organization's structure in an attempt to improve performance. There is no one best structure that meets the needs of all circumstances. Structure must be addressed in a contingency fashion; as environments and situations change, structures must often be changed too. To make good choices, a manager must know the alternatives and be familiar with current trends and developments.

FORMAL STRUCTURE

You may know the concept of structure best in the form of an **organization chart.** This is a diagram that shows the formal arrangement of work positions within an organization.[4] A typical organization chart identifies various positions and job titles as well as the lines of authority and communication between them. This is the **formal structure,** or the structure of the organization in its official state. It represents the way the organization is intended to function. *Manager's Notepad 10.1* identifies some of the things that you can learn by reviewing an organization chart.

• An **organization chart** describes the basic arrangement of work positions within an organization.

• **Formal structure** is the official structure of the organization.

INFORMAL STRUCTURE

Behind every formal structure typically lies an **informal structure.** This is a "shadow" organization made up of the unofficial, but often critical, working relationships between organizational members. If the informal structure could be drawn, it would show who talks to and interacts regularly with whom regardless of their formal titles and relationships. The lines of the informal structure would cut across levels and move from side to side. They would show people meeting for coffee, exercise groups, and in friendship cliques, among other possibilities. Importantly, no organization can be fully understood without gaining insight into the informal structure as well as the formal one.[5]

It is important to recognize that informal structures can be very helpful in getting needed work accomplished in any organization. This is especially true during times of change when out-of-date formal structures may simply not provide the support people need to deal with new or unusual situations. And because it takes time to change or modify formal structures, this is a common situation. Through the emergent and spontaneous relationships of informal structures, people benefit by gaining access to interpersonal networks of emotional support and friendship that satisfy important social needs. They also benefit in task performance by being in personal contact with others who can help

• **Informal structure** is the set of unofficial relationships among an organization's members.

● **Informal learning** occurs as people interact informally throughout the work day.

them get things done when necessary. In fact, what is known as **informal learning** is increasingly recognized as an important resource for organizational development. This is learning that takes place as people interact informally throughout the work day and in a wide variety of unstructured situations.

When the Center for Workforce Development conducted a study at a Siemens factory in North Carolina, the focus was on informal learning. What they found was that the cafeteria was a "hotbed" of learning as workers shared ideas, problems, and solutions with one another over snacks and meals. Says the Director of Training for Siemens, Barry Blystone: "The assumption was made that this was chitchat, talking about the golf game. But there was a whole lot of work activity." For Blystone and others the lesson is to mobilize informal learning opportunities as a resource for organizational improvement.[6]

Of course, informal structures also have potential disadvantages. Because they exist outside the formal authority system, the activities of informal structures can sometimes work against the best interests of the organization as a whole. They can also be susceptible to rumor, carry inaccurate information, breed resistance to change, and even divert work efforts from important objectives. Also, "outsiders" or people who are left out of informal groupings may feel less a part of daily activities and suffer a loss of satisfaction. Some American managers of Japanese firms, for example, at times complain about being excluded from the "shadow cabinet." This is an informal group of Japanese executives who hold the real power to get things done in the firm and sometimes do so without the participation of others.[7]

 ## TRADITIONAL ORGANIZATION STRUCTURES

A traditional principle of organizing is that performance gains are possible when people are allowed to specialize and become expert in certain jobs or tasks. Given this division of labor, however, decisions must then be made on how to group work positions into formal teams or departments and then link them together in a coordinated fashion within the larger organization. These decisions involve a process called **departmentalization** and it has traditionally resulted in three major types of organizational structures — the functional, divisional, and matrix structures.[8]

● **Departmentalization** is the process of grouping together people and jobs into work units.

FUNCTIONAL STRUCTURES

● A **functional structure** groups together people with similar skills who perform similar tasks.

In **functional structures,** people with similar skills and performing similar tasks are formally grouped together. Members of functional departments share technical expertise, interests, and responsibilities. The example in *Figure 10.2* shows a common business structure, in this case with senior management arranged by the functions of marketing, finance, production, and human resources. In this functional structure, manufacturing problems are the responsibility of the production vice president, marketing problems are the province of the marketing vice presi-

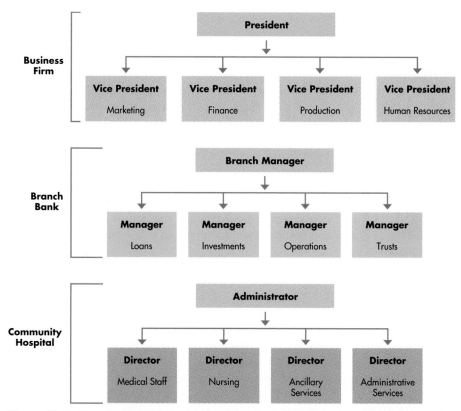

Figure 10.2 Functional structures in a business, branch bank, and community hospital.

dent, and so on. The key point is that members of each function work within their areas of expertise. If each function does its jobs properly, the expectation is that the business will operate successfully.

Functional structures are not limited to businesses. *Figure 10.2* also shows how this form of departmentalization can be used in other types of organizations such as banks and hospitals. These types of structures typically work well for small organizations that produce only one or a few products or services. They also tend to work best in relatively stable environments where problems are predictable and little demands for change and innovation occur. The major *advantages of a functional structure* include the following:

- Economies of scale with efficient use of resources.
- Task assignments consistent with expertise and training.
- High-quality technical problem solving.
- In-depth training and skill development within functions.
- Clear career paths within functions.

There are also *potential disadvantages of functional structures.* Foremost among these is something that is often called the **functional chimneys problem.** This refers to the lack of communication, coordination, and problem solving across functions. Because the functions become formalized not only on an organization chart but also in the mind-sets of people, the sense of cooperation and common purpose breaks down. When functional units develop self-centered and narrow viewpoints they lose the total system perspective. When problems occur with another unit, they are too often referred up to higher levels for resolution rather than being addressed at the level of action or operations. This slows decision making and problem solving and can result in a loss of advantage in competitive situations. Other problems with functional structures involve the possible

Advantages of functional structures

- The **functional chimneys problem** is a lack of communication and coordination across functions.

loss of clear responsibility for cost containment, product or service quality and timeliness, and innovation in response to environmental changes.

When Ford took over as the new owner of Jaguar, it had to resolve many quality problems. Although the "Jaguar" automobile enjoyed cachet, it had also developed a reputation for maintenance problems. The quality turnaround at Jaguar took longer than Ford anticipated, in part because of what Jaguar's chairman called "excessive compartmentalization." In building cars, the different departments did very little talking and working with one another. Ford's response was to push for more interdepartmental coordination, consensus decision making, and cost controls, an approach that is now paying off. [9]

DIVISIONAL STRUCTURES

● A **divisional structure** groups together people who work on the same product, work with similar customers, or who work in the same area or processes.

A second organizational alternative is the **divisional structure.** It groups together people who work on the same product or process, serve similar customers, and/or are located in the same area or geographical region. As illustrated in *Figure 10.3,* divisional structures are common in complex organizations that have multiple and differentiated products and services, pursue diversified strategies, and/or operate in various and different competitive environments.

Divisional structures attempt to avoid problems common to functional structures. They are especially popular among organizations with diverse operations that extend across many products, territories, customers and work processes.[10] The *potential advantages of divisional structures* include the following:

Advantages of divisional structures

● More flexibility in responding to environmental changes.
● Improved coordination across functional departments.

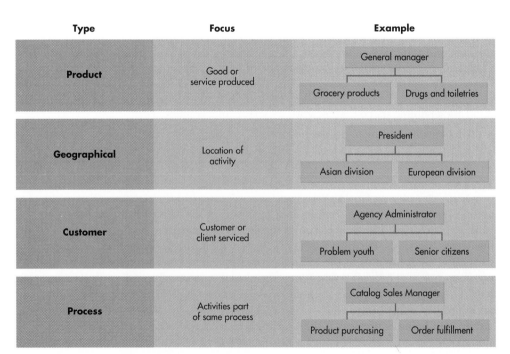

Figure 10.3   Divisional structures based on product, geography, customer, and process.

- Clear points of responsibility for product or service delivery.
- Expertise focused on specific customers, products, and regions.
- Greater ease in changing size by adding or deleting divisions.

As with other structural alternatives, however, divisional structures also have *potential disadvantages.* They can reduce economies of scale and increase costs through the duplication of resources and efforts across divisions. They can also create unhealthy rivalries as divisions compete for resources and attention, and as they emphasize division needs and goals to the detriment of the goals of the organization as a whole.

Product Structures

Product structures group together jobs and activities working on a single product or service. They clearly identify costs, profits, problems, and successes with a central point of accountability. Consequently, managers are encouraged to be responsive to changing market demands and customer tastes. Common in large organizations, product structures may even extend into global operations. At Worthington Industries, the corporate philosophy specifically addresses the advantage of performance accountability in this type of structure. It states: "We believe in a divisionalized organizational structure with responsibility for performance resting with the head of each operation."[11]

- A **product structure** groups together people and jobs working on a single product or service.

Geographical Structures

Geographical structures, sometimes called *area structures,* group together jobs and activities being performed in the same location or geographical region. They are typically used when there is a need to differentiate products or services in various locations, such as in different regions of a country. They are also quite common in international operations, where they help to focus attention on the unique cultures and requirements of particular regions.

- A **geographical structure** groups together people and jobs performed in the same location.

Customer Structures

Customer structures group together jobs and activities that are serving the same customers or clients. American Hospital Supply Corporation uses customer structures to give separate attention to its hospital and laboratory customers. Many business firms use them to give separate customer attention to industrial firms and consumers. Banks use them to give separate attention to consumer and commercial customers for loans. The example used in *Figure 10.3* is of a government agency serving different client populations. The major appeal of these structures is the ability to serve the special needs of the different customer groups.

- A **customer structure** groups together people and jobs that serve the same customers or clients.

Process Structures

A work **process** is a group of tasks related to one another that collectively create something of value to a customer.[12] An example is order fulfillment as when you telephone a catalog retailer and request a particular item. The process of order fulfillment takes the order from point of initiation to point of fulfillment. A **process structure** groups together jobs and activities that are part of the same processes. In the example of *Figure 10.3,* this might take the form of product purchasing teams, order fulfillment teams, and systems support teams for the mail-order catalog business.

- A **process** is a group of related tasks creating something of value to a customer.

- A **process structure** groups jobs and activities that are part of the same processes.

MATRIX STRUCTURES

● A **matrix structure** combines functional and divisional approaches to emphasize project or program teams.

The **matrix structure,** often called the *matrix organization,* is a combination of the functional and divisional structures just described. In effect, it is an attempt to gain the advantages of the two structures by using permanent cross-functional teams to integrate functional expertise with a divisional focus.[13] As shown in *Figure 10.4,* workers in a matrix structure belong to at least two formal groups at the same time — a functional group and a product, program, or project team. They also report to two bosses — one within the function and the other within the team.

The matrix organization has gained a strong foothold in the workplace, with applications in such diverse settings as manufacturing (e.g., aerospace, electronics, pharmaceuticals), service industries, (e.g., banking, brokerage, retailing), professional fields (e.g., accounting, advertising, law), and the nonprofit sector (e.g., city, state, and federal agencies, hospitals, universities).[14] Matrix structures are also found in multinational corporations, where they offer the flexibility to deal with regional differences as well as multiple product, program, or project needs. Matrix structures are common in organizations pursuing growth strategies in dynamic and complex environments.

The main contribution of matrix structures to organizational performance lies in the use of permanent cross-functional teams. Team members work closely together to share expertise and information in a timely manner to solve problems. The *potential advantages of matrix structures* include the following:

Advantages of a matrix structure

- Better interfunctional cooperation in operations and problem solving.
- Increased flexibility in adding, removing, and/or changing operations to meet changing demands.
- Better customer service since there is always a program, product, or project manager who is fully informed and available to answer questions.
- Better performance accountability through the program, product, or project managers.
- Improved decision making as problem solving takes place at the team level, where the best information is available.
- Improved strategic management since top managers are freed from unnecessary problem solving to focus time on strategic issues.

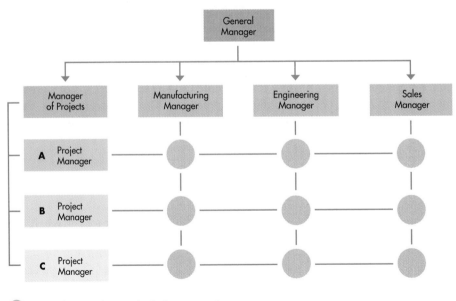

Functional personnel assigned to both projects and their respective functional departments

Figure 10.4 Matrix structure in a small multi-project business firm.

Predictably, the matrix structure also has *potential disadvantages*. The two-boss system is susceptible to power struggles, as functional supervisors and team leaders vie with one another to exercise authority. Members of the matrix may suffer task confusion when taking orders from more than one boss. Teams may develop "groupitis," or strong team loyalties that cause a loss of focus on larger organizational goals. And the requirements of adding the team leaders to a matrix structure can result in increased costs.[15]

DEVELOPMENTS IN ORGANIZATION STRUCTURES

The realities of a global economy and strategies driven by hyper-competition are putting increasing pressures on organizations. Managers everywhere are continually searching for structures that can meet the demands of environments that are ripe with complexity and constant change. Structural innovation is an important part of the search for productivity improvement and performance advantage in the workplace. New developments are emphasizing structures that promote integration and cross-functional teamwork and that take advantage of networking opportunities in an age of high technology.

TEAM STRUCTURES

In organizations that operate with **team structures,** both permanent and temporary teams are used extensively to accomplish tasks.[16] Importantly, these are often **cross-functional teams** composed of members from different areas of work responsibility.[17] The intention is to break down the functional chimneys or barriers and create more effective lateral relations for ongoing problem solving and work performance. As illustrated in *Figure 10.5,* a team structure involves teams of various types working together as needed to solve problems and explore opportunities, either on a full- or part-time basis.

Organizations like American Express, General Electric, and Ford, for example, are trying to utilize teams as basic building blocks of new organizational structures. They are dismantling more traditional vertical structures in favor of more horizontal ones.[18] They are doing so to avoid disadvantages common to functional and divisional approaches.

There are many *potential advantages of team structures.* They are frequently tried when an organization experiences difficulties with communication and decision making due to the functional chimneys problem earlier described. At the same time that team assignments help to break down barriers between op-

- A **team structure** uses permanent and temporary cross-functional teams to improve lateral relations.

- A **cross-functional team** brings together members from different functional departments.

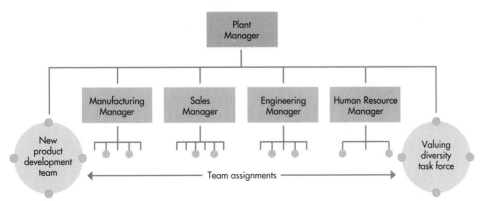

Figure 10.5   How a team structure uses cross-functional teams for improved lateral relations.

● **KPMG Peat Marwick LLP**
http://www.kpmg.com

The accounting and consulting giant KPMG Peat Marwick LLP abandoned a functional organization for an integrated team approach. Within industry-focused lines of business, regional areas have their own teams that draw upon both local and national information technology resources to serve customer needs.

● **A network structure** consists of a central business core that works with networks of outside suppliers and service contractors.

erating departments, they can also boost morale as people from different parts of an organization get to know more about one another. Because the teams focus shared knowledge and expertise on specific problems, they can also improve the speed and quality of decisions in many situations.

All organizational structures should harness the full talents of the workforce. However, in team structures this goal is pursued relentlessly and with full recognition of the value of group as well as individual contributions. Within teams and under the guidance of formal and informal leaders, individuals are expected to work together through cooperation, shared commitments to a common purpose, and consensus.[19] After a research team at Polaroid Corporation developed a new medical imaging system called Helios in 3 years, when most had predicted it would take 6, a senior executive said, "Our researchers are not any smarter, but by working together they get the value of each other's intelligence almost instantaneously."[20]

The complexities of teams and teamwork are discussed in Chapter 17. They contribute to the *potential disadvantages of team structures.* These include conflicting loyalties among members to both team and functional assignments. They also include issues of time management and group process. By their very nature, teams spend a lot of time in meetings. Not all of this time is productive. How well team members spend their time together often depends on the quality of interpersonal relations, group dynamics, and team management.

NETWORK STRUCTURES

Organizations using variations of the **network structure** operate with a central core that is linked through "networks" of relationships with outside contractors and suppliers of essential services. With the great advantages offered by communications and information technology today, new emphasis is being given to *boundaryless organizations* and *virtual corporations.*[21] These are network organizations that utilize the latest technologies while engaging in a shifting variety of strategic alliances and business contracts that sustain operations without the costs of "owning" all supporting functions.

June Holley, president of the Appalachian Center for Economic Networks (ACEnet), uses network organization concepts to support economic development in rural America. The Athens, Ohio, center serves as a networking hub for small businesses, "microenterprises," to come together to share expertise and connections in order to develop new business initiatives. ACEnet offers information and business incubator support, including a large community kitchen. Some 100 area farmers and entrepreneurs have so far rented kitchen space to test new products. As they cook, they rub elbows with one another. When Chris Chmiel started experimenting with a wild local fruit, pawpaws, he ended up talking with someone from the local Casa Nueva restaurant. Now the restaurant serves "pawpaw coladas." Networking works for ACEnet. Holley says that "poverty is due to isolation. So we set up a networking hub."[22]

Figure 10.6 illustrates a network structure as it might work for a mailorder company selling lawn and deck furniture through a catalog. The firm itself is very

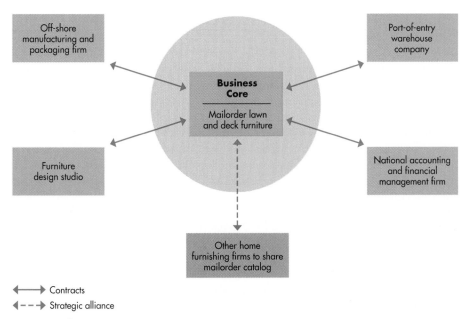

Figure 10.6 A network structure for a catalog-based retail business.

small, consisting of a relatively few full-time employees working from a central headquarters. Beyond that, it is structured as a series of business relationships. Merchandise is designed on contract with a furniture design firm; its manufacture and packaging are contracted to "off-shore" companies; stock is maintained and shipped from a contract warehouse; and all of the accounting and financial details are managed on contract with an outside firm. The quarterly catalog is designed, printed, and mailed as a strategic alliance with two other firms that sell different home furnishings with a related price appeal.

The creative use of technology adds to the *potential advantages of network structures.* With the technological edge the mailorder company can operate with fewer full-time employees and less complex internal systems. They can develop and maintain the linkages necessary to work with partners across great distances rather than face to face. Such arrangements are increasingly common in the international arena, where the Internet, Email, and other computer networks bring the advantages of global operations into easy reach at minimum cost. Networks can also help organizations stay cost competitive through reduced overhead and increased operating efficiency.

Within the operating core of a network structure, a variety of interesting jobs are created for those who must coordinate the entire "system" of relationships. In fact, the *potential disadvantages of network structures* largely lie with the demands of this responsibility. The more complex the business or mission of the organization, the more complicated the network of contracts and relationships that must be maintained. It may be difficult to control and coordinate between them. If one part of the network breaks down or fails to deliver, the entire system suffers the consequences.

As information technology continues to develop and as the concept of network structures becomes better understood, the future will very likely see such network structures grow in number and range of applications. They are great for smaller businesses and organizations, including entrepreneurial ones. They are also appropriate components in larger organizational structures. Many corporations, for example, are using network concepts internally as they contract out specialized business functions rather than maintain full-time staff to do them.[23] A bank may contract with local firms to provide mailroom, cafeteria, and legal services; an airline might contract out customer service jobs at various airports.

Intel is a major player in the dynamic computer chip industry. It is a fast-moving company, and it operates in a fast-moving environment. To stay ahead of its competitors, Intel relies on a team organization in which most workers are assigned to one or more projects under the direction of team leaders. The traditional hierarchy of organizations takes a back seat to the focus on team activities and project accomplishments. Team members feel responsible for meeting performance targets and act accordingly. Says one team member, "We report to each other."

ORGANIZING TRENDS IN THE MODERN WORKPLACE

Change is part of organizational life. Even as traditional structures are modified, refined, and abandoned in the search for new ones, the organizing practices that create and implement them must change too. In Chapter 1 the concept of the "upside-down pyramid" was introduced as an example of the new directions in management. By putting customers on top, served by workers in the middle, who are in turn supported by managers at the bottom, this notion tries to refocus attention on the marketplace and customer needs. Although more of a concept than a depiction of an organization structure, such thinking is representative of forces shaping new trends and directions in how the modern workplace is organized. Among the organizing trends to be discussed next, a common theme runs throughout—making the adjustments needed to streamline operations for cost efficiency and to allow increased participation by workers.

SHORTER CHAINS OF COMMAND

● The **chain of command** links all persons with successively higher levels of authority.

A typical organization chart shows the **chain of command,** or the line of authority that vertically links all persons with successively higher levels of management. The classical school of management suggested that the chain of command should operate according to the *scalar principle:* There should be a clear and unbroken chain of command linking every person in the organization with successively higher levels of authority up to and including the top manager.

When organizations grow in size they tend to get taller, as more and more levels of management are added to the chain of command. This increases overhead costs; it increases distance in communication, understanding, and access between top and bottom levels; it can greatly slow decision making; and it can lead to a loss of contact with the client or customer. These are all reasons why "tall" organizations with many levels of management are often criticized for inefficiencies and poor productivity. The current trend in organizing seeks to address this problem directly.

Current Trend Organizations are being "streamlined" by cutting unnecessary levels of management; flatter structures are viewed as a competitive advantage.

Nucor Corp., for example, is a successful "mini-mill" steel company with a reputation for cost efficiency and streamlined management. Under the leadership of Chairman F. Kenneth Iverson, the firm operates with a minimum of staff; Iverson's philosophy is to put daily decision making into the hands of operating people. Larger steel companies typically have eight or nine "levels" of management; Nucor operates with half as many with close to 7000 employees. "I'm a firm believer in having the fewest number of management levels and in delegating authority to the lowest level possible," says Iverson. This includes an emphasis on decentralization, with plant managers given substantial operating autonomy. Iverson doesn't believe in corporate jets, company cars, reserved parking spaces, or executive dining rooms either. Says Iverson, "We're trying to get our employees to feel they're a real part of the company and that what they do makes the company successful. . . . We've tried to eliminate any differences between management and the rest of our employees."[24]

LESS UNITY OF COMMAND

Another classical management principle describes how the chain of command should operate in daily practice. The *unity-of-command principle* states that each person in an organization should report to one and only one supervisor. This notion of one person/one boss is a foundation of the traditional pyramid form of organization. It is intended to avoid the confusion potentially created when a person gets work directions from more than one source. Unity of command is supposed to ensure that everyone clearly understands assignments and does not get conflicting instructions. It is violated, for example, when a senior manager bypasses someone's immediate supervisor to give him or her orders. This can create confusion for the subordinate and also undermine the supervisor's authority.

The "two-boss" system of matrix structure is a clear violation of unity of command. Whereas the classical advice is to avoid creating multiple reporting relationships, the matrix concept creates them by design. It does so in an attempt to improve lateral relations and teamwork in special programs or projects. Unity of command is also less predominant in the team structure and in other arrangements that emphasize the use of cross-functional teams or task forces. Clearly, the current trend is for less, not more, unity of command in organizations.

Current Trend Organizations are using more cross-functional teams, task forces, and horizontal structures, and they are becoming more customer conscious; as they do so, employees often find themselves working for more than one "boss."

WIDER SPANS OF CONTROL

The **span of control** is the number of persons reporting directly to a manager. When span of control is "narrow," only a few people are under a manager's immediate supervision; a "wide" span of control indicates that the manager supervises many people. There was a time in the history of management thought when people searched for the ideal span of control. Although the magic number was never found, this *span-of-control principle* evolved: There is a limit to the number of people one manager can effectively supervise; care should be exercised to keep the span of control within manageable limits.

Figure 10.7 shows the relationship between span of control and the number of levels in the hierarchy of authority. Organizations with wider spans of control tend to be flat — they have few levels of management; those with narrow spans of

> ● **Span of control** is the number of subordinates reporting directly to a manager.

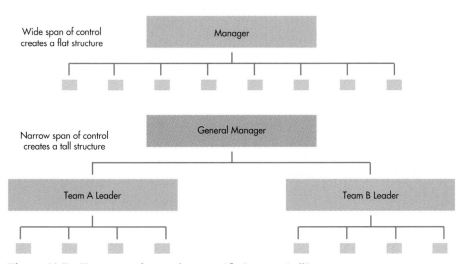

Figure 10.7 How span of control creates "flat" versus "tall" structures.

• **Delegation** is the process of distributing and entrusting work to other persons.

When H. J. Heinz's new CEO, William Johnson, became concerned about the company's international performance he decided to change the structure. The former structure, which emphasized countries and regions, was changed to global product divisions. Johnson believes this structure will bring the best brand management to all countries and increase cooperation around the world within product businesses.

control tend to be tall — they have many levels of management. Because tall organizations have more managers, they are more costly. They are also generally viewed as less efficient, less flexible, and less customer sensitive than flat organizations. Before making spans of control smaller, therefore, serious thought should always be given to both the cost of the added management overhead and the potential disadvantages of lengthening the chain of command. When spans of control are increased, by contrast, overhead costs are reduced, and workers may benefit from less direct supervision and more independence.[25] The trend today is clear.

Current Trend Many organizations are shifting to wider spans of control as chains of command are shortened and "empowerment" gains prominence; individual managers are taking responsibility for larger numbers of subordinates who operate with less direct supervision.

MORE DELEGATION AND EMPOWERMENT

All managers must decide what work they should do themselves and what should be left for others. At issue here is **delegation** — the process of distributing and entrusting work to other persons. There are three steps to delegation. In *step 1, the manager assigns responsibility* by carefully explaining the work or duties someone else is expected to do. This responsibility is an expectation for the other person to perform assigned tasks. In *step 2, the manager grants authority to act.* Along with the assigned task, the right to take necessary actions (for example, to spend money, direct the work of others, use resources) is given to the other person. Authority is a right to act in ways needed to carry out the assigned tasks. In *step 3, the manager creates accountability.* By accepting an assignment, the person takes on a direct obligation to the manager to complete the job as agreed upon. This is accountability, originally defined in Chapter 1 as the requirement to answer to a higher level manager for performance results.

A classical principle of organization warns managers not to delegate without giving the subordinate sufficient authority to perform. When insufficient authority is delegated, it will be very hard for the subordinate to live up to performance expectations. They simply don't have the authority needed to get the job done. The *authority-and-responsibility principle* states: Authority should equal responsibility when work is delegated from a supervisor to a subordinate. Useful guidelines for delegating are offered in *Manager's Notepad 10.2.*[26]

M a n a g e r ' s   N o t e p a d   1 0 . 2
Ground Rules for Effective Delegation
• Carefully choose the person to whom you delegate.
• Define the responsibility; make the assignment clear.
• Agree on performance objectives and standards.
• Agree on a performance timetable.
• Give authority; allow the other person to act independently.
• Show trust in the other person.
• Provide performance support.
• Give performance feedback.
• Recognize and reinforce progress.
• Help when things go wrong.
• Don't forget *your* accountability for performance results.

A common management failure is unwillingness to delegate. Whether due to a lack of trust in others or to a manager's inflexibility in the way things get done, failure to delegate can be damaging. It overloads the manager with work that could be done by others; it also denies others many opportunities to fully utilize their talents on the job. When done well, by contrast, delegation leads to empowerment, in that people have the freedom to contribute ideas and do their jobs in the best possible ways. This involvement can increase job satisfaction for the individual and frequently results in better job performance.

Current Trend Managers in progressive organizations are delegating more and finding more ways to empower people at all levels so they can make more decisions affecting themselves and their work.

DECENTRALIZATION WITH CENTRALIZATION

A question frequently asked by managers is "Should most decisions be made at the top levels of an organization, or should they be dispersed by extensive delegation throughout all levels of management?" The former approach is referred to as **centralization;** the latter is called **decentralization.** There is no classical principle on centralization and decentralization. The traditional pyramid form of organization may give the impression of being a highly centralized structure, and to be sure decentralization is characteristic of newer structures and many recent organizing trends. But the issue doesn't have to be framed as an "either/or" choice. Today's organizations can operate with greater decentralization without giving up centralized control. This is facilitated by developments in information technology.

- **Centralization** is the concentration of authority for most decisions at the top level of an organization.

- **Decentralization** is the dispersion of authority to make decisions throughout all levels of the organization.

With computer networks and advanced information systems managers at higher levels can more easily stay informed about a wide range of day-to-day performance matters. Because they have information on results readily available, they can allow more decentralization in decision making.[27] If something goes wrong, presumably the information systems will sound an alarm and allow corrective action to be taken quickly. At BancOne, Inc., for example, the demands of growth and an expanding geographical base have not blurred the lines of authority and accountability. Individual banks in geographically dispersed locations are closely monitored for performance results. With the guiding theme of "centralizing paper and decentralizing people," BancOne has decentralized its branch bank operations while retaining central control.[28]

Current Trend Whereas empowerment and related forces are contributing to more decentralization in organizations, advances in information technology simultaneously allow for the retention of centralized control.

REDUCED USE OF STAFF

When it comes to coordination and control in organizations, the issue of line-staff relationships is important. Chapter 1 described the role of staff as providing expert advice and guidance to line personnel. This can help ensure that performance standards are maintained in areas of staff expertise. **Specialized staff** perform a technical service or provide special problem-solving expertise for other parts of the organization. This could be a single person, such as a corporate safety director, or a complete unit, such as a corporate safety department. Many organizations rely on staff specialists to maintain coordination and control over a variety of matters. In a large retail chain, such as Kmart or J.C. Penney, line managers in each store make daily operating decisions regarding direct sales of merchandise. But staff specialists at the corporate or regional levels provide direction

- **Specialized staff** provide technical expertise for other parts of the organization.

and support so that all the stores operate with the same credit, purchasing, employment, and advertising procedures.

- **Personal staff** are "assistant-to" positions that support senior managers.

Delta Airlines
http://www.delta-air.com

When Leo F. Mullin became CEO of Delta Airlines he took steps to restore the airline's reputation and performance. Rebuilding began at once and with a new focus on employees. Mullin met with workers all over the system to gather ideas and rebuild morale and started decentralizing. His goal is to give managers more day-to-day decision-making power to speed problem solving and improve service.

Organizations may also employ **personal staff,** individuals appointed in "assistant-to" positions with the purpose of providing special support to higher level managers. Such assistants help by following up on administrative details and performing other duties as assigned. They can benefit also in terms of career development through the mentoring relationships that such assignments offer. An organization, for example, might select promising junior managers as temporary administrative assistants to senior managers. This helps them gain valuable experience at the same time that they are facilitating the work of executives.[29]

Problems in line-staff distinctions can and do arise. In too many cases, organizations find that the staff grows to the point where it costs more in administrative overhead than it is worth. This is why staff cutbacks are common in downsizing and other turnaround efforts. There are also cases where conflicts in line-staff relationships cause difficulties. This often occurs when line and staff managers disagree over the extent of staff authority. At the one extreme, staff has purely *advisory authority* and can "suggest" but not "dictate." At the other extreme, it has *functional authority* to actually "require" that others do as requested within the boundaries of staff expertise. For example, a human resource department may advise line managers on the desired qualifications of new workers when hiring (advisory authority); the department may require the managers to follow equal-employment-opportunity hiring guidelines (functional authority).

There is no one best solution to the problem of how to divide work between line and staff responsibilities. What is best for any organization will be a cost-effective staff component that satisfies, but doesn't overreact to, needs for specialized technical assistance to line operations. The current trend is toward minimal use of staff as organizations are being restructured to increase productivity and reduce staff costs.

Current Trend Organizations are reducing the size of staff; they are seeking increased operating efficiency by employing fewer staff personnel and using smaller staff units.

CHAPTER REVIEW

This section should be used as an end-of-chapter "study guide." The *Summary* helps to put the chapter's content into overall perspective. The list of *Key Terms* allows you to double-check your familiarity with basic concepts and definitions. *Self-Test 10* gives you the opportunity to test your basic comprehension of the chapter using sample test questions.

SUMMARY

What is organizing as a management function?

- Organizing is the process of creating work arrangements of people and resources, be it for a small unit, a large division, or an entire enterprise.

- To organize a work setting, decisions must be made about how to divide up the work that needs to be done, allocate people and resources to do it, and coordinate results to achieve productivity.

- Structure is the system of tasks, reporting relationships, and communication that links together the people and positions within an organization.

- Formal structure, such as shown on an organization chart, describes how an organization is supposed to work.

- The informal structure of organization consisting of the unofficial working relationships among members.

What are the major types of organization structures?

- Departmentalization is the process of creating structure by grouping people together in formal work units or teams.

- In functional structures, people with similar skills who perform similar activities work together under a common manager.

- In divisional structures, people who work on a similar product, work in the same geographical region, serve the same customers, or participate in the same work process are grouped together under common managers.

- A matrix structure combines the functional and divisional approaches to create permanent cross-functional project teams.

What are the new developments in organization structures?

- Increasing complexity and greater rates of change in the environment are challenging the performance capabilities of traditional organization structures.

- New developments include the growing use of team structures that create horizontal organizations using cross-functional teams and task forces to improve lateral relations and improve problem solving at all levels.

- New developments are also underway in respect to network structures, sometimes called boundaryless or virtual organizations, that cluster systems of contracted services and strategic alliances around a "core" business or organizational center.

What organizing trends are changing the workplace?

- Traditional vertical command-and-control structures are giving way to more horizontal structures strong on employee involvement and flexibility.

- Many organizations today are operating with shorter chains of command and less unity of command.

- Many organizations today are operating with wider spans of control and fewer levels of management.

- The emphasis in more organizations today is on effective delegation and empowerment.

- Advances in information technology are making it possible to operate with decentralization while still maintaining centralized control.

- Reduction in the size of staff is a trend in organizations seeking greater efficiency and productivity.

KEY TERMS

Centralization (p. 217)

Chain of command (p. 214)

Cross-functional teams (p. 211)

Customer structure (p. 209)

Decentralization (p. 217)

Delegation (p. 216)

Departmentalization (p. 206)

Divisional structure (p. 208)

Formal structure (p. 205)

Functional chimneys problem (p. 207)

Functional structure (p. 206)

Geographical structure (p. 209)

Informal learning (p. 206)

Informal structure (p. 205)

Matrix structure (p. 210)

Network structure (p. 212)

Organization chart (p. 205)

Organization structure (p. 204)

Organizing (p. 204)

Personal staff (p. 218)

Process (p. 209)

Process structure (p. 209)

Product structure (p. 209)

Span of control (p. 215)

Specialized staff (p. 217)

Team structure (p. 211)

SELF-TEST 10

Take this test much as you would in a normal classroom situation. It should offer you a good way to check your basic comprehension of chapter material. Answers may be found at the end of the book.

MULTIPLE-CHOICE QUESTIONS:

1. _____ is the system of communication and authority that links together the various parts of an organization. (a) Structure (b) Empowerment (c) Decentralization (d) Differentiation

2. An organization chart shows the _____ structure of an organization. (a) personal (b) impersonal (c) formal (d) informal

3. Good organizing _____. (a) clarifies who is supposed to do what (b) identifies who is in charge of whom (c) establishes official channels of communication (d) all of these

4. An organization chart showing vice presidents of marketing, finance, manufacturing, and purchasing all reporting to the president is depicting a _____ structure. (a) functional (b) matrix (c) network (d) product

5. The "two boss" system of reporting relationships is found in the _____ structure. (a) functional (b) matrix (c) geographical (d) product

6. A manufacturing business with a functional structure has recently developed two new product lines. The president of the company might consider shifting to a _____ structure to gain a stronger product focus for operations. (a) functional (b) matrix (c) divisional (d) network

7. Better lower level teamwork and more top-level strategic management are among the expected advantages in a _____ structure. (a) divisional (b) matrix (c) geographical (d) product

8. "Tall" organizations tend to have long chains of command and _____ spans of control. (a) wide (b) narrow (c) informal (d) centralized

9. The unity-of-command principle is intentionally violated in the _____ structure.
   (a) divisional (b) matrix (c) geographical (d) product

10. In delegation, _____ is the right of a subordinate to act in ways needed to carry out the assigned tasks. (a) authority (b) responsibility (c) accountability (d) centrality

TRUE-FALSE QUESTIONS:

11. Organizing is the most important management function. T F

12. Managers should not waste their time trying to understand informal structures in their organizations. T F

13. A matrix structure is a combination of the functional and divisional structures. T F

14. A process structure is the same thing as a customer structure. T F

15. A potential disadvantage of the divisional structure is that divisions will become self-centered and lose focus on organizationwide goals. T F

16. The use of teams and cross-functional task forces is the central element in the virtual corporation. T F

17. Organizations cannot operate with both centralization and decentralization. T F

18. Many organizations today are finding that a large staff component increases productivity. T F

19. Empowerment is a desired outcome of delegation. T F

20. A wider span of control for the manager can mean greater job autonomy for the subordinates. T F

SHORT-RESPONSE QUESTIONS:

21. What is the difference between a product divisional structure and a geographical or area division structure?

22. What are some of the symptoms that might indicate a functional structure is causing problems for the organization?

23. Explain by example the concept of a network organization structure.

24. What positive results might be expected when levels of management are reduced and the chain of command shortened in an organization?

APPLICATION QUESTION:

25. Faisal Sham supervises a group of seven project engineers. His unit is experiencing a heavy workload as the demand for different versions of one of his firm's computer components is growing. Faisal finds that he doesn't have time to follow up on all design details for each version. Up until now he has tried to do this all by himself. Two of the engineers have shown interest in helping him coordinate work on the various designs. As a consultant, what would you advise Faisal in terms of delegating work to them?

CHAPTER ELEVEN

Organizational Design and Work Processes

Planning Ahead—Chapter 11 Study Questions

- What are the essentials of organizational design?
- How do contingency factors influence organization design?
- What are the major issues in subsystems design?
- How can work processes be reengineered?
- How is operations technology influencing design?

Design for Integration and Empowerment

Fortune magazine calls Nestle a "Swiss powerhouse . . . racing across the developing world, building roads, farms, factories, and whatever else it needs to capture new markets." The largest branded food company in the world, Nestle, is a truly global company still looking for opportunities. The firm pursues growth by adapting its strategies to fit regional conditions and by allowing managers autonomy to pursue opportunities specific to their countries and regions. The company is building a strong cadre of local managers who transfer around regions and continuously share new ideas for improved operations. Nestle Thailand's "Red Hot Sales Force" operates with self-management ideas gained at the firm's Switzerland training center and uses a high-tech inventory control system.[1]

Like Nestle, many organizations are changing and adapting their structures to best meet competitive demands. They seek improved teamwork, more creativity, shorter product development cycles, better customer service, and higher productivity overall. Changing times require more flexible and well-integrated organizations that can deliver high-quality products and services while still innovating for sustained future performance. We already know that team structures and network organizations are gaining in popularity.[2] Yet organizations face widely varying problems and opportunities, and there is no one best way to structure and manage them. The key to success is finding the best design to master the unique situational needs and challenges for each organization.[3]

ORGANIZATIONAL DESIGN ESSENTIALS

● **Organizational design** is the process of creating structures that best organize resources to serve mission and objectives.

Organizational design is the process of choosing and implementing structures that best arrange resources to serve the organization's mission and objectives.[4] The ultimate purpose of organizational design is to put into place structures that facilitate the implementation of strategies. Importantly, the process of organizational design is a problem-solving activity that should be approached in a *contingency* fashion. That is, structures must be designed to fit the unique needs of an organization or subunit.

DIRECTIONS FOR CHANGE

Change is the ever-present fact of life in organizations today.[5] The various trends in organization and management practices that were described in the last chapter are resulting in fundamental changes in the way organizations are designed and operated. As these trends make their way into the operations of organizations, one finds more sharing of tasks, reduced emphasis on hierarchy, greater emphasis on lateral communication, more teamwork, and more decentralization of decision making and empowerment.

The virtual organization is reality at Rickard Group, Inc., which was founded by Wendy Rickard to produce magazines, collateral materials, web sites, videos, and marketing plans. The only people going to work in the Victorian house that serves as corporate headquarters are Wendy and two staff members. The Internet and on-line computer services allow Rickard to interact electronically with art directors, designers, and technical associates around the country. Her latest venture makes ultimate sense—publishing the magazine on the Internet.

A unique example is provided by the directions being set at a new London-based advertising agency, St. Luke's. If you look at the firm's stationery you will see everyone's name listed — right from the creative director to receptionist. The focus is on achieving creativity and work space is designed so that everyone shares common areas to maximize interaction and connectivity. The culture is informal; each of the 35 employees is a part owner; a six-member board elected by staff members overseas the company. Everyone focuses on great service to customers. One member of the firm describes working there as like "the difference between going to grade school and going to the university. At school the bell goes 'ding' and tells you what to do. We have no bell. Like the university, as long as you create great stuff, we don't care how you do it."[6]

As suggested in the example, key directions for changes in organizations today involve a basic shift in attention away from a traditional emphasis on more vertical or authority-driven structures to ones that are more horizontal and task-driven. In management theory, these developments are framed by an important distinction between bureaucratic designs that are mechanistic and vertical in nature, and adaptive designs that are more organic and horizontal in nature.

BUREAUCRATIC DESIGNS

As introduced in Chapter 4, a *bureaucracy* is a form of organization based on logic, order, and the legitimate use of formal authority. Originally described by sociologist Max Weber as "ideal" organizational forms, bureaucracies are supposed to be orderly, fair, and highly efficient.[7] Their features include a clear-cut division of labor, strict hierarchy of authority, formal rules and procedures, and promotion based on competency. However, many people view them in a negative sense, and today we recognize that there are limits to bureaucracy.[8] If organizations rely too much on rules and procedures, they become unwieldy and too rigid. This makes them slow in responding to changing environments.

Instead of viewing all bureaucratic structures as inevitably flawed, however, management theory takes a contingency perspective and asks these critical questions: When is a bureaucratic form a good choice for an organization? What alternatives exist when it is not a good choice? A basis for answering these questions lies in research conducted in England during the early 1960s by Tom Burns and George Stalker.[9]

After investigating 20 manufacturing firms, Burns and Stalker concluded that two quite different organizational forms could be successful, depending on the nature of a firm's external environment. A more bureaucratic form, which Burns and Stalker called "mechanistic," thrived when the environment was stable. It experienced difficulty when the environment was rapidly changing and uncertain. In dynamic situations, a much less bureaucratic form, called "organic," performed best. *Figure 11.1* portrays these two approaches as opposite extremes on a continuum of organizational design alternatives.

Mechanistic designs are highly bureaucratic in nature. As shown in *Figure 11.1,* they typically operate with more centralized authority, many rules and procedures, a precise division of labor, narrow spans of control, and formal means of coordination. Mechanistic designs are described as "tight" structures of the traditional "pyramid" form.[10] An example is your local McDonald's restaurant. A relatively small operation, each store operates quite like every other and under the close guidance of corporate management. Local personnel work in orderly and disciplined ways, guided by the many rules and procedures. Crew leaders in special uniforms work alongside counter personnel and cooks, each of whom knows exactly what to do but always does it under the watchful eye of a supervisor.[11]

> • A **mechanistic design** is highly bureaucratic, with centralized authority, many rules and procedures, a clear-cut division of labor, narrow spans of control, and formal coordination.

ADAPTIVE DESIGNS

In many settings, the limits of bureaucracy are increasingly apparent, and adjustments in organizational design are being made. Enlightened managers are helping

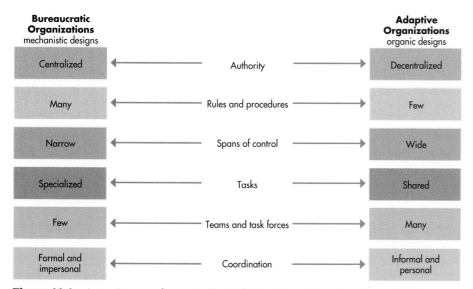

Figure 11.1 A continuum of organizational design alternatives: from bureaucratic to adaptive organizations.

organizations reconfigure into new forms that emphasize flexibility and speed, without losing sight of important performance objectives. In her book *The Change Masters,* Rosabeth Moss Kanter notes that the ability to respond quickly to shifting challenges in today's rapidly changing environment often distinguishes successful organizations from less successful ones. Specifically, Kanter states,

> The organizations now emerging as successful will be, above all, flexible; they will need to be able to bring particular resources together quickly, on the basis of short-term recognition of new requirements and the necessary capacities to deal with them. . . . The balance between static plans — which appear to reduce the need for effective reaction — and structural flexibility needs to shift toward the latter.[12]

"It's a millennial change," says Dee Hock the founder of Visa International. "We can't run 21st-century society with 17th century notions of organization." What Hock is referring to is the growing emphasis on what some call "self-organization." These are organizations in which employees are given the freedom to do what they can do best — get the job done. The focus in self-organization is to free otherwise capable people from unnecessarily centralized control and restrictions. It means letting workers take over production scheduling and problem solving; it means letting workers set up their own control techniques; it means letting workers use their ideas to improve customer service. Above all, adaptive organizations are built upon trusting that people will do the right things on their own initiative. [13]

● An **adaptive organization** operates with a minimum of bureaucratic features and encourages worker empowerment and teamwork.

● An **organic design** is decentralized with fewer rules and procedures, more open divisions of labor, wide spans of control, and more personal coordination.

The organizational design trend is now toward more **adaptive organizations** that operate with a minimum of bureaucratic features and with cultures that encourage worker empowerment and participation.[14] They display features of the **organic designs** portrayed in *Figure 11.1,* including more decentralized authority, fewer rules and procedures, less precise division of labor, wider spans of control, and more personal means of coordination. They are described as relatively loose systems in which a lot of work gets done through informal structures and networks of interpersonal contacts.[15] Organic designs recognize and legitimate these linkages and give them the resources they need to operate best. This works well for organizations facing dynamic environments that demand flexibility in dealing with changing conditions. They are also increasingly popular in the new workplace, where the demands of total quality management (TQM) and competitive advantage place more emphasis on internal teamwork and responsiveness to customers.

CONTINGENCIES IN ORGANIZATIONAL DESIGN

Good organizational design decisions should result in supportive structures that satisfy situational demands and allow all resources to be used to best advantage. This is true contingency thinking. Among the contingency factors that should receive managerial attention (see *Manager's Notepad 11.1*) are the environment, strategy, technology, size and life cycle, and human resources.

Manager's Notepad 11.1

Organizational Design Checklist

Check 1: Does the design fit well with the major problems and opportunities of the external environment?

Check 2: Does the design support the implementation of strategies and the accomplishment of key operating objectives?

Check 3: Does the design support core technologies and allow them to be used to best advantage?

Check 4: Can the design handle changes in organizational size and different stages in the organizational life cycle?

Check 5: Does the design support and empower workers and allow their talents to be used to best advantage?

ENVIRONMENT

The organization's external environment and the degree of uncertainty it offers are of undeniable importance in organizational design.[16] A *certain environment* is composed of relatively stable and predictable elements. As a result, an organization can succeed with relatively few changes in the goods or services produced or in the manner of production over time. Bureaucratic organizations and mechanistic designs are quite adequate under such conditions. An *uncertain environment* will have more dynamic and less predictable elements. Changes occur frequently and may catch decision makers by surprise. As a result, organizations must be flexible and responsive over relatively short time horizons. This requires more adaptive organizations and organic designs. *Figure 11.2* summarizes these relationships, showing how increasing uncertainty in organizational environments calls for more horizontal and adaptive designs.

STRATEGY

The nature of organizational strategies and objectives should influence the choice of structure. Research on these contingency relationships is often traced to the pioneering work of Alfred Chandler Jr., who analyzed the histories of DuPont, General Motors, Sears, and Standard Oil of New Jersey in depth.[17] Chandler's conclusion that "structure follows strategy" is an important premise of organizational design. An organization's structure must support its strategy if the desired results are to be achieved.[18]

When strategy is stability oriented, the choice of this structure should be based on the premise that little significant change will be occurring in the exter-

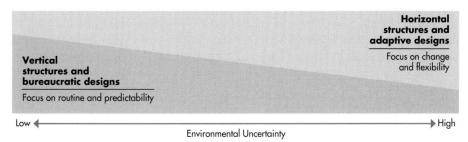

Horizontal structures and adaptive designs

Focus on change and flexibility

Vertical structures and bureaucratic designs

Focus on routine and predictability

Low ← Environmental Uncertainty → High

Figure 11.2 Influences of environmental uncertainty on organizational design.

nal environment. It also means that operations and plans can be programmed and implemented routinely. To best support this strategic approach, the organization's structure must be well defined and predictable. This is most typically found in bureaucratic organizations using more mechanistic design alternatives.

When strategy is growth oriented, the situation as a whole becomes more complex, fluid, and uncertain. Operating objectives are likely to include the need for innovation and flexible responses to changing competition in the environment. Operations and plans are likely to require considerable change over time. The most appropriate structure is one that can facilitate and support the inevitable modifications. This will likely require more decentralization as is found in adaptive organizations using more organic design alternatives.

TECHNOLOGY

- **Technology** is the combination of equipment, knowledge, and work methods that transforms inputs into outputs.

- **Small-batch production** manufactures a variety of products crafted to fit customer specifications.

- **Mass production** manufactures a large number of uniform products with an assembly-line type of system.

- In **continuous-process production** raw production materials continuously move through an automated system.

- **Intensive technology** focuses the efforts and talents of many people to serve clients.

- **Mediating technology** links together people in a beneficial exchange of values.

- In **long-linked technology** a client moves from point to point during service delivery.

Technology is the combination of knowledge, equipment, and work methods used to transform resource inputs into organizational outputs. It is the way tasks are accomplished using tools, equipment, techniques, and human know-how. The availability of appropriate technology is a cornerstone of productivity, and the nature of the core technologies in use must be considered in organizational design.

In the early 1960s, Joan Woodward conducted a study of technology and structure in over 100 English manufacturing firms. She classified core manufacturing technology into three categories.[19] In **small-batch production,** such as a racing bicycle shop, a variety of custom products are tailor-made to order. Each item or batch of items is made somewhat differently to fit customer specifications. The equipment used may not be elaborate, but a high level of worker skill often is needed. In **mass production,** the organization produces a large number of uniform products in an assembly-line system. Workers are highly dependent on one another, as the product passes from stage to stage until completion. Equipment may be sophisticated, and workers often follow detailed instructions while performing simplified jobs. Organizations using **continuous-process production** produce a few products by continuously feeding raw materials — such as liquids, solids, and gases — through a highly automated production system. Such systems are equipment intensive but can often be operated by a relatively small labor force. Classic examples are automated chemical plants and oil refineries.

Woodward found that the right combination of structure and technology was critical to organizational success. The best small-batch and continuous-process plants in her study had more flexible structures; the best mass-production operations were more rigidly structured. The implications of this research have become known as the *technological imperative:* Technology is a major influence on organizational structure.

The importance of technology for organizational design applies in services as well as manufacturing, although the core service technologies are slightly different.[20] In health care, education, and related services, an **intensive technology** focuses the efforts of many people with special expertise on the needs of patients or clients. In banks, real estate firms, insurance companies, employment agencies, and others like them, a **mediating technology** links together parties seeking a mutually beneficial exchange of values — typically a buyer and seller. Finally, a **long-linked technology** can function like mass production, where a client is passed from point to point for various aspects of service delivery.

SIZE AND LIFE CYCLE

Typically measured by number of employees, organizational size is another contingency factor in organizational design.[21] Although research indicates that larger organizations tend to have more mechanistic structures than smaller ones, it is clear that this is not always best for them.[22] In fact, a perplexing managerial concern is that organizations tend to become more bureaucratic as they grow in size and subsequently have more difficulty adapting to changing environments.

It is especially important for today's managers to understand the design implications of **organizational life cycle,** or the evolution of an organization over time through different stages of growth. Whereas the actual pattern will vary from one organization to the next, most will encounter these four stages:

1. *Birth stage:* When the organization is founded by an entrepreneur.
2. *Youth stage:* When the organization starts to grow rapidly.
3. *Mid-life stage:* When the organization has grown large with success.
4. *Maturity stage:* When the organization stabilizes at a large size.[23]

In its birth stage the founder usually runs the organization. It stays relatively small, and the structure is quite simple. The organization starts to grow rapidly during the youth stage and management responsibilities extend among more people. Here, the simple structure begins to exhibit the stresses of change. An organization in the mid-life stage is even larger, with a more complex and increasingly formal structure. More levels appear in the chain of command, and the founder may have difficulty remaining in control. In the maturity stage, the organization stabilizes in size, typically with a mechanistic structure. It runs the risk of becoming complacent and slow in competitive markets. Bureaucratic tendencies toward stability may lead an organization at this stage toward decline. Steps must be taken to counteract these tendencies and allow for needed creativity and innovation.

One way of coping with the disadvantages of bigness is *downsizing,* that is, taking actions to reduce the scope of operations and number of employees. This response is often used when top management is challenged to reduce costs quickly and increase productivity.[24] But, perhaps more significantly, good managers in many organizations find unique ways to overcome the disadvantages of large size before the crisis of downsizing hits. They are creative in fostering *intrapreneurship,* described in Chapter 8 as the pursuit of entrepreneurial behavior by individuals and subunits within large organizations.[25] They also find ways for smaller units to operate with considerable autonomy within the larger organizational framework. **Simultaneous structures,** for example, employ both mechanistic and organic designs to meet the need for production efficiency and continued innovation.[26] This loose-tight concept in organizational design is depicted in *Figure 11.3.*

• In the **organizational life cycle** an organization passes through different stages of growth over time.

• **3M**
http://www.mmm.com

3M is saving hundreds of thousands of dollars annually by making use of the new RP or rapid prototyping machines. The technology turns CAD drawings into working prototypes and parts for a variety of 3M production systems. The firm even has a rapid prototype center that adds to competitive advantage.

• A **simultaneous structure** uses mechanistic and organic designs to accomplish both production efficiency and innovation.

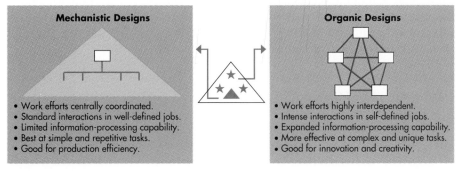

Figure 11.3 Simultaneous "loose-tight" properties of team structures support efficiency and innovation.

PEOPLE

Another contingency factor in organizational design is people—the human resources that staff the organization for action. A good organizational design provides people with the supporting structures they need to achieve both high performance and satisfaction in their work. Modern management theory views people-structure relationships in a contingency fashion. The prevailing argument is that there should be a good "fit" between organization structures and the people who staff them.[27]

Especially in the age of information and knowledge workers, organic designs with their emphasis on empowerment are important. When IBM purchased the software firm Lotus, for example, the intention was to turn it into a building block for the firm's networking business. But Lotus was small and IBM was huge. The whole thing had to be carefully handled or IBM might lose many of the talented people who created the popular LotusNotes and related products. The solution was to adapt the design to fit the people. IBM gave Lotus the space it needed to retain the characteristics of a creative software house. Says the firm's head of software, John Thompson: "You have to keep the people, so you have to ask yourself why it is they like working there."[28]

SUBSYSTEMS DESIGN AND INTEGRATION

• A **subsystem** is a work unit or smaller component within a larger organization.

Subsystems, such as a department or work unit headed by a manager, operate as smaller parts of larger organizations. Ideally, their work serves the needs of the larger organization. Ideally, too, the work of each subsystem supports the work of others. Things don't always work out this way, however. Another challenge of organizational design is to create subsystems and coordinate relationships so that the entire organization's interests are best met.

Important research in this area was reported in 1967 by Paul Lawrence and Jay Lorsch of Harvard University.[29] They studied 10 firms in three different industries—plastics, consumer goods, and containers. The firms were chosen because they differed in performance. The industries were chosen because they faced different levels of environmental uncertainty. The plastics industry was uncertain; containers was more certain; consumer goods was moderately uncertain. The results of the Lawrence and Lorsch study can be summarized as follows.

First, the total system structures of successful firms in each industry matched their respective environmental challenges. Successful plastics firms in uncertain environments had more organic designs; successful container firms in certain environments had more mechanistic designs. Second, subsystem structures in the successful firms matched the challenges of their respective subenvironments. Subsystems within the successful firms assumed different structures to accommodate the special problems and opportunities of their operating situations. Third, subsystems in the successful firms worked well with one another, even though some had very different structures.

DIFFERENTIATION

• **Differentiation** is the degree of difference between subsystems in an organization.

Figure 11.4 depicts operating differences between three divisions in one of the firms studied by Lawrence and Lorsch. The illustration shows how research and development, manufacturing, and sales subunits may operate differently in response to unique needs. This illustrates **differentiation,** which is the degree of difference that exists between the internal components of the organization.

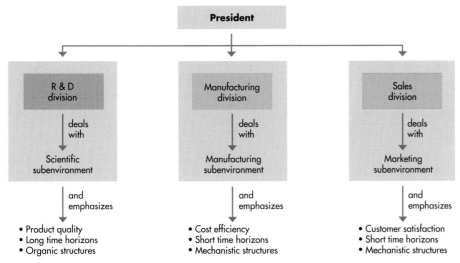

Figure 11.4 Differentiation among research and development (R&D), manufacturing, and sales divisions.

There are four common sources of differentiation among subsystems. The planning and action horizons of managers vary from short term to long term. Sometimes these *differences in time orientation* become characteristic of work units themselves. In a business firm, for example, the manufacturing subsystem may have a shorter term outlook than does the research and development group. These differences can make it difficult for personnel from the two units to work well together. The different tasks assigned to work units may also result in *differences in objectives.* For example, cost-conscious production managers and volume-conscious marketing managers may have difficulty agreeing on solutions to common problems.

Differences in interpersonal orientation can affect subsystem relations. To the extent that patterns of communication, decision making, and social interaction vary, it may be harder for personnel from different subsystems to work together. *Differences in formal structure* can also affect subsystem behaviors. Someone who is used to flexible problem solving in an organic setting may find it very frustrating to work with a manager from a mechanistic setting who is used to strict rules.

INTEGRATION

Integration is the level of coordination achieved among an organization's internal components. Organizational design involves the creation of both differentiated structures and appropriate integrating mechanisms. A basic paradox, however, makes this a particularly challenging managerial task: Increased differentiation among organizational subsystems creates the need for greater integration. However, integration becomes harder to achieve as differentiation increases.

Manager's Notepad 11.2 identifies several mechanisms for achieving subsystem integration.[30] The first integrating mechanisms listed in the notepad rely more on vertical coordination and the use of authority relationships in the chain of command. The use of rules and procedures, hierarchical referral, and planning, work best when differentiation is low. Integrating mechanisms that emphasize horizontal coordination and improved lateral relations work better when differentiation is high.[31] They include the use of direct contact between managers, liaison roles, task forces, teams, and matrix structures.

- **Integration** is the level of coordination achieved between subsystems in an organization.

Manager's Notepad 11.2

How to Improve Subsystems Integration

- *Rules and procedures:* Clearly specify required activities.
- *Hierarchical referral:* Refer problems upward to a common superior.
- *Planning:* Set targets that keep everyone headed in the same direction.
- *Direct contact:* Have subunit managers coordinate directly.
- *Liaison roles:* Assign formal coordinators to link subunits together.
- *Task forces:* Form temporary task forces to coordinate activities and solve problems on a timetable.
- *Teams:* Form permanent teams with the authority to coordinate and solve problems over time.
- *Matrix organizations:* Create a matrix structure to improve coordination on specific programs.

WORK PROCESS DESIGN

- **Process reengineering** systematically analyzes work processes to design new and better ones.

The emphasis on subsystems integration and more cross-functional collaboration in organizational design has come a popular development known as business **process reengineering.**[32] This is defined by consultant Michael Hammer as the systematic and complete analysis of work processes and the design of new and better ones.[33] The goal of a reengineering effort is to focus attention on the future, on customers, and on improved ways of doing things. It tries to break people and mindsets away from habits, preoccupation with past accomplishments, and tendencies to continue implementing old and outmoded ways of doing things. Simply put, reengineering is a radical and disciplined approach to changing the way work is carried out in organizations.

At the Coleman Company, the Wichita, Kansas maker of stoves and camping equipment, adaptation, flexibility, and quality are important. In the past, the firm was slow and bureaucratic at a time when Rubbermaid, Igloo, and other competitors were beginning to take its market share. At one time, it took up to 16 signatures to proceed in a slow and tedious process of new product development. Then, consultants recommended dramatic organizational changes—all to emphasize speed. Coleman needed to become faster at making old products, developing new ones, and getting both in their customers' hands. Now, product development teams make most decisions on their own, and development time has been cut in half. The firm makes and ships new orders to Wal-Mart and its other retail customers within one week.[34]

WHAT IS A WORK PROCESS?

- A **work process** is a related group of tasks that together create a value for the customer.

In his book *Beyond Reengineering,* Michael Hammer defines a **work process** as "a related group of tasks that together create a result of value for the customer."[35] He goes further to highlight the following key words in this definition and their implications: (1) *group* — tasks are viewed as part of a group rather than in isolation; (2) *together* — everyone must share a common goal: (3) *result* — the focus is on what is accomplished not on activities; (4) *customer* — processes serve customers and their perspectives are the ones that really count.

The concept of **workflow,** or the movement of work from one point to another in the manufacturing or service delivery processes, is central to the understanding of processes.[36] The various aspects of a work process must all be completed to achieve the desired results, and they must typically be completed in a given order. An important starting point for a reengineering effort is to diagram or map these workflows as they actually take place. Then each step can be systematically analyzed to determine whether or not it is adding value and to consider ways of streamlining to improve efficiency. Since some form of computer support is typically integral to organizational workflows today, special attention should be given to maximizing the contribution of this technology to processes. At PeopleSoft, for example, the goal is to eliminate paper forms as much as possible. Employees are even able to order their own supplies through a direct Web link to Office Depot. Says the firm's chief information officer: "Nobody jumps out of bed in the morning and says, 'I want to go to work and fill out forms.' We create systems that let people be brilliant rather than push paper."[37]

- **Workflow** is the movement of work from one point to another in a system.

HOW TO REENGINEER CORE PROCESSES

In reengineering, a process is viewed as a "black box" with inputs and outputs. The process is what turns the inputs into outputs, and the outputs should have greater value coming out than did the inputs as they went in. Given the mission, objectives and strategies of an organization, business process reengineering can be used to regularly assess and fine tune work processes to ensure that they directly add value to operations. Through a technique called **process value analysis,** core processes are identified and carefully evaluated for their performance contributions. Each step in a workflow examined. Unless a step is found to be important, useful, and contributing to the value-added, it is eliminated. Process value analysis typically involves the following steps.[38]

- **Process value analysis** identifies and evaluates core processes for their performance contributions.

← Steps in process value analysis

1. Identify the core processes.

2. Map the core processes in respect to workflows.

3. Evaluate all tasks for the core processes.

4. Search for ways to eliminate unnecessary tasks or work.

5. Search for ways to eliminate delays, errors, and misunderstandings.

6. Search for efficiencies in how work is shared and transferred among people and departments.

Figure 11.5, for example, shows how reengineering and better use of computer technology can streamline a purchasing operation. A purchase order should result in at least three value-added outcomes: order fulfillment, a paid bill, and a satisfied supplier. Work to be successfully accomplished includes such things as ordering, shipping, receiving, billing, and payment. A traditional business system might have purchasing, receiving, and accounts payable as separate functions, with each communicating with each other and the supplier. Alternatively reengineering might design a new purchasing support team whose members handle the same work more efficiently and with the support of the latest computer technology.[39]

Customers, teamwork, and efficiency are central to Hammer's notion of process reengineering. He describes the case of Aetna Life & Casualty Company where a complex system of tasks and processes once took as much as 28 days to accomplish.[40] Customer service requests were handled in step-by-step fashion by

Before reengineering

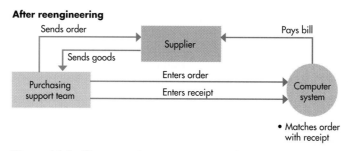

After reengineering

Figure 11.5   How reengineering can streamline core business processes.

many different persons. After an analysis of workflows, the process was re-designed into a "one and done" format where a single customer service provider handled each request from start to finish. One of Aetna's customer account managers said after the change was made: "Now we can see the customers as individual people. It's no longer 'us' and 'them.' "[41]

Hammer also describes reengineering at GTE Corporation of Florida. Before reengineering, customer inquiries for service and repairs required extensive consultation between technicians and their supervisors. After process value analysis technicians were formed into geographical teams which handled their own scheduling, service delivery, and reporting. They were given celluar telephones and laptop computers to assist in managing their work, resulting in the elimination of a number of costly supervisory jobs. The technicians responded enthusiastically to the changes and opportunities. Says one: "The fact that you've got four or five people zoned in a certain geographical area means that we get personally familiar with our customers' equipment and problems."[42]

The prior examples describe the essence of process reengineering. The approach tries to redesign processes to center control for them with an identifiable group of people, and to focus the entire system on meeting customer needs and expectations. It tries to eliminate duplications of work and systems bottlenecks, and in so doing tries to reduce costs and streamline operations efficiency.

OPERATIONS TECHNOLOGY AND DESIGN

As organizations change with the times, and as the emphasis on systems integration continues to gain in importance in newer horizontal and adaptive structures, technology plays an increasingly important role in operations design. Not only are computers and related technological developments changing the nature of work, they are also changing how workflows and systems are organized. At one extreme, technology substitutes for people. We see this in the way ATM's satisfy many of our banking needs, in the convenience of automated credit card billing at gasoline pumps, in the burgeoning use of on-line retail catalogs available through the Internet, in the sophisticated robots used in automobile assemblies, and more. At the other extreme, technology makes work easier, quicker, more efficient, and basically more productive in a wide variety of manufacturing and service settings.

A load of steel parts arrives every 90 minutes at the Dana Corp. plant in Stockton, California. They come from Toyota in Japan, and they must be assembled into truck chassis. Each chassis has some 180 parts requiring 115 feet of welding done both by robots and by hand. Completed chassis are shipped to a nearby Toyota facility for final assembly. To get the business, plant manager Mark Schmink had to promise Toyota a price cut. To enable it he formed an employee team to study ways of improving the assembly process. They questioned everything and were able to speed the production process. The result was a reduced price to Toyota — an important effort in keeping the customer happy, and a new culture of commitment to improved work processes by everyone throughout the plant.[43]

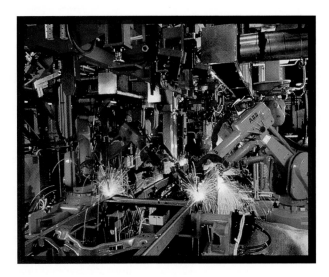

MANUFACTURING APPLICATIONS

There is no doubt that an important strategic direction in operations management is the broad-based utilization of technology. The concept of competitive advantage was linked in Chapter 2 to such manufacturing innovations as lean production, flexible manufacturing, agile manufacturing, and mass customization.[44] They are part of continuing technological developments that include a range of applications. *Computer-aided process planning* uses computers to plan operations and determine the best routing for parts through a series of machines. *Computer numerical control* uses computers to store instructions on various machine operations and to control changes in machine settings and movements. *Group technology* uses computers to help code and classify parts into families that get similar handling in storage and manufacturing. *Robotics* uses computers to guide multi-functional robots in the performance of work tasks otherwise performed by human operators.

In the important area of design, *computer-aided design (CAD)* uses computers to help create engineering designs and change them rapidly as needed. *Computer-aided manufacturing (CAM)* uses computers to monitor the production process, link various machines and operations to one another, and provide feedback for control. A promising new development called *rapid prototyping*, or "RP," is improving on the CAD-CAM linkage. Previously, CADs were turned into prototypes and working parts through complex and time-consuming hand work. With RP software, many CAD designs can be turned directly into prototypes with great time and cost savings. A related development called *rapid manufacturing* is even starting to use the technology to allow for the manufacture of salable end products directly from the CADs. Clearly, the trends are toward ever more sophisticated technology utilization in all types and facets of manufacturing applications.

• Patricia Seybold Group
http://www.psgroup.com

At Patricia Seybold Group of Boston, vice president Ronni Marshak specializes in work group products. To improve a process she determines how it works, the sequence of activities or tasks involved, the responsibilities of the people involved, and the rules of the process or conditions under which it might change. This is often done with the assistance of consultants and special software tools.

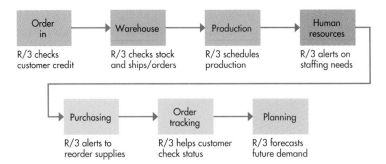

Figure 11.6   Enterprise-wide integration with support of SAP's R/3 systems.

ENTERPRISE-WIDE INTEGRATION

Integration is one of the dominant themes in organizational design today. When it comes to operations, furthermore, one of the goals is to achieve enterprise-wide integration of business and support systems. Once again technology is leading us in new and promising directions, and things should only get better in the future. Consider technology that is already available through the German software company SAP. As shown in *Figure 11.6,* SAP's powerful R/3 computer programs provide for complex integration of diverse processes and systems from point of customer order to inventory management, staffing, production scheduling, materials purchasing, and more.[45]   With SAP's R/3 software activity in any part of the system is automatically integrated with the needs of supporting systems. The result is improved operations efficiency. At Monsanto, for example, SAP's R/3 systems resulted in reduced time for production planning, lower inventories, and reduced needs for working capital. The company estimates that it has saved some $200 million annually due to the integration of enterprise-wide operations systems.[46]

CHAPTER REVIEW

This section should be used as an end-of-chapter "study guide." The *Summary* helps to put the chapter's content into overall perspective. The list of *Key Terms* allows you to double-check your familiarity with basic concepts and definitions. *Self-Test 11* gives you the opportunity to test your basic comprehension of the chapter using sample test questions.

SUMMARY

What are the essentials of organizational design?

- Organizational design is the process of choosing and implementing structures that best arrange resources to serve organizational mission and purpose.

- Bureaucratic or mechanistic organizational designs are vertical in nature and perform best for routine and predictable tasks.

- Adaptive or organic organizational designs are horizontal in nature and perform best in conditions requiring change and flexibility.

Which contingency factors influence organization design?

- Environment, strategy, technology, size, and people are all contingency factors influencing organizational design.

- Certain environments lend themselves to more vertical and mechanistic organizational designs. Uncertain environments require more horizontal and adaptive organizational designs.

- Technology—including the use of knowledge, equipment, and work methods in the transformation process, is an important consideration in organizational design.

- Although organizations tend to become more mechanistic as they grow in size, designs must be used to allow for innovation and creativity in changing environments.

What are the major issues in subsystems design?

- Organizations are composed of subsystems that must work well together.

- Differentiation is the degree of difference that exists between various subsystems; integration is the level of coordination achieved among them.

- As organizations become more highly differentiated they have a greater need for integration, but as differentiation increases integration is harder to accomplish.

- Low levels of differentiation can be handled through authority relationships and more vertical organizational designs.

- Greater differentiation requires more intense coordination through horizontal organizational designs, with an emphasis on cross-functional teams and lateral relations.

How can a work processes be reengineered?

- A work process is a related group of tasks that together create value for a customer.

- Business process engineering is the systematic and complete analysis of work processes and the design of new and better ones.

- In reengineering the workflows of an organization are diagramed to identify how work moves from one point to another throughout a system.

- In process value analysis all elements of a process and its workflows are examined to identify their exact contributions to key performance results.

How is operations technology influencing design?

- Computer and information technologies are having an important impact on the design of organizations and their component operations.

- In manufacturing the developments with computer applications include lean production, flexible manufacturing, mass customization, among other possibilities.

- In the important area of enterprise-wide integration of operating systems and processes, SAP computer programs are examples of new technological directions in the search for potential competitive advantage.

KEY TERMS

Adaptive organization (p. 224)

Continuous-process technology (p. 226)

Differentiation (p. 228)

Integration (p. 229)

Intensive technology (p. 226)

Long-linked technology (p. 226)

Mass production (p. 226)

Mechanistic design (p. 223)

Mediating technology (p. 226)

Organic design (p. 224)

Organizational design (p. 222)

Organizational life cycle (p. 227)

Process reengineering (p. 230)

Process value analysis (p. 231)

Simultaneous structures (p. 227)

Small-batch production (p. 226)

Subsystem (p. 228)

Technology (p. 226)

Workflow (p. 231)

Work process (p. 230)

SELF-TEST 11

Take this test much as you would in a normal classroom situation. It should offer you a good check of your basic comprehension of chapter material. Answers may be found at the end of the book.

MULTIPLE-CHOICE QUESTIONS:

1. The bureaucratic organization described by Max Weber is similar in nature to the _____ organization described by Burns and Stalker. (a) adaptive (b) mechanistic (c) organic (d) adhocracy

2. Teamwork, less emphasis on hierarchy and wide spans of control are typical in _____. (a) mechanistic structures (b) bureaucracies (c) centralized structures (d) adaptive organizations.

3. The production method characteristic of an oil refinery is a good example of what Woodward referred to as the _____ technology. (a) intensive (b) continuous-process (c) mass-production (d) small-batch

4. As organizations grow in size, they tend to become more _____ in design, although this is not always best for them. (a) mechanistic (b) organic (c) adaptive (d) flexible

5. A basic paradox in subsystem design is that as differentiation increases the need for _____ also increases, but it is harder to accomplish. (a) cost efficiency (b) innovation (c) integration (d) transformation

6. A/an _____organizational design works best in _____ environments. (a) flexible, stable (b) organic, uncertain (c) mechanistic, dynamic (d) adaptive, certain

7. The important contingency factors in organizational design include _____. (a) organizational strategy and structure (b) organizational size and life cycle (c) human resources of the organization (d) all of these

8. A work process is defined as a related group of tasks that together create a result of value for _____. (a) shareholders (b) customers (c) workers (d) society

9. The first step in process value analysis is to _____. (a) look for ways to eliminate unnecessary tasks (b) map or diagram the workflows (c) identify core processes (d) look for efficiencies in transferring work among people and departments

10. The R/3 software made available by the German firm SAP is most useful in _____. (a) helping achieve enterprise-wide integration of systems (b) mapping workflows (c) allowing lean production (d) facilitating mass customization

TRUE-FALSE QUESTIONS:

11. A key trend in organizations today is the emphasis on horizontal integration and teamwork. T F

12. Organizations should never use simultaneous structures involving both mechanistic and organic designs. T F

13. A small machine shop making high-performance racing engines for motorcycles operates with what Woodward would call a small-batch technology. T F

14. In organizational design, a basic principle is that strategy should always follow and support structure. T F

15. In complex organizations, subunit differences in structure and time orientation may cause integration problems. T F

16. The use of teams and task forces is an example of how integration is achieved by emphasizing vertical aspects of organizational design. T F

17. Once a new organization gets an effective structure, it should continue to use this structure through all stages of its life cycle. T F

18. Short term horizons by a manufacturing unit and long term horizons by a R&D unit illustrate differentiation among subsystems. T F

19. Business process reengineering focuses on customers and improved ways of doing things. T F

20. The process reengineering approach is not a good fit with current organizational interests in teamwork. T F

SHORT-RESPONSE QUESTIONS:

21. "Organizational design should always be addressed in contingency fashion." Explain this statement.

22. What difference does environment make in organizational design?

23. Describe the relationship between differentiation and integration as issues in subsystems design.

24. If you were a reengineering consultant, how would you describe the steps in a typical approach to process value analysis?

APPLICATION QUESTION:

25. Two business women, former college roommates, are discussing their jobs and careers over lunch. You overhear one saying to the other: "I work for a large corporation. It is bureaucratic and very authority driven. However, I have to say that it is also very successful. I like working there." Her friend commented somewhat differently. She said: "My, I wouldn't like working there at all. In my organization things are very flexible and the structures are loose. We have a lot of freedom and the focus on operations is much more horizontal than vertical. And, we too are very successful." After listening to the conversation and using insights from management theory, how can these two very different "success stories" be explained?

Human Resource Management

Planning Ahead—Chapter 12 Study Questions

- What is strategic human resources management?
- How do organizations attract a quality workforce?
- How do organizations develop a quality workforce?
- How do organizations maintain a quality workforce?

Make People Your Top Priority

At Coopers & Lybrand (C&L), human resource development is a top priority. The firm is committed to hiring and retaining talented people who have the abilities, knowledge, and ideas to match the demands of a challenging 21st-century environment. Chairman and CEO Nicholas C. Moore says, "Attracting and retaining the highest intellectual capital are critical objectives of Coopers & Lybrand." The firm's commitment to talent is backed by a strong diversity program that includes a C&L mentoring initiative. In this program the top 100 partners in the company serve as mentors to at least one female or minority manager. The program seeks to increase their success rate in achieving partner status. Moore chairs a Diversity Advisory Group with the goal of fully understanding diversity as it relates to the business.[1]

People are precious as the human resources of organizations. No one's talents can be wasted in the quest for high performance. Like Coopers & Lybrand, progressive employers everywhere are taking steps to unlock the full potential of their workforces as they respond to the pressures of today's competitive environments. In principle, at least, the following organizational slogans say it all: "*People* are our most important asset"; "It's *people* who make the difference"; "It's the *people* who work for us who . . . determine whether our company thrives or languishes."[2]

Such testimonials are found in newspaper and television ads, annual reports, corporate recruiting literature, executive speeches, and organizational newsletters. They communicate a very specific understanding: Even with the guidance of a clear mission and the best strategies, and even with the support of appropriate structures and work designs, an organization must be well staffed with capable and committed people if it is to fully achieve its objectives. Today, and perhaps more than ever before, the pressures of global competition and social change have led to what *Fortune* magazine refers to as "a human resources revolution" that affects organizations of all types and sizes.[3]

The implications of this human resource revolution not only apply to organizations but to all of us who seek careers within them. The watchwords and buzzwords of changing organizations are all around — reengineering, delayering, rightsizing, outsourcing, empowering, and the like. You should be reading and thinking seriously about them. They are already bringing about fundamental changes in the employer-employee relationship. And they are changing the terms of your future career. "Build a portfolio of skills," "Protect your mobility," "Take charge of your destiny," "Add value to your organization" advise the modern career gurus. But let's turn to the tough question: "Are you ready?"[4] Test yourself by asking and answering these even more specific career readiness questions: Who am I? What do I want? What have I done? What do I know? What can I do? Why should someone hire me?

STRATEGIC HUMAN RESOURCE MANAGEMENT

● **Human resource management** is the process of attracting, developing, and maintaining a talented and energetic workforce.

The process of **human resource management** involves attracting, developing, and maintaining a talented and energetic workforce to support organizational mission, objectives, and strategies. This is a strategic process that makes an irreplaceable contribution to the readiness of any organization to perform up to expectations. In order for corporate, business, and functional strategies to be well implemented, workers with relevant skills and enthusiasm are needed. It is the task of strategic human resource management to make them available. A marketing manager at Ideo, a Palo-Alto based industrial design firm says, for example: "If you hire the right people . . . if you've got the right fit . . . then everything will take care of itself."[5]

HUMAN RESOURCE MANAGEMENT

There are three major responsibilities in the human resource management process. First is the responsibility of *attracting a quality workforce.* This is a process of human resource planning, recruitment, and selection. Second is *developing a quality workforce.* This is the responsibility for employee orientation, training and development, and career planning and development. Third is *maintaining a quality workforce.* This involves management of employee retention and turnover, performance appraisal, and compensation and benefits.

Human resource specialists often assist line managers in fulfilling these three responsibilities. A human resource department appears on many organization charts and is often headed by a senior manager reporting directly to the chief executive officer. It is also increasingly common to find organizations outsourcing various technical aspects of the human resource management process. There are a growing number of career opportunities with consulting firms that provide such specialized services as recruiting, compensation planning, outplacement, and the like. In a dynamic environment complicated by legal issues, labor shortages, economic turmoil, changing corporate strategies, new organization and job designs, high technology, changing personal values and expectations, human resource specialists become ever more important.

COMPLEX LEGAL ENVIRONMENT

Human resource management must be accomplished within the framework of government regulations and laws. In most countries, the legal environment grows increasingly complex as old laws are modified and new ones are added. These developments affect any and all employers operating in a particular setting, whether the employer is a domestic or a foreign operation. For example, the United States Supreme Court has ruled that American workers can sue their foreign employers for compliance with U.S. employment laws. This ruling once cost Japanese-owned Sumitomo Corporation of America $2.7 million to settle a sex discrimination suit by female secretaries, who successfully argued that male Japanese coworkers were given preferences in promotions and pay raises.[6]

The American legal and regulatory environment covers human resource management activities related to pay, employment rights, occupational health and safety, retirement, privacy, vocational rehabilitation, and related areas. A sample of major U.S. laws relating to human resource management is provided in *Figure 12.1*. An important cornerstone of protection for employees' rights to fair treatment was established by *Title VII of the Civil Rights Act of 1964*, as amended by the *Equal Employment Opportunity Act of 1972* and the *Civil Rights Act of 1991*. They provide for **equal employment opportunity (EEO)** — the right to employment without regard to race, color, national origin, religion, gender, age, or physical and mental ability. EEO is federally enforced by the Equal Employment Opportunity Commission (EEOC) and generally applies to all public and private organizations employing 15 or more people.

These and related laws are designed to protect people from **employment discrimination,** or the use of criteria that are not job-relevant when hiring or promoting someone into a position. As a general rule, the statutes do not restrict an employer's right to establish *bona fide occupational qualifications.* These are criteria for employment that can be clearly justified as being related to a person's capacity to perform a job. But, the laws do require careful consideration of job requirements vis-à-vis an applicant's capabilities. For example, the Americans With Disabilities Act, passed in 1990, prevents discrimination against people with disabilities. The law forces employers to focus on abilities and what a person can do and, increasingly, persons with disabilities are gaining in employment opportunities. The popular musician Stevie Wonder, blind since birth, has joined with SAP America — an enterprise-integration software company, to offer the Stevie Wonder Vision Awards. These will go to companies that promote employment opportunities for the visually impaired.[7]

All managers are expected to act within the law and equal opportunity principles. Failure to do so is not only unjustified in a free society, it can also be a very expensive mistake resulting in fines and penalties. When discrimination in any of the above-mentioned areas is encountered, legal charges can be filed and court action taken to resolve complaints. Organizations doing business with the federal

● **Johnson & Johnson**
http://www.jnj.com

Johnson & Johnson's new ethics credo includes the importance of families: "We must be mindful of ways to help our employees fulfill their family responsibilities." J&J's managers have training in diversity and family issues, with a special focus on the needs of nontraditional families. The company offers family care leave, on-site day care, eldercare referral, and other services.

● **Equal employment opportunity (EEO)** is the right to employment and advancement without regard to race, sex, religion, color, or national origin.

● **Employment discrimination** occurs when non-job relevant criteria are used for hiring and job placements.

Equal Pay Act of 1963 →	Prohibits pay differences for men and women doing equal work.
Title VII of the Civil Rights → *Act of* 1964 (as amended)	Prohibits discrimination in employment based on race, color, religion, sex, or national origin.
Age Discrimination Employment → *Act of* 1967 (as amended)	Prohibits discrimination in employment against persons over 40; restricts mandatory retirement.
Occupational Safety and → *Health Act of* 1970 (OSHA)	Establishes mandatory safety and health standards in workplaces.
Vocational Rehabilitation → *Act of* 1973	Prohibits discrimination in employment based on physical or mental disability.
Pregnancy Discrimination → *Act of* 1978	Prohibits employment discrimination against pregnant workers.
Immigration Reform and → *Control Act of* 1986	Prohibits knowing employment of illegal aliens.
Americans with Disabilities → *Act of* 1990	Prohibits discrimination against a qualified individual on the basis of disability.
Civil Rights Act of 1991 →	Reaffirms Title VII of the 1964 Civil Rights Act, reinstates burden of proof by employer, and allows for punitive and compensatory damages.
Family and Medical Leave → *Act of* 1993	Allows employees up to 12 weeks of unpaid leave with job guarantees for childbirth, adoption, or family illness.

Figure 12.1   A sample of U.S. laws influencing human resource management.

● An **affirmative action program** tries to increase employment opportunities for women and minorities.

government must also have **affirmative-action programs** promoting the employment opportunities of women and other minorities, including veterans, the aged, and the disabled. The intent of such programs is to ensure that women and other minorities are represented in the workforce in proportion to their actual availability in the area labor market. Organizations that fail to meet these proportions must pursue assigned affirmative action goals to increase the hiring and/or advancement of minorities. Failure to comply can result in the loss of federal funding and contracts. Controversy over affirmative action is in the news, with the pros and cons being debated at both the federal and state levels. The debates involve such issues as hiring quotas and the potential for reverse discrimination to interfere with the individual rights of members of majority populations.

● **Strategic human resource planning** analyzes staffing needs and identifies actions to fill those needs.

STRATEGIC HUMAN RESOURCE PLANNING

Any organization should at all times have the right people available to do the required work. This requires a commitment to **strategic human resource plan-**

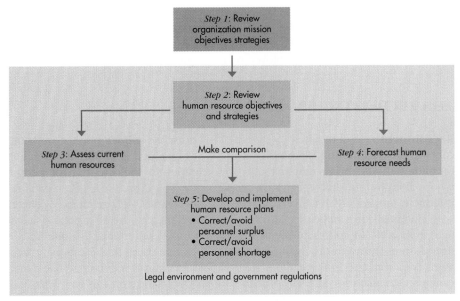

Figure 12.2 Steps in the human resource planning process.

ning, a process of analyzing staffing needs and planning how to satisfy these needs in a way that best serves organizational mission, objectives, and strategies.[8]

The elements in strategic human resource planning are shown in *Figure 12.2.* The process begins with a review of organizational mission, objectives, and strategies. This establishes a frame of reference for forecasting human resource needs and labor supplies, both within and outside the organization. Ultimately, the planning process should help managers identify staffing requirements, assess the existing workforce, and determine what additions and/or replacements are required to meet future needs. It is no secret, for expample, that high-tech workers are in great demand today and many organizations are experiencing or are anticipating difficulty in meeting their staffing needs. At GE Medical, a multigenerational staffing plan is used to help resolve the problem. For every new product plan there is a human resource plan associated with it, and one that covers all generations of the product's anticipated life. This plan helps focus recruiters on key staffing needs within GE Medical; it is also a basis for holding them accountable for producing the desired results.[9]

The foundations for human resource planning are set by **job analysis.** This involves the orderly study of just *what* is done, *when, where, how, why,* and by *whom* in existing or potential new jobs.[10] The job analysis provides useful information that can then be used to write and/or update **job descriptions.** These are written statements of job duties and responsibilities. The information in a job analysis can also be used to create **job specifications.** These are lists of the qualifications — such as formal education, prior work experience, and skill requirements, that should be met by any person hired for or placed in a given job.

● **Job analysis** is an orderly study of job requirements and facets that can influence performance.

● A **job description** details the duties and responsibilities of a job holder.

● A **job specification** lists the qualifications required of a job holder.

 ATTRACTING A QUALITY WORKFORCE

With a human resource plan prepared, the process of attracting a quality workforce begins. An excerpt from a public relations advertisement once run by the Motorola Corporation clearly identifies the goal of this aspect of human resource management: "Productivity is learning how to hire the person who is *right* for the job." To attract the right people to its workforce, an organization must first know exactly what it is looking for — it must have a clear understanding of the jobs to be done and the talents required to do them well. Then it must have the systems in place to excel at employee recruitment and selection.

THE RECRUITING PROCESS

- **Recruitment** is a set of activities designed to attract a qualified pool of job applicants.

Recruitment is a set of activities designed to attract a *qualified* pool of job applicants to an organization. Emphasis on the word qualified is important. Effective recruiting should bring employment opportunities to the attention of people whose abilities and skills meet job specifications. The three steps in a typical recruitment process are (1) advertisement of a job vacancy, (2) preliminary contact with potential job candidates, and (3) initial screening to create a pool of qualified applicants. In collegiate recruiting, for example, advertising is done by the firm posting short job descriptions in print or on-line through the campus placement center and/or in the campus newspaper. Preliminary contact is made after candidates register for interviews with company recruiters on campus. This typically involves a short 20- to 30-minute interview, during which the candidate presents a written resume and briefly explains his or her job qualifications. As part of the initial screening, the recruiter shares interview results and resumes from the campus visits with appropriate line managers. Decisions will then be made about who to include in the final pool of candidates to be invited for further interviews during a formal visit to the organization.

External versus Internal Recruitment

The collegiate recruiting example is one of *external recruitment* in which job candidates are sought from outside the hiring organization. Newspapers, employment agencies, colleges, technical training centers, personal contacts, walk-ins, employee referrals, and even persons in competing organizations are all sources of external recruits. Not all recruiting is done this way, however. *Internal recruitment* seeks applicants from inside the organization. This involves notifying existing employees of job vacancies through job postings and personal recommendations. Most organizations have a procedure for announcing vacancies through newsletters, electronic bulletin boards, and the like. They also rely on managers to recommend subordinates as candidates for advancement.

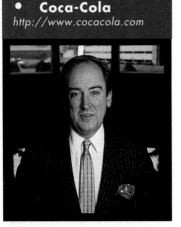

- **Coca-Cola**
http://www.cocacola.com

One of the most famous "salarymen" in recent American corporate history was the late Robert Goizueta. CEO of Coca-Cola when he died, Goizueta owned over $1 billion of the company's stock. He worked his way up to the top position over a 43-year career in the firm. Employee loyalty and hard work paid off for this respected business leader.

Both recruitment strategies offer potential advantages and disadvantages. External recruiting brings in outsiders with fresh perspectives. It also provides access to specialized expertise or work experience not otherwise available from insiders. Internal recruitment is usually less expensive. It also deals with persons whose performance records are well established. A history of serious internal recruitment can also be encouraging to employees; it shows that one can advance in the organization by working hard and achieving high performance at each point of responsibility. Procter & Gamble, for example, is known for its commitment to internal recruitment. The firm tries to hire the best young people out of college and then provide them with career-long challenges and opportunities. And at Citibank, a human resource information system keeps track of some 10,000 employees world-wide for career development purposes.[11]

Realistic Job Previews

There is another important recruitment issue that must be considered. In what may be called *traditional recruitment,* the emphasis is on selling the organization to job applicants. In this case, only the most positive features of the job and organization are communicated to potential candidates. Bias may even be introduced as these features are exaggerated while negative features are concealed. This form of recruitment is designed to attract as many candidates as possible. The problem is that it may create unrealistic expectations that result in early job turnover when new hires leave prematurely. This turnover can be very costly. In one survey of the job-turnover tab, including lost productivity, search fees, and recruiting costs, some 30% of companies reported a per-person cost exceeding $20,000.[12]

Realistic job previews, by contrast, try to provide the candidate with *all* pertinent information about the job and organization without distortion and *before* the job is accepted.[13] Instead of "selling" only positive features of a job, this approach tries to be realistic and balanced in the information provided. It tries to be fair in depicting actual job and organizational features. With a more complete view of the job and organization, new employees should have more "realistic" job expectations. A healthy perspective on the employment relationship, higher levels of early job satisfaction, and less premature turnover are the anticipated benefits.

- **Realistic job previews** provide the job candidate with all pertinent information about a prospective job and the employing organization.

MAKING SELECTION DECISIONS

Selection is the process of choosing from a pool of applicants the person or persons who offer the greatest performance potential. Steps in a typical selection process are shown in *Figure 12.3.* They are (1) completion of a formal application form, (2) interviewing, (3) testing, (4) reference checks, (5) physical examination, and (6) final analysis and decision to hire or reject. Again, the best employers exercise extreme care in the selection process. At Federal Express, for example, psychological testing is used to identify what the firm calls "risk taking and courage of conviction."[14] It is important to know that all aspects of the selection process should meet the test of **validity.** That is, there should be a demonstrable relationship between a person's score or rating on any selection device and their eventual job performance. In simple terms, a good score should predict good performance.

- **Selection** is the process of choosing from a pool the best qualified applicants.

- **Validity** is a demonstrated link between a selective device and job performance.

Application Forms

The *application form* declares the individual to be a formal candidate for a job. It documents the applicant's personal history and qualifications. The personal resume is often included with the job application. This important document should accurately summarize an applicant's special qualifications. As a job applicant, you

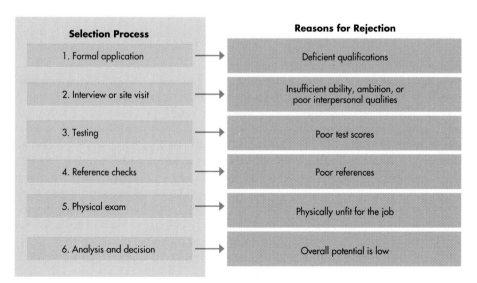

Figure 12.3 Steps in the typical selection process: the case of a rejected job applicant.

> **Manager's Notepad 12.1**
>
> **How to Conduct Job Interviews**
>
> - *Plan ahead.* Review the job specifications and job description as well as the candidate's application; allow sufficient time for a complete interview.
> - *Create a good interview climate.* Allow sufficient time; choose a quiet place; be friendly and show interest; give the candidate your full attention.
> - *Conduct a goal-oriented interview.* Know what information you need and get it; look for creativity, independence, and a high energy level.
> - *Avoid questions that may imply discrimination.* Focus all questioning on the job applied for and the candidate's true qualifications for it.
> - *Answer the questions asked of you . . . answer others that may not be asked.* Do your part to create a realistic job preview.
> - *Write notes on the interview immediately upon completion.* Document details and impressions for later deliberation and decision making.

● **Southwest Airlines**
http://www.iflyswa.com

Over 150,000 resumes are received each year by Southwest Airlines. Only 5,000 of the applicants are hired, and they go through a rigorous process of selection. Even humor counts; it goes with the coporate culture. An interviewee who appears a bit too tight may be asked to "tell a joke." It's a serious requirement—you can't work for the company if you can't pass the levity test.

● An **assessment center** is a selection technique that examines candidates' handling of simulated job situations.

should exercise great care in preparing your resume for job searches. See the Career Advancement Portfolio section in the end-of-text *Career Readiness Workbook* for advice on resume preparation. As a recruiter, you should also learn how to screen applications and resumes for insights that can help you make good selection decisions. Importantly, the application should only request information that is directly relevant to the job and the applicant's potential job success.

Interviews

Interviews are extremely important in the selection process because of the information exchange they allow.[15] It is a time when both the job applicant and potential employer can learn a lot about one another. However, interviews are also recognized as potential stumbling blocks in the selection process. Sometimes interviewers ask the wrong things, sometimes they talk too much, sometimes the wrong people do the interviewing, and other times the interviewer falls prey to personal biases and makes a judgement that fails to fully consider the applicant's capabilities. Among the recommendations for how to interview a job applicant are those shown in the *Manager's Notepad 12.1*.

Employment Tests

Testing is often used in the screening of job applicants. Some common employment tests are designed to identify intelligence, aptitudes, personality, and interests. Whenever tests are used and in whatever forms, however, the goal should be to gather information that will help predict the applicant's eventual performance success. Like any selection device, an employment test should meet the criterion of *validity* and measure exactly what it intends to relative to the job specification—for example, written communication skills or manual dexterity. It should also meet the criterion of *reliability* by yielding approximately the same results over time if taken by the same person. Any employment test used in the selection process, furthermore, should be legally defensible on the grounds that it actually measures an ability required to perform the job.

New developments in testing extend the process into actual demonstrations of job-relevant skills and personal characteristics. An **assessment center** evaluates a person's potential by observing his or her performance in experiential activities designed to simulate daily work. *Computerized testing* is becoming more common today, aided by specialized software that includes interactive and multi-media approaches. Such computerized tests often ask the applicant to indicate how he or she would respond to a series of job-relevant situations. Another form of this testing approach is *work sampling,* which directly assesses a person's performance on a set of tasks that directly replicate those required in the job under consideration. Here, applicants are asked to work on actual job tasks while being graded by observers on their performance.

When Mercedes opened its new plant in Alabama, it had over 45,000 applicants for 1,500 jobs. To help make its selection decisions the firm set up job-specific exercises to determine who had the best of the required skills and attitudes. One was a tire-changing test, with color-coded bolts and a set of instructions. As Charlene Paige took the test she went slow and carefully followed directions. Two men that went with her changed the tires really fast. She got the job because the firm wanted people who would follow directions and work for quality. Now Charlene has worked into the position of team leader in an assembly shop.[16]

Reference and Background Checks

Reference checks are inquiries to previous employers, academic advisors, coworkers, and/or acquaintances regarding the qualifications, experience, and past work records of a job applicant. Although they may be biased if friends are prearranged "to say the right things if called," reference checks can be helpful. They can reveal important information on the applicant that was not discovered elsewhere in the selection process. The Society for Human Resources Management (SHRM), for example, estimates that 25 percent of job applications and resumes contain errors.[17] The references given by a job applicant can also add credibility to an application if they include a legitimate and even prestigious list of persons.

Physical Examinations

Many organizations ask job applicants to take a physical examination. This health check helps ensure that the person is physically capable of fulfilling job requirements. It may also be used as a basis for enrolling the applicant in health-related fringe benefits such as life, health, and disability insurance programs. A recent and controversial development in this area is the emerging use of drug testing. This has become part of preemployment health screening and a basis for continued employment at some organizations. At a minimum, care must be exercised that any required test is job relevant and does not discriminate in any way against the applicant.

Final Decisions to Hire or Reject

The best selection decisions are most likely to be those involving extensive consultation among the manager or team leader, potential coworkers, and human resource staff. Importantly, the emphasis in selection must always be comprehensive and focus on all aspects of the person's capacity to perform in a given job. After all, the selection decision poses major consequences for organizational performance and for the internal environment or work climate. Just as a "good fit" can produce long term advantage, a "bad fit" can be the source of many and perhaps long term problems. Sometimes the people who know this lesson best are those that run small businesses. Says one dairy store owner who knew the importance of customer service in retail sales, "If applicants have a good attitude, we can do the rest . . . but if they have a bad attitude to start with, everything we do seems to fail."[18]

DEVELOPING A QUALITY WORKFORCE

- **Socialization** is the process of systematically changing the expectations, behavior, and attitudes of a new employee.

When people join an organization, they must "learn the ropes" and become familiar with "the way things are done." It is important that newcomers be helped fit into the work environment in a way that furthers their development and performance potential. **Socialization** is the process of influencing the expectations, behavior, and attitudes of a new employee in a way considered desirable by the organization.[19] The intent of socialization in the human resource management process is to help achieve the best possible fit between the individual, the job, and the organization.

EMPLOYEE ORIENTATION

- **Orientation** makes new employees familiar with their jobs, coworkers, and organizational policies, rules, objectives, and services.

Socialization of newcomers begins with **orientation**—a set of activities designed to familiarize new employees with their jobs, coworkers, and key aspects of the organization as a whole. This includes clarifying the organizational mission and culture, explaining operating objectives and job expectations, communicating policies and procedures, and identifying key personnel.

The first 6 months of employment are often crucial in determining how well someone is going to perform over the long run. It is a time when the original expectations are tested, and patterns are set for future relationships between an individual and employer. Unfortunately, orientation is sometimes neglected and newcomers are often left to fend for themselves. They may learn job and organizational routines on their own or through casual interactions with coworkers, and they may acquire job attitudes the same way.[20] The result is that otherwise well-intentioned and capable persons may learn inappropriate attitudes and/or behaviors. Good orientation, by contrast, enhances a person's understanding of the organization and adds purpose to his or her daily job activities. Increased performance, greater job satisfaction, and greater commitment to the job and organizational culture are the desired results.

At Walt Disney World Resort in Buena Vista, Florida, some 20,000 of the resort's 35,000-member workforce have direct customer service responsibilities. Each is carefully selected and trained to provide high-quality customer service as a "cast member." During orientation, newly hired employees are taught the corporate culture. They learn that everyone employed by the company, regardless of her or his specific job—be it entertainer, ticket seller, or groundskeeper—is there "to make the customer happy." The company's interviewers say that they place a premium on personality. Says director of casting Duncan Dickson, "We can train for skills. We want people who are enthusiastic, who have pride in their work, who can take charge of a situation without supervision."[21]

TRAINING AND DEVELOPMENT

Training is a set of activities that provides the opportunity to acquire and improve job-related skills. This applies both to the initial training of an employee and to upgrading or improving someone's skills to meet changing job requirements. A major and current concern of American employers is the lack of educational preparation of some workers for jobs, often high-technology jobs, in the new workplace. These concerns even extend to the basic skills of reading, writing, and arithmetic.[22] The more progressive organizations offer extensive training programs to ensure that their workers always have the skills needed to perform well.

> • **Training** provides learning opportunities to acquire and improve job-related skills.

On-the-Job Training

On-the-job training takes place in the work setting while someone is doing a job. *Job rotation* allows people to spend time working in different jobs and thus expand the range of their job capabilities. *Coaching* occurs when an experienced person gives specific technical advice to someone else. This can be done on a formal and planned basis by a supervisor or coworkers. It can also occur more informally in the form of help spontaneously offered in teams. *Apprenticeship* involves a work assignment wherein a person serves as understudy or assistant to someone who already has the desired job skills. Through this relationship, an apprentice learns a job over time and eventually becomes fully qualified to perform it.

Modeling is the process by which someone demonstrates through personal behavior what is expected of others. One way to learn managerial skills, for example, is to observe and practice the techniques of good managers. **Mentoring,** occurs when new or early-career employees are formally assigned as protégés to senior persons who then coach, model, and otherwise assist them to develop job skills and get a good start in their careers. This approach is evident in the diversity commitments of Coopers & Lybrand senior partners as described in the chapter-opening example.

> • **Modeling** demonstrates through personal behavior that which is expected of others.
>
> • **Mentoring** is the sharing of experiences and insights between an experienced and an inexperienced person.

Off-the-Job Training

Off-the-job training is accomplished outside the work setting. It may be done within the organization at a separate training room or facility or at an off-site location. Examples of the latter include attendance at special training programs sponsored by universities, trade or professional associations, or consultants. The willingness of organizations to invest in training is a good indicator of their commitment to the people they hire. At Intel, for example, some 6 percent of its payroll—an amount in excess of $160 million, is annually spent on training through the firm's in-house university.[23]

Management development is a special form of off-the-job training designed to improve a person's knowledge and skill in the fundamentals of management. For example, *beginning managers* often benefit from training that emphasizes delegating duties; *middle managers* may benefit from training to better understand multifunctional viewpoints; *top managers* may benefit from advanced management training to sharpen their decision-making and negotiating skills and to expand their awareness of corporate strategy and direction. At the Center for Creative Leadership, for example, managers learn by participating in the "Looking Glass" simulation that models the pressures of daily work. The simulation is followed by extensive debriefings and discussion in which participants give feedback to one another. One participant commented, "You can look in the mirror but you don't see yourself. People have to say how you look."[24]

> • **Management development** is training to improve knowledge and skills in the fundamentals of management.

PERFORMANCE MANAGEMENT

- A **performance management system** sets standards, assesses results, and plans actions to improve future performance.

- **Performance appraisal** is the process of formally evaluating performance and providing feedback.

The continuous development and improvement of human resource potential requires a successful **performance management system.** This is a system that ensures performance standards and objectives are set, that performance is regularly assessed for accomplishments, and that actions are taken to improve performance potential in the future. The process of formally assessing someone's work accomplishments and providing feedback is **performance appraisal** and it serves two basic purposes in the maintenance of a quality workforce. The *evaluation purpose* is intended to let people know where they stand relative to performance objectives and standards. The *development purpose* is intended to assist in their training and continued personal development.[25]

With respect to the evaluation, purpose performance appraisal focuses on past performance and measures results against standards. Performance is documented for the record and to establish a basis for allocating rewards. The manager acts in a *judgmental role* in which he or she gives a direct evaluation of another person's accomplishments. The development purpose of performance appraisal, by contrast, focuses on future performance and the clarification of success standards. It is a way of discovering performance obstacles and identifying training and development opportunities. Here the manager acts in a *counseling role,* focusing on a subordinate's developmental needs.

Like employment tests, any performance appraisal method should meet the criteria of reliability and validity.[26] To be reliable, the method should consistently yield the same result over time and/or for different raters; to be valid, it should be unbiased and measure only factors directly relevant to job performance. Both these criteria are especially important in today's complex legal environment. A manager who hires, fires, or promotes someone is increasingly called upon to defend such actions—sometimes in specific response to lawsuits alleging that the actions were discriminatory. At a minimum, written documentation of performance appraisals and a record of consistent past actions will be required to back up any contested evaluations.

Performance management plays an important role in any organization. At American Cyanamid, for example, a survey once revealed that employees viewed the company as "conservative, bureaucratic, and not sufficiently people-oriented." Part of the problem was traced to a performance appraisal system in which managers had to compare the performance of subordinates with one another and were required to discuss their subordinates' shortcomings. The company devised a new system focusing more on employee strengths and limiting discussions of shortcomings to those within the individuals' capacity to change.[27] Performance appraisal methods commonly used in organizations include the following.

Graphic Rating Scales

- A **graphic rating scale** uses a checklist of traits or characteristics to evaluate performance.

As shown in *Figure 12.4,* **graphic rating scales** offer checklists of traits or characteristics thought to be related to high performance outcomes in a given job. A manager rates the individual on each trait using a numerical score. The primary appeal of graphic rating scales is that they are relatively quick and easy to complete. Their reliability and validity are questionable, however, because the categories and scores are subject to varying interpretations.

Narrative Technique

- **The narrative technique** uses a written essay approach to describe a person's performance.

The **narrative technique** is a written essay description of a person's job performance. The commentary typically includes actual descriptions of performance, discusses an individual's strengths and weaknesses, and provides an overall evalu-

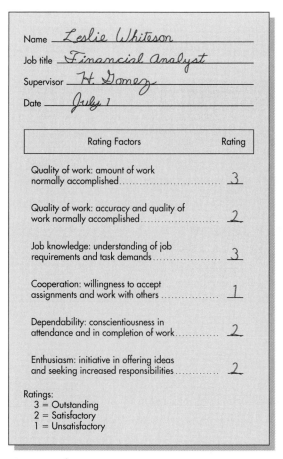

Rating Factors	Rating

Name *Leslie Whiteson*

Job title *Financial Analyst*

Supervisor *H. Gomez*

Date *July 1*

Quality of work: amount of work normally accomplished............................ **3**

Quality of work: accuracy and quality of work normally accomplished...................... **2**

Job knowledge: understanding of job requirements and task demands.................. **3**

Cooperation: willingness to accept assignments and work with others................ **1**

Dependability: conscientiousness in attendance and in completion of work............. **2**

Enthusiasm: initiative in offering ideas and seeking increased responsibilities............. **2**

Ratings:
3 = Outstanding
2 = Satisfactory
1 = Unsatisfactory

Figure 12.4 Example of a graphic rating scale for performance appraisal.

ation. Free-form narratives are sometimes used in combination with other performance appraisal methods, such as the graphic rating scale.

Behaviorally Anchored Rating Scales

A **behaviorally anchored rating scale (BARS)** offers rating scales for actual behaviors that exemplify various levels of performance achievement. Look at the case of a customer service representative illustrated in *Figure 12.5*. "Extremely poor" performance is clearly defined as rude or disrespectful treatment of a customer. Because performance assessments are anchored to specific descriptions of work behavior, a BARS is more reliable and valid than the graphic rating scale. The behavioral anchors can also be helpful in training people to master job skills of demonstrated performance importance.

● A **behaviorally anchored rating scale (BARS)** uses specific descriptions of actual behaviors to rate various levels of performance.

Critical-Incident Technique

The **critical-incident technique** involves keeping a running log or inventory of effective and ineffective job behaviors. By creating a written record of positive and negative performance examples, this method documents success or failure patterns that can be specifically discussed with the individual. Using the case of the customer service representative again, a critical-incidents log might contain the following types of entries: *Positive example* — "Took extraordinary care of a customer who had purchased a defective item from a company store in another city"; *negative example* — "Acted rudely in dismissing the complaint of a customer who felt that a sale item was erroneously advertised."

● The **critical incident technique** involves keeping a running log of effective and ineffective job behaviors.

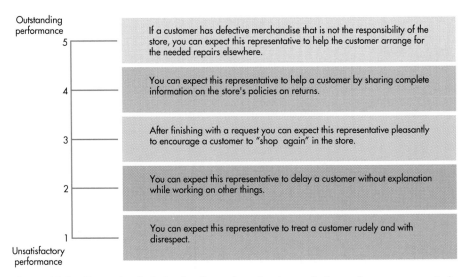

Figure 12.5   Example of a behaviorally anchored rating scale for performance appraisal: the case of a customer-service representative.

Multiperson Comparisons

• **A multiperson comparison** compares one person's performance with that of others.

An increasingly popular approach to performance appraisal involves the use of **multiperson comparisons,** which formally compare one person's performance with that of one or more others. Such comparisons can be used on their own or in combination with some other method. They can also be done in different ways. In *rank ordering,* all persons being rated are arranged in order of performance achievement, the best performer at the top of the list, the worst performer at the bottom; no ties are allowed. In *paired comparisons,* each person is formally compared to every other person and rated as either the superior or the weaker member of the pair. After all paired comparisons are made, each person is assigned a summary ranking based on the number of superior scores achieved. In *forced distribution,* each person is placed into a frequency distribution that requires that a certain percentage fall into specific performance classifications, such as top 10 percent, next 40 percent, next 40 percent, and bottom 10 percent.

MAINTAINING A QUALITY WORKFORCE

Human resource management should result in the maintainance of a qualified workforce at all times, even in a dynamic and changing environment with shifting work demands. It is not enough to attract and develop a qualified workforce; the workforce must be successfully nurtured and managed for long-term effectiveness. This requires proper attention to such issues as career development, retention and turnover, and compensation and benefits.

CAREER DEVELOPMENT

In his book *The Age of Unreason,* British scholar and consultant Charles Handy discusses dramatic new developments in the world of work and careers. Specifically, Handy says, "The times are changing and we must change with them."[28] Each of us should take Handy's advice and take charge of our careers. The Career

Advancement Portfolio section of the end-of-book *Career Readiness Workbook* is a useful resource in helping you to meet this challenge.

Formally defined, a *career* is a sequence of jobs and work pursuits that constitute what a person does for a living. For many of us, a career begins on an anticipatory basis with our formal education. From there it progresses into an initial job choice and any number of subsequent choices that may involve changes in task assignments, employing organizations, and even occupations. A *career path* is a sequence of jobs held over time during a career. Career paths vary between those that are pursued internally with the same employers and those pursued externally among various employers. Whereas many organizations place great emphasis on making long-term career opportunities available to their employees, Handy's view of the future is that external career paths will be increasingly important.

Career planning is the process of systematically matching career goals and individual capabilities with opportunities for their fulfillment. It involves answering such questions as "Who am I?," "Where do I want to go?," "How do I get there?" While some suggest that a career should be allowed to progress in a somewhat random but always opportunistic way, others view a career as something to be rationally planned and pursued in a logical step-by-step fashion. In fact, a well-managed career will probably include elements of each. The carefully thought-out plan can point you in a general career direction; an eye for opportunity can fill in the details along the way.

- **Career planning** is the process of systematically matching career goals and individual capabilities with opportunities for their fulfillment.

When you think about adult life stages or transitions, you should note that sooner or later most people's careers level off. A **career plateau** is a position from which someone is unlikely to move to a higher level of work responsibility.[29] Three common reasons for career plateaus are personal choice, limited abilities, and limited opportunities. For some, the plateau may occur at a point in life when it suits their individual needs; for others, the plateau may be unwanted and frustrating.

- **A career plateau** is a position from which someone is unlikely to move to a higher level of work responsibility.

WORK-LIFE BALANCE

Today's fast-paced and complicated life styles bring with them inevitable pressures on the balance between work and personal time. This issue of **work-life balance** deals with how people balance the demands of careers with their personal and family needs, with "family" including not just children but also elderly parents and other relatives in need of care. Among progressive employers human resource policies and practices that support a healthy work-life balance are increasingly viewed as positive investments. Although not all employers have yet responded to the call, benchmarks are available and they are growing in number. At First Union Bank in Charlotte, North Carolina, for example, employees have access to on-site day care as well as such additional services as medical and dental offices, dry cleaning, and even video rentals. All of this is aimed at improving employee welfare and productivity through an organizational commitment to work-life balance.[30]

- **Work-life balance** involves balancing career demands with personal and family needs.

Included among work-life balance concerns are the unique needs *single parent*— who must balance complete parenting responsibilities with a job, and *dual-career couples* — who must balance the career needs and opportunities of each partner. The special needs of both working mothers and working fathers are also being recognized.[31] Not surprisingly, the "family-friendliness" of an employer is now frequently and justifiably used as a screening criterion by job candidates. *Business Week* magazine has started an annual survey of "Work and Family Strategies in Corporate America." A recent rating had MBNA America, Motorola, Barnett Banks, Hewlett-Packard and Unum in the top five.[32] All top ranked companies shared a commitment to job flexibility in meeting employee's diverse family needs. Similar rankings are found in *Working Mother, Fortune,* and in a U.S. Department of Labor report.[33]

Family friendliness is evident at Autodesk, a software maker. The firm was rated highly by its employees in a *Business Week* annual survey. The fact that you can bring dogs, cats, and even iguana to work with co-workers' approval is a bit extreme. But the job flexibility offered by the firm isn't. It offers opportunities for balance between work and family. The company atmosphere is informal, employees are allowed to set their own work schedules, and almost half spend one day a week working from their homes. Support comes from the top . . . by example. CEO Carol Bartz makes it a point to stay home a week after long trips to be with her young daughter.[34]

RETENTION AND TURNOVER

- **Replacement** is the management of promotions, transfers, terminations, layoffs, and retirements.

The several steps in the human resource management process both conclude and recycle with **replacement,** that is, the management of promotions, transfers, terminations, layoffs, and retirements. Any replacement situation should be approached as an opportunity to review human resource plans, update job analyses, rewrite job descriptions and job specifications, and ensure that the best people are selected to perform the required tasks. Some replacement decisions shift people between positions within the organization. *Promotion* is movement to a higher level position; *transfer* is movement to a different job at a similar level of responsibility.

Another set of replacement decisions relates to *retirement,* something most people look forward to . . . until it is close at hand. Then the prospect of being retired often raises fears and apprehensions. Many organizations offer special counseling and other forms of support for preretirement employees, including advice on company benefits, money management, estate planning, and use of leisure time. Downsizing is sometimes accompanied by special offers of early retirement, that is, retirement before formal retirement age but with special financial incentives. Where this is not possible, a growing number of organizations provide outplacement services to help terminated employees find other jobs.

The most extreme replacement decisions involve *termination,* the involuntary and permanent dismissal of an employee. For the person being dismissed accepting the fact of termination is difficult. The termination notice may come by surprise and without the benefit of advance preparation for either the personal or the financial shock. The experts' advice, though, is to ask at least three tough questions of the ex-boss: "Why am I being fired?" "What are my termination benefits?" "Can I have a good reference?" Advice for the manager who must do the firing is offered in *Manager's Notepad 12.2.*

COMPENSATION AND BENEFITS

- **Base compensation** is a salary or hourly wage paid to an individual.

When properly designed and implemented, compensation and benefit systems help attract qualified people to the organization and retain them. This issue was introduced in our discussion of organizational control systems in Chapter 9. **Base compensation** in the form of salary or hourly wages can make the organization a desirable place of employment. It can help get the right people into jobs to begin with, and by making outside opportunities less attractive it can also help keep them there. Unless an organization's prevailing wage and salary structure is competitive, it will be difficult to attract and retain a staff of highly competent work-

---

M a n a g e r ' s   N o t e p a d   1 2 . 2

Things to Remember when Handling a Dismissal

- Dismissal can be as personally devastating as a divorce or the death of a loved one.
- Dismissal should always be legally defensible and done in complete compliance with organizational policies.
- Dismissal should not be delayed unnecessarily; it is best done as soon as the inevitability of the dismissal is known.
- Dismissal should include offers of assistance to help the former employee reenter the labor market.

---

ers. A basic rule of thumb is to study the labor market carefully and pay at least as much as, and perhaps a bit more than, what competitors are offering.

The organization's employee-benefit program also plays a role in attracting and retaining capable workers. **Fringe benefits** are the additional nonwage or nonsalary forms of compensation provided to an organization's workforce. They now constitute some 30 percent or more of a typical worker's earnings. Benefit packages usually include various options on disability protection, health and life insurance, and retirement plans. At the executive level, these benefits may extend into such additional "perks" as company cars and expenses, deferred compensation, supplemental retirement benefits, and personal tax and financial planning.

The ever-rising cost of fringe benefits, particularly employee medical benefits, is a major worry for employers. Some are attempting to gain control over health-care costs by becoming more active in their employees' choices of health-care providers and by encouraging healthy lifestyles. An increasingly common approach overall is **flexible benefits,** sometimes known as *cafeteria benefits,* which let the employee choose a set of benefits within a certain dollar amount. The employee gains when such plans are better able to meet individual needs; the employer gains from being more responsive to a wider range of needs in a diverse workforce.

- **Fringe benefits** are nonmonetary forms of compensation (e.g., health plans, retirement plans, etc.).

- A **flexible benefits** program allows employees to choose a range of benefit options.

MANAGEMENT RELATIONS

A final aspect of human resource management relates to the influence of organized labor. **Labor unions** are organizations to which workers belong that deal with employers on the workers' behalf.[35] Although they used to be associated primarily with industrial and business occupations, labor unions increasingly represent such public sector employees as teachers, police officers, and government workers. They are important forces in the modern workplace both in the United States and around the world. Today, slightly over 16 percent of American non-farm workers belong to a union; the figures are over 30 percent for Canada and some 25 percent for Great Britain.[36] Such unions act as bargaining agents who negotiate legal contracts that affect many aspects of human resource management. These **labor contracts** specify the rights and obligations of employees and management with respect to wages, work hours, work rules, seniority, hiring, grievances, and other aspects or conditions of employment.

The foundation of any labor and management relationship is **collective bargaining,** which is the process of negotiating, administering, and interpreting labor contracts. Labor contracts and the collective bargaining process — from negotiating a new contract to resolving disputes under an existing one, are major influences on human resource management in unionized work settings. They are also governed closely in the United States by a strict legal framework. For example, the *Wagner Act of 1935* protects employees by recognizing their rights to

- A **labor union** is an organization to which workers belong and that deals with employers on their collective behalf.

- A **labor contract** is a formal agreement between a union and the employing organization that specifies the rights and obligations of each party with respect to wages, work hours, work rules, and other conditions of employment.

- **Collective bargaining** is the process of negotiating, administering, and interpreting a labor contract.

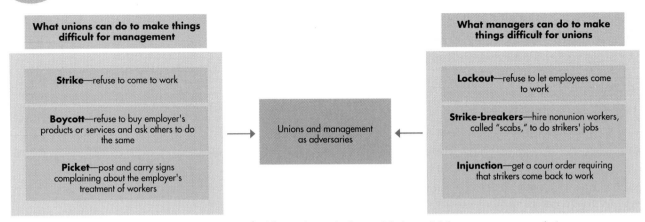

What unions can do to make things difficult for management

Strike—refuse to come to work

Boycott—refuse to buy employer's products or services and ask others to do the same

Picket—post and carry signs complaining about the employer's treatment of workers

Unions and management as adversaries

What managers can do to make things difficult for unions

Lockout—refuse to let employees come to work

Strike-breakers—hire nonunion workers, called "scabs," to do strikers' jobs

Injunction—get a court order requiring that strikers come back to work

Figure 12.6 The traditional adversarial view of labor-management relations.

● **Xerox Corporation**
http://www.xerox.com

Labor-management cooperation helped Xerox Corporation bring home to America jobs it had previously performed abroad. The firm is trying new team manufacturing concepts developed with the assistance of the union representing its copier assemblers, the Amalgamated Clothing & Textiles Workers Union. Says CEO Paul A. Allaire: ". . . if we have a cooperative model, the union movement will be sustained and the industries it's in will be more competitive."

join unions and engage in union activities; the *Taft-Hartley Act of 1947* protects employers from unfair labor practices by unions and allows workers to decertify unions; and the *Civil Service Reform Act Title VII of 1978* clarifies the rights of government employees to join and be represented by labor unions.

The collective bargaining process typically occurs in face-to-face meetings between labor and management representatives. During this time, a variety of demands, proposals, and counter proposals are exchanged. Several rounds of bargaining may be required before a contract is reached or a dispute over a contract issue is resolved. And, as you might expect, the process can lead to adversarial relationships.

In *Figure 12.6,* labor and management are viewed as "win-lose" adversaries, destined to be in opposition and possessed of certain weapons with which to fight one another. *If* labor-management relations take this form, a lot of energy on both sides can be expended in prolonged conflict. For years, the bargaining between Ford, General Motors, Chrysler, on the one hand, and the strong, demanding leadership of the United Auto Workers (UAW) on the other, had an adversarial character. Unions perceived management as aloof and uncaring in dealing with the needs of auto workers. The resulting labor contracts tried to protect worker interests through complex work rules and expensive compensation packages. While all this was happening, the competitiveness of the automakers was eroding. Many layoffs and plant closings occurred.

The traditional adversarial model of labor-management relations is, to some extent, giving way to a new and more progressive era of greater cooperation. Even the automakers and the UAW have tried to work more closely together to reduce production costs while maintaining basic worker rights and benefits.[37] Each side seems more willing to understand that the productivity and future survival of the industry depend on cooperation and mutual adjustment to new and challenging times. Today's union leaders appear to recognize that unions must adapt to changing conditions if they are to survive and prosper in the years ahead. The International Association of Machinists, for example, has cooperated with Aluminum Company of America in developing a high performance work system. To get started, the company sent three managers to be trained at the union's week-long training course of labor-management partnerships.[38] In today's competitive and challenging global economy, cooperation between unions and employers seems to be gaining headway.

CHAPTER REVIEW

This section should be used as an end-of-chapter "study guide." The *Summary* helps to put the chapter's content into overall perspective. The list of *Key Terms* allows you to double-check your familiarity with basic concepts and definitions. *Self-Test 12* gives you the opportunity to test your basic comprehension of the chapter using sample test questions.

SUMMARY

Why is human resource management important?

- The human resource management process is the process of attracting, developing, and maintaining a quality workforce.

- A complex legal environment influences human resource management, giving special attention to equal employment opportunity.

- Human resource planning is the process of analyzing staffing needs and identifying actions to satisfy these needs over time.

- The purpose of human resource planning is to make sure the organization always has people with the right abilities available to do the required work.

How do organizations attract quality workers?

- Recruitment is the process of attracting qualified job candidates to fill vacant positions.

- Recruitment can be both external and internal to the organization.

- Recruitment should involve realistic job previews that provide job candidates with accurate information on the job and organization.

- Managers typically use interviews, employment tests, and references to help make selection decisions; the use of assessment centers and work sampling is becoming more common.

How do organizations develop quality workers?

- Orientation is the process of formally introducing new hires to their jobs, performance requirements, and the organization.

- On-the-job training may include job rotation, coaching, apprenticeship, modeling, and mentoring.

- Off-the-job training may include a range of formal courses and programs, as well as simulations and other training specifically to tailored job needs.

- Performance management systems focus on the establishment of work standards and the assessment of results through performance appraisal.

- Common performance appraisal methods are graphic rating scales, narratives, behaviorally anchored rating scales, and multiperson comparisons.

How do organizations maintain a quality workforce?

- Career planning systematically matches individual career goals and capabilities with opportunities for their fulfillment.

- Programs that address work-life balance and the complex demands of job and family responsibilities are increasingly important in human resource management.

- Whenever workers must be replaced over time because of promotions, transfers, retirements, and terminations, the goal should be to treat everyone fairly while ensuring that jobs are filled with the best personnel available.

- Compensation and benefits packages must be continually updated so the organization maintains a competitive position in external labor markets.

- Where labor unions exist, labor-management relations should be positively approached and handled with all due consideration of applicable laws.

KEY TERMS

Affirmative action program (p. 242)

Assessment center (p. 246)

Base compensation (p. 254)

Behaviorally anchored rating scale (BARS) (p. 251)

Career planning (p. 253)

Career plateau (p. 253)

Collective bargaining (p. 255)

Critical-incident technique (p. 251)

Equal employment opportunity (p. 241)

Employment discrimination (p. 241)

Flexible benefits (p. 255)

Fringe benefits (p. 255)

Graphic rating scale (p. 250)

Human resource management (p. 240)

Job analysis (p. 243)

Job description (p. 243)

Job specification (p. 243)

Labor contract (p. 255)

Labor union (p. 255)

Management development (p. 249)

Mentoring (p. 249)

Modeling (p. 249)

Multiperson comparison (p. 252)

Narrative technique (p. 250)

Orientation (p. 248)

Performance appraisal (p. 250)

Performance management system (p. 250)

Realistic job preview (p. 245)

Recruitment (p. 244)

Replacement (p. 254)

Selection (p. 245)

Socialization (p. 248)

Strategic human resource planning (p. 242)

Training (p. 249)

Validity (p. 245)

Work-life balance (p. 253)

SELF-TEST 12

Take this test much as you would in a normal classroom situation. It should offer you a good way to check your basic comprehension of chapter material. Answers may be found at the end of the book.

MULTIPLE-CHOICE QUESTIONS:

1. Formally described, the staffing or human resource management process involves _____, developing, and maintaining a high-quality workforce. (a) attracting (b) compensating (c) appraising (d) testing

2. A _____ is a criterion that can be legally justified for use in screening candidates for employment. (a) job description (b) bona fide occupational qualification (c) job evaluation (d) occupational benchmark

3. _____ programs are designed to improve employment opportunities for minorities. (a) Realistic recruiting (b) External recruiting (c) Affirmative action (d) Labor-management cooperation

4. An employment test that fails to yield similar results over time when taken by the same person would be considered _____. (a) nonspecific (b) unstable (c) contradictory (d) unreliable

5. The assessment center approach to employee selection relies heavily on _____. (a) pencil and paper tests (b) simulations and experiential exercises (c) the review of written resumes (d) formal one-on-one interviews

6. _____ is a form of on-the-job training wherein an individual learns by observing others who demonstrate desirable job behaviors. (a) Case study (b) Work sampling (c) Modeling (d) Simulation

7. The first step in human resource planning is to _____. (a) forecast human resource needs (b) forecast labor supplies (c) assess the existing workforce (d) review organizational mission, objectives, and strategies

8. In the American legal environment, the _____ Act of 1947 protects employers from unfair labor practices by unions. (a) Wagner (b) Taft-Hartley (c) Labor Union (d) Hawley-Smoot

9. Socialization of newcomers occurs during the _____ step of the staffing process. (a) recruiting (b) orientation (c) selecting (d) training

10. Performance appraisal should _____ . (a) serve only evaluation purposes (b) not be done through forced comparisons (c) use reliable and valid methods (d) all of these.

TRUE-FALSE QUESTIONS:

11. In the United States, the legal environment affecting the staffing process is not very complicated. T F

12. In human resource planning, a job analysis determines exactly what is done in existing jobs. T F

13. The job specification identifies the qualifications required for someone to fill a job successfully. T F

14. External recruitment is always better than internal recruitment. T F

15. In a realistic job preview, a job applicant is provided with accurate information about a job and/or organization, even if it has negative aspects. T F

16. Collective bargaining is the process of negotiating, administering, and interpreting a labor contract. T F

17. The evaluation purpose of performance appraisal is served by managers acting in counseling roles. T F

18. An adversarial relationship in labor-management relations improves productivity in unionized work settings. T F

19. Flexible benefit programs are becoming less important today. T F

20. Career plateaus can create problems as organizations try to maintain a quality workforce. T F.

SHORT-RESPONSE QUESTIONS:

21. How do internal recruitment and external recruitment compare in terms of advantages and disadvantages for the employer?

22. Why is orientation an important part of the staffing process?

23. What is the difference between the graphic rating scale (BARS) as performance appraisal methods?

24. How does mentoring work as a form of on-the-job training?

APPLICATION QUESTION:

25. Sy Smith is not doing well in his job. The problems began to appear shortly after Sy's job was changed from a manual to a computer-based operation. He has tried but is just not doing well in terms of learning to use the computer and meet the performance expectations. As a 55-year-old employee with over 30 years with the company, Sy is both popular and influential among his work peers. Along with his performance problems you have also noticed the appearance of some negative attitudes — a tendency for Sy to "badmouth" the firm. As Sy's manager, what options would you consider in terms of dealing with the issue of his retention in the job and in the company? What would you do and why?

Leading – To Inspire Effort

Planning Ahead—Chapter 13 Study Questions

▬ What is leadership?

▬ How do leaders gain and use power?

▬ What are the important leadership traits and behaviors?

▬ What are the contingency theories of leadership?

▬ What are current issues in leadership development?

You Have to Believe in People

What is great leadership? At Herman Miller, Inc., the innovative Michigan-based maker of office furniture, the answer lies in a belief in people. Max DePree, the firm's chairperson and the son of its founder, tells the story of a millwright who worked for his father. The millwright held an important job in the plant. He was responsible for keeping all of the machines supplied with power from a central boiler.

When the man died, DePree's father, wishing to express his sympathy to the family, went to their home. There he listened as the widow read some beautiful poems, which, he was surprised to learn, had been written by the millwright. To this day, DePree says, he and his father still wonder, "Was he a poet who did millwright's work, or was he a millwright who wrote poetry?"

Max DePree summarizes the lesson of the chapter opening story this way: "It is fundamental that leaders endorse a concept of persons. This begins with an understanding of the diversity of people's gifts, talents, and skills." According to DePree, when we recognize the unique qualities of others, we become less inclined to believe that we alone know what is best. By valuing diversity, not only do we learn what may be needed to provide others with meaningful work and opportunities, we also benefit by allowing everyone's contribution to have an influence on the organization. Under DePree's leadership, and using techniques such as participative ownership and teamwork, Herman Miller has achieved the rank of one of *Fortune*'s "most admired" American corporations.[1]

THE NATURE OF LEADERSHIP

It is time to think seriously about the many demands made on those who serve as leaders in the new workplace. Part of this chapter's theme relates to the distinction between management and leadership.[2] Warren Bennis, a respected leadership scholar and consultant, claims that too many American corporations are "overmanaged and under led."[3] Grace Hooper, another management expert and the first female admiral in the U.S. Navy says, "You manage things; you lead people."[4]

> **Leadership** is the process of inspiring others to work hard to accomplish important tasks.

A glance at the shelves in your local bookstore will quickly confirm that **leadership** — the process of inspiring others to work hard to accomplish important tasks, is one of the most popular management topics. As shown in *Figure 13.1*, it is also one of the four functions that constitute the management process. With the rapid technological change, intense global competition, and workforce diversity of the new workplace leadership is essential to management. Planning sets the direction and objectives; organizing brings the resources together to turn plans into action; *leading* builds the commitments and enthusiasm needed for people to apply their talents fully to help accomplish plans; and controlling makes sure things turn out right. To succeed as a leader in this action context, one must be good at dealing with all aspects of communication, interpersonal relations, motivation, job design, teamwork, and change — all topics covered in this part of the book.[5]

LEADERSHIP AND VISION

> **Vision** is a term used to describe a clear sense of the future.

"Great leaders," it is said, "get extraordinary things done in organizations by inspiring and motivating others toward a common purpose."[6] More and more frequently great leadership is associated with **vision.** The term is generally used to describe someone who has a clear sense of the future and an understanding of the actions needed to get there successfully. But there is more. Leading requires turning vision into results. At GE, for example, the top management team says:

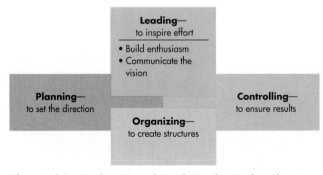

Figure 13.1   Leading viewed in relationship to the other management functions.

Manager's Notepad 13.1

Five Principles of Visionary Leadership

1. *Challenge the process:* Be a pioneer — encourage innovation and support people who have ideas.

2. *Be enthusiastic:* Inspire others through personal enthusiasm to share in a common vision.

3. *Help others to act:* Be a team player and support the efforts and talents of others.

4. *Set the example:* Provide a consistent role model of how others can and should act.

5. *Celebrate achievements:* Bring emotion into the workplace and rally "hearts" as well as "minds."

"At the leadership level, an "A" is a man or woman with vision and the ability to articulate that vision to the team, so vividly and powerfully that it also becomes their vision."[7]

The accompanying *Manager's Notepad 13.1* offers five principles for meeting the challenges of visionary leadership.[8] Note that the suggestions go beyond a manager's responsibilities for making long-term plans and drafting budgets. They go beyond putting structures in place and assigning people jobs. And they go beyond making sure that results are consistent with the original plan. Leadership with vision means doing all these things and more. It means beginning with a clear vision; it requires communicating that vision to all concerned; and it involves getting people motivated and inspired to pursue the vision in their daily work. This is the ultimate test for Max DePree at Herman Miller, for managers at GE, as well as others in dynamic leadership settings around the world. Leadership, simply put, involves both having a vision and being able to turn it into reality.

LEADERSHIP AND POWER

The foundations of effective leadership lie in the way a manager uses power to influence the behavior of other people. **Power** is the ability to get someone else to do something you want done. It is the ability to make things happen the way you want them to.[9] Research recognizes that a need for power is essential to executive success.[10] But this need for power is not a desire to control for the sake of personal satisfaction; it is a desire to influence and control others for the good of the group or organization as a whole. This "positive" face of power is the foundation of effective leadership. *Figure 13.2* shows one set of power sources that is based in the position a person holds and a second set that is based in one's personal qualities.[11]

- **Power** is the ability to get someone else to do something you want done or to make things happen the way you want.

Sources of power...

Power of the POSITION: *Based on things managers can offer to others.*	Power of the PERSON: *Based on the ways managers are viewed by others.*
Rewards: "If you do what I ask, I'll give you a reward."	**Expertise**—as a source of special knowledge and information.
Coercion: "If you *don't* do what I ask, I'll punish you."	**Reference**—as a person with whom others like to identify.
Legitimacy: "Because I am the boss; you *must* do as I ask."	

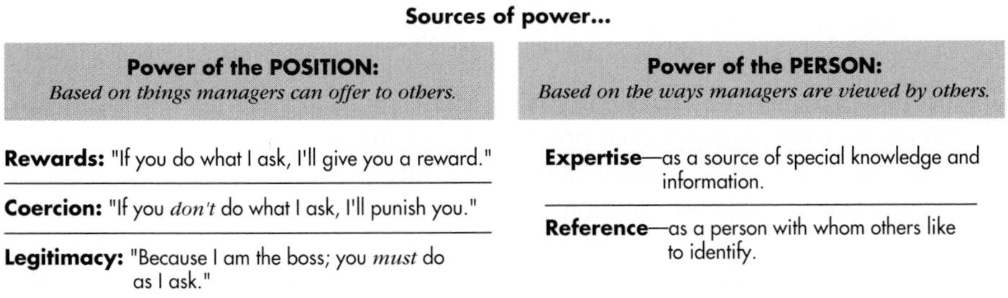

Figure 13.2 Sources of position power and personal power used by managers.

Sources of Position Power

One important source of power is a manager's official status, or position, in the organization's hierarchy of authority. Whereas anyone holding a managerial position theoretically has this power, how well it is used will vary from one person to the next. Consequently, leadership success will vary as well. The three bases of *position power* are reward power, coercive power, and legitimate power.

Reward power is the ability to influence through rewards. It is the capability to offer something of value — a positive outcome, as a means of influencing the behavior of other people. This involves the control of rewards or resources such as pay raises, bonuses, promotions, special assignments, and verbal or written compliments. To mobilize reward power, a manager says, in effect, "If you do what I ask, I'll give you a reward."

- **Reward power** is the capacity to offer something of value as a means of influencing other people.

Coercive power is the ability to influence through punishment. It is the capacity to punish or withhold positive outcomes as a way to influence the behavior of other people. A manager may attempt to coerce someone by threatening him or her with verbal reprimands, pay penalties, and even termination. To mobilize coercive power, a manager says, in effect, "If you don't do what I want, I'll punish you."

- **Coercive power** is the capacity to punish or withhold positive outcomes as a means of influencing other people.

Legitimate power is the ability to influence through *authority* — the right by virtue of one's organizational position or status to exercise control over persons in subordinate positions. It is the capacity to influence the behavior of other people by virtue of the rights of office. To mobilize legitimate power, a manager says, in effect, "I am the boss and therefore you are supposed to do as I ask."

- **Legitimate power** is the capacity to influence other people by virtue of formal authority, or the rights of office.

Sources of Personal Power

Another source of power lies in the individual manager and the unique personal qualities she or he brings to a leadership situation. This is a very important source of power that a truly successful leader cannot do without. Two bases of *personal power* are expert power and referent power.

Expert power is the ability to influence through special expertise. It is the capacity to influence the behavior of other people because of one's knowledge, understanding, and skills. Expertise derives from the possession of technical know-how or information pertinent to the issue at hand.[12] This is developed by acquiring relevant skills or competencies or by gaining a central position in relevant information networks. It is maintained by protecting one's credibility and not overstepping the boundaries of true understanding. When a manager uses expert power, the implied message is, "You should do what I want because of my special expertise or information."

- **Expert power** is the capacity to influence other people because of specialized knowledge.

Referent power is the ability to influence through identification. It is the capacity to influence the behavior of other people because they admire you and want to identify positively with you. Reference is a power derived from charisma or interpersonal attractiveness. It is developed and maintained through good interpersonal relations that encourage the admiration and respect of others. When a manager uses referent power, the implied message is, "You should do what I want in order to maintain a positive self-defined relationship with me."

- **Referent power** is the capacity to influence other people because of their desire to identify personally with you.

TURNING POWER INTO INFLUENCE

To succeed at leadership, anyone must be able to both acquire and appropriately use position power and personal power.[13] *Centrality* is important. Managers, for example, must establish a broad network of interpersonal contacts and get involved in the important information flows within them. They must avoid becoming isolated. *Criticality* is also important. To gain power, managers must take good care of others who are dependent on them. They should take care to support them exceptionally well by doing things that add value to the work setting.

Power is also enhanced by *visibility.* It helps to become known as an influential person in the organization. Good managers don't hesitate to make formal presentations, participate in key task forces or committees, and pursue special assignments that can display their leadership talents and capabilities.

It is important to remember that position power alone is often insufficient to achieve needed influence. This is particularly true in influencing the behavior of peers and superiors in the organization. In such cases, personal power must be developed through good interpersonal skills. Four points to keep in mind are (1) there is no substitute for expertise, (2) likable personal qualities are very important, (3) effort and hard work breed respect, and (4) personal behavior must support expressed values.[14]

Chester Barnard's *acceptance theory of authority* identifies four conditions that determine whether a leader's directives will be followed and true influence achieved:[15] (1) The other person must truly understand the directive. (2) The other person must feel capable of carrying out the directive. (3) The other person must believe that the directive is in the organization's best interests. (4) The other person must believe that the directive is consistent with personal values. One application of this theory relates to ethics and the limits to power.

When the complexities of ethical dilemmas were discussed in Chapter 6, it was noted that many such dilemmas begin when leaders and managers pressure followers to do questionable things. Using the acceptance theory of authority as a starting point, the ethical question one must always be prepared to ask is "Where do I (or will I) draw the line; at what point do I (or will I) refuse to comply with requests?" Someday you may face a situation in which you are asked by someone in authority to do something that violates personal ethics and/or even the law. Can you . . . will you . . . when will you . . . say "no"? After all and as Barnard said, it is "acceptance" that establishes the limits of managerial power.

• **Harley-Davidson**
http://www.harley-davidson.com

The success of Harley-Davidson owes a debt to visionary leadership and a commitment to quality. Harley today appeals to customers worldwide. The firm promotes its high-quality product through an emphasis on both image and safety. And it still has its competition on the run.

LEADERSHIP AND EMPOWERMENT

At many points in this book, we have talked about *empowerment,* the process through which managers enable and help others to gain power and achieve influence within the organization. Effective leaders empower others. They know that when people feel powerful, they are more willing to make the decisions and take the actions needed to get their jobs done. They also realize that power in organizations is not a "zero-sum" quantity. That is, they realize that in order for someone to gain power, it isn't necessary for someone else to give it up. Indeed, to master the complexity and pace of challenges faced in today's environments, an organization's success may well depend on how much power can be mobilized throughout all ranks of employees.

When *Working Woman* was looking for a role model of business leadership in the 21st century it turned to Patricia Gallup, CEO of PC Connection. Gallup co-founded the computer mail-order firm in 1982 and has since gained a reputation for first-class leadership. She is considered the new breed of leader who emphasizes integration, teamwork, collaboration, and consensus rather than command and control. Of course it's hard work and the hours are long—some 60 or more in Gallup's typical week. She communicates via Email and directly with the firm's 284 employees, greets employees by name in the hallways, and prefers working with others out on the floor rather than spending time alone in her office.[16]

Manager's Notepad 13.2

How to Empower Others

- Get others involved in selecting their work assignments and the methods for accomplishing tasks.
- Create an environment of cooperation, information sharing, discussion, and shared ownership of goals.
- Encourage others to take initiative, make decisions, and use their knowledge.
- When problems arise, find out what others think and let them help design the solutions.
- Stay out of the way; give others the freedom to put their ideas and solutions into practice.
- Maintain high morale and confidence by recognizing successes and encouraging high performance.

Manager's Notepad 13.2 offers tips on how to empower others.[17] There are many benefits for managers who are successful at doing so. On the one hand, empowerment allows people to act independently and feel more "adult" in their work activities. On the other hand, a manager who empowers others tends to gain power too. Having a high-performing work unit certainly helps establish the criticality, centrality, and visibility of one's position. The very act of empowering others may create a positive relationship and build reference power. And what better way to demonstrate expertise than to show that one's team does a great job?

Returning to the Herman Miller example, Max DePree praises leaders who are willing to focus on what is best for the organization and "permit others to share ownership of problems—to take possession of the situation."[18] DePree is talking about leadership through empowerment; he is talking about helping others use their knowledge and judgment to make a real difference in daily workplace affairs. This occurs as people work in responsible jobs, as they participate in cross-functional task forces and teams, and as they function in work environments that respect them as capable and creative human beings. It occurs anywhere that managers truly empower others by supporting initiative, respecting individual talents, and sharing power at all levels of operations.

LEADERSHIP TRAITS AND BEHAVIORS

For centuries, people have recognized that some persons perform very well as leaders, whereas others do not. The question still debated is "Why?" Historically, the trait, behavioral, and contingency approaches shown in *Figure 13.3* have taken slightly different tacks in attempting to answer this question.

SEARCH FOR LEADERSHIP TRAITS

One direction in leadership research has involved a search for universal traits that separate effective and ineffective leaders.[19] Given such a list, it would be easy to select for leadership positions only those people whose characteristics matched the profile and who would therefore surely succeed. Overall, however, re-

Why are some people more effective leaders than others?

Trait approach	Focus on leader's personal characteristics
Behavioral approach	Focus on leader's behavior vis-à-vis followers
Contingency approach	Focus on match between leader behavior and situational characteristics
Charismatic approach	Focus on visionary, inspirational, and empowering qualities of "superleaders"

Figure 13.3 Directions in leadership research: the trait, behavioral, contingency, and charismatic approaches.

searchers have been unable to isolate a definitive profile of traits that consistently accounts for leadership success. The results of many years of research can be summarized as follows. Physical traits such as a person's height, weight, and physique make no difference in determining leadership success. On the other hand, followers do appear to admire certain things about leaders. In one study of over 3,400 managers, for example, the most respected leaders were described as honest, competent, forward-looking, inspiring, and credible.[20] Such positive feelings may enhance a leader's effectiveness, particularly with respect to creating vision and a sense of empowerment. Among the personal traits now considered important as personal foundations for leadership success are drive, desire to lead, motivation, honesty and integrity, self-confidence, intelligence, knowledge, and flexibility.[21]

FOCUS ON LEADERSHIP BEHAVIORS

Recognizing that the possession of certain traits alone does not guarantee leadership success, researchers turned their attention to a leader's behavior vis-à-vis followers. The behavioral theories of leadership sought to determine which **leadership style** — the recurring pattern of behaviors exhibited by a leader, worked best. Given a preferred style, the goal was to be able to train leaders to become skilled at using it to best advantage.

• **Leadership style** is the recurring pattern of behaviors exhibited by a leader.

Now president of the Child Care Action Campaign, Faith Wohl was one of DuPont's first senior female managers. When she took over as the director of workforce partnering for the firm, she was committed to making the firm "family friendly." She advocated policies that help employees balance work and family needs, such as job sharing and Flextime schedules, day-care programs, elder care, and related matters. Knowing she needed management support to make them work, Wohl made data-filled presentations, held well-publicized meetings with employees to discuss the programs, met frequently with managers to determine their needs, set up "work life" committees to solicit employee suggestions, and made sure the CEO regularly expressed his public support.[22]

The world took notice when Bernard J. Ebbers, CEO of WorldCom, outbid competitors for MCI Communications. With the deal's approval WorldCom will become the second-largest player in the world's telecommunications industry. But the deal will also bring important leadership and management challenges for Ebbers as he tries to forge the union into a powerhouse company.

Task and People Concerns

Most research in the leader behavior tradition focused on the degree to which a leader's style displays concern for the task to be accomplished and/or concern for the people doing the work. The terminology used to describe these dimensions of leader behavior varies among the many available studies. *Concern for task* is sometimes addressed as initiating structure, job-centeredness, and task orientation; *concern for people* is also referred to as consideration, employee-centeredness, and relationship orientation. But regardless of the terminology, the behaviors characteristic of each dimension are quite clear. A leader high in concern for task plans and defines work to be done, assigns task responsibilities, sets clear work standards, urges task completion, and monitors performance results. By contrast, a leader high in concern for people acts warm and supportive toward followers, develops social rapport with them, respects their feelings, is sensitive to their needs, and shows trust in them.

When these behaviors are used in different combinations the following leadership styles have been identified.[23] An *abdicative* or *laissez-faire leader* shows low concern for both people and tasks. Managers with this style turn most decisions over to the work group and show little interest in the work process or its results. A *directive* or *autocratic leader* shows high concern for the task and low concern for people. Managers with this style make most of the decisions for the work group, give directions, and expect their orders to be followed. A *supportive* or *human relations leader* shows high concern for people and low concern for tasks. Managers with this style are warm in interpersonal relationships, avoid conflict, and seek harmony in decision making. A *participative* or *democratic leader* shows high concern for both people and tasks. Managers with this style share decisions with the work group, encourage participation, and support the work efforts of others.

Research and Training Insights

The results of leader behavior research at first suggested that followers of people-oriented leaders would be more productive and satisfied than those working for more task-oriented leaders.[24] Later results, however, suggested that truly effective leaders were high in both concern for people and concern for task. *Figure 13.4* describes one of the popular versions of this conclusion, the Blake and Mouton leadership grid.[25] This approach uses assessments to first determine where someone falls with respect to people and task concerns. Then a training program is designed to help shift the person's style in the preferred direction of a "team leader" who scores high in both areas. Similar to the participative leader previously described, a team leader shares decisions with subordinates, encourages participation, and supports the teamwork needed for high levels of task accomplishment. In today's terminology, this could also be a manager who "empowers" others.

CONTINGENCY APPROACHES TO LEADERSHIP

As leadership research continued to develop, interest emerged in yet another question: "When and under what circumstances is a particular leadership style preferable to others?" This is the essence of the *contingency approach* to leadership, which attempts to understand the conditions for leadership success in widely varying situations.

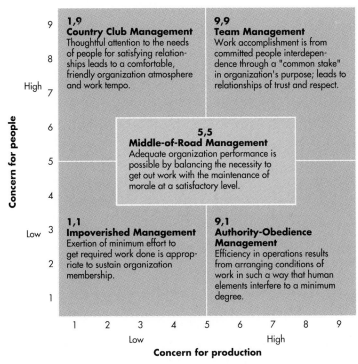

Figure 13.4 The leadership grid. *Source:* From Robert R. Blake and Anne Adams McCanse, *Leadership Dilemmas — Grid Solutions* (Houston: Gulf, 1991), 29. Copyright © 1991, by Scientific Methods, Inc. Reproduced by permission of the owners.

FIEDLER'S CONTINGENCY MODEL

An early contingency leadership theory developed by Fred Fiedler was based on the premise that good leadership depends on a match between leadership style and situational demands.[26] Leadership style is measured on what Fiedler calls the *least-preferred coworker scale* (available as a self-assessment in the end-of-book *Career Readiness Workbook*). It describes the tendencies of a leader to be either task motivated or relationship motivated. This either/or concept is important. Fiedler believes that leadership style is part of one's personality; therefore, it is relatively enduring and difficult to change. Instead of trying to train a task-motivated leader to be relationship motivated, or vice versa, Fiedler suggests that the key to leadership success is putting the existing styles to work in situations for which they are the best "fit."

Understanding Leadership Situations

In Fiedler's theory, the amount of control a situation allows the leader is a critical issue in determining the correct style-situation fit. Three contingency variables are used to diagnose situational control. The *quality of leader-member relations* (good or poor) measures the degree to which the group supports the leader. The *degree of task structure* (high or low) measures the extent to which task goals, procedures, and guidelines are clearly spelled out. The *amount of position power* (strong or weak) measures the degree to which the position gives the leader power to reward and punish subordinates.

Figure 13.5 shows eight leadership situations that result from different combinations of these variables. They range from the most favorable situation of high control (good leader-member relations, high task structure, strong position

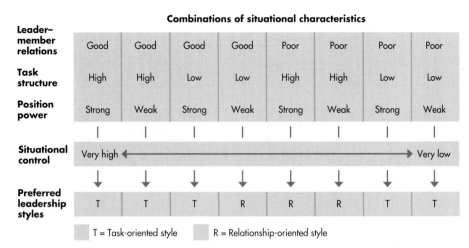

Figure 13.5   Matching leadership style and situation: summary predictions from Fiedler's contingency theory.

power), to the least favorable situation of low control (poor leader-member relations, low task structure, weak position power).

Matching Leadership Style and Situation

Figure 13.5 also summarizes Fiedler's extensive research on the contingency relationships between situation control, leadership style, and leader effectiveness. Neither the task-oriented nor the relationship-oriented leadership style is effective all the time. Instead, each style appears to work best when used in the right situation. The results can be stated as two propositions. *Proposition 1* is that a task-oriented leader will be most successful in either very favorable (high-control) or very unfavorable (low-control) situations. *Proposition 2* is that a relationship-oriented leader will be most successful in situations of moderate control.

Fiedler believes that leadership success depends on a good match between style and situation. This means that prospective leaders should actively seek situations for which their predominant style is most appropriate. Assume, for example, that you are the leader of a team of bank tellers. The tellers seem highly supportive of you, and their job is clearly defined regarding what needs to be done. You have the authority to evaluate their performance and to make pay and promotion recommendations. This is a high-control situation consisting of good leader-member relations, high task structure, and high position power. *Figure 13.6* shows that a task-motivated leader would be most effective in this situation.

Now take another example. Suppose that you are chairperson of a committee asked to improve labor-management relations in a manufacturing plant. Although the goal is clear, no one can say for sure how to accomplish it. Task structure is low. Because committee members are free to quit anytime they want, the chairperson has little position power. Because not all members believe the committee is necessary; poor leader-member relations are apparent. According to *Figure 13.6,* this low-control situation also calls for a task-motivated leader.

Finally, assume that you are the new head of a retail section in a large department store. Because you were selected over one of the popular sales clerks you now supervise, leader-member relations are poor. Task structure is high since the clerk's job is well defined. Your position power is low because the clerks work under a seniority system and fixed wage schedule. *Figure 13.6* shows that this moderate-control situation requires a relationship-motivated leader.

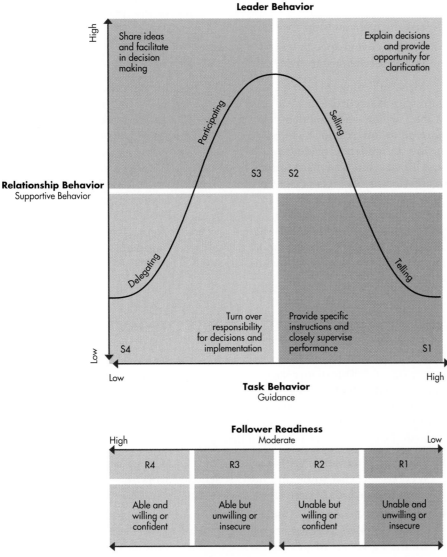

Figure 13.6 The Hersey-Blanchard model of situational leadership. *Source:* Paul Hersey and Kenneth H. Blanchard, *Management of Organizational Behavior* (Englewood Cliffs, N.J.: Prentice-Hall, 1988), p. 171. Used by permission.

HERSEY-BLANCHARD SITUATIONAL LEADERSHIP MODEL

The Hersey-Blanchard situational leadership model suggests that successful leaders adjust their styles depending on the readiness of followers to perform in a given situation.[27] "Readiness," in this sense, is based on how able, willing, and confident followers are to perform required tasks. As shown in *Figure 13.6,* the possible leadership styles that result from different combinations of task- oriented and relationship-oriented behaviors are as follows:

- *Delegating:* Allowing the group to make and take responsibility for task decisions; a low-task, low-relationship style.

- *Participating:* Emphasizing shared ideas and participative decisions on task directions; a low-task, high-relationship style.

Leadership styles in the situational theory

- *Selling:* Explaining task directions in a supportive and persuasive way; a high-task, high-relationship style.

- *Telling:* Giving specific task directions and closely supervising work; a high-task, low-relationship style.

Managers using this model must be able to implement the alternative leadership styles as needed. The *delegating style* works best in high-readiness situations of able, willing, and confident followers; the *telling style* works best at the other extreme of low readiness. In between, the *participating style* is recommended for low to moderate readiness and the *selling style* for moderate to high readiness. Hersey and Blanchard further believe that leadership styles can and should be adjusted as followers in a given situation change over time. The model also implies that if the correct styles are used in lower readiness situations, followers will "mature" and grow in ability, willingness, and confidence. Not only is this a positive result in itself, it also allows the leader to become less directive. Although the Hersey-Blanchard model is popular in management training programs and is intuitively appealing, limited research has been accomplished on it to date.[28]

HOUSE'S PATH-GOAL LEADERSHIP THEORY

A third contingency leadership approach is the path-goal theory advanced by Robert House.[29] This theory suggests that an effective leader is one who clarifies paths through which followers can achieve both task-related and personal goals. A good leader helps people progress along these paths, removes any barriers, and provides appropriate rewards for task accomplishment. House identifies four leadership styles that may be used in this "path-goal" sense:

Leadership styles in the path-goal theory

- *Directive leadership:* Letting subordinates know what is expected; giving directions on what to do and how; scheduling work to be done; maintaining definite standards of performance; clarifying the leader's role in the group.

- *Supportive leadership:* Doing things to make work more pleasant; treating group members as equals; being friendly and approachable; showing concern for the well-being of subordinates.

- *Achievement-oriented leadership:* Setting challenging goals; expecting the highest levels of performance; emphasizing continuous improvement in performance; displaying confidence in meeting high standards.

- *Participative leadership:* Involving subordinates in decision making; consulting with subordinates; asking for suggestions from subordinates; using these suggestions when making a decision.

Predictions and Managerial Implications

The path-goal leadership theory is summarized in *Figure 13.7*. It advises a manager always to use leadership styles that *complement* the needs of situations. This means that the leader "adds value" by contributing things that are missing from the situation or that need strengthening; she or he specifically avoids redundant behaviors. The important contingencies for making good path-goal leadership choices include the work environment (tasks, authority, and group) and subordinate personal characteristics (ability, experience, and locus of control). For example, when *job assignments* are unclear, the effective manager provides directive leadership to clarify task objectives and expected rewards. When *worker self-confidence* is low, the effective manager provides supportive leadership to clarify individual abilities and offers needed task assistance. When *performance incentives* are poor, the effective manager provides participative leadership to

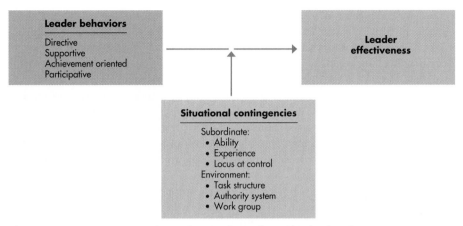

Figure 13.7 Contingency relationships in the path-goal leadership theory.

identify individual needs and appropriate rewards. When *task challenge* is insufficient, the effective manager provides achievement-oriented leadership to raise performance aspirations.

Substitutes for Leadership

Path-goal theory has also contributed to the recognition of what some theorists call **substitutes for leadership.**[30] These are aspects of the work setting and the people involved that can reduce the need for a leader's personal involvement. In effect, they make leadership from the "outside" unnecessary because leadership is already built into the situation. Possible substitutes for leadership include *subordinate characteristics* such as ability, experience, and independence; *task characteristics* such as routineness and availability of feedback; and *organizational characteristics* such as clarity of plans and formalization of rules and procedures. When substitutes are present, managers should avoid redundant leadership behaviors and concentrate on things that truly require outside attention.

● **Substitutes for leadership** are factors in the work setting that direct work efforts without the involvement of a leader.

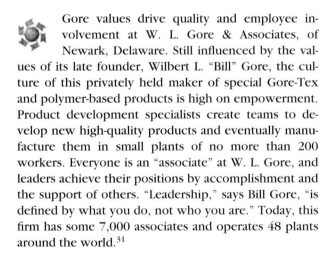

Gore values drive quality and employee involvement at W. L. Gore & Associates, of Newark, Delaware. Still influenced by the values of its late founder, Wilbert L. "Bill" Gore, the culture of this privately held maker of special Gore-Tex and polymer-based products is high on empowerment. Product development specialists create teams to develop new high-quality products and eventually manufacture them in small plants of no more than 200 workers. Everyone is an "associate" at W. L. Gore, and leaders achieve their positions by accomplishment and the support of others. "Leadership," says Bill Gore, "is defined by what you do, not who you are." Today, this firm has some 7,000 associates and operates 48 plants around the world.[31]

VROOM-JAGO LEADER-PARTICIPATION THEORY

The Vroom-Jago theory is designed to help a leader choose for any problem situation the best decision-making method — the individual or authority decision, the

- An **authority decision** is a decision made by the leader and then communicated to the group.

- A **consultative decision** is a decision made by a leader after receiving information, advice, or opinions from group members.

- A **group decision** is a decision made with the full participation of all group members.

consultative decision, or the group or consensus decision.[32] An **authority decision** is one made by the leader and then communicated to the group. No input is asked of group members other than to provide specific information on request. A **consultative decision** is made by the leader after asking group members for information, advice, or opinions. In some cases, group members are consulted individually; in others, the consultation occurs during a meeting of the group as a whole. In a **group decision,** all members participate in making a decision and work together to achieve a consensus regarding the preferred course of action. This approach to decision making is a form of empowerment, and it is successful to the extent that each member is ultimately able to accept the logic and feasibility of the final group decision.[33]

A single contingency proposition underlies the Vroom-Jago leader-participation model: Effective leadership results when the decision method used correctly matches the characteristics of the problem to be solved. There will be times when each of the three decision methods is most appropriate. For a manager who wants to be successful at leading through participation, therefore, the challenge is twofold: (1) to know when each decision method is the best approach and (2) to be able to implement each well when needed.

In general, a more group-oriented and participative decision method is recommended when leaders lack sufficient information to solve a problem by themselves, the problem is unclear and help is needed to clarify the situation, acceptance of the decision by others is necessary for its implementation, and adequate time is available to allow for true participation. On the other hand, a more authority-oriented leadership style can be used when leaders personally have the expertise needed to solve the problem, they are confident and capable of acting alone, others are likely to accept the decision they make, and little or no time is available for discussion.

 ## ISSUES IN LEADERSHIP DEVELOPMENT

- A **charismatic leader** is a leader who develops special leader-follower relationships and inspires followers in extraordinary ways.

- **Transformational leadership** is inspirational leadership that gets people to do more in achieving high performance.

- **Transactional leadership** is leadership that directs the efforts of others through tasks, rewards, and structures.

Current trends in leadership thinking seek to integrate and extend the insights discussed so far in this chapter.[34] This is the era of "superleaders" who, through vision and strength of personality, have a truly inspirational impact on others.[35] Their leadership efforts result in followers not only meeting performance expectations but performing above and beyond them. These are **charismatic leaders** who develop special leader-follower relationships and inspire their followers in extraordinary ways. The presence of charismatic leadership is reflected in followers who are enthusiastic about the leader and his or her ideas, who work very hard to support them, who remain loyal and devoted, and who seek superior performance accomplishments.[36]

WHAT IS TRANSFORMATIONAL LEADERSHIP?

The term **transformational leadership** describes someone who uses charisma and related qualities to raise aspirations and shift people and organizational systems into new high-performance patterns. This is distinguished from **transactional leadership** in which a leader adjusts tasks, rewards, and structures to help followers meet their needs while working to accomplish organizational objectives.[37] Although important, such transactional leadership meets only part of an organization's requirements in today's dynamic environment. Additional impetus to achieve extraordinary performance, through transformational leadership, is also essential.

The notion of transformational leadership offers a distinct management challenge. It is not enough to possess leadership traits, know the leadership behaviors, and understand leadership contingencies. From these foundations of transactional leadership, the manager must also lead in an inspirational way and with a compelling personality. The transformational leader provides a strong aura of vision and contagious enthusiasm that substantially raises the confidence, aspirations, and commitments of followers. The transformational leader arouses followers to be more highly dedicated, more satisfied with their work, and more willing to put forth extra effort to achieve success in challenging times.

Who hasn't heard about Mary Kay Ash, described by a Harvard leadership professor as an "opportunity-generating machine"? As founder of the cosmetics firm Mary Kay, she built a $600-million firm with a global reach on a straightforward leadership approach—the power of employee recognition. At the annual awards banquet in Dallas, extraordinary success on the part of top sales representatives is rewarded with pink Cadillacs, trips abroad, diamonds, and more. They also receive the emotional support of a caring and considerate leadership figure who emphasizes a personal relationship with her employees. Knowing full well that "Mary K" might telephone to inquire about a sick child, representatives act the same way in their relationships with customers—for example, sending birthday cards and demonstrating concern. Mary Kay's enthusiasm is contagious, and the success of the firm reflects the power of employee recognition.[38]

The special qualities that are often characteristic of transformational leaders include the following:

Attributes of transformational leaders

- *Vision:* Having ideas and a clear sense of direction; communicating them to others; developing excitement about accomplishing shared "dreams."

- *Charisma:* Arousing others' enthusiasm, faith, loyalty, pride, and trust in themselves through the power of personal reference and appeals to emotion.

- *Symbolism:* Identifying "heroes," offering special rewards, and holding spontaneous and planned ceremonies to celebrate excellence and high achievement.

- *Empowerment:* Helping others develop, removing performance obstacles, sharing responsibilities, and delegating truly challenging work.

- *Intellectual stimulation:* Gaining the involvement of others by creating awareness of problems and stirring their imagination to create high-quality solutions.

- *Integrity:* Being honest and credible, acting consistently out of personal conviction, and by following through commitments.[39]

GENDER AND LEADERSHIP

One of the leadership themes of continuing interest deals with the question of whether or not gender influences leadership effectiveness. Sara Levinson, President of NFL Properties, Inc. of New York, for example, explored the question di-

• The Gap

http://www.gap.com

The Gap's Jeanne P. Jackson led the charge to resurrect success at the firm's troublesome Banana Republic stores. She pursued a strategy of differentiating Banana Republic from other Gap stores and pushed the store into upscale clothes for young professionals and even home furnishings. And she's leading the company back to the catalog business.

rectly in a conversation with the all male members of her management team. "Is my leadership style different from a man's?" she asked. "Yes," they replied, suggesting that the very fact that she was asking the question of them helped to demonstrate the difference. They also indicated that her leadership style emphasized communication and the gathering ideas and opinions from others. When Levinson probed further by asking the team members "Is this a distinctly 'female' trait?," they said that they thought it was.[40]

The evidence clearly supports that both women and men can be effective leaders. As suggested by the prior example, however, they may tend toward somewhat different styles.[41] Women may be more prone to behaviors typically considered democratic and participative—such as showing respect for others, caring for others, and sharing power and information with others. This style is sometimes referred to as *interactive leadership,* focusing on the building of consensus and good interpersonal relations through communication and involvement. It also has qualities in common with the transformational leadership just discussed.[42] Men, by contrast, may be more transactional in their leadership tendencies—tending toward more directive and assertive behaviors, and toward using authority in a traditional "command and control" sense.

Given the emphasis on shared power, communication, cooperation, and participation in the new-form organizations of today, these results are provocative. Gender issues aside, the interactive leadership style seems to be an excellent fit with the demands of a diverse workforce and the new workplace. Regardless of whether the relevant behaviors are displayed by women or men, it seems clear that future leadership success will rest more often on one's capacity to lead through positive relationships and empowerment than through aloofness and formal authority. The chapters that follow on leading through motivation, communication, interpersonal relations, group dynamics and teamwork, and innovation and planned change, are highly relevant to this issue.

"GOOD OLD-FASHIONED" LEADERSHIP

Peter Drucker offers another very pragmatic approach to leadership in the new workplace. It is based on what he refers to as a "good old-fashioned" view of the plain hard work it takes to be a successful leader. Consider, for example, Drucker's description of a telephone conversation with a potential consulting client who was the human resources vice president of a big bank: "We'd want you to run a seminar for us on how one acquires charisma," she said. Drucker's response was not what she expected. He advised her to tell the VP that there's more to leadership than the popular emphasis on personal qualities that offer a sense of personal "dash" or charisma. In fact, he said that "leadership . . . is work."[43]

Drucker's observations on leadership offer a useful complement to the transformational leadership ideas just discussed. He identifies the following three essentials of leadership. First, Drucker believes that the foundation of effective leadership is *defining and establishing a sense of mission.* A good leader sets the goals, priorities, and standards. A good leader keeps them all clear and visible and maintains them. In Drucker's words, "The leader's first task is to be the trumpet that sounds a clear sound." Second, he believes in *accepting leadership as a responsibility rather than a rank.* Good leaders surround themselves with talented people. They are not afraid to develop strong and capable subordinates. And they do not blame others when things go wrong. As Drucker says, "The buck stops here" is still a good adage to remember. Third, Drucker stresses the importance of *earning and keeping the trust of others.* The key here is the leader's personal integrity. The followers of good leaders trust them. This means that they believe the leader means what he or she says and that his or her actions will be consistent with what is said. In Drucker's words again, "Effective leadership . . . is not based on being clever; it is based primarily on being consistent."

ETHICAL ASPECTS OF LEADERSHIP

Firmly embedded in the concept of transformational leadership and good old-fashioned leadership is "integrity" — the leader's honesty, credibility, and consistency in putting values into action. Leaders have an undeniable responsibility to set high ethical standards to guide the behavior of followers. For managers, the ethical aspects of leadership are important and everyday concerns. At General Electric, for example, the concept of the "A" leader clearly includes an ethical component. Described as someone with "the instinct and courage to make the tough calls," GE's "A" leader also does so "decisively, but with fairness and absolute integrity."[44]

Concerned about what he perceives as a lack of momentum in organizational life, John Gardner talks about the "moral aspects" of leadership.[45] "Most people in most organizations most of the time," he writes, "are more stale than they know, more bored than they care to admit." Leaders, according to Gardner, have a moral obligation to supply the necessary spark to awaken the potential of each individual — to urge each person "to take the initiative in performing leader-like acts." He points out that high expectations tend to generate high performance. It is the leader's job to remove "obstacles to our effective functioning — to help individuals see and pursue shared purposes."

Gardner's *moral leadership* view is based on a premise that people with a sense of ownership of their jobs will naturally outperform those who feel they are outsiders. Good leaders, accordingly, should instill ownership by being the kind of leaders who are truly willing to let others do their best.[46] Returning once again to the Herman Miller example that opened the chapter, the words of Max DePree provide a useful final reminder: "Nobody is common. Everybody has a right to be an insider."[47]

CHAPTER REVIEW

This section should be used as an end-of-chapter "study guide." The *Summary* helps to put the chapter's content into overall perspective. The list of *Key Terms* allows you to double-check your familiarity with basic concepts and definitions. *Self-Test 13* gives you the opportunity to test your basic comprehension of the chapter using sample test questions.

SUMMARY

What is leadership?

- Leadership is the process of inspiring others to work hard to accomplish important tasks.

- An effective leader influences other people to work enthusiastically to achieve performance objectives.

- Vision, or a clear sense of the future, is increasingly considered to be an essential ingredient of effective leadership.

- Visionary leaders are able to communicate their vision to others and build the commitments needed to perform the required work.

How do leaders gain and use power?

- Power, the ability to get others to do what you want them to do, is an essential ingredient of effective leadership.

- Managerial power may be gained through the formal position in the organization and/or through personal sources of influence.

- Sources of position power include rewards, coercion, and legitimacy or formal authority.

- Sources of personal power include expertise and reference.

- Effective leaders empower others — that is, they help and allow others to take action and make job-related decisions on their own.

What are the important leadership traits and behaviors?

- Early leadership research searched unsuccessfully for a definitive set of personal traits that differentiated successful and unsuccessful leaders.

- Traits that seem to have a positive impact on leadership include drive, integrity, and self-confidence, among others.

- Research on leader behaviors focused on alternative leadership styles that involved concerns for task and concerns for people.

- One suggestion of leader-behavior researchers is that effective leaders will be good at team based or participative leadership that is high in both task and people concerns.

What are the contingency theories of leadership?

- Contingency leadership approaches point out that no one leadership style always works best; rather, the best style is one that properly matches the demands of each unique situation.

- Fiedler's contingency theory describes how situational differences in task structure, position power, and leader-member relations may influence which leadership style works best.

- House's path-goal theory points out that leaders should add value to situations by responding with supportive, directive, achievement-oriented, and/or participative styles as needed.

- The Hersey-Blanchard situational model recommends using task-oriented and people-oriented behaviors, depending on the "maturity" of the group a manager is attempting to lead.

- The Vroom-Jago leader-participation theory advises leaders to choose decision-making methods — individual, consultative, group, that best fit the problems they are trying to resolve.

What are current issues in leadership development?

- Transactional leadership focuses on tasks, rewards, and structures to influence follower behavior.

- Charismatic leadership creates a truly inspirational relationship between leader and followers.

- Transformational leaders use charisma and related qualities to inspire extraordinary efforts in support of innovation and large-scale change.

- The interactive leadership style seems consistent with the demands of the new workplace and the emphasis on communication, involvement, and interpersonal respect.

- All leadership is "hard work" that always requires a personal commitment to meeting the highest ethical and moral standards.

KEY TERMS

Authority decision (p. 274)

Charismatic leader
   (p. 274)

Coercive power (p. 264)

Consultative decision
   (p. 274)

Expert power (p. 264)

Group decision (p. 274)

Leadership (p. 262)

Leadership style
   (p. 267)

Legitimate power
   (p. 264)

Power (p. 263)

Referent power (p. 264)

Reward power (p. 264)

Substitutes for leadership
   (p. 273)

Transactional leadership
   (p. 274)

Transformational
   leadership (p. 274)

Vision (p. 262)

SELF-TEST 13

Take this test much as you would in a normal classroom situation. It is a good way to check your basic comprehension of chapter material. Answers may be found at the end of the book.

MULTIPLE-CHOICE QUESTIONS:

1. Someone with a clear sense of the future and the actions needed to get there is considered a _____ leader. (a) task-oriented (b) people-oriented (c) transactional (d) visionary

2. Managerial power = _____ power + _____ power. (a) reward, punishment (b) reward, expert (c) legitimate, position (d) position, personal

3. A manager who says "Because I am the boss you must do what I ask" is relying on _____ power. (a) reward (b) legitimate (c) expert (d) referent

4. Among the personal traits now considered important for managerial success is _____. (a) self-confidence (b) gender (c) age (d) height

5. According to research into leader behaviors, the most successful leader is one who acts with a _____. (a) high initiating structure (b) high consideration (c) high concern for task and high concern for people (d) low job centeredness and high employee centeredness

6. In Fiedler's contingency theory, both highly favorable and highly unfavorable leadership situations are best dealt with by a _____ leader. (a) task-oriented (b) democratic (c) participative (d) relationship-oriented

7. Directive leadership and achievement-oriented leadership are among the options in House's _____ theory of leadership. (a) trait (b) path-goal (c) transformational (d) life-cycle

8. Vision, charisma, integrity, and symbolism are all on the list of attributes typically associated with _____ leaders. (a) contingency (b) informal (c) transformational (d) transactional

9. _____ leadership theory suggests that leadership success is achieved by correctly matching leadership style with situations. (a) Path-goal (b) Fiedler's (c) Transformational (d) Blake and Mouton's

10. In the leader-behavior approaches to leadership, someone who does a very good job of planning work, setting standards, and monitoring results would be considered a _____ leader. (a) task-oriented (b) control-oriented (c) achievement-oriented (d) employee-centered

TRUE-FALSE QUESTIONS:

11. A good leader will always be a good manager. T F

12. Possession of so-called leadership traits guarantees that a person will be a successful leader. T F

13. Referent power is developed and maintained in part through good interpersonal skills. T F

14. One outcome of the leader-behavior approach is the belief that people can be trained to acquire and utilize a successful leadership style. T F

15. In Fiedler's contingency leadership approach, a person's leadership style is considered very flexible and easy to modify from one situation to the next. T F

16. A major point of path-goal theory is that a leader's contributions should complement or "add value" to a situation. T F

17. In the Vroom-Jago leader-participation theory, all decisions should be made by group consensus. T F

18. A charismatic leader is someone who is very successful with the transactional aspects of leadership. T F

19. Managers who empower their subordinates to make more decisions are losing power themselves. T F

20. The only leadership theory now considered correct is the Hershey-Blanchard situational theory. T F

SHORT-RESPONSE QUESTIONS:

21. Why does a person need both position power and personal power to achieve long-term managerial effectiveness?

22. What is the major insight offered by the Vroom-Jago leader-participation theory?

23. What are the three variables that Fiedler's contingency theory uses to diagnose the favorability of leadership situations, and what does each mean?

24. How does Peter Drucker's view of "good old-fashioned leadership" differ from the popular concept of transformational leadership?

APPLICATION QUESTION:

25. When Rod Henry took over as leader of a new product development team, he was both excited and apprehensive. "I wonder," he said to himself on the first day in his new assignment, "if I can meet the challenges of leadership." Later that day, Rod shares this concern with you during a coffee break. Based on the insights of this chapter, how would you describe to him the essential implications for his personal leadership development of the current thinking on charismatic or transformational leadership?

CHAPTER FOURTEEN

Motivation and Rewards

Planning Ahead—Chapter 14 Study Questions

- Why is motivation important?

- What are the different types of individual needs?

- What are the insights of process theories of motivation?

- What role does reinforcement play in motivation?

- What are the trends in motivation and compensation?

Value Diversity and Individual Differences

Why do some people outperform others in their work? What can be done to ensure that maximum performance is achieved by each and every employee? These questions are, or should be, asked by managers in all work settings, and they will continue to be important in the dynamic environment of the 21st century. Good answers to them will rest on a foundation of true respect for people, with all of their talents and diversity, as the human resources of organizations. The best managers already know this; their leadership approaches reflect an awareness that "productivity through people" is a key and irreplaceable ingredient for long-term success. The corporate philosophy of Dana Corporation is a well-known example. It states, in part, "People. . . . We are dedicated to the belief that our people are our most important asset. We will encourage all of them to contribute and to grow to the limit of their desire and ability. We believe people respond to recognition, freedom to contribute, opportunity to grow, and to fair compensation."[1]

Human nature is always both fascinating and complex, and all of its intricate facets come into play in the workplace. At a packaging plant in California, for example, senior executive Kevin Kelley learned that a supervisor was starting to retire on the job. The man had worked his twenty years and felt it was time to slow down. He was unresponsive to gentle "nudging" from co-workers and managers. Kelley politely confronted him with the facts, saying: "We need your talent, your knowledge of those machines." The supervisor responded with new vigor in his work and earned the praise of his peers. For his part, Kelley claims that "motivating the go-getters isn't hard." He believes in employee involvement and claims that one of the best motivators is information on the firm's competitive environment. With information, so to speak, comes the motivation to work hard and keep the company competitive.[2]

IMPORTANCE OF MOTIVATION

- **Motivation** accounts for the level, direction, and persistence of effort expended at work.

This chapter contains many ideas on how managers like Kevin Kelley can exercise leadership in ways that encourage other people to work hard in their jobs. The concept of **motivation** is central to this goal. The term is used in management theory to describe forces within the individual that account for the level, direction, and persistence of effort expended at work. Simply put, a highly motivated person works hard at a job; an unmotivated person does not. A manager who leads through motivation does so by creating conditions under which other people feel inspired to work hard. Obviously, a highly motivated workforce is indispensable if high-performance outcomes are to be achieved consistently in organizations.

MOTIVATION AND REWARDS

- An **extrinsic reward** is provided by someone else.

Formally defined, a *reward* is a work outcome of positive value to the individual. A motivational work setting is rich in rewards for people whose performance accomplishments help meet organizational objectives. **Extrinsic rewards** are externally administered. They are valued outcomes given to someone by another person, typically, a supervisor or higher level manager. Common workplace examples are pay bonuses, promotions, time off, special assignments, office fixtures, awards, verbal praise, and the like. In all cases, the motivational stimulus of extrinsic rewards originates outside of the individual.[3]

- An **intrinsic reward** occurs naturally during job performance.

Intrinsic rewards are self-administered. They occur "naturally" as a person performs a task and are, in this sense, built directly into the job itself. The major sources of intrinsic rewards are the feelings of competency, personal development, and self-control people experience in their work.[4] In contrast to extrinsic rewards, the motivational stimulus of intrinsic rewards is internal and does not depend on the actions of some other person. They offer the great advantage and power of "motivating from within."[5] An air traffic controller, for example, says, "I don't know of anything I'd rather be doing. I love working the airplanes."[6]

REWARDS AND PERFORMANCE

Starbucks, the popular coffee house chain, seems to have the recipe right — for rewards and performance that is. The company offers a stock option plan to all its employees. Called "bean stock," the incentive plan offers employees stock options linked to their base pay. This means they can buy the company's stock at a fixed price in the future; if the market value is higher than the price of their option, they gain. CEO Howard Schulz says the plan had an immediate impact on attitudes and performance. The phrase "bean-stocking it" came to be used by employees when they found ways to reduce costs or increase sales. Schulz is committed to the motivational value of the innovative reward plan.[7]

There are many possible ways to creatively link rewards and performance in the new workplace. To take full advantage of the possibilities, however, managers must (1) respect diversity and individual differences, (2) clearly understand what people want from work, and (3) allocate rewards to satisfy the interests of both individuals and the organization. Among the insights into this complex process that are available, the *content theories of motivation* help us to understand human needs and how people with different needs may respond to different work situations. The *process theories of motivation* offer additional insights into how people give meaning to rewards and then respond with various work-related behaviors. Another approach is found in the *reinforcement theory of motivation,* which focuses attention on the environment as a major source of rewards and influence on human behavior.

CONTENT THEORIES OF MOTIVATION

Needs are the unfulfilled physiological or psychological desires of an individual. Content theories of motivation use individual needs to explain the behaviors and attitudes of people at work. Although each of the following theories discusses a slightly different set of needs, all agree that needs cause tensions that influence attitudes and behavior. Good managers and leaders establish conditions in which people can satisfy important needs through their work. They also take action to eliminate things that can block or interfere with the satisfaction of important needs.

- A **need** is an unfulfilled physiological or psychological desire.

HIERARCHY OF NEEDS THEORY

Abraham Maslow's theory of human needs was introduced in Chapter 4 as an important foundation of the history of management thought. Recall that according to his hierarchy of human needs, **lower order needs** include physiological, safety, and social concerns, and **higher order needs** include esteem and self-actualization concerns.[8] Whereas lower order needs are desires for social and physical well-being, the higher order needs represent a person's desires for psychological development and growth.

Two principles are central to Maslow's theory about how these needs affect human behavior. The *deficit principle* holds that a satisfied need is not a motivator of behavior. People are expected to act in ways that satisfy deprived needs — that is, needs for which a "deficit" exists. The *progression principle* holds that a need at one level does not become activated until the next lower level need is already satisfied. People are expected to advance step by step up the hierarchy in their search for need satisfactions. At the level of self-actualization, the more these needs are satisfied, the stronger they are supposed to grow. According to Maslow, a person should continue to be motivated by opportunities for self-fulfillment as long as the other needs remain satisfied.

Although research has not verified the strict deficit and progression principles just presented, Maslow's ideas are very helpful for understanding the needs of people at work and for determining what can be done to satisfy them. His theory advises managers to recognize that deprived needs may negatively influence attitudes and behaviors. By the same token, providing opportunities for need satisfac-

- **Lower order needs** are physiological, safety, and social needs in Maslow's hierarchy.

- **Higher order needs** are esteem and self-actualization needs in Maslow's hierarchy.

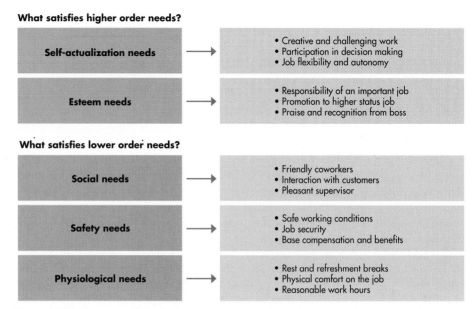

What satisfies higher order needs?

Self-actualization needs →
- Creative and challenging work
- Participation in decision making
- Job flexibility and autonomy

Esteem needs →
- Responsibility of an important job
- Promotion to higher status job
- Praise and recognition from boss

What satisfies lower order needs?

Social needs →
- Friendly coworkers
- Interaction with customers
- Pleasant supervisor

Safety needs →
- Safe working conditions
- Job security
- Base compensation and benefits

Physiological needs →
- Rest and refreshment breaks
- Physical comfort on the job
- Reasonable work hours

Figure 14.1   Opportunities for satisfaction in Maslow's hierarchy of human needs.

tion may have positive motivational consequences. *Figure 14.1* gives some examples of how managers can use Maslow's ideas to better meet the needs of their subordinates. Notice that the higher order self-actualization needs are served entirely by intrinsic rewards. The esteem needs are served by both intrinsic and extrinsic rewards. Lower order needs are served solely by extrinsic rewards.

ERG THEORY

One of the most promising efforts to build on Maslow's work is the ERG theory proposed by Clayton Alderfer.[9] To begin, his theory collapses Maslow's five needs categories into three. *Existence needs* are desires for physiological and material well-being. *Relatedness needs* are desires for satisfying interpersonal relationships. *Growth needs* are desires for continued psychological growth and development. Alderfer's ERG theory also differs from Maslow's theory in other respects. This theory does not assume that lower level needs must be satisfied before higher level needs become activated. According to ERG theory, any or all of these three types of needs can influence individual behavior at a given time. Alderfer also does not assume that satisfied needs lose their motivational impact. Rather, ERG theory contains a unique *frustration-regression principle,* according to which an already satisfied lower level need can become reactivated and influence behavior when a higher level need cannot be satisfied. Alderfer's approach offers an additional means for understanding human needs and their influence on people at work.

TWO-FACTOR THEORY

Frederick Herzberg's two-factor theory offers another framework for understanding the motivational implications of work environments.[10] The theory was developed from a pattern identified in the responses of almost 4,000 people to questions about their work. When questioned about what "turned them on," they tended to identify things relating to the nature of the job itself. Herzberg calls these **satisfier factors.** When questioned about what "turned them off," they tended to identify things relating more to the work setting. Herzberg calls these **hygiene factors.**

- A **satisfier factor** is found in job content, such as a sense of achievement, recognition, responsibility, advancement, or personal growth.

- A **hygiene factor** is found in the job context, such as working conditions, interpersonal relations, organizational policies, and salary.

Job Dissatisfaction	Job Satisfaction
Influenced by *job context,* or *hygiene factors*	Influenced by *job content,* or *motivator factors*
• Working conditions • Interpersonal relations • Organizational policies • Quality of supervision • Base wage or salary	• Sense of achievement • Feelings of recognition • Sense of responsibility • Opportunity for advancement • Feelings of personal growth
Rule Poor job context increases dissatisfaction.	*Rule* Good job content increases satisfaction.

Figure 14.2   Herzberg's two-factor theory.

As shown in *Figure 14.2,* the two-factor theory associates hygiene factors, or sources of job *dis*satisfaction, with aspects of *job context.* That is, "dissatisfiers" are considered more likely to be a part of the work setting than of the nature of the work itself. The *hygiene factors* include such things as working conditions, interpersonal relations, organizational policies and administration, technical quality of supervision, and base wage or salary. It is important to remember that Herzberg's two-factor theory would argue that improving the hygiene factors, such as by adding piped-in music or implementing a no-smoking policy, can make people less dissatisfied with these aspects of their work. But they would not in themselves contribute to increases in satisfaction. That requires attention to an entirely different set of factors and managerial initiatives.

To really improve motivation, Herzberg advises managers to give proper attention to the satisfier factors. As part of *job content* the satisfier factors deal with what people actually *do* in their work. By making improvements in what people are asked to do in their jobs, Herzberg suggests that job satisfaction and performance can be raised. The important *satisfier factors* include such things as a sense of achievement, feelings of recognition, a sense of responsibility, the opportunity for advancement, and feelings of personal growth.

Scholars have criticized Herzberg's theory as being method-bound and difficult to replicate.[11] For his part, Herzberg reports confirming studies in countries located in Europe, Africa, the Middle East, and Asia.[12] At the very least, the two-factor theory remains a useful reminder that there are two important aspects of all jobs: *job content*—what people do in terms of job tasks, and *job context*—the work setting in which they do it. Furthermore, Herzberg's advice to managers is still timely: (1) Always correct poor context to eliminate actual or potential sources of job dissatisfaction; and (2) be sure to build satisfier factors into job content to maximize opportunities for job satisfaction. The two-factor theory cautions managers not to expect too much by way of motivational improvements from investments in such things as special office fixtures, attractive lounges for breaks, and even high base salaries. Instead, it focuses on the nature of the job itself and directs attention toward such things as responsibility and opportunity for personal growth and development. These directions are very consistent with themes in the new workplace.

• Roppe Corporation
http://www.roppe.com

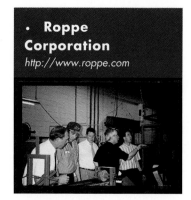

Owner Don Miller of the $50+ million Roppe Corporation wanted to encourage his workers to do better than their average of 75 percent of quotas. So, he offered a novel incentive: On any day you hit a new quota, 10 percent higher than the old, he would pay 10 percent more and let them go home early. Productivity in the plant increased and Miller has since negotiated new quotas as more efficient technologies are installed.

ACQUIRED NEEDS THEORY

In the late 1940s, David McClelland and his colleagues began experimenting with the Thematic Apperception Test (TAT) as a way of examining human needs. The TAT asks people to view pictures and write stories about what they see. The stories are then content analyzed for themes that display individual needs.[13] From

- **Need for Achievement (nAch)** is the desire to do something better, to solve problems, or to master complex tasks.

- **Need for Power (nPower)** is the desire to control, influence, or be responsible for other people.

- **Need for Affiliation (nAff)** is the desire to establish and maintain good relations with people.

this research, McClelland identified three needs that are central to his approach to motivation. **Need for Achievement (nAch)** is the desire to do something better or more efficiently, to solve problems, or to master complex tasks. **Need for Power (nPower)** is the desire to control other people, to influence their behavior, or to be responsible for them. **Need for Affiliation (nAff)** is the desire to establish and maintain friendly and warm relations with other people.

According to McClelland, people acquire or develop these needs over time as a result of individual life experiences. In addition, he associates each need with a distinct set of work preferences. Managers are encouraged to recognize the strength of each need in themselves and in other people. Attempts can then be made to create work environments responsive to them. People high in the need for achievement, for example, like to put their competencies to work, they take moderate risks in competitive situations, and they are willing to work alone. As a result, the work preferences of high need achievers include (1) individual responsibility for results, (2) achievable but challenging goals, and (3) feedback on performance.

Through his research McClelland concludes that success in top management is not based on a concern for individual achievement alone. It requires broader interests that also relate to the needs for power and affiliation. People high in the need for power are motivated to behave in ways that have a clear impact on other people and events. They enjoy being in control of a situation and being recognized for this responsibility. A person with high need for power prefers work that involves control over other persons, has an impact on people and events, and brings public recognition and attention.

Importantly, McClelland distinguishes between two forms of the power need. The *need for "personal" power* is exploitative and involves manipulation for the pure sake of personal gratification. This type of power need is not successful in management. By contrast, the *need for "social" power* is the positive face of power. It involves the use of power in a socially responsible way, one that is directed toward group or organizational objectives rather than personal ones. This need for social power is essential to managerial leadership.

People high in the need for affiliation seek companionship, social approval, and satisfying interpersonal relationships. They take a special interest in work that involves interpersonal relationships, work that provides for companionship, and work that brings social approval. McClelland believes that people very high in the need for affiliation alone may not make the best managers. For these managers, the desire for social approval and friendship may complicate managerial decision making. There are times when managers and leaders must decide and act in ways that other persons may disagree with. To the extent that the need for affiliation interferes with someone's ability to make these decisions, managerial effectiveness will be sacrificed. Thus, the successful executive, in McClelland's view, is likely to possess a high need for social power that is greater than an otherwise strong need for affiliation.

QUESTIONS AND ANSWERS ON THE CONTENT THEORIES

Figure 14.3 shows how the human needs identified by Maslow, Alderfer, Herzberg, and McClelland compare to one another. Although the terminology varies, there is a lot of common ground. The insights of the theories can and should be used together to add to our understanding of human needs in the workplace. By way of summary, the following questions and answers further clarify the content theories and their managerial implications.[14]

"How many different individual needs are there?" Research has not yet identified a perfect list of individual needs at work. But, as a manager, you can use the ideas of Maslow, Alderfer, Herzberg, and McClelland to better understand the various needs that people may bring with them to the work setting.

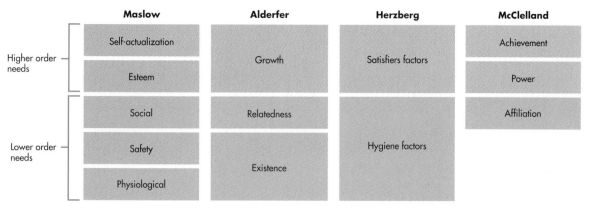

Figure 14.3   Comparison of Maslow's, Alderfer's, Herzberg's, and McClelland's motivation theories.

"Can a work outcome or reward satisfy more than one need?" Yes, work outcomes or rewards can satisfy more than one need. Pay is a good example. It is a source of performance feedback for the high need achiever. It can be a source of personal security for someone with strong existence needs. It can also be used indirectly to obtain things that satisfy social and ego needs.

"Is there a hierarchy of needs?" Research does not support the precise five-step hierarchy of needs postulated by Maslow. It seems more legitimate to view human needs as operating in a flexible hierarchy, such as the one in Alderfer's ERG theory. However, it is useful to distinguish between the motivational properties of lower order and higher order needs.

"How important are the various needs?" Research is inconclusive as to the importance of different needs. Individuals vary widely in this regard. They may also value needs differently at different times and at different ages or career stages. This is another reason that managers should use the insights of all the content theories to understand the differing needs of people at work.

PROCESS THEORIES OF MOTIVATION

Although the details vary, each of the content theories described in the last section can help managers understand individual differences better and deal positively with workforce diversity. Another set of theories, the process theories, adds to this understanding. The equity, expectancy, and goal-setting theories each offer advice and insight on how people actually make choices to work hard or not, based on their individual preferences, the available rewards, and possible work outcomes.

EQUITY THEORY

The equity theory of motivation is known best through the work of J. Stacy Adams.[15] The essence of the theory is that perceived inequity is a motivating state. That is, when people believe that they have been inequitably treated in comparison to others, the theory suggests they will try to eliminate the discomfort and restore a sense of equity to the situation.

Figure 14.4 shows the equity comparison. It typically occurs whenever managers allocate extrinsic rewards, especially monetary incentives or pay increases.

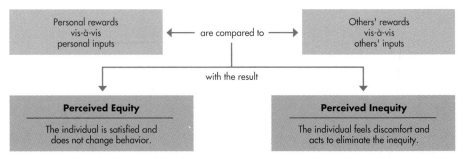

Figure 14.4 Equity theory and the role of social comparison.

Inequities occur whenever people feel that the rewards received for their work are unfair given the rewards other persons appear to be getting. The comparison points may be coworkers in the group, workers elsewhere in the organization, and even persons employed by other organizations. Adams predicts that the ways people deal with perceived inequity include the following:

Possible responses to perceived inequity

- Change their work inputs by putting less effort into their jobs.
- Change the rewards received by asking for better treatment.
- Change the comparison points by finding ways to make things seem better.
- Change the situation by transferring or quitting the job.

The research of Adams and others has largely been accomplished in the laboratory. It is most conclusive with respect to perceived negative inequity, a condition that most managers would want to avoid. People who feel underpaid and perceive negative inequity, for example, tend to reduce their work efforts to compensate for the missing rewards. They are less motivated to work hard in the future. People who feel overpaid and perceive positive inequity by contrast, have been found to increase the quantity or quality of their work. However, many questions involving this particular issue remain to be answered.

Equity theory is another good reminder of a key point to be discussed in Chapter 16 — people behave according to their perceptions. In the current case, the issue is the way rewards are perceived by their recipients. It is not the reward's absolute value or what a manager thinks that counts, it is what the recipient perceives that determines motivational outcomes. Rewards perceived as equitable should have a positive result on satisfaction and performance; those perceived as inequitable may create dissatisfaction and cause performance problems.

It is every manager's responsibility to ensure that any negative consequences of the equity comparison are avoided, or at least minimized, when rewards are allocated. Informed managers anticipate perceived negative inequities whenever especially visible rewards such as pay or promotions are allocated. Instead of letting equity concerns get out of hand, they carefully communicate the intended value of rewards being given, clarify the performance appraisals upon which they are based, and suggest appropriate comparison points.

Pay is a common source of equity controversies in the workplace. Consider the issue of *gender equity*. It is well established that women on the average only earn about 75 percent as much as men. This difference is most evident in occupations traditionally dominated by men, such as the legal professions, but it also includes ones where females have traditionally held most jobs, such as teaching. An additional equity question relates to the issue of *comparable worth*. This is the concept that people doing jobs of similar value based on required education, training, and skills (such as nursing and accounting) should receive similar pay. Advocates of comparable worth claim that it corrects historical pay inequities

• **Silicon Graphics**
http://www.sgi.com

At Silicon Graphics, employees can receive "spirit" awards for things like "encouraging creativity" and "seeking solutions rather than blame." Fifty awards are given annually. Winners get trips to Hawaii for two and a year-long appointment to the management advisory group.

and is a natural extension of the "equal-pay-for-equal-work" concept. Critics claim that "similar value" is too difficult to define and that the dramatic restructuring of wage scales would have a negative economic impact on society as a whole.

EXPECTANCY THEORY

Victor Vroom introduced to the management literature another process theory of work motivation that has made an important contribution.[16] The expectancy theory of motivation asks a central question: What determines the willingness of an individual to work hard at tasks important to the organization? In response to this question, expectancy theory suggests that "people will do what they can do when they want to do it." More specifically, Vroom suggests that the motivation to work depends on the relationships between the *three expectancy factors,* depicted in *Figure 14.5:*

- **Expectancy:** A person's belief that working hard will result in a desired level of task performance being achieved (this is sometimes called *effort-performance expectancy*).

- **Instrumentality:** A person's belief that successful performance will be followed by rewards and other potential outcomes (this is sometimes called *performance-outcome expectancy*).

- **Valence:** The value a person assigns to the possible rewards and other work-related outcomes.

Expectancy theory posits that motivation (M), expectancy (E), instrumentality (I), and valence (V) are related to one another in a multiplicative fashion: $M = E \times I \times V$. In other words, motivation is determined by expectancy times instrumentality times valence. The multiplier effect has important managerial implications. Mathematically speaking, a zero at any location on the right side of the equation (that is, for E, I, or V) will result in zero motivation. Managers are thus advised to act in ways that maximize all three components of the following equation—not one can be left unattended.

$$\text{Motivation} = \text{Expectancy} \times \text{Instrumentality} \times \text{Valence}$$

Suppose, for example, that a manager is wondering whether or not the prospect of earning a promotion will be motivational to a subordinate. A typical assumption is that people will be motivated to work hard to earn a promotion. But is this necessarily true? Expectancy theory predicts that a person's motivation to work hard for a promotion will be low if any one or more of the following three conditions apply. First, *if expectancy is low motivation will suffer.* The person may feel that he or she cannot achieve the performance level necessary to get promoted. So why try? Second, *if instrumentality is low motivation will suf-*

Three expectancy factors

- **Expectancy** is a person's belief that working hard will result in high task performance.

- **Instrumentality** is a person's belief that various outcomes will occur as a result of task performance.

- **Valence** is the value a person assigns to work-related outcomes.

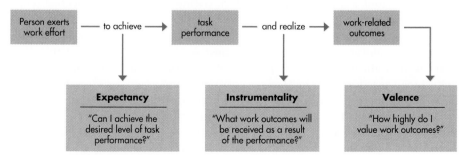

Figure 14.5   Elements in the expectancy theory of motivation.

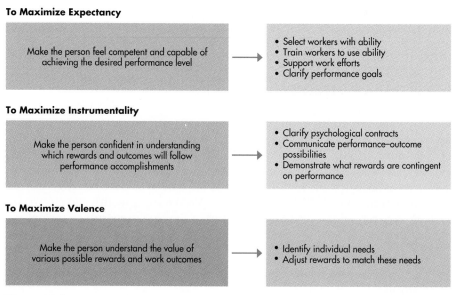

Figure 14.6 Managerial implications of expectancy theory.

fer. The person may lack confidence that a high level of task performance will result in being promoted. So why try? Third, *if valence is low motivation will suffer.* The person may place little value on receiving a promotion. It simply isn't much of a reward. So, once again, why try?

Expectancy theory makes managers aware of such issues. It can help them better understand and respond to different points of view in the workplace. As shown in *Figure 14.6,* the management implications include being willing to work with each individual and trying to maximize his or her expectancies, instrumentalities, and valences in ways that support organizational objectives. Stated a bit differently, a manager can apply the insights of expectancy theory by clearly linking effort and performance, linking performance to work outcomes, and choosing work outcomes valued by the individual.

GOAL-SETTING THEORY

• **Task goals** are performance targets for individuals or groups.

Task goals, in the form of clear and desirable performance targets, form the basis of Edwin Locke's goal-setting theory.[17] The theory's basic premise is that task goals can be highly motivating — *if* they are properly set and *if* they are well managed. Goals give direction to people in their work. Goals clarify the performance expectations between a supervisor and subordinate, between coworkers, and across subunits in an organization. Goals establish a frame of reference for task feedback. Goals also provide a foundation for behavioral self-management.[18] In these and related ways, Locke believes goal setting can enhance individual work performance and job satisfaction.

To achieve these benefits, however, research by Locke and his associates indicates that managers and team leaders must work with others to set the right goals in the right ways. The key issues and principles in managing this goal-setting process are described in *Manager's Notepad 14.1,* and "participation" is an important element. The degree to which the person expected to do the work is involved in setting the performance goals can influence his or her satisfaction and performance. Research indicates that a positive impact is most likely to occur when the participation (1) allows for increased understanding of specific and difficult goals and (2) provides for greater acceptance and commitment to them.

Manager's Notepad 14.1

How to Make Goal Setting Work for You

- *Set specific goals:* They lead to higher performance than more generally stated ones, such as "Do your best."

- *Set challenging goals:* As long as they are viewed as realistic and attainable, more difficult goals lead to higher performance than do easy goals.

- *Build goal acceptance and commitment:* People work harder for goals that they accept and believe in; they tend to resist goals forced on them.

- *Clarify goal priorities:* Make sure that expectations are clear as to which goals should be accomplished first and why.

- *Reward goal accomplishment:* Don't let positive accomplishments pass unnoticed; reward people for doing what they set out to do.

The concept of *management by objectives* (MBO), first introduced in Chapter 7 on planning, is a good illustration of a participative approach to joint goal setting by supervisors and subordinates. The MBO process helps to unlock and apply the motivational power of goal-setting theory. In addition to MBO, managers should also be aware of the participation options. It may not always be possible to allow participation when selecting exactly which goals need to be pursued, but it may be possible to allow participation in the decisions about how to best pursue them. Furthermore, the constraints of time and other factors operating in some situations may not allow for participation. In these settings, research suggests that workers will respond positively to externally imposed goals if the supervisors assigning them are trusted and if the workers believe they will be adequately supported in their attempts to achieve them.

REINFORCEMENT THEORY OF MOTIVATION

The content and process theories described so far use cognitive explanations of behavior. They are concerned with explaining "why" people do things in terms of satisfying needs, resolving felt inequities, and/or pursuing positive expectancies and task goals. Reinforcement theory, by contrast, views human behavior as determined by its environmental consequences.[19] Instead of looking within the individual to explain motivation and behavior, it focuses on the external environment and the consequences it holds for the individual. The basic premises of the theory are based on Thorndike's **law of effect:** Behavior that results in a pleasant outcome is likely to be repeated; behavior that results in an unpleasant outcome is not likely to be repeated.[20]

> - The **law of effect** states that behavior followed by pleasant consequences is likely to be repeated; behavior followed by unpleasant consequences is not.
>
> - **Operant conditioning** is the control of behavior by manipulating its consequences.
>
> - **Organizational behavior modification** is the application of operant conditioning to influence human behavior at work.

REINFORCEMENT STRATEGIES

The late psychologist B. F. Skinner popularized the concept of **operant conditioning** as the process of applying the law of effect to control behavior by manipulating its consequences.[21] You may think of operant conditioning as learning by reinforcement. **Organizational behavior modification,** or "OB Mod," for short, is a term that describes the application of operant conditioning techniques to influence human behavior in the workplace.[22] Its goal is to use reinforcement

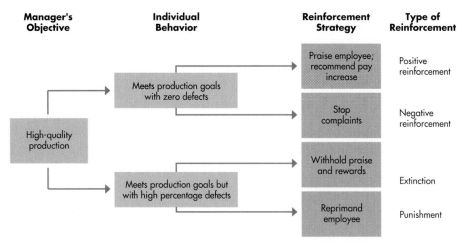

Figure 14.7   Reinforcement strategies in total quality management.

principles to systematically reinforce desirable work behavior and discourage undesirable work behavior.

There are four reinforcement strategies. **Positive reinforcement** strengthens or increases the frequency of desirable behavior by making a pleasant consequence contingent on its occurrence. *Example:* A manager nods to express approval to someone who makes a useful comment during a staff meeting. **Negative reinforcement** increases the frequency of or strengthens desirable behavior by making the avoidance of an unpleasant consequence contingent on its occurrence. *Example:* A manager who has been nagging a worker every day about tardiness does not nag when the worker comes to work on time one day. **Punishment** decreases the frequency of or eliminates an undesirable behavior by making an unpleasant consequence contingent on its occurrence. *Example:* A manager issues a written reprimand to an employee who reports late for work one day. **Extinction** decreases the frequency of or eliminates an undesirable behavior by making the removal of a pleasant consequence contingent on its occurrence. *Example:* A manager observes that a disruptive employee is receiving social approval from coworkers; the manager counsels coworkers to stop giving this approval.

These four reinforcement strategies are applied in *Figure 14.7* to a total quality management (TQM) situation. Note how the supervisor uses each of them to influence employees toward continuous improvement practices. Note, too, that both positive and negative reinforcement strengthen desirable behavior when it occurs. Punishment and extinction weaken or eliminate undesirable behaviors.

- **Positive reinforcement** strengthens a behavior by making a desirable consequence contingent on its occurrence.

- **Negative reinforcement** strengthens a behavior by making the avoidance of an undesirable consequence contingent on its occurrence.

- **Punishment** discourages a behavior by making an unpleasant consequence contingent on its occurrence.

- **Extinction** discourages a behavior by making the removal of a desirable consequence contingent on its occurrence.

POSITIVE REINFORCEMENT

Positive reinforcement should be a central part of any manager's motivational strategy. One of the best examples of how this approach has been used with great success is the classic story of Mary Kay Cosmetics. Most everyone knows that the legendary pink Cadillac has been a sought after prize by top sellers for many years. But how many know that rewards are carefully linked to specified performance results in the following ways: top producers = pink Cadillac, next best = pink Pontiac, next best = red Grand Am? More recently and to keep pace with changing times, Mary Kay has added a sport vehicle, white GMC Jimmy, as an option to the Grand Prix. Of course, all the cars are awarded with great ceremony at a gala celebration.[23]

Two laws of positive reinforcement must be understood. The *law of contingent reinforcement* states: "For a reward to have maximum reinforcing value, it must be delivered only if the desired behavior is exhibited." The *law of imme-*

Manager's Notepad 14.2

Guidelines for Positive Reinforcement . . . and Punishment

Positive reinforcement:
- Clearly identify desired work behaviors.
- Maintain a diverse inventory of rewards.
- Inform everyone what must be done to get rewards.
- Recognize individual differences when allocating rewards.
- Follow the laws of immediate and contingent reinforcement.

Punishment:
- Tell the person what is being done wrong.
- Tell the person what is being done right.
- Make sure the punishment matches the behavior.
- Administer the punishment in private.
- Follow the laws of immediate and contingent reinforcement.

diate reinforcement states "The more immediate the delivery of a reward after the occurrence of a desirable behavior, the greater the reinforcing value of the reward." Managers should take full advantage of the everyday value and power of these laws as they pursue positive reinforcement. Several useful guidelines are presented in *Manager's Notepad 14.2.*

The power of positive reinforcement can and should be applied through a process known as **shaping.** This is the creation af a new behavior by the positive reinforcement of successive approximations to it. The timing of positive reinforcement can also make a difference in its impact. *Continuous reinforcement* administers a reward each time a desired behavior occurs. *Intermittent reinforcement* rewards behavior only periodically. In general, a manager can expect that continuous reinforcement will elicit a desired behavior more quickly than will intermittent reinforcement. Also, behavior acquired under an intermittent schedule will be more permanent than will behavior acquired under a continuous schedule. To succeed with a shaping strategy, for example, reinforcement should be given on a continuous basis until the desired behavior is achieved. Then an intermittent schedule should be used to maintain the behavior at the new level.

- **Shaping** is positive reinforcement of successive approximations to the desired behavior.

PUNISHMENT

Punishment is a means of eliminating undesirable behavior by administering an unpleasant consequence upon the occurrence of that behavior. To punish an employee, a manager may deny the individual a valued reward, such as verbal praise or merit pay, or the manager may administer an unpleasant outcome, such as a verbal reprimand or pay reduction. Like positive reinforcement, punishment can be done poorly or it can be done well. *Manager's Notepad 14.2* offers guidance on handling punishment as a reinforcement strategy. Remember, too, that punishment most often should be combined with positive reinforcement.

Workers at Rocky Shoes & Boots in Nelsonville, Ohio, know the goals. A goal clock prominently displays actual performance versus the daily goal for the factory's production of shoes and boots. With new modular technologies and a focus on teams, plant efficiency and profitability has increased.

ETHICAL ISSUES IN REINFORCEMENT

The use of reinforcement techniques in work settings has produced many success stories of improved safety, decreased absenteeism and tardiness, and increased productivity.[24] But there are also debates over the ethics of controlling human behavior. There is concern, for example, that use of operant conditioning principles ignores the individuality of people, restricts their freedom of choice, and ignores the fact that people can be motivated by other things than externally administered rewards.

Advocates of the reinforcement orientation attack the problem straight on. They agree that reinforcement involves the control of behavior, but they argue that control is part of every manager's job. The real question may be not whether it is ethical to control behavior but whether it is ethical not to control behavior well enough so the goals of both the organization and the individual are well served. Even as research continues, the value of reinforcement techniques seems confirmed. This is especially true when they are combined with the insights of the other motivation theories discussed in this chapter.[25]

MOTIVATION AND COMPENSATION

By way of summary, *Figure 14.8* offers an integrative view of motivation. It shows how the insights of various theories in this chapter can be combined into one model of motivational dynamics in the workplace. In this figure motivation leads to effort that, along with appropriate individual abilities and organizational support, leads to performance. The motivational impact of any rewards received for this performance depends on equity and reinforcement considerations. Ultimately, satisfaction with rewards should lead to increased motivation to work hard in the future.

Of the motivation issues that can be addressed within this framework, perhaps none receives as much attention as the special case of compensation.[26] There are many advantages, both individual and organizational, to be gained from a truly motivational compensation scheme. In general, the success of any such system lies in its ability to apply the alternative motivation theories in positive and credible ways. In practice, however, the link between motivation and compensation is usually very complicated.

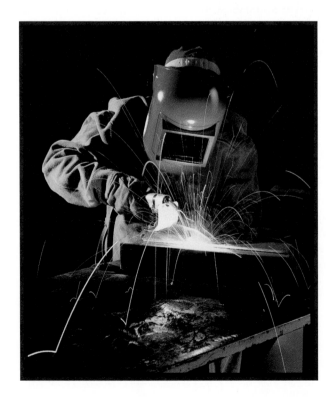

One example of a company whose approach to compensation has attracted attention over the years is Lincoln Electric. Founded in 1895, the Cleveland-based manufacturer of welding products and industrial motors uses an incentive pay system based on a low base salary coupled with bonuses that are tied to company profitability and individual performance ratings. To promote quality and to impart a sense of responsibility, employees are held accountable for the pieces they've produced. Pieces are "signed," or marked, so that defective ones are easily traced. Rejects and returns are noted on employees' merit ratings, which affect the year-end bonuses. When Lincoln's domestic workers complained because their bonuses were threatened by the costs of the firm's international expansion, former CEO Donald Hastings described the problem this way: "We did it too fast, paid too much; we didn't understand foreign markets and cultures." In Brazil, Lincoln ran into a legal problem. Any bonuses paid for two consecutive years become part of an employee's base salary. Lincoln faces hard questions about the transcultural applications of the company's unique incentive pay system.[27]

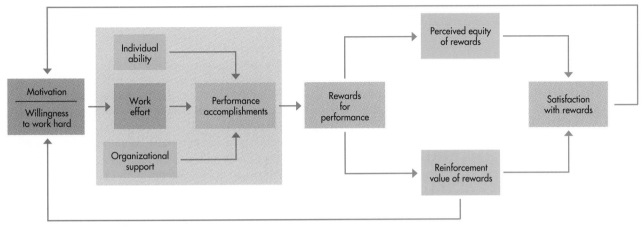

Figure 14.8 An integrated approach to motivational dynamics.

PAY FOR PERFORMANCE

Pay for performance is a concept that is consistent with the equity, expectancy, and reinforcement theories. Formally defined, **merit pay** is a compensation system that awards pay increases in proportion to individual performance contributions. By allocating pay increases in this way managers are attempting to recognize and positively reinforce high performers and to encourage them to work hard for similar accomplishments in the future. They are also attempting to remind low performers of their lack of achievement and send a signal that they must do better in the future.

The concept of merit pay is a logical extension of the motivation theories. In principle at least, it makes sense to reward people in proportion to their work contributions. Because of the difficulty of actually linking pay with performance in a truly contingent and equitable manner, however, merit pay does not always achieve the desired results. A successful merit pay system must have a solid foundation in agreed-upon and well-defined "performance measures." Any weakness in the performance appraisal methods can undermine a merit pay system. And, lack of consistency in applying merit pay at all levels of the organization can jeopardize its credibility. There is concern, for example, that the pay of CEO's isn't adequately linked to performance. The impression of some is that CEOs are well-rewarded no matter how well the company performs. Apple Computer, for example, reportedly lost $2 billion during Gilbert Amelio's 17-month tenure as CEO. When he was ousted by the board he took away $2 million in salary and bonus for a year plus a $6.7 million severance package.[28]

For these and related reasons, not everyone believes in merit pay. John Whitney, author of *The Trust Factor* and Director of the W. Edwards Deming Center for Quality Management at Columbia University, suggests that pay-for-performance may not work very well when it comes to promoting total quality management and continuous improvement. While pointing out that market forces should determine base pay, Whitney believes that organizations might benefit by making the annual merit increase an equal percentage of base. This communicates a universal sense of importance and helps to avoid frustrations and complaints when merit increases are tied to performance differences. Says Whitney: "Quibbling over whether someone should get a 4.7% raise or 5.1% is a colossal waste of time."[29]

- **Merit pay** awards pay increases in proportion to performance contributions.

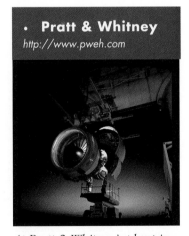

• Pratt & Whitney
http://www.pweh.com

At Pratt & Whitney's plant in Maine, employee pay is tied to skills and results-sharing bonuses are available. Based on recommendations from an employee team, pay increases are tied to training and job responsibilities. Results-sharing bonuses are earned plant-wide when annual targets for cost-cutting and on-time delivery are exceeded.

INCENTIVE COMPENSATION SYSTEMS

Today, employees at all levels in more and more organizations benefit from special incentive compensation systems of many forms. Examples include bonus pay plans, profit-sharing plans, gain-sharing plans, and employee stock ownership plans.[30]

Bonus Pay

• A **bonus pay plan** provides cash bonuses based on achievement of specific performance targets.

Bonus pay plans provide one-time or lump-sum payments to employees based on the accomplishment of specific performance targets or some other extraordinary contribution, such as an idea for a work improvement. They typically do not increase base salary or wages. Bonuses have been most common at the executive level, but they are now being used more extensively. Corning Glass Works, for example, has tried rewarding individual achievements with on-the-spot bonuses of 3 to 6 percent of someone's pay. Peter Maier, director of risk management and prevention for the firm, gave about 40 percent of his subordinates individual bonuses in a year. He says, "If someone has done a spiffy job, you need to recognize them."[31]

Profit Sharing

• A **profit-sharing plan** distributes a proportion of net profits to employees.

Profit-sharing plans distribute to some or all employees a proportion of net profits earned by the organization during a stated performance period. The exact amount varies according to the level of profits and each person's base compensation. For example, at Vatex America, CEO Jerry Gorde instituted a profit-sharing program to help "democratize the work environment" in his $9 million T-shirt and sweatshirt manufacturing firm. The program distributes 10 percent of pretax profits to employees each month and an additional amount at the end of the year. The exact share depends on an individual's monthly attendance, tardiness, and performance as rated by supervisors.[32]

Gain Sharing

• A **gain-sharing plan** allows employees to share in gains from lower costs and increased productivity.

Gain-sharing plans extend the profit-sharing concept by allowing groups of employees to share in any savings or "gains" realized through their efforts to reduce costs and increase productivity. Specific formulas are used to calculate both the performance contributions and gain-sharing awards. A classic example is the *Scanlon plan,* which usually results in 75 percent of gains being distributed to workers and 25 percent being kept by the company.

Employee Stock Ownership

• An **employee stock ownership plan** (ESOP) allows employees to share ownership of their employing organization through the purchase of stock.

Employee stock ownership plans involve employees in ownership through the purchase of stock in the companies that employ them. Whereas formal "ESOP" plans are often used as financing schemes to save jobs and prevent business closings, stock ownership by employees is an important performance incentive. It can be motivating to have an ownership share in one's place of employment. An approach to employee ownership through *stock options* gives the option holder the right to buy shares of stock at a future date at a fixed price. This links ownership directly with a performance incentive, since employees holding stock options presumably are motivated to work hard to raise the price of the firm's stock. When the price has risen they can exercise their option and buy the stock at a discount, thus realizing a financial gain. Stock options are most common in senior executive compensation, but their use is spreading to include lower-level employees. Recently, the Hay Group reports that the most admired companies in America are also ones that offer stock options to a greater proportion of their work forces. At two of the firms, Intel and Federal Express, all employees have access to options.[33]

Pay for Knowledge

In addition to paying for performance, some organizations now emphasize paying for knowledge. A concept called **skills-based pay,** for example, pays workers according to the number of job-relevant skills they master. Federal Express uses this approach in its pay-for-knowledge reward system. Federal Express's customer-contact employees must periodically take and pass written job knowledge tests. Test scores are incorporated into the employee's performance appraisals, and pay can be increased for employees scoring highly. Skill-based pay systems are common in self-managing teams where part of the "self-management" includes responsibilities for the training and certification of coworkers in job skills.

Another creative pay practice is **entrepreneurial pay.** Individuals put their knowledge to work and part of their compensation at risk in return for the rights to pursue entrepreneurial ideas and participate in any resulting profits. AT&T encourages new venture development through such a plan. Interested employees have contributed from 12 to 15 percent of their salaries for the opportunity to apply their efforts in this way and for the prospect of future income gains.

- **Skills-based pay** is a system of paying workers according to the number of job-relevant skills they master.

- **Entrepreneurial pay** involves workers putting part of their compensation at risk in return for the right to pursue entrepreneurial ideas and share in any resulting profits.

CHAPTER REVIEW

This section should be used as an end-of-chapter "study guide." The *Summary* helps to put the chapter's content into overall perspective. The list of *Key Terms* allows you to double-check your familiarity with basic concepts and definitions. *Self-Test 14* gives you the opportunity to test your basic comprehension of the chapter using sample test questions.

SUMMARY

Why is motivation important?

- Motivation involves the level, direction, and persistence of effort expended at work; simply put, a highly motivated person works hard.

- Extrinsic rewards are given by another person; intrinsic rewards derive naturally from the work itself.

- To maximize the motivational impact of rewards, they should be allocated in ways that respond to both individual and organizational needs.

- The three major types of motivation theories are the content, process, and reinforcement theories.

What are the different types of individual needs?

- Maslow's hierarchy of human needs suggests a progression from lower order physiological, safety, and social needs to higher order ego and self-actualization needs.

- Alderfer's ERG theory identifies existence, relatedness, and growth needs.

- Herzberg's two-factor theory points out the importance of both job content and job context factors in satisfying human needs.

- McClelland's acquired needs theory identifies the needs for achievement, affiliation, and power, all of which may influence what a person desires from work.

- Managers should respect individual differences and diversity to create motivating work environments.

What are the insights of process theories of motivation?

- Adams's equity theory recognizes that social comparisons take place when rewards are distributed in the workplace.

- People who feel inequitably treated are motivated to act in ways that reduce the sense of inequity; perceived *negative* inequity may result in someone working less hard in the future.

- Vroom's expectancy theory states that Motivation = Expectancy × Instrumentality × Valence.

- Expectancy theory encourages managers to make sure that any rewards offered for motivational purposes are both achievable and individually valued.

- Locke's goal-setting theory emphasizes the motivational power of goals; people tend to be highly motivated when task goals are specific rather than ambiguous, difficult but achievable, and set through participatory means.

What role does reinforcement play in motivation?

- Reinforcement theory recognizes that human behavior is influenced by its environmental consequences.

- The law of effect states that behavior followed by a pleasant consequence is likely to be repeated; behavior followed by an unpleasant consequence is unlikely to be repeated.

- Reinforcement strategies used by managers include positive reinforcement, negative reinforcement, punishment, and extinction.

- Positive reinforcement works best when applied according to the laws of contingent and immediate reinforcement.

What are the trends in motivation and compensation?

- The area of compensation provides a good test of a manager's ability to integrate and apply the various insights of the motivation theories.

- Pay for performance in the form of merit pay plans ties pay increases to performance increases.

- Various incentive compensation programs, such as bonuses, gain sharing, and profit sharing, allow workers to benefit materially from improvements in profits and productivity.

- Pay-for-knowledge systems typically link pay to the mastery of job-relevant skills.

KEY TERMS

Bonus pay plans (p. 298)

Employee stock ownership (p. 298)

Entrepreneurial pay (p. 299)

Expectancy (p. 291)

Extinction (p. 293)

Extrinsic rewards (p. 284)

Gain sharing (p. 298)

Higher order needs (p. 287)

Hygiene factors (p. 286)

Instrumentality (p. 291)

Intrinsic rewards (p. 284)

Law of effect (p. 293)

Lower order needs (p. 285)

Merit pay (p. 297)

Motivation (p. 284)

Natural rewards (p. 284)

Need (p. 285)

Need for achievement (p. 288)

Need for affiliation (p. 288)

Need for power (p. 288)

Negative reinforcement (p. 293)

Operant conditioning (p. 293)

OB Mod (p.293)

Positive reinforcement (p. 294)

Profit-sharing plans (p. 298)

Punishment (p. 293)

Reward (p. 284)

Satisfier factors (p. 286)

Shaping (p. 295)

Skills-based pay (p. 299)

Task goals (p. 292)

Valence (p. 291)

SELF-TEST 14

Take this test much as you would in a normal classroom situation. It is a good way to check your basic comprehension of chapter material. Answers may be found at the end of the book.

MULTIPLE CHOICE QUESTIONS:

1. Lower order needs in Maslow's hierarchy correspond to _____ needs in ERG theory. (a) growth (b) affiliation (c) existence (d) achievement

2. A worker high in need for _____ power in McClelland's theory tries to use power for the good of the organization. (a) position (b) expert (c) referent (d) social

3. In the _____ theory of motivation, an individual who feels underrewarded relative to a coworker might be expected to reduce his or her performance in the future. (a) ERG (b) acquired needs (c) two-factor (d) equity

4. Which of the following is a correct match? (a) McClelland-ERG theory (b) Skinner-reinforcement theory (c) Vroom-equity theory (d) Locke-expectancy theory

5. The expectancy theory of motivation says that: motivation = expectancy $\times$ _____ $\times$ _____. (a) rewards, valence (b) instrumentality, valence (c) equity, instrumentality (d) rewards, valence

6. The law of _____ states that behavior followed by a positive consequence is likely to be repeated, whereas behavior followed by an undesirable consequence is not likely to be repeated. (a) reinforcement (b) contingency (c) goal setting (d) effect

7. _____ is a positive reinforcement strategy that rewards successive approximations to a desirable behavior. (a) Extinction (b) Negative reinforcement (c) Shaping (d) Merit pay.

8. A/an _____ pay plan gives bonuses based on the savings in costs or increases in productivity workers help to generate. (a) merit (b) gain-sharing (c) entrepreneurial (d) skills-based

9. In Herzberg's two-factor theory, base pay is considered a _____ factor. (a) valence (b) satisfier (c) equity (d) hygiene

10. Jobs high in _____ rewards naturally provide workers with higher-order need satisfactions. (a) intrinsic (b) extrinsic (c) monetary (d) profit-sharing

TRUE-FALSE QUESTIONS:

11. By definition, a highly motivated worker will always be a high-performing worker. T F

12. The ego need is the highest level need in Maslow's need hierarchy. T F

13. Pay is an example of a work outcome that can satisfy more than one type of need. T F

14. In goal-setting theory, goals that are easy to accomplish have the strongest motivational impact. T F

15. Reinforcement theory relies on cognitive explanations of human behavior. T F

16. Pay and verbal praise are good examples of intrinsic rewards. T F

17. A person with a high expectancy believes that she or he can perform a task at a desired high level. T F

18. Someone high in need for achievement would have strong social needs in Maslow's hierarchy. T F

19. Research has confirmed the existence of the hierarchy of needs first described by Abraham Maslow. T F

20. Punishment should never be used along with positive reinforcement. T F

SHORT-RESPONSE QUESTIONS:

21. What types of preferences does a person high in the need for achievement bring with him or her to the workplace?

22. Why is participation important to goal-setting theory?

23. What is motivation to work?

24. What is the managerial significance of Herzberg's distinction between factors in the job content and job context?

APPLICATION QUESTION:

25. How can a manager combine the powers of goal setting and positive reinforcement to create a highly motivational work environment for a group of workers with high needs for achievement?

CHAPTER FIFTEEN

Individual Performance and Job Design

Planning Ahead—Chapter 15 Study Questions

▬ What is the meaning of work?

▬ What are important issues in job design?

▬ How can job designs be enriched?

▬ What are alternative work arrangements?

▬ How can job and workplace stress be managed?

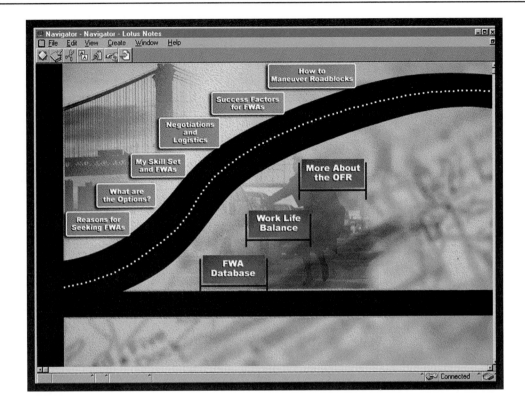

Unlock Everyone's Performance Potential

As the top accounting firms vie for first place in their industry, they are also battling for reputation as the most family-friendly employer. A growing economy challenges everyone with problems of finding and retaining the best skilled professionals. Among the recruiting and retention tools that work well are flexible work arrangements that allow employees more choice in scheduling their job duties. At Ernst & Young, an Office of Retention was created to oversee the new push toward flexibility in work and career management, and a computer data base was developed to help employees choose work schedules that are best for them.[1] These and related trends in worker empowerment and involvement are indicative of efforts to help all levels of employees find opportunities for respect and self-fulfillment at work.

Managers at businesses and organizations of all types and sizes, both for-profit and not-for-profit, are seeking higher productivity through organizational and work designs that make better use of human resources. Although the approaches vary, the roles of both the individual contributors and work teams are central to developments taking place. All this, of course, is especially crucial as employers struggle to come to grips with the implications of workforce diversity, the global economy, total quality demands, and related challenges. The pressure is on every employer to develop a talented pool of human resources and to then use all the available talents to their fullest potential. Indeed, unlocking the performance potential of each person in every job is the order of the day for the modern manager. This chapter is about work and the jobs people are asked to perform in organizations.[2] A central premise, consistent with the entire book, is that when work is well designed both high performance and a high-quality work life can be achieved.

THE MEANING OF WORK

What do you think about when you see or hear the word *work?* Is it a "turn-on" or a "turn- off"? When Dolly Parton sang "Working 9 to 5; what a way to make a living," she reminded us of an unfortunate reality — that work is not a positive experience for everyone. Dolly's song continued: "Barely getting by; it's all taking and no giving. They just use your mind, and they never give you credit. It's enough to drive you crazy if you let it."[3] Isn't it a shame when this is what *work* really means to someone? Some years ago, Karen Nussbaum founded an organization called "9 to 5" that was devoted to improving women's salaries and promotion opportunities in the workplace. She started the business after leaving her job as a secretary at Harvard University. Describing what she calls "the incident that put her over the edge," Nussbaum says, "One day . . . I was sitting at my desk at lunchtime, when most of the professors were out. A student walked into the office and looked me dead in the eye and said, 'Isn't *anyone* here?' "[4] Nussbaum founded 9 to 5 to support her personal commitment to "remake the system so that it does not produce these individuals."

Although in different ways and through different mediums, Parton and Nussbaum direct our attention toward an unfortunate fact of life in the modern workplace — some people, too many people, work under conditions that fail to provide them with respect and satisfaction. It does not have to be this way. More and more employers are coming to the same conclusion: People are the foundation for high performance in the workplace. By valuing people and by creating jobs and work environments that respect their needs and potential, everyone gains.

PSYCHOLOGICAL CONTRACTS

• A **psychological contract** is the set of expectations held by an individual about working relationships with the organization.

Work should involve a positive give and take, or exchange of values, between the individual and the organization. This sense of mutual benefit is expressed in the concept of a **psychological contract,** which is defined as an informal understanding about what an individual gives to and receives from an organization as part of the employment relationship.[5] The ideal work situation is one in which the exchange of values in the psychological contract is considered fair. When the psychological contract is broken, however, morale problems easily develop. This problem surfaced in Japan where workers historically enjoyed high job security and, in return, put in long work hours at great personal sacrifice. But when the Japanese economy experienced difficulty and companies cut back on job protections, worker morale declined. The psychological contract shared between worker and employer had been damaged.[6]

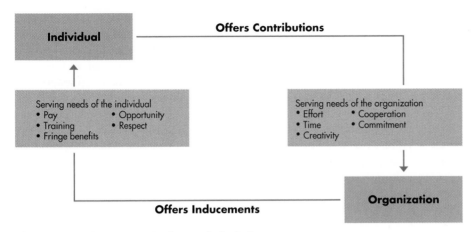

Figure 15.1 Components in the psychological contract.

As shown in *Figure 15.1,* a healthy psychological contract offers a balance between contributions made to the organization and inducements received in return. A person offers *contributions,* or valued work activities, such as effort, time, creativity, and loyalty. These are among the things that make the individual a desirable resource. *Inducements* are things of value that the organization gives to the individual in exchange for these contributions. Typical inducements include pay, fringe benefits, training, and opportunities for personal growth and advancement. Such inducements should be valued by employees and should make it worthwhile for them to work hard for the organization.

WORK AND THE QUALITY OF LIFE

The term *quality of work life,* or QWL, was first used in Chapter 1 to describe the overall quality of human experiences in the workplace. Most people spend many hours a week, and many years of their lives, at work. What happens to them at work, how they are treated, and what their work is like can all have an influence on their overall lives. Simply put, the quality of work is an important component in the quality of life for most of us.[7] Anyone who serves as a manager, therefore, must accept that this job carries a high level of social responsibility. The way managers treat people at work may have consequences extending far beyond the confines of the actual work setting. Our experiences at work can and often do spill over to affect our nonwork activities and lives, just as our nonwork experiences sometimes affect our attitudes and performance at work. Poor management practices can diminish a person's overall quality of life, not just the quality of work life; good management, by contrast, has the potential to enhance both. And if you think the preceding comments are an overstatement, consider the implications of this steelworker's compelling words to noted American author Studs Terkel:[8]

> When I come home, know what I do for the first twenty minutes? Fake it. I put on a smile. I got a kid three years old. Sometimes she says, "Daddy, where've you been?" I say, "Work." I could have told her I'd been in Disneyland. What's work to a three-year-old kid? If I feel bad, I can't take it out on the kid. Kids are born innocent of everything but birth. You can't take it out on your wife either. That is why you go to a tavern. You want to release it there rather than do it at home. What does an actor do when he's got a bad movie? I got a bad movie every day.

Today's managers are increasingly expected to focus their attention on creating work environments within which people can have positive experiences while performing to high levels of expectation. A term increasingly used in this

Marriott Hotels
http://www.marriott.com

Marriott Hotels's customer services associates program redefined the job of doorman into that of a "guest service associate." This new role was described by one worker as "a bellman, a doorman, a front-desk clerk, and a concierge all rolled into one. I have more responsibilities. I feel better about my job, and the guests get better service." The new job's multiple tasks all focus on a common result—quality customer service.

respect is *work-life balance,* first described in Chapter 12 as the fit between one's job or work responsibilities and personal or family needs. When job demands get to the point of interfering with personal responsibilities and vice-versa, stress and performance problems are likely results. The goal, of course, is to achieve a productive and satisfying balance of career and family pursuits. The themes of this chapter all relate in one way or another to this goal, with many examples of how progressive employers can increase employee involvement through better job designs and become more family friendly through alternative work schedules and stress management assistance. Work-life balance was important, for example, to Trudy Desilets whose position as manager of marketing systems at Eddie Bauer offered a way to satisfy both personal needs and career aspirations. The job not only challenged her professionally, but also allowed flexibility in scheduling hours around her daughter's school activities.[9]

JOB DESIGN ISSUES

● A **job** is the collection of tasks a person performs in support of organizational objectives.

A *job* is a collection of tasks performed in support of organizational objectives. The process of **job design** is one of creating or defining jobs by assigning specific work tasks to individuals and groups. It should contribute to the accomplishment of two major goals—job satisfaction and job performance. All managers should consider both as key results to be achieved by people at work. One without the other is simply insufficient to meet the high standards expected of today's workplace. There is no reason why you or anyone else cannot experience personal satisfaction while making high-performance contributions to an employer. Jobs can and should be designed so that satisfaction and performance go hand in hand.

● **Job design** is the allocation of specific work tasks to individuals and groups.

JOB SATISFACTION

● **Job satisfaction** is the degree to which an individual feels positively or negatively about a job.

One measure of quality of work life is **job satisfaction.**[10] This is the degree to which an individual feels positively or negatively about various aspects of the job. We have all heard someone criticized for having a "bad attitude." In the present context, job satisfaction is an important attitude that can and does influence behavior at work. The question becomes: How can we develop job satisfaction and positive work attitudes? In answering this question satisfaction with such things as pay, tasks, supervision, coworkers, work setting, and advancement opportunities must be considered. These are all facets of job satisfaction that can be addressed through job design in the attempt to improve attitudes and raise the quality of work life.

Hewitt Associates is a consulting firm that does employee-satisfaction surveys for clients. In one 6,000-worker credit card processing company, a survey revealed that workers had concerns about the quality of their work lives and didn't feel valued by their employer. They liked the employer's good benefits but disliked the lack of privacy at their workstations and the poor relationships with managers. In response to the consultant's report, company executives provided more private workstations, gave more attention to management training and selection, and reemphasized teamwork. An evaluation of the changes reported a decrease in employee turnover from 35 percent to 15 percent, making it well worth the consulting costs.[11]

Researchers know that there is a strong relationship between job satisfaction and *absenteeism*. Workers who are more satisfied with their jobs attend more regularly; they are absent less often than those who are dissatisfied. There is also a relationship between job satisfaction and *turnover*. Satisfied workers are more likely to stay and dissatisfied workers are more likely to quit their jobs. Both of these findings are important since absenteeism and turnover are costly in terms of the additional recruitment and training that are needed to replace workers as well as in the productivity lost while new workers are learning how to perform up to expectations.

Closely related to job satisfaction are two other concepts with quality of work life implications. *Job involvement* is defined as the extent to which an individual is dedicated to a job. Someone with high job involvement, for example, would be expected to work beyond expectations to complete a special project. *Organizational commitment* is defined as the loyalty of an individual to the organization itself. Someone with a high organizational commitment would identify strongly with the organization and take pride in considering themselves a member. Importantly, a Gallup Organization survey of 55,000 American workers found evidence that attitudes reflecting job involvement and commitment correlated with higher profits for their employers. The four attitudes that counted most were: believing one has the opportunity to do best every day, believing one's opinions count, believing fellow workers are committed to quality, and believing there is a direct connection between one's work and the company's mission.[12]

In a poll of American workers, *The Wall Street Journal* asked this question: How satisfied are you with your current job? The responses are as follows — 37%, completely satisfied, 47% somewhat satisfied, 10% somewhat dissatisfied, 4% completely dissatisfied, 2% not sure. The same poll went on to identify that some 36% of workers are "workbodies" who feel more fulfilled at work than at home, while another 34% were clearly "homebodies" who felt just the opposite.[13] Interestingly, the survey does indicate that a majority of the American workers were satisfied to some extent with their jobs. In an international comparison, however, U.S. workers scored relatively lower in job satisfaction (65%) than their counterparts in Switzerland (82%) and Canada (73%) but higher than those in Japan (44%).[14]

● **International Survey Research**
http://www.irsurveys.com

A report from Chicago-based International Survey Research indicates that Japanese workers were less satisfied with their jobs than workers from Switzerland, Canada, Mexico, Germany, the United States, and the United Kingdom. Compared to job satisfaction in Switzerland (82%) and the U.S. (65%), only 44 percent of Japanese workers responded positively.

JOB PERFORMANCE

Somewhere in Michigan near a Ford Motor Company plant, the following sign once hung in a tavern: "I spend forty hours a week here — am I supposed to work too?" The message in these words is an important one in management: It is one thing for people to come to work; it is quite another for them to perform at high levels while they are on the job. Formally defined, **job performance** is the quantity and quality of tasks accomplished by an individual or group at work. Performance, as is commonly said, is the "bottom line" for people at work. It is a cornerstone of productivity, and it should contribute to the accomplishment of organizational objectives. Indeed, a *value-added criterion* is being used in more and more organizations to evaluate the worthwhileness of jobs and/or jobholders. The performance of every job should add value to the organization's production of useful goods and/or services.

As earlier examples have shown, however, some workers achieve a sense of personal satisfaction from their jobs and others do not. Some workers achieve high levels of task performance and others do not. The test of a manager's skill in building value-added jobs is to discover what work means to other people and then to create jobs and work environments that help them achieve high levels of both performance and satisfaction. Fortunately, many insights are available. Consider, for example, this **high-performance equation:**

● **Job performance** is the quantity and quality of task accomplishment by an individual or group.

$$Performance = Ability \times Support \times Effort$$

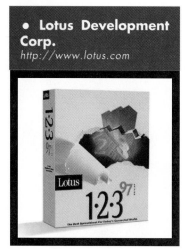

● Lotus Development Corp.
http://www.lotus.com

The search for meaning in one's work took center stage when Lotus Development Corp., a division of IBM, formed a "soul committee" to find ways to improve employee morale. Out of the group emerged recommendations for flexible working hours and more employee involvement in senior managers' performance appraisals.

If high performance is to be achieved in any work setting, the individual contributor must possess the right abilities (creating the *capacity to perform*), work hard at the task (showing the *willingness to perform*), and have the necessary support (creating the *opportunity to perform*).[15] All three factors are important and necessary; failure to provide for any one or more is likely to cause performance losses and establish limited performance ceilings. Simply put, jobs must be designed and staffed to meet the requirements of ability, support, and effort.

Performance Begins with Ability

Ability counts. As the basic foundation of aptitudes and skills it establishes an individual's capacity to perform at a high level of accomplishment. This is the central issue in human resource management, as discussed in Chapter 12. Proper employee selection brings people with the right abilities to a job; poor selection does not. Good training and development keeps peoples' skills up to date and their jobs relevant; poor or insufficient training does not.

The goal of maintaining and increasing the ability of workers in every job should be central to all human resource development initiatives and policies. The best managers never let a job vacancy or training opportunity pass without giving it serious attention. The best managers make sure everyday that all jobs under their supervision are staffed up to the moment with talented people. By renewing and redoubling their commitments to the ability factor and best practices in human resource management, managers can make substantial contributions to performance development.

Performance Requires Support

The support factor in the high-performance equation can easily be neglected in day-to-day management practice. But such oversight comes at a high cost. Even the most capable and hard-working individual will not achieve the highest performance levels unless proper support is available. Support creates a work environment rich in opportunities to apply one's talents to maximum advantage. To fully utilize their abilities workers need sufficient resources, clear goals and directions, freedom from unnecessary rules and job constraints, appropriate technologies, and performance feedback. Providing these and other forms of direct work support is a basic managerial responsibility. Doing it right, however, requires a willingness to get to know the jobs to be done and the people doing them. The best information on the need for support, of course, comes from the workers themselves. Wouldn't it be nice to hear more managers speak the following words in everyday conversations with their subordinates: "How can I help you today?"

Performance Involves Effort

Without any doubt, effort — the willingness to work hard at a task, is an irreplaceable component of the high-performance workplace. Even the most capable workers won't achieve consistent high performance unless they are willing to try hard enough. But the decision by anyone to work hard or not rests squarely on the shoulders of the individual alone. This is the ultimate test of the motivation theories discussed in Chapter 14. All any manager (or teacher, or parent) can do is attempt to create the conditions under which the answer to the all-important question — "Should I work hard today?" is more often "Yes!" than "No!" And quite frankly, the most powerful and enduring "Yes" is the one driven by forces within the individual — intrinsic motivation, rather than by outside initiatives such as supervisory appeals, offers of monetary reward, or threats of punishment. Good managers understand this reality.

JOB DESIGN ALTERNATIVES

Job design is in many ways an exercise in "fit." A good job design is one that provides a good fit between the individual worker and the task requirements. To explore this notion further, consider a short case.[16] Datapoint Corporation manufactures a line of personal computers. Jackson White has just been employed by Datapoint. He is a competent person who enjoys interpersonal relationships. He also likes to feel helpful or stimulating to others. How do you think he will react to each of the following job designs?

In *Job 1,* Jackson reports to a work station on the computer assembly line. A partially assembled circuit board passes in front of him on a conveyor belt every 90 seconds. He adds 2 pieces to each board and lets the conveyor take the unit to the next work station. Quality control is handled at a separate station at the end of the line. Everyone gets a 10-minute break in the morning and afternoon and a 30-minute lunch period. Jackson works by himself in a quiet setting.

In *Job 2,* Jackson works on the same assembly line. Now, however, a circuit board comes to his station every 12 minutes, and he performs a greater number of tasks. He adds several pieces to the board, adds a frame, and installs several electric switches. Periodically, Jackson changes stations with one of the other workers and does a different set of tasks on earlier or later stages of the same circuit board. In all other respects, the work setting is the same as in the first job described.

In *Job 3,* Jackson is part of a team responsible for completely assembling circuit boards for the computers. The team has a weekly production quota but makes its own plans for the speed and arrangement of the required assembly processes. The team is also responsible for inspecting the quality of the finished boards and for correcting any defective units. These duties are shared among the members and are discussed at team meetings. Jackson has been selected by the team as its plant liaison. In addition to his other duties, he works with people elsewhere in the plant to resolve any production problems and achieve plant-wide quality objectives.

These three job design alternatives are identified in *Figure 15.2* as job simplification, job enlargement and rotation, and job enrichment, respectively. Each varies in how specialized the division of labor becomes — that is, in how narrowly job tasks are defined. And although not every one of these designs may be a good choice for maximizing Jackson White's job performance and satisfaction, each has a role to play in the modern workplace.

Job Simplification

Job simplification involves standardizing work procedures and employing people in well-defined and highly specialized tasks. This is an extension of the scientific management approach discussed in Chapter 4. Simplified jobs are narrow in **job scope** — that is, the number and variety of different tasks a person performs. Jackson White's first job on the assembly line was highly simplified. He isn't

- **Job simplification** employs people in clearly defined and very specialized tasks.

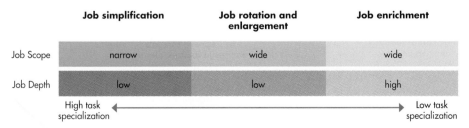

Figure 15.2 A continuum of job-design alternatives.

• **Automation** is the total mechanization of a job.

alone. Many employees around the world earn their livings working at highly simplified tasks. The most extreme form of job simplification is *automation,* or the total mechanization of a job.

The logic of job simplification is straightforward: Because the jobs don't require complex skills, workers should be easier and quicker to train, less difficult to supervise, and easy to replace if they leave. Furthermore, because tasks are precisely and narrowly defined, workers should become good at doing the same tasks over and over again. This logic has caused Kawasaki Steel Corporation in Japan to adopt a very different job design approach for its programmers than is typical in American industry. At Kawasaki, software programmers work in an assembly-line fashion according to rigid guidelines and with continuous review and monitoring. Management claims this has improved software productivity 2.5 times.[17]

Situations don't always work out this well in highly simplified jobs. Productivity can suffer as unhappy workers drive up costs through absenteeism and turnover and through poor performance caused by boredom and alienation. Although simplified jobs appeal to some people, disadvantages can develop with the structured and repetitive tasks. For example, in the Datapoint case, White's social need is thwarted in Job 1 because the assembly line prevents interaction with coworkers. We would predict low satisfaction, occasional tardiness and absenteeism, and boredom, which may cause a high error rate. White's overall performance could be just adequate enough to prevent him from being fired. This is hardly sufficient for a computer maker trying to maintain a high-performance edge in today's competitive global economy.

JOB ROTATION AND JOB ENLARGEMENT

• **Job rotation** increases task variety by periodically shifting workers between jobs involving different tasks.

• **Job enlargement** increases task variety by combining into one job two or more tasks previously assigned to separate workers.

One way to move beyond job simplification is to expand job scope by increasing the number and variety of tasks performed by a worker. This can be done through job rotation and/or job enlargement. **Job rotation** increases task variety by periodically shifting workers between jobs involving different task assignments. Job rotation can be done on a regular schedule; it can also be done periodically or occasionally. The latter approach is often used in training to broaden people's understanding of jobs performed by others.

Job enlargement increases task variety by combining two or more tasks that were previously assigned to separate workers. Often these are tasks done immediately before or after the work performed in the original job. *Figure 15.3* shows how such *horizontal loading* — pulling prework and/or later work stages into the job, can be used to enlarge jobs. In this job design strategy the old job is permanently changed through the addition of new tasks.

Jackson White's second job on the modified assembly line is an example of job enlargement with occasional job rotation. Instead of doing only one task, he now

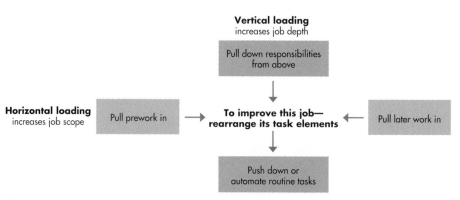

Figure 15.3 How to change job design by horizontal and vertical loading.

Manager's Notepad 15.1

Job Enrichment Checklist

Check 1: Remove controls that limit people's discretion in their work.
Check 2: Grant people authority to make decisions about their work.
Check 3: Make people understand their accountability for results.
Check 4: Allow people to do "whole" tasks or complete units of work.
Check 5: Make performance feedback available to those doing the work.

does three. And he occasionally switches jobs to work on a different part of the assembly. Because job enlargement and rotation can reduce some of the monotony in otherwise simplified jobs, we would expect an increase in White's satisfaction and performance. Satisfaction should remain only moderate, however, because the job still does not respond completely to his social needs. Although White's work quality should increase as boredom is reduced, some absenteeism is likely.

JOB ENRICHMENT

Frederick Herzberg, whose two-factor theory of motivation was discussed in Chapter 14, questions the true value of the job design approaches just discussed. "Why," he asks, "should a worker become motivated when one or more meaningless tasks are added to previously existing ones or when work assignments are rotated among equally meaningless tasks?" By contrast, he says, "If you want people to do a good job, give them a good job to do."[18] **Job enrichment** is the practice of building more opportunities for satisfaction into a job by expanding its content.

> • **Job enrichment** increases job depth by adding work planning and evaluating duties normally performed by the supervisor.

In contrast to job enlargement and rotation, job enrichment focuses not just on job scope but also on **job depth** — that is, the extent to which task planning and evaluating duties are performed by the individual worker rather than the supervisor. As depicted in *Figure 15.3,* changes designed to increase job depth are sometimes referred to as *vertical loading*. Herzberg's recommendations for enriching jobs through vertical loading are found in *Manager's Notepad 15.1.*

There are some elements of job enrichment in Job 3 in the Datapoint case, where Jackson White works in a team assembly process. White's team is responsible for task planning and evaluation duties as well as actual product assembly. White should respond well to the challenges of this arrangement. It provides opportunities to satisfy his social needs, and he should get added satisfaction from acting as the team's plant liaison. Higher performance and satisfaction are the predicted results.

 ## DIRECTIONS IN JOB ENRICHMENT

Job enrichment is an important strategy with the potential to improve individual performance and satisfaction in the new workplace. But modern management theory takes job enrichment a step beyond the suggestions of Frederick Herzberg. Most importantly, it adopts a contingency perspective and recognizes that job enrichment may not be best for everyone. Among the directions in job design, the job characteristics model developed by Richard Hackman and his associates offers a way for managers to create jobs, enriched or otherwise, that best fit the needs of people and organizations.[19]

THE JOB CHARACTERISTICS MODEL

The model described in *Figure 15.4* offers a diagnostic approach to job enrichment. Five core job characteristics are identified as task attributes of special importance. A job that is high in the core characteristics is considered enriched; the lower a job scores on the core characteristics, the less enriched it is. The five core job characteristics are as follows:

Five core job characteristics

- *Skill variety:* The degree to which a job requires a variety of different activities to carry out the work and involves the use of a number of different skills and talents of the individual.

- *Task identity:* The degree to which the job requires completion of a "whole" and identifiable piece of work, that is, one that involves doing a job from beginning to end with a visible outcome.

- *Task significance:* The degree to which the job has a substantial impact on the lives or work of other people elsewhere in the organization or in the external environment.

- *Autonomy:* The degree to which the job gives the individual substantial freedom, independence, and discretion in scheduling the work and in determining the procedures to be used in carrying it out.

- *Feedback from the job itself:* The degree to which carrying out the work activities required by the job results in the individual obtaining direct and clear information on the results of his or her performance.

According to *Figure 15.4,* this model of job design views job satisfaction and performance as being influenced by three critical psychological states of the individual: (1) experienced meaningfulness of the work; (2) experienced responsibility for the outcomes of the work; and (3) knowledge of actual results of work activities. These psychological states, in turn, are influenced by the presence or absence of the five core job characteristics. In true contingency fashion, however, the core characteristics will not affect all people in the same way. Generally speaking, people who respond most favorably to enriched jobs will have strong higher-order needs and appropriate job knowledge and skills. They will also be

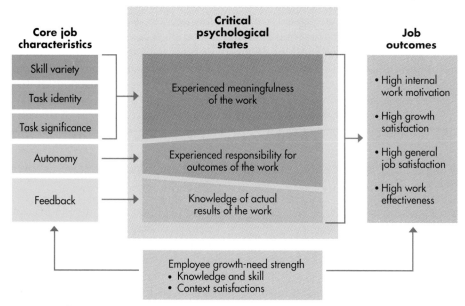

Figure 15.4 Core job characteristics and individual work outcomes in a diagnostic model of job design. *Source:* Reprinted by permission from J. Richard Hackman and Greg R. Oldham, *Work Redesign* (Reading, MA: Addison-Wesley, 1980), p. 90.

otherwise satisfied with job context. One of the key contingency variables is **growth-need strength,** described in Alderfer's ERG theory (see Chapter 14) as the degree to which an individual seeks psychological growth in his or her work. The expectation is that people with strong growth needs will respond most positively to enriched jobs.

When job enrichment is a good job design choice, Hackman and his colleagues recommend five ways to improve the core characteristics. First, you can *form natural units of work.* Make sure that the tasks people perform are logically related to one another and provide a clear and meaningful task identity. Second, try to *combine tasks.* Expand job responsibilities by pulling together into one larger job a number of smaller tasks previously done by others. Third, *establish client relationships.* Put people in contact with others who, as clients inside and/ or outside the organization, use the results of their work. Fourth, *open feedback channels.* Provide opportunities for people to receive performance feedback as they work and to learn how performance changes over time. Fifth, *practice vertical loading.* Give people more control over their work by increasing their authority to perform the planning and controlling previously done by supervisors.

- **Growth-need strength** is the desire to achieve psychological growth in one's work.

TECHNOLOGY AND JOB ENRICHMENT

An important issue of job enrichment involves the impact of technology on job design.[20] The managerial challenge is quite clear: Job design should proceed with the goal of increasing productivity through integrated **sociotechnical systems.** These are job designs that use technology to best advantage while still treating people with respect and allowing their human talents to be applied to their fullest potential.[21] The continuing inroads made by computers into the workplace provide a good case in point. We know that they are changing structures, workflows, and the mix of skills needed in many settings.

- A **sociotechnical system** integrates technology and human resources in high-performance systems.

Consider the special case of *robotics*—the use of computer-controlled machines to automate completely work tasks previously performed by hand. As mentioned earlier, such automation of work is the most extreme form of job simplification. It takes exactly the opposite approach to job enrichment and, in this respect, has both its limits and critics.[22] On the positive side, technology offers an opportunity to take over many routine tasks previously assigned to individuals and thereby frees human talents for more enriched job assignments. In this and other ways, technology utilization and job enrichment can be complimentary strategies.

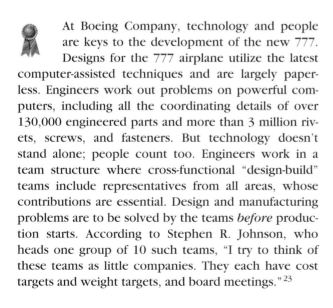 At Boeing Company, technology and people are keys to the development of the new 777. Designs for the 777 airplane utilize the latest computer-assisted techniques and are largely paperless. Engineers work out problems on powerful computers, including all the coordinating details of over 130,000 engineered parts and more than 3 million rivets, screws, and fasteners. But technology doesn't stand alone; people count too. Engineers work in a team structure where cross-functional "design-build" teams include representatives from all areas, whose contributions are essential. Design and manufacturing problems are to be solved by the teams *before* production starts. According to Stephen R. Johnson, who heads one group of 10 such teams, "I try to think of these teams as little companies. They each have cost targets and weight targets, and board meetings."[23]

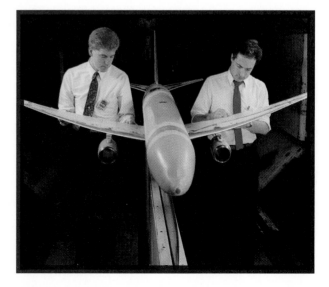

QUESTIONS AND ANSWERS ON JOB ENRICHMENT

"Is it expensive to implement job enrichment?" Job enrichment can be costly. The cost grows as the required changes in technology, workflow, and other facilities become more complex.

"Will people demand more pay for doing enriched jobs?" Herzberg believes that if people are being paid truly competitive wages (i.e., if pay dissatisfaction does not already exist), the satisfactions of performing enriched tasks will be adequate compensation for the increased work involved. But a manager must be cautious on this issue. Any job-enrichment program should be approached with due recognition that pay may be an important issue for the people involved.[24]

"Should everyone's job be enriched?" No, contingency counts. The people most likely to respond favorably to job enrichment are those seeking higher order or growth-need satisfactions at work and who have the levels of training, education, and ability required to perform the enriched job.

"What do the unions say about job enrichment?" It is hard to speak for all unions. Suffice it to say that the following comments of one union official are worth consideration.

> Better wages, shorter hours, vested pensions, a right to have a say in their working conditions, the right to be promoted on the basis of seniority, and all the rest. That's the kind of job enrichment that unions believe in. And I assure you that that's the kind of job enrichment that we will continue to fight for.[25]

ALTERNATIVE WORK ARRANGEMENTS

Not only is the content of jobs changing for individuals and groups in today's workplace, the context is changing too. Among the more significant developments is the emergence of a number of alternative ways for people to schedule their work time. This is especially important as employers deal with work-life balance issues affecting today's highly diverse workforce. Many are finding that alternative work schedules can help attract and retain the best workers. The top three reasons employers give for initiating such plans are as a response to employee requests, to support a responsible corporate image, and as part of a work-family assistance program.[26] It is popular in this sense to talk about a new and more "flexible" workplace in which alternative work schedules such as the compressed workweek, flexible working hours, job sharing, telecommuting, and part-time work are more and more common.

At Aetna Life & Casualty Company, a Work/Family Strategies unit was formally charged with the task of helping the firm respond to employees' work-family concerns. Before the unit was created, Aetna lost many talented female employees who did not return to full-time work after pregnancies. The head of the unit convinced Aetna management that it was cheaper and more responsible to keep trained workers on reduced schedules if they didn't want to work full-time. Aetna estimates that some $1 million in training costs is saved annually by allowing workers to pursue flexible schedules. It has also earned the reputation as a top "family-friendly" company.[27]

THE COMPRESSED WORKWEEK

A **compressed workweek** is any work schedule that allows a full-time job to be completed in less than the standard 5 days of 8-hour shifts.[28] Its most common form is the "4-40," that is, accomplishing 40 hours of work in four 10-hour days. One advantage of the 4-40 schedule is that the employee receives 3 consecutive days off from work each week. This benefits the individual through more leisure time and lower commuting costs. The organization should also benefit through lower absenteeism and any improved performance that may result. Potential disadvantages include increased fatigue and family adjustment problems for the individual, as well as increased scheduling problems, possible customer complaints, and union objections for the organization. At USAA, a diversified financial services company, nearly 75 percent of the firm's San Antonio workforce is on a 4-day schedule, with some working Monday through Thursday and others working Tuesday through Friday. Company benefits include improved employee morale, lower overtime costs, less absenteeism, and less sick leave.[29]

> • A **compressed workweek** allows a full-time, 40-hour-per-week job to be completed in less than 5 days.

FLEXIBLE WORKING HOURS

The term **flexible working hours,** also called *flexitime* or *flextime,* describes any work schedule that gives employees some choice in the pattern of their daily work hours. A sample flexible working schedule offers choices of starting and ending times, such as the program depicted in *Figure 15.5.* Employees in this example work 4 hours of "core" time, or the time they must be present at work. In this case, core time falls between 9 and 10 A.M. and 1 and 3 P.M. They are then free to choose another 4 work hours from "flextime" blocks. Such flexible schedules give employees greater autonomy while ensuring that they maintain work responsibility. Early risers may choose to come in earlier and leave earlier, while still completing an 8-hour day; late sleepers may choose to start later in the morning and leave later. In between these extremes are opportunities to attend to personal affairs, such as dental appointments, home emergencies, visits to children's schools, and so on.

> • **Flexible working hours** give employees some choice in the pattern of daily work hours.

The advantages of flexible working hours are especially important to members of a diverse workforce. By offering flexibility, organizations can attract and hold employees with special nonwork responsibilities. The work schedule is important to many dual-career couples who face the complications of managing careers and other responsibilities, including parenting. Single parents with young children and employees with elder-care responsibilities also find it very attractive to have the option of adjusting work schedules to allow for other obligations to be met. The added discretion flextime provides may also encourage workers to have more positive attitudes toward the organization.

Flex time	Core time*	Flex time	Core time*	Flex time

6 A.M.   9 A.M.   11 A.M.   1 P.M.   3 P.M.   6 P.M.

Sample Schedules

Early schedule   7:00–3:00
Standard schedule 8:00–4:30
Late schedule   9:00–5:30
*Everyone must work during "core" time.

Figure 15.5 A sample flexible working hours schedule.

JOB SHARING

● **Job sharing** splits one job between two people.

Another important development for today's workforce is **job sharing,** whereby one full-time job is split between two or more persons. Job sharing often involves each person working one-half day, but it can also be done on weekly or monthly sharing arrangements. When it is feasible for jobs to be split and shared, organizations can benefit by employing talented people who would otherwise be unable to work. The qualified specialist who is also a parent may be unable to stay away from home for a full workday but may be able to work a half day. Job sharing allows two such persons to be employed as one. Although there are sometimes adjustment problems, the arrangement can be good for all concerned.

Job sharing is sometimes viewed skeptically by those who don't believe two workers can perform a shared job as productively as one person alone. However, when such concerns were investigated at Lotus Development Corporation early in the life of its job-sharing program, the results turned out to be just the opposite. When performance was studied, none of the initial 9 teams of job sharers had to apologize to anybody. They were among the top performers in annual merit pay appraisals.[30]

Job sharing should not be confused with a more controversial concept called *work-sharing.* This involves an agreement between employees who face layoffs or terminations to cut back their work hours so they can all keep their jobs. Instead of losing 20 percent of a firm's work force to temporary layoffs in an unexpected business downturn, for example, a work-sharing program would cut everyone's hours by 20 percent to keep them all employed. This allows employers to retain trained and loyal workers even when forced to economize temporarily by reducing labor costs. For employees whose seniority might otherwise protect them from layoff, the disadvantage is lost earnings. For those who would otherwise be terminated, however, it provides continued work — albeit with reduced earnings, and with a preferred employer. Some unions endorse this concept, and it is now legal in many states. It is prohibited in others, however, because of legal complications relating to unemployment compensation and benefits.

Catalyst, the New York-based research organization, claims there are some 28 million dual-career couples in the American workforce. A recent Catalyst survey reports that both men and women support more flexible working schedules. Respondents indicate interest in having the freedom to "come in early, leave late, go to the school play or a soccer game" and to do so without fear of damaging one's career. Almost 50 percent of male respondents would use flexible hours as a screening criterion in searching for employment.

TELECOMMUTING

● **Telecommuting** or **flexiplace** involves working at home or other places using computer links to the office.

Another significant development in work scheduling is the growing popularity of a variety of ways for people to work away from a fixed office location. This includes alternatives ranging from self-employment and entrepreneurship based at home to utilizing the latest in computer and information technology to maintain a "virtual" office. **Telecommuting,** sometimes called **flexiplace,** is a work arrangement that allows at least a portion of scheduled work hours to be completed outside of the office, with work-at-home one of the options. Often this is facilitated by advances in information technology and computer linkages to clients or customers and a central office. The United States has experienced a tripling of telecommuters since 1990 to some 11 million workers; one survey reports that the number of companies that already have or are developing the option is up to 74%.[31]

Telecommuting frees the jobholder from the normal constraints of commuting, fixed hours, special work attire, and even direct contact with supervisors. It is popular, for example, among computer programmers and is found increasingly in such diverse areas as marketing, financial analysis, and administrative support. New terms are becoming associated with telecommuting practices. We speak of *hoteling* when telecommuters come to the central office and use temporary office facilities; we are immersed in a world of *telemarketing* where customers are contacted and orders taken by service personnel working in diverse locations; and we often refer to *virtual offices* that include everything from an office at home to mobile workspace in automobiles.

All these options offer both advantages and disadvantages from a job design and management perspective. When asked what they liked about these alternatives, a survey of "home workers" conducted by the *Wall Street Journal* reported increased productivity, fewer distractions, the freedom to be your own boss, and the benefit of having more time for yourself. On the negative side, they cited working too much, having less time to yourself, difficulty separating work and personal life, and having less time for family.[32] Other considerations for the individual include feelings of isolation and loss of visibility for promotion. Managers, in turn, may be required to change their routines and procedures to accommodate the challenges of supervising people from a distance. Such problems tend to be magnified in situations where employees feel forced into these work arrangements rather than opting for them voluntarily.[33]

PART-TIME WORK

The growing use of temporary workers is another striking trend, and it has a controversial side. **Part-time work** is done on any schedule that is less than the standard 40-hour work week and does not qualify the individual as a full-time employee. Increasingly, employers are relying on **contingency workers.** These are part-time workers who supplement the full-time workforce, often on a long-term basis. These *permatemps,* for example, are important at the Lamson & Sessions Company's plastics plant in Bowling Green, Ohio. The firm is in continuous operation and operates with a core group of full-time employees who comprise about 50 percent of the total workforce. The other 50 percent consists of temporaries as well as some independent contractors located outside the plant. Summer workers and other part-timers are hired as needed.[34]

- **Part-time work** is temporary and requires less than the standard 40-hour workweek.

- **Contingency workers** are employed on a part-time and temporary basis to supplement a permanent workforce.

Contingency workers now constitute some 30 percent of the American workforce.[35] No longer limited to the traditional areas of clerical services, sales personnel, and unskilled labor, these workers serve an increasingly broad range of employer needs. It is now possible to hire on a part-time basis everything from executive support, such as a chief financial officer, to such special expertise as engineering, computer programming, and market research.

Because part-time or contingency workers can be easily hired, contracted with, and/or terminated in response to changing needs, many employers like the flexibility they offer in controlling labor costs and dealing with cyclical demand. On the other hand, some worry that temporaries lack the commitment of permanent workers and may lower productivity. Perhaps the most controversial issue of the part-time work trend relates to the different treatment part-timers may receive from employers. They may be paid less than their full-time counterparts, and they often fail to receive important benefits, such as health care, life insurance, pension plans, and paid vacations. The social and economic implications of the growing role of part-time and contingent employment are fast gaining the attention of concerned policymakers.[36]

JOB STRESS AND STRESS MANAGEMENT

The jobs that people are asked to perform, and the relationships and circumstances under which they have to do them are often causes of significant stress. Formally defined, **stress** is a state of tension experienced by individuals facing extraordinary demands, constraints, or opportunities.[37] Any look ahead toward your future work career would be incomplete without considering stress as a challenge you are sure to encounter along the way—and a challenge you must be prepared to help others learn to deal with. The United States Bureau of Labor Statistics, for

- **Stress** is a state of tension experienced by individuals facing extraordinary demands, constraints, or opportunities.

example, reports that women are working 223 hours a year more than in 1976 and that men are working 100 additional yearly hours.[38] It is not surprising, therefore, that concerns for work-life balance are on the rise and that people are experiencing more stress in their daily lives. Job-related stress, in particular, goes hand in hand with the dynamic and sometimes uncertain nature of the managerial role. Think about this statement by a psychologist who works with top-level managers who have alcohol abuse problems: "All executives deal with stress. They wouldn't be executives if they didn't. Some handle it well, others handle it poorly."[39]

SOURCES OF STRESS

> • A **stressor** is anything that causes stress.

Various **stressors,** or sources of stress, originate in work, personal, and nonwork situations that can influence a person's work attitudes and behavior. *Work factors* have an obvious potential to create job stress. Some 46 percent of workers in one survey reported that their jobs were highly stressful; 34 percent said that their jobs were so stressful that they were thinking of quitting.[40] Such job-related stress can result from excessively high or low task demands, role conflicts or ambiguities, poor interpersonal relations, or career progress that is too slow or too fast. When asked what factors caused them the most stress on the job, workers in another survey identified the following: not doing the kind of work they wanted to (34%), coping with their current job (30%), working too hard (28%), colleagues at work (21%), a difficult boss (18%).[41] Stress also tends to be high during periods of work overload, when office politics are common, and among persons working for organizations undergoing staff cutbacks and downsizing. This latter situation and lack of "corporate loyalty" to the employee can be especially stressful, especially to someone with major financial responsibilities and/or approaching retirement age.

A variety of *personal factors* are also sources of potential stress for people at work. Such individual characteristics as needs, capabilities, and personality can influence how one perceives and responds to the work situation. Researchers, for example, identify a **Type A personality** that is high in achievement orientation, impatience, and perfectionism. Type A persons are likely to create stress in circumstances that others find relatively stress-free. Type As, in this sense, bring stress on themselves. The stressful behavior patterns of Type A personalities include the following:[42]

> • A **Type A personality** is a person oriented toward extreme achievement, impatience, and perfectionism.

> Characteristics of a Type A personality ⟶

- Always moving, walking, and eating rapidly.
- Acting impatient, hurrying others, disliking waiting.
- Doing, or trying to do, several things at once.
- Feeling guilty when relaxing.
- Trying to schedule more in less time.
- Using nervous gestures such as a clenched fist.
- Hurrying or interrupting the speech of others.

Finally, *nonwork factors* may "spill over" and influence the stress an individual experiences at work. Stressful life situations including such things as family events (e.g., the birth of a new child), economics (e.g., a sudden loss of extra income), and personal affairs (e.g., a preoccupation with a bad relationship) are often sources of emotional strain. Depending upon the individual and his or her ability to deal with them, preoccupation with such situations can affect one's work and add to the stress of work-life conflicts.

CONSEQUENCES OF STRESS

The discussion of stress so far may give the impression that stress always acts as a negative influence on our lives. But, like conflict, stress actually has two faces—

one constructive and one destructive. **Constructive stress** acts in a positive way for the individual and/or the organization. Low to moderate levels of stress can be energizing. They can encourage increased effort, stimulate creativity, and enhance diligence in one's work. Individuals with a Type A personality, for example, are likely to work long hours and to be less satisfied with poor performance. Heavy task demands imposed by a supervisor may elicit higher levels of task accomplishment. Even nonwork stressors such as new family responsibilities may cause an individual to work harder in anticipation of greater financial rewards. The difficult question, however, is "When is a little stress *too much* stress?"

Destructive stress is dysfunctional for the individual and/or the organization. High stress can overload and break down a person's physical and mental systems. Productivity can suffer as people react to very intense stress through turnover, absenteeism, errors, accidents, dissatisfaction, and reduced performance. Medical research is also concerned that too much stress can reduce resistance to disease and increase the likelihood of physical and/or mental illness. It may contribute to health problems such as hypertension, ulcers, substance abuse, overeating, depression, and muscle aches, among others. The multiple and varied symptoms of excessive stress include changes in eating habits, restlessness, irritability, and stomach upset.

STRESS MANAGEMENT STRATEGIES

There are at least four reasons that managers should also be skilled at dealing with workplace stress so that it rarely, if ever, reaches the point of causing dysfunction.[43] The first is humanitarianism. To the extent that managerial awareness and action can enhance employee health, managers have a humanitarian responsibility to do so. The second is productivity. Healthy employees are absent less often, make fewer errors, and must be replaced less frequently than less healthy ones. The third is creativity. Persons in poor health tend to be less creative and are less likely to take reasonable risks than their healthy counterparts. The fourth is return on investment. When poor health reduces or removes the individual's contribution to the organization, return on the time and money invested in human resources is lost.

Managers should obviously be alert to signs of excessive stress in themselves and the people with whom they work. The best stress management alternative is to prevent it from ever reaching excessive levels in the first place. Stressors emerging from personal and nonwork factors must be recognized so that action can be taken to prevent them from adversely affecting the work experience. Family difficulties may be relieved by a change of work schedule, or the anxiety they cause may be reduced by an understanding supervisor.

Among the work factors with the greatest potential to cause excessive stress are role ambiguities, conflicts, and overloads. Role clarification through a management-by-objectives (MBO) approach can work to good advantage here. By bringing the supervisor and subordinate together in face-to-face task-oriented communications, MBO offers an opportunity to spot stressors and take action to reduce or eliminate them. Self-awareness and a realistic approach to one's responsibilities can also help prevent the stress brought on by simply "working too much." Understanding the **survivor syndrome,** that is, the stress experienced by persons who fear for their jobs in organizations that are reducing staff through downsizing and layoffs, is also important. As more managers become aware of this phenomenon, they are developing formal programs to help those employees who remain employed to better cope after major staff cutbacks have occurred.

Personal wellness is a term used to describe the pursuit of one's physical and mental potential through a personal health-promotion program.[44] This concept recognizes the individual's responsibility to enhance his or her personal health through a disciplined approach to such things as smoking, alcohol use,

- **Constructive stress** acts in a positive way to increase effort, stimulate creativity, and encourage diligence in one's work.

- **Destructive stress** impairs the performance of an individual.

- **Personal wellness** is the pursuit of one's full potential through a personal-health promotion program.

> ## Manager's Notepad 15.2
>
> **How to Cope with Workplace Stress**
>
> - *Take control of the situation:* Do your best, know your limits, and avoid unrealistic deadlines.
> - *Pace yourself:* Plan your day to do high-priority things first, but stay flexible and try to slow down.
> - *Open up to others:* Discuss your problems, fears, and frustrations with those who care about you.
> - *Do things for others:* Think about someone else's needs, and try to help satisfy those needs.
> - *Exercise:* Engage in regular physical activity as recommended by your physician.
> - *Balance work and recreation:* Schedule time for recreation, including vacations from your work.

maintaining a nutritious diet, and engaging in a regular exercise and physical-fitness program. The essence of personal wellness is a lifestyle that reflects a true commitment to health.

Personal wellness makes a great deal of sense as a personal stress-management strategy. Those who aggressively maintain their personal wellness are better prepared to deal with the inevitable stresses of work and work-life conflicts. They may be able to deal with levels of workplace stress that are higher than others can tolerate; they may also have more insight into the personal wellness needs of their subordinates. Indeed, many organizations are now formally sponsoring wellness programs for employees. Among the health promotion activities typically offered are smoking control, health risk appraisals, back care, stress management, exercise/physical fitness, nutrition education, high blood pressure control, and weight control. The expectations are that investments in such programs benefit both the organization and its employees. Ultimately, though, it is important to know how to help yourself. Some guidelines for coping with workplace stress are suggested in the accompanying *Manager's Notepad 15.2.*[45]

CHAPTER REVIEW

This section should be used as an end-of-chapter "study guide." The *Summary* helps to put the chapter's content into overall perspective. The list of *Key Terms* allows you to double-check your familiarity with basic concepts and definitions. *Self-Test 15* gives you the opportunity to test your basic comprehension of the chapter using sample test questions.

SUMMARY

What is the meaning of work?

- Work is an activity that produces value for people; it is something people do to "earn a living."

- Work is an exchange of values between individuals who offer contributions such as time and effort to organizations that offer monetary and other inducements in return.

- A healthy psychological contract occurs when a person believes that his or her contributions and inducements are in balance; it is one component in a high quality of work life.

- Quality of work life (QWL) is an important issue in creating opportunities for positive work-life balance.

What are important issues in job design?

- Job design is the process of creating or defining jobs by assigning specific work tasks to individuals and groups.

- Jobs should be designed so workers enjoy high levels of both job performance and job satisfaction.

- The high performance equation states: Performance = Ability $\times$ Support $\times$ Effort.

- Job simplification creates narrow and repetitive jobs consisting of well-defined tasks with many routine operations, such as the typical assembly-line job.

- Job enlargement allows individuals to perform a broader range of simplified tasks; job rotation allows individuals to transfer between different jobs of similar skill levels on a rotating basis.

- Job enrichment results in more meaningful jobs that involve more autonomy in decision making and broader task responsibilities.

How can jobs be enriched?

- The diagnostic approach to job enrichment involves analyzing jobs according to five core characteristics: skill variety, task identity, task significance, autonomy, and feedback.

- Jobs deficient in one or more of these core characteristics can be redesigned to improve their level of enrichment.

- Jobs can be enriched by forming natural work units, combining tasks, establishing client relationships, opening feedback channels, and vertically loading to give workers more planning and controlling responsibilities.

- Job enrichment does not work for everyone; it works best for people with a high growth-need strength — the desire to achieve psychological growth in their work.

What are alternative work arrangements?

- Alternative work schedules can make work hours less inconvenient and enable organizations to respond better to individual needs and personal responsibilities.

- The compressed workweek allows 40 hours of work to be completed in only 4 days' time.

- Flexible working hours allow people to adjust the starting and ending times of their daily schedules.

- Job sharing allows two people to share one job.

- Telecommuting allows people to work at home or in mobile offices through computer links with their employers and/or customers.

- An increasing number of people work on part-time schedules; more and more organizations are employing part-timers or contingency workers to reduce their commitments to full-time positions.

How can job and work stress be managed?

- Stress occurs as the tension accompanying extraordinary demands, constraints, or opportunities.

- Stress can be destructive or constructive; a moderate level of stress typically has a positive impact on performance.

- Stressors are found in a variety of work, personal, and nonwork situations.

- For some people, having a Type A personality creates stress as a result of continual feelings of impatience and pressure.

- Stress can be effectively managed through both prevention and coping strategies, including a commitment to personal wellness.

KEY TERMS

Automation (p. 312)
Compressed workweek (p. 317)
Constructive stress (p. 321)
Contingency workers (p. 319)
Destructive stress (p. 321)
Flexible working hours (p. 317)
Flexiplace (p. 318)
Growth-need strength (p. 315)

Job (p. 308)
Job design (p. 308)
Job enlargement (p. 312)
Job enrichment (p. 313)
Job performance (p. 309)
Job rotation (p. 312)
Job satisfaction (p. 308)
Job sharing (p. 318)
Job simplification (p. 311)

Part-time work (p. 319)
Personal wellness (p. 321)
Psychological contract (p. 306)
Sociotechnical systems (p. 315)
Stress (p. 319)
Stressors (p. 320)
Telecommuting (p. 318)
Type A personality (p. 320)
Work-at-home (p. 318)

SELF-TEST 15

Take this test much as you would in a normal classroom situation. It is a good way to check your basic comprehension of chapter material. Answers may be found at the end of the book.

MULTIPLE-CHOICE QUESTIONS:

1. Which statement about QWL is incorrect? (a) QWL can influence work-life balance. (b) Managers should create high QWL environments. (c) QWL is related to the worker's overall quality of life. (d) QWL is the only important job design consideration.

2. A manager's job design goals should be to establish the conditions for workers to achieve both high levels of both task performance and _____. (a) financial gain (b) social interaction (c) job satisfaction (d) job security

3. Vertical loading of a job is most associated with _____. (a) bringing prework into the job (b) bringing later work stages into the job (c) bringing higher level or managerial work into the job (d) increasing the quantity of output expected from a job

4. The _____ strategy of job design allows workers to shift regularly between a variety of jobs requiring essentially the same skills. (a) job simplification (b) job enlargement (c) job rotation (d) job sharing

5. The addition of more planning and evaluating responsibilities to a job is an example of the _____ job design strategy. (a) job enrichment (b) job enlargement (c) job rotation (d) job sharing

6. _____ is one of the core characteristics that should be improved upon in order to enrich a job. (a) Work-life balance (b) Task significance (c) Growth need strength (d) Automation

7. Workers in a compressed workweek typically work 40 hours in _____ days. (a) 3 (b) 4 (c) 5 (d) a flexible number of

8. Another term used to describe part-time workers is _____. (a) contingency workers (b) virtual workers (c) flexible workers (d) secondary workers

9. _____ is where two workers split one job on an arranged work schedule; _____ is where a group of workers accept reduced individual work hours in order to avoid layoffs. (a) Job rotation, job sharing (b) Job sharing, work sharing (c) Job enrichment, job sharing (d) Job splitting, job reduction

10. Hoteling is a development associated with the growing importance of _____ in the new workplace. (a) personal wellness (b) telecommuting (c) compressed work-weeks (d) Type A personalities

TRUE-FALSE QUESTIONS:

11. It is not a manager's responsibility to deal with the psychological contracts of people at work. T F

12. It is safe to say that improvements in job satisfaction should result in lower absenteeism. T F

13. The contingency approach to job design rules out any use of job simplification. T F

14. Job enlargement is a good example of job enrichment for an individual worker. T F

15. The basic idea of sociotechnical systems is to replace all human effort with machines. T F

16. Job enrichment is good for everyone. T F

17. Part-time work is increasing in importance in the American economy. T F

18. Flexible working hours are proving useful in "family-friendly" companies trying to meet the needs of diverse workforces. T F

19. Stress can have positive as well as negative effects on work performance. T F

20. The "spill over effect" helps explain how stressful life situations can adversely affect one's work. T F

SHORT-RESPONSE QUESTIONS:

21. What is a "healthy" psychological contract?

22. What difference does growth-need strength make in the job enrichment process?

23. Why is it important for a manager to understand the Type A personality?

24. Why might an employer *not* be interested in offering employees the option of working on a compressed workweek schedule?

APPLICATION QUESTION:

25. Kurt Swenson has just attended a management development program in which the following "high performance equation" was discussed: Performance = Ability $\times$ Support $\times$ Effort. As a plant manager, he is interested in implementing the concept. He plans to hold a meeting for all of his team leaders to explain the implications of this equation. If you were Kurt, how would you explain the importance of each performance factor — ability, support, effort, and how would you explain the significance of the multiplication signs in the equation?

Communication and Interpersonal Skills

Planning Ahead—Chapter 16 Study Questions

- What is the communication process?
- How can communication be improved?
- How does perception influence behavior?
- How can conflict be constructively managed?
- How can agreements be negotiated successfully?

CENTER FOR CREATIVE LEADERSHIP
MAIN ENTRANCE

When in Doubt, Communicate

Communication and interpersonal skills are indispensable to leadership success and effective motivation. Yet, some 30 percent or more of managers report difficulties in dealing with communication and interpersonal relations. Helping them to do something about such problems is what the Center for Creative Leadership, a well-known management training center, is all about. Richard S. Herlich came to the Center after being promoted to director of marketing for his firm. "I thought I had the perfect style," he said. He learned through role-playing that others viewed him as an aloof and poor communicator. After returning to his job and meeting with his subordinates to discuss his style, Herlich became more involved in their work projects. Another participant, Robert Siddall, received feedback that he was too structured and domineering. Center instructors worked with him to develop more positive relationships and to display a more "coaching" style of management. After returning to his job Siddall's performance ratings went up, and his relationships with coworkers improved. He says, "If I start screaming and yelling, they say—'Old Bob, old Bob.'"[1]

The ability to communicate well, both orally and in writing, is a critical managerial skill and a foundation of effective leadership.[2] Through communication people exchange and share information with one another, and influence one another's attitudes, behaviors, and understandings. Communication allows managers to establish and maintain interpersonal relationships, listen to others, and otherwise gain the information needed to create an inspirational workplace. No manager can handle conflict, negotiate successfully, and succeed at leadership without being a good communicator. It is no wonder that "communication skills" often top the list of attributes employers look for in job candidates. Any career portfolio should include adequate testimony to one's abilities to communicate well in interpersonal relationships, in various forms of public speaking, and increasingly through the electronic medium of the computer.

THE COMMUNICATION PROCESS

• **Communication** is the process of sending and receiving symbols with meanings attached.

Formally defined, **communication** is an interpersonal process of sending and receiving symbols with messages attached to them. The key elements in the communication process are shown in *Figure 16.1*. They include a *sender,* who is responsible for encoding an intended *message* into meaningful symbols, both verbal and nonverbal. The message is sent through a *communication channel* to a *receiver,* who then decodes or interprets its meaning. This interpretation, importantly, may or may not match the sender's original intentions. *Feedback,* when present, reverses the process and conveys the receiver's response back to the sender. Another way to view the communication process is as a series of questions. "Who?" (sender) "says what?" (message) "in what way?" (channel) "to whom?" (receiver) "with what result?" (interpreted meaning).

WHAT IS EFFECTIVE COMMUNICATION?

• In **effective communication** the intended meaning of the source and the perceived meaning of the receiver are identical.

• **Efficient communication** occurs at minimum cost.

Effective communication occurs when the intended message of the sender and the interpreted meaning of the receiver are one and the same. Although this should be the goal in any communication attempt, it is not always achieved. **Efficient communication** occurs at minimum cost in terms of resources expended. Time, in particular, is an important resource in the communication process. Picture your instructor taking the time to communicate individually with each student about this chapter. It would be virtually impossible. Even if it were possible, it would be costly. This is why managers, for example, often leave voice mail messages and interact by Email rather than visit their subordinates personally.

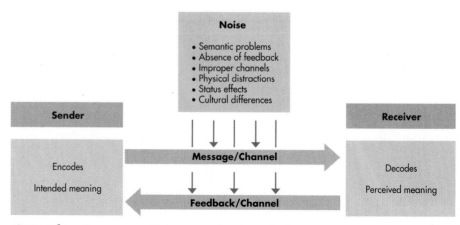

Figure 16.1 The process of interpersonal communication.

Simply put, these alternatives are more efficient ways to communicate than through one-on-one and face-to-face communications.

One problem is that efficient communications are not always effective. A low-cost approach such as an Email note to a distribution list may save time, but it does not always result in everyone getting the same meaning from the message. Without opportunities to ask questions and clarify the message, erroneous interpretations are possible. By the same token, an effective communication may not always be efficient. If a work team leader visits each team member individually to explain a new change in procedures, this may guarantee that everyone truly understands the change. But it may also be very costly in the demands it makes on the leader's time. A team meeting would be more efficient. In these and other ways, potential trade-offs between effectiveness and efficiency must be recognized in communication.

BARRIERS TO EFFECTIVE COMMUNICATION

Effective communication is a two-way process that requires effort and skill on the part of both the sender and the receiver. **Noise,** as *Figure 16.1* shows, is anything that interferes with the effectiveness of the communication process. For example, when Mazda president Yoshihiro Wada met with representatives of the firm's American joint venture partner Ford, he had to communicate through an interpreter. He estimated that between him and his interpreter, 20 percent of his intended meaning was lost. He expected another 20 percent to be lost between the interpreter and the Americans with whom he was ultimately trying to communicate.[3] In addition to these obvious problems when different languages are involved in a communication attempt, common sources of noise include poor choice of channels, poor written or oral expression, failure to recognize nonverbal signals, physical distractions, and status effects.

- **Noise** is anything that interferes with communication effectiveness.

Poor Choice of Channels

A **communication channel** is the medium through which a message is conveyed from sender to receiver. Good managers choose the right communication channel, or combination of channels, to accomplish their intended purpose in a given situation.[4] In general, written channels are acceptable for simple messages that are easy to convey and for those that require extensive dissemination quickly. They are also important, at least as follow-up communications, when formal policy or authoritative directives are being conveyed. Oral channels work best for messages that are complex and difficult to convey, where immediate feedback to the sender is valuable. They are also more personal and can create a supportive, even inspirational, emotional climate.

- A **communication channel** is the medium through which a message is sent.

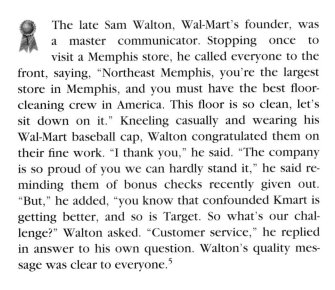 The late Sam Walton, Wal-Mart's founder, was a master communicator. Stopping once to visit a Memphis store, he called everyone to the front, saying, "Northeast Memphis, you're the largest store in Memphis, and you must have the best floor-cleaning crew in America. This floor is so clean, let's sit down on it." Kneeling casually and wearing his Wal-Mart baseball cap, Walton congratulated them on their fine work. "I thank you," he said. "The company is so proud of you we can hardly stand it," he said reminding them of bonus checks recently given out. "But," he added, "you know that confounded Kmart is getting better, and so is Target. So what's our challenge?" Walton asked. "Customer service," he replied in answer to his own question. Walton's quality message was clear to everyone.[5]

Poor Written or Oral Expression

Communication will be effective only to the extent that the sender expresses a message in a way that can be clearly understood by the receiver. This means that words must be well chosen and properly used to express the sender's intentions. When they are not, semantic barriers to communication occur as encoding and decoding errors and as mixed messages. Consider the following "bafflegab" found among some executive communications. *The report said:* "Consumer elements are continuing to stress the fundamental necessity of a stabilization of the price structure at a lower level than exists at the present time." (*Translation:* Consumers keep saying that prices must go down and stay down.) *The manager said:* "Substantial economies were effected in this division by increasing the time interval between distribution of data-eliciting forms to business entities." (*Translation:* The division was saving money by sending fewer questionnaires to suppliers.)

Both written and oral communication require skill. It isn't easy, for example, to write a concise letter or to express one's thoughts in a computer Email report. Any such message can easily be misunderstood. It takes practice and hard work to express yourself well. The same holds true for oral communication that takes place via the spoken word in telephone calls, face-to-face meetings, formal briefings, video conferences, and the like. The accompanying *Manager's Notepad 16.1* identifies guidelines for a common and important oral communication situation faced by managers—the executive briefing or formal presentation.[6]

Failure to Recognize Nonverbal Signals

• **Nonverbal communication** takes place through gestures and body language.

Nonverbal communication takes place through such things as hand movements, facial expressions, body posture, eye contact, and the use of interpersonal space. It can be a powerful means of transmitting messages. Eye contact or voice intonation can be used intentionally to accent special parts of an oral communication. The astute observer notes the "body language" expressed by other persons. At times our body may be "talking" for us even as we otherwise maintain si-

---

Manager's Notepad 16.1

How to Make a Successful Presentation

- *Be prepared:* Know what you want to say; know how you want to say it; and rehearse saying it.

- *Set the right tone:* Act audience centered; make eye contact; be pleasant and confident.

- *Sequence points:* State your purpose; make important points; follow with details; then summarize.

- *Support your points:* Give specific reasons for your points; state them in understandable terms.

- *Accent the presentation:* Use good visual aids and provide supporting "handouts" when possible.

- *Add the right amount of polish:* Attend to details; have the room, materials, and other arrangements ready to go.

- *Check your technology:* Check everything ahead of time; make sure it works and know how to use it.

- *Don't bet on the Internet:* Beware of plans to make real-time Internet visits; save your sites on a disk and then use a browser to open the file.

- *Be professional:* Be on time; wear appropriate attire; and act organized, confident, and enthusiastic.

lence. And when we do speak, our body may sometimes "say" different things than our words convey. A **mixed message** occurs when a person's words communicate one message while his or her actions, body language, appearance, or situational use of interpersonal space communicate something else. Watch how people behave in a meeting. A person who feels under attack may move back in a chair or lean away from the presumed antagonist, even while expressing verbal agreement. All of this is done quite unconsciously, but it sends a message to those alert enough to pick it up.

Nonverbal channels probably play a more important part in communication than most people recognize. One researcher indicates that gestures alone may make up as much as 70 percent of communication.[7] In fact, a potential side effect of the growing use of electronic mail, computer networking, and other communication technologies is that gestures and other nonverbal signals that may add important meaning to the communication event are lost.

- A **mixed message** results when words communicate one message while actions, body language, or appearance communicate something else.

Physical Distractions

Any number of physical distractions can interfere with the effectiveness of a communication attempt. Some of these distractions, such as telephone interruptions, drop-in visitors, and lack of privacy, are evident in the following conversation between an employee, George, and his manager:

> Okay, George, let's hear your problem [phone rings, boss picks it up, promises to deliver a report "just as soon as I can get it done"]. Uh, now, where were we — oh, you're having a problem with your technician. She's [manager's secretary brings in some papers that need his immediate signature; secretary leaves] . . . you say she's overstressed lately, wants to leave. . . . I tell you what, George, why don't you [phone rings again, lunch partner drops by] . . . uh, take a stab at handling it yourself. . . . I've got to go now.[8]

- **BankBoston Corp.**
http://www.bankboston.com

At Community Banking Group of BankBoston Corp., group executive Gail Snowden holds "town meetings" to stay in touch with her 600-plus employees. At the executive level it's hard for her to meet personally with everyone. She holds the town meetings to give them a chance to ask questions and express opinions.

Besides what may have been poor intentions in the first place, the manager in this example did not do a good job of communicating with George. This problem could be corrected easily. If George has something important to say, he should set aside adequate time for the meeting. Additional interruptions such as telephone calls and drop-in visitors could be eliminated by issuing appropriate instructions to the secretary. Many communication distractions can be avoided or at least minimized through proper planning.

Status Effects

"Criticize my boss? I don't have the right to." "I'd get fired." "It's her company, not mine." As suggested in these comments, the hierarchy of authority in organizations creates another potential barrier to effective communications. Consider the "corporate cover-up" once discovered at an electronics company. Product shipments were being predated and papers falsified to meet unrealistic sales targets set by the president. His managers knew the targets were impossible to attain, but at least 20 persons in the organization cooperated in the deception. It was months before the top found out. What happened in this case is **filtering** — the intentional distortion of information to make it appear favorable to the recipient.

Such filtering of information is often seen in the communication between lower and higher levels in organizations. Tom Peters, the popular management author and consultant, calls such information distortion "Management Enemy Number 1."[9] Simply put, it most often involves someone "telling the boss what he or she wants to hear." Whether the reason behind this is a fear of retribution for bringing bad news, an unwillingness to identify personal mistakes, or just a

- **Filtering** is the intentional distortion of information to make it appear most favorable to the recipient.

general desire to please, the end result is the same. The person receiving filtered communications can end up making poor decisions because of a biased and inaccurate information base.

IMPROVING COMMUNICATION

A number of things can be done to overcome barriers and improve the process of communication. They include active listening, making constructive use of feedback, opening upward communication channels, understanding proxemics and the use of space, utilizing technology, and valuing diversity.

ACTIVE LISTENING

• **Active listening** helps the source of a message say what he or she really means.

Managers must be very sensitive to their listening responsibility. When people "talk," they are trying to communicate something. That "something" may or may not be what they are saying. **Active listening** is the process of taking action to help the source of a message say exactly what he or she really means. There are five rules for becoming an active listener:[10]

Rules for active listening

1. *Listen for message content* — try to hear exactly what content is being conveyed in the message.
2. *Listen for feelings* — try to identify how the source feels about the content in the message.
3. *Respond to feelings* — let the source know that her or his feelings are being recognized.
4. *Note all cues* — be sensitive to nonverbal and verbal messages; be alert for mixed messages.
5. *Paraphrase and restate* — state back to the source what you think you are hearing.

Different responses to the following two questions contrast how a "passive" listener and an "active" listener might act in real workplace conversations. Put yourself in the position of the questioner in each case; then consider how you would react to each listener's response. Question 1: "Don't you think employees should be promoted on the basis of seniority?" *Passive listener's response:* "No, I don't!" *Active listener's response:* "It seems to you that they should, I take it?" Question 2: "What does the supervisor expect us to do about these out-of-date computers?" *Passive listener's response:* "Do the best you can, I guess." *Active listener's response:* "You're pretty disgusted with those machines, aren't you?"

The prior examples should give you a sense of how the active listening approach can facilitate and encourage communication in difficult circumstances, rather than discourage it. *Manager's Notepad 16.2* offers an additional set of useful guidelines for good listening.

CONSTRUCTIVE FEEDBACK

• **Feedback** is the process of telling someone else how you feel about something that person did or said.

The process of telling other people how you feel about something they did or said, or about the situation in general, is called **feedback.** The art of giving feedback is an indispensable skill, particularly for managers who must regularly give

Manager's Notepad 16.2
Ten Steps to Good Listening
1. Stop talking.
2. Put the other person at ease.
3. Show that you want to listen.
4. Remove any potential distractions.
5. Empathize with the other person.
6. Don't respond too quickly; be patient.
7. Don't get mad; hold your temper.
8. Go easy on argument and criticism.
9. Ask questions.
10. Stop talking.

feedback to other people. Often this takes the form of performance feedback given as evaluations and appraisals. When poorly done, such feedback can be threatening to the recipient and cause resentment. When properly done, feedback — even performance criticism, is listened to, accepted, and used to good advantage by the receiver.[11]

There are ways to help ensure that feedback is useful and constructive rather than harmful. To begin with, the sender must learn to recognize when the feedback he or she is about to offer will really benefit the receiver and when it will mainly satisfy some personal need. A supervisor who berates a computer operator for data analysis errors, for example, actually may be angry about personally failing to give clear instructions in the first place. Also, a manager should make sure that any feedback is considered from the recipient's point of view as understandable, acceptable, and plausible. Usefully accepted guidelines for giving "constructive" feedback include:[12]

- First, give feedback directly and with real feeling, based on trust between you and the receiver.

- Second, make sure that feedback is specific rather than general; use good, clear, and preferably recent examples to make your points.

- Third, give feedback at a time when the receiver seems most willing or able to accept it.

- Fourth, make sure the feedback is valid and limit it to things the receiver can be expected to do something about.

- Fifth, give feedback in small doses; never give more than the receiver can handle at any particular time.

Constructive feedback guidelines

OPEN COMMUNICATION CHANNELS

Status effects, as described earlier, can limit communication between levels in organizations. For those in managerial or leadership positions, however, there are a number of steps that can be taken to keep communication channels open. A popular approach is called **management by wandering around**, or **MBWA**, for short. This means dealing directly with subordinates by regularly spending time walking around and talking with them about a variety of work-related matters.

Instead of relying on formal channels to bring information to your attention, MBWA involves finding out for yourself what is going on. The basic objectives

- In **management by wandering around (MBWA)** workers at all levels talk with bosses about a variety of work-related matters.

Twice a year Scott's Co., makers of the well-known lawn care products of the same name, holds large employee meetings to thank employees for their work, tell them the results of the firm's financial performance, and celebrate teamwork. The food is good and plentiful, there is music and entertainment, and a lot of information is shared. These meetings demonstrate top management's commitment to an informed and involved workforce.

● **360-degree feedback** involves upward appraisals from subordinates as well as additional feedback from peers, internal and external customers, and higher managers.

are to break down status barriers, increase the frequency of interpersonal contact, and get more and better information from lower level sources. Of course, this requires a trusting relationship. Patricia Gallup, CEO of PC Connection, is well known for her interactive style of leadership and emphasis on communication. She makes herself available by Email and greets employees by name as she walks the hallways. MBWA is clearly part of her style. She spends as much time as possible out of her office and on the floor where she can be close to workers in the various departments.[13]

Any comprehensive approach to open channels and improve upward communications often involves *open office hours,* whereby busy senior managers like Gallup set aside time in their calendars to welcome walk-in visits during certain hours each week. A program of formal *employee group meetings* is also useful. Here, a rotating schedule of "shirtsleeve" meetings brings top managers into face-to-face contact with mixed employee groups throughout an organization. In some cases, a comprehensive communications program includes an *employee advisory council* composed of members elected by their fellow employees. Such a council may meet with top management on a regular schedule to discuss and react to new policies and programs that will affect employees. And there is always a place for the traditional *suggestion box,* electronic or other, which is another way to encourage all employees to communicate ideas or complaints.

When bosses suspect they are having communication problems, *communication consultants* can be hired to conduct interviews and surveys of employees in their behalf. At his 49-member public relations firm, for example, Lou Hoffman found that a consultant's assistance in surveying his staff helped identify communication problems. Working with the consultant, Hoffman kept track of improvements from one year to the next.[14] Marc Brownstein, also president of a public relations and advertising firm, had a similar experience. He was surprised when managers in an anonymous survey complained that he was a poor listener and gave them insufficient feedback. They also felt poorly informed about the firm's financial health. In other words — poor communication was hurting staff morale. With help from consultants, Brownstein now holds more meetings and works more aggressively to share information and communicate regularly with the firm's employees.[15]

Another communication approach that seeks to broaden the awareness of "bosses" regarding the feelings and perceptions of other people that they work closely with is called **360-degree feedback.** This typically involves upward appraisals done by a manager's subordinates as well as additional feedback from peers, internal and external customers, and higher-ups. A self-assessment is also part of the process. Often this feedback is gathered through questionnaires in which respondents can remain anonymous. The goal of "360 feedback" is to provide the manager with information that can be used for constructive improvement. Managers who have participated in the process often express surprise at what they learn. Some have found themselves perceived as lacking vision, having bad tempers, being bad listeners, lacking flexibility, and the like.[16] True success with the "360" group technique, however, requires a commitment to improve communication and relationships in the future.

PROXEMICS AND SPACE DESIGN

● **Proxemics** is the use of interpersonal space.

An important but sometimes neglected part of communication involves **proxemics,** or the use of interpersonal space.[17] The distance between people conveys varying intentions in terms of intimacy, openness, and status. And, the proxemics or physical layout of an office is an often overlooked form of nonverbal communication. Check it out. Offices with two or more chairs available for side-by-side seating, for example, convey different messages from those where the manager's chair sits behind the desk and those for visitors sit facing in front.

Office or workspace architecture is becoming increasingly recognized for its important influence on communication and behavior. If you visit Sun Microsystems in San Jose, California, for example, you will see many public spaces designed to encourage communication among persons from different departments. At the firm's Sunsoft Experimental Space on the research campus you can't get to a private office without passing through a public space. Most meeting areas have no walls and most of the walls that exist are glass. Ann Bamesberger, manager of planning and research says: "We were creating a way to get these people to communicate with each other more." Importantly, the Sun project involved not only the assistance of expert architectural consultants, but also extensive inputs and suggestions from the employees themselves. The results seem to justify the effort. A senior technical writer, Terry Davidson says: "This is the most productive workspace I have ever been in."[18]

TECHNOLOGY UTILIZATION

Communication in organizations can benefit greatly from advancements in information technology. As discussed earlier in this book, employees in the new workplace are expected to be computer literate and willing to use the new technologies to maximum advantage. The new age of communication is one of Email, voice mail, videoconferencing, computer-mediated meetings, and more. For Andy Grove, Chairman and former CEO of Intel, Email is a must for any progressive and quality-oriented company. Sitting at a computer in his open-office cubicle, Grove considers Email a primary channel of communication. He trades "volleys" with Email correspondents throughout his firm, even taking to the computer mails during breaks from person-to-person meetings. Email enables Grove to hold meetings with people at widely dispersed locations, and further allows the meeting to proceed "right to the point" and without interpersonal distractions.[19]

Another related and important development is the growing use of in-house Intranets to provide opportunities for increased communication and collaboration. At CompuServe, for example, a variety of on-line forums are available for internal communication among employees. However, the firm also has a secure Intranet site that allows employees to share ideas and opinions without the threat of management evesdropping. The purpose is to encourage freewheeling communication, and to provide a source of up-to-date information on the company and important projects. When the firm was in merger negotiations with World-Com, this site was used to allow communication about the merger and to offer official information regarding employee benefits and severance packages.[20]

By making it easier and faster to move information from top to bottom in an organization and across great distances, technology is contributing to the flattening of organization structures. Fewer middle managers are needed to serve in information transfer roles now that computers are able to do it for them. New information departments or centers are appearing on organization charts. They represent the importance staff expertise plays in information technology and its growing role in day-to-day organizational affairs. And as managers adapt to the new technologies and the expanded availability of information, their roles are changing too. At the same time that computers help empower lower level personnel with more and better information, their capacity to process information allows for improved control and accountability.

But whereas technology allows people to work together across great distances in "real time" through "electronic networks," legitimate concerns may be raised over the loss of the personal side of group decision making and the risks of being too focused on data alone. Indeed, a critical test of the *new* manager may be his or her ability to utilize new information technology, such as Email, while still maintaining a leadership edge based on good interpersonal relationships.

Alcoa
http://www.alcoa.com

Faster decision making is one of the goals behind Alcoa's new-form executive suites. Senior executives work in "cockpit offices" with special furniture and short, movable walls. This is designed to promote interaction and spontaneous association. The new executive offices include a common "coffee kitchen" complete with chalkboards for jotting down ideas that pop up in informal conversations.

VALUING CULTURE AND DIVERSITY

Workforce diversity and the global economy are two of the most talked-about trends in modern society. Communicating under conditions of diversity, where the sender and receiver are part of different cultures, is certainly a significant challenge. A major source of difficulty is *ethnocentrism,* the tendency to consider one's culture superior to any and all others. Ethnocentrism can adversely affect communication in at least three major ways: (1) it may cause someone to *not* listen well to what others have to say; (2) it may cause someone to address or speak with others in ways that alienate them; and (3) it may lead to the use of inappropriate stereotypes when dealing with persons from another culture.[21]

When Hyatt chairman Darryl Hartley-Leonard speaks to the firm's employees, to industry groups, and to other business-people, his message communicates a common theme: Value diversity and fulfill your social responsibilities. Says Hartley-Leonard, "No longer can we hide from the social, educational, and cultural challenges taking place in this country." Hyatt encourages employees to take up to 4 days leave per year for volunteer services. The firm works in Chicago with inner-city schools to help train students for careers in the hotel industry. This is part of business today, says Hartley-Leonard: "We all need to accept the fact that there is no longer a difference between what's good for society and what's good for business."[22]

For years, cultural challenges have been recognized by international travelers and executives. But as we know, you don't have to travel abroad to come face to face with communication and cultural diversity. Just going to work is a cross-cultural journey for most of us today. The workplace abounds with subcultures based on gender, age, ethnicity, race, and other factors. As a result, the importance of cross-cultural communication skills applies at home just as well as it does in a foreign country. And cultural skills are gained by reaching out, crossing cultural boundaries, and embracing differences.

PERCEPTION, COMMUNICATION, AND BEHAVIOR

• **Perception** is the process through which people receive, organize, and interpret information from the environment.

The process through which people receive and interpret information from the environment is called **perception.** It is the way we form impressions about ourselves, other people, and daily life experiences and the way we process information into the decisions that ultimately guide our actions.[23]

As shown in *Figure 16.2,* perception acts as a screen or filter through which information must pass before it has an impact on communication, decision making, and action. The results of this screening process vary because individual perceptions are influenced by such things as values, cultural background, and other circumstances of the moment. Simply put, people can and do perceive the same things or situations very differently. And importantly, people behave according to their perceptions. Unless the potential for alternative perceptions is recognized and understood, this important influence on individual behavior at work may be neglected.

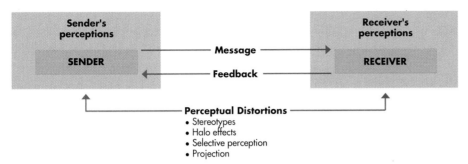

Figure 16.2 Perception and communication.

ATTRIBUTION ERRORS

It is natural for people to try to explain what they observe and the things that happen to them. This process of developing explanations for events is called *attribution*. The fact that people can perceive the same things quite differently has an important influence on attributions and their ultimate influence on behavior. In social psychology, attribution theory describes how people try to explain the behavior of themselves and other people.[24] Applications of attribution theory are particularly important in work settings. The theory suggests that individual performance will be judged as being internally or externally caused and that tendencies toward systematic errors of attribution are common.

Fundamental **attribution error** occurs when observers blame another person's performance failures or problems more on internal factors relating to the individual than on external factors relating to the environment. In the case of someone who is producing poor-quality work, for example, a supervisor might blame a lack of job skills or laziness — an unwillingness to work hard enough. These internal explanations of the performance deficiency, moreover, are likely to lead the supervisor to try to resolve the problem through training, motivation, or even replacement. The attribution error leads to the neglect of possible external explanations that might suggest, for example, that the poor-quality work was caused by unrealistic time pressures or substandard technology. Opportunities to improve upon these factors through managerial action will thus be missed.

The **self-serving bias,** by contrast, occurs because individuals tend to blame their personal failures or problems on external causes and attribute their successes to internal causes. In this instance, the individual may give insufficient attention to the need for personal change and development. Instead, he or she may be prone to take credit for successes and focus on the environment to explain away failures.

- **Attribution error** overestimates internal factors and underestimates external factors as influences on someone's behavior.

- **Self-serving bias** explains personal success by internal causes and personal failures by external causes.

PERCEPTUAL TENDENCIES AND DISTORTIONS

In addition to the tendency to make attribution errors in assigning causes to events, a variety of perceptual distortions can also affect human behavior in the workplace. Of particular interest are the use of stereotypes, halo effects, selectivity, and projection when we deal with and judge other people.

Stereotypes

A **stereotype** occurs when someone is identified with a group or category, and then oversimplified attributes associated with the group or category are linked back to the individual. Common stereotypes are those of young people, old people, teachers, students, union members, males, and females, among others. The

- A **stereotype** is when attributes commonly associated with a group are assigned to an individual.

phenomenon, in each case, is the same: A person is classified into a group on the basis of one piece of information, such as age, for example. Characteristics commonly associated with the group are then assigned to the individual. What is generalized about the group (e.g., "Young people dislike authority") may or may not be true about the individual.

Stereotypes based on such factors as gender, age, and race can, and unfortunately still do, bias the perceptions of people in some work settings. The *glass ceiling,* mentioned in Chapter 1, as an invisible barrier to career advancement, still exists in some places.[25] Legitimate questions can be asked about *racial stereotypes* and about the slow progress of African-American managers into America's corporate mainstream. Their numbers in the executive ranks remain disappointingly low, despite clear advances in the recent past.[26] Although employment barriers caused by *gender stereotypes* are falling, women may still suffer from false impressions and biases imposed on them. Consider this example: *Case*—"*He's* talking with coworkers." (*Interpretation:* He's discussing a new deal.); "*She's* talking with coworkers." (*Interpretation:* She's gossiping.)[27] And *age stereotypes* also exist in the workplace. Their inappropriate use may place older workers at a disadvantage in various work situations. A talented older worker may not be promoted to fill an important and challenging job, for example, because a manager assumes older workers lack creativity, are cautious, and tend to avoid risk.

Halo Effects

● A **halo effect** occurs when one attribute is used to develop an overall impression of a person or situation.

A **halo effect** occurs when one attribute is used to develop an overall impression of a person or situation. When meeting someone new, for example, the halo effect may cause one trait, such as a pleasant smile, to result in a positive first impression. By contrast, a particular hairstyle or manner of dressing may create a negative reaction. Halo effects cause the same problem for managers as do stereotypes; that is, individual differences become obscured. This is especially significant with respect to a manager's view of subordinates' work performance. One factor, such as a person's punctuality, may become the "halo" for a positive overall performance evaluation. Even though the general conclusion seems to make sense, it may or may not be true in a given circumstance.

Selectivity

● **Selective perception** is the tendency to define problems from one's own point of view.

Selective perception is the tendency to single out for attention those aspects of a situation or person that reinforce or appear consistent with one's existing beliefs, values, or needs.[28] What this often means in an organization is that people from different departments or functions—such as marketing and manufacturing, tend to see things from their own points of view and tend not to recognize other points of view. Like the other perceptual distortions just discussed, selective perception can bias a manager's view of situations and individuals. One way to reduce its impact is to gather additional opinions from other people. When the alternative perceptions prove contradictory, efforts should be made to check one's original impression to create the most appropriate basis for decision making and action.

Projection

● **Projection** is the assignment of personal attributes to other individuals.

Projection is the assignment of personal attributes to other individuals. A classic projection error is to assume that other persons share our needs, desires, and values. Suppose, for example, that you enjoy a lot of responsibility and challenge in your work. Suppose, too, that you are the newly appointed supervisor for people whose work you consider dull and routine. You might move quickly to start a program of job enrichment to help them experience more responsibility and challenge. This may not be a good decision. Instead of designing jobs to best fit *their* needs, you have designed their jobs to fit *yours*. In fact, your subordinates may be quite satisfied and productive doing jobs that, to you, seem routine. Such projection errors can be controlled through self-awareness and a willingness to communicate and empathize with other persons, that is, to try to see things through their eyes.

COMMUNICATION AND CONFLICT MANAGEMENT

Communication and related "people" skills must be at the forefront of any attempt to develop managerial and leadership expertise. The former CEO of Arthur Andersen, Lawrence A. Weinback, says, "Pure technical knowledge is only going to get you to a point. Beyond that, interpersonal skills become critical." [29] Among these essential skills, the ability to deal with interpersonal conflicts is critical. Formally defined, **conflict** is a disagreement between people on substantive or emotional issues.[30] Managers and leaders spend a lot of time dealing with conflicts of various forms. **Substantive conflicts** involve disagreements over such things as goals; the allocation of resources; the distribution of rewards, policies and procedures; and job assignments. **Emotional conflicts** result from feelings of anger, distrust, dislike, fear, and resentment, as well as from personality clashes. Both forms of conflict can cause problems in the workplace. But when managed well, they can be helpful in promoting high performance, creativity, and innovation.

- **Conflict** is a disagreement over issues of substance and/or an emotional antagonism.

- **Substantive conflict** involves disagreements over goals, resources, rewards, policies, procedures, and job assignments.

- **Emotional conflict** results from feelings of anger, distrust, dislike, fear, and resentment as well as from personality clashes.

FUNCTIONAL AND DYSFUNCTIONAL CONFLICT

Whether or not conflict benefits people and organizations depends on two factors: (1) the intensity of the conflict and (2) how well the conflict is managed. The inverted "U" curve depicted in *Figure 16.3* shows that conflict of moderate intensity can be good for performance. This **functional conflict,** or *constructive conflict,* stimulates people toward greater work efforts, cooperation, and creativity. At very low or very high intensities **dysfunctional conflict,** or *destructive conflict,* occurs. Too much conflict is distracting and interferes with other more task-relevant activities; too little conflict may promote complacency and the loss of a creative, high-performance edge. The dysfunctions of too much conflict can be illustrated by two employees who are unable to work together because of

- **Functional conflict** is constructive and helps task performance.

- **Dysfunctional conflict** is destructive and hurts task performance.

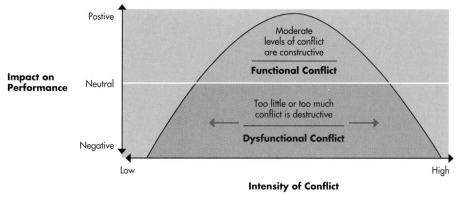

Figure 16.3 The relationship between conflict and performance.

Differences in perception are evident in a Coopers & Lybrand/F.W. Dodge/McGraw-Hill study of 6,800 senior managers and 450,000 employees. Although some 75 percent of managers agreed that company management is interested in workers' well-being, only 52 percent of employees believed this was the case. Over a six-year period, this perception gap is widening.

interpersonal hostilities (an emotional conflict) or by members of a committee who can't agree on common goals (a substantive conflict).

CONFLICT ANTECEDENTS

Conflict in organizations may arise for a variety of reasons. Indeed, the following antecedent conditions can make the eventual emergence of conflict very likely. *Role ambiguities* set the stage for conflict. Unclear job expectations and other task uncertainties increase the probability that some people will be working at cross-purposes, at least some of the time. *Resource scarcities* cause conflict. Having to share resources with others and/or compete directly with them for resource allocations creates a potential situation conflict, especially when resources are scarce. *Task interdependencies* cause conflict. When individuals or groups must depend on what others do to perform well themselves, conflicts often occur. *Competing objectives* are opportunities for conflict. When objectives are poorly set or reward systems are poorly designed, individuals and groups may come into conflict by working to one another's disadvantage. *Structural differentiation* breeds conflict. Differences in organization structures and in the characteristics of the people staffing them may foster conflict because of incompatible approaches toward work. And *unresolved prior conflicts* tend to erupt in later conflicts. Unless a conflict is fully resolved, it may remain latent in the situation as a lingering basis for future conflicts over the same or related matters.

CONFLICT RESOLUTION

When any one or more of these antecedent conditions is present, an informed manager expects conflicts to occur. And when they do, the conflicts then can either be "resolved," in the sense that the sources are corrected, or "suppressed," in that the sources remain but the conflict behaviors are controlled. Suppressed conflicts tend to fester and recur at a later time. They can also contribute to other conflicts over the same or related issues. True **conflict resolution** eliminates the underlying causes of conflict and reduces the potential for similar conflicts in the future.

● **Conflict resolution** is the removal of the substantial and/or emotional reasons for a conflict.

    Managers can try several approaches to restructure situations in order to resolve conflicts between individuals or groups.[31] There are times when an *appeal to superordinate goals* can focus the attention of conflicting parties on one mutually desirable end state. The appeal to higher level goals offers all parties a common frame of reference against which to analyze differences and reconcile disagreements. Conflicts whose antecedents lie in the competition for scarce resources can also be resolved by *expanding the resources available* to everyone. Although costly, this technique removes the reasons for the continuing conflict. By *altering one or more human variables*—that is, by replacing or transferring one or more of the conflicting parties, conflicts caused by poor interpersonal relationships can be eliminated. The same holds true if a manager can *alter the physical environment* by rearranging facilities, work space, or workflows to decrease opportunities for conflict.

    The *use of integrating devices* or coordinating mechanisms, introduced in Chapter 11, is another useful approach in many settings. In particular, the use of liaison personnel, special task forces, and cross-functional teams, and even the matrix form of organization, can change interaction patterns and assist in conflict management. *Changes in reward systems* may reduce the competition between individuals and groups for rewards. Creating systems that reward cooperation can encourage behaviors and attitudes that promote teamwork and keep conflict within more constructive limits. *Policies and procedures* may be used to direct behavior in ways that minimize the likelihood of unfortunate conflict situations. Finally, *training* can help prepare people to communicate and work more effectively in situations that are conflict prone.

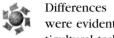 Differences in conflict management styles were evident when IBM participated in a multicultural task force in an ambitious project to develop a 21st-century computer chip. "Triad" team members from America, Germany, and Japan had to learn to manage the conflict of cultures. The Japanese found it difficult to work in small groups and in English; the Americans complained about the Germans planning too much and the Japanese taking too much time to review ideas. Before leaving home, the Germans were briefed on what was called the American "hamburger style of management." When it comes to giving criticism, their trainer said, Americans start soft (the top of the bun), then criticize (the meat), and then end with encouragement (the bottom of the bun). Germans, by contrast, only give the meat and the Japanese only give the bun—you have to "smell" the meat.[32]

CONFLICT MANAGEMENT STYLES

People respond to conflict by placing different emphases on cooperativeness and assertiveness.[33] *Cooperativeness* is the desire to satisfy another party's needs and concerns; *assertiveness* is the desire to satisfy one's own needs and concerns. *Figure 16.4* shows five interpersonal styles of conflict management that result from various combinations of the two. Briefly stated, these conflict management styles involve the following behaviors:

- **Avoidance:** Being uncooperative and unassertive; downplaying disagreement, withdrawing from the situation, and/or staying neutral at all costs.

- **Accommodation,** or *smoothing:* Being cooperative but unassertive; letting the wishes of others rule; smoothing over or overlooking differences to maintain harmony.

Five conflict management styles

- **Avoidance** pretends that a conflict doesn't really exist.

- **Accommodation** or **smoothing** plays down differences and highlights similarities to reduce conflict.

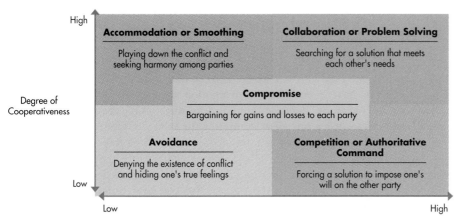

Figure 16.4 Alternative conflict management styles.

- **Competition** or **authoritative command** uses force, superior skill, or domination to "win" a conflict.

- **Compromise** occurs when each party to the conflict gives up something of value to the other.

- **Collaboration** or **problem solving** involves working through conflict differences and solving problems so everyone wins.

- In **lose-lose conflict** no one achieves his or her true desires and the underlying reasons for conflict remain unaffected.

- In **win-lose conflict** one party achieves its desires and the other party does not.

- In **win-win conflict** the conflict is resolved to everyone's benefit.

- **Competition,** or *authoritative command:* Being uncooperative but assertive; working against the wishes of the other party, engaging in win-lose competition, and/or forcing through the exercise of authority.

- **Compromise:** Being moderately cooperative and assertive, bargaining for "acceptable" solutions in which each party wins a bit and loses a bit.

- **Collaboration** or *problem solving:* Being both cooperative and assertive; trying to satisfy everyone's concerns fully by working through differences; finding and solving problems so that everyone gains.[34]

The various conflict management styles can have quite different outcomes.[35] Conflict management by avoidance or accommodation often creates **lose-lose conflict.** No one achieves her or his true desires and the underlying reasons for conflict often remain unaffected. Although a lose-lose conflict may appear settled or may even disappear for a while, it tends to recur in the future. Avoidance is an extreme form of nonattention. Everyone pretends that conflict doesn't really exist and hopes that it will simply go away. Accommodation or smoothing plays down differences and highlights similarities and areas of agreement. Peaceful coexistence through a recognition of common interests is the goal. In reality, smoothing may ignore the real essence of a conflict.

Competition, or authoritative command, and compromise tend to create **win-lose conflict.** Here, each party strives to gain at the other's expense. In extreme cases, one party achieves its desires to the complete exclusion of the other party's desires. Because win-lose methods fail to address the root causes of conflict, future conflicts of the same or a similar nature are likely to occur. In competition, one party wins, as superior skill or outright domination allows his or her desires to be forced on the other. In authoritative command, the forcing is accomplished by a higher level supervisor who simply dictates a solution to subordinates. Compromise occurs when trade-offs are made such that each party to the conflict gives up and gains something of value. As a result, neither party is completely satisfied, and antecedents for future conflicts are established.

Collaboration, or problem solving, tries to reconcile underlying differences and is often the most effective conflict management style. It is a form of **win-win conflict** whereby issues are resolved to the mutual benefit of all conflicting parties. This is typically achieved by confronting the issues and through the willingness of those involved to recognize that something is wrong and needs attention. Win-win conditions are created by eliminating the underlying causes of the conflict. All relevant issues are raised and discussed openly. Win-win methods are clearly the most preferred of the interpersonal styles of conflict management.

COMMUNICATION AND NEGOTIATION

Put yourself in the following situations. How would you behave, and what would you do? (1) You have been offered a promotion and would really like to take it. However, the pay raise being offered is less than you hoped. (2) You have enough money to order one new computer for your department. Two of your subordinates have each requested a new computer for their individual jobs.[36]

These are but two examples of the many negotiation situations that involve managers and other people in the typical workplace. **Negotiation** is the process of making joint decisions when the parties involved have different preferences. Stated a bit differently, it is a way of reaching agreement when decisions involve more than one person or group. People negotiate over such diverse matters as salary, merit raises and performance evaluations, job assignments, work schedules, work locations, special privileges, and many other considerations. All such

- **Negotiation** is the process of making joint decisions when the parties involved have different preferences.

situations are susceptible to conflict and require exceptional communication skills.

NEGOTIATION GOALS AND APPROACHES

There are two important goals in negotiation. *Substance goals* are concerned with outcomes; they are tied to the "content" issues of the negotiation. *Relationship goals* are concerned with processes; they are tied to the way people work together while negotiating and how they (and any constituencies they represent) will be able to work together again in the future.

Effective negotiation occurs when issues of substance are resolved and working relationships among the negotiating parties are maintained or even improved in the process.[37] The three criteria of effective negotiation are (1) *quality* — negotiating a "wise" agreement that is truly satisfactory to all sides; (2) *cost* — negotiating efficiently, using up minimum resources and time; and (3) *harmony* — negotiating in a way that fosters, rather than inhibits, interpersonal relationships.

The way each party approaches a negotiation can have a major impact on its outcome.[38] **Distributive negotiation** focuses on "claims" made by each party for certain preferred outcomes. This can take a competitive form in which one party can gain only if the other loses. In such "win-lose" conditions, relationships are often sacrificed as the negotiating parties focus only on their respective self-interests. It may also become accommodative if the parties defer to one another's wishes simply "to get it over with."

Principled negotiation, often called **integrative negotiation,** is based on a "win-win" orientation.[39] The focus on substance is still important, but the interests of all parties are considered. The goal is to base the final outcome on the merits of individual claims and to try to find a way for all claims to be satisfied if at all possible. No one should "lose," and relationships should be maintained in the process.

● **Distributive negotiation** focuses on "win-lose" claims made by each party for certain preferred outcomes.

● **Principled/integrative negotiation** uses a "win-win" orientation to reach solutions acceptable to each party.

GAINING INTEGRATIVE AGREEMENTS

In their book *Getting to Yes,* Roger Fisher and William Ury point out that truly integrative agreements are obtained by following four negotiation rules:[40]

● Separate the people from the problem.

● Focus on interests, not on positions.

● Generate many alternatives before deciding what to do.

● Insist that results are based on some objective standard.

Four rules of principled negotiation

Proper attitudes and good information are important foundations for such integrative agreements. The attitudinal foundations of integrative agreements involve the willingness of each negotiating party to trust, share information with, and ask reasonable questions of the other party. The informational foundations of integrative agreements involve each party knowing what is really important to them and finding out what is really important to the other party. In addition, each should understand his or her personal *b*est *a*lternative *t*o a *n*egotiated *a*greement, or **BATNA.** This is an answer to the question "What will I do if an agreement can't be reached?"

● **BATNA** is the best alternative to a negotiated agreement.

Figure 16.5 introduces a typical case of labor-management negotiations over a new contract and salary increase. This helps to illustrate elements of classic two-party negotiation as they occur in many contexts.[41] To begin, look at the figure and case from the labor union's perspective. The union negotiator has told her management counterpart that the union wants a new wage of $12.00 per

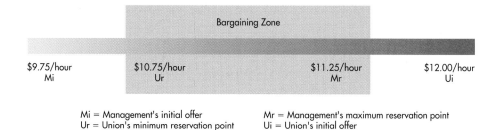

Mi = Management's initial offer
Ur = Union's minimum reservation point

Mr = Management's maximum reservation point
Ui = Union's initial offer

Figure 16.5 The bargaining zone in classic two-party negotiation.

• A **bargaining zone** is the area between one party's minimum reservation point and the other party's maximum reservation point.

hour. This expressed preference is the union's *initial offer.* However, she also has in mind a *minimum reservation point* of $10.75 per hour. This is the lowest wage rate that she is willing to accept for the union. But the management negotiator has a different perspective. His *initial offer* is $9.75 per hour, and his *maximum reservation point,* the highest wage he is prepared eventually to offer to the union, is $11.25 per hour.

In classic two-party negotiation of this type, the **bargaining zone** is defined as the zone between one party's minimum reservation point and the other party's maximum reservation point. The bargaining zone of $10.75 per hour to $11.25 per hour in this case is a "positive" one since the reservation points of the two parties overlap. If the union's minimum reservation point were greater than management's maximum reservation point, no room would exist for bargaining. Whenever a positive bargaining zone exists, there is room for true negotiation.

A key task for any negotiator is to discover the other party's reservation point. Until this is known and each party becomes aware that a positive bargaining zone exists, it is difficult to proceed effectively. When negotiation does move forward, each negotiator typically tries to achieve an agreement that is as close as possible to the other party's reservation point. Returning to *Figure 16.5,* the union negotiator would like to get an offer as close to $12.00 per hour as possible. The management negotiator would like to get a contract for as close to $9.75 per hour as possible.

AVOIDING NEGOTIATION PITFALLS

The negotiation process is admittedly complex, and negotiators must guard against common mistakes. Four negotiator pitfalls that can be avoided by proper discipline and personal attention should be recognized. The first is the tendency of *falling prey to the myth of the "fixed pie."* This involves acting on the distributive assumption that in order for you to gain, the other person must give something up. Negotiating this way fails to recognize the integrative assumption that the "pie" can sometimes be expanded and/or utilized to everyone's advantage. A second negotiation error is the *nonrational escalation of conflict.* The negotiator in this case becomes committed to previously stated "demands" and allows concerns for "ego" and "face saving" to increase the perceived importance of satisfying these demands. The third error is *overconfidence and ignoring the other's needs.* The error here is becoming overconfident that your position is the only correct one and failing to see the needs of the other party and the merits in its position. The fourth error is the tendency to do *too much "telling" and too little "hearing."* When committing the "telling" problem, parties to a negotiation don't really make themselves understood to each other. When committing the "hearing" problem they don't "listen" sufficiently to understand what the other is saying.[42]

It may not always be possible to achieve integrative agreements. When disputes reach the point of impasse, mediation and arbitration can be useful. **Mediation** involves a neutral third party who tries to improve communication between negotiating parties and keep them focused on relevant issues. This *mediator* does not issue a ruling or make a decision, but can take an active role in discussions. This may include making suggestions in an attempt to move the parties toward agreement. **Arbitration,** such as salary arbitration in professional sports, is a stronger form of dispute resolution. It involves a neutral third party, the *arbitrator,* who acts as a "judge" and issues a binding decision. This usually includes a formal hearing in which the arbitrator listens to both sides and reviews all facets of the case before making a ruling.

Some organizations formally provide for a process called *alternative dispute resolution.* This approach utilizes mediation and/or arbitration but only after direct attempts to negotiate agreements between the conflicting parties have failed. Often an *ombudsperson,* or designated neutral third party who listens to complaints and disputes, plays a key role in the process.

- In **mediation** a neutral party tries to help conflicting parties improve communication to resolve their dispute.

- In **arbitration** a neutral third party issues a binding decision to resolve a dispute.

ETHICAL ISSUES IN NEGOTIATION

Managers, and anyone else involved in negotiation, should maintain high standards of ethical conduct even when they are personally engaged in a dynamic and challenging situation. The motivation to behave unethically sometimes arises from an undue emphasis on the profit motive. This may be experienced as a desire to "get just a bit more" or to "get as much as you can" from a negotiation. The motivation to behave unethically may also result from a sense of competition. This may be experienced as a desire to "win" a negotiation just for the sake of it or as a misguided belief that someone else must "lose" in order for you to gain.

When unethical behavior occurs in negotiation, the persons involved sometimes attempt to rationalize or explain it away. We first discussed such rationalizations for unethical conduct in Chapter 6. In a negotiation situation, the following comments may be indicative of inappropriate rationalizing: "It was really unavoidable," "Oh, it's harmless," "The results justify the means," or "It's really quite fair and appropriate."[43] Moral issues aside, tendencies to use or accept such explanations can be challenged by the possibility that any short-run gains may be accompanied by long-run losses. Unethical parties should also realize that they may be targeted for later "revenge" from those disadvantaged by their tactics. Furthermore, once people behave unethically in one situation, they may have a tendency to consider such behavior acceptable in similar circumstances in the future.

CHAPTER REVIEW

This section should be used as an end-of-chapter "study guide." The *Summary* helps to put the chapter's content into overall perspective. The list of *Key Terms* allows you to double-check your familiarity with basic concepts and definitions. *Self-Test 16* gives you the opportunity to test your basic comprehension of the chapter using sample test questions.

SUMMARY

What is the communication process?

- Communication is the interpersonal process of sending and receiving symbols with messages attached to them.

- Effective communication occurs when the sender and the receiver of a message both interpret it in the same way; efficient communication occurs when the message is sent at low cost for the sender.

- Noise is anything that interferes with the effectiveness of communication; it occurs in the form of poor utilization of channels, poor written or oral expression, physical distractions, and status effects, among other possibilities.

How can communication be improved?

- Active listening, through reflecting back and paraphrasing, can help overcome communication barriers.

- Upward communication may be improved through MBWA—managing by wandering around, and by the use of structured meetings, suggestion systems, advisory councils, and the like.

- Space can be used and designed to improve communication in organizations.

- The appropriate use of information technology, such as Email and Intranets, can improve communication in organizations.

- Greater cross-cultural awareness and sensitivity can help reduce the difficulties of communication and diversity.

How does perception influence behavior?

- Perception acts as a filter through which all communication passes as it travels from one person to the next.

- Because people tend to perceive things differently, the same message may be interpreted quite differently by different people.

- Attribution is the process of assigning explanations to events.

- Attribution theory identifies tendencies toward fundamental attribution errors when judging the performance of others and self-serving bias when judging the performance of ourselves.

- Common perceptual distortions that may reduce communication effectiveness include stereotypes, projections, halo effects, and selective perception.

How can managers deal positively with conflict?

- Conflict occurs as disagreements over substantive or emotional issues.

- Managers should support functional conflict that facilitates a high-performance edge and creativity; they should avoid the harmful effects of too little or too much conflict that becomes dysfunctional.

- Conflict may be managed through structural approaches that involve changing people, goals, resources, or work arrangements.

- Personal conflict management "styles" include avoidance, accommodation, compromise, competition, and collaboration.

- True conflict resolution involves problem-solving through a win-win collaborative approach.

How can managers negotiate agreements?

- Negotiation is the process of making decisions in situations in which the participants have different preferences.

- Both substance goals, those concerned with outcomes, and relationship goals, those concerned with processes, are important in successful negotiation.

- Effective negotiation occurs when issues of substance are resolved and the process results in good working relationships.

- Distributive approaches to negotiation emphasize win-lose outcomes and are usually harmful to relationships.

- Integrative approaches to negotiation emphasize win-win outcomes and the interests of all parties.

KEY TERMS

Accommodation (p. 341)
Active listening (p. 332)
Arbitration (p. 345)
Attribution error (p. 337)
Authoritative command (p. 342)
Avoidance (p. 341)
BATNA (p. 343)
Collaboration (p. 342)
Communication (p. 328)
Communication channel (p. 329)
Competition (p. 342)
Compromise (p. 342)
Conflict (p. 339)
Conflict resolution (p. 340)
Distributive negotiation (p. 343)
Dysfunctional conflict (p. 339)

Effective communication (p. 328)
Efficient communication (p. 328)
Emotional conflict (p. 339)
Feedback (p. 332)
Filtering (p. 331)
Functional conflict (p. 339)
Halo effect (p. 338)
Integrative negotiation (p. 343)
Lose-lose conflict (p. 342)
Management by Wandering Around (MBWA) (p. 333)
Mediation (p. 345)
Mixed message (p. 331)
Negotiation (p. 342)
Noise (p. 329)

Nonverbal communication (p. 330)
Perception (p. 336)
Principled negotiation (p. 343)
Problem solving (p. 342)
Projection (p. 338)
Proxemics (p. 334)
Selective perception (p. 338)
Self-serving bias (p. 337)
Smoothing (p. 341)
Stereotype (p. 337)
Substantive conflict (p. 339)
360-degree feedback (p. 334)
Win-lose conflict (p. 342)
Win-win conflict (p. 342)

SELF-TEST 16

Take this test much as you would in a normal classroom situation. It is a good way to check your basic comprehension of chapter material. Answers may be found at the end of the book.

MULTIPLE-CHOICE QUESTIONS:

1. In communication the use of paraphrasing and reflecting back is characteristic of _____. (a) mixed messages (b) active listening (c) passive listening (d) ethno-centrism

2. When the intended meaning of the sender and the interpreted meaning of the receiver are the same, communication is _____. (a) effective (b) perceived (c) selective (d) efficient

3. Constructive feedback is _____. (a) general rather than specific (b) indirect rather than direct (c) given in small doses (d) given any time the sender is ready

4. When a manager uses Email to send a message that is better delivered face to face, the communication process suffers from _____. (a) semantic problems (b) a poor choice of communication channels (c) physical distractions (d) status effects

5. _____ may be used to minimize the risk of status effects in upward communication. (a) Projection (b) One-way communication (c) MBWA (d) Impression management

6. Cross-cultural communication may run into difficulties because of _____, or the tendency to consider one's culture superior to others. (a) multiculturalism (b) ethnocentrism (c) mixed messages (d) projection

7. An appeal to superordinate goals is an example of a/an _____ approach to conflict management. (a) avoidance (b) structural (c) assertiveness (d) compromise

8. The conflict management style with the greatest potential for true conflict resolution involves _____. (a) compromise (b) competition (c) smoothing (d) collaboration

9. When a person is highly cooperative but not very assertive in approaching conflict, the conflict management style is referred to as _____. (a) avoidance (b) authoritative (c) smoothing (d) collaboration

10. The three criteria of an effective negotiation are quality, cost, and _____. (a) harmony (b) timeliness (c) acceptability (d) durability

TRUE-FALSE QUESTIONS:

11. Effective communication is always efficient. T F

12. Of the 10 rules for good listening described in the chapter, "stop talking" is the first and the tenth. T F

13. Semantic problems in communication may involve a poor choice of words in a written message. T F

14. Senior managers can be highly confident that information received from lower levels is unbiased. T F

15. Proxemics deals with the use of space. T F

16. One-way communications such as Email are often efficient, but they are not always effective. T F

17. The best conflict management style is one of high assertiveness and low cooperativeness. T F

18. Substantive conflicts are of managerial concern, but emotional conflicts are not. T F

19. Win-lose claims are common in distributive negotiation. T F

20. Arbitration involves a neutral third party acting as a judge to resolve a negotiation. T F

SHORT-RESPONSE QUESTIONS:

21. Describe briefly what a manager would do to be an "active listener" when communicating with subordinates.

22. What is the difference between the halo effect and selective perception?

23. How do tendencies toward assertiveness and cooperativeness in conflict management result in win-lose, lose-lose, and win-win outcomes?

24. What is the difference between substance and relationship goals in negotiation?

APPLICATION QUESTION:

25. After being promoted to store manager for a new branch of a large department store chain, Harold Welsch was concerned about communication in the store. Six department heads reported directly to him, and 50 full-time and part-time sales associates reported to them. Given this structure, Harold worried about staying informed about all store operations, not just those coming to his attention as senior manager. What steps might Harold take to establish and maintain an effective system of upward communication in his store?

CHAPTER SEVENTEEN

Teams and Teamwork

Planning Ahead—Chapter 17 Study Questions

- How do teams contribute to organizations?
- What are current trends in the use of teams?
- How do teams work?
- How do teams make decisions?
- How can leaders build high performance teams?

Teams are Worth the Hard Work

A boy scout camp in central Ohio has found a new purpose in life. In addition to its traditional work with the scouts, Camp Lazarus is host to unique team-building exercises for many corporations. On a fall day, for example, a team of employees from American Electric Power (AEP) worked to solve the problem of how to get 6 members through a spider-web maze of bungee cords strung 2 feet above the ground. When her colleagues lifted Judy Gallo into their hands to pass her over the obstacle, she was nervous. But a trainer told the team this was just like solving a problem together at the office. The spider web was just another performance constraint like difficult policies or financial limits they might face at work. After swapping "high-fives" for making it through the web, Judy's team went on to jump tree stumps together, pass hula hoops while holding hands, and more. Says one team trainer, "We throw clients into situations to try and bring out the traits of a good team."[1]

Today's managers are expected to create work environments within which people can achieve high performance not only as individual contributors but also as members of work teams. Indeed, finding the best use of groups and teams as resources for organizations is an increasingly important goal in the new workplace. The ability to lead through teamwork is an increasingly important managerial responsibility, but not an easy one to achieve. Just the words *group* and *team* alone elicit both positive and negative reactions in the minds of many people. Although it is said that "two heads are better than one," we are also warned that "too many cooks spoil the broth." The true skeptic can be heard to say, "A camel is a horse put together by a committee." But against this somewhat humorous background lies a most important point: Many if not most tasks in organizations are beyond the capabilities of people operating alone. True managerial success entails mobilizing and utilizing teams as essential organizational resources. The new organizational designs and cultures require it, as does a comprehensive commitment to empowerment and employee involvement.[2] And the tasks of knowledge worker—such as creating a new product, developing an advertising strategy, and reengineering core work process, are often beyond individual capabilities. Teams, simply put, are indispensable to the new workplace.

TEAMS IN ORGANIZATIONS

- A **team** is a collection of people who regularly interact to pursue common goals.

- **Teamwork** is the process of people actively working together to accomplish common goals.

Formally defined, a **team** is a small group of people with complimentary skills, who work together to achieve a shared purpose, and hold themselves mutually accountable for its accomplishment.[3] **Teamwork** is the process of people working together to accomplish these goals. The ability to lead through teamwork requires a special understanding of how teams operate and the commitment to use that understanding to help them achieve high levels of task performance and membership satisfaction.

SYNERGY AND USEFULNESS OF TEAMS

- **Synergy** is the creation of a whole greater than the sum of its individual parts.

A special benefit of teamwork is **synergy**—the creation of a whole that is greater than the sum of its parts. The presence of synergy means that a team is using its membership resources to the fullest and is achieving through collective performance far more than could otherwise be achieved. This is obviously an important advantage for organizations facing the many pressures and demands of increasingly complex operating environments. But teams are also useful in other ways. Being part of a team can have a strong influence on individual attitudes and behaviors. When the experience is positive, working in and being part of a team helps satisfy important individual needs. Sometimes these are needs that may be difficult to meet in the regular work setting. Teams, simply put, can be very good for both organizations and their members. The usefulness of teams includes the following contributions:[4]

How teams help organizations

- Increasing resources for problem solving.
- Fostering creativity and innovation.
- Improving the quality of decision making.
- Enhancing members' commitments to tasks.
- Raising motivation through collective action.
- Helping control and discipline members.
- Satisfying individual needs as organizations grow in size.

WHAT CAN GO WRONG IN TEAMS?

There is no guarantee that teams will always be successful. Who hasn't encountered **social loafing,** that is, the presence of "free-riders" who slack off because responsibility is diffused in teams and others are present to do the work?[5] And who hasn't heard people complain about having to attend what they consider to be another "time-wasting" meeting?[6]

Things don't have to be this way. In fact, they must not be if teams are to make their best contributions to organizations. The time we spend in groups can be productive and satisfying, but to make it so we must understand the complex nature of groups and their internal dynamics. An important part of a manager's job, in particular, is knowing *when* a team is the best choice for a task. The second is to know *how* to work with and manage the team to best accomplish that task.

As we more closely examine these and related issues, keep in mind these four problems commonly encountered in small teams: (1) *personality conflicts* — Individual differences in personality and work style can disrupt the team; (2) *task ambiguity* — unclear agendas and/or ill-defined problems can cause teams to work too long on the wrong things; (3) *poor readiness to work* — time can be wasted when meetings lack purpose and structure and when members come unprepared; (4) *poor teamwork* — failures in communication, conflict, and decision making may limit performance and/or hurt morale.

- **Social loafing** is the tendency of some people to avoid responsibility by "free-riding" in groups.

FORMAL WORK TEAMS

The teams officially recognized and supported by the organization for specific purposes are **formal teams.** They are part of the formal structure and are created to perform essential tasks. A good example is the **functional team** consisting of a manager and her or his subordinates, or a team leader and team member. These formal building blocks of organizations are often called *departments* (e.g., market research department), *units* (e.g., product assembly unit), or *divisions* (e.g., office products division).

Organizations may be viewed as interlocking networks of functional teams. The managers and leaders of these teams serve important "linking pin" roles.[7] For example, each manager acts as a superior in one work team and a subordinate in another at the next higher level. In the latter, the manager interacts not only with a "boss" but also with "peers" who are in charge of other work units themselves. The resulting vertical and horizontal linkages, if well maintained, help integrate activities and accomplishments of teams throughout an organization.

- A **formal team** is officially recognized and supported by the organization.

- A **functional team** is a formally designated work team with a manager or team leader.

INFORMAL GROUPS

Standing in contrast to the formal teams just described are the **informal groups** which are also important in every organization. These informal groups are not recognized on organization charts and are not officially created to serve an organizational purpose. They emerge as part of the informal structure and from natural or spontaneous relationships among people. You might recognize these as *interest groups* in which workers band together to pursue a common cause or special position, such as a concern for poor working conditions. Some emerge as *friendship groups* that develop for a wide variety of personal reasons, including shared nonwork interests. Others emerge as *support groups* in which the members basically help one another do their jobs.

Two points about informal groups are especially important to understand. First, informal groups are not necessarily bad. Indeed, they can have a positive

- An **informal group** is unofficial and emerges from relationships and shared interests among members.

impact on work performance. In particular, the relationships and connections made possible by informal groups may actually help speed the workflow or allow people to "get things done" in ways not possible within the formal structure. Second, informal groups can help satisfy social needs that members find otherwise thwarted or left unmet in the formal work setting. Among other things, members of informal groups often find that the groups offer social satisfactions, security, support, and a sense of belonging.

TRENDS IN THE USE OF TEAMS

The trend toward greater empowerment in organizations is associated with several developments in the utilization of teams. In previous chapters, we noted the growing use of cross-functional committees or task forces to improve integration. A variety of employee involvement teams, including quality circles, are increasingly more commonplace as managers seek to expand opportunities for broad-based participation in workplace affairs. And developments in information technology are creating further opportunities for people to work together in computer-mediated or virtual teams.

COMMITTEES AND TASK FORCES

- A **committee** is a formal team designated to work on a special task on a continuing basis.

Two common and important types of teams used in organizations are "committees" and "task forces." Although serving somewhat different purposes, each brings people together outside of their daily job assignments to work in small teams for a specific purpose. They typically operate with task agendas and are led by a designated head or chairperson, who, in turn, is held accountable for committee or task force results. A **committee** usually operates with an ongoing purpose; its membership may change over time even as the committee remains in existence. Organizations usually have a variety of permanent or standing committees dedicated to a wide variety of concerns. Many committees are used to improve lateral coordination. In addition, committees are often formed to involve different constituencies when important policies and procedures are developed.

- A **task force** is a formal team convened for a specific purpose and expected to disband when that purpose is achieved.

A **task force** usually operates on a more temporary basis. Its official tasks are very specific and time defined.[8] Once its stated purpose has been accomplished, the task force may disband. Creativity and innovation are very important since task forces are often convened to handle particularly difficult or troublesome problems or to establish directions that will take best advantage of opportunities. Like committees, task forces are increasingly used to bring together people from various parts of an organization to work on common problems, such as a new product development project. But to achieve the desired results, any task force must be carefully established and then well run. Some task force management guidelines are found in the accompanying *Manager's Notepad 17.1.*

CROSS-FUNCTIONAL TEAMS

Organizational design today emphasizes adaptation and horizontal integration. It emphasizes problem solving and information sharing. It also tries to eliminate the functional chimneys problem, described in Chapter 10 as the tendency of workers to remain within their functions and restrict communication with other parts of an organization. The **cross-functional team** whose members come from different functional units and parts of an organization is indispensable to fulfillment

Manager's Notepad 17.1

Guidelines for Managing a Task Force

- *Select appropriate task force members* who will be challenged by the assignment, who have the right skills, and who seem able to work well together.
- *Clearly define the purpose of the task force* to ensure that members and important outsiders know what is expected, why, and on what timetable.
- *Carefully select a task force leader* who has good interpersonal skills, can respect the ideas of others, and is willing to do what needs to be done.
- *Periodically review progress* to ensure that all task force members feel collectively accountable for results, and that they receive performance feedback.

of these design goals. At ABB Industrial Systems, Inc., cross-functional teams are specifically created to knock down the "walls" separating departments within the firm. Representation on a team might consist, for example, of engineers, buyers, assemblers, and shipping clerks.[9]

Typically, the members of a cross-functional team, task force, or committee come together to work on a specific problem or task and to do so with the needs of the whole organization in mind. They are expected to share information, explore new ideas, seek creative solutions, meet project deadlines, and importantly, not to be limited in performance by purely functional concerns and demands. Rather, the team members collectively and individually are to think and act cross-functionally and in the best interests of the total system.

Increasing the level of diversity in the workforce is an important initiative at American Express. Employee diversity teams help ensure that differences among people are recognized and valued. The firm's diversity initiatives are supported and integrated into company-wide diversity strategy by a Diversity Council made up of senior executives. Employee networks are also recognized by the company as a way to promote diversity. Says one executive: "A lot of the initiatives underway are, in part, because employees at all levels feel empowered to foster change that will advance our vision to be the world's most respected service brand."[10]

Valuing Diversity℠ www.americanexpress.com

EMPLOYEE INVOLVEMENT TEAMS

Another development in today's organizations is the formation of various types of **employee involvement teams.** These are groups of workers who meet on a regular basis outside of their formal assignments, with the goal of applying their expertise and attention to important workplace matters. The general purpose of employee involvement teams is continuous improvement. Using a problem-solving framework, the teams try to bring the benefits of employee participation to bear on a wide variety of performance issues and concerns.

- An **employee involvement team** meets on a regular basis to use its talents to help solve problems and achieve continuous improvement.

● A **quality circle** is a team of employees who meet periodically to discuss ways of improving work quality.

A popular form of employee involvement team is the **quality circle,** a group of workers that meets regularly to discuss and plan specific ways to improve work quality.[11] Usually it consists of 6 to 12 members from a work area. After receiving special training in problem solving, team processes, and quality issues, members of the quality circle try to come up with suggestions that can be implemented to raise productivity through quality improvements. Quality circles became popular in U.S. industry in part because of their place in Japanese management. Along with other types of involvement teams, they are now found in organizations where empowerment and participation are valued as keys to high performance.

Recycling car parts is the goal of the RAT pack at Ford Motor Company. The firm's Recycle Action Team meets once a week to find new ways to use recycled materials and to recycle as much as possible of the firm's products. Take scrap tires, for example. Ford vehicles now are incorporating parts made from recycled tires, soda bottles, and even used carpeting from homes. A special project of Ford's environmental outreach and strategy program, RAT is a good example of applying team creativity and initiative to solve important problems.[12]

VIRTUAL TEAMS

● Members of a **virtual team** work together and solve problems through computer-based interactions.

A new form of group that is increasingly common in today's organizations is the **virtual team,** sometimes called a *computer-mediated group* or *electronic group network.* This is a team of people who work together and solve problems through largely computer-mediated rather than face-to-face interactions. Chapter 3, on information and decision making, highlighted the role of new technology in today's organizations. Among the many developments, the sophistication of networking technologies and groupware programs are highly significant. As organizations become increasingly global in their operations and perspectives, the opportunity to utilize virtual teams whose members are dispersed around the world is highly advantageous.

The use of intranets and special software support for computerized meetings is changing the way many committees, task forces, and other problem-solving teams function.[13] Working in virtual environments, team members address problems and seek consensus on how to best deal with them. Such electronic team meetings can cause problems, particularly when members' working relationships are depersonalized and some of the advantages of direct interaction are lost.[14] But the approach also has many potential advantages that make it increasingly important. Members of computer-mediated teams can deal collectively with issues in a time-efficient fashion and without some of the interpersonal difficulties that might otherwise occur — especially when the issues are controversial. A vice president for human resources at Marriott, for example, has called electronic meetings "the quietest, least stressful, most productive meetings you've ever had." In one 2-month period, Marriott's electronic meeting room was used by over 1,000 people who collectively identified over 10,000 ideas as they worked on problems via computer mediation. It is estimated that the same accomplishments would have taken up to 12 times longer if normal team meeting procedures had been followed.[15]

SELF-MANAGING WORK TEAMS

In a growing number of organizations the functional team consisting of a first-level supervisor and his or her immediate subordinates is disappearing. It is being replaced with a new organizational form based around **self-managing work teams.** Sometimes called autonomous work groups, these are teams of workers whose jobs have been redesigned to create a high degree of task interdependence and who have been given authority to make many decisions about how they go about doing the required work.[16]

Self-managing teams operate with participative decision making, shared tasks, and the responsibility for many of the managerial tasks performed by supervisors in more traditional settings. The "self-management" responsibilities include planning and scheduling work, training members in various tasks, sharing tasks, meeting performance goals, ensuring high quality, and solving day-to-day operating problems. In some settings, the team's authority may even extend to "hiring" and "firing" its members when necessary. A key feature is *multi-tasking,* in which team members each have the skills to perform several different jobs. As shown in *Figure 17.1,* typical characteristics of self-managing teams are as follows:

- Members are held collectively accountable for performance results.
- Members have discretion in distributing tasks within the team.
- Members have discretion in scheduling work within the team.
- Members are able to perform more than one job on the team.
- Members train one another to develop multiple job skills.
- Members evaluate one another's performance contributions.
- Members are responsible for the total quality of team products.

The structural implications of self-managing teams are also depicted in *Figure 17.1.* Members of a self-managing team report to higher management through a team leader rather than a formal supervisor, making the traditional role of first-line supervisor unnecessary. This is an important change in structure.

> • Members of a **self-managing work team** have the authority to make decisions about how they share and complete their work.

> ◀ Characteristics of self-managing teams

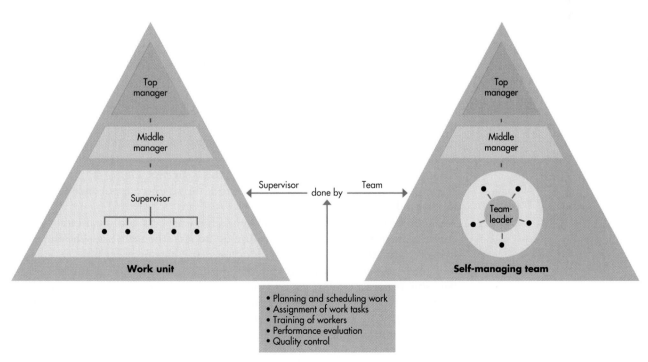

Figure 17.1 Organizational and management implications of self-managing work teams.

Each self-managing team handles the supervisory duties on its own, and each team leader handles the upward reporting relationships. Higher level managers to whom self-managing teams report must learn to work with teams rather than individual subordinates. This can be a difficult challenge for some managers who are used to more traditional operating methods. As the concept of self-managing teams spreads globally, researchers are also examining the receptivity of different cultures to self-management concepts.[17] Such cultural dimensions as high power distance and individualism, for example, may generate resistance that must be considered when implementing this and other team-based organizational practices.

Within a self-managing team the emphasis is always on participation. The leader and members are expected to work together not only to do the required work but also to make the decisions that determine how it gets done. A true self-managing team emphasizes team decision making, shared tasks, high involvement, and collective responsibility for accomplished results. The expected advantages include better performance, decreased costs, and higher morale.

HOW TEAMS WORK

- **Human resource maintenance** is a team's ability to maintain its social fabric so that members work well together.

Regardless of its form and purpose, any team must achieve two key results — perform tasks and satisfy members. On the *performance* side, a work group or team is expected to transform resource inputs (such as ideas, materials, and objects) into product outputs (such as a report, decision, service, or commodity) that have some value to the organization. On the satisfaction side, any team should also provide for **human resource maintenance.** This is the team's ability to maintain its interpersonal fabric and to keep its members willing and able to work well together again and again over time.

TEAM EFFECTIVENESS

- An **effective team** achieves high levels of both task performance and membership satisfaction.

An **effective team** is one that achieves and maintains high levels of both task performance and human resource maintenance.[18] *Figure 17.2* shows how any team can be viewed as an open system that transforms various resource inputs into these two outputs. The figure also indicates that a team's ability to be effective depends on the strength of its internal or group process and the quality of its inputs.

- **Group process** is the way team members work together to accomplish tasks.

The way the members of any team actually work together as they transform inputs into outputs is called the **group process.** It includes how well team members communicate with one another, make decisions, and handle conflicts, among other things. When group process breaks down and the internal dynamics fail in any way, team effectiveness can suffer. But although good process is essential to team effectiveness, it does not guarantee success. *Figure 17.2* also clearly shows that any team must have available to it the resource inputs needed to deal best with the task at hand.

Four input factors that can influence group process and team effectiveness are the organizational setting, the nature of the task, the team size, and the membership characteristics.[19] The *organizational setting* can affect how team members relate to one another and apply their skills toward task accomplishment. A key issue is the amount of support provided in terms of information, material resources, technology, spatial arrangements, organization structures, and available rewards. The *nature of the task* is also important. It affects how well a team can focus its efforts and how intense the group process needs to be to get the job done. Clearly defined tasks make it easier for team members to focus their work efforts. Complex tasks require more information exchange and intense interaction than do simpler tasks.

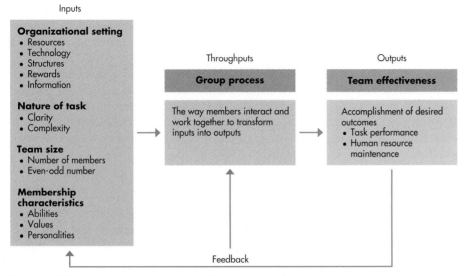

Inputs

Organizational setting
- Resources
- Technology
- Structures
- Rewards
- Information

Nature of task
- Clarity
- Complexity

Team size
- Number of members
- Even-odd number

Membership characteristics
- Abilities
- Values
- Personalities

Throughputs

Group process

The way members interact and work together to transform inputs into outputs

Outputs

Team effectiveness

Accomplishment of desired outcomes
- Task performance
- Human resource maintenance

Feedback

Figure 17.2   An open systems model of work team effectiveness.

Team size affects how members work together, handle disagreements, and reach agreements. The number of potential interactions increases geometrically as teams increase in size, and communications become more congested. Teams larger than about 6 to 7 members can be difficult to manage for the purpose of creative problem solving. When voting is required, teams with odd numbers of members are often preferred so as to prevent "ties."

In all teams, *membership characteristics* are important. The ability of members to work well together to accomplish tasks depends on the blend of competencies and personalities. Whereas heterogeneity in the mix of individual skills, values, and personalities broadens the resource base of the team, it also adds complexity to members' interpersonal relationships. Membership diversity, sometimes referred to as team demography, should be recognized as a potential influence on team effectiveness.[20] This influence may be especially evident in cross-cultural work settings.[21] Research suggests, for example, that culturally diverse work teams have more difficulty learning how to work well together than do culturally homogeneous ones. This is true, even though the diverse teams eventually prove more creative than the homogeneous ones.[22]

STAGES OF TEAM DEVELOPMENT

A synthesis of research on small groups suggests that there are five distinct phases in the life cycle of any team:[23]

- *Forming:* A stage of initial orientation and interpersonal testing. Stages of team development
- *Storming:* A stage of conflict over tasks and ways of operating as a team.
- *Norming:* A stage of consolidation around task and operating agendas.
- *Performing:* A stage of teamwork and focused task performance.
- *Adjourning:* A stage of task accomplishment and eventual disengagement.

Forming Stage

The forming stage involves the initial entry of individual members into a team. This is a stage of initial task orientation and interpersonal testing. As individuals come together for the first time or two, they ask a number of questions: "What can or does the team offer me?" "What will I be asked to contribute?" "Can my needs be met while my efforts serve the task needs of the team?"

When Angel Martinez, chief executive of Rockport Co., wanted to implement change and refocus employees on new performance norms, he expanded the top management team. New vice presidents of sales, international, and brand marketing were brought in. Says Martinez, "The easiest thing is getting rid of everyone, but that can create many more problems in the long run."

In the forming stage, people begin to identify with other members and with the team itself. They are concerned about getting acquainted, establishing interpersonal relationships, discovering what is considered acceptable behavior, and learning how others perceive the team's task. This may also be a time when some members rely on or become temporarily dependent on another member who appears "powerful" or especially "knowledgeable." Such things as prior experience with team members in other contexts and individual impressions of organization philosophies, goals, and policies may also affect member relationships in new work teams. Difficulties in the forming stage tend to be greater in more culturally and demographically diverse teams.

Storming Stage

The storming stage of team development is a period of high emotionality. Tension often emerges between members over tasks and interpersonal concerns. There may be periods of outright hostility and infighting. Coalitions or cliques may form around personalities or interests. Subteams form around areas of agreement and disagreement involving group tasks and/or the manner of operations. Conflict may develop as individuals compete to impose their preferences on others and to become influential in the group's status structure.

Important changes occur in the storming stage as task agendas become clarified and members begin to understand one another's interpersonal styles. Here attention begins to shift toward obstacles that may stand in the way of task accomplishment. Efforts are made to find ways to meet team goals while also satisfying individual needs. Failure in the storming stage can be a lasting liability, whereas success in the storming stage can set a strong foundation for later team effectiveness.

Norming Stage

Cooperation is an important theme of teams in the norming stage. At this point, members of the team begin to become coordinated as a working unit and tend to operate with shared rules of conduct. The team feels a sense of leadership, with each member starting to play useful roles. Most interpersonal hostilities give way to a precarious balancing of forces as norming builds initial integration. Harmony is emphasized, but minority viewpoints may be discouraged.

In the norming stage, members are likely to develop initial feelings of closeness, a division of labor, and a sense of shared expectations. This helps protect the team from disintegration. Holding the team together may become even more important than successful task accomplishment.

Performing Stage

Teams in the performing stage are more mature, organized, and well functioning. This is a stage of total integration in which team members are able to deal in creative ways with both complex tasks and any interpersonal conflicts. The team operates with a clear and stable structure, and members are motivated by team goals.

The primary challenges of teams in the performing stage are to continue refining the operations and relationships essential to working together as an integrated unit. Such teams need to remain coordinated with the larger organization and adapt successfully to changing conditions over time. A team that has achieved total integration will score high on the criteria of team maturity presented in *Figure 17.3*.

Adjourning Stage

The final stage of team development is one in which team members prepare to disband. It is especially common for temporary groups that operate in the form of committees, task forces, and projects. Ideally, the team disbands with a sense

A mature group possesses:

1. Adequate mechanisms for getting feedback

Poor feedback
mechanisms
1 2 3 4 5
Average
Excellent feedback
mechanisms

2. Adequate decision-making procedure

Poor decision-
making procedure
1 2 3 4 5
Average
Very adequate
decision making

3. Optimal cohesion

Low cohesion
1 2 3 4 5
Average
Optimal cohesion

4. Flexible organization and procedures

Very inflexible
1 2 3 4 5
Average
Very flexible

5. Maximum use of member resources

Poor use of
resources
1 2 3 4 5
Average
Excellant use of
resources

6. Clear communications

Poor
communication
1 2 3 4 5
Average
Excellant
communication

7. Clear goals accepted by members

Unclear goals—
not accepted
1 2 3 4 5
Average
Very clear goals–
accepted

8. Feelings of interdependence with authority person

No
interdependence
1 2 3 4 5
Average
High
interdependence

9. Shared participation in leadership functions

No shared
participation
1 2 3 4 5
Average
High shared
participation

10. Acceptance of minority views and persons

No acceptance
1 2 3 4 5
Average
High acceptance

Figure 17.3 Criteria for assessing the maturity of a team. *Source:* Edgar H. Schein, *Process Consultation Volume I: Its Role in Organization Development* (Reading Mass.: Addison-Wesley, 1988), pp. 81–82. Reprinted with permission.

that important goals have been accomplished. Members are acknowledged for their contributions and the group's overall success.

This may be an emotional time, and disbandment should be managed with this possibility in mind. For members who have worked together intensely for a period of time, breaking up the close relationships may be painful. In all cases, the team would like to disband with members feeling they would work with one another again sometime in the future if another need or opportunity to do so arises.

NORMS AND COHESIVENESS

A **norm** is a behavior expected of team members.[24] It is a "rule" or "standard" that guides their behavior. When violated, a norm may be enforced with reprimands and other sanctions. In the extreme, violation of a norm can result in a member being expelled from a team or socially ostracized by other members. The *performance norm,* which defines the level of work effort and performance that team members are expected to contribute, is extremely important. It can have positive or negative implications for team performance and organizational productivity. In

● A **norm** is a behavior, rule, or standard expected to be followed by team members.

general, work groups and teams with positive performance norms are more successful in accomplishing task objectives than are teams with negative performance norms. Other important team norms relate to such things as helpfulness, participation, timeliness, and innovation.

Enthusiasm and high-performance norms rule the day at Motorola's Penang, Malaysia, operation. A team spirit rallies the plant's workers, who in one year alone submitted 41,000 suggestions for improvement and saved the firm some $2 million. Now Motorola is trying to import the Malaysian team spirit to its Plantation, Florida, operation. New applicants are carefully screened for their attitudes toward teamwork. A quality team at the Florida plant suggested ways to streamline workflow and increased output by 150 percent. Still, the Malaysian plant sets a high benchmark. Says one manager who recently spent 3 years working there, "The whole plant in Penang had this craving for learning."[25]

Because a team's norms are largely determined by the collective will of its members, it is difficult for a manager or designated leader simply to dictate which norms will be adopted. Instead, the concerned manager or team leader must help and encourage members to develop norms that support organizational objectives. During forming and storming steps of development, for example, norms relating to membership issues such as expected attendance and levels of commitment are important. By the time the stage of performing is reached, norms relating to adaptability and change become most relevant. Guidelines for how to build positive norms are as follows:

How to build positive norms ➝

- Act as a positive role model.
- Reinforce the desired behaviors with rewards.
- Control results by performance reviews and regular feedback.
- Train and orient new members to adopt desired behaviors.
- Recruit and select new members who exhibit the desired behaviors.
- Hold regular meetings to discuss progress and ways of improving.
- Use team decision-making methods to reach agreement.[26]

● **Cohesiveness** is the degree to which members are attracted to and motivated to remain part of a team.

Norms vary in the degree to which they are accepted and adhered to by team members. Conformity to norms is largely determined by the strength of **cohesiveness,** defined as the degree to which members are attracted to and motivated to remain part of a team. Persons in a highly cohesive team value their membership and strive to maintain positive relationships with other team members. Because of this, highly cohesive teams are good for their members, who experience satisfaction from team identification and interpersonal relationships. Highly cohesive teams can also be very good for organizations, but *not* always. It all depends on the performance norm that the cohesiveness is paired with.

A basic rule of group dynamics is that the more cohesive the team, the greater the conformity of members to team norms. Look at *Figure 17.4.* When

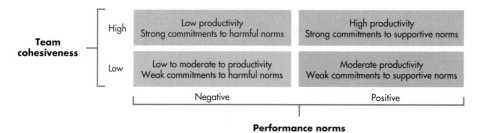

Figure 17.4 Productivity and the relationship between team cohesiveness and performance norms.

the performance norm of a team is positive, high cohesion and the resulting conformity to norms has a beneficial effect on productivity. This is a "best-case" scenario for both the manager and the organization. Competent team members work hard and reinforce one another's task accomplishments while experiencing satisfaction with the team. But when the performance norm is negative in a cohesive team, high conformity to the norm can have undesirable results. The figure shows this as a "worst-case" scenario where productivity suffers from restricted work efforts. Between these two extremes are mixed situations of moderate to low productivity.

To achieve and maintain the best-case scenario shown in *Figure 17.4,* managers should be skilled at influencing both the norms and cohesiveness of any team. They will want to build and maintain cohesiveness in teams whose performance norms are positive. Guidelines on how to increase cohesion include the following:

How to increase team cohesiveness

- Induce agreement on team goals.
- Increase membership homogeneity.
- Increase interactions among members.
- Decrease team size.
- Introduce competition with other teams.
- Reward team rather than individual results.
- Provide physical isolation from other teams.

TASK AND MAINTENANCE NEEDS

Research on the social psychology of groups identifies two types of activities that are essential if team members are to work well together over time.[27] **Task activities** contribute directly to the team's performance purpose, whereas **maintenance activities** support the emotional life of the team as an ongoing social system. Although a person with formal authority, such as a chairperson or supervisor, will often handle them, the responsibility for both types of activities should be shared and distributed among all team members. Any member can help lead a team by taking actions that help satisfy its task and maintenance needs. This concept of *distributed leadership in teams* thus makes every member continually responsible for recognizing when task and/or maintenance activities are needed and then stepping in to provide them.

Figure 17.5 offers useful insights on distributed leadership in teams. Leading through task activities involves making an effort to define and solve problems and apply work efforts in support of accomplishing tasks. Without relevant task activities, such as initiating agendas, sharing information, and others listed in the figure, teams will have difficulty accomplishing their objectives. Leading through

- A **task activity** is an action taken by a team member that contributes directly to the group's performance purpose.

- A **maintenance activity** is an action taken by a team member that supports the emotional life of the group.

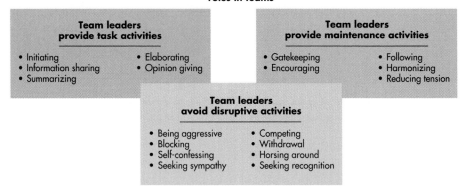

Figure 17.5 Distributed leadership helps a team meet its task and maintenance needs.

maintenance activities, by contrast, helps strengthen and perpetuate the team as a social system. When the maintenance activities such as encouraging others and reducing tensions, are performed well good interpersonal relationships are achieved and the ability of the team to stay together over the longer term is ensured.

Both team task and maintenance activities stand in distinct contrast to the dysfunctional activities also described in *Figure 17.5*. Activities such as withdrawing and horsing around are usually self-serving to the individual member. They detract from, rather than enhance, team effectiveness. Unfortunately, very few teams are immune to dysfunctional behavior by members. Everyone shares in the responsibility for minimizing its occurrence and meeting the distributed leadership needs expressed in this equation:

$$\text{Team results} = \text{Task Gains} + \text{Maintenance Gains} - \text{Self-serving Losses}$$

COMMUNICATION NETWORKS

Figure 17.6 depicts three interaction patterns and communication networks that are common in teams.[28] When teams are interacting intensively and their members are working closely together on tasks, close coordination of activities is needed. This need is best met by a **decentralized communication network** in which all members communicate directly with one another. Sometimes this is called the all-channel or star communication network.[29] At other times and in other situations team members work on tasks independently, with the required work being divided up among them. Activities are coordinated and results pooled by a central point of control. Most communication flows back and forth between individual members and this hub or center point. This creates a **centralized communication network** as shown in the figure. Sometimes this particular network is called a wheel or chain communication structure.

When teams are composed of subgroups experiencing issue-specific disagreements, such as a temporary debate over the best means to achieve a goal, the resulting interaction pattern involves a *restricted communication network.* Here, the polarized subgroups contest one another and engage in sometimes antagonistic relations. Communication between the subgroups is often limited and biased, with the result that problems can easily occur.

- A **decentralized communication network** allows all members to communicate directly with one another.

- In a **centralized communication network** communication flows only between individual members and a hub or center point.

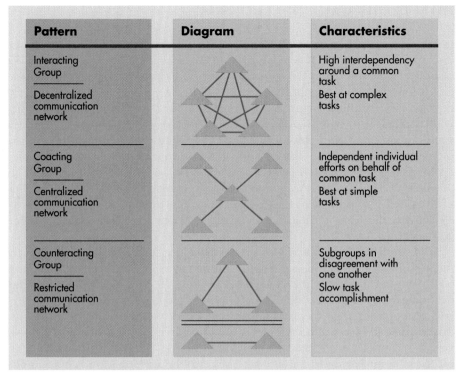

Pattern	Diagram	Characteristics
Interacting Group Decentralized communication network		High interdependency around a common task Best at complex tasks
Coacting Group Centralized communication network		Independent individual efforts on behalf of common task Best at simple tasks
Counteracting Group Restricted communication network		Subgroups in disagreement with one another Slow task accomplishment

Figure 17.6 Interaction patterns and communication networks in teams. *Source:* John R. Schermerhorn, Jr., James G. Hunt and Richard N. Osborn, *Organizational Behavior,* Sixth Edition (New York: John Wiley & Sons, 1997), p. 351. Used by permission.

The best teams use communication networks in the right ways, at the right times, and for the right tasks. In general, centralized communication networks seem to work better on simple tasks. These tasks require little creativity, information processing, and problem solving and lend themselves to more centralized control. They tend to be performed faster and more accurately by coacting groups. The reverse is true for more complex tasks, where interacting groups do better. Here, the decentralized networks work well since they are able to support the more intense interactions and information sharing required to perform under such task conditions. Interacting groups tend to be the top performers when tasks get complicated. When subgroups have difficulty communicating with one another, task accomplishment typically suffers for the short run at least. If the team is able to restore good communication between subgroups, it can benefit from the creativity and critical evaluation that typically accompanies conflict. If the subgroups drift further and further apart, negative dynamics set in and the team may suffer long term damage.

DECISION MAKING IN TEAMS

Decision making is one of the most important group processes, and decisions in teams can be made in several different ways. Edgar Schein, a respected scholar and consultant, notes that teams make decisions by at least 6 methods: lack of response, authority rule, minority rule, majority rule, consensus, and unanimity.[30]

HOW TEAMS MAKE DECISIONS

In *decision by lack of response,* one idea after another is suggested without any discussion taking place. When the team finally accepts an idea, all others have been bypassed and discarded by simple lack of response rather than by critical evaluation. In *decision by authority rule,* the leader, manager, committee head or some other authority figure makes a decision for the team. This can be done with or without discussion and is very time efficient. Whether the decision is a good one or a bad one, however, depends on whether the authority figure has the necessary information and on how well this approach is accepted by other team members. In *decision by minority rule,* two or three people are able to dominate or "railroad" the team into making a mutually agreeable decision. This is often done by providing a suggestion and then forcing quick agreement by challenging the team with such statements as "Does anyone object? . . . Let's go ahead then."

One of the most common ways teams make decisions, especially when early signs of disagreement arise, is *decision by majority rule.* Here, formal voting may take place, or members may be polled to find the majority viewpoint. This method parallels the democratic political system and is often used without awareness of its potential problems. The very process of voting can create coalitions; that is, some people will be "winners" and others will be "losers" when the final vote is tallied. Those in the minority — the "losers" — may feel left out or discarded without having had a fair say. They may be unenthusiastic about implementing the decision of the "majority," and lingering resentments may impair team effectiveness in the future.

Another alternative is *decision by consensus.* Formally defined, consensus is a state of affairs whereby discussion leads to one alternative being favored by most members and the other members agreeing to support it. When a consensus is reached, even those who may have opposed the chosen course of action know that they have been heard and have had an opportunity to influence the decision outcome. Consensus, therefore, does not require unanimity. But it does require that team members be able to argue, engage in reasonable conflict, and yet still get along with and respect one another.[31] And, it requires that there be the opportunity for any dissenting members to feel they have been able to speak — and that they have been listened to.

A *decision by unanimity* may be the ideal state of affairs. Here, all team members agree on the course of action to be taken. This is a "logically perfect" method for decision making in teams, but it is also extremely difficult to attain in actual practice. One of the reasons that teams sometimes turn to authority decisions, majority voting, or even minority decisions, in fact, is the difficulty of managing the team process to achieve consensus or unanimity.

ASSETS AND LIABILITIES OF GROUP DECISIONS

The best teams don't limit themselves to just one decision-making method. Instead, they change methods to best fit the problems at hand. An important team leadership skill is helping a team choose the "right" decision method — one that provides for a timely and quality decision and one to which the members are highly committed. This reasoning is consistent with insights of the Vroom-Jago leader-participation model as discussed in Chapter 13.[32] This model indicates that good leaders utilize the full range of individual, consultative and group decision methods as they resolve daily problems. To do this well, however, team leaders must understand both the potential assets and potential liabilities of more group-oriented decisions.[33]

• Telespan Publishing Corporation
http://www.telespan.com

TeleSpan Publishing Corporation reports that electronic meetings using computer-mediated conferencing and collaboration tools are growing 50 to 70 percent a year. Electronic team meetings are easy ways to meet across large distances, share documents and spreadsheets, and examine databases and information sources together.

The potential advantages of group decision making are highly significant, and they should be actively sought whenever time and other circumstances permit. Team decisions make greater amounts of information, knowledge, and expertise available to solve problems. They expand the number of action alternatives that are examined; they help to avoid tunnel vision and consideration of only limited options. Team decisions increase the understanding and acceptance of outcomes by members. And importantly, team decisions increase the commitments of members to final plans. Simply put, team decisions can result in quality decisions that all members work hard to implement.

The potential disadvantages of team decision making trace largely to the difficulties that can be experienced in group process. In a team decision there may be social pressure to conform. That is, individual members may feel intimidated or compelled to go along with the apparent wishes of others. There may be minority domination, where some members feel forced or "railroaded" to accept a decision advocated by one vocal individual or small coalition. Also, there is no doubt that the time required to make team decisions can sometimes be a disadvantage. As more people are involved in the dialogue and discussion, decision making takes longer. This added time may be costly, even prohibitively so, in certain circumstances.[34]

GROUPTHINK

A high level of cohesiveness can sometimes be a disadvantage during decision making. Members of very cohesive teams may publicly agree with actual or suggested courses of action, while privately having serious doubts about them. Strong feelings of team loyalty can make it hard for members to criticize and evaluate one another's ideas and suggestions. Desires to hold the team together and avoid disagreements may result in poor decisions. Psychologist Irving Janis calls this phenomenon **groupthink,** the tendency for highly cohesive groups to lose their critical evaluative capabilities.[35] He identifies the following as possible symptoms that groupthink may be occurring during team decision making.

- *Illusions of invulnerability*: members assume the team is too good for criticism or beyond attack.

- *Rationalizing unpleasant and disconfirming data*: members refuse to accept contradictory data or to consider alternatives thoroughly.

- *Belief in inherent group morality:* members act as though the group is inherently right and above reproach.

- *Stereotyping competitors as weak, evil, and stupid:* members refuse to look realistically at other groups.

- *Applying direct pressure to deviants to conform to group wishes:* members refuse to tolerate anyone who suggests the team may be wrong.

- *Self-censorship by members:* members refuse to communicate personal concerns to the whole team.

- *Illusions of unanimity:* members accept consensus prematurely, without testing its completeness.

- *Mind guarding:* members protect the team from hearing disturbing ideas or outside viewpoints.

Groupthink can occur anywhere. In fact, Janis ties a variety of well-known historical blunders to the phenomenon, including the lack of preparedness of the United States' naval forces for the Japanese attack on Pearl Harbor, the Bay of Pigs invasion under President Kennedy, and the many roads that led to the

> • **Groupthink** is a tendency for highly cohesive teams to lose their evaluative capabilities.

Symptoms of groupthink

Manager's Notepad 17.2
How To Avoid Groupthink
• Assign the role of critical evaluator to each team member; encourage a sharing of viewpoints.
• Don't, as a leader, seem partial to one course of action; do absent yourself from meetings at times to allow free discussion.
• Create subteams to work on the same problems and then share their proposed solutions.
• Have team members discuss issues with outsiders and report back on their reactions.
• Invite outside experts to observe team activities and react to team processes and decisions.
• Assign one member to play a "devil's advocate" role at each team meeting.
• Hold a "second-chance" meeting after consensus is apparently achieved to review the decision.

United States' involvement in Vietnam. When and if you encounter groupthink, Janis suggests taking action along the lines shown in *Manager's Notepad 17.2.*

CREATIVITY AND TEAM DECISION MAKING

Among the potential benefits of teams in organizations is their potential to increase creativity in the workplace. Two team techniques that are particularly helpful in decision making are brainstorming and the nominal team technique, both of which can now be pursued in computer-mediated or virtual team discussions as well as in face-to-face meetings.

In **brainstorming,** teams of 5 to 10 members meet to generate ideas. Brainstorming teams typically operate within these guidelines. *All criticism is ruled out* — judgment or evaluation of ideas must be withheld until the idea-generation process has been completed. *"Freewheeling" is welcomed* — the wilder or more radical the idea, the better. *Quantity is important* — the greater the number of ideas, the greater the likelihood of obtaining a superior idea. *Building on one another's ideas is encouraged* — participants should suggest how ideas of others can be turned into better ideas, or how two or more ideas can be joined into still another hybrid idea.

By prohibiting criticism, the brainstorming method reduces fears of ridicule or failure on the part of individuals. Ideally, this results in more enthusiasm, involvement, and a freer flow of ideas among members. But there are times when team members have very different opinions and goals. The differences may be so extreme that a brainstorming meeting might deteriorate into antagonistic arguments and harmful conflicts. In such cases, a **nominal group technique** could help. This approach uses a highly structured meeting agenda to allow everyone to contribute ideas without the interference of evaluative comments by others. It allows for many alternatives to be generated and evaluated without risk of inhibitions or hostilities.

The basic steps for running a nominal group session are easy to implement.[36] Participants are first asked to work alone and respond in writing with possible solutions to a stated problem. Ideas are then shared in round-robin fashion without any criticism or discussion; all ideas are recorded as they are presented. Ideas are

• **Goodyear**
http://www.goodyear.com

A Goodyear engineer worked for years to develop an innovative tire that you can drive on after it has been punctured and loses air. Called the EMT, the tire is a major product innovation. The many complications of manufacturing a tire that runs well flat, can be produced in large quantities, and is cost efficient were solved through dedication and teamwork.

next discussed and clarified in round-robin sequence, with no evaluative comments allowed. Next, members individually and silently follow a written voting procedure which allows for all alternatives to be rated or ranked in priority order. Finally, the last two steps are repeated as needed to further clarify the process.

LEADERSHIP AND HIGH PERFORMANCE TEAMS

When we think of the word "team," sporting teams often come to mind. And we know these teams certainly have their share of problems. Members slack off or become disgruntled; even world champion teams have losing streaks; and, the most highly talented players sometimes lose motivation, quibble with other team members, and lapse into performance slumps. When these things happen, the owners, managers, and players are apt to take corrective action to "rebuild the team" and restore what we have called team effectiveness. Work teams are teams in a similar sense. And even the most mature work team is likely to experience problems over time. When such difficulties arise, "team building" can help.

THE TEAM-BUILDING PROCESS

Team building is a sequence of planned activities used to gather and analyze data on the functioning of a team and to implement constructive changes to increase its operating effectiveness.[37] Most systematic approaches to team building follow the steps described in *Figure 17.7*. The cycle begins with the awareness that a problem may exist or may develop within the team. Members then work together to gather and analyze data so that the problem is finally understood. Action plans are made by members and collectively implemented. Results are evaluated in similar fashion by team members working together. Any difficulties or

- **Team building** is a sequence of collaborative activities to gather and analyze data on a team and make changes to increase its effectiveness.

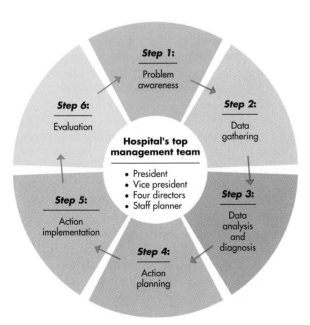

Figure 17.7 Steps in the team-building process: case of the hospital top management team.

new problems that are discovered serve to recycle the team-building process. Consider this added detail on the case featured in *Figure 17.7:*

> The consultant received a call from the hospital's director of personnel. He indicated that a new hospital president felt the top management team lacked cohesiveness and was not working well together as a team. The consultant agreed to facilitate a team-building activity that would include a day-long retreat at a nearby resort hotel. The process began when the consultant conducted interviews with the president and other members of the executive team. During the retreat, the consultant reported these results to the team as a whole. She indicated that the hospital's goals were generally understood by all but that they weren't clear enough to allow agreement on action priorities. Furthermore, she reported that interpersonal problems between the director of nursing services and the director of administration were making it difficult for the team to work together comfortably. These and other issues were addressed by the team at the retreat. Working sometimes in small subteams, and at other times together as a whole, they agreed first of all that action should be taken to clarify the hospital's overall mission and create a priority list of objectives for the current year. Led by the president, activity on this task would involve all team members and was targeted for completion within a month. The president asked that progress on the action plans be reviewed at each of the next three monthly executive staff meetings. Everyone agreed.

This example introduces team building as a way to assess a work team's functioning and take corrective action to improve its effectiveness. This can and should become a regular work routine. There are many ways to gather data on team functioning, including structured and unstructured interviews, questionnaires, team meetings, and written records. Regardless of the method used, the principle of team building requires that a careful and collaborative assessment of the team's inputs, processes and results be made. All members should participate in the data-gathering process, assist in the data analysis, and collectively decide to take action to resolve and/or prevent problems that interfere with team effectiveness.

The ultimate goal of team building is to create more and better teamwork among group members. Sometimes teamwork can be improved when people share the challenges of unusual and even physically demanding experiences, such as the one featured in the chapter opening example. Many creative alternatives are possible. At Eagle Group USA, Inc., a small automotive consulting firm in Michigan, the management team once went to a laser-tag arena for a day-long session of planning followed by a laser-tag session. Says client services director Deborah Iafrate, "We decided that it would be better to have battles on the court than in the boardroom."[38]

LEADERSHIP CHALLENGES

Among the many developments in the workplace today, the continuing effort to refine and apply creative team concepts should be at the forefront of any progressive manager's action agendas. But harnessing the full potential of teams involves special challenges. We know, for example, that high-performance teams generally share common characteristics. These include a clear and elevating goal, a task-driven and results-oriented structure, competent and committed members who work hard, a collaborative climate, high standards of excellence, external support and recognition, and strong and principled leadership.[39]

At Worthington Industries, the innovative Ohio steelmaker, applicants for new positions must pass the team test. They interview with members of their potential teams and then must serve a 90-day probation period before being voted on by an employee council of coworkers. Because the company operates on the basis of profit sharing, a willingness to be a team player gets extra emphasis.

The last point on this list—the need for strong and principled leadership, may be the key to them all. In their book *Teamwork: What Can Go Right/What Can Go Wrong,* Carl Larson and Frank LaFasto state: "The right person in a leadership role can add tremendous value to any collective effort, even to the point of sparking the outcome with an intangible kind of magic."[40] They further point out that leaders of high-performing teams share many characteristics with the "transformational leader," examined in Chapter 13.

According to Larson and LaFasto, effective team leaders *establish a clear vision of the future.* This vision serves as a goal that inspires hard work and the quest for performance excellence; it creates a sense of shared purpose. Effective team leaders help to *create change.* They are dissatisfied with the status quo, influence team members toward similar dissatisfaction, and infuse the team with the motivation to change in order to become better. Finally, effective team leaders *unleash talent.* They make sure the team is staffed with members who have the right skills and abilities. And they make sure these people are highly motivated to use their talents to achieve the group's performance objectives.

You don't get a high performing team by just bringing a group of people together and giving them a shared name or title. Leaders of high-performance teams create supportive climates in which team members know what to expect from the leader and each other, and know what the leader expects from them. They empower team members. By personal example, they demonstrate the importance of setting aside self-interests to support the team's goals. And, they use team building on a relatively continuous basis viewing it as an ongoing leadership responsibility.

Teams take hard work, but they are worth it.[41] That's part of any manager's leadership challenge.

CHAPTER REVIEW

This section should be used as an end-of-chapter "study guide." The *Summary* helps to put chapter content into overall perspective. The list of *Key Terms* allows you to double-check your familiarity with basic concepts and definitions. *Self-Test 17* gives you the opportunity to test your basic comprehension of the chapter using sample test questions.

SUMMARY

How do teams contribute to organizations?

- A team is a collection of people who work together to accomplish a common goal.

- Organizations operate as interlocking networks of formal work teams, which offer many benefits to the organizations and to their members.

- Teams help organizations through synergy in task performance, the creation of a whole that is greater than the sum of its parts.

- Teams help satisfy important needs for their members, providing various types of support and social satisfactions.

- Social loafing and other problems can limit the performance of teams.

What are current trends in the use of teams?

- Teams are important mechanisms of empowerment and participation in the workplace.

- Committees and task forces are used to facilitate operations and allow special projects to be completed with creativity.

- Cross functional teams bring members together from different departments and help improve lateral relations and integration in organizations.

- Employee involvement teams, such as the quality circle, allow employees to provide important insights into daily problem solving.

- New developments in information technology are also making virtual teams, or computer-mediated teams, more commonplace.

- Self-managing teams are changing organizations by allowing team members to perform many tasks previously reserved for their supervisors.

How do teams work?

- An effective team achieves high levels of both task performance and human resource maintenance.

- Important team input factors include the organizational setting, nature of the task, size, and membership characteristics.

- A team matures through various stages of development, including forming, storming, norming, performing, and adjourning.

- Norms are the standards or rules of conduct that influence the behavior of team members; cohesion is the attractiveness of the team to its members.

- In highly cohesive teams, members tend to conform to norms; the best situation for a manager or leader is a team with positive performance norms and highly cohesiveness.

- Distributed leadership in serving a team's task and maintenance needs helps in achieving long term effectiveness.

- Effective teams make use of alternative communication networks to best complete tasks.

How do teams make decisions?

- Teams can make decisions by lack of response, authority rule, minority rule, majority rule, consensus, and unanimity.

- The potential advantages of more team decision making include having more information available and generating more understanding and commitment.

- The potential liabilities to team decision making include social pressures to conform and greater time requirements.

- Groupthink is a tendency of members of highly cohesive teams to lose their critical evaluative capabilities and make poor decisions.

- Techniques for improving creativity in team decision making include brainstorming and the nominal group technique.

What can leaders build for high-performance teams?

- Team building helps team members develop action plans for improving the way they work together and the results they accomplish.

- The team-building process should be data based and collaborative, involving a high level of participation by all team members.

- High-performance work teams have a clear and shared sense of purpose as well as strong internal commitment to its accomplishment.

KEY TERMS

Centralized
    communication
    network (p. 364)
Cohesiveness (p. 362)
Committee (p. 354)
Decentralized
    communication
    network (p. 364)
Effective team (p. 358)
Employee involvement
    team (p. 355)
Formal team (p. 353)

Functional team (p. 353)
Group process (p. 358)
Groupthink (p. 367)
Human resource
    maintenance (p. 358)
Informal group (p. 353)
Maintenance activities
    (p. 363)
Norm (p. 361)
Quality circle
    (p. 356)

Self-managing work teams
    (p. 357)
Social loafing (p. 353)
Synergy (p. 352)
Task activities (p. 363)
Task force (p. 354)
Team (p. 352)
Team building (p. 369)
Teamwork (p. 352)
Virtual team (p. 356)

SELF-TEST 17

Take this test much as you would in a normal classroom situation. It is a good way to check your basic comprehension of chapter material. Answers may be found at the end of the book.

MULTIPLE-CHOICE QUESTIONS:

1. Teams are good for organizations because they may _____. (a) increase creativity in problem solving (b) help control and discipline members (c) satisfy individual needs (d) all of these

2. In an organization operating with self-managing teams, the traditional role of _____ is replaced by the role of team leader. (a) chief executive officer (b) first-line supervisor (c) middle manager (d) general manager

3. An effective team is defined as one that achieves high levels of both _____ and _____. (a) task performance, resource efficiency (b) member satisfaction, resource efficiency (c) task performance, human resource maintenance (d) task performance, creativity

4. In the open-systems model of teams, the _____ is an important input factor. (a) communication network (b) decision-making method (c) performance norm (d) membership characteristics

5. A basic rule of team dynamics states that the greater the _____ in a team, the greater the conformity to norms. (a) membership diversity (b) cohesiveness (c) task structure (d) competition among members

6. Groupthink is most likely to occur in teams that are _____. (a) large in size (b) diverse in membership (c) high performing (d) highly cohesive

7. Gatekeeping is an example of a _____ activity that can help teams work effectively over time. (a) task (b) maintenance (c) team-building (d) decision-making

8. Members of a team tend to become more motivated and able to deal with conflict during the _____ stage of team development. (a) forming (b) norming (c) performing (d) adjourning

9. One way for a manager to build positive norms within a team is to _____. (a) act as a positive role model (b) adjourn the team (c) introduce groupthink (d) isolate the team from others

10. When teams are highly cohesive _____. (a) members are high performers (b) members tend to be satisfied with their team membership (c) members have positive norms (d) all of these

TRUE-FALSE QUESTIONS:

11. Informal groups should be eliminated because they create problems for organizations. T F

12. Cross-functional committees and task forces can be used to improve lateral coordination. T F

13. Teams larger than 7 or so members may have difficulty solving problems together. T F

14. The only important norm in a work team is the performance norm. T F

15. A work team with a negative performance norm and low cohesiveness is the worst case for managers. T F

16. Self-censorship by members during team discussions is an indicator that groupthink is not operating. T F

17. Team building occurs when a manager tells a team what to do to improve performance. T F

18. Teams that must document decisions by voting are better off with an odd number of members. T F

19. Increasing the homogeneity of team membership is likely to increase team cohesiveness. T F

20. Multiskilling is a typical characteristic of self-managing teams. T F

SHORT-RESPONSE QUESTIONS:

21. How can a manager improve team effectiveness by modifying inputs?

22. What is the relationship between a team's cohesiveness, performance norm, and performance results?

23. How would a manager know that her team was suffering from groupthink [give two symptoms] and what could she do about it [give two responses]?

24. What makes a self-managing team different from a traditional work team?

APPLICATION QUESTION:

25. Marcos Martinez has just been appointed manager of a production team operating the 11 P.M. to 7 A.M. shift in a large manufacturing firm. An experienced manager, Marcos is concerned that the team members really like and get along well with one another, but they also appear to be restricting their task outputs to the minimum acceptable levels. What could Marcos do to improve things in this situation and why should he do them?

Innovation and Change Management

Planning Ahead—Chapter 18 Study Questions

- What is the nature of innovation?
- What are the challenges of organizational change?
- How can planned organizational change be managed?
- What is organization development?
- How do you build career readiness in a change environment?

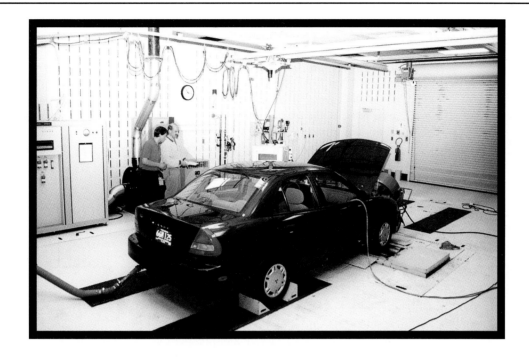

Innovation = Competitive Advantage

When a group of Japanese students drove out of Tokyo one day, the event wouldn't have seemed remarkable to bystanders. But when they arrived some 900 kilometers later on the northern island of Hokkaido, Mitsubishi's president was sure pleased. The students' car, powered by a new Gasoline Direct Engine (GDI) technology, had made the trip without refueling! In fact, there was fuel to spare in the gas tank.

The engine and its success were an important breakthrough for the company. Says President Takemune Kimura, "For many years engineers knew it would be technically possible, but they didn't know how. . . . Our computers finally found the answer." Mitsubishi's push for engine innovation is part of its commitment to safeguarding the environment. It also helps in its quest for advantage in a highly competitive global industry.[1]

● A **learning organization** utilizes people, values, and systems to continuously change and improve its performance.

Learning was obviously an important part of the process through which Mitsubishi developed the GDI engine. Indeed, we are in the age of the *learning organization,* first described in Chapter 3 as one that by virtue of people, values, and systems is able to continuously change and improve its performance based upon the lessons of experience."[2] And in this age the watchwords of the day are, and will remain for some time to come — *change, change* and *change.* But change in organizations, simply said, is not always easy to accomplish. In his book *The Circle of Innovation,* in fact, consultant Tom Peters argues that we must refocus the attention of managers and leaders away from past accomplishments and toward the role of innovation as the primary source of competitive advantage. In support, he cites this statement by Hewlett Packard CEO Lew Platt: "Whatever made you successful in the past *won't* in the future."[3] In this final chapter of the book the future is the issue, and our inquiry is into innovation and the dynamics of organizational change.

THE NATURE OF INNOVATION

Organizations and their managers must continually innovate and adapt to new situations if they are to survive and prosper over the long run. Max DePree, CEO of Herman Miller Company and cited in Chapter 13 for his leadership accomplishments, says it well: "You have to have an environment where the body of people are really amenable to change and can deal with the conflicts that arise out of change and innovation."[4] Consultant Peter Senge, author of the popular book *The Fifth Discipline,* further describes this environment as one in which managers stimulate and lead change in order to create learning organizations with the following characteristics — everyone sets aside old ways of thinking, everyone becomes self-aware and open to others, everyone learns how the whole organization works, everyone understands and agrees to a plan of action, and everyone works together to accomplish the plan.[5]

CREATIVITY

● **Creativity** is ingenuity and imagination that results in a novel solution to a problem.

Formally defined, **creativity** is the display or use of ingenuity and imagination to create a novel approach to things or a unique solution to a problem.[6] Creativity is an essential fuel for the learning organization. It is indispensable to those who must master the demands of complex and changing environments. In progressive work settings, good managers use all of the advantages of participation, involvement, and empowerment to stimulate individual and group creativity. Yet in far too many others, poor management and cumbersome organizational practices stifle people's creative abilities. Consider these words penned by an executive who once put his frustrations into rhyme:[7]

> Along this tree
> From root to crown
> Ideas flow up
> And vetoes flow down.

This verse certainly doesn't describe a learning organization that is ready to meet the tests of competition and environmental change. Quite the contrary. It creates the impression of an organization that loses the advantages of alertness and imagination at its lower levels due to rigidity, resistance to change, and a lack

Manager's Notepad 18.1

Ten Ways to Increase Creativity

1. Look for more than one "right" answer or "one best way."
2. Avoid being too logical; let your thinking roam.
3. Challenge rules; ask "why"; don't settle for the status quo.
4. Ask "what if" questions.
5. Let ambiguity help you and others see things differently.
6. Don't be afraid of error; let trial and error be a path to success.
7. Take time to play and experiment; let them be paths to discovery.
8. Open up to other viewpoints and perspectives.
9. Support nonconformity; let differences exist.
10. Believe in creativity; make it a self-fulfilling prophecy.

of foresight at the top. While the internal resources required for creativity are readily available, "for the asking" so to speak, top management is apparently discouraging instead of encouraging their utilization. This is a costly oversight to say the least.

By the way, take a moment to test your creativity. Each of the following puzzles symbolizes a familiar word or phrase. See if you can name each.

1. SAND   2. MIND   3. 0   4. DICE
                 ————   ————   +
                 MATTER   M.D.   DICE
                                    PH.D.
                                    D.D.

To solve these puzzles, you must be creative and look at things with a fresh and unrestrained eye. The correct answers are (1) "sandbox," (2) "mind over matter," (3) "three degrees below zero," and (4) "paradise." And just as the puzzles probably look easier in retrospect, creativity is something that can be enhanced through discipline and good judgment. *Manager's Notepad 18.1* introduces a number of other techniques that can be used to enhance creative thinking. All are designed to help you look at problems more creatively.

THE INNOVATION PROCESS

Innovation is the process of creating new ideas and putting them into practice.[8] It is the act of converting new ideas into usable applications. In organizations these applications occur in two forms: (1) *process innovations,* which result in better ways of doing things; and (2) *product innovations,* which result in the creation of new or improved goods and services.

The management of both process and product innovations includes supporting *invention,* the act of discovery, and *application,* the act of use. Invention relates to the development of new ideas. Managers need to be concerned about building new work environments that stimulate creativity and an ongoing stream of new ideas. Application, on the other hand, deals with the utilization of inventions to take the best advantage of ideas. Here, managers must make sure that good ideas for new or modified work processes are actually implemented. They must also make sure that the commercial potential of ideas for new products or services is fully realized.

- **Innovation** is the process of taking a new idea and putting it into practice.

Innovation is critical at Rubbermaid Incorporated, which creates a new product every day. CEO Wolfgang Schmitt says this isn't easy to accomplish. The firm uses the latest management approaches in its quest for innovativeness. Cross-functional teams facilitate new product development. People are hired from different countries to bring new ideas into the firm. Employees travel to trade shows — Schmitt himself came up with the ideas for a heat-resistant plastic spatula in China and a new container lid while touring the British Museum's Egyptian exhibit. Environmental trends are closely watched. Spotting increased interest in toy safety, the company builds plastic playground equipment; spotting the work-at-home trend, the firm builds office equipment for small spaces; spotting an increased interest in home gardening, the firm builds assemble-it-yourself plastic tool sheds. Schmitt aims to keep the ideas flowing, with an emphasis on intuition and good judgement. He says: "Where people go wrong is by spending too much time analyzing." [9]

While creativity and innovation are key operating objectives for progressive organizations like Rubbermaid, there are many organizations that should be innovating but fail to do so. As dramatic technological, economic, political, and social changes continue to characterize the world at large, however, the necessity for these organizations to stimulate, support, and achieve innovation is becoming inescapable. One of the best examples of a process for promoting change is found in the four steps of the product innovation process:

Four steps in product innovation

1. *Idea creation:* New knowledge forms around basic discoveries, extensions of existing understanding, or spontaneous creativity made possible by individual ingenuity and communication with others.

2. *Initial experimentation:* Ideas are initially tested in concept by discussions with others; referrals to customers, clients, or technical experts; and/or in the form of prototypes or samples.

3. *Feasibility determination:* Practicality and financial value are examined in formal feasibility studies, which also identify potential costs and benefits as well as potential markets or applications.

4. *Final application:* A new product is finally commercialized or put on sale in the open market, or a new process is implemented as part of normal operating routines. [10]

Figure 18.1 uses the example of new product development to highlight these steps and show the business significance of *commercializing innovations.* This is the process of turning new ideas into products or processes that can make a difference in sales, profits, and/or costs. One of the major features of organizational innovation, as shown in *Figure 18.1,* is that the entire process must be related to the needs of the organization and its marketplace. New ideas alone are not sufficient to guarantee success in this setting; they must be implemented effectively in order to contribute to organizational performance. For example, 3M Corporation generates over one-third of its revenues from products that didn't exist four years ago. The firm, for whom product innovation is a way of life, owes its success to the imagination of employees like Art Fry. He's the person whose creativity turned an adhesive that "wasn't sticky enough" into the blockbuster product known worldwide today as Post-It Notes. [11]

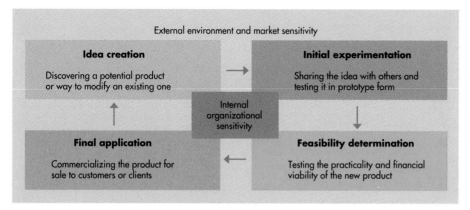

Figure 18.1 Process of innovation in organizations: the case of new product development.

At Olympus Optical, one of Japan's well-known multinational companies, President Masatoshi Kishimoto tries to encourage creativity and innovation. A corporate vision called "Focus 21" will improve quality assurance, not only in products but in all aspects of company services and operations. The goal is to better meet the needs of all its customers around the world.

CHARACTERISTICS OF INNOVATIVE ORGANIZATIONS

Innovative organizations like 3M and Rubbermaid are mobilized to support creativity and entrepreneurship, and their managers take active roles in leading the process.[12] In highly innovative organizations, *the corporate strategy and culture support innovation.* The strategies of the organization, the visions and values of senior management, and the framework of policies and expectations emphasize an entrepreneurial spirit. Innovation is expected, failure is accepted, and the organization is willing to take risks. For example, Johnson & Johnson CEO James Burke has said, "I try to give people the feeling that it's okay to fail, that it's important to fail."[13] The key here is for managers to eliminate risk-averse climates and replace them with organizational cultures in which innovation is expected and failure is accepted.

In highly innovative organizations, *organization structures support innovation.* More and more large organizations are trying to capture the structural flexibility of smaller ones. That is, they are striving for more organic operations with a strong emphasis on lateral communications and cross-functional teams and task forces. In particular, research and development, historically a separate and isolated function, is being integrated into a team setting. As Peter Drucker points out, "Successful innovations . . . are now being turned out by cross-functional teams with people from marketing, manufacturing, and finance participating in research work from the very beginning."[14] Innovative organizations are also reorganizing to create many smaller divisions that allow creative teams or "skunk works" to operate and to encourage "intrapreneurial" new ventures.

In highly innovative organizations, *the organization's staffing supports innovation* well. Organizations need different kinds of people to succeed in all stages of the innovation process. The critical innovation roles to be filled include the following:

← Innovation roles in organizations

- *Idea generators:* People who create new insights from internal discovery or external awareness, or both.

- *Information gatekeepers:* People who serve as links between people and groups within the organization and with external sources.

- *Product champions:* People who advocate and push for change and innovation in general and for the adoption of specific product or process ideas in particular.

- *Project managers:* People who perform the technical functions needed to keep an innovative project on track with all the necessary resource support.

Manager's Notepad 18.2
Spotting Barriers to Innovation
• *Top management isolation* fosters misunderstandings and contributes to a "risk-averse" climate.
• *Intolerance of differences* denies uniqueness, creates homogeneity, and brands as "troublemakers" those who question the status quo.
• *Vested interests* focus on the "parts" rather than the "whole" and emphasizes the defense of one's "turf" against inroads by outsiders.
• *Short time horizons* emphasizes short-term goals rather than the potential for new ideas to generate long-term gains.
• *Overly rational thinking* tries to make creativity a systematic process and emphasizes schedules over results.
• *Inappropriate incentives* use rewards and controls to reinforce routines; discourage surprises and differences linked to innovation.
• *Excessive bureaucracy* gives allegiance to rules, procedures, and efficiency that frustrate creativity and innovation.

• *Innovation leaders:* People who encourage, sponsor, and coach others to keep the innovation values and goals in place and channel energies in the right directions.[15]

In highly innovative organizations, *top management supports innovation.* In the case of 3M, for example, many top managers have been the innovators and product champions of the company's past. They understand the innovation process, are tolerant of criticisms and differences of opinion, and take all possible steps to keep the goals clear and the pressure on. The key, once again, is to allow the creative potential of people to operate fully. As Max DePree of Herman Miller again states, "If you want the best things to happen in corporate life, you have to find ways to be hospitable to the unusual person."[16] Finally, an enlightened top management helps break down the possible barriers to innovation listed in *Manager's Notepad 18.2.*[17]

 ## CHALLENGES OF ORGANIZATIONAL CHANGE

"Change" is an essential part of the processes of organizational creativity and innovation. Especially today, many people say that change is inevitable and a way of life. But is it? Rockport CEO Angel Martinez says that "the one constant factor in business today is that we live in a perpetual hurricane season." Yet when as a new CEO Martinez sought to change traditional ways in his company he encountered resistance from those he said "gave lip service to my ideas and hoped I'd go away."[18] And consider what once happened at BankAmerica. After the company announced a large quarterly operating loss, its new CEO at the time, Samuel Armacost, complained about the lack of "agents of change" among his top managers. Claiming that the managers seemed more interested in taking orders than initiating change, Armacost said, "I came away quite distressed from my first couple of management meetings. Not only couldn't I get conflict, I couldn't even get comment. They were all waiting to see which way the wind blew."[19]

CHANGE LEADERSHIP

A **change agent** is a person or group who takes leadership responsibility for changing the existing pattern of behavior of another person or social system. Change agents make things happen, and part of every manager's job is to act as a change agent in the work setting. This requires being alert to situations or to people needing change, being open to good ideas, and being able to support the implementation of new ideas in actual practice. *Figure 18.2* contrasts, for example, a change leader with a status quo manager. The former is forward-looking, proactive and embraces new ideas; the latter is backward-looking, reactive, and comfortable with habit. Obviously, the new workplace demands change leadership.

In the last chapter on teams and teamwork, we discussed the concept of distributed leadership in groups. The point was that everyone in a group has the potential to lead by serving group needs for task and maintenance activities. The same general notion applies when it comes to change leadership in organizations — the responsibilities for change leadership are ideally distributed and shared top to bottom. In *top-down change,* strategic and comprehensive changes are initiated with the goal of comprehensive impact on the organization and its performance capabilities. But change that is driven from the top runs the risk of being perceived as insensitive to the needs of lower level personnel. It can easily fail if implementation suffers from excessive resistance and insufficient commitments to change. The success of top-down change is usually determined by the willingness of middle- and lower-level workers to actively support top-management initiatives.

Bottom-up change is also important in organizations. In such cases, the initiatives for change come from persons throughout an organization and are supported by the efforts of middle- and lower-level managers acting as change agents. Bottom-up change is essential to organizational innovation and is very useful in terms of adapting operations and technologies to the changing requirements of work. It is made possible by empowerment, involvement, and participation as discussed in earlier chapters. For example, at Johnson Controls, Inc., Jason Moncer is often called "Mr. Kaizen" by his co-workers. The nickname refers to a Japanese practice of continuous improvement. Moncer earned the nickname through his willingness to offer numerous ideas for changes in his work area. At his plant, workers contributed some 221 suggestions that were implemented in just one year alone. The company is committed to the belief that workers should be encouraged to use their job knowledge and common sense to improve things. In other words, when the workers talk managers listen.[20]

● A **change agent** tries to change the behavior of another person or social system.

● Toro
http://www.toro.com

When a new molding technique didn't work, Toro lost mower sales. Members of the engineering team responsible for the technique were called to CEO Kendrick Melrose's office. Instead of "pink slips," they were met with a party that included balloons and a cake. The celebration was in honor of the risk they had taken. Later, it was found that the technique could be used successfully in the production of other Toro products.

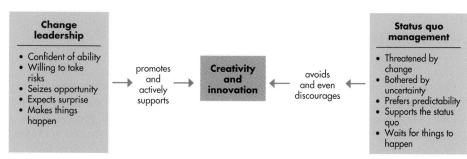

Figure 18.2   Change leadership versus status quo management.

PLANNED VERSUS UNPLANNED CHANGE

● **Planned change** occurs as a result of specific efforts by a change agent.

We are particularly interested in **planned change** that occurs as a result of the specific efforts of a change agent. Planned change is a direct response to a person's perception of a *performance gap,* or a discrepancy between the desired and actual state of affairs. Performance gaps may represent problems to be resolved or opportunities to be explored. In each case, managers as change agents should be ever alert to performance gaps and take action to initiate planned changes to deal with them.

● A **performance gap** is a discrepancy between the desired and actual state of affairs.

● **Unplanned change** occurs spontaneously and without a change agent's direction.

But, **unplanned changes** are important too. They occur spontaneously or randomly and without the benefit of a change agent's attention. Unplanned changes may be disruptive, such as a wildcat strike that results in a plant closure, or beneficial, such as an interpersonal conflict that results in a new procedure on interdepartmental relations. The appropriate goal in managing unplanned change is to act immediately once it is recognized in order to minimize negative consequences and maximize possible benefits.

FORCES AND TARGETS FOR CHANGE

The impetus for change can arise from a variety of external forces.[21] These include the global economy and market competition, local economic conditions, government laws and regulations, technological developments, market trends, and social forces, among others. As an organization's general and specific environments develop and change over time, the organization must adapt as well. Internal forces for change are important too. Indeed, any change in one part of the organization as a complex system — perhaps a change initiated in response to one or more of the external forces just identified, can often create the need for change in another part of the system.

The many organizational targets for planned change are found among all the aspects of organizations already discussed in this book. These targets for change — including tasks, people, culture, technology, structure, are highly interrelated:[22]

Organizational targets for change

● *Tasks:* The nature of work as represented by organizational mission, objectives, and strategy and the job designs for individuals and groups.

● *People:* The attitudes and competencies of the employees and the human resource systems that support them.

● *Culture:* The value system for the organization as a whole and the norms guiding individual and group behavior.

● *Technology:* The operations and information technology used to support job designs, arrange workflows, and integrate people and machines in systems.

● *Structure:* The configuration of the organization as a complex system, including its design features and lines of authority and communications.

 ## MANAGING PLANNED CHANGE

Change is a complicated phenomenon in any setting, and human nature always stands at the heart of it. People tend to act habitually and in stable ways over time. They may *not* want to change even when circumstances require it. As a manager and change agent, you will need to recognize and deal with such tendencies. It helps to understand the phases of planned change and their implications.

When Vice Chairman Martin McGuinn of Mellon Bank faced resistance to change in the bank's retail division, he consistently communicated a compelling message: "We want to be the best retailer in financial services." McGuinn spent a lot of time at the branches. He told employees, "If something isn't working, it's okay to say so." With persistence, the support of his top managers, and a willingness to let staffers voice their concerns about change, he managed a major overhaul of the division.[23]

THE PHASES OF PLANNED CHANGE

Kurt Lewin, a noted psychologist, recommends that any planned-change effort be viewed as the three-phase process shown in *Figure 18.3*.[24] Lewin's three phases of planned change are (1) *unfreezing*—preparing a system for change; (2) *changing*—making actual changes in the system; and (3) *refreezing*—stabilizing the system after change.

Unfreezing

In order for change to be successful, people must be ready for it. Planned change has little chance for long-term success unless people are open to doing things differently. **Unfreezing** is the stage in which a situation is prepared for change and

• **Unfreezing** is the phase during which a situation is prepared for change.

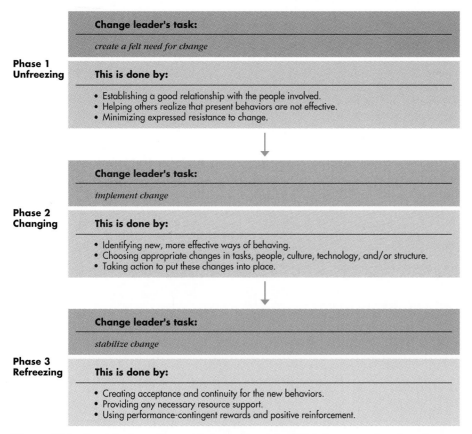

Figure 18.3 Lewin's three phases of planned organizational change: unfreezing, changing, and refreezing.

felt needs for change are developed. It can be facilitated in several ways: through environmental pressures for change, declining performance, the recognition that problems or opportunities exist, and through the observation of behavioral models that display alternative approaches. When handled well, conflict can be an important unfreezing force in organizations. It often helps people break old habits and recognize alternative ways of thinking about or doing things.

Changing

● **Changing** is the phase where a planned change actually takes place.

In the **changing** phase, something new takes place in a system, and change is actually implemented. This is the point at which managers initiate changes in such organizational targets of tasks, people, culture, technology, and structure. Ideally, all change is done in response to a good diagnosis of a problem and a careful examination of alternatives. However, Lewin believes that many change agents enter the changing phase prematurely, are too quick to change things, and therefore end up creating resistance to change. When managers implement change before people feel a need for it, there is an increased likelihood of failure.

Refreezing

● **Refreezing** is the phase at which change is stabilized.

The final stage in the planned-change process is **refreezing.** Here, the manager is concerned about stabilizing the change and creating the conditions for its long-term continuity. Refreezing is accomplished by appropriate rewards for performance, positive reinforcement, and providing necessary resource support. It is also important to evaluate results carefully, provide feedback to the people involved, and make any required modifications in the original change. When refreezing is done poorly, changes are too easily forgotten or abandoned with the passage of time. When it is done well, change can be more long lasting.

CHOOSING A CHANGE STRATEGY

Managers use various approaches when trying to get others to adopt a desired change. *Figure 18.4* summarizes three common change strategies known as force-coercion, rational persuasion, and shared power.[25]

Force-Coercion Strategies

● A **force-coercion strategy** pursues change through formal authority and/or the use of rewards or punishments.

A **force-coercion strategy** uses the power bases of legitimacy, rewards, and punishments as the primary inducements to change. As *Figure 18.4* shows, the

Change Strategy	Power Bases	Managerial Behavior	Likely Results	
Force–Coercion Using position power to create change by decree and formal authority	Legitimacy Rewards Punishments	*Direct forcing and unilateral action* *Political maneuvering and indirect action*	Fast	Temporary compliance
Rational Persuasion Creating change through rational persuasion and empirical argument	Expertise	*Informational efforts using credible knowledge, demonstrated facts, and logical argument*		
Shared power Developing support for change through personal values and commitments	Reference	*Participative efforts to share power and involve others in planning and implementing change*	Slow	Longer term Internalization

Figure 18.4   Alternative change strategies and their managerial implications.

likely outcomes of force-coercion are immediate compliance but little commitment.

Force-coercion can be pursued in at least two ways, both of which can be commonly observed in organizations. In a *direct forcing* strategy, the change agent takes direct and unilateral action to "command" that change take place. This involves the exercise of formal authority or legitimate power, offering special rewards, and/or threatening punishment. In *political maneuvering,* the change agent works indirectly to gain special advantage over other persons and thereby make them change. This involves bargaining, obtaining control of important resources, or granting small favors.

In both versions, the force-coercion strategy produces limited results. Although it can be implemented rather quickly, most people respond to this strategy out of fear of punishment or hope for a reward. This usually results in only temporary compliance with the change agent's desires. The new behavior continues only so long as the opportunity for rewards and punishments is present. For this reason, force-coercion is most useful as an unfreezing device that helps people break old patterns of behavior and gain initial impetus to try new ones.

A change agent that seeks to create change through force-coercion believes that people who run things are basically motivated by self-interest and by what the situation offers in terms of potential personal gains or losses. This change agent believes that people change only in response to such motives, tries to find out where their vested interests lie, and then puts the pressure on. If the change agent has formal authority, she or he uses it along with whatever rewards and punishments are available. Once a weakness is found, it is exploited. This change agent is always quick to work "politically" by building supporting alliances wherever possible.[26]

Rational Persuasion Strategies

Change agents using a **rational persuasion strategy** attempt to bring about change through persuasion backed by special knowledge, empirical data, and rational argument. The likely outcome is eventual compliance with reasonable commitment. This is an informational strategy that assumes that rational people will be guided by facts, reason, and self-interest when deciding whether or not to support a change.

- A **rational persuasion strategy** pursues change through empirical data and rational argument.

A manager using rational persuasion must convince others that the cost-benefit value of a planned change is high and that it will leave them better off than before. Accomplishing this depends to a large extent on the presence of expert power. This can come directly from the change agent if she or he has personal credibility as an "expert." If not, it can be obtained in the form of consultants and other outside experts or from credible demonstration projects. When successful, a rational persuasion strategy helps unfreeze and refreeze a change situation. Although slower than force-coercion, it tends to result in longer lasting and internalized change.

A change agent following this strategy believes that people are inherently rational and are guided by reason in their actions and decision making. Once a specific course of action is demonstrated to be in a person's self-interest, the change agent assumes that reason and rationality will cause the person to adopt it. Thus, he or she uses information and facts to communicate the essential desirability of change. If the logic is sound, the change agent is confident that the person will adopt and support the proposed change.

Shared Power Strategies

A **shared power strategy** engages people in a collaborative process of identifying values, assumptions, and goals from which support for change will naturally

- A **shared power strategy** pursues change by participation in assessing values, needs, and goals.

• **Hyatt Hotels**
http://www.hyatt.com

Hyatt Hotels has used surveys for many years to examine organizational climate and effectiveness. A 100-item questionnaire is distributed annually to all employees. Seven items, including "Tell us what you think of management," create a General Morale Index that is closely watched by senior management. A computer program compares the results from various operating locations.

emerge. The process is slow, but it is likely to yield high commitment. Sometimes called a *normative-reeducative strategy,* this approach is based on empowerment and is highly participative in nature. It relies on involving others in examining personal needs and values, group norms, and operating goals as they relate to the issues at hand. Power is shared by the change agent and other persons as they work together to develop a new consensus to support needed change.

Managers using shared power as an approach to planned change need reference power and the skills to work effectively with other people in group situations. They must be comfortable allowing others to participate in making decisions that affect the planned change and the way it is implemented. Because it entails a high level of involvement, a normative-reeducative strategy is often quite time consuming, but it is likely to result in a longer lasting and internalized change.

A change agent who shares power begins by recognizing that people have varied needs and complex motivations. He or she believes people behave as they do because of sociocultural norms and commitments to the expectations of others. Changes in organizations are understood to inevitably involve changes in attitudes, values, skills, and significant relationships, not just changes in knowledge, information, or intellectual rationales for action and practice. Thus, when seeking to change others, this change agent is sensitive to the way group pressures can support or inhibit change. In working with people, every attempt is made to gather their opinions, identify their feelings and expectations, and incorporate them fully into the change process.

DEALING WITH RESISTANCE TO CHANGE

Change typically brings with it resistance. When people resist change, furthermore, they are defending something important and that appears to them as threatened by the attempted change. A change of work schedules for the 600 workers in Cherry Semiconductor's Rhode Island plant, for example, may not have seemed like much to top management. But to the workers it was significant enough to bring about an organizing attempt by the Teamster's Union. When management delved into the issues, they found that workers viewed changes in weekend work schedules as threatening to their personal lives. With inputs from the workers, the problem was resolved satisfactorily.[27]

Resistance is often viewed by change agents and managers as something that must be "overcome" in order for change to be successful. This is not necessarily true. Resistance is better viewed as feedback that the informed change agent can use to constructively modify a planned change to better fit situational needs and goals. When resistance appears, it usually means that something can be done to achieve a better "fit" between the planned change, the situation, and the people involved. Going back to the issue of work schedules once again, this conversation with a manager is reported by Jim Stam, a shift work consultant with Circadian Technologies: *Manager* — "Come on, Jim, there must be one schedule that's the right schedule for this industry." *Jim* — "Yes, it's the one the people in the plant pick."[28]

There are any number of reasons why people in organizations may resist planned change. Some of the more common ones are shown in the *Manager's Notepad 18.3.*

Once resistance to change is recognized and understood, it can be dealt with in various ways. Among the alternatives for effectively managing resistance, the *education and communication* approach uses discussions, presentations, and demonstrations to educate people beforehand about a change. *Participation and involvement* allows others to contribute ideas and help design and implement the change. The *facilitation and support* approach involves providing encouragement and training, actively listening to problems and complaints, and helping

Manager's Notepad 18.3

Why People May Resist Change

- *Fear of the unknown:* Not understanding what is happening or what comes next.

- *Disrupted habits:* Feeling upset when old ways of doing things can't be followed.

- *Loss of confidence:* Feeling incapable of performing well under the new ways of doing things.

- *Loss of control:* Feeling that things are being done "to" you rather than "by" or "with" you.

- *Poor timing:* Feeling overwhelmed by the situation or that things are moving too fast.

- *Work overload:* Not having the physical or psychic energy to commit to the change.

- *Loss of face:* Feeling inadequate or humiliated because it appears that the "old" ways weren't "good" ways.

- *Lack of purpose:* Not seeing a reason for the change and/or not understanding its benefits.

to overcome performance pressures. *Facilitation and agreement* provides incentives that appeal to those who are actively resisting or ready to resist. This approach makes trade-offs in exchange for assurances that change will not be blocked. *Manipulation and co-optation* tries to influence others covertly by providing information selectively and structuring events in favor of the desired change. *Explicit and implicit coercion* forces people to accept change by threatening resistors with a variety of undesirable consequences if they do not go along as planned.[29] Obviously, the last two approaches carry great risk and potential for negative side effects.

TECHNOLOGICAL CHANGE

Technological change is common in today's organizations, but it also brings special challenges to change leaders. For the full advantages of new technologies to be realized, a good fit must be achieved with work needs, practices, and people. This, in turn, requires sensitivity to resistance and continual gathering of information so that appropriate adjustments can be made all during the time a new technology is being implemented. In this sense, the demands of managing technological change have been described using the analogy of Trukese and European navigators.[30]

The European navigator works from a plan, relates all moves during a voyage to the plan, and tries to always stay "on course." When something unexpected happens, the plan is revised systematically, and the new plan followed again until the navigator finds the ship to be off course. The Trukese navigator, by contrast, starts with an objective and moves off in its general direction. Always alert to information from waves, clouds, winds, etc., the navigator senses subtle changes in conditions and steers and alters the ship's course continually to reach the ultimate objective.

Like the Trukese navigator, technological change may best be approached as an ongoing process that will inevitably require improvisation as things are being implemented. New technologies are often designed external to the organization in which they are to be used. The implications of such a technology for a local

• Motorola
http://www.mot.com

Motorola implemented a program called "internal readiness" to help make sure that women and minorities get the assistance they need to move up the firm's ladder of corporate success. A corporate vice president calls the change plan a business initiative. She says, "We're talking about competitive advantage. If everybody else is stuck in the muck and mire of sexism and racism and we can blow out of that, look at all the people who will be available to us who the competition can't get."

application may be difficult to anticipate and plan for ahead of time. A technology that is attractive in concept may appear complicated to the new users; the full extent of its benefits and/or inadequacies may not become known until it is tried. This, in turn, means that the change leader and manager should be alert to resistance, should continually gather and process information relating to the change, and should be willing to customize the new technology to best meet the needs of the local situation.[31]

ORGANIZATION DEVELOPMENT

● **Organization development** is a comprehensive effort to improve an organization's ability to deal with its environment and solve problems.

Among consulting professionals **organization development,** or **OD** for short, is known as a comprehensive approach to planned organizational change that involves the application of behavioral science in a systematic and long-range effort to improve organizational effectiveness.[32] Organization development is supposed to help organizations cope with environmental and other pressures for change while also improving their internal problem-solving capabilities. OD, in this sense, brings the quest for continuous improvement to the planned change process.

There will always be times when the members of organizations should sit together and systematically reflect on strengths and weaknesses as well as performance accomplishments and failures. Organization development is one way to ensure that this happens in a supportive and action-oriented environment. OD is an important avenue through which leaders can advance planned-change agendas, foster creativity and innovation, and more generally assist people and systems to continuously improve organizational performance. It often involves the assistance of an external consultant or an internal staff person with special training. But importantly, all managers should have the skills and commitment to utilize the various elements of OD in their continuous improvement agendas. The notion of organization development dovetails nicely with the popular concepts of total quality management (TQM) and employee involvement discussed throughout this book. In fact, the OD approach may offer added opportunities to utilize them to the best advantage.[33]

● **Clorox**
http://www.clorox.com

Daniel Simpson, Director of Strategy and Planning for Clorox says the firm tries to avoid chasing new management fads. "You need to be fairly selective and consistent over time so you're not upsetting your organization over the tool of the month," he says. When top management is linked to fads, confidence is easily undermined in the employee ranks.

GOALS OF ORGANIZATION DEVELOPMENT

In organization development two goals are pursued simultaneously. The *outcome goals of OD* focus on task accomplishments, while the *process goals of OD* focus on the way people work together. It is this second goal that strongly differentiates OD from more general attempts at planned change in organizations. You may think of OD as a form of "planned change plus," with the "plus" meaning that change is accomplished in such a way that organization members develop a capacity for continued self-renewal. That is, OD tries to achieve change while helping organization members become more active and self-reliant in their ability to continue changing in the future. What also makes OD unique is its commitment to strong humanistic values and established principles of behavioral science. OD is committed to improving organizations through freedom of choice, shared power and self-reliance, and by taking the best advantage of what we know about human behavior in organizations.

A GENERAL MODEL OF ORGANIZATION DEVELOPMENT

Figure 18.5 presents a general model of OD and shows its relationship to Lewin's three phases of planned change. To begin the OD process successfully, any con-

Organization Development Process

Diagnosis	**Intervention**	**Evaluation**
Gathering and analyzing data, setting change objectives	Taking collaborative action to implement desired change	Following up to reinforce and support change

Establish a change relationship

Create links with members of client system

Achieve a terminal relationship

Withdraw to leave members of client system self reliant

Unfreezing   *Changing*   *Refreezing*

Planned change process

Figure 18.5 Organization development and the planned change process.

sultant or facilitator must *establish a working relationship* with members of the client system. The next step is *diagnosis* — gathering and analyzing data to assess the situation and set appropriate change objectives. This helps with unfreezing as well as pinpointing appropriate directions for action. Diagnosis leads to active *intervention,* wherein change objectives are pursued through a variety of specific interventions, a number of which will be discussed shortly.

Essential to any OD effort is *evaluation.* This is the examination of the process to determine if things are proceeding as desired and if further action is needed. Eventually, the OD consultant or facilitator should *achieve a terminal relationship* that leaves the client able to function on its own. If OD has been done well, the system and its members should be prepared to manage their ongoing need for self-renewal and development better.

The success or failure of any OD program lies in part in the strength of its methodological foundations. As shown in *Figure 18.6,* these foundations rest on **action research** — the process of systematically collecting data on an organization, feeding it back to the members for action planning, and evaluating results by collecting more data and repeating the process as necessary. Action research is initiated when someone senses a performance gap and decides to analyze the situation to understand its problems and opportunities. Data gathering can be

● **Action research** is a collaborative process of collecting data, using it for action planning, and evaluating the results.

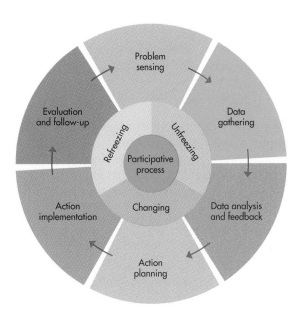

Figure 18.6 Action research as the methodological foundation of organization development.

done in several ways. Interviews are a common means of gathering data in action research. Formal written surveys of employee attitudes and needs are also growing in popularity. Many such "climate," "attitude," or "morale" questionnaires have been tested for reliability and validity. Some have even been used so extensively that norms are available so that one organization can compare its results with those from a broad sample of counterparts.

ORGANIZATION DEVELOPMENT INTERVENTIONS

The foundations of organization development include respect for people and a commitment to their full participation in self-directed change processes. It is employee involvement in action. OD rallys an organization's human resources through teamwork and in support of constructive change. This process is evident in the variety of **OD interventions** or activities that are initiated to directly facilitate the change processes. Importantly, these interventions are linked to concepts and ideas discussed elsewhere in this book and that are well represented in the practices and approaches of the new workplace.

● An **OD intervention** is a structured activity that helps create change in organization development.

Individual Interventions

Concerning individuals, organization development practitioners generally recognize that the need for personal growth and development are most likely to be satisfied in a supportive and challenging work environment. They also accept the premise that most people are capable of assuming responsibility for their own actions and of making positive contributions to organizational performance. Based on these principles, some of the more popular *OD* interventions designed to help improve individual effectiveness include the following:

Individual OD interventions

- *Sensitivity training (T-groups):* Unstructured group sessions where participants learn interpersonal skills and increased sensitivity to other people.

- *Management training:* Structured educational opportunities for developing important managerial skills and competencies.

- *Role negotiation:* Structured interactions to clarify and negotiate role expectations among people who work together.

- *Job redesign:* Realigning task components to better fit the needs and capabilities of the individual.

- *Career planning:* Structured advice and discussion sessions to help individuals plan career paths and programs of personal development.

Team Interventions

The team plays a very important role in organization development (OD). OD practitioners recognize two principles in this respect. First, teams are viewed as important vehicles for helping people satisfy important needs. Second, it is believed that improved collaboration within and among teams can improve organizational performance. Selected OD interventions designed to improve team effectiveness include the following:

Team OD interventions

- *Team building:* Structured experiences to help team members set goals, improve interpersonal relations, and become a better functioning team.

- *Process consultation:* Third-party observation and advice on critical team processes (e.g., communication, conflict, and decision making).

- *Intergroup team building:* Structured experiences to help two or more teams set shared goals, improve intergroup relations, and become better coordinated.

Organization-wide Interventions

At the level of the total organization, OD practitioners operate on the premise that any changes in one part of the system will also affect other parts. The organization's culture is considered to have an important impact on member attitudes and morale. And it is believed that structures and jobs can be designed to bring together people, technology, and systems in highly productive and satisfying working combinations. Some of the OD interventions often applied with an emphasis on organizational effectiveness include the following:

- *Survey feedback:* Comprehensive and systematic data collection to identify attitudes and needs, analyze results, and plan for constructive action.

- *Confrontation meeting:* One-day intensive, structured meetings to gather data on workplace problems and plan for constructive actions.

- *Structural redesign:* Realigning the organization structure to meet the needs of environmental and contextual forces.

- *Management by objectives (MBO):* Formalizing MBO throughout the organization to link individual, group, and organizational objectives.

Organization-wide OD interventions

CHANGE AND CAREER READINESS

Now is a final chance for us to raise once again the issue of your career. And when it comes to success in a career during changing times, one thing is without a doubt true — what happens is up to you.

EARLY CAREER ADVICE

The best early career advice returns again and again to the same message — what happens is up to you. Don't let yourself down. Step forward and take charge of your learning. Begin building what author and consultant Tom Peters refers to as the "brand called 'you.'"[34] Peters advises each of us to continually work hard to create and maintain a unique and timely package of skills and capabilities with career potential. In Peters words, your personal brand should be "remarkable, measurable, distinguished, and distinctive" relative to the competition—others like you.[35]

In times of great change, the early career challenge is even more dramatic. Like organizations that must innovate and adapt to achieve competitive advantage, you and your brand must also be flexible and change with the times. According to another noted author and consultant Stephen Covey, this means that you must be prepared to step forward in a career and always (1) behave like an entrepreneur, (2) seek feedback on your performance continually, (3) set up your own mentoring systems, (4) get comfortable with teamwork, (5) take risks to gain experience and learn new skills, (6) be a problem solver, and (7) keep your life in balance.[36]

BUILDING THE BRAND CALLED "YOU"

The following section contains a *Career Readiness Workbook.* It is designed to help you begin the process of brand building and to prepare your credentials for success in a world of dynamic employment opportunities. Hopefully you have already taken advantage of the learning activities offered in the workbook. Its many

● A **career portfolio** documents academic and personal accomplishments for external review.

options are well worth serious attention. Don't neglect the Career Advancement Portfolio section. It provides the template for a **career portfolio** that documents, in paper or electronic form, your academic and personal accomplishments for external review. This is a great resource that can help you frame and summarize your credentials for potential internship sources and full time employers. Take advantage of the option to build an electronic career portfolio and put it on-line as a means of further distinguishing yourself from the competition. Once started, your career portfolio can be easily maintained as a continuing resource for self-assessment and personal development, as well as brand communication.

Management 6/E has been rich with insights into the new workplace, the nature of managerial work, and the great challenges organizations face in a highly competitive global economy. As you move forward in this exciting world of work, you must continue the process of brand building and continue to strengthen your potential for satisfying life-long career advancement. Don't ever forget that what you do with your career is up to you. Many foundations for career success have been set during your introductory study of management. Please put them to good use!

CHAPTER REVIEW

This section should be used as an end-of-chapter "study guide." The *Summary* helps to put the chapter's content into overall perspective. The list of *Key Terms* allows you to double-check your familiarity with basic concepts and definitions. *Self-Test 18* gives you the opportunity to test your basic comprehension of the chapter using sample test questions.

SUMMARY

What is the nature of innovation?

● A learning organization is one in which people, values, and systems support innovation and continuous change based upon the lessons of experience.

● Creativity, essential to innovation, is the use of ingenuity and imagination to provide unique solutions to problems.

● Innovation allows creative ideas to be turned into products and/or processes that benefit organizations and their customers.

● Highly innovative organizations tend to have supportive cultures, strategies, structures, staffing, and top management.

● The possible barriers to innovation in organizations include a lack of top management support, excessive bureaucracy, short time horizons, and vested interests.

What are the challenges of organizational change?

● A change agent is someone who takes leadership responsibility for helping to change the behavior of people and organizational systems.

- Managers should be able to spot change opportunities and lead the process of planned change in their areas of work responsibilities.

- Although organizational change can proceed with a top-down emphasis, inputs from all levels of responsibility are essential to achieve successful implementation.

- The many possible targets for change include organizational tasks, people, cultures, technologies, and structures.

How can planned organizational change be managed?

- Lewin identified three phases of planned change: unfreezing — preparing a system for change; changing — making a change; and refreezing — stabilizing the system with a new change in place.

- Good change agents understand the nature of force-coercion, rational persuasion, and shared power change strategies.

- People resist change for a variety of reasons, including fear of the unknown and force of habit.

- Good change agents deal with resistance positively and in a variety of ways, including education, participation, facilitation, manipulation, and coercion.

- The special case of technological change requires an openness to resistance and willingness to improvise as implementation proceeds.

What is organization development?

- Organization development (OD) is a comprehensive approach to planned organization change that uses principles of behavioral science to improve organizational effectiveness over the long term.

- OD has both outcome goals, with a focus on improved task accomplishment, and process goals, with a focus on improvements in the way people work together to accomplish important tasks.

- The OD process involves action research wherein people work together to collect and analyze data on system performance and decide what actions to take to improve things.

- OD interventions are structured activities that are used to help people work together to accomplish change; they may be implemented at the individual, group, and/or organizational levels.

How do you build career readiness in a change environment?

- What happens in your career is up to you; take responsibility for building and maintaining a competitive "brand called 'you.'"

- Take charge of your learning; create a career portfolio that documents at all times your career readiness by displaying critical skills and accomplishments.

- Use the insights, examples, and concepts from *Management 6/E* and your introductory management course as a strong foundation for life-long personal development and career advancement.

KEY TERMS

Action research (p. 391)
Career portfolio (p. 394)
Change agent (p. 383)
Changing (p. 386)
Creativity (p. 378)
Force-coercion strategy
(p. 386)
Innovation (p. 379)

Learning organization
(p. 378)
OD interventions (p. 392)
Organization development
(OD) (p. 390)
Performance gap (p. 384)
Planned change (p. 384)

Rational persuasion
strategy (p. 387)
Refreezing (p. 386)
Shared power strategy
(p. 387)
Unfreezing (p. 385)
Unplanned change (p. 384)

SELF-TEST 18

Take this test much as you would in a normal classroom situation. It is a good way to check your basic comprehension of chapter material. Answers may be found at the end of the book.

MULTIPLE-CHOICE QUESTIONS:

1. In organizations, both product innovation, creating new goods or services, and _____ innovation, creating new ways of doing things, are important. (a) content (b) process (c) quality (d) task

2. The first step in product innovation is _____. (a) idea creation (b) initial experimentation (c) feasibility determination (d) final application

3. In an innovative organization, _____ support(s) innovation. (a) strategy and culture (b) structure (c) top management (d) all of these.

4. A manager using a force-coercion strategy will rely on _____ to bring about change. (a) expertise (b) reference (c) rewards, punishments, or authority (d) information

5. The most participative of the planned change strategies is _____. (a) force-coercion (b) rational persuasion (c) shared power (d) command

6. Trying to covertly influence others, offering only selective information, and/or structuring events in favor of the desired change are ways of dealing with resistance by _____. (a) participation (b) manipulation and cooptation (c) force-coercion (d) facilitation

7. In organization development (OD), both _____ and _____ goals are important. (a) task, maintenance (b) management, labor (c) outcome, process (d) profit, market share

8. Sensitivity training and role negotiation are examples of organization development interventions at the _____ level. (a) individual (b) group (c) systemwide (d) organization

9. The concept of empowerment is most often associated with the _____ strategy of planned change. (a) market-driven (b) rational persuasion (c) direct forcing (d) normative-reeducative

10. Unfreezing occurs during the _____ step of organizational development. (a) diagnosis (b) intervention (c) evaluation (d) termination

TRUE-FALSE QUESTIONS:

11. According to consultant Peter Senge, today's leaders and managers should create "learning" organizations. T F

12. The management of innovation involves supporting both invention and application. T F

13. Managers fulfill their responsibilities for change leadership by accepting the status quo. T F

14. Successful change in organizations occurs only in bottom-up and never in top-down fashion. T F

15. Unplanned change can be good for organizations. T F

16. Successful technological change often involves improvisation and adjustments during the change process. T F

17. Organization development (OD) is a short-run approach to improving organizational effectiveness. T F

18. Organizations always require outside consultants in order to continue with organization development. T F

19. The confrontation meeting is an OD intervention to improve organizational effectiveness. T F

20. In a changing environment there is little anyone can do to maintain career readiness. T F

SHORT-RESPONSE QUESTIONS:

21. Identify and explain the importance of three internal targets for organizational change.

22. What are the three phases of change described by Lewin, and what do they mean?

23. What are the major differences in potential outcomes achieved by managers using the force-coercion, rational persuasion, and shared power strategies of planned change?

24. What does the statement "OD equals planned change *plus*" mean?

APPLICATION QUESTION:

25. As a newly appointed manager in any work setting, you are liable to identify things that "could be done better" and to have many "new ideas" that you would like to implement. Based on the ideas presented in this chapter, how should you go about effecting successful planned change in such situations?

THE CAREER
READINESS
WORKBOOK

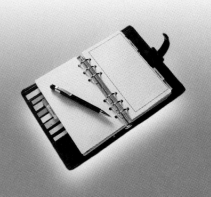

Cases for Critical Thinking

Chapter/Case	Overview	Cross-References and Integration
1. *Coca-Cola*	Describes the challenges and decisions Coca-Cola has made in entering and building foreign markets and expanding its international base.	competitive advantage, international management, social responsibility, strategic management, leadership
2. *Saturn*	Explains General Motors' efforts to reinvent the manner in which automobiles are assembled, with an emphasis on employee/management cooperation based on an incentive-based reward system.	historical foundations of management, organizational design and work systems, human resource management, motivation and rewards, individual performance and job design
3. *Netscape*	Analyzes the evolution and development of a legendary Silicon Valley startup, in addition to confronting new challenges from Microsoft for domination in the Internet browser market.	dynamic new workplace, planning, strategic management, leading, innovation and change management
4. *Harley-Davidson*	Describes the Harley corporate culture and international business strategies in addition to increasing competition from a host of imitators in the large-bike market.	competitive advantage, global economy, strategic management, leading, innovation and change
5. *Eastman Kodak*	Describes Kodak's difficulties in meeting international competition from Fuji in addition to the challenges a manager faces in trying to change a strong corporate culture.	competitive advantage, strategic management and entrepreneurship, leading, teams, change management
6. *Tom's of Maine*	Introduces Tom Chappell's personal views of ethical business behavior and social responsibility and their application to his personal care products company.	decision making, entrepreneurship, human resource management, leading, motivation and rewards, communication and interpersonal skills, teams
7. *Wal-Mart*	Provides a discussion of Wal-Mart's "grand strategy" for the next decade as the largest retailer in the world attempts to continue its spectacular growth.	information and decision making, strategic management, human resource management, motivation and rewards, communication, teams
8. *Nucor*	Describes Nucor's decentralized organization structure and how the firm substitutes incentive-based reward systems for levels of management control.	historical foundations, planning, controlling, human resource management, teams
9. *United Parcel Service*	Examines United Parcel Service and their commitment to customer service by examining its sophisticated control.	information and decision making, planning, organizing, innovation and change
10. *AT&T*	Looks at the difficulties AT&T has experienced in moving from a regulated monopoly to an extremely competitive marketplace for communication services.	dynamic new workplace, global economy, strategic management, leading, innovation and change

Chapter/Case	Overview	Cross-References and Integration
11. *Price Waterhouse/ Coopers & Lybrand*	Analyzes the mega-merger between the two accounting firms and suggests consequences for the accounting/consulting industry.	competitive advantage, global economy, communication and interpersonal skills, teams, change
12. *Ben & Jerry's*	Identifies the human resource management policies Ben and Jerry employ to gain acceptance and commitment of improved quality among its workforce and examines competitive consequences of this stance in the premium ice cream market.	ethical behavior and social responsibility, strategic management, leading, motivation and rewards, communication, change
13. *Duke Basketball*	Examines Duke basketball coach Mike Krzyzewski's no-nonsense approach to leadership, while exploring issues of motivation and commitment.	ethical behavior, human resource management, motivation and rewards, communication, teams and teamwork
14. *Black Entertainment Television*	Chronicles Robert Johnson's rise from poverty to the head of the largest African-American cable company in America.	ethical behavior and social responsibility, planning, organizing, communication and interpersonal skills, innovation
15. *Boeing*	Describes the role top management plays in the communication process at Boeing as the firm attempts to radically alter the way in which it manufactures planes.	historical foundations, planning, controlling, organizational design, teams, change
16. *Southwest Airlines*	Describes the unique corporate culture at Southwest Airlines and the ways in which management motivates its employees as well as the motivational problems the airline faces as it continues to expand.	dynamic new workplace, competitive advantage, historical foundations of management, strategic management, leading, teams
17. *Steinway Piano*	Examines Steinway's unique approach to craftsmanship in the design and production of its world-famous concert pianos.	strategic management, controlling, individual performance and job design, innovation
18. *Disney/ABC*	Follows the evolution of Walt Disney from a small production company into one of the largest integrated entertainment firms in the world today.	dynamic new workplace, competitive advantage, planning, strategic management, leading, communication

Integrative Learning Activities

Integrative Activity	Suggested Book Parts	Cross-References and Integration
1. In-Basket Exercise	Useful in all parts	A leadership in-basket exercise requiring participants to make and justify decisions while integrating insights from the entire management process. Useful applications in all book parts.
2. Cross-Functional Integrated Video Case	Useful in all parts	A cross-functional text and video case that examines the experience of Outback Steakhouse in entering new markets and adjusting strategies, structures, and operations in a highly competitive environment. Useful applications in all book parts.

Exercises in Teamwork

Exercises	Suggested Chapter	Cross-References and Integration
1. My Best Manager	1 The Dynamic New Workplace	management history, ethics, strategic management, leading, motivation, communication, career readiness
2. What Managers Do	1 The Dynamic New Workplace	planning, organizing, leading, controlling, career readiness
3. Defining Quality	2 Environment and Competitive Advantage	management history, strategic management, work systems, leading
4. Leading Through Participation	3 Information Technology and Decision Making	leading, teams and teamwork, communication, conflict, negotiation
5. What Would the Classics Say?	4 Historical Foundations of Management	organizing, human resource management, leading, motivation, rewards
6. The Great Management History Debate	4 Historical Foundations of Management	organizing, human resource management, leading, motivation, rewards
7. What Do You Value in Work?	5 Global Dimensions of Management	motivation, rewards, diversity, management history
8. Confronting Ethical Dilemmas	6 Ethical Behavior and Social Responsibility	decision making, planning, leading, human resource management, career readiness
9. Beating the Time Wasters	7 Planning — To Set Direction	managerial activities and skills, strategic management, individual performance
10. Personal Career Planning	7 Planning — To Set Direction	managerial skills, learning, strategic management, career readiness
11. Strategic Scenarios	8 Strategic Management and Entrepreneurship	planning, controlling, leading, managerial skills, communication, organizational design, innovation
12. The MBO Contract	9 Controlling — To Ensure Results	planning, strategic management, leading, communication, managerial skills
13. The Future Workplace	10 Organizing — To Create Structures	competitive advantage, global economy, strategic management, organizational design, innovation

Exercises	Suggested Chapter	Cross-References and Integration
14. *Dots and Squares Puzzle*	11 Organizational Design and Work Processes	creativity, innovation, decision making, teams and teamwork
15. *Interviewing Job Candidates*	12 Human Resource Management	communication, conflict, negotiation management skills
16. *Work vs. Family — You Be the Judge*	12 Human Resource Management	new workplace, motivation, rewards, individual performance, organizational design, job design, ethics, social responsibility
17. *Compensation and Benefits Debate*	12 Human Resource Management	competitive advantage, decision making, motivation, rewards, individual performance
18. *Sources and Uses of Power*	13 Leading — To Inspire Effort	managerial activities and roles, management skills, communication, conflict, strategic management
19. *Empowering Others*	13 Leading — To Inspire Effort	organizing, managerials activities and roles, management skills, human resource management, communication, motivation
20. *Gender Differences in Management*	13 Leading — To Inspire Effort	diversity, culture, subcultures, perception, attribution, individual performance
21. *Why Do We Work?*	14 Motivation and Rewards	diversity, culture, management history, organizing, job design, individual performance, job design
22. *The Case of the Contingency Workforce*	15 Individual Performance and Job Design	human resource management, organizing, ethics, social responsibility, motivation, rewards
23. *The "Best" Job Design*	15 Individual Performance and Job Design	organizing, human resource management, motivation, rewards, teams and teamwork
24. *Upward Appraisal*	16 Communication and Interpersonal Skills	human resource management, managerial activities and roles, management skills, controlling, leading, career readiness
25. *Feedback and Assertiveness*	16 Communication and Interpersonal Skills	leading, planning, controlling, human resource management, managerial activities and roles, management skills, career readiness
26. *How To Give, and Take, Criticism*	16 Communication and Interpersonal Skills	managerial activities and roles, management skills, leading, planning, controlling, human resource management, career readiness
27. *Work Team Dynamics*	17 Teams and Teamwork	decision making, organizational design, job design, communication, conflict, negotiation, leading
28. *Lost at Sea*	17 Teams and Teamwork	decision making, communication, conflict, negotiation, perception, leading
29. *Creative Solutions*	18 Innovation and Change Management	information processing, perception, entrepreneurship, strategic management, managerial skills, planning
30. *Force-Field Analysis*	18 Innovation and Change Management	decision making, information processing, strategic management, perception

Management Skills Assessments

Assessment	Suggested Chapter	Cross-References and Integration
1. *A 21st-Century Manager?*	1 The Dynamic New Workplace	career readiness, environment, information systems, global economy, leading
2. *Which Organizational Culture Fits You?*	2 Environment and Competitive Advantage	culture, strategic management, organizational design, job design, leading
3. *Decision-Making Biases*	3 Information Technology and Decision Making	teams and teamwork, communication, perception
4. *What Are Your Managerial Assumptions?*	4 Historical Foundations of Management	leading, perception, motivation, rewards, controlling
5. *Cultural Attitudes Inventory*	5 Global Dimensions of Management	diversity, management skills, perception, communication, leading
6. *Global Readiness Index*	5 Global Dimensions of Management	diversity, culture, leading, perception, management skills, career readiness
7. *Diversity Awareness*	6 Ethical Behavior and Social Responsibility	culture, leading perception, management skills, career readiness
8. *Your Intuitive Ability*	7 Planning — To Set Direction	decision making, perception, strategic management, management skills
9. *Time Management Profile*	7 Planning — To Set Direction	management skills, controlling, communication, conflict
10. *Entrepreneurship Orientation*	8 Strategic Management and Entrepreneurship	management skills, entrepreneurship, strategic management, perception, communication, leading, innovation
11. *Internal/External Control*	9 Controlling — To Ensure Results	perception, management history, leading, information processing
12. *Organizational Design Preference*	10 Organizing — To Create Structures	organizational cultures, management history, motivation, perception, diversity, culture
13. *Performance Appraisal Assumptions*	12 Human Resource Management	communication, perception, conflict, decision making, leading, management skills
14. *"T-P" Leadership Questionnaire*	13 Leading — To Inspire Effort	management skills, management history, communication, perception, teams and teamwork
15. *"T-I" Leadership Style*	13 Leading — To Inspire Effort	management skills, learning, new workplace, communication, teams and teamwork, innovation
16. *Least Preferred Coworker Scale*	13 Leading — To Inspire Effort	motivation, perception, management skills, communication
17. *Two-Factor Profile*	14 Motivation and Rewards	management history, perception, job design, culture, human resource management
18. *Job Design Preference*	15 Individual Performance and Job Design	motivation and rewards, culture, perception, diversity
19. *Conflict Management Styles*	16 Communication and Interpersonal Skills	leading, human resource management, teams and teamwork

Assessment	Suggested Chapter	Cross-References and Integration
20. *Facts and Inferences*	17 Teams and Teamwork	decision making, information processing, perception, planning
21. *Stress Self-Test*	18 Innovation and Change Management	individual performance, organizational design, human resource management, communication, ethics, environment, career readiness

Research and Presentation Projects

Projects	Suggested Book Parts
1. *Diversity Lessons — What Have We Learned?*	Part 1 — Management Today
2. *Corporate Culture — Can It Be Changed?*	Part 1 — Management Today
3. *Foreign Investment in America — What Are the Implications?*	Part 2 — Context
4. *Corporate Social Responsibility — What's the Status?*	Part 2 — Context
5. *Entrepreneurship — Is It for You?*	Part 3 — Mission
6. *Total Quality Management — Is It Working?*	Part 3 — Mission
7. *Re-engineering — Does It Work?*	Part 4 — Organization
8. *Affirmative Action — Where Do We Go from Here?*	Part 4 — Organization
9. *Fringe Benefits — Can They Be Managed?*	Part 4 — Organization
10. *CEO Pay — Is It Too High?*	Part 5 — Leadership
11. *Managing Your Boss — "Possible or Not?"*	Part 5 — Leadership
12. *Self-Managing Teams — How Good Are They?*	Part 5 — Leadership
13. *Virtual Teams — Does Groupware Work?*	Part 5 — Leadership

CAREER ADVANCEMENT PORTFOLIO

David S. Chappell and John R. Schermerhorn, Jr.
Ohio University

[Note: An online version of this section with all referenced Internet links is available at the Management 6/E web site at <http://www.wiley.com/college/scherman6e>.]

What Is a Career Advancement Portfolio?

A **Career Advancement Portfolio,** or CAP, is a paper or electronic collection of documents that summarizes your academic and personal accomplishments in a way that communicates effectively with academic advisors and potential employers. The purpose of a CAP is twofold—academic assessment and career readiness.

1. *Academic Assessment Goal* The CAP serves as an ongoing academic assessment tool that documents your learning and career readiness throughout your university stay. As you progress through a curriculum, the portfolio depicts the progress you are making in acquiring the skills and competencies necessary to be successful in lifelong career pursuits. Over time, it will become increasingly sophisticated in the range and depth of capabilities and accomplishments that are documented. A well-documented CAP is a very effective way of summarizing your academic achievements in consultation with both faculty advisors and professors.

2. *Career Readiness Goal* The CAP serves as an important means of communicating your resume and credentials to potential employers as you search for internship and full-time job opportunities. Here, the portfolio evolves into an effective career tool that offers insight far beyond the standard resume. Potential employers can readily examine multiple aspects of your accomplishments and skill sets in order to make a desired match. A professional and complete CAP allows potential employers to easily review your background and range of skills and capabilities. It may convey your potential to a much greater depth and with a more positive impression than a traditional resume. There is no doubt that a professional and substantive CAP can help set you apart from the competition and attract the interest of employers.

What Goes into a Career Advancement Portfolio?

A CAP should document, in a progressive and developmental manner, your credentials and accomplishments as they build throughout your academic career. As you progress through the curriculum in your major and supplementary fields of study, the CAP should be refined and materials added to display your most up-to-date skills, competencies, and accomplishments. The closer you get to graduation, the entries in your CAP should become more specific to your job and career goals. In this way, your personal CAP becomes a dynamic and evolving career tool with value far beyond that of the standard resume.

In Chapter 1, for example, the CAP created and maintained by Ronald Larimer, a student at Ohio University, was introduced at <http://www.wiley.com/college/scherman6e>. Ronald began his CAP early in his junior year and has since used it successfully to pursue internship and full-time job opportunities. His CAP includes a very professional resume that documents his program of study, leadership activities, work experiences, and his special computer skills. In addition, Ronald's portfolio includes an actual sample of his skills at computer programming, his use of spreadsheet and database software, his writing skills in the form of a one-page executive memorandum and a research report, and even an Excel data analysis and a PowerPoint presentation. These are just a few examples of the many different types of materials that you can consider for inclusion in your personal CAP.

The supplementary resource materials available with *MANAGEMENT 6/E* support the development of your personal CAP in either paper or electronic versions. In both cases, the basic portfolio consists of (1) a professional resume and (2) a compendium of coursework samples that display your skills and capabilities.

Paper Portfolio

The easiest way to organize a paper portfolio is with a three-ring binder. This binder should be professional in appearance and have an attractive cover page that clearly identifies it as your CAP. The binder should be indexed with dividers that allow a reader to easily browse the resume and other materials to gain a complete view of your special credentials. To help you get started with a paper portfolio, the following sections offer a sample resume as well as examples of coursework materials that other students have placed in their CAPs. Also, you can download a resume template in Microsoft Works 97 format from the *MANAGEMENT 6/E* web site at <http://www.wiley.com/college/scherman6e>.

Electronic Portfolio

In today's age of information technology and electronic communication, it is highly recommended that you develop an online or electronic CAP. A Career Advancement Portfolio in this format allows you to communicate easily and effectively through the Internet with employers offering potential internship and job placements. An online version of your CAP can be displayed either on your personal web site or on one provided by your university. Once you have created an electronic portfolio, it is easy to maintain. It is also something that will impress reviewers and help set you apart from the competition. At the very least, the use of an electronic CAP communicates to potential employers that you are a full participant in this age of information technology. Easy-to-use instructions and templates for building your personal and electronic CAP are available on the *MANAGEMENT 6/E* web site, at <http://www.wiley.com/college/scherman6e>.

Note: *The annotations indicate positive reactions by a prospective employer to the information being provided.*

[*Web site support for building your personal resume is provided at <http://www.wiley.com/college/scherman6e>*]

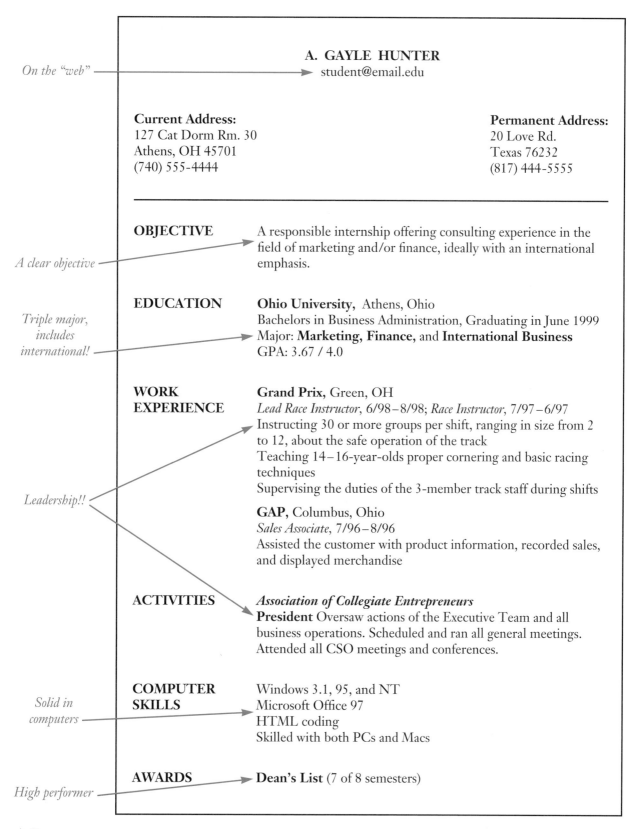

A. GAYLE HUNTER
student@email.edu

On the "web"

Current Address:
127 Cat Dorm Rm. 30
Athens, OH 45701
(740) 555-4444

Permanent Address:
20 Love Rd.
Texas 76232
(817) 444-5555

OBJECTIVE

A responsible internship offering consulting experience in the field of marketing and/or finance, ideally with an international emphasis.

A clear objective

EDUCATION

Ohio University, Athens, Ohio
Bachelors in Business Administration, Graduating in June 1999
Major: **Marketing, Finance,** and **International Business**
GPA: 3.67 / 4.0

Triple major, includes international!

WORK EXPERIENCE

Grand Prix, Green, OH
Lead Race Instructor, 6/98–8/98; *Race Instructor,* 7/97–6/97
Instructing 30 or more groups per shift, ranging in size from 2 to 12, about the safe operation of the track
Teaching 14–16-year-olds proper cornering and basic racing techniques
Supervising the duties of the 3-member track staff during shifts

GAP, Columbus, Ohio
Sales Associate, 7/96–8/96
Assisted the customer with product information, recorded sales, and displayed merchandise

Leadership!!

ACTIVITIES

Association of Collegiate Entrepreneurs
President Oversaw actions of the Executive Team and all business operations. Scheduled and ran all general meetings. Attended all CSO meetings and conferences.

COMPUTER SKILLS

Windows 3.1, 95, and NT
Microsoft Office 97
HTML coding
Skilled with both PCs and Macs

Solid in computers

AWARDS

Dean's List (7 of 8 semesters)

High performer

Executive Memorandum

Professional format

MEMORANDUM

Date:
To: Professor Chappell
From:
Re: MGT300 Internet Report on Novell, Inc.

**Novell:
The
Networking
Company**

Novell is the world's leading network software provider. Novell makes possible the connected enterprise, bringing structure to the Internet to make it a serious business tool. Novell empowers customers to take charge of the changes brought on by the proliferation of the Internet and intranets.

Novell software solutions include server-operating environments, network applications, and distributed network services. These solutions enable businesses of all sizes to integrate the diverse information resources within their organizations and to access the global Internet. Businesses deploy Novell networks to make more efficient use of information technology, improve customer service, and enhance communication and collaboration both internally and with customers, partners, and suppliers.

Incorporated in 1983, Novell helped create the local-area network (LAN) market by delivering the first server-based software ~~ducts to connec~~ ~~rsonal comp~~ ~~~~

Clear, easy to understand

Good written expression!

Written Assignment in French

**La Conception
de L'Amour
Pendant toute
L'Histoire**

La conception de l'amour pendant toute l'histoire est tres interresant de voir. Pendant l'histoire, les formes de l'amour ont change un peu, mais l'idee le plus de base reste la meme. Dans les ouvrages au XVIeme siecle, on peut trouver les idees de l'amour qui sont semblable a la conception de l'amour dans notre societe moderne. Avec un comparaison entre la poesie de Louise Labe et Ronsard au XVIeme siecle, et le film Indochine, que Regis Wargnier a realise a 1992, on peut voir la conception de l'amour pendant l'histoire.

Pour bien comprendre la comparaison de l'amour entre le film moderne est les ouvrages au XVIeme siecle, on doit savoir un petit resume du film. La guerre a Indochine n'arretait pas pour le francais jusqu'a le mai, 1954. Pendant cette periode, une fille

Second language skill!!

Special International Virtual Teamwork Project

Shows high initiative!

In my management course I volunteered for a special assignment called the "International Virtual Teamwork Project." Through this experience I learned about cross-cultural issues in management and had the opportunity to experience the challenges of working as a member of a virtual team. The instructor's description of the project completed by my international virtual team follows.

Project Overview and Deliverables

Experienced with groupware

This project requires extra effort to participate in an *international virtual team*. The virtual team will be mediated by the Lotus Notes Domino software located on the College of Business server. Students from each participating university will form into 4–5 person teams. Each team will complete a "domestic" project (Part A) and then participate in an "international" comparison project working with a team from the other university (Part B). A final report will be created by each pair of teams working together. The same final report will be submitted for grading by the Ohio University and Bangkok University instructors. The final report will also be posted on the course website.

Part A— "Domestic" Comparisons

1. At the end of each part of *Management* by Schermerhorn, there are sets of self-assessment instruments. Your first task is to reach agreement with your counterpart team at the other university on a set of 5 assessments which you will both work with from the following list.

Self awareness— GOOD

- What are your managerial assumptions?
- Your intuitive ability.
- Time management profile.
- Organizational design preference.
- "TT" leadership style.
- Least preferred coworker scale.
- Conflict management styles.

2. Working individually, each member of the two teams should individually complete the self-assessments according to textbook instructions. Each member should then have the same set of assessments completed by five additional students who are not part of the management class.

3. Results from #2 should be entered into an Excel spreadsheet and analyzed to provide descriptive statistics that compare (a) differences between team members and the additional students, as well as (b) differences among team members. These results should be summarized in well-chosen tabular and graphical forms suitable for Power Point presentation.

Can handle Excel! and PowerPoint

4. Team members should discuss results, identify insightful patterns in the data and summarize findings in a 1–2 page single-spaced memorandum addressed to the instructor.

Part B— "International" Activities

Cross-cultural awareness

1. Teams from each university should share their results in Part A with their counterpart team at the other university. They should compare both the data and interpretations for each

Nice design choices →

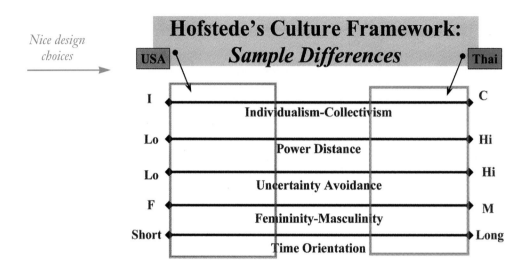

Hofstede's Culture Framework:
Sample Differences

USA		Thai
I	Individualism-Collectivism	C
Lo	Power Distance	Hi
Lo	Uncertainty Avoidance	Hi
F	Femininity-Masculinity	M
Short	Time Orientation	Long

"T-T" LEADERSHIP

Shows good presentation skills →

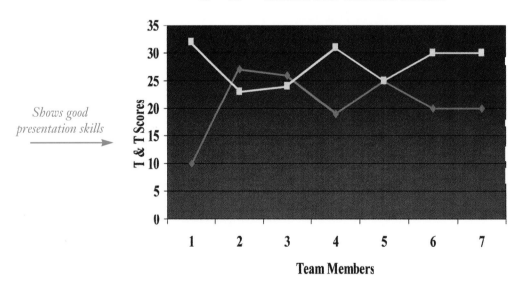

Spreadsheet Analysis

Group Member

Sample No.	Manage. Assump.		Your Intuitive Ability			Time Management	TT Leadership	
	X	Y	A	B	A+B		Transform	Transact.
1	5	3	4	3	7	6	28	22
2	6	4	3	5	8	6	27	23
3	3	5	5	6	11	8	33	17
4	6	6	3	2	5	6	26	24
5	2	5	4	3	7	4	29	21
Average	4.40	4.60	3.80	3.80	7.60	6.00	28.60	21.40
Std. Diviation	1.82	1.14	0.84	1.64	2.19	1.41	2.70	2.70

Additional Students

Shows ability to work with data →

Sample No.	Manage. Assump.		Your Intuitive Ability			Time Management	TT Leadership	
	X	Y	A	B	A+B		Transform	Transact.
1	5	6	4	5	9	6	19	31
2	5	5	4	4	8	9	28	22
3	2	6	4	3	7	8	30	20
4	1	6	4	3	7	6	28	22
5	4	3	3	6	9	7	26	24
6	2	5	4	2	6	9	29	21
7	3	3	3	3	6	6	28	22
8	2	4	4	1	5	6	23	27
9	4	6	3	4	7	6	25	25
10	5	6	2	3	5	5	28	22
11	6	5	4	3	7	7	31	19
12	5	6	4	3	7	8	30	20
13	2	7	4	3	7	6	30	20
14	3	5	2	3	5	8	27	23

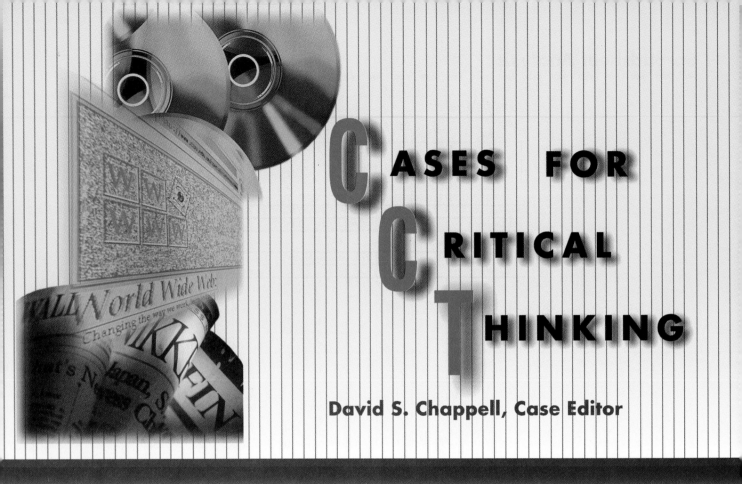

CASES FOR CRITICAL THINKING

David S. Chappell, Case Editor

CASE 1

The Coca-Cola Company: A Global Presence

As one of the world's best-known brands, Coca-Cola* has endured some important changes in the latter half of the 1990s. Its CEO of 17 years, Roberto Goizueta, passed away in October 1997 of lung cancer. During Mr. Goizueta's tenure at Coca-Cola, the company's market value dramatically increased from $4 billion in 1981 to nearly $150 billion. This makes him one of the greatest value creators in history. Former chief financial officer Douglas Ivester was appointed as his replacement. The question on many investors' minds is can Mr. Ivester continue Coke's incredible pace in the global soft drink market?

Coca-Cola's Global Dominance

The larger a company is, the harder it is to continue to grow at a steady pace. This was the major challenge facing the Coca-Cola Company in the mid-1990s. The U.S. market had already been

well developed, with an average of 296 8-ounce servings of Coke products consumed by every man, woman, and child annually.[1] But the company had not introduced a major new product in nearly 10 years. Demand for diet drinks— the fastest growing soft drink category of the 1980s—had leveled

off, and demand for cola-flavored drinks had begun to decrease.[2] According to a former Coke executive, "The problem was that Diet Coke was driving the engine and everybody was living off that."[3]

Meanwhile, the competition had not been sleeping. Pepsi was

*Note: The blue underscored words/phrases in the cases indicate Internet links provided in the online versions. See the *MANAGEMENT 6/E* website at http://www.wiley.com/college/scherman6e.

test marketing a colorless cola, Crystal Pepsi, in response to consumers' interest in clear flavored waters and seltzers. It had also come out with a new advertising campaign and slogan. Neither company appeared to be particularly concerned about competition from other soft drink manufacturers. However, consumers were drinking more and more new types of beverages, and traditional juice companies such as Very Fine and Ocean Spray had begun to package their products in single-serving cans in addition to the traditional bottles or juice boxes. Snapple, owned by Quaker Oats, developed a new process for bottling tea that required no preservatives and expanded its product line from juices into seltzers and other natural sodas.[4]

Roberto Goizueta recognized the problem. He challenged now company president Douglas Ivester, to rejuvenate the Coke brand. Under Ivester's direction, Coke's advertising agency was given the freedom to develop different messages and marketing campaigns aimed at different groups of consumers. Previously, Coke had been advertised with a single theme and image, which was intended to appeal to everyone. Ivester also rehired Sergio Zyman as head of marketing. This surprised many people since Zyman had been largely responsible for "New Coke," a reformulation of Coca-Cola with a new taste that was designed to compete more closely with Pepsi but had proved highly unpopular among Coke drinkers.

Zyman led the introduction of new packaging—the plastic contour bottle, based on Coke's traditional glass shape.[5] He also emphasized the importance of marketing the product with more than just traditional advertising. One new idea was "fast-lane merchandisers"—coolers of Coke at the end of checkout counters designed to attract people standing in line.[6] The company also signed

an agreement with Rutgers University in New Jersey, paying the school $10 million for 10-year rights to be the exclusive supplier of soft drinks and juices, including vending machines, cafeterias, convenience stores, and student centers.[7] A similar Pepsi contract with Pennsylvania State University was expected to earn Pepsi $14 million over 10 years. In addition to their sales, both companies valued these contracts because they offered the opportunity to reach and influence younger cola drinkers.

The Coca-Cola Company also began to actively develop new products.[8] It introduced Power-Ade, challenging Gatorade in the $1.2-billion sports drink market and promoted it with free samples at the World Cup soccer matches throughout the United States. OK Soda, a lightly carbonated drink was targeted at "Generation Xers," consumers in their late teens and early twenties. The company also developed Fruitopia drinks, mixtures of fruit flavors such as cranberry lemonade, for the alternative beverage market.

CEO Goizueta and president Ivester were also concerned with expanding Coke's international base. In 1993, more than 6.3 billion unit cases of Coke and Coke Classic were sold worldwide in more than 195 countries. Diet Coke, also known as Coke Light, was the number one low-calorie soda in the world, available in 117 countries. However, 80 percent of the 6.3 billion unit cases was sold in only four markets, all English speaking. Fanta was the only global brand in orange sodas, available in 170 countries, and Sprite, available in 168 countries, was the fifth-largest selling brand in the world. Coke was also the largest marketer of juice and juice drink products in both the United States (with such brands as Minute Maid and Hi-C) and the world. However, Goizueta felt that there was still room to grow.

To manage the scope of its business, the company is divided into two soft drink business sectors, the North America Business Sector and the International Business Sector. The North America Business Sector is made up of Coca-Cola USA, which operates in the United States; Coca-Cola Ltd., which is responsible for soft drink operations in Canada; and Houston-based Coca-Cola Foods, which produces and markets juices and juice drinks.

The International Business Sector is divided into four operating groups, each of which is responsible for a geographic region of the globe. The Greater Europe Group manages the countries of the European Union, Central and Eastern Europe, Scandinavia, and the former Soviet Union. The Latin America Group oversees Mexico and Central and South America; the Middle and Far East Group manages the countries of the Pacific and the Middle East. The Africa Group is responsible for sub-Saharan Africa.

Traditionally, the Coca-Cola Company's main technique for entering and building foreign markets was through independent bottlers, to whom it sold its "secret formula" in the form of syrup or concentrate. However, this meant relying on the local bottlers to distribute and market Coke products. Soon after he became CEO, Goizueta was asked by John Hunter, his regional manager in the Philippines, to consider becoming an active partner in the Philippine bottler, which had been neglecting Coke and concentrating on the beer it bottled. Coke invested $13 million to become the controlling partner in a joint venture with the bottler. Goizueta and his managers made this their model for international expansion. When entering a new market, the company would seek to establish distribution of Coke products in key population centers and develop relationships with the important retail channels. It would look for "well-capitalized business partners with local know-how and visibility." The workforce would come from the local area and would be extensively trained and eligible for promotion.

These strong, experienced partner companies helped Coke move quickly into Eastern Europe in the 1990s. On one tour, Goizueta attended the opening of plants in Prague (with anchor bottler Coca-Cola Amatil of Australia), Warsaw (with anchor bottler Ringnes of Norway), and Bucharest. When the United States ended its trading ban with Vietnam in 1994, Coca-Cola had already signed a joint venture agreement for at least two plants and was prepared to start operations within weeks. Coke reentered the market in India in late 1993, having left the country many years earlier when the Indian government pushed for local ownership. This time, Coke formed a strategic alliance with Parle Exports, a local company with its own soft drink brands and a network of 60 bottling plants. The company saw India's 896 million people and fast-growing middle class as a significant growth opportunity. Coke also began a joint venture with the Swiss Company Nestle to produce and market canned coffee and tea drinks.

Coke's Continued International Expansion

The Coca-Cola Company is the global soft drink industry leader. Every day in 1994, consumers enjoyed an average of more than 773 million servings of Coca-Cola (known as Coca-Cola Classic in the United States and Canada), Diet Coke (known as Coca-Cola Light in some countries), Sprite, Fanta, and other products of the Coca-Cola Company. Syrups, concentrates, and beverage bases for Coca-Cola, the company's flagship brand, as well as other company soft drinks are manufactured and sold by the Coca-Cola Company and its subsidiaries in more than 195 countries around the world.[9;10]

One of Ivester's first threats as CEO was the currency crisis across Southeast Asia in late 1997. Rather than view the situation as a setback, the new chairman saw it as an opportunity to bolster its business in these areas. The strength of the dollar against other major currencies is a primary concern because Coke receives 80 percent of its profit from overseas—15 percent to 17 percent from Japan alone. Coca-Cola learned from the peso crisis in Mexico in 1994 and used that situation to build its business there and now has a market share in Mexico much larger than it was in 1994. Ivester's decision to restructure Coca-Cola's global bottling system by lashing together hundreds of small bottlers into a handful of well-capitalized "anchor" bottlers with strong local ties and distribution systems is paying off handsomely.[11]

In a continued sign of its global emphasis, in December 1997 Coca-Cola signed an agreement to purchase the Orangina brands and four bottling and concentrate plants in France from Pernod Ricard SA for a price of $700 million. This action represents both Coke's and Pepsi's expansion of their soft drink brands beyond colas. With its addition of Surge and Citra, Coke is acknowledging the movement of the U.S. market away from colas (72 percent in 1990 to 64 percent in 1996), with the fastest-growing brands now including Sprite, Mountain Dew, and Dr. Pepper.[12]

Review Questions

1. What are the management functions performed by Mr. Goizueta, Mr. Hunter, and Mr. Ivester? How do their responsibilities differ?
2. Describe the changes in Coca-Cola's environment when Mr. Goizueta became CEO and after his death.
3. How has the Coca-Cola Company changed to adapt to its environment?

CASE 2

Saturn: A New Kind of Car

Saturn, the General Motors car division that brought new production and marketing concepts to American car manufacturers, faces tough questions in an increasingly competitive global market. Its reliance on a limited offering of compact models hurts its performance in the face of declining sales. Can it continue to set the standards for customer satisfaction and reliability without delivering consistent profits?

The Saturn Story

Jack Smith Jr., appointed CEO and president of General Motors Corporation in 1992 after a revolt of the outside members of the board of directors, noted that the firm had turned around its losing ways by focusing on its customers. In a speech to auto dealers in Michigan, he cited the success of the Saturn Division of GM for setting the standard for "hassle-free purchasing and services, and . . . exceeding customer expectations." Smith further noted that this success had led to the addition of a third shift at the Spring Hill, Tennessee, complex that produced Saturns. Moreover, Saturn dealers continued to lead all dealer organizations in the United States in unit sales per outlet.[1]

The original plan, developed in 1982, was given to Richard LeFauve, who was named president of Saturn Corporation after its first president died shortly after the company was set up. The plan called for a $5 billion investment in a series of plants that would produce up to 350,000 cars per year. By 1988, when the plant was just about completed, the investment had been trimmed to approximately $3 billion.

The Saturn complex was comprised of a series of six interconnected buildings. Four of the six buildings were manufacturing and assembly plants. The remaining two were a maintenance and utilities facility and a training and administration building. The complex had a rated production capacity of 240,000 cars per year. This was to be expanded to 310,000 with the addition of a third shift in 1993.

The Saturn Corporation was the first new automotive division of General Motors since 1918. The purpose of developing a new division was to meet the competition of the Japanese, particularly at the lower end of the product line.[2] GM had seen its share of the U.S. market fall throughout the 1970s. This was especially true for lower-priced cars. U.S. auto consumers no longer had confidence in the ability of GM to be able to produce a low-priced, high-quality car. Roger Smith, then CEO of GM, felt that the only way to overcome this perception was to launch an entirely new line of cars. The technology, labor policies, work rules, and marketing of this new product were to be developed from scratch; there would be no preconceived notions concerning any of these areas brought in from the existing organization structure or culture.[3]

The initial phase of planning for the Saturn Corporation was carried out by bringing together managers and workers from 55 plants in 17 GM divisions. The "Group of 99"—so named because it consisted of 99 United Auto Workers (UAW) members, GM mangers, and staff personnel—started meeting in 1984.[4] The group quickly split into separate research teams to study all aspects of the new operation. One of the teams realized that labor relations would be a critical factor in the development and implementation of a successful new offering. GM entered into separate negotiations with the UAW to develop a new contract strictly for the Saturn Corporation.

The rest of GM was covered by a master contract with the United Auto Workers, which covered not only wages, benefits, and hours of work but also a complex series of work rules that restricted GM's ability to transfer workers from one task to another on the production line. GM felt that the effectiveness of the new Saturn Corporation would be dependent on more flexible work rules. Management wanted the ability to develop the kind of work flexibility found in most Swedish and Japanese auto plants. The UAW finally agreed to a system of self-governing work teams on the production line at the Saturn assembly plant. These teams would be designed to follow the construction of an automobile unit throughout the entire assembly line. Under the terms of the contract, workers would be cross-trained so that the members of each team could switch off on the various tasks required to complete the assembly of each individual unit.

Saturn uses a "risk-and-reward system" that puts 12 percent of a worker's pay at risk, contingent on the following:

1. 5 percent risk on quality—a threshold, measured in reduction of sample defects per vehicle, that must be met before the reward portion, which also contains a quality goal, can kick in;
2. 5 percent risk on training; and
3. 2 percent risk on team skills.

All Saturn workers are paid at a rate equal to 88 percent of average GM compensation. The 12 percent at risk brings pay "up to a line" roughly equal with industry averages, with the reward portion providing possibilities "above the line."[5] The basis for the reward portion contains provisions regarding schedules, productivity, and quality. Saturn uses the Uniform Vehicle Evaluation system, an international standard in which auditors enter the plant and select 20 to 25 cars at random and evaluate these for sample defects.[6] With the American public's present loss of appetite for small cars, the system may need to be revamped for cost reduction rather than output. In early 1998, the Saturn union voted to retain the innovative system, 4,052 in favor with 2,120 opposed.[7]

In many ways, this was similar to the assembly process employed by Volvo at some of its auto plants, which had led to increased quality, decreased boredom, and increased job satisfaction on the part of its workers. Each member of the Saturn work team was put through an extensive training program before joining the assembly line. The 350 hours of training were designed to cover both technical and team-building aspects of the job.

Richard LeFauve was selected as the new president of Saturn Corporation because of his experience within GM. He had spent two years in charge of GM's Adam Opel unit in Germany, where he had supervised the development of a sporty new Kadett model. Moreover, LeFauve had gained experience with the German labor-management system. Under German codetermination laws, labor is required to have a say in decision making, and management is required to grant labor a position on the board of directors. This, it was felt, would give LeFauve better insight into the problems that might develop as the new labor contract was implemented.

GM management sought and developed new technology and machinery consistent with the new labor agreement. A great many robots and other forms of automation were incorporated into the production line to help reduce employee boredom and fatigue and to help ensure high quality standards. Furthermore, company engineers developed a platform that was designed to move along with the car. In this manner, workers no longer needed to walk at a steady pace beside the car to be able to complete their tasks; instead, workers and the car moved together on the new platform.

The new organization was built around several key factors. They included the following:

- Quality as a top priority
- Ownership by all
- Equality of all
- Total trust
- People orientation
- Union-management partnership
- Authority commensurate with responsibility

These factors were put to the test in 1991. Unfortunately, the results of the first year of operation indicated that the Saturn plant would not meet its goals. Under the terms of the Saturn/UAW contract, workers could suffer penalties that would mean their salary would equal approximately 80 percent of the average GM worker's annual wages. There was concern that the workers would find this unacceptable since some of the failure was not their fault. Furthermore, there had been quality lapses in the initial products. While many had been caught and corrected before the autos left the plant, other cars had to be recalled. All of these factors led to lower production, productivity, and quality standards than had originally been planned for the first year.

Management decided to share the responsibility for falling short of the first-year goals. It relaxed the terms of the contract and essentially granted bonuses that brought Saturn salaries to approximately 95 percent of an hourly worker's average annual wage. Management hoped this would convince the workers that the company planned to live up to the seven key points outlined earlier.

It was still unclear, however, whether the Saturn cars being sold were replacing Japanese sales or cars that would have been sold by other GM units. Moreover, GM management realized that sales of Saturn cars could not possibly recoup the original $3 billion investment in the new unit. They would have to be able to transfer the ideas, technology, concepts, and labor relations developed for the Saturn plants to other parts of the GM organization to make the investment worthwhile.

To compound problems, the new workers that were being added to the Saturn workforce were being recruited from closed GM plants, under an agreement with the UAW. These new workers were being rushed onto the production line with only one-third the training time of the original Saturn workers. Many managers and original members of the Saturn union felt that these two factors might reduce morale at the Saturn complex and could lead to a decline in the quality standards that had contributed to the success of this unit. Both Smith and LeFauve knew that the continued growth and quality of the Saturn projects and service would be key factors in the success of GM as a whole.

Saturn's Future

The Saturn story has been one of alternating success and failure in the 1990s. IntelliChoice ranked the 1997s L1, SL2, SC1, and SC2 models as the "Best Overall Values" in their respective classes. J.D. Power put Saturn in first place for sales satisfaction and seventh in customer satisfaction. (The top six were all luxury cars—Lexus, Infiniti, Acura, Mercedes-Benz, Cadillac, and Jaguar.)

At the same time, the competition in the 1998 small car market is increasing dramatically. Experts claim that Saturn's limited lineup is holding back sales, with the car company only offering a coupe, sedan, and wagon—all small cars based on the same architecture and looking pretty much the same. Saturn is bringing a new midsize car on line in 1999 and is expected to add a sport-utility vehicle in 2001.[8] Because of these limitations, Saturn has been forced to reduce prices on its 1998 models by as much as $300, even though prices had been mostly unchanged from its 1997 lineup.[9]

New initiatives include an attempt to open foreign markets, with Japan targeted with 80 dealerships. In addition, GM wants Saturn to market its electric vehicle, the EV-1.[10] Mike Bennett, head of the UAW Local 1853 at Saturn, states, "We're going to be a 100-year car company, right? Well, if we're going to be a 100-year car company, we need to be a learning organization."[11]

Review Questions

1. Describe the changes that GM is trying to implement at Saturn Corporation.
2. What are the critical factors in developing the management of the Saturn Corporation plants?
3. What problems might GM management face in trying to transplant the Saturn concept to other GM units?

CASE 3

Netscape: Taking on Goliath

n early 1995, with the World Wide Web still new to most people, Netscape was just another Silicon Valley startup in danger of heading down the road to oblivion. With its $12 million in seed money running out, cofounders James Clark and Marc Andreesson laid off a dozen workers, froze hiring, and hoped new chief executive officer Jim Barksdale, having served previously with AT&T and Federal Express, had some fresh ideas. Vice president Richard Schell recalled: "Jim walked in the door and said, 'This rocket is going to take off, or it's going to crash into the ground. So, ladies and gentlemen, strap it on!'"[1]

The decision was historic; as the Web took off in 1995, so did Netscape Communications. It's sales for its first full year of operations in 1995 hit $81 million, a faster rise than any software company in history. Just 16 months after its founding, Netscape's initial public offering (IPO) in August 1995 turned a company with only $20 million in sales and no profit into a Wall Street darling with a market capitalization of $2 billion. By 1996, the firm employed over 2,000 people and earned $21 million on sales of $346 million. The firm's milestones have been impressive, to say the least.[2]

In this business, a year's worth of change happens in a couple of months, a phenomenon known as "Internet Time." Over 50 million copies of Netscape's popular Internet browser were distributed in two years, making it the number two program in the world, right behind Windows. While Microsoft's founder Bill Gates originally was slow to react to the Internet, he has now focused a daunting amount of Microsoft's resources behind the development of his own browser, Internet Explorer, first introduced in August 1995. Since then, Gates has integrated the browser into his Windows operating system, a move that has allowed Microsoft to capture roughly 50 percent of the browser market.[3]

In the Beginning

Shortly after meeting and forming the company in April 1994, Clark and Andreesson visited the National Center for Supercomputing Applications at the University of Illinois. Within days, they hired nearly the entire team that developed Mosaic, the first user-friendly Web browser. Having completed the first version of

Navigator in the next few months, Andreesson insisted that the company release a new version of the product every six months, an almost unheard of pace.[4]

To get the product to market as quickly and as widely as possible, Andreesson proposed another revolutionary idea—give the browser away free over the Web (the way Mosaic had been distributed). On October 14, 1994, just six months after Netscape began, a free test version of Navigator was posted on the Netscape Web site. By the spring of 1995, 6 million copies had been downloaded.[5] This new distribution medium not only had profound effects on Netscape but portended huge changes in the computer software business itself.

Today, Netscape still gives away trial copies of its browser but is still able to generate 51 percent of its revenue from browser sales. In addition, with over 4 million visitors every day to its Web site, the Netscape home page is the most sought after advertising space on the Web, generating millions of dollars in fees. The pace at the company is so fast it utilizes what it calls "surround-sound" management: An issue is identified, key people assemble, and a decision is concluded in about 20 minutes.[6]

With Success Comes Competition

Although Netscape was largely alone in developing the Web browser market, it did not take long for Microsoft to take notice and react with its own browser offering—Microsoft Internet Explorer. In 1996, Microsoft spent $750 million to acquire or invest in 20 Internet-related companies. Caught off guard at the start, Gates now claims that the Internet is driving everything at Microsoft.[7] Other firms, including IBM/Lotus with its Lotus Notes offering, only add to the competitive fever driving the industry.

This is a problem with many Internet upstarts; their initial success attracts the attention of more experienced and more capitalized rivals. Amazon.com was an early and successful provider of online books, but Barnes and Noble is entering Internet commerce in competition with Amazon. Kevin Landis, manager of the Technology Leaders Fund in San Jose, California, says that the key to the success of many early movers is to remain on the cutting edge. "As soon as innovation slows down, they are playing a game the Goliaths have been playing for a long time. There are going to be companies along the way that get crushed in the process."[8] Additional Internet companies including Cybercash, Spyglass, and CompuServe have suffered as increased competition erodes their profits.

Another problem with Netscape is its drive to evolve beyond a one-product company. Its decisions to enter groupware and Email for intranets force it to compete with the likes of Microsoft and IBM. Bill Gates is particularly critical of Netscape's decision to enter the groupware market: "IBM has decided this market is strategic, meaning they are willing to take noneconomic returns, hoping it will help them imagewise or marginwise in other businesses. Microsoft has decided that Exchange [its Email product] is 'strategic.' This means we are willing to take noneconomic returns. So you'd call this space hypercompetitive between IBM and Microsoft. It is kind of surprising to have somebody else come along and say, "Oh, yeah, me too.'"[9]

Can Netscape Survive?

Microsoft's entry into the browser market has not been without controversy. Its decision to link its Explorer browser into its Windows operating system caused the Justice Department to launch an inquiry into the practice, an investigation that eventually resulted in Microsoft backing down from this strategy. However, with massive advertising behind its product offerings, Microsoft can outspend Netscape at every turn.

Microsoft's new version of Explorer is designed to give users almost seamless integration between the World Wide Web and the user's PC hard disk. By bundling its browser into its market-dominant Windows operating system, Microsoft is pushing a multitude of corporate partners, including Disney, Time Warner, Pointcast, and others through the use of an "Active Desktop" control panel or "dashboard."[10] The feature makes it possible to reach these and other popular Internet locations with a single mouse click.

Netscape's legacy to the computer software market will remain regardless of whether or not it survives as an independent entity. More than any other company, Netscape pioneered downloading software on the Web, a practice that today is followed by every major software provider. Netscape continues to attempt to reinvent itself—it is investigating the possibility of turning its online site into a web "portal" brimming with links to many content-driven amenities available at other providers.[11]

Netscape's Netcenter is the second most-visited site on the Web, with 23.1 million discrete users, behind Yahoo.com with 31.3 million. Microsoft's home site, in comparison, receives 17.9 million users. This strategy attempts to capitalize on the realization that Internet activity clusters around a few major hubs.[12] In addition to advertising, Netscape receives payments from search engine companies licensing positions on its Web site. The Netscape home page generated $18 million in fees in the first nine months of 1996 alone.[13]

To stay competitive, Netscape must continue to innovate into new product offerings and new market niches. Having popularized the Web through the development of its landmark browser, can the firm stay ahead of the increasingly competitive marketplace? Many Netscape fans are starting to ask if the company that seemed destined for an Oracle-like future is more likely to end up like Borland, once a key Microsoft competitor but now known mostly as the great disappointment.[14]

Review Questions

1. What was Netscape's impact on the Internet in particular and the business community in general?
2. Can Netscape survive as an independent entity?
3. Can Netscape continue by giving away its primary product?

CASE 4

Harley-Davidson: The Harley Way of Life

Brought back from near death, Harley-Davidson Motorcycles represents a true American success story. Reacting to global competition, Harley has been able to reestablish itself as the dominant maker of big bikes in the United States. However, success often breeds imitation, and Harley faces a mixture of domestic and foreign competitors encroaching on its market. Can it meet the challenge?

Harley-Davidson

When Harley-Davidson was founded in 1903, it was one of over 100 firms producing motorcycles in the United States. The U.S. government became an important customer for the company's high-powered, reliable bikes, using them in both world wars. By the 1950s, Harley-Davidson was the only remaining American manufacturer.[1]

But British competitors were beginning to enter the market with faster, lighter-weight bikes. Honda Motor Company of Japan began marketing lightweight bikes in the United States, moving into middleweight vehicles in the 1960s. Harley initially tried to compete by manufacturing smaller bikes but had difficulty making them profitably. The company even purchased an Italian motorcycle firm, Aermacchi, but many of its dealers were reluctant to sell the small Aermacchi Harleys.[2] American Machine and Foundry Co. (AMF) took over Harley in 1969, expanding its portfolio of recreational products. AMF increased production from 14,000 bikes to 50,000 bikes per year. This rapid expansion led to significant problems with quality, however, and better built Japanese motorcycles began to take over the market. Harley's share of its major U.S. market—heavyweight motorcycles—fell to 23 percent.[3]

In 1981, a group of 13 managers bought Harley-Davidson back from AMF and began to turn the company around. Richard Teerlink, CEO of Harley since 1987, joined the company that year as chief financial officer. He described the problem the new management faced: "The problem was us. The problem was the guys in the white shirts and ties." He explained that "our solution was to get back to detail. The key was to know the business, know the customer, and pay attention to de-tail."[4] The key comments in this process were increasing quality and improving service to customers and dealers. Management kept the classic Harley style and focused on the company's traditional strength—heavyweight and super-heavyweight bikes. Once Harley's quality image had been restored, the company slowly began to expand production. The company made only 280 bikes per day in January 1992, increasing output to 345 by the end of the year. Despite increasing demand, production was scheduled to reach only 420 per day, approximately 100,000 per year, by 1996.[5]

The popularity of the motorcycles continued to increase throughout the 1980s. The average Harley purchaser was in his late thirties, with an average household income of over $40,000. Teerlink didn't like the description of his customers as "aging" baby boomers: "Our customers want the sense of adventure that they get on our bikes. . . . Harley-Davidson doesn't sell transportation, we sell transformation. We sell excitement, a way of life."[6] Managers participated in this lifestyle, many riding their bikes to work and participating in rallies.[7] The company built on the enthusiasm of its customers by creating the Harley Owners Group (H.O.G.). H.O.G. members receive a bimonthly magazine, emergency road service, Harley rental programs for trips, and opportunities to meet and ride with other Harley owners.

Although the company had been exporting motorcycles ever since it was founded, it wasn't until the late 1980s that Harley-Davidson management began to think seriously about international markets. Traditionally, the company's ads had been translated word for word into foreign languages. Now, ads were developed specifically for different markets, and rallies were adapted to fit local customs. In 1993, a branch office of H.O.G. was set up in Frankfurt, Germany, to serve European owners and fans. According to Wilke, "As the saying goes, we needed to think global but act local."[8]

The company also began to actively recruit and develop dealers in Europe and Japan. It purchased a Japanese distribution company and built a large parts warehouse in Germany to support its European operations.[9] The bikes proved to be as popular abroad as in the United States. Japanese owners ranged from middle-aged men who had first seen Harleys ridden by American soldiers just after World War II, to younger riders who were intrigued by the mechanics or the American image. It was an expensive interest, with bike prices overseas ranging up to $25,000.[10] Foreign dealers were just as enthusiastic as their customers. At the ninetieth birthday rally, the general manager of a chain of Harley-Davidson dealerships in Greece summed up his feelings about his product: "You can own a Suzuki or a Kawasaki, but you can only love a Harley. It's the only bike you can develop a relationship with."[11]

Harley-Davidson continued to look for ways to expand its activities. On a biking tour in Europe, Wilke realized that German motorcyclists rode at high speeds, often more than 100 mph. As a result, the company began to study ways to give Harleys a smoother ride. It also began to emphasize accessories that would give riders more protection.[12] The company also created a line of Harley Motor Clothes, available through dealers and a catalog, all adorned with the Harley-Davidson logo. These jackets, caps, T-shirts, and other items became popular with nonbikers as well. In fact, the clothing and parts had a higher profit margin than the motorcycles; nonbike products made up as much as half of sales at some dealers.

Despite pressure from customers and dealers, Harley-Davidson's top management resisted the temptation to expand at a faster pace. Teerlink explained that, although the company had looked into manufacturing overseas, "our customers are buying a piece of the American dream. Overseas manufacturing just wouldn't work for them."[13] The company reaffirmed its long-term strategic objectives: to be number one in consumer satisfaction in the United States and abroad, to develop the ability to produce and market more than 100,000 units per year by 1996, and to support those sales with parts, accessories, and merchandise.[14]

International Efforts

Harley continues to make inroads in overseas markets. Important events include a joint venture it has launched with Porsche AG of Stuttgart, Germany, in which they will "source and assemble powertrain components for use in potential new motorcycle products."[15] Also noteworthy is the June 23, 1997, announcement that Jeffrey L. Bleustein had taken over as Harley-Davidson's president and CEO. Richard Teerlink remained the chairman.[16]

One interesting area of development is Japan. Harley-Davidson Japan KK estimates that 51,000 of its bikes can be found on the roads and that that number is increasing rapidly. One event assisting this rise is the government's removal of a restriction that required drivers to pass a stringent National Police Agency examination for bikes over 401 cc. Drivers now must pass only a local driving school test. The next step in promoting Harleys will be to persuade the police to permit two to ride on a bike on highways, a practice that is presently illegal. As a result of these initiatives, Harley-Davidson expects 50,000 new large motorbike licenses to be granted in 1997, almost double that of a year before.[17]

Harley motorcycles are among America's fastest-growing exports to Japan. Japanese bikers bought 4,387 Harleys from January through August 1997, up 27 percent from a year before. To rev up sales, Harley's Japanese subsidiary is obsessing over details by customizing its marketing approach to Japanese tastes. Harley also offers shinier and more complete tool kits than those offered in the United States.[18]

Harley bikes have long been considered symbols of prestige in Japan. Before World War II, they were built under a licensing arrangement by a small company called Rikuo. Toshiaki Iijima, 56, the president of a construction company, has shelled out $54,000 on his 1340-cc red Ultra Classic Electric Glide, including $28,000 for a sidecar to help him keep his balance. Consistent with their U.S. counterparts, many Japanese enthusiasts see themselves as rebels on wheels.

Success Breeds Imitation

A handful of new U.S. motorcycle manufacturers are trying to catch a ride with Harley-Davidson's "Made in America" craze. With Harley-Davidson's control of 47 percent of the domestic market for heavyweight machines (chrome-laden cruisers, aerodynamic rocket bikes mostly produced by the Japanese, and oversize touring motorcycles), its dominance remains secure. However, with manufacturers such as Big Dog Motorcycles, Polaris Industries and Excelsior-Henderson starting to produce larger bikes, Harley's success is certainly stimulating new ventures.[19]

Industry analyst Don Brown of DJB Associates estimates that the U.S.-retained sales of street bikes will exceed 231,000 in 1997, up 44 percent since 1991. Worldwide, heavyweight motorcycles represent a $4.8 billion market. Harley has been steadily increasing production, from 118,000 bikes in 1996 to 131,000 in 1997, with a new production plant on the way as well.[20]

Big Dog represents the high end, building customized bikes that run upward of $22,000 each, compared to $16,000 for a Harley. Its 55 employees will turn out about 300 bikes in 1997. Polaris, a $1.2 billion snowmobile manufacturer, is aiming its $12,500 Victory at its present all-terrain vehicle and personal watercraft consumers. Excelsior is providing the Super X, due out in 1998, for between $16,000 to $20,000, with an annual capacity of 20,000 motorcycles produced in its Belle Plaine, Minnesota, plant. It remains to be seen what impact these new producers will have on Harley.[21]

Review Questions

1. Describe Harley-Davidson's international business strategy. Would you consider Harley to be a multinational corporation?

2. If you were Harley's top management, in which regions of the world would you consider expanding?

3. Evaluate Harley-Davidson's decision not to produce overseas. What would be the advantages of overseas production? What problems might the company encounter if it does manufacture abroad?

Eastman Kodak: A Company in Transition

When Eastman Kodak Company appointed a new CEO in October 1993, the company's top management expected him or her to turn the 113-year-old company around. Morale among employees and managers was low. The company's core business—photographic products—was potentially threatened by digital imaging, but no one seemed sure how to deal with this new competition. Further, the company had borrowed heavily to finance the purchase of Sterling Drug, Inc., in 1988, which it had not yet fully integrated. One of the biggest challenges facing new CEO George Fisher, however, was how to turn around the company's attitude to make it as innovative and cost competitive as it had been until the 1970s.

Kodak in Transition

The hiring of a new CEO, the first from outside the company, was not the first attempt top management had made to change Kodak's direction; there had been no less than *five* major restructuring programs in the previous decade. In 1990 top managers had developed a strategic direction plan to determine how Kodak could make the transition to the new digital technologies. The strategy had never been implemented, however, because, as a former manager described it, "People thought that it was too big a risk, that we didn't have the skills to succeed."[1] Instead, Kay Whitmore, CEO at the time, concentrated on restructuring and trying to solve short-term problems.

New CEO Fisher praised the company's brand and products. "Kodak has a great franchise, and my hope is to build on that to get exciting growth," he said.[2] Fisher started not with extensive cost cutting but by emphasizing the opportunities facing the company. In his previous position as CEO of Motorola, Fisher had managed this mix of efficiency and technology-based growth and had understood that concentrating on lower costs by eliminating expenses or jobs could actually make Kodak's problems worse. He quickly sold Sterling Drug and the household prod-

ucts division and paid off much of the company's debt. He then focussed attention on Kodak's traditional film products, created a separate digital technology division, and concentrated on changing the company's culture.

Two of Fisher's complaints were that decision making was too slow and that people were afraid to take risks. He attributed part of the problem to the company's previous management style: "It was so hierarchically oriented that everybody looked to the guy above him for what needed to be done. . . . You have a different mental attitude when you drive for growth. You don't just try to figure out how to manage your way through existing markets."[3] Fisher wanted to encourage employees at all levels to take more responsibility. To overcome the rigid hierarchy, he made himself visible and accessible. He ate breakfast in the company cafeteria and personally answered Email messages from employees.

1983 With profits lagging, Eastman Kodak Co. laid off 3,100 employees; another 5,000 took a buyout plan.

1986 Kodak said it would reduce its workforce by 10 percent, or 12,000.

1988 Kodak bought Sterling Drug for $5.1 billion, the biggest move yet in its efforts

to diversify during the 1980s. Kodak earned a record $1.4 billion for the fiscal year.

1989 Consolidation during the year eventually led to the departure of 6,000 workers.

1991 Kodak eliminated 3,000 jobs, primarily in its business information divisions.

1993 Kodak said in January it would cut 2,000 jobs and reduce R&D spending. In August, CEO Kay Whitmore was fired because he had failed to act to cut debt. Weeks later, the company said it would lay off 10,000 workers by 1995. George Fisher was named chairman, chief executive, and president in October.

1994 In May, Fisher announced plans to concentrate on the film and camera business, selling other units.

1995 Fisher cut 4,000 jobs but stopped short of a major restructuring.

January 1997 Kodak said it would cut 3,900 jobs over the next 18 months, mainly in Europe and Latin America.

November 1997 Under price-cutting pressure from Fuji Film, Kodak said it would eliminate 20,000 jobs to help cut costs by $1 billion.

Source: Columbus Dispatch, November 12, 1997, G1.

Fisher stressed the issue of accountability among his managers. "How can you hold a person accountable when you've had three overrides on his decision?" he asked.[4] He worked with executives to help them set realistic goals during the annual planning process. It was up to the executives to work out how to reach those goals, but Fisher emphasized that they would be held responsible for achieving them. He planned to provide further incentives with a plan linking managerial pay to performance. One area in which Fisher's new approach has already produced results is in the film division. Consumers appeared to have developed new patterns, taking pictures at different times and for different reasons. Fisher personally picked a team to address this challenge. Members came from manufacturing, as well as consumer research and sales. None were executives, but top management insisted that team members be allowed to take as much time as they needed from their "real" jobs to focus on this issue. Their goal was to understand why customer demand was changing and to develop products to serve this new market.

The team discovered that many customers want quality pictures of special events, such as birthdays, weddings, and graduations. For these occasions, the price of the film is not as important as the quality of the prints and enlargements. By using new technologies, the team was able to develop professional quality film for this "special occasion" market segment. It also developed the manufacturing process and the marketing campaign. The new product, Royal Gold film, was an immediate success. Betty Noonan, a team member whose "real" job is United States marketing manager for film, described the process as "wonderful and painful." She was enthusiastic about the team's ability to define a new product and make it come to life. But she acknowledged that it was also painful because "it was risky . . . I was afraid our strategy would be useless by the time we were finished."[5]

Just one year after Fisher's appointment, the company had already produced a number of new products. In addition to new film and improved single-use cameras, Kodak had created one-stop photo print centers where customers could make copies and enlargements directly from pictures. Shifting its emphasis from film to imaging, Kodak has made technology a centerpiece of its new strategy, as evidenced by the firm's foray into digital cameras and digital imaging. However, in many departments, decision making remains slow, and some employees are still confused about Kodak's strategic direction. Kodak's core businesses of amateur film, photographic paper, and cameras continue to generate half its profits.[6] Although Kodak continues to push digital technology, its 1997 projected loss in digital photography is $400 million.

Fuji's Onslaught

One area for concern is the continued inroads that Tokyo-based FujiFilm has made in the U.S. market, particularly in the core area of film. Using aggressive pricing, Fuji has successfully captured 20 percent of the American market—while it continues to dominate its home market back in Japan. Kodak charged Fuji with unfair practices and claimed that it keeps Kodak out of its home Japanese photography markets. This claim was formalized in 1996 when the U.S. government requested that the World Trade Organization (WTO) resolve the dispute. In late 1997, the WTO ruled against Kodak, leaving the firm with a large number of difficult decisions.

The immediate problem for Kodak is its inability to compete in a new global marketplace. Daniel Carp, Kodak's COO, argues that "It's not our intention to lead prices downward in the U.S. market, but we're not going to allow that value gap to open up and rise to levels that we saw this [1997] summer.[7] Another problem in late 1997 was the strength of the dollar against the yen. The weakening yen, having moved from 80 to 125 to the dollar, provided Fuji with a tremendous pricing advantage.

When Fisher arrived at Kodak, he attempted to apply the same principles of high technology that had served him so well at Motorola. However, Fuji's market share has moved from 14 percent in 1996 to 19.4 percent in 1997; conversely, Kodak has only 10 percent of the picture-taking Japanese market. Fuji is making these gains by pricing their film up to 30 percent below Kodak's and their sales per employee are twice that of Kodak. While Fisher contends that he has made significant cuts at Kodak, Wall Street is pressing him to lay off as many as 20,000 of Kodak's 94,800 employees and cut $1 billion from its $4.5 billion in annual expenses.[8]

Critics complain that Fisher refuses to address Kodak's basic internal problems: a corporate culture caught in a mind-set left over from an earlier manufacturing age and excessive costs.[9] Much of the trouble is that Kodak's move into the digital arena forces it to confront more nimble competition such as Canon and Hewlett-Packard. The biggest test for Fisher's digital strategy comes in 1998 when he'll unveil the core product—a global network of digital printing stations or kiosks called Image Magic.[10]

Confronted with Fuji's competition, Kodak faces more layoffs. Fisher is cutting 10,000 more jobs in an effort to save $1 billion in costs. In addition to the reduction in workforce, Kodak is reducing its 1998 R&D budget of $1 billion by $100 to $150 million, much of it in the digital arena. Whether this is drastic enough remains to be seen. As *U.S. News and World Report* magazine put it, "Before Fisher can enjoy any Kodak moments, he's going to have to slog it out one yellow box at a time."[11]

Review Questions

1. What strategy has Kodak adopted to enter the global arena?
2. How has Kodak reacted to its global competition?
3. An October 20, 1997, *Business Week* cover story asked the question "Can George Fisher Fix Kodak?" How would you respond to that question?

Tom's of Maine: Not Your Average Toothpaste

Tom's of Maine represents one of the first natural health care companies to distribute their product beyond the normal channels of health food stores. While it continues to grow, the owners, Tom and Katie Chappell, continue to emphasize the values that got them started over 28 years ago. The question becomes, can a small firm stay true to its founding principles and continue to grow in a fiercely competitive environment?

Tom's of Maine

For its first 15 years, Tom's of Maine looked a lot like many other new businesses. It was started in 1970 by Tom and Katie Chappell, two people with an idea they believed in and felt others would also buy into, and financed by a small loan. Like many business start-ups, the company's first product was not successful. Its phosphate-free detergent was environmentally friendly but, according to founder Tom Chappell, "it didn't clean so well."[1] Consumers did appear to be interested in "green" or environmentally friendly products, however, and the fledgling company's next products, toothpaste and soap, were more successful.

All Tom's of Maine products were made with all-natural ingredients and packaged using recycled materials whenever possible. New personal care products, including shampoo and deodorant, were developed while avoiding the controversial practice of animal testing.[2] This refusal caused Tom's to have to wait seven years and shell out about 10 times the usual sum to get the American Dental Association's seal of approval for its fluoride toothpastes.

In 1992, Tom's deodorant accounted for 25 percent of its business. Chappell reformulated the product for ecological reasons (replacing petroleum with vegetable glycerin), but the new formulation "magnified the human

bacteria that cause odor" in half its customers. After much agonizing, Chappell ordered the deodorant taken off the shelves at a cost of $400,000, or 30 percent of the firm's projected profits for the year. Dissatisfied consumers were sent refunds or the new product, along with a letter of apology.

Tom's of Maine recovered from this experience, but founder Tom Chappell was not happy. The company's products were a success in health food stores, and Chappell was beginning to think in terms of national distribution. He had hired a team of marketing people who had experience at major companies. At the same time, he felt that something was missing; he was "tired of creating new brands and making money.[3]"

One pivotal event was the introduction of a baking soda toothpaste. The product was gritty and didn't have the sweet flavor typical of commercial toothpastes, and the marketing manager told Chappell, "In all candor I don't know how we're going to sell it."[4] Chappell insisted that the product be test marketed. It proved to be a best seller and was quickly copied by Arm and Hammer and Proctor and Gamble.[5] It also appeared that a new product's sales potential had become more important to the company than the qualities of the product itself. "We were working for the numbers, and we got the numbers. But I was confused by success, unhappy with success" said Chappell.[6] He later wrote, "I

had made a real go of something I'd started. What more could I do in life except make more money? Where was the purpose and direction for the rest of my life?"[7] As a result of this line of thinking in the fall of 1986 the successful businessman Tom Chappell entered Harvard Divinity School.[8]

The years that Chappell spent as a part-time student at the Divinity School brought him to a new understanding of his role. "For the first time in my career, I had the language I needed to debate my bean-counters" he explained.[9] He realized that his company was his ministry. "I'm here to succeed. But there's a qualifier. It's not to succeed at all costs, it's to succeed according to my principles."[10]

One tangible result was a mission statement for the company. This document spelled out the values that would guide the company in the future. It covered the types of products ordered and the need for natural ingredients and high quality. It also included respect for employees and the need for meaningful work as well as fair pay. It pointed out the need to be concerned with the community and even the world. Finally, it called for Tom's of Maine "to be a profitable and successful company, while acting in a socially responsible manner."[11] Some of the company's programs were the result of decisions made by top management. The company began donating 10 percent of its pretax profits to charities ranging from art organizations to environmental groups. These included funds donated to state and local curbside recycling programs and a pledge of $100,000 for the Rainforest Alliance.

The company also urged its employees to get involved in charitable causes. It set up a program that allowed employees to donate 5 percent of their work time to volunteer activities. Employees enthusiastically took advantage of the opportunity. When one employee began teaching art classes for emotionally disturbed children, others became interested, until almost all of the company's employees were involved.[12] One tangible result was a cardboard totem pole, which decorated the corporate hallways.[13] Other employees worked in soup kitchens and homeless shelters. Employees formed their own teams to work on projects or used the company's matching service. Tom's even created the position of "vice president of community life."

The volunteer program did have its costs, however. Other employees had to pitch in to cover volunteers' absences, which amounted to the equivalent of 20 days a month. However, Colleen Myers, the VP of community life, felt that the volunteer activities were valuable to the company as well as the community. "After spending a few hours at a soup kitchen or a shelter you're happy to have a job. It's a morale booster, and better morale translates pretty directly into better productivity."[14] Sometimes the company even benefited directly from these activities. Chappell explained, "The woman who headed up those art classes—she discovered she's a heck of a project manager. We found that out, too."[15]

Employee benefits were not strictly psychological. The company offered flexible four-day scheduling and subsidized day care. Even coffee breaks were designed with employee preferences

in mind, providing them with fresh fruit. The company also worked with individual employees, helping them earn their high school equivalency degrees and develop skills for new positions.[16]

By 1993, Tom's of Maine was moving beyond health food stores and into supermarkets—where 70 percent of toothpaste is purchased—and drugstores. Its products are widely distributed on the East Coast and are moving up the West Coast from California; the brand is carried in 30,000 mass-market outlets nationwide, including Wal-Mart, Katie Sisler, vice president of marketing, felt that the company's marketing strategy was low key. "We just tell them our story. We tell them why we have such a loyal base of consumers who vote with their dollars ever day. A number of trade accounts appreciate our social responsibility and are willing to go out on a limb with us.[17] Tom Chappell agreed: "We're selling a lot more than toothpaste; we're selling a point of view—that nature is worth pro-tecting."[18]

By the mid-1990s, Tom's of Maine was facing increasing competition. Its prices were similar to those of its national competitors for baking soda toothpaste but 20 to 40 percent higher for deodorant and mouthwash. Tom Chappell did not appear worried, however. He felt that "You have to understand from the outset that they have more in the marketing war chest than you. That's not the way you're going to get market share, you're going to get it by being who you are."[19] He explained his philosophy: "A small business obviously needs to distinguish itself from the commodities. If we try to act like commodities, act like a toothpaste, we give up our souls. Instead, we have to be peculiarly authentic in everything we do."[20] This authenticity is applied to both ingredients and advertising decisions. "When you start doing that customers are very aware of

your difference. And they like the difference."[21]

By 1997, total sales approached $20 million. Of its 250 all-natural products, including shampoo, deodorant, and mouthwash, toothpaste still provides the bulk of the sales, with a contribution between $10 million and $12 million. While behemoth Proctor and Gamble produces 250 million tubes of toothpaste annually, Tom's produces 8 million tubes. Nationally, Tom's has grabbed a 0.7 percent market share; in major markets such as New York, Boston, and the Rockies, the company claims the share is between 2 and 3 percent.[22]

In addition, Chappell's message is starting to draw the attention of several Fortune 500 companies. Ralph Larsen, chairman and CEO of Johnson and Johnson (J & J), a $20 billion company with 87,000 employees in 160 subsidiaries, says that Chappell is "charting a new course" and recently invited him to address his top management team at J&J's New Brunswick, New Jersey, headquarters.[23] Robert Reich, former secretary of labor, says, "The debate that sounds as if it's about maximizing shareholder returns versus being socially responsible usually comes down to whether a top manager is paying attention only to very short-term performance or is taking a longer-term view."[24] Arnold Hiatt, former president and CEO of Stride Rite, agrees with Chappell's brand of "common-good capitalism," particularly as it impacts employees. Hiatt now serves as cochair of Business for Social Responsibility, whose 900 member companies include Ben and Jerry's, Home Depot, Levi Strauss, and Reebok.[25]

Interesting Facts

- Chappell's name is pronounced "chapel."
- Tom's of Maine gives away 10 percent of its pretax profits to charities, gives three months' maternity leave, provides

child-care subsidies, and encourages employees to spend 5 percent of their paid work time doing volunteer service— with nearly 80 percent of its employees participating.

- The manufacturing plant is housed in an old converted railway station.
- Toothpaste is mixed in 3,000-pound batches.
- As an 11-year old, Tom served as a model for a Norman Rockwell portrait of a choirboy.

Review Questions

1. Which way of thinking about ethical behavior best describes Tom's of Maine and its founder, Tom Chappell?
2. What potential dilemma did Tom Chappell face in the mid-1980s?
3. How important were Tom Chappell's personal views in helping Tom's of Maine to be successful?

He felt that the traditional format of organization, employee commitment, cost control, carefully planned locations for new stores, and attention to customer needs and desires would enable Wal-Mart to meet Sam's lofty prediction. In addition to its main objectives, Wal-Mart has stayed true to its basic values and beliefs. Its success originated in three fundamental principals: *Respect for the Individual, Service for our Customers*, and *Striving for Excellence*.

Wal-Mart has grown by paying careful attention to its market niche of customers looking for quality at a bargain price. Customers do not have to wait for a sale to realize savings. Many of its stores are located in smaller towns, primarily throughout the South and Midwest. Glass knew that although the traditional geographical markets served by Wal-Mart were not saturated, growth in these areas was limited and any strategy to achieve continuing growth would have to include expansion into the Northeast and the West Coast. It might also have to include new product lines and higher-priced products to allow existing stores to achieve year-to-year sales growth. By mid-1994, the company had a firm base in New England, and it was growing rapidly in the West. The geographical areas Wal-Mart has recently been expanding into have different demographics than those in which the company has traditionally grown. These were large urban areas where entrenched competition was offered by such companies as Kmart and Target.

CASE 7

Wal-Mart: Always the Low Price

Wal-Mart has grown to be the dominant discount merchandise retailer in the United States and is now branching out overseas. It accomplished this feat by locating in primarily small, rural communities—away from competitors. People who put $1,000 into Wal-Mart stock when it went public in 1970 saw that investment grow to nearly $2 million by 1993.[1] The question becomes, can Wal-Mart continue to expand and succeed in an increasingly hostile retail environment?

Out of Arkansas

Wal-Mart was first opened in 1962 by Sam Walton in Bentonville, Arkansas. Since then it has become the largest retailer in the United States, with over 3,300 Wal-Mart stores, and has become the largest online retailer. It has also experienced some of the best customer approval scores in retail history. Wal-Mart employs 728,000 individuals, and in 1996 reached sales of $105 billion dollars. Together Kmart, Target, and Wal-Mart hold over 85 percent of the discount store market share. Despite the death of its founder Sam Walton Wal-Mart continues to be successful. Under his successor, CEO David Glass, the little discount store chain started in Arkansas has become one the largest corporations in the world. It is already on its way to achieving Sam Walton's 1991

prediction of $125 billion sales by the turn of the century.[2]

In his 1990 letter to Wal-Mart stockholders, CEO David Glass laid out the company's philosophy: "We approach this new exciting decade of the '90s much as we did in the '80s—focused on only two main objectives, (1) providing the customers what they want, when they want it, all at a value, and (2) treating each other as we would hope to be treated, acknowledging our total dependency on our associate-partners to sustain our success."[3]

1996 Sales	% of Total
Hard goods (hardware, housewares)	25
Soft goods/domestics	25
Stationery and candy	11
Records and electronics	10
Pharmaceuticals	9
Sporting goods and toys	9
Health and beauty aids	7
Jewelry and shoes	4

Source: Hoovers, 1996

In 1993, the company added the 91-store Pace Membership Warehouse chain, which it had purchased from Kmart.[4] Competition was increasing as smaller regional chains such as Costco and Price Club merged and opened stores in many of the same markets as Wal-Mart.[5] The company began to experiment with one-stop shopping in 1987, when it opened Hypermart* USA, a Wal-Mart/supermarket combination. Wal-Mart is now made up of five retail divisions: Wal-Marts, Wal-Mart Supercenters (Wal-Mart with grocery), SAM's Clubs (membership warehouse clubs), Bud's Discount City (discount warehouse outlets), and an International Division.

Wal-Mart has a lean corporate staff. Its buyers are known as tough negotiators who ascribe to the corporate policy "Buy American whenever possible." The company has set up an extensive control procedure based on a satellite communication system that links all stores with the Bentonville, Arkansas, headquarters. The satellite system is also used to transmit messages from headquarters, training materials, and communications between stores and can even be used to track the company's delivery trucks. In addition, Wal-Mart has an online system with its suppliers. This system has linked Wal-Mart's computer systems with its suppliers. The showroom employees also have "Magic Wands," which are small handheld computers linked by radio frequency to the store's computer terminals. Given that a typical Wal-Mart store contains more than 70,000 standard items in stock, these innovative devices help to keep up-to-the-minute track of inventory, deliveries, and backup merchandise in stock. Because of its innovative technology, Wal-Mart has gained a **competitive advantage** in the speed with which it delivers goods to the customer.

While each new Wal-Mart brings in new jobs, it can also bring detrimental effects to the community as well. A 1991 *Wall Street Journal* article noted that many small retailers are forced to close after Wal-Mart opens nearby.[6] In one Wisconsin town, even J.C. Penny lost 50 percent of its Christmas sales and closed down when Wal-Mart opened up. In an Iowa town, four clothing and shoe stores, a hardware store, a drug store, and a dime store all went out of business. In 1994, the voters in Greenfield, Massachusetts, forced Wal-Mart to withdraw its building plans by using a few simple rules of engagement. It also had to give up plans to build in Bath, Maine; Simi Valley, California; and two towns in Pennsylvania. Vermont successfully resisted all Wal-Mart plans to locate in that state.

Even Wal-Mart's "Bring it home to the USA" buying program produced controversy when an NBC news program found clothing that had been made abroad on racks under a "Made in the USA" sign in 11 stores. In addition, the program showed a tape of children sewing at a Wal-Mart supplier's factory in Bangladesh. Wal-Mart insisted that its supplier was obeying local labor laws, which allowed 14-year-olds to work. A company official had also paid a surprise visit to the factory and had not found any problems. CEO Glass stated that "I can't tell you today that [illegal child labor] hasn't happened someplace, somewhere. All we can do is try our best to prevent it."[7]

Meanwhile, Wal-Mart began considering international expansion. In March 1994, the company bought 122 Canadian Woolco stores, formerly owned by Woolworth Corp. and were the largest single purchase Wal-Mart had ever made.[8] In 1997, Wal-Mart opened six stores abroad, bringing the number of international units to 207, with the largest concentration in Canada followed by Mexico. In addition, Wal-Mart has gone to places such as Brazil, Puerto Rico, San Luis Potosi, Asia, China, Indonesia, and South America.

Even in a global economy the jobs are always local, and the products are "made right here" whenever possible. These international stores reported $5 billion in sales in 1996. Wal-Mart employees now show pride in their company by shouting the Wal-Mart Cheer, which can be heard in many different languages in the many different regions of the world.[9]

Wal-Mart is proud to have various philosophies, called Culture Stories. First, the Sundown Rule means Wal-Mart strives to answer requests by sundown on the day it receives them. Next, the Ten-Foot Attitude promises that if a employee comes within ten feet of a customer the employee must look the customer in the eye and ask if the person would like to be helped. Every Day Low Prices is another philosophy. Wal-Mart believes that by lowering markup, they will earn more because of increased volume, thereby bringing consumers added value for the dollar everyday. Also, customers have been known to send letters to individual associates for giving exceptional service. This is what Wal-Mart calls Exceeding Customer Expectations.

Wal-Mart believes in bringing people from diverse backgrounds together, which is the idea behind the Minority- and Women-Owned Development Program. It helps minority- and women-owned businesses provide goods and services in the retail sector. Wal-Mart knows that cultural diversity translates into customer satisfaction. A key to Wal-Mart's popularity with customers is its hometown identity. People Greeters welcome shoppers at the entrance of each store.

Customer service and community support go hand in hand. Wal-Mart strives to enhance the quality of life in each town in which it operates by implementing community outreach programs, led by local associates living in the town. Also, Wal-Mart has created projects to help the national community as well with such efforts as the Competitive Edge Scholarship Fund, raising funds for the Children's Miracle Network Telethon, raising money and providing manpower for fundraisers benefiting such organizations as the Boy and Girl Scouts, and donating funds from bake sales to benefit charities.

In the past few years, Wal-Mart has made a commitment to the environment in its communities. It recycles over 700,000 tons of cardboard, paper, and plastic each year. Wal-Mart has opened three "EcoStores," which serve as laboratories for ideas that can potentially be used in future stores. These stores are energy efficient and environmentally friendly. The chains' Green Coordinators are knowledgeable about environmental issues and share information with Wal-Mart associates and customers.

Increasing the shareholders' value is very important to the corporation. In their 1997 Annual Report Wal-Mart stated that it had generated over $3 billion in free cash flow, which enabled it to enhance shareholder value.[10] This cash flow increased the dividend by 29 percent while also increasing the size of its share repurchase program. It will also help the company to reach its targeted annual total shareholder return of 15 percent.[11]

This rate of return has been accomplished by cutting inventories by over $2 billion, thereby saving $150 million in interest costs. Overseas expansion added $9.5 billion in sales in 1997, with a profit of more than $100 million.[12] Wal-Mart has an extensive online-shopping site on the Web as well. And Glass has a prototype for a green and white Wal-Mart convenience store on his desk in Bentonville.

Still, the company faces stiff competition from old and new rivals alike. Privately owned Meijers, is one of the 16 fastest-growing companies in the coun-try and the nation's fifth-largest discount retailer. Having enjoyed double-digit annual growth for so long, Wal-Mart now seems ready to admit to a slower (15 percent, versus 25 percent in earlier days) but still profitable growth strategy.[13] Over 100 supercenters, totaling 180,000 square feet in floor space (and generating $65 million in sales on average), are replacing smaller 90,000 square feet ($25 million average sales) Wal-Mart stores, in addition to promoting Wal-Mart's entry into the $450 billion grocery business.[14]

As CEO, David Glass has to determine whether any changes to the organization's style, culture, and structure will be necessary to carry the company to a higher level. In essence, he must decide whether the company's past strategy will allow Wal-Mart to continue to dominate as a retailer into the 21st century. He put it best in the 1997 annual report: "so if anyone wonders where our next $100 billion will come from—it will come from customers who recognize value throughout the world and from our associates who deliver it with a smile."[15]

Review Questions

1. Who are Wal-Mart's major external stakeholders?
2. Do a SWOT analysis of Wal-Mart. What are the company's distinctive competencies?
3. How would you describe Wal-Mart's "Grand" strategy for the next decade? In terms of Porter's generic strategies? In terms of Miles and Snow's adaptive model (see Chapter 9)?

CASE 8

Can Nucor Handle Growth and Control?

Nucor achieved its position as one of the largest steel producers in the United States by carefully monitoring costs and paying attention to the needs of its markets. This strategy of providing its customers with a competitive product at competitive prices has brought Nucor success and growth in sales, income, and stock price. Recently, however, the control of the organization has been brought into question. The recent announcement of a joint venture between Nucor and U.S. Steel to develop, test, and bring on line a new method for turning iron ore into steel added to the concern over the ability of company management to maintain the entrepreneurial spirit for which the company is famous.

Background

Nucor is the second-largest steel producer (second in assets, first in profits) in the United States. Its profits of $123 million have made it one of the most efficient firms in the steel industry. Nucor achieved that position by focusing on the manufacturing segment known as minimills—the relatively small, electrically powered mills that melt down scrap metal to produce steel. This process saves on costly labor, raw materials, and the capital-intensive machinery necessary to produce steel from iron ore. A major concern of minimill steel manufacturers is maintaining quality, since their raw material consists of scrap steel of varying quality and containing a variety of alloys and impurities. Another concern is the recent rising price of scrap steel.

Nucor started out by manufacturing steel for the beams and posts produced in company-owned structural steel manufacturing plants and then expanded by selling its low-cost steel to other firms. Outside customers gradually became the primary outlet for sales by the minimills. Nucor was able to expand sales from the minimills by keeping costs below those of its competitors, both in the United States and abroad. Nucor has consistently sought ways to lower costs while broadening markets. During the latter part of the 1980s, much of the company's efforts focused on developing technology for manufacturing sheet—flat-rolled steel of the type used by automotive and appliance manufacturers—which had traditionally been the sole domain of the Big Steel companies and foreign competitors. Ken Iverson, CEO of Nucor, risked several hundred million dollars in adapting an untested German process for manufacturing this flat steel. Fortunately, the gamble paid off, increasing the company's growth in both sales and profits.

Iverson determined that one means of maintaining both quality control and costs was a highly decentralized organizational structure. Corporate staff was kept to a minimum. All decisions involving operations were delegated to the individual plants. Iverson believed that the managers closest to the action should be given the responsibility to develop plans to allow the plants, and the firm, to adapt to any changes in the environment. Iverson also gave plant-level managers the authority to make and implement the decisions necessary to make these adaptations. Each plant manager gave a brief monthly report to headquarters and received a report comparing the divisions' performance. Major expenditures and changes were made by consensus at the periodic meetings of all plant and corporate managers.

Iverson took pride in Nucor's lean corporate structure. But the lack of corporate staff appeared to become a problem as Nucor expanded. By 1994 the company was operating 16 plants, and the new flat-rolled steel plants increased the diversity of the operations reporting to the president. Nucor president John Correnti noted, "My biggest fear is even though we're now a $3.3 billion company, we've still got to act, feel, and smell like a $300 million company."[1] Some steel industry analysts remained concerned over how Iverson would continue to control the growth of a company that was attempting to diversify its product line.

Iverson is not overly concerned with how Nucor will cope. He delights in highlighting Nucor's seeming incongruities:

- Nucor's 7,000 employees are the best-paid workers in our industry, yet Nucor has the lowest labor cost per ton of steel produced.
- Nucor is a Fortune 500 company with sales in excess of $3.6 billion, yet we have a total of just 22 people working at our corporate headquarters and just four layers of management from the CEO to the frontline worker.
- Nucor operates in a "rust belt" industry that lost one out of every two jobs over a 25-year span, yet Nucor has never laid off an employee or shut down a facility for lack of work, nor have we lost money in any business quarter for more than 30 consecutive years.
- We are in a labor-intensive and technology-intensive business, yet we've built most of our manufacturing facilities in areas that have more cows than people.
- We track and manage costs more closely than just about any business you can name, yet we anticipate and accept that roughly half of our investments in new ideas and new technologies will yield no usable results.
- Nucor pays hourly wages and salaries that run about 66 percent to 75 percent of the average for our industry—the rest of our employees' income comes from "at risk" bonuses—yet we regularly have large pools of qualified applicants for every job opening.
- Our company is broken up into 21 independently operated businesses, each with almost complete local autonomy, yet we have an unusually active and free exchange of ideas and solutions across divisional, geographical, and functional boundaries.
- We have no R&D department or corporate engineering group, yet we were America's first major operator of "minimills," the first to demonstrate that minimills could make flat-rolled steel (a high-end steel product formerly made only by the Big Steel companies), the first to apply thin-slab casting (a technology Big Steel had written off as impractical), and the first to commercially produce iron carbide (an energy-efficient substitute for the scrap metal from which minimills make steel).

Source: "How Nucor Works," *New Steel,* November 1997.

Nucor replaces many control features common to most companies with an incentive program that focuses on productivity. As Ted Kuster of *New Steel* notes, "What Nucor management has been able to do is get workers to identify their own interests fundamentally with those of management, something managers have been attempting to do, not very successfully, since the dawn of industry."[2] Iverson stresses four clear-cut principles:

1. Management is obligated to manage the company in such a way that employees will have the opportunity to earn

according to their productivity.

2. Employees should feel confident that if they do their jobs properly, they will have a job tomorrow.
3. Employees have the right to be treated fairly and must believe that they will be.
4. Employees must have an avenue of appeal when they believe they are being treated unfairly.[3]

The question becomes, can this management arrangement continue as the company grows?

Questions facing Nucor management in the late 1990s revolved around issues of staffing, control, communications, and planning. As the span of control of top management increased, concern over whether operations were becoming unwieldy and uncomfortable became evident. Iverson was proud of the fact that there were only three layers between the president and workers on the floor. Managers were being rewarded for meeting short-

term goals of increased sales, decreased costs, and quality maintenance. For example, Nucor managers would set standards for quality and output for groups of 25 to 30 employees and reward them with weekly bonuses.

Nucor top management maintained that this highly decentralized and lean organizational structure was necessary to meet foreign competition. According to top management, this structure would allow the firm to take advantage of those growth opportunities available in the environment. The risk was that the lower levels of management would follow short-term goals at the expense of long-term corporate objectives and coordination.

The Future

Industry analysts were also concerned that Nucor's joint venture with U.S. Steel would hinder the quick decision making typical at

Nucor. Iverson had gambled by committing to the first phase of the new process on his own, without first testing the process in a pilot plant on a small scale. The next stage was to complete the new process with a plant in the United States, relying on the high level of research and development skills at U.S. Steel and the ability of Nucor to pioneer new methods. Analysts wondered whether Nucor could coexist with U.S. Steel, with its large, hierarchical structure and strong union. This challenge was especially important since the new venture was felt to be the focal point for the continued growth of Nucor.

Review Questions

1. Evaluate Nucor's strategy using Porter's competitive strategies model.
2. Evaluate Nucor based on Miles and Snow's adaptive model.
3. Is Nucor capable of continuing its entrepreneurial spirit as it grows larger?

CASE 9

United Parcel Service: Technology to the Rescue

- -

United Parcel Service (UPS), the world's largest package distribution company, transports more than 3.1 billion parcels and documents annually. With over 500 aircraft, 147,000 vehicles, and 2,400 facilities providing service in over 200 countries, the firm has a worldwide commitment to serving the needs of the global marketplace. How does the company control such a vast and extended enterprise?

Corporate History

In 1907 there was a great need in America for private messenger and delivery services. With few private home telephones, luggage, packages, and personal messages had to be carried by hand. The U.S. Postal Service would not begin the parcel post system for another six years. To help meet this need, an

enterprising 19-year-old, James E. ("Jim") Casey, borrowed $100 from a friend and established the American Messenger Company in Seattle, Washington. Despite stiff competition, the company did well, largely because of Jim Casey's strict policies: customer courtesy, reliability, round-the-clock service, and low rates. These principles, which guide UPS even today, are summarized by

Jim's slogan: "Best Service and Lowest Rates."[1]

Obsessed with efficiency from the beginning, the company pioneered the concept of consolidated delivery—combining packages addressed to certain neighborhoods onto one delivery vehicle. In this way, manpower and motorized equipment could be used more efficiently. The

1930s brought more growth. By this time, UPS provided delivery services in all major West Coast cities, and a foothold was established on the other end of the country with a consolidated delivery service in the New York City area. Many innovations were adopted, including the first mechanical system for package sorting, and a 180-foot-long conveyor belt installed in Los Angeles. During this time, accountant George D. Smith joined the firm and helped make financial cost control the cornerstone of all planning decisions. The name United Parcel Service was adopted: "United" because shipments were consolidated and "Service" because "Service is all we have to offer." All UPS vehicles were painted the now-familiar Pullman brown color because it was neat, dignified, and professional.[2]

In 1953, UPS resumed air service, which had been discontinued during the Depression, offering two-day service to major cities on the East and West Coasts. Packages flew in the cargo holds of regularly scheduled airlines. Called UPS Blue Label Air, the service grew, until by 1978 it was available in every state, including Alaska and Hawaii. The demand for air parcel delivery increased in the 1980s, and federal deregulation of the airline industry created new opportunities for UPS. But deregulation caused change, as established airlines reduced the number of flights or abandoned routes altogether. To ensure dependability, UPS began to assemble its own jet cargo fleet—the largest in the industry. With growing demand for faster service, UPS entered the overnight air delivery business, and by 1985 UPS Next Day Air service was available in all 48 states and Puerto Rico. Alaska and Hawaii were added later. That same year, UPS entered a new era with international air package and document service, linking the United States and six European nations.

UPS Today

In 1988 UPS received authorization from the FAA (Federal Aviation Administration) to operate its own aircraft, thus officially becoming an airline. Recruiting the best people available, UPS merged a number of cultures and procedures into a seamless operation called UPS Airline. UPS Airline was the fastest-growing airline in FAA history, formed in little more than one year with all the necessary technology and support systems. Today, UPS Airline is among the ten largest airlines in the United States. UPS Airline features some of the most advanced information systems in the world, like the COMPASS (Computerized Operations Monitoring, Planning, and Scheduling System), which provides information for flight planning, scheduling, and load handling. The system, which can be used to plan optimum flight schedules up to six years in advance, is unique in the industry.

Today, the UPS system moves over 11.5 million packages and documents daily around the globe. From pickup at over 50,000 drop-off locations packages are transported by 157,000 brown trucks to over 2,400 centralized "hubs" where a combined workforce of over 338,000 employees sorts and distributes packages around the world. A huge technology support system that supports over 1 million cellular calls per day allows UPS to track all its packages electronically. Over $1.5 billion has been invested in technology systems in the past five years alone. Nonetheless, analysts suggest that UPS trails rival Federal Express by over one year in technology applications.[3]

Innovations at UPS

Tom Weidemeyer, president and chief operating officer of UPS Airline, likes to say that UPS likes to take the really long-term view about investments in its infrastructure. Technology at UPS spans an incredible range, from specially designed package delivery vehicles to global computer and communications systems. For example, UPSnet is a global electronic data communications network that provides an information processing pipeline for international package processing and delivery. UPSnet, which has more than 500,000 miles of communications lines, including a UPS satellite, links more than 1,300 distribution sites in 46 countries. The system tracks 821,000 packages daily.[4]

Weidemeyer introduced three additional changes. First, the entire airfleet of over 206 aircraft has been raised to meet Stage 3 noise requirements, three years ahead of the 1999 U.S. compliance deadline, at a cost of over $500 million. Second, he has introduced heads-up displays (HUDs) on all of UPS's 59 Boeing 727s. "In this business, it goes almost beyond reliability to criticality. There is only one launch, and if you miss that then you miss it. The HUDs will help us get even higher reliability."[5] Third, Weidemeyer has UPS in the charter passenger service. UPS has five 727s that have been converted to a dual cargo/passenger configuration. On Fridays, in three hours the planes can be converted from freight to 113 passenger seats. Vacation Express, an Atlanta travel agency, charters the aircraft, complete with UPS pilots, for weekend flights.[6]

UPS's commitment to technology is reflected in the upgrades it undertook for its Louisville international hub. The Atlanta-based delivery giant will spend $275 million to build a 2.7 million-square-foot facility that has been dubbed "Hub 2000." The name reflects the high-tech nature of the building and the $584 million UPS will invest in equipment and furnishings to replace the existing 1-million-square-foot sorting center. The new building, with three peninsulas jutting out from the main section, will have 42 bays where airplanes can pull up much as in truck docks at conventional factories and warehouses. Computerized overhead scanners will read "smart labels" and determine the direction packages will take along conveyor belts en route to the airplanes. Rather than replace workers, UPS will hire an additional 6,000 sorters as the hub is expanded.[7]

Three Trends Driving the Industry

Frederick Smith of Fed Ex identifies three trends driving the package business. *Globalization* will cause the world express-transportation market to explode from today's $12 billion to more than $150 billion. While DHL Worldwide Express is a major player in the international market, UPS and Fed Ex are expanding at a rapid pace. The fastest-growing segments of UPS's business are the express and international markets, whose revenues leapt by almost 25 percent in 1997. Lee Hibbets of Air Cargo Management Group in Seattle states that "FedEx is seen as more aggressive, whereas UPS is a little bit more methodical and long-term."[8]

Cost cutting among firms—primarily by cutting inventory—fits into the package firms' delivery systems. Technology plays a part in every company's future, but Fed Ex has a distinct edge in this area. It has installed computer terminals for 100,000 customers and given proprietary software to another 650,000. As a result, shippers now label 60 percent of their own packages, with Fed Ex receiving electronic notifications for pickup and delivery.[9]

Internet commerce, rather than a threat to the shippers, turns out to be a vast opportunity. Electronic commerce generates a huge need for shipping, and the package deliverers hope to capture the lion's share of the business. Fed Ex's recent $2.7 merger of Caliber System, with its RPS trucking subsidiary comprising 13,000 trucks, puts it in even closer competition with UPS.

It remains to be seen who will win out in the package delivery wars, but Fed Ex and UPS are both leaders in the market. Their ability to track packages around the world is a testament to the value of technology in the workplace. With innovations generating higher productivity, the future for package delivery remains bright.

Review Questions

1. How does performance appraisal assist control, and how does it relate to UPS?
2. How has UPS used the Internet, and how does this strategy apply to control?
3. The fourth management function is controlling; explain it and relate it to UPS.

CASE 10

AT&T: Reorganization for Performance

or 100 years AT&T believed that bigger was always better. It spent decades buying up local phone companies to create the Bell System and then fought off the government's effort to break up the monopoly it had created. Finally, in 1984, the divestiture order was finally realized, and AT&T spun off seven regional Bell operating companies known as the Baby Bells. However, 11 years after the divestiture ended its monopoly, the firm had still not found its role in the fiercely competitive telecommunications environment. In an effort to adjust, AT&T is restructuring itself to meet the new challenges.[1]

Ma Bell to AT&T

"Mr. Watson. Come here. I want you" remains one of the historic moments in American invention. After he uttered these words, Alexander Graham Bell perfected his telephone, originally meant to aid the deaf, in 1876. By 1877,

Bell's backers founded Bell Telephone, followed by New England Telephone in 1878. These two operating units were consolidated in 1879 into National Bell Telephone.[2]

From the start, Bell made every attempt to protect its franchise. After much litigation, National Bell barred rival Western Union from entering the telephone business in 1879. In 1882, the Bell company gained control of Western Electric, the United States's number one electrical equipment manufacturer, once again from Western Union.[3]

As Bell's patents expired in the 1890s, many independent localized phone companies raced into the market. Concentrating on evolving long distance, Bell changed its name to American Telephone and Telegraph and moved its headquarters to New York in 1899. In 1913, in reaction to the Kinsbury Commitment, AT&T agreed to buy no more independent phone companies and to grant independents access to its networks.

Although it long enjoyed monopoly status, competition has been slowly encroaching on AT&T's environment. FCC regulations stripped AT&T of its telephone equipment monopoly in 1968 and allowed specialized carriers such as MCI to hook their microwave-based systems into phone networks, injecting competition into the long-distance market.[4]

In 1984, succumbing to a government lawsuit, the firm spun off its seven regional Bell companies. AT&T was allowed to keep long-distance service and Western Electric. In reaction to new firms entering its long-distance market (Sprint, Alltel), AT&T has attempted to diversify itself through some high-profile purchases.

In 1991, for example, AT&T completed a hostile takeover of National Cash Register (NCR) for $7.5 billion. The $110 per share price for a hobbled computer maker has turned out to be an expensive blunder by the firm. NCR has run up billions in losses and untold billions in opportunity cost. Salomon's Jack Grubman suggests that "AT&T has blown at least $11 billion on NCR."[5] He goes on to emphasize "the opportunity they blew to extend their core business" by investing that $7 billion of equity in infrastructure, such as local fiber-optic networks in the United States and Europe.[6]

Another questionable investment came with AT&T's 1993 purchase of McCaw Cellular for $11.5 billion and the 1995 purchase of LIN Broadcasting stock for $3.3 billion. AT&T's costs for entry into wireless compares poorly with competitors. Ma Bell paid in the low $300 to $350 range per POP (estimated market population) in buying McCaw and LIN. By comparison, Sam Ginn, the CEO of Airtouch Communications, paid $10 per POP in the San Francisco Bay area, $17 in Dallas, and $17 in Atlanta.[7]

However, in 1995, 90 percent of AT&T's earnings continued to come from its core long-distance service. They still control over 60 percent of long-distance service, but Joseph Kraemer, a consultant with consulting firm A.T. Kearney, sees its market share dropping to below 50 percent within 18 to 24 months of the late-1997 entry of the Baby Bells into the long distance market.

New Challenges

The Telecommunications Act of 1996 substantially changed the U.S. communications market. Regional phone companies can now provide long-distance service, long-distance companies can offer local service, and cable companies can get into the phone business. This is in addition to increased rivalry from the Internet and wireless communications.[8] AT&T complains that the regional Bells are conspiring to keep it out of the local markets.

In anticipation of this development, CEO Robert Allen announced a trivestiture plan that splits AT&T into three operating units: AT&T Services is the largest entity, with the long-distance and cellular operations. Its 1996 revenues were $53.3 billion. AT&T Network Equipment is the second largest telecom equipment manufacturer in the world, with 1996 revenues of $24.5 billion with Lucent, has been particularly successful after the spinoff. The third unit is AT&T Global Information Systems, which represents the old NCR. It's 1996 revenues are $8.3 billion.

CEO Allen has raised many complaints concerning his strategic choices for AT&T. After bringing in John Walter from R.R. Donnelley as his handpicked successor, Allen led a charge to replace him. Many argued that Walter lacked the technology background necessary to run the new AT&T. New CEO C. Michael Armstrong, the first outsider to head AT&T in nearly 80 years, has brought in an "invest or divest" strategy that focuses back on the core businesses. Known as a slasher, Armstrong has his work cut out, as selling, general, and administrative expenses—30 percent of revenue—are the highest in the telecom industry, with MCI at 27 percent and Sprint at 22 percent.[9] He vows to cut the figure to 22 percent in two years with a necessary $3 to $3.5 billion reduction in annual costs.[10]

Armstrong's First 100 Days

- **Sold** AT&T's Universal Card Services, its credit card division with 18 million accounts, to Citibank for $3.5 billion.
- **Sold** AT&T's Solutions Customer Care unit, which provides outsourcing and consulting for call centers, to Cincinnati Bell for $625 million.
- **Bought** Teleport Communications Group, an upstart local phone company with strong management, for $11.3 billion. The deal will let AT&T package together long-distance and local phone service. AT&T will hawk the bundle to business customers. Armstrong retained Teleport's top execs.
- **Restructured** compensation for AT&T's top management, closely linking performance to salary.

Source: *Fortune*, February 16, 1998.

Armstrong's boldest move may be his merger with Teleport Communications Group in early 1998. Prior to this action, AT&T had attempted to exist in the local market primarily as a reseller of the local Bell services. Abandoning that strategy, the new CEO places AT&T firmly in the local telephone market, with TCG's 490,000 lines in 65 cities. He is causing the "Bellheads"—the term people use for insiders who rose to the top through telephone service—to rethink everything.[11]

The biggest impact Armstrong is having at AT&T is to shake up the old bureaucratic ways and shorten decision-making cycles. His most immediate impact has been to improve the morale within the organization. Having performed a relatively similar miracle at Hughes Electronics, the next three years should be most interesting.

Review Questions

1. Analyze AT&T's organization based on functional and divisional structures.
2. Would a matrix structure be more effective for AT&T?
3. What is the purpose of the headquarters staff now that AT&T has split into three businesses?

CASE 11

Price Waterhouse and Coopers & Lybrand: A Megamerger

Since the late 1980s, the national accounting/consulting industry has been dominated by the Big Six firms of Arthur Andersen & Co., Coopers & Lybrand LLP, Deloitte and Touche, Ernst & Young, KPMG, and Price Waterhouse. Together, they charged more than $45 billion in fees in 1996. In September 1997, Price Waterhouse and Coopers & Lybrand announced plans to merge their operations into what will represent the second-largest firm behind Andersen. What does this combination portend for both the firms and the industry in general?

Firm	1996 Fees (Billions)	% Change 1995–96
Arthur Andersen	$9.5	16.8
Ernst & Young	$7.7	13.0
KPMG Peat Marwick	$7.4	8.0
Coopers & Lybrand	$6.8	9.7
Deloitte and Touche	$6.5	9.5
Price Waterhouse	$5.0	12.6
BDO Seidman	$1.3	8.1
Grant Thornton	$1.3	7.1
McGladrey & Pullen	$0.9	8.4

Source: U.S. Industry and Trade Outlook 1998. (New York, McGraw-Hill)

From Six to Five

Mergers are not new to the accounting industry. Once known as the Big Eight, the mergers in the late 1980s of Deloitte Haskins & Sells with Touche Ross & Company to form Deloitte & Touche and Ernst & Whinney with Arthur Young & Company to form Ernst and Young, shrank the industry to the Big Six.[1] Price Waterhouse attempted to merge with Deloitte in 1984, but talks were canceled. In 1989, Price Waterhouse once again was set to merge, this time with Arthur Andersen, but the deal fell apart after quarrels over a new name.[2]

However, Price remained under pressure to combine with a larger player. In September of 1997, it announced that it intended to merge with Coopers & Lybrand in a deal that creates a firm with combined worldwide revenues of $12 billion, over 130,000 employees, and more than 8,500 partners. As the fifth- (Coopers) and sixth- (Price) largest players in the accounting/consulting market, their combination may have been inevitable. "Had Price Waterhouse not done this deal, they were in danger of fast becoming a niche player as the smallest of the Big Six," claimed Arthur Bowman, editor of *Bowman's Accounting Reports.*[3]

In addition to its U.S. operation, Price is active in Asia and South America. Price represents such industries as chemicals, entertainment and media, and energy. Coopers has a strong presence in Europe and specializes in consumer products, manufacturing, and communications on an international scale. The need to develop a larger presence in consulting appears to have been one of the main motivations for the merger.[4] In 1996, for the first time, the 100 biggest accountancy firms in the United States earned more from consulting ($8.3 billion) than they did from either auditing ($7.9 billion) or tax consulting ($5 billion).[5]

While previous mergers in the industry have been motivated by the need to reduce the size of the firms and reduce overhead, the Price/Coopers union is motivated by the need for global support and seamless business consulting. Shortly after the Price/Coopers announcement, KPMG and Ernst and Young announced that they too would be merging. However, in early March of 1998, they announced they had abandoned their proposed $18 billion merger after four tumultuous months of negotiations.

The need for economies of scale is starkly evident when revenues per partner are compared across the firms in the industry. On average, Price Waterhouse's 3,300 partners generated $1.5 million apiece in 1996, with Coopers' 5,200 partners averaging $1.3 million. By comparison, Arthur Andersen's 2,611 partners generated an average of $3.6 million each.

A number of forces in the rapidly changing accounting/consulting industry are both supporting and aggravating such combinations. The market for professional business services is growing more rapidly overseas than it is in the United States.[6] Globalization of the industry is expected to become increasingly prevalent throughout this century and into the next. The *U.S. Industry and Trade Outlook* forecasts that demand for U.S. management, consulting, and public relations services overseas will continue to grow at 14 to 15 percent annually into the 21st century, compared to a domestic growth rate averaging 5.4 percent annually.[7]

Another cause for concern is legal liability. All Big Six accounting firms have become limited liability partnerships (LLP)

in an effort to protect their partners from litigation. Especially now as the firms strengthen their global presence, partners in Britain for example, do not wish to be sued for the alleged errors of their colleagues in California. Even more pervasive is the conflict between accountants and consultants, which tends to pull the two major revenue sources in opposite directions. Indeed, many clients have problems with the new one-stop firms, as conflicts of interest arise when they are independently audited by the same firm providing them with professional business advice.

The Future

One of the biggest problems with any merger as large as Price and Coopers is the potential for clashing cultures. A former Coopers & Lybrand partner likens Price Waterhouse to a Roman legion: pristine, well-equipped, and efficiently drilled. Alternatively, Coopers "are the Visigoths of the industry throwing stones from the tops of trees."[8] Price has a strong team culture; new business at Coopers is fought over "tooth and nail" internally.[9] Andersen Worldwide recently voted to split off its consulting and accounting arms.

Howard Schilit, an accounting professor who is president of the Center for Financial Research and Analysis, worries that "each of the firms has a very special culture and it will be difficult to merge the two together."[10] James Wadia, managing director and head of Arthur Andersen, the accounting arm of Andersen Worldwide notes that "These megamergers are difficult to do. The firms get distracted, and there's tremendous opportunity in the turmoil." Andersen lost its top-ranked spot during the last merger wave, only to reclaim it a few years later. Wadia insists that internal growth, not mergers, is the way to grow and hopes to pick up disgruntled partners from the merged firms.[11]

Review Questions

1. Compare the cultures of Price and Coopers. Are there differences?
2. What pressure does this merger put on the rest of the industry?
3. Would you classify the accounting/consulting work design as small batch, mass production, or continuous process according to Joan Woodward's classification?

CASE 12

Ben & Jerry's Ice Cream: Leading with Values

Ben & Jerry's Ice Cream, long viewed as one of the most socially active, countercultural companies in America, faces increasing competition in the premium ice cream market, where they remain a high-cost, inefficient producer paying high wages and using expensive, chemical-free milk. Coupled with a new emphasis on international expansion, the firm must continue to generate sufficient profits to keep its investors happy. Can this "quasi-corporate Woodstock" continue to flourish and remain true to its founding values?[1]

From Humble Beginnings

Ben & Jerry's Homemade, Inc. has often been viewed as an ideal working environment from the

employees' perspective. Jerry Greenfield, cofounder and a director of the company, was fond of saying of the work the company does, "If it's not fun, why do it?" But not too long ago both Greenfield and Ben Cohen, cofounder and company CEO, became concerned that running the company was no longer fun. Greenfield had already withdrawn from management of the company when Cohen announced, in the summer of 1994, that the company would be looking for a new CEO. Greenfield's departure raised the question of what impact the change at the top would have on the culture and style of the working environment at Ben & Jerry's.

Greenfield and Cohen had decided at the outset that their company would be different— this would be a company where the employees would be treated well. As such, they hoped that the company would be more likely to provide a product that would meet its customers' needs in terms of quality and cost. The founders set up a human resources department that was designed to help develop and foster an environment consistent with the desire to provide a good place for people to work. Kathy Chaplin, personnel operations manager, stated, "We make decisions based on what's really best for our workers, not on the dollar amount. We ask ourselves, 'How is it going to improve employees lives.'"[2] One way to achieve this end was to provide an open system of communications within the company. Employees were encouraged and expected to provide annual evaluations of their supervisors, and the personnel department set up training sessions to help employees understand both the purpose and process of these evaluations.

Employees were also involved in the development of the benefits package available at Ben & Jerry's. For example, when some employees noted that there was a lack of day-care opportunities near the company's main facilities, company man-

agement agreed to help set up such an operation. But instead of doing so from the top down, the company created a worker committee to decide just how the day-care facility should be set up and operated. Chaplin noted that while this process of employee involvement was more work for her department and the company as a whole, the results were worth it. She noted, "I think people feel good that they have some say about what they're getting."[3]

Management then set workers up in teams that were charged with designing their own work procedures. This process was extended to include team input into the design of the new distribution center and manufacturing facilities the company needed to bring on line during the early 1990s to meet increased customer demand. The open communications and shared decision making were viewed by management as key factors in reducing the cost of building and equipping the new facilities. It was believed that the ideas provided by the worker teams would also lower the operating costs of the facilities once they were on line.

The concept of team building and decision making also extended to the hiring process. New hire prospects first had to be interviewed by the people the prospective employee would be working with. If the new person was replacing a departing employee, even that person would be part of the interviewing team. The team members would have a major say in determining who would be added to their group. In this way, as Greenfield noted, "the new person would be surrounded by people who would have a vested interest in his or her success."[4]

Greenfield credits several of these extensions of the human relations management process to Chuck Lacy, president of Ben & Jerry's. Lacy was brought in to

help in the transition during Greenfield's gradual withdrawal from active management of the company. Greenfield stated that Lacy brought a "sense of how to treat people and make it a part of our daily work."[5] This concept was extended to all aspects of the human relations process, including establishing a friendly work environment. This involved adding music to the production area. The music was piped in from one of three local radio stations, and the choice of stations was rotated on a continual basis. The process also involved expanding the benefits program to include a flexible spending program that allowed employees to pick and choose among various alternatives based on their specific needs and wants. An employee might even choose to elect out of the health-care program if his or her spouse were already covered by an equal or better program in another company. The money saved from this election could then be applied to other benefits, such as child care. Dave Barash, former director of human relations and current director of social ventures, noted that "the role of the HR people in this company is to act as coaches and resource people to give people the tools they need and to teach them how to use them.[6]

In 1995, Ben Cohen announced the appointment of Robert Holland Jr. as the new company CEO. Holland had come not from the general call for applicants but from an executive search firm hired by Ben & Jerry's to recruit top management prospects. Ben & Jerry's had already abandoned its policy of limiting the top manager's salary to no more than seven times that of the average total compensation (including benefits) of the lowest level employee in anticipation of hiring a new CEO. Despite the apparent consistency between Holland's beliefs and those of the company's founders, some were concerned whether he would, or could, allow the independence that had been encouraged to date to continue, especially given the simultaneous announcement that the company would incur its first quarterly loss since going public.

A New CEO

On Thursday, January 2, 1997, Ben & Jerry's issued a news release announcing the selection of their new CEO. Ben Cohen, cofounder and chairman of Ben & Jerry's, announced the selection of Perry D. Odak as chief executive officer.

Odak comes to Ben & Jerry's with 25 years of senior management experience in a variety of consumer product and retailing businesses. Among these businesses is Armour-Dial, a Fortune 500 company. Mr. Odak started his career in the food division of Armour-Dial and went on to become senior vice president of Worldwide Operations for all divisions. At Jovan, Inc., an innovative fragrance and cosmetic company, he was part of the start-up and served as general manager in charge of marketing sales and distribution. Other companies in which Perry Odak worked are Atari, where he was president of the Consumer Product Group and responsible for new product development; Dellwood Foods, where he completed a successful buyout and merger with Tuscan Dairy; and most recently U.S. Repeating Arms Co. (Winchester) and Browning, a manufacturer of outdoor and recreation sporting goods, where he was part of the companies' senior management teams.

Cohen notes, "We feel incredibly lucky to have found a person of Perry's caliber to lead our company at this time. Perry has proven business skills, an eye for both the top and bottom line, and extensive experience in con-sumer product businesses." "As someone who has worked with consumer brands for most of my professional life," said Odak, "I am really excited about the chance to work with so fine a brand—and company—as Ben & Jerry's. There is a lot to do here, and I view the tasks at hand as being great opportunities both for Ben & Jerry's and for me."

Can Odak continue Ben and Jerry's unique emphasis on values and apply more traditional business concepts? While he envisions that the company's social mission will remain intact, "we've had to bring some new balance to that and focus on making the economic side of the company stronger."[7]

Review Questions

1. What human resource management policies does Ben & Jerry's employ to gain acceptance of and commitment to improved quality within the workforce?

2. What recruiting and staffing innovations does Ben & Jerry's use to improve employee morale and motivation?

3. What reactions might occur as the founders turn over operational control to a new CEO from outside the company?

CASE 13

Mike Krzyzewski: Duke Basketball's No-nonsense Leader

Duke University basketball coach Mike Krzyzewski (pronounced *Shuh-SHEF-ski*) is considered a symbol of everything that is right about college basketball. He is a no-nonsense leader of a major college basketball program that is highly admired and scandal free while ensuring that almost all of its players earn their degrees in four years.[1] He is a true leader to his university, his team, and his profession.

The Early Years

Mike Krzyzewski was born on February 13, 1947, and raised in a two-family dwelling in northwest Chicago. Exhibiting an early affinity for basketball, he led the city-wide Catholic basketball league in scoring for two of his years at Weber High School. Upon graduation, he enrolled in West Point Military Academy to learn basketball under the tutelage of legendary coach Bobby Knight. As a fierce competitor and taskmaster, Knight turned Krzyzewski into a defensive specialist and playmaker by warning him that Knight would "break his arm" if he attempted to shoot the ball.[2] When he graduated, Krzyzewski was a three-year letterman who had played in the National Invitational Tournament (NIT) three times; he captained the team his senior year.

After serving his required tour of duty in the army, Krzyzewski began his career in basketball as a graduate assistant at Indiana University for his former coach, Bobby Knight. In 1975, he was chosen from a field of 120 applicants to be the head basketball coach at his alma mater, West Point. From a 1974 season in which the team had only won 3 out of 25 games, Krzyzewski compiled a five-year record of 73 wins and 59 losses and two NIT bids.

At the end of the 1979–80 basketball season, Krzyzewski was approached by Tom Butters, Duke University's athletic director, who, on the advice of Bobby Knight, offered him the head coaching position at Duke. Echoing Knight's high praise,

Butters declared Duke had hired "the most brilliant young basketball coach in the country."[3] Even so, Krzyzewski's appointment was greeted by Duke's student newspaper with the headline "THIS IS NOT A TYPO."[4]

Krzyzewski took the Duke Blue Devils team to a 17–13 record in his first year, but in the following recruiting season he and his assistants failed to sign a single high school senior. The next two years were marked by back-to-back 17-loss seasons, as the new coach was initiated into the competitive atmosphere of the Atlantic Coast Conference (ACC), one of basketball's premier leagues.[5] Sportswriter Keith Drum claimed that Krzyzewski grew "thin-skinned"—"He could be stubborn, and he wasn't very patient. . . . There's no way what he'd done previously prepared him for the ACC."[6]

Krzyzewski's first break came with his recruitment of Johnny Dawkins, an event that opened a pipeline between Duke and the talented Washington, D.C., area. This was followed by Tommy Amaker, Danny Ferry, Christian Laettner, and Bobby Hurley. These individuals represent the epitome of the student-athlete because Duke's rigorous admissions policies and high classroom standards are not compromised for hotshot recruits.[7]

The exploits of Krzyzewski have earned him the well-recognized moniker of Coach K. However, despite his four Final Four appearances (1986, 1988–90) in the NCAA Tournament the Duke program was getting the reputation of being the classy bridesmaid but never the bride. With the help of Laettner, Hurley, and freshman Grant Hill, Duke won its first National Championship with a 72-65 win over Kansas in 1991. This was followed the next year with a repeat championship in the finals over Michigan.

Throughout this experience, Coach K continued to require high standards of both himself and his players. He refused to raise the team's 1990 Final Four banner in Duke's Cameron Indoor Stadium until two ungraduated members of the squad obtained their degrees.[8] Indeed, Krzyzewski has been criticized has being overly rigorous. Coach K responds that his program's success had neither compromised nor overshadowed the school's academic mission.

However, the success came with a price. The *Washington Post's* Tony Kornheiser claims that since winning the back-to-back titles in 1991 and 1992, Krzyzewski had grown "so concerned that he wouldn't appear to be big-timing anyone after his success, that he went out of his way to say 'yes' to every request: from his fellow coaches, from his recruits, from the media."[9] He served as spokesman for the National Association of Basketball Coaches and was an assistant coach for the gold-medal American men's basketball team at the 1992 Olympics Games in Barcelona.

In 1993, Coach K signed an endorsement package with Nike that paid him $6.6 million over 15 years and is reportedly the most lucrative deal ever inked by a college basketball coach.[10] While Coach K has been criticized for this contract, he is likely to give substantial support to the university, just as he did with his earlier $250,000 per year contract with Adidas.[11]

After the 1994–95 season, which saw Duke lose in the championship game to Arkansas, Coach K started suffering lower back pain because of a bulging disk. The coach had to opt for surgery on October 22, and while doctors recommended a month of inactivity followed by two months of limited activity, Coach K returned almost immediately to work. In early January of 1995, Krzyzewski informed his team that he needed to take time off due to pain and exhaustion.[12] He handed over responsibility to his longtime assistant, Pete Gaudet, who guided the team through the last 19 games. The combination of a young team and the loss of its head coach resulted in the worst season for Duke basketball in decades.

Returning to his coaching responsibilities at the start of the 1995–96 basketball season, Coach K was able to take a team short on talent and motivate them to win 18 of 31 games and return to the NCAA tournament. This was followed by a 24–9 season in 1996–97 and 30–3 in 1997–98, in which they lost to Kentucky in the South Regional Final.[13]

In 1990, pondering an offer to coach in the NBA with the Boston Celtics, Coach K remarked, "I realized I'm not just a basketball coach. And if I were in the NBA, that's what I'd be. I want to be a teacher and work with kids and see them grow up. What's neat is that I can win a lot of basketball games while I'm doing that."[14] As coach Bobby Knight likes to say about the Blue Devils, they are "doing what has to be done. . . . and doing it with college students."[15]

Review Questions

1. Describe Coach Krzyzewski's leadership style according to House's Path-Goal Leadership Theory.
2. Analyze Coach K's leadership approach using Blake and Mouton's leadership grid and the Hershey-Blanchard situational leadership model. Which of the two models provides more insight into this case?
3. Would you describe Coach K's style as more representative of transactional or transformational leadership?

Black Entertainment Television (BET): Rags to Riches

R obert Johnson, born the ninth of ten children in Hickory, Mississippi, is a true rags-to-riches success story. His father, Archie, chopped wood while his mother taught school, and their search for a better life led them to Freeport, Illinois, a predominantly white working-class neighborhood. Archie supplemented his factory jobs by operating his own junkyard on the predominantly black east side of town. Edna Johnson got a job at Burgess Battery, and although she eventually secured a job for her son Robert at the battery firm, he knew it wasn't for him.[1]

Bobby Johnson showed an enterprising nature at an early age, delivering papers, mowing lawns, and cleaning out tents at local fairs. At Freeport High School, Robert was an honors student and was able to enter the University of Illinois upon graduation. Virgil Hemphill, his freshman roommate, commented that "He was not overly slick, overly smooth. He was kind of innocent and naive. His strength was being able to talk to different types of people. I went to Freeport with him, and he could communicate with the regular people and with the suit-and-tie people."[2]

Johnson did well at Illinois, studying history, holding several work-study jobs, and participating at Kappa Alpha Psi, a black fraternity. After graduation in 1968, Johnson was admitted to Princeton University's Woodrow Wilson School of Public and International Affairs, a two-year program with a full scholarship plus expenses. However, he dropped out after the first semester to marry his college sweetheart, Sheila Crump, a former cheerleader and gifted violinist. He eventually returned to Princeton to earn his master's degree in public administration in 1972.[3]

He moved on to Washington to work at the Corporation for Public Broadcasting, followed by the Washington Urban League,

where the director, Sterling Tucker, was leading the struggle for District home rule. Tucker appreciated Johnson's ability to think both "microly and macro-ly" while still "thinking like a visionary" in pursuing larger goals.[4] Having moved on to the Congressional Black Caucus, Johnson became impressed with the possibilities for black power that lay in television and cable in particular. In 1976, he moved on to work as a lobbyist for the National Cable Television Association (NCTA), where he gained invaluable insight into the cable industry.

At the NCTA's 1979 convention, Johnson met Bob Rosencrans, president of UA-Columbia Cablevision. While Bob Johnson had a strong idea in providing cable programming to minority audiences, he had no satellite time; Rosencrans owned some unused slots on one of the three cable TV satellites and was looking for programs to support his local franchises. "I just said, 'Bob, you're on. Let's go.' I don't think we even charged him. We knew he couldn't afford much, and for us, it was a plus because it gave us more ammunition to sell cable . . . The industry was not attracting minority customers.[5]

With $15,000 from a consulting contract that he received upon his departure from NCTA, Robert Johnson launched Black

Entertainment Television (BET) at 11 PM on January 8, 1980. The first show bounced off an RCA satellite and into 3.8 million homes served by Rosencrans's franchises. Johnson received his first crucial financing from John Malone of TCI in the form of a $380,000 loan plus $120,000 to purchase 20 percent of BET.[6]

Johnson's original staff at BET included Vivian Goodier, who came over from NCTA and assisted Johnson with the original BET business plan. In addition, Johnson hired his secretary, Carol Coody, and his older sister Polly. The BET staff approached cable companies, subscribers, and others at industry shows, using a little 10-by-10 booth with a collapsible table and display. After a decade of learning the finer points of cable industry, Johnson went public with BET and raised $70 million.

However, this did not occur without controversy. In 1992, Goodier, Coody, and Polly Johnson all sued Robert Johnson, claiming that he had promised them shares of the company in exchange for their hard work. These claims were eventually settled, with $900,000 each going to Coody and Polly and more than $2 million for Goodier, who claimed a personal relationship with Bob Johnson.[7]

To raise capital in the

1980s, Johnson sold off pieces of BET to Time Inc. and Taft Broadcasting for over $10 million. However, controversy over programming has followed Johnson from the start because of his heavy reliance on music videos (60 percent of total programming), gospel and religious programs, infomercials, and reruns of older shows such as *Sanford and Son* and *227*.[8] Lydia Cole, BET vice president for programming, does not let her young daughters watch BET, claiming, "We don't watch BET. I'm concerned about the images portrayed of young girls."[9]

Johnson lives on a $4.3 million, 133-acre horse farm in Virginia, and while he supports a large number of black causes, he declines to be identified as a role model. "I don't want to be seen as a hero to younger people. I want to be seen as a good solid business guy who goes out and does a job, and the job is to build a business. . . . What are my responsibilities to black people at large? If I help my family get over and deal with the problems they might confront, then I have achieved that one goal that is my responsibility to society at large."[10]

Although Johnson professes to want to produce original programming, he continues to suffer from low fees compared to other cable offerings. Early in BET's existence, Johnson was earning only 2 cents per subscriber, while major networks such as TNT and USA were getting 15 to 20 cents. Johnson has won the battle for higher fees, which jumped from 2.5 cents to 5 cents in 1989 and eventually to 15.5 cents in the next five years. BET is watched by 52 million households, 142,000 in any given minute, and ranks nineteenth among 28 cable channels tracked by Nielsen data.[11] Subscriber fees generated $50.4 million in 1996, compared to $60 million through infomercials and advertising.[12]

The Future

Robert Johnson continues to have grand plans for BET, seeking to turn the enterprise into what marketers call an umbrella brand.[13] The firm publishes two national magazines that reach 250,000 readers combined: *Young Sisters and Brothers* for teens and *Emerge* for affluent adults, and it has interests in film production, electronic retailing, and radio.[14] The first BET Sound Stage restaurant opened in suburban Washington, with another opening in Disney World in Orlando. With Hilton as a partner, Johnson hopes to open a casino in Las Vegas, Nevada.[15]

Johnson wants to capture some of the black consumers' disposable income—valued at $425 billion annually. To do this, he partners primarily with such big names as Disney, Hilton, Blockbuster, Microsoft, and others.

"You simply cannot get big anymore by being 100 percent black-owned anything," Johnson claims.[16] Reaching 98 percent of all black cable homes, his BET cable station provides the perfect medium to influence this increasingly affluent black audience.

In September 1997, Delano E. Lewis, a director of BET, was appointed to serve on a special independent committee of the BET board of directors to consider and make recommendations to the board concerning a September 10, 1997, proposal by Robert Johnson and TCI's Liberty Media Group to purchase all of the outstanding shares of BET common stock not already owned by them for a price of $48 per share. In early 1998, Lewis reported that the $48-per-share offer was inadequate.[17]

• The first BET show was a 1974 African safari movie, *Visit to a Chief's Son*. Initially, BET aired for only two hours on Friday nights.

Review Questions

1. How does motivation influence performance and is this evident at BET?
2. What role does reinforcement play in motivation?
3. What is happening in the area of motivation and compensation?

CASE 15

Boeing: Faster-Better-Cheaper

Boeing, based in Seattle, Washington, has remained the world's #1 commercial aircraft manufacturer for more than 30 years, with more than 60 percent of the world market share. A major exporter, its aircraft, which range from the popular 737 to the Jumbo 747, are flown by every major airline in the world. However, even in the face of success, Boeing is under intense pressure to reinvent the way it develops and manufactures aircraft.

A Proud History

William Boeing built his first airplane in 1916 with navy office Conrad Westervelt. His Seattle factory, originally named Pacific Aero Products, changed its name to Boeing Airplane Company the following year. The company produced training planes for the U.S. Navy in World War 1. After the war, Boeing began the first international airmail service between Seattle and Victoria, British Columbia, with its B-1 flying boat.[1]

Between the wars, Boeing created the United Aircraft and Transport Corporation to facilitate its manufacturing and transportation concerns. The company introduced the first all-metal airliner in 1933. The following year, due to changes in airmail rules, the firm was forced to sell its airline operations (the predecessor of today's United Airlines) and concentrate on aircraft manufacturing.[2]

Boeing has always been a leader in aircraft innovations, introducing the Model 314 Clipper (flying boats) used by Pan Am, the Model 307 Stratoliner (the first aircraft with a pressurized cabin), and the B-17 bomber during World War 2. However, it was the introduction in 1954 of the Boeing 707 that redefined the aircraft industry as we know it today. For over the following 40 years, Boeing added to its line of aircraft, including the Jumbo 747, its popular 737, and the more recent 777, to meet the increasing needs of airline travel both in the United States and around the world.

After recent mergers with McDonnell Douglas in 1997 and the space and defense divisions of Rockwell International in 1996, Boeing is suffering from the problems associated with such mergers. With orders for new aircraft at an all-time high, the firm faces problems keeping up with production demands. The situation got so bad that the company actually closed down its 737 and 747 production lines for a month in 1997 in order to gain control of its needs, problems that caused it to write off a $1.6 billion charge in the third quarter and face over $300 million in penalties from customers for late deliveries. As a result, Boeing announced a radical new development strategy in early 1998.

The Need for Change

Boeing is an example of what can happen to a company that is overwhelmed by good fortune. Record orders required that Boeing ramp up its production from 18 jets a month in 1995 to 43 by early 1998. In an attempt to hire and train 41,000 new workers, the company often raided its own suppliers, aggravating an already strained supply chain. In May of 1997, the FAA warned Boeing about improper paperwork on its 737s, and as a result it stepped up its inspections of Boeing assembly lines.[3]

Meanwhile, Boeing faces stiff rivalry from Airbus Industrie, a European consortium that builds the A300 aircraft family. In early 1998, France, Germany, Britain, and Spain agreed to a merger for the consortium to eliminate inefficient assembly methods and make the company more competitive with Boeing.[4] The European jet maker's market share edged up to 30 percent as it booked record orders. Boeing's production delays and costly overhead structure makes it increasingly difficult to compete in a market dominated by a concern for cost. As Byron Callan, aerospace analysis for Merrill Lynch, emphasizes "the name of the game is cost."[5]

As a result of these and other problems, Boeing CEO Philip Condit formed a project team called the Aircraft Creation Process Strategy (ACPS), nicknamed by suppliers as "faster-better-cheaper."[6] The goal is to curb the production time of aircraft from 60 months to 12 and cut the costs from around $6.5 billion to $1 billion.[7] Headed by Walter Gillette, the program is conducted in close association with Boeing's suppliers and airlines. Since 1960, the price per seat of transport aircraft has increased more than 140 percent, while yield per passenger mile has dropped by about half. Time-to-market for new aircraft during the same period increased from 3 to almost 4.5 years from the "first order" date.[8]

With no new airplanes on its drawing boards, Boeing has only one place to look for a competitive advantage—the factory floor.[9] The new scheme is intended to supplant a system of engineering, manufacturing, and parts procurement that dates back to the production of B-17 and B-29 bombers in the 1940s. Over the years, the system has grown more and more complex; it does not necessarily produce more airplanes but definitely produces more paperwork.[10]

An additional problem is the extraordinary choice Boeing offers its customers on aircraft configurations. On the 747 alone, there are four bulkhead options that can result in the placement or repositioning of 2,500 parts and the modification of 900 pages of drawings. Computers help track some of these problems, but every factory has its own computer system, and parts lists are maintained on over 400 different databases. Robert Hammer, V.P. of production process reform, observes that "You know the Baldridge prize for the best manufacturing processes. Well, if there was a prize for the opposite, this system would win it hands down." So, can the systems be fixed? No way, says Hammer. "We're going to kill it."[11]

ACPS envisions a number of improvements to the present system. Key strategies include reuse of existing components and reducing parts counts with integrated, monolithic structures. Common, modular, and integrated systems also would be employed. Aircraft catalog options will be reduced with financial incentives to limit aircraft customization. Production changes include building multiple models of aircraft on a single production line, with the aircraft flyable almost immediately to "last-stage customization" centers for interiors and paint application.[12]

Emphasis is also being placed on how workers actually do their jobs on the assembly line, a process Boeing calls "lean manufacturing."[13] To this end, the firm retained the consulting firm Shinijutsu, run by Yoshiki Iwata, a former Toyota engineer who speaks no English. Iwata's first step was to identify piles of unnecessary inventory. Boeing's factories turn their stocks only 2 to 3 times per year, while an efficient manufacturing operation might turn stock 12 times a year. Boeing holds about $18 billion in gross inventories, equivalent to about 35 percent of its total revenues. If it can trim that figure to 25 percent, the average for American industry, it can free up $6 billion in free cash flow annually.[14]

Another minor but symbolic innovation involved ladders. Airline fuselages are curved, but to gain access to them on the factory floor a worker used a straight ladder. The closer the worker got to the top of the ladder, the farther he/she had to stretch to reach the fuselage. Iwata's conclusion was to use a ladder that's shaped like an upside-down J.[15] Indeed, Boeing is introducing many reforms American automobile manufacturers were forced to make 10 years ago because of competition from Japan. Employees contribute by huddling in five-day "accelerated improvement workshops" where they brainstorm on how to do their jobs more efficiently.[16]

Boeing's challenge is one it should be prepared for: For decades it has succeeded at designing, building, marketing, and servicing very big and very complex machines on a global scale. As Condit notes, "Large-scale systems integration is what we do. Airplanes, space stations, launch vehicles. Things with lots of parts."[17] What could be a more challenging test of Boeing than the integration of itself?[18]

However, doubts persist as to whether Boeing can accomplish all it intends with this new program. Gordon Bethune, chairman and CEO of Continental Airlines and a former Boeing executive, states that "This company is trying to do so much at the same time—increase production, make its manufacturing lean, and deal with mergers. It's like a guy who's juggling eggs, and then somebody tosses him an orange. It's easy to drop something."[19]

Review Questions

1. Interpret Boeing's work design based on the core job characteristics of the Job Characteristics Model presented in this chapter.
2. Interpret "old" versus "new" trends in the workplace in regard to Boeing's shift away from 1940s methods to new, more modern work designs.
3. Do environmental conditions assist or hinder Boeing's attempts to restructure its work force?

CASE 16

Having Fun at Southwest Airlines

The U.S. airline industry experienced problems in the early 1990s. From 1989 through 1993, the largest airlines, including American, United, Delta, and USAir, lost billions of dollars. Only Southwest Airlines remained profitable throughout that period. CEO and co-founder Herb Kelleher pointed out that, "we didn't make much for a while there. It was like being the tallest guy in a tribe of dwarfs."[1] Nevertheless, his company had sales of $3.8 billion in 1997, an increase over 1996 of 12 percent, and profits of $317 million. This is particularly noteworthy since Southwest is not a nationwide air carrier; 85 percent of its flights are under 500 miles.[2] How did a little airline get to be so big? Its success is due to its key values, developed by Kelleher and carried out daily by his 25,000 employees. These core values are humor, altruism, and "luv" (the company's stock ticker symbol).[3]

One of the things that makes Southwest so unique is its short-haul focus. The airline doesn't assign seats or sell tickets through the reservation systems used by travel agents. Many passengers buy tickets at the gate. The only food served is peanuts or crackers. But passengers don't seem to mind. In fact, serving "Customers" (at Southwest, always written with a capital C) is the focus of the company's employees. As the executive vice president for customers, Colleen Barrett, said, "We will never jump on employees for leaning too far toward the customer, but we come down on them hard for not using common sense."[4] As *Fortune* magazine summarized, "treating the customer right is a lot easier when employees are treating one another that way." Southwest's core values produce employees who are highly motivated and who care about the customers and about one another.

One way in which Southwest carries out this philosophy is by treating employees and their ideas with respect. Executive vice president Barrett formed a "culture committee," made up of employees from different functional areas and levels, who meet quarterly to come up with ideas for maintaining Southwest's corporate spirit and image. All managers, officers, and directors are expected to "get out in the field," meet and talk to employees, and understand their jobs. Employees are encouraged to use their creativity and sense of humor to make their jobs and the customers' experience more enjoyable. Gate agents, for example, are given a book of games to play with waiting passengers when a flight is delayed. Flight agents might do an imitation of Elvis or Mr. Rogers while making announcements. Other have jumped out of the overhead luggage bins to surprise boarding passengers.[5]

CEO Kelleher knows that not everyone would be happy as a Southwest employee, however: "What we are looking for, first and foremost, is a sense of humor. Then we are looking for people who have to excel to satisfy themselves and who work well in a collegial environment." He feels that the company can teach specific skills but a compatible attitude is most important. When asked to prove that she had a sense of humor Mary Ann Adams, hired in 1997 as a finance executive, recounted a practical joke in which

she turned an unflattering picture of her boss into a screen saver for her department.[6]

To encourage employees to treat one another as well as they treat their customers, departments examine linkages within Southwest to see what their internal "customers" need. The provisioning department, for example, whose responsibility is to provide the snacks and drinks for each flight, selects a flight attendant as "customer of the month." The department's own board of directors makes the selection decision, as well as other managerial decisions, for the provisioning department. Kelleher and Barrett are invited to these board meetings, and both feel that it is important to attend. Other departments have sent their internal "customers" pizza and ice cream. Employees write letters commending the work of other employees or departments, and these letters are valued as much as those from customers. When problems do occur between departments, the employees work out solutions in supervised meetings.

Employees exhibit the same attitude of altruism and "luv" (Southwest's term for its relationship with its customers) to other groups as well. Nearly 25 percent of Southwest employees volunteered their time at Ronald McDonald Houses throughout Southwest's territory. When the company purchased a small regional airline, employees personally sent cards and company T-shirts to their new colleagues to welcome them to the Southwest family. They demonstrate similar caring to the company itself. As gasoline prices rose during the period of the Gulf War in the early 1990s, many of the employees created the "Fuel from the Heart Program," donating fuel to the company by deducting the cost of one or more gallons from their paychecks.

Acting in the company's best interests is also directly in the in-

terest of its employees. Southwest has a profit-sharing plan in which approximately 15 percent of net profit is distributed to employees, and unlike many of its competitors Southwest consistently has profits to share. Employees also own 13 percent of Southwest stock. Although 80 percent unionized, the company has a history of good labor relations. In fact, the firm and the pilots union have recently agreed to an unusual 10-year contract under which the pilots will receive stock options to buy millions of shares, as well as profit sharing, but will receive no wage increase during the first five years.[7]

According to Harvard University professor John Kotter, setting the standard for low costs in the airline industry does not mean Southwest is "cheap." "Cheap is trying to get your prices down by nibbling costs off everything. . . . [Firms like Southwest Airlines] are thinking 'efficient,' which is very different. . . . They recognize that you don't necessarily have to take a few pennies off of everything. Sometimes you might even spend more."[8] By buying one type of plane—the Boeing 737—Southwest saves both on pilot training and on maintenance costs. The "cheap" paradigm would favor used planes; Southwest's choice results in the youngest fleet of airplanes in the industry because the model favors high productivity over lower expenses.

By utilizing its planes an average of 11 hours and 20 minutes each day, Southwest is able to make more trips with less planes than any other airline. Its ground turnaround time of 17 minutes is the best in the industry. Not serving meals and cooperation from its ground and flight crews make this amazing statistic possible.

Keeping labor costs low is one of the ways in which Southwest maintains its competitive advantage. Employees' productivity is higher than that of any other airline. As of 1994, the company had won its eleventh "Triple crown" for being number one in the industry in on-time performance, baggage handling, and customer satisfaction. However, management also worried about the effects on morale of limited opportunities for promotion. The company has created "job families" with different grade levels so that employees can work their way up within their job category. However, as executive V.P. Barrett notes, "some jobs are worth only so much money," and after five or six years employees begin to hit the maximum for their job category.

Southwest's management has other concerns for the future. The addition of Baltimore, Chicago, and Cleveland has increased routes, personnel, and distance. As the company continues to grow, it is becoming more difficult for employees in outlying locations to get to meetings and events at its Dallas headquarters. Recently, problems

with delivery of 737-700 aircraft from the Boeing Company hobbled some of Southwest's expansion plans.

Another issue is how to maintain the culture of caring and fun while expanding rapidly into new markets. Southwest's success has been built with the enthusiasm and hard work of its employees; as CEO Kelleher said, "The people who work here don't think of Southwest as a business. They think of it as a crusade."[9] Cultivating that crusading atmosphere must be a continuing priority for the company.

The Southwest Story
Hoover's Company Capsule
Corporate Ranking
Airline industry
Stock market Performance
Yahoo Profile

1997 Fun Facts:

- Southwest answered 83 million reservations calls

- Southwest served 87.4 million bags of peanuts
- Southwest served 12 million bags of raisins
- Southwest received 105,583 job applications
- Southwest hired 3,006 new employees
- Southwest utilized approximately 65.6 million gallons of jet fuel per month
- Southwest had 993 married couples. In other words, 1,986 Southwest Employees have spouses who work for the company.

Review Questions

1. What needs were Southwest's employees able to meet through their jobs?
2. How did Southwest motivate its employees?
3. What are the principle motivational problems facing Southwest as it continues to expand?

CASE 17

Steinway: A History of Quality

Steinway & Sons remains one of the best-known producers of concert pianos in the world. Throughout its great history the company has shown a distinctive talent at innovation and quality workmanship, as evidenced by its 114 patents. In an age of mass production, Steinway continues to manufacture a limited number of handmade pianos in a unique testament to individual craftsmanship. However, Steinway's dominance in the concert piano market is being challenged by several rivals. Can Steinway continue its cherished ways, or will it need to adjust to new circumstances?

A Long History

Steinway & Sons was founded in 1853 by German immigrant Henry Engelhard Steinway in a

Manhattan loft on Varick Street. Henry was a master cabinetmaker who built his first piano in the kitchen of his Seesen, Germany, home. By the time Henry established Steinway & Sons, he had built 482 pianos. The first piano produced by the company, number 483, was sold to a New York family for $500. It is now displayed at New York City's Metropolitan Museum of Art.

Steinway's unique quality became obvious early in the history of the firm, as is evidenced by its winning gold medals in several American and European exhibitions in 1855. The company gained international recognition in 1867 at the Paris Exhibition when it was awarded the prestigious "Grand Gold Medal of Honor" for excellence in manufacturing and engineering.[1] Henry Steinway developed his pianos with emerging technical and scientific research, including the acoustical theories of the renowned physicist Hermann von Helmhotz.

In the early 1890s, Steinway moved to its current location in the Astoria section of Queens, New York, and built Steinway Village. Virtually its own town, Steinway Village had its own foundries, factory, post office, parks, and housing for employees. It's factory today still uses many of the craftsmanship techniques handed down from previous generations. Steinway produces approximately 5,000 pianos annually worldwide, with over 900 prominent concert artists bearing the title of Steinway Artist.[2]

New Competition

Yamaha Corporation of America has sold pianos in the United States since 1960 and remains the preferred brand for top jazz and pop artists. But in the late 1980s, Yamaha chose to enter the concert piano market in direct competition with Steinway. Developing grand pianos such as the CFIIIS provided Yamaha with the product offering to attack Steinway's 95 percent market share in concert sales. Yamaha created its Concert and Artist Service—similar to Steinway's—to supply pianos across the country.

Steinway was owned in the 1970s by CBS, and many concert artists complained that the quality had suffered as a result of that ownership. Pianists talked of the "Teflon controversy," when Steinway replaced some fabric innards with Teflon (it now coats the Teflon with fabric). Steinway was sold by CBS in 1985, and many experts voiced the opinion that Steinway's legendary quality was returning. Larry Fine, a piano expert, argues that "a Steinway has a kind of sustained, singing tone that a Yamaha doesn't have. Yamaha has a more brittle tone in the treble that some jazz pianists prefer."[3]

Even with increased competition, the Steinway Tradition continues. Every grand piano takes over a year to complete and incorporates over 1,000 details that set a Steinway apart from competitors. A tour of the Steinway factory is a trip back through time, as many of the manufacturing techniques have not changed since 1853.

Recently, Steinway developed Boston Piano in an attempt to broaden its market. Boston pianos—designed by Steinway & Sons with the latest computer technology—are manufactured in Japan by Kawai, the second-largest Japanese piano maker. At first, Boston intended to ship all of its pianos to markets outside of Japan, but when Kawai expressed interest in distributing them throughout Japan, Steinway took a different tack.

Boston's success in Japan is a result of an unorthodox method called "guerrilla marketing." This approach involved developing new dealers, referrals, and direct-mail programs. But the strategy also brought into play "selection events." With display space at a premium in Japan's cramped cities, displaying 65 grand pianos in one location was something quite new. Using telemarketing and direct mail, Boston's Japanese distributor attracted 260 people to a selection event in Osaka . . .

and sold 100 pianos. Boston Piano now accounts for 10 percent of the Japanese market.[4]

By transferring its quality and knowledge of building pianos to Boston, Steinway is able to open up a whole new market to exploit. Its core competence of hand craftsmanship can be applied in a newer, high-technology manner to a lower-priced market niche.

A New Partnership

On May 25, 1995, Steinway & Sons merged with The Selmer Company, manufacturer of brass wind, woodwind, percussion, and stringed instruments, to form Steinway Musical Instruments, Inc. The new company's strategy strives to capitalize on its strong brand names and leading market positions. The company's net sales of $258 million for 1996 were split between Steinway piano sales (53 percent) and sales of Selmer band and orchestral instruments (47 percent). In addition, the purchase of William Lewis Violin and the Emerson Flute Company adds to the band and musical instrument line.

On August 1, 1996, an initial public offering (IPO) of common stock raised $63 million in new equity capital. This money allowed the firm to repay over $54 million of senior secured notes, thereby greatly improving the financial flexibility of the new company.

Steinway's piano sales are influenced by general economic conditions in the United States and Europe, demographic trends, and general interest in music and the arts. Steinway's operating results are primarily influenced by grand piano sales. Given the total number of grand pianos sold by Steinway in any year (3,066 in 1996), a decrease of a relatively small number of units sold by Steinway can have a material impact on its business and operating results.

Domestic grand piano unit sales have increased 32.2 percent

from 1993 to 1996, largely because of the economic recovery in the United States and increased selling and marketing efforts. Grand piano unit sales to international markets have remained relatively flat over the same period, primarily as a result of the weakness of the European economies. In 1996, approximately 54 percent of Steinway's net sales were in the United States, 33 percent in Europe, and the remaining 13 percent primarily in Asia.[5]

Unlike many of its competitors in the piano industry, Steinway does not provide extended financing arrangements to its dealers. To facilitate the long-term financing required by some dealers, Steinway has arranged for financing through a third-party provider, which generally involves no guarantee by Steinway.

The question remains, can Steinway continue to operate in the way that has proved successful over the past 140 years? The re-cent merger with The Selmer Company creates a stronger and more diversified firm.

Review Questions

1. How have group norms developed in Steinway?
2. How does Steinway's piano manufacturing process exhibit the need for teamwork?
3. Suggest how a new employee might work his or her way through the Stages of Group Development.

CASE 18

The Walt Disney Company: Undergoing Change

The Walt Disney Company has evolved from a wholesome family-oriented entertainment company into a massive multimedia conglomerate Its July 31, 1991, acquisition of ABC Network is the most recent of a number of changes in the organization. With this purchase, Disney moves beyond being a mere producer of media into the distribution of its and others' media products through a variety of channels. Has CEO Michael Eisner changed his mind from his earlier vision that "Content is King" to a realization that control of distribution may be where the new value lies?

Disney through the Years

After his first film business failed, artist Walt Disney and his brother Roy started a film studio in Hollywood in 1923. The first Mickey Mouse cartoon, *Plane Crazy*, was completed in 1928, and the first cartoon with a soundtrack, *Steamboat Willie*, was the studio's third production. The studio's first animated feature film was *Snow White* in 1937, followed by *Fantasia* and *Pinocchio* in the 1940s. Disneyland, the theme park developed largely by Walt, opened in 1955 in Anaheim, California. The television series, *The Mickey Mouse Club*, was produced from 1955 to 1959, and the Disney weekly television series (under different names, in-

cluding *The Wonderful World of Disney*) ran for 29 straight years.[1]

Walt Disney died in 1966 of lung cancer. Disney World in Orlando, Florida, opened in 1971, the same year that Roy Disney died. His son, Roy E., took over the organization, but without the creative leadership of brothers Walt and Roy Disney, the firm fell on hard times. Walt's son-in-law, Ron Miller became president in 1980. Many industry watchers felt that Disney had lost its creative energy and sense of direction because of lackluster corporate leadership. In 1984, the Bass family, in alliance with Roy E. Disney, bought a controlling interest in the company. Their decision to bring in new CEO

Michael Eisner from Paramount and a new president, Frank Wells, from Warner Brothers ushered in a new era in the history of Disney.[2]

Work the Brand

Michael Eisner has been involved in the entertainment industry from the start of his career (interestingly, beginning at ABC Television in the 1960s). He exhibits a knack for moving organizations from last place to first through a combination of hard work and timely decisions. From ABC, Eisner moved on to Paramount Pictures in 1976, which at the time was dead last of the six major motion picture studios. During his reign as president, it moved to first with blockbusters such as *Raiders of the Lost Ark*, *Trading Places*, *Beverly Hills Cop*, and *Airplane*, along with other megahits. By applying lessons he learned in television to keep costs down, the average cost of a Paramount picture during his tenure was $8.5 million, while the industry average was $12 million.[3]

Eisner viewed Disney as a greatly underutilized franchise identified by millions throughout the world. In addition to reenergizing film production, Eisner wanted to extend the brand recognition of Disney products through a number of new avenues. Examples of his efforts included the Disney Channel (cable), Tokyo Disneyland (Disney receives a management fee only), video distribution, Disney Stores, Broadway shows (*Beauty and the Beast*) and additional licensing arrangements for the Disney characters.

Disney represents movie production assets (Buena Vista Television, the Disney Channel, Miramax Film Company, and Touchstone Pictures), theme parks, publication companies (Disney Press, Mouse Works, Hyperion Press), and professional sports franchises (the Mighty Ducks hockey team and part of the California Angels baseball team).

However, in the early 1990s problems began emerging for Disney. An attempt to build a theme park in Virginia based on a Civil War theme was defeated by local political pressure. EuroDisney, the firm's theme park in France caused over $500 million in losses for Disney due to miscalculations on attendance and concessions. In 1994, Eisner underwent emergency open heart bypass surgery, and Frank Wells, long working in the shadows of his boss but increasingly viewed as integral for the success of Disney, died in a helicopter crash.

Eisner's choice to succeed Wells, Michael Ovitz from Creative Artists Agency, did not work out and Ovitz soon left. Stories of Eisner's dictatorial management style brought succession worries to shareholders.

Capital Cities/ABC

Once again, Eisner ushered in a new era at Disney by announcing the $19 billion takeover of Capital Cities/ABC on July 31, 1995. The deal came in the same week as Westinghouse Electric Corporation's $5.4 billion offer for CBS Inc. Disney represents one of several consolidations of the media conglomerates that are increasingly controlling the distribution of entertainment programming in the United States. Eisner appreciated the importance of both programming content and the distribution assets needed to deliver it.[4] As a result of many of his decisions, Disney has transformed from a sleepy film production studio into a major entertainment giant, with its revenues of over $2 billion in 1987 increasing to $22 billion in 1997.[5] Its stock price has multiplied over 15 times, creating enormous wealth for both stockholders and executives of Disney.

Mickey meets ABC

Source: Business Week, August 14, 1995.

PRODUCTION

Walt Disney Pictures
Touchstone Pictures
ABC Productions

CABLE

ESPN
Lifetime
A&E
Disney Channel

DISTRIBUTION

11 company-owned TV stations
228 TV affiliates
21 radio stations

PUBLISHING

Newspapers in 13 states
Fairchild Publications
Chilton Publications

One of the biggest questions arising from the ABC deal is whether Disney paid too dearly for declining network assets. Viewership among all the major networks continues to decline on a regular basis. Michael Jordan, the CEO of CBS, complains that "the pure network television business is basically a low-margin to breakeven business."[6] The networks are squeezed by having to pay extravagantly for programming while attracting an audience of older viewers who are scorned by advertisers.

However, another way to look at networks is as the lifeblood of the global, vertically integrated entertainment giants that own them, as loss leaders that act to promote their parent's more lucrative operations. In this scenario, ABC acts as Disney's megaphone to tell the masses about Disney movies, theme parks, Disney-made shows, and toys. Indeed, rather than shrinking, Rupert Murdoch's Fox, Paramount's UPN, and Time Warner's WB are three of the newest networks, with Barry Diller and Lowell Paxson planning to launch networks of their own.

Synergy is one key in today's network economies. ABC is able to turn 50 percent profit margins on its 10 network-owned stations and will realize a profit of over $550 million, largely because of local news shows and syndicated shows like *Oprah* and *Wheel of Fortune*. The other big payday comes when networks own and syndicate a hit show, something they could not do before they were deregulated in the mid-1990s. By owning more of their own shows, the networks avoid increasing license fees from the production companies.[7]

One risk in this strategy is that a network will miss out on a hit by favoring its own shows. Disney has blocked out certain parts of the week for its own shows. Fox and Disney appear best situated to exploit their platforms, with Fox injecting new life into an old brand, and Disney providing diverse production assets to feed its network.[8] This strategy works as long as networks remain big; since 1992, ABC and CBS have lost 25 percent and 23 percent of their viewers, respectively. The networks have cushioned this problem by investing more in their cable holdings.

Eisner remains committed to integrating the ABC Network into the greater Disney picture. "It sounds funny, but I am thinking about the millennium change. I've got to protect the Disney brand well into the future."[9]

Review Questions

1. Examine the internal and external forces for change faced by Disney.
2. How have external forces in the entertainment industry affected Disney's need for change?
3. What changes do you foresee in the entertainment industry in the next five years?

Integrative Learning Activities

In-Basket Exercise

Student Instructions for the Broadway Management Company In-Basket Exercise:

Bonnie Fremgen, Ph.D., Associate Professor, Department of Management, University of Notre Dame

You are Mitch Morris, vice president of productions for Broadway Management Company (BMC). Broadway Management Company manages Broadway musicals and currently has three in production: "Dogs," "Mortgage," "My Average Gentleman," with a fourth one, "Charlie" to open at the end of this year. The four managers of these productions report directly to you (see organizational chart). They supervise the musicians and performers who are all covered by a union contract. You started work with BMC as a company manager 12 years ago and became the VP for productions 5 years ago. You are in line to succeed Richard Reynolds as president of the company when he retires.

You have been out of the country on a month-long vacation. You are leaving town early Monday morning for a week's trip to Toronto to solve legal problems with the Toronto Theatre Company. At the end of the week you will be flying on the Seattle for a week to negotiate the opening of the company's new musical, "Charlie."

You have dropped by your office on Sunday evening to catch up on your in-basket. You have been out of touch with your office and your secretary, Jean, while you were on vacation. The office is deserted when you arrive at 7 p.m. and because of a power failure in New York City, the telephone system is temporarily down. To further complicate matters, the files are locked and you have forgotten to bring your set of keys. A new computer system was installed during your absence, and your old access code is denied. Therefore, you will only be able to communicate with your secretary and others by written memorandum.

You have two hours before leaving to catch your plane for Toronto. The following memos and correspondence are waiting for you in your in-basket. An organizational chart is provided for your information. Make a list of instructions (To Do list) for your secretary. Responses to some of the memos can be written directly on the memo. Any letters you wish to send can be handwritten for your secretary to type. The date is July 1.

450

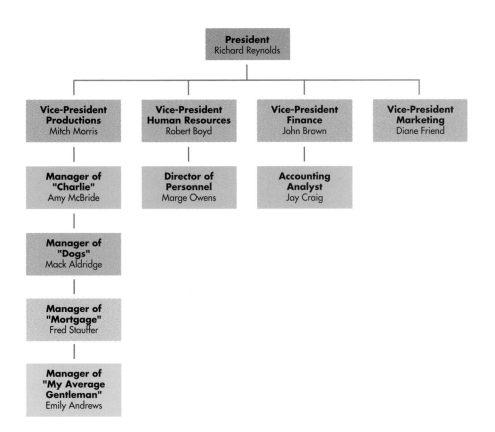

Organizational Chart

President
Richard Reynolds

Vice-President Productions
Mitch Morris

Vice-President Human Resources
Robert Boyd

Vice-President Finance
John Brown

Vice-President Marketing
Diane Friend

Manager of "Charlie"
Amy McBride

Director of Personnel
Marge Owens

Accounting Analyst
Jay Craig

Manager of "Dogs"
Mack Aldridge

Manager of "Mortgage"
Fred Stauffer

Manager of "My Average Gentleman"
Emily Andrews

MEMO 1

TO: Mitch
FROM: Jean
DATE: June 29
RE: Welcome Back!

I have to leave town quite unexpectedly today to take care of my father. I'm not sure when I'll be back, but I've left instructions with Alice, a temp from the ABC Employment Agency, on how you like things handled. I'm sure she'll work out fine for you.

MEMO 2

TO: Mitch Morris
FROM: Marge—Personnel Office
DATE: June 29
RE: Employee complaint

Called to discuss a grievance that was filed against one of your managers by Betty Black, a costume designer.

MEMO 3

TO: Mitch Morris
FROM: Jim Campbell—your broker
DATE: June 28
RE: Call him ASAP

MEMO 4

TO: Mitch Morris
FROM: Bob Boyd
DATE: June 29
RE: Attached letter

Please see attached letter that arrived during your absence. Let's discuss as soon as you return.

Attachment to Memo 4

- -

June 15

Mr. Mitchell Morris
Vice President for Productions
Broadway Management Company
1212 Broadway
New York, NY 10011

Dear Mr. Morris:

I am writing to you to express my extreme frustration over a recent incident involving the hiring of the new head costume designer, Lee Adams.

I have been a costume designer for this company for 25 years. I trained under Grace Foster and even filled in for her as acting head designer during her recent illness. All of my performance evaluations were above average, and I was told that I would be in line to get the head designer job.

Lee Adams is a personal friend of Diane Friend. The rumor mill has it that Lee got the job because of her friendship with Diane. The position was not even posted or advertised.

I'm writing to you, Mr. Morris, because you have always treated me fairly when I worked on your productions. I want you to be aware of the kind of underhanded deals that are being made by Ms. Friend.

If you don't respond to this letter, as much as I regret doing so, I will have to file a grievance with the union against Broadway Management Company. I will take this matter to court if necessary.

Sincerely,

Betty Black

TO: Mitch Morris
FROM: Jay Craig, Accounting Analyst
DATE: June 29
RE: FYI

Attached are the cumulative budget expenditures for your area of responsibility. This is based on your own line-item budget projections as stated in the far-right column. Please examine each line item to determine your status at mid-year and call with any questions.

Attachment to Memo 5

	Cumulated Actual Expenditures To June 30	Budget for Year Ending December 31
Salaries	400,000	800,000
Benefits	75,000	150,000
Travel	60,000	80,000
Advertising	450,000	600,000
Training	45,000	600,000
Supplies	10,000	40,000
Maintenance & Repairs	20,000	60,000
Communications	30,000	42,000
Rent	60,000	120,000
TOTAL	$1,150,000	$1,942,000

TO: Mitch Morris
FROM: Bob Boyd, Human Resources
DATE: June 27

Confidential

I think I've found the answer to your dilemma over filling the manager position for "Charlie." I've talked with a friend of mine who would be willing to take the job if we can bring the salary up just another 8 percent. She's extremely qualified, having just recently left a position as manager of "The Sound of Merger." I was able to observe her work on that production when she and I had a close personal relationship. That relationship is now over, but I believe that she would be an excellent choice for the position.

I know what a bind you are in with the new production of "Charlie" getting ready to open. Just give me the "go-ahead," and I can bring her on board. It would be a good move since she would bring her contacts on the union negotiation team along with her.

TO: Mitch Morris
FROM: Richard Reynolds
DATE: June 27
RE: Revenue Projections for "Charlie"

Can you get me some projected revenue figures for "Charlie" ASAP? Our investors are getting nervous since the opening of the show has been delayed. What shall I tell them to try to allay their fears?

TO: Mitch
FROM: Mack Aldridge
          Manager, "Dogs" musical
DATE: June 26

I would like your advice on handling some tough problems here at the Boston production of "Dogs." Your speedy response would be greatly appreciated since these problems are getting out of hand.

1. As you know the production company has always had our musicians and performers stay at the Hutton Hotels while they were traveling with a show. With the recent need to curtail spending we put the entire troop at the Red Road Inn. I'm also staying at this motel and find the accommodations to be fine. However, the performers have made numerous threats to file grievances if the accommodations are not upgraded. What do I do?

2. We have been using a national firm to transport our sets by overland trucks. This has resulted in less-than-good service. We have experienced numerous damages to sets, the loss of costumes, and late arrivals. My niece is married to someone who runs his own delivery service, with individualized attention paid to customers needs. I would like to give him the contract for all the wardrobe and set transport needs for "Dogs." What do you think?

MEMO 9

TO: Mitch Morris
FROM: Jay Craig—Financial Analyst
DATE: June 25

Mitch—I would like to thank you for offering to do everything in your power to get our numbers under control. Making some of the necessary administrative decisions can be difficult. Since I am new on the job and spent most of my career in public accounting auditing manufacturing companies, I am not acquainted with accounting practices in the music production business.

Since Mr. Reynolds has mandated strict enforcement regarding budget overruns, and your budget appears to be in the greatest need of curtailment, could we meet as soon as possible to discuss how we might reverse the situation?

MEMO 10

TO: All Vice Presidents, Managers, Department Heads
FROM: Richard Reynolds—President
DATE: June 22
RE: Performance Evaluations

As you know, Broadway Management Company has implemented a Performance Rating System this year. Please indicate in writing what steps you have taken to implement this performance rating system.

MEMO 11

TO: Mitch Morris
FROM: Bob Boyd
DATE: June 22

Confidential

The "boss" wants me to develop an analysis of how we can keep our employees happy. I told him they were interested in better lunchroom facilities, more attention and appreciation from their managers, and perks such as an indoor exercise track and day-care facility. He said, "That's all bull! All they really want is more money."

I don't know how to convince him. What do you think?

Incidentally, I'm really pushing for the indoor track so that we can all cancel our personal club memberships.

TO: Mitch Morris
FROM: Richard Reynolds
DATE: June 20
RE: Time Chart

I'm really worried that we won't open "Charlie" on time. Can you give me an estimated time chart representing this project? It'll make me a lot more comfortable if I can see where we are.

I pulled your projected schedule from my file and had my secretary attach it to this memo. My understanding is that we are still set to open on August 1.

Attachment to Memo 12

Activities	Time Required
Final costume fittings	2 weeks
Ticket presales	4 weeks
Advertising	6 weeks before opening
Assembly of set	1 week
Safety check	1 day
Inspection before opening	2 days
Dress rehearsal	4 days before opening
Carpentry work to prepare for set	5 days
Telephone installation (needed 2 weeks ahead of time)	2 days
Electrical installations (need before dress rehearsals)	3 days
All contracts signed (2 weeks before opening)	1 week
Tickets printed (6 weeks before opening)	3 days

TO: Mitch Morris
FROM: Emily Andrews
      Manager of "My Average Gentleman"
DATE: June 19

I know that we are making every attempt to get a better balance of personnel in our hiring practices. This musical has far more male parts than female parts. I wonder if you and I could discuss how we might address the issue of increasing the minority hiring within our productions.

TO: Mitch Morris
FROM: Diane Friend
DATE: June 20

Confidential

- -

Mitch—I wonder if you would help me out. I have a great opportunity for a job. I need to have a reference from someone who is highly placed here. Since I have had a couple of problems with Reynolds I'm not sure he would give me the recommendation I want. Can you write me a good reference? You know, the usual stuff: "conscientious, great worker, able to follow-through, fair, etc."

Thanks so much. I'll do the same for you if you ever need it.

TO: Mitch Morris
FROM: Richard Reynolds
DATE: June 18
RE: Budget Forecast

Your budget forecast is outstanding! I was able to incorporate it into my board report without any alterations. Keep up the good work.

TO: All Vice Presidents
FROM: Richard Reynolds
DATE: June 15
RE: Federal Regulations

We have had far too many grievances filed by employees who are saying their rights and safety are not being protected by the Broadway Musical Company. I've instructed Bob Boyd to bring in a training consultant to discuss the federal regulations that everyone in this business must know. All VPs, managers, and department heads are expected to attend the seminars.

Remember, we are just like any other big company. We're all guided by the same regulations. Please get a memo back to me ASAP with your reaction to the regulations that should be discussed in these seminars.

MEMO 17

TO: Mitch Morris
FROM: Diane Friend
DATE: June 14

We are very unhappy about the marketing support we are getting from the public relations company we are using for the musical "Mortgage." They have overcharged us by $12,000.

They don't seem to be able to relate to me. I think it's that gender thing again. Could you handle this? Thanks so much.

MEMO 18

TO: Mitch Morris
FROM: Mack Aldridge
         Manager, "Dogs" musical
DATE: June 25
RE: Late delivery of sets

Once again, we had a late delivery of sets from ACME trucking. This has happened in just about every city we have traveled to. ACME is getting more and more unreliable. What should I do?

MEMO 19

TO: Mitch Morris
FROM: Fred Stauffer
         Manager of "Mortgage"
DATE: June 12
RE: FYI

Just an informational memo to let you know about a recent incident that occurred when we opened the show in Cleveland. I've enclosed a couple of newspaper clips that appeared the day after we opened the show. As you know, the musical has explicit lyrics that some writers have labeled as "aggressive and hostile." We have limited admittance for adults 18 years and older. I held an interview with a local news station that went very well. I used some of the material out of the two articles, which I am attaching to this memo. Everything seemed to go well.

TO: Mitch Morris
FROM: John Brown—Finance
DATE: June 11
RE: Five-year Budget Forecast

I was glad to hear that the revised budget you requested made it in time for Reynold's board report. My staff put in a lot of overtime on this one. But I think it looks good and was worth the effort.

TO: All Vice Presidents
FROM: Richard Reynolds
DATE: June 7
RE: Journal article on Union Negotiations

In light of the recent concern over the negotiations for a new union contract, I thought you might find this article informative.
Attachment: "Union Negotiations"

TO: Mitch Morris
FROM: Richard Reynolds
DATE: June 6
RE: Gunpowder Incident

We have received a letter from the city of Madrid, Illinois, informing us that we have violated the Clean Air Act with the gunpowder we use in the battle scene of "Charlie." Get back to me on this.

MEMO 23

TO: Mitch Morris
FROM: Emily Andrews
DATE: June 6
RE:

We're still in the planning stage for taking the production of "My Average Gentleman" to Japan. I'm getting information from my sources in Japan that the management practices over there are quite different from our own. Since we will be hiring many Japanese musicians and actors, I'm wondering if we should try to implement their management practices. For example:

There are morning pep talks by supervisors.
All management and workers wear the same uniform.
After-work socializing with coworkers is greatly encouraged.
All managers and workers eat together in the same cafeteria.
No layoffs.
Direct orders to employees are avoided whenever possible. They prefer consensus
    decision making.
Company loyalty is cherished above all else.
Physical exercise is available for all employees every morning.
Bonuses are paid to all for extraordinary performance.

What do you think, Mitch?

MEMO 24

TO: All Vice Presidents, Managers, Department Heads
FROM: Richard Reynolds
DATE: June 6
RE: Budget Concerns

Broadway Management Company is in the process of recovering from a bleak, financially troubled year. We are currently preparing for new productions during the next fiscal year. Because of the uncertainty regarding some of the projects, all managers are advised to build in a 10 percent across-the-board budget cut for the next fiscal year.

MEMO 25

TO: Mitch
FROM: Jean
DATE: June 5
RE:

I know you are on vacation—but I wanted to remind you that you are scheduled to speak at a summer conference at your alma mater on July 10.

TO: Mitch Morris
FROM: John Brown—Finance
DATE: June 5

Our legal department has advised us that there may be a conflict with our use of the title "Charlie." I know we did an extensive research of this title already. What do you think we should do?

TO: Mitch Morris
FROM: Richard Reynolds
DATE: June 5
RE: Employee Reference

I received the attached request to provide a recommendation for one of your managers, Fred Stauffer, who is trying to get a mortgage. Please handle. Thanks.

Attachment to Memo 27

Federal National Mortgage Bank
June 1, 1997

Mr. Richard Reynolds
President
Broadway Management Company
1212 Broadway
New York, NY 10011

Dear Rich,

It was good to see you at the benefit last week. I hope your family is well and you've been able to get away to play a little golf this summer.

I wonder if you would do me a favor by providing some background information on one of your employees, Fred Stauffer, who is applying for a large mortgage loan. Can you tell me if he has any financial, emotional, or health problems? Do you anticipate that his income will increase on a regular basis? Has he been dependable for you?

Any help you can give me would be great. I really want to help your employee out if we can, but you know how careful we have to be when we make these large loans.

I look forward to our getting together to discuss financing for that new musical you spoke to me about.

Sincerely,
Frank Lynch
Vice President
Lending

Integrative
Learning
Activities

Cross-Functional Integrated Video Case

Outback Steakhouse, Inc.
Fueling the fast-growth company

‒ ‒ ‒ ‒ ‒ ‒ ‒ ‒ ‒ ‒ ‒ ‒ ‒ ‒ ‒ ‒

Marilyn L. Taylor, D.B.A., Gottlieb-Missouri, Distinguished Professor of Business Strategy, Henry W. Bloch School of Business and Public Administration, University of Missouri—Kansas City, Kansas City, MO 64110

Krishnan Ramaya, Ph.D., Henry W. Bloch School of Business and Public Administration, University of Missouri—Kansas City, Kansas City, MO 64110

George M. Puia, Ph.D., School of Business, Indiana State University, Terre Haute, IN 47809, Tel: (812) 237-2090

Support for the development of this case and its accompanying video were provided by

Center for Entrepreneurial Leadership
Ewing Marion Kauffman Foundation
Kansas City, MO

The authors express deep appreciation to the following individuals at the Ewing Marion Kauffman Foundation: Dr. Ray Smilor, vice president of the Center for Entrepreneurial Leadership Inc.; Ms. Pam Kearney, communications specialist, Communications Department; and Ms. Judith Cone, ETI professional with the Center for Entrepreneurial Leadership Inc. In addition, the authors wish also to express appreciation to Outback executives Chris Sullivan, chairman and CEO; Bob Basham, president and COO; Tim Gannon, sr. vice president; Bob Merritt, sr. vice President, CFO, and treasurer; Nancy Schneid, vice president of marketing; Ava Forney, assistant to the chairman and CEO; as well as the other Outback officers, executives, and employees who gave so enthusiastically and generously of their time, knowledge, and skills to make this case study possible.

Contact Person: George M. Puia, Ph.D.

Exhibits may be found in the Instructor's Manual.

Outback Steakhouse: Fueling the Fast-Growth Company

Since the company's initial public offering in June of 1991, Wall Street observers had continually predicted a downturn in the price of Outback's stock. Indeed, most analysts viewed Outback as just another fad in an intensely competitive industry where there are plenty of imitators. They continued to caution that Outback was in a saturated market and that the company could not continue growing at its existing pace. The December 1994 issue of *Inc.* magazine declared Outback's three founders as winners of the coveted Entrepreneur of the Year award. The company was profiled in 1994 and early 1995 by the business press as one of the biggest success stories in corporate America in recent years.[1]

At 5:00 P.M. on a Saturday in early 1995 in Brandon, a suburb outside Tampa, the lines had already begun to form in a strip mall outside Outback Steakhouse. Customers waited anywhere from half an hour to almost two hours for a table.

The firm's founders, Chris Sullivan, Bob Basham, and Tim Gannon, organized Outback in August 1987 with the expectation of building five restaurants and spending increased leisure time on the golf course and with their families. In 1988 the company had sales of $2.7 million from its two restaurants. By year-end 1994 the chain exceeded all of the founders' expectations, with over 200 restaurants and $549 million in systemwide sales (see Exhibits 1 and 2 for financial data) and had formed a joint venture partnership with Texas-based Carrabbas Italian Grill to enter the lucrative Italian restaurant segment, currently dominated by General Mill's Olive Garden. A 1994 national survey of the country's largest restaurant chains ranked

Outback first in growth (52.9%), second by sales per unit ($3.3 million), sixth by market share (5.9%), and tenth by number of units (205), all of which was accomplished in less than six years (see Exhibit 3).[2]

The founders expected that Outback could grow into a 550–600-unit chain in the continental United States. During 1995 alone, the company expected to add 65 to 70 new restaurants, maintain overall sales growth comparable to 1994, and continue to increase its same-store sales. In spite of the company's past success and future plans, however, analysts and other industry observers questioned how long Outback could continue its astounding growth, whether the company could maintain its strong momentum while pursuing multiple major strategic thrusts to propel its growth, and whether and how the culture of the company could be maintained. Skepticism about Outback's continued growth was clearly evident in the way Wall Street analysts viewed the company. By the end of 1994, Outback's stock was one of the most widely held stocks on the short sellers' list.[3] Adjusted for stock splits, Outback's share price rose from $3.50 to almost $30 over a three-year period. Exhibits 4 and 5 provide information on Outback's stock performance as well as samples of analysts' perspectives on Outback's continued growth during 1994.

The French Restaurant Legacy

The French coined the term *restaurant*, meaning "a food that restores," and were the first to create a place that could be defined as a restaurant by modern standards.[4] Before the French Revolution most culinary experiences were the exclusive domain of the nobility. The French

Revolution dispersed the nobility and their chefs. The chefs, denied the patronage of the nobles, scattered throughout Europe, taking the restaurant concept with them.

In contrast, American restaurants grew up in response to the need to serve the burgeoning 19th-century U.S. workforce. The rapid growth of U.S. cities, fueled by the influx of European immigrants, provided the initial impetus for the American restaurant industry. Initially, restaurants were single family-owned operations and consisted of two broad categories.[5] The first category, fine dining, had facilities that were affordable only to the wealthy and were located primarily in major cities. The second category catered primarily to industrial workers. This latter category included concepts such as lunch wagons and soda fountains, which later evolved into coffee shops and luncheonettes. These grew rapidly in response to the continuous expansion of urban areas. The American obsession with efficiency propelled yet another restaurant concept, the self-service restaurant, to become a central theme for 20th-century American restaurants.

Retail and theater chains emerged with the new century. The first large U.S. restaurant chain organization was the brainchild of Frederick Henry Harvey, an English immigrant.[6] After his Harvey House opened in 1876 in Topeka, Kansas, restaurant chains too quickly became part of the American scene.

The restaurant industry's $290 billion revenues in 1993 accounted for 4.3 percent of U.S. GDP.[7] The industry's 100 largest chains accounted for 40 percent of total industry sales. U.S. restaurants in the latter part of the twentieth century could broadly be classified into three segments—fast-food, casual dining, and fine dining. However, within these three broad categories were highly fragmented subsegment markets. The fast-food segment was primarily catered to by major chains such as McDonald's, Wendy's, Burger King, Hardee's, and Kentucky Fried Chicken. Casual dining catered to the cost conscious and typically priced menu entrees between fastfood and fine dining restaurants. Fine dining establishments catered to affluent customers and were located primarily in major metropolitan areas. Fine dining establishments were mostly single-unit businesses. In the early 1990s 75 percent of all casual dining establishments were still mom-and-pop operations.[8] The industry was characterized by high failure rates. Approximately 75 percent of all establishments failed within the first year; 90 percent within five years. Failure in the restaurant industry was attributed to a plethora of factors, including undercapitalization, poor location, poor food quality, underestimation of the effort needed to be successful, the effect of changing demographics segments, and government regulations.[9]

Restaurant operations are highly labor-intensive businesses. However, aspiring restaurant owners often seriously underestimated their capitalization requirements, that is, the funds needed for leasehold improvements and equipment. Indeed, new restaurants are often seriously undercapitalized. The owners might also fail to plan for other startup funds such as the first year's working capital, preopening expenses, advertising, and inventory costs.

Location choice was another common error. A restaurant location had to attract sufficient traffic to sustain operations. The demographics required for appropriate fine dining restaurant sites were different from those required for casual dining establishments, which differed again from fast-food establishments such as McDonald's. The availability of suitable locations especially in major cities had become an important factor in the success or failure of restaurants.

Aspiring restaurant owners also often underestimated *the effort required* to make a restaurant successful. Running a restaurant was hard work and could easily involve 80 to 100 hours of work each week. *Changing demographics* affected not only location choices but also the theme and type of restaurant. What had once been easily definable segments had fundamentally changed. It had become increasingly difficult to clearly define targetable segments. *American Demographics* magazine referred to the current situation as "particle markets."[10] Examples of such particle markets included empty nesters, step-families, the baby boomlet, immigrants, the disabled, savers, the affluent, the elderly, and others. The restaurant industry was also one of the country's most *regulated industries*. A myriad of regulations on such issues as hygiene, fire safety, and the consumption of alcoholic beverages governed daily operations.

Still another requirement for a successful restaurant was the maintenance of consistent *food quality*. Maintaining a level of consistent food quality was challenging. Any variability in food quality was typically viewed as deficient.

Founding Outback Steakhouse—From Down Under to Where?

In March 1987 three friends—Chris Sullivan, Bob Basham, and Tim Gannon—opened their first two Outback restaurants in Tampa, Florida. Each of the three had started early in their careers in the restaurant industry—Chris as a busboy, Bob as a dishwasher, and Tim as a chef's assistant. Between them they had more than sixty years of restaurant experience, most in the casual dining segment. The three met when they went to work for Steak & Ale, a Pillsbury subsidiary, shortly after they completed college in the early 1970s. Chris and Bob went to executive roles in the Bennigan's restaurant group, part of the Steak & Ale group. The two men met their mentor and role model in casual dining legend Norman Brinker. Brinker had headed Pillsbury's restaurant subsidiary. When Brinker left Pillsbury to form Brinker International, Chris and Bob followed him. Among Brinker International's casual dining chains was Chili's. Brinker helped the two men finance a chain of 17 Chili's restaurants in Florida and Georgia. Chris and Bob described their contribution as "sweat equity."[11] Brinker was considered a leading pioneer in the development of the causal dining industry.[12] Brinker International, the restaurant holding company that Brinker created, was widely considered an industry barometer for the casual dining segment.

Brinker International, the parent company, acquired Chris and Bob's interest in the Chili's franchise for $3 million in Brinker stock. With about $1.5 million each, Chris and Bob turned their attention to a long-standing dream—their own entrepreneurial venture. They considered several options, finally settling on the idea of a startup venture consisting of a small chain of casual dining restaurants. Each of the two men brought special skills to the table—Chris in his overall strategic sense and Bob in his strong skills in operations and real estate.

In early fall 1987 the two men asked Tim Gannon to join Outback as its chief chef. Tim had left Steak & Ale in 1978 to play a significant entrepreneurial role in several restaurant chains and single-establishment restaurants, primarily in the New Orleans area. His last venture was a restaurant with Pete Fountain at the New Orlean's World's Fair. The venture at the World's Fair had experienced early success and then suddenly encountered severe financial difficulties, leaving Tim with virtually no financial resources. In fact, when Gannon accepted Chris and Bob's invitation to join them, he had to sell his one remaining prized possession, a saddle, in order to buy gas money to travel from New Orleans to Tampa.

Tim brought with him recipes drawn from 25 years of experience. His first tutelage had been under a French chef in Aspen, Colorado. Concerning his initial teacher, Tim said:

I was an Art History major (who) found his way to Colorado to Aspen to ski. My first job was as a cook. That job became exciting because the man I worked for was a chef from Marseilles who had a passion for great foods. I grew to love the business. . . . I have made the restaurant industry my whole life.

Bob Basham especially wanted a restaurant concept that focused on steaks. The three men recognized that in the United States in-home consumption of beef had declined over the years, primarily because of health concerns. However, they also noted that the upscale steak houses and the budget steak houses were extremely popular in spite of all the concerns about red meat. That observation came from their market research, which Bob Basham described as follows:

We visited restaurants to see what people were eating. We talked to other people in the industry. Basically we observed and read trade magazines. That is the kind of research I am talking about. We did not hire a marketing research crew to go out and do a research project. It was more hands-on research. . . . "the

experts said people will eat less red meat, but we saw them lining up to get in. We believed in human behavior, not market research."

The partners concluded that people were cutting in-home red meat consumption but were still very interested in going out to a restaurant for a good steak. They saw an untapped opportunity between high-priced and budget steakhouses to serve quality steaks at an affordable price.

Outback operated in the dinner house category of the casual dining segment where 75 percent of all such establishments were family-owned and operated. The top fifteen dinner house chains accounted for approximately $9 billion dollars in total sales.[13] Dinner house chains usually had higher sales volumes than fast-food chains. However, dinner houses typically cost more to build and operate.[14]

The initial investment for Outback came from the sale of the Chili's restaurant franchise. Both men were able to forego taking cash salaries from Outback for the company's first two years. Funding for the early restaurants came from their own resources, relatives, and the sale of limited partnerships. During 1990 the founders turned to venture capitalists for about $2.5 million. Just as the venture capital deal was materializing, Bob Merritt was hired as CFO. Trained as an accountant, Merrit had extensive experience with the financial side of the restaurant business. Prior to joining Outback, Merritt served as the vice president of finance for JB's Restaurants. Merritt had IPO experience, and the founders later decided a public offering was warranted. The company went public in June 1991. The market had a general aversion toward restaurant stocks during the mid- and late 1980s. However, Outback's share offering, contrary to expectations, traded at premium. CFO Merritt

recalled his efforts to borrow funds in 1990 even after the venture-capital infusion:

In November 1990, Outback was really taking off. . . . The most significant limitation was capital. . . . So, I shaved off my beard—because Tampa is a fairly conservative community—and went from bank to bank. I spent every day trying to borrow. I think we were asking for $1.5M so that we could finance that year's crop of equipment packages for the restaurants. We basically met with dead ends. . . . [It was] very frustrating. . . . So Chris and I started talking about where the market was. One strategy, I felt, was to sell a little bit of the company to finance maybe 18 months of growth, get a track record in the Street and come back with another offering with credibility. [So] we priced the transaction at about a 20 percent discount relative to the highest-flying restaurant stock we could find and, of course, the stock traded up from 15 to 22 on the first day. At that point we were trading at a premium for restaurant stocks.

Outback's continuing success made possible two additional stock offerings during the following eighteen months. All together, a total of $68 million was raised. By the end of 1994, the founders owned almost 24 percent of the company, which was valued at approximately $250 million.

Outback's Strategy and Structure—"No rules—just right"

The Theme—"Cheerful, comfortable, enjoyable, and fun!"

The three partners debated for some time about the appropriate theme and name for their restaurants. They wanted a casual theme but felt that the western theme was overused by budget steak houses. Ultimately, they focused on an Australian theme. None of the partners had ever been to Australia, but U.S. attention was focused there. Bob Basham explained:

In late 1987–88 when we started there was a lot of hype about Australia. We had just lost the Americas Cup not long before that. They were celebrating their bicentennial. The movie Crocodile Dundee had just come out. [So, there] was a lot of interest in Australia when we were looking for a theme . . . that was probably one of our hardest decisions . . . (we) wanted to stay away from a western theme. . . . [We] started talking about Australia [which] is perceived as very casual and we wanted to be a casual steakhouse. It is a good marketing niche tool and we continue to take advantage of it in our ads.

Bob's wife, Beth, ultimately wrote the name "Outback" with her lipstick on a mirror. As Tim Gannon put it, the name epitomized:

[What] we wanted to convey. We wanted to be a hearty good-fun atmosphere and [the name] represents our personalities too. The three of us live robust, fun lives.

The founders of Outback were convinced that any enduring concept must place a heavy emphasis upon fun, family, quality food, and community. Bob Basham explained:

I don't care what business you are in, if you aren't having fun, you shouldn't be in that business. . . . Chris, Tim, and I have a lot of fun doing what we are doing, and we want our people to have a lot of fun doing what they are doing. We try to set it up so they can do that.

Tim, whom the other two partners described as being the "hospitality" part of the team, elaborated on the entertainment aspect of the Outback theme:

We are in the business of entertainment and the way we entertain is through flavors. Service is a big component of that. We want our customers—someone who comes in at 7 P.M. and waits until 9 P.M. and leaves at 10:30 P.M.—to view us as their entertainment. We owe it to them!

Outback employees who waited on customers typically handled only three tables at a time, and this allowed closer customer attention.

Choosing the Menu— "Kookaburra Wings, Victoria's Filet, Chocolate Thunder Down Under"

The company gave Australian theme names to many of the menu items. For example, Buffalo chicken were called "Kookabura wings," a filet mignon was called "Victoria's Filet," and a rich chocolate sauce dessert was titled, "Chocolate Thunder Down Under." The menu also included a wide variety of beverages, including a full liquor service featuring Australian beer and wine. The menu for the trio's casual dining operation featured specially seasoned steaks and prime rib and also included chicken, ribs, fish, and pasta entrees. Tim explained the menu selections for Outback:

At Outback we don't look at other menus or trends. . . . [The] best things I learned in a lifetime I put in the menu.

The company's house specialties included its "'Aussie-Tizers'. . . and delectable desserts."[15] The company's signature trademark quickly became its best-selling "Aussie-Tizer," the "Bloomin' Onion." The idea for a large single-hearted onion cut to resemble a blooming flower, dipped in batter, and fried was originally developed by a New

Orleans chef from a picture in a Japanese book. Tim added seasonings and enlarged it to "Outback size." The company expected to serve nine million "Bloomin' Onions" in 1995.

The menu, attention to quality from suppliers, and the emphasis on exceeding customer expectations all contributed to the high food quality. At about 40 percent of total costs, Outback's food costs were among the highest in the industry. "If we didn't have the highest food costs in the industry," explained Bob Basham, "we would be worried."

Outback's founders paid particular attention to the flavor profiles of the food. As Bob Merritt put it:

One of the important reasons for our success is that we took basic American meat and potatoes and enhanced the flavor profile so that it fit with the aging population. . . . Just look at what McDonald's and Burger King did in their market segment. They tried to add things to their menu that were more flavorful. McDonald's put the Big Mac on their menu because they found that as people aged, they wanted more flavor. McDonald's could not address that customer need with an old cheeseburger which tastes like cardboard. . . . That's why Tex Mex is such a great segment. That's why Italian is such a great segment because Italian food tends to have higher flavor profiles. It's not happenstance. It's a science. There's too much money at risk in this business not to know what's going on with customer taste preferences.

The founders knew that as people age, their taste buds also age. Thus, they recognized that their baby-boomer customers, those born in the 1946 to 1964 period, would demand more flavor in their food.

The 1995 menu remained essentially the same in character as originally envisioned in 1987. The price range of appetizers was about $2 to $6 with entrees ranging between $8 and $17. The average check per person was approximately $15 to $16.[16] The changing of menu items was done with care. For example, a new item planned for 1995 was the rack of lamb. As Tim Gannon explained, the menu was an issue to which all three founders turned their attention:

Where we all come together is on the menu. Bob comes to the plate thinking how the kitchen can put this out and how it can be stored. Chris will look at it from how the customer is going to view it. Is it of value? I come to it from a flavor point of view. Is it an exciting dish? We all add something to the final decision.

Tim and the staff at the company's original restaurant located on Henderson Avenue in Tampa, Florida, undertook most of the company's R&D. The founders approved any menu changes only after paying careful attention to development. For example, Tim and the Henderson staff had worked for a number of months on the rack of lamb entree. Tim explained:

We have been working with it [the rack of lamb entree] for some time on the operational side trying to get the cook times down. The flavors are there. Chris is excited although it [the rack] is not a mainstream product. It is an upscale product for us. . . . We are still fine-tuning the operational side to be sure it is in balance with other things we are doing. We are serving 800 dinners a night, and you can't have a menu item that throws the chemistry of the kitchen off.

Quality Fanatics— "We won't tolerate less than the best"

Outback executives and restaurant managers were staunchly committed to the principle that good food required outstanding ingre-

dients. Tim explained the company's attention to the suppliers:

I have been to every onion grower from Oregon, Idaho, and all the way to Mexico looking for a continuous supply of single-hearted onions. I talk to the growers.. . . . If it's a product you serve, you cannot rely on the words of a distributor to say, "This is what we have." I have to get into the fields and see what they have. If I am going to take 50 percent of the crop like that, I have to get into the fields to know, to see, how the crop is developed. So that took me into the fields of Idaho to see what makes onions get that big and what makes double hearts because they are hard for us to use. We do that with everything, the species of shrimp, which boats have the ice, what's the best safety standards. [I go] with the guys who purchase the cattle and learn to look for what they look for. . . . That's the only way you can produce great food.

Supplier relationships were long-standing. The company made beef purchases centrally for the entire Outback system. The company's original menu was designed by Tim Gannon with help from Warren LeRuth, one of New Orleans's premier chefs. LeRuth recommended Bruss, a Chicago-based meatpacking company, as a source of high-quality beef. Tim explained why Bruss was such a great partner as a supplier:

We couldn't even get samples [from the others]. We were on a low budget at the time. This company believed in us. They sent us samples after samples. . . . Their cutters were more like craftsman; the sense of pride that the Chicago butchers have about their product is really what we wanted in our restaurants. Bruss was at about $37 million at the time. Today, they are at $100 million, and we represent $75 to $80 million of that. We've been a great partner for them as they have been for us.

In 1994 Outback had two major suppliers of beef, but Bruss

continued to supply over half of the Outback restaurants. About 60 percent of Outback's menu items were red meat entrees, and its best-selling steak alone accounted for about 25 percent of entrees sold. The attention to quality extended, however, to all suppliers. Vanilla, used only for the whipped cream in just one dessert item, was the "real thing" from the island of Madagascar. Olive oil was imported from Tuscany and wheels of parmesan cheese from Italy. Tim explained the company policy:

. . . if any supplier replaces our order with a cheap imitation, I will know about it and they will not supply us anymore. . . . I will not tolerate anything less than the best.

The attention to quality and detail was also evidenced at the individual restaurant level. For example, croutons were made daily at each restaurant with 17 different seasonings, including fresh garlic and butter, and cut by hand into irregular shapes so that customers would recognize they were handmade.

In addition to his oversight of supplier quality, Tim Gannon also focused on continual training of the restaurant staff throughout the Outback system. He held about ten meetings a year in various parts of the country with staff members from various regional restaurants. Typically, about 50 kitchen managers and other kitchen staff attended these meetings. There was a presentation from a special guest with half of the group in the front of the restaurant. In the meantime, the other half of the group worked on "the basics" in the kitchen. Then the two groups exchanged places. Tim felt these meetings were critical for generating new ideas, sometimes from very new kitchen staff employees. For example, one new employee had urged attention to the dessert sauces. Discussion of this issue ultimately resulted in a reformulation of the sauces so that they did not so easily crystallize as well as the installation of the warmers that held the sauces at a constant temperature. This innovation allowed the restaurants to serve desserts more quickly.

The restaurant general managers also emphasized food quality. This commitment was illustrated by Joe Cofer, manager of the Henderson Street restaurant in Tampa, when he said:

We watch the food as it comes out of the kitchen, touching every single plate to make sure every single plate is perfect—that's our commitment to this restaurant [i.e.,] to watch the food. We can take care of every single table by watching the food. If we have a problem at a table, we go to talk to them.

Designing a Restaurant—"Bob Basham's memorial kitchen"

Facility design was also a critical component in quality food preparation. Bob Basham especially paid attention to kitchen design, so much so that Chris and Tim termed Outback's kitchen design Bob's "Memorial Kitchen." Fully 45 percent of Outback's restaurant unit was generally dedicated to the kitchen. Analysts and other industry observers had pointed out that Outback could enlarge the dining area and reduce wait times for customers. However, Bob Basham explained the logic behind the company's restaurant design:

Restaurants get busy on a Friday night or a Saturday night when most people go out to eat. That's when you are trying to make the best impression on people. [But] physically, the kitchen cannot handle the demand. So if you have standards in your operation of a 12-minute cook time. . . . [it's] impossible to exe-

cute that way. We all decided we would not have it happening in our restaurant. So we underdesigned the front of the house and overdesigned the back of the house. That has worked very, very well for us. To this day we limit the number [of tables]. Even in our busiest restaurants where people tell us we could be twice as big and do twice the sales, we still discipline ourselves to build our restaurants one size.

The interior design was a "subtle decor featuring blond woods, large booths and tables [with] Australian memorabilia— boomerangs, surfboards, maps, and flags."[17] A typical Outback occupied over 6,000 square feet, featuring a dining room and an island bar. The restaurant area had 30 to 35 tables and could seat about 160 patrons. The bar had about six to nine tables with seating for about 35.

Location Is Everything?—"You're going to put a restaurant where? For dinner only?!"

The company's first restaurant was located on a site that had held several restaurants before Bob and Chris leased it. Early Outback restaurants were all located in strip shopping centers or were retrofits of existing freestanding restaurant sites. When the company first started, lease costs for retrofits were lower than the cost of constructing and owning a building. Bob Basham explained the rationale behind Outback's location strategy:

. . . We call it our A-market B-location. . . . we didn't have enough money to go to the corner of Main and Main. So we felt that if we went to a great market [that] had great demographics that we needed, and got in what we called a B-location, that typically most restaurant companies would think of

as a B-location, we felt we could be successful there if we executed great, and that strategy continues today.

However, as the company expanded into other parts of the country, the cost structure shifted. In 1993 the company developed a prototype that was being constructed in most new locations. The company devoted significant effort to site evaluation efforts that focused on area demographics, target population density, household income levels, competition, and specific site characteristics such as visibility, accessibility, and traffic volume.

Conventional wisdom in the restaurant industry suggested that facilities should be utilized as long as possible during the day. However, Outback restaurants were open daily for seven hours from 4:30 to 11:30 P.M. This dinner-only approach had been highly successful. The dinner-only concept had led to the effective utilization of systems, staff, and management. By not offering lunch, Outback avoided restaurant sites in high-traffic, high-cost city centers. Furthermore, the dinner-only theme minimized the strain on staff. Tips were typically much higher for dinner than for lunch or breakfast service. Outback restaurants averaged 3,800 customers per week and were usually filled shortly after opening. In an industry where a sales-to-investment ratio of 1.2 : 1 was considered strong, Outback's restaurants generated $2.10 in sales for every $1 invested in the facility.

Operating Structure— "No organization charts here"

Management remained informal in 1995. Corporate headquarters were located on the second floor of an unpretentious office building near the Tampa airport. The headquarters offices were about two miles from the original store on Henderson Boulevard. Headquarters staff numbered approximately 80. Corporate existed as a service center. As Bob Merritt put it:

We exist here to service the restaurants. . . . There is nothing I can do from Tampa, Florida, to make sure the customer has a great experience in Kansas City, nothing except to put in management people who have great attitudes, who like to take care of people, who are highly motivated economically, and make sure they have hired the best and most highly motivated people, and trained them to get the job done. It is absolutely our point of differentiation. You can get at the food and all the other stuff, but in the end what makes this company work is its decentralized nature and our willingness, particularly Chris and Bob's willingness, to live with the mistakes of their subordinates and look at those mistakes as opportunities to teach, not opportunities to discipline. That is the pervasive element of our corporate culture that makes it work.

There was no human resources department at corporate. However, Trudy Cooper, vice president for training and development, had been involved in the hiring of associates at most new restaurants until 1994. In 1994 Cooper added two coordinators who helped with new restaurant openings. One of the coordinators supervised training in the front operations and the other supervised the kitchen. Each selected 15 other high-quality employees from restaurants throughout the system to work on a temporary, one to one basis with the new employees during an opening. The two coordinators and the special training staff all returned to their home restaurants assignments once an opening was completed.

Training at a new restaurant site took place over a two-week period. Outback absorbed all the costs related to an opening into the marketing/advertising budget. The restaurant staff had four practice nights. On the first night, a Friday, the guests were family members of the staff. On the second and third nights, Saturday and Sunday, the invited guests were community members, including construction workers, vendors, and other VIP guests. The fourth night, Monday, was charity night. Trudy Cooper described a new restaurant opening:

We have those people on site for about two weeks. We have classroom sessions, then a food show and a wine show. We do a mock night. We do two nights of role play. We do a night with the media followed by a charity function. All of the proceeds go to charity. It is $10 a person for heavy hors d'oeuvres and an open bar. We make quite a bit of money on that night for the charity chosen by the restaurant manager.

Local press representatives were invited to a special briefing session an hour in advance of the opening night. All the proceeds from opening night went to a charity of the restaurant manager's choice.

A typical Outback restaurant staff consisted of a general manager, one assistant manager, and a kitchen manager plus 50 to 70 hourly employees, many of whom worked part-time. Job candidates for the restaurant staff were required to pass an aptitude test that assessed basic skills such as making change at the till. Every applicant interviewed with two managers. A friendly and outgoing disposition was a critical job requirement. The company also used psychological profile tests to better understand an applicant's personality.

Outback placed a great degree of emphasis upon learning and personal growth throughout the company. Trudy Cooper called it "Our learn-teach-learn approach." Chris Sullivan further explained:

I was given the opportunity to make a lot of mistakes and learn, and we try to do that today. We try to give our people a lot of opportunity to make some mistakes, learn, and go on.

"Every worker an owner . . ."

The three founders keenly remembered their early desire to own their own restaurant. Consequently, Outback provided ownership opportunities at three levels in the organization: at the individual restaurant level; through multiple store arrangements (joint venture and franchise opportunities); and through the newly formed employee stock ownership plan.

Top management selected the joint venture partners and franchisees. As franchisee Hugh Connerty put it, "There is no middle management here. All franchisees report directly to the president." Franchisees and joint venture partners in turn hired the general managers at each restaurant. All of the operating partners and general managers were required to complete a comprehensive 12-week training course that emphasized the company's operating strategy, procedures, and standards.

From the beginning, the founders wanted ownership opportunities for each restaurant general manager and formed the limited partner arrangement. Each restaurant general manager committed to a five-year contract and invested $25,000 for a 10 percent stake in the restaurant. Initially, the arrangement was in the form of a limited partnership. However, the company was in the process of converting all agreements to general partnerships backed with liability insurance.

Under the program, the restaurant general manager received a base salary of $45,000 plus 10 percent of the pre-rent "cash flow" from the restaurant. "Pre-rent" cash flow for Outback restaurants was calculated monthly and defined as earnings before taxes, interest, and depreciation.[18] Each manager's name appeared over the restaurant door with the designation, "Proprietor." An average Outback generated $3.2 million in sales and a pre-rent "cash flow" of $736,000. Average total compensation for managing partners exceeded $100,000, including an average $73,600 share of the restaurant profits. If the manager chose to leave the company at the end of five-year period, Outback bought out the manager's ownership. If managers chose to stay with Outback, they could sign up for five additional years at the same restaurant or invest another $25,000 in a new store. After the company went public in 1991, the company began to give restaurant managers nonqualified stock options at the time they became managing partners. The options vested at the end of five years. Each manager received about 4,000 shares of stock over the five-year period. Outback's attractive arrangements for restaurant general managers resulted in a 1994 management turnover of 5 percent compared to 30 percent to 40 percent industrywide.

By early 1995, eleven stores had celebrated their five-year anniversaries (see Exhibit 3). Of the eleven managers, two had left the company. One later returned. Four had gone on to new stores in which they invested $25,000 with the same repeat deal. Five stayed with their same stores, renewing their contract with additional options that would vest at the end of the second five-year period. Joe Cofer, manager of the Henderson Street Outback in Tampa, indicated how his position as general manager of the restaurant affected his life:

I have been with the Outback for about 4 1/2 years now. I started out as a manager. Sixteen months ago I was offered a partnership in the Henderson store. I grew up in Tampa, right down the street, and have lived here nearly my whole life. So when they offered me this store, it was perfect. . . . If you walk in the restaurant and look at the name on the sign, some people I went to high school with say, "How in the heck did this happen?". . . . The other organization [I worked for] had long hours when you were open from 11:30 in the morning until 1 or 2 in the evening. Those hours have a tendency to burn people out. . . . At Outback, from the [supplier] level all the way down to the dishwasher level we all work as a team. That is another difference between Outback and the organization I used to work for. . . . Here at Outback we don't have those rules and regulations . . . Chris always claims he plays a lot of golf in the daytime and has a lot of fun. . . . He will come up to you and ask, "Are you having fun?" [We say] "Oh, we're having a great time." He says, "Okay, that's the way you need to run this stuff."

Multiple-store ownership occurred through franchises, joint venture partnership arrangements, and sometimes a combination. The founders' original plan did not include franchises. However, in 1990 a friend who owned several restaurants in Kentucky asked to put Outback franchises in two of his restaurants that had not done very well. The founders reluctantly awarded the KY franchise. The two franchised restaurants quickly became successful. Under a franchise arrangement, the franchisees paid 3 percent of gross revenues to Outback.

After the IPO the company began to form joint venture partnerships with individuals who had strong operating credentials but not a lot of funds to invest. Under a joint venture arrangement a joint venture partner invested

$50,000 and in return received a $50,000 base salary, plus 10 percent of the "cash flow" generated by the restaurants in his/her group after the restaurant general managers were paid their 10 percent. Therefore, a joint venture partner who operated ten Outbacks generating $600,000 each would end up with $54,000 per unit or $540,000 total plus the $50,000 base. Since Outback's general managers were experienced restaurateurs, the joint venture partners focused primarily on area development, including site research for new locations and hiring and training new managers. The company instituted its employee stock ownership plan in 1993 for employees at the restaurant level. At the time the ESOP was established, all employees received stock proportional to their time in service. Each employee received a yearly statement. The stock ownership program required no investment from the employees and vested after five years.

Advertising and Promotion—"We have always established that Outback is quality product at a great value"

Vice president of marketing Nancy Schneid came to Outback in 1990. Before working for Outback, Schneid had been first a media buyer in a large advertising agency and then an advertising sales representative for Tampa's dominant radio station. She met Chris and Bob while she was at the radio station and they were running their Chili's franchise. Although Chili's advertising strategy did not usually include radio advertising, Chris and Bob chose to use a significant level of local radio advertising.

Nancy was well aware of Chris and Bob's success with Chili's. When they established

Outback, she became an early investor in the form of a limited partnership. She explained how the radio station she worked with was able to help the three entrepreneurs with advertising:

When they first opened Outback they were struggling. Our radio station was expensive to advertise on. . . . So I made an opportunity for them to go on radio on a morning show that had a 35 percent share of the market and an afternoon show that had a 28 percent share of the market. That gave them the opportunity to tell the Tampa Bay community about the concept [which was] in a very B location on Henderson. Tim Gannon came at 5:00 A.M. and set up a cooking station downstairs. He cooked and ran food upstairs while Chris and Bob talked to the DJ. They basically owned the morning show.

Outback used very little print media. Print advertisements typically appeared only if a charity or sports event offered space as part of its package. Thus, Outback ads might appear in the American Cancer Magazine or a golf tournament program. Billboards were used to draw customers to specific restaurant locations. TV advertising began in 1991 after the local advertising agency, the West Group in Tampa, was selected. The company produced about three or four successful TV advertisements per year. Although not a company spokesman, well-known model Rachel Hunter had participated in several of the ads and had become identified with Outback. Hunter's New Zealand origin was generally interpreted by audiences to be Australian.

Except for the development of the TV advertisements, advertising and marketing efforts were decentralized. As VP Schneid put it:

We are very much micro-managers when it comes to the spending of our media dollars. . . . We are very responsive to the needs of the commu-nity, for example, Big Sisters and Brothers. . . . [Our advertising, marketing, and community involvement efforts] help us build friends and an image of great food at a great price.

Community Involvement— "We have been rewarded . . . out of proportion to our needs, and we want to give some of that back"

Central to Outback's operating strategy was a high degree of visibility and involvement in the community. Outback sponsored the Outback Bowl that first aired on ESPN on New Year's afternoon 1996. In addition, the company was involved in a number of charity golf tournaments with a unique format involving food preparation and service at each hole. Community involvement involved not only top management but everyone at Outback. Each new store opening involved community participation and community service to charities. Other community involvement took various forms. The Tampa-based corporate staff included a full-time special events person with a staff that catered to charity as well as for-profit events in the Tampa area. For many charity events Outback provided the food while staff donated their time.

For example, a black-tie dinner for 400 was scheduled for May 1995 at Tampa's Lowry Park Zoo, a special interest of Outback's three top executives.

Every local restaurant managing partner was likely to have a Little League or other sports sponsorship. Basham explained:

We are really involved in the community. . . . I think you have to give back. We have been very, very fortunate, we have been re-warded . . . out of proportion to our needs, and we want to give some of that back to the community. . . . I think if more people did that we would have a lot less problems in this country than we have right now . . . I have certainly been rewarded out of proportion to any contribution I feel I have made, and I just feel I should give something back. That goes throughout our company.

The Founders' Relationship— "The three of us kind of stay on each other, challenging each other, kid each other a lot, but more than anything support each other to make this thing work"

The three founders contributed in different ways to running the company. Each shared his perspective on his own as well the others' roles. Chris gave his view of the trio:

. . . Bob and I became corporate-type restaurant people, and sometimes that is more systems-oriented and not so much hospitality-oriented. Tim really brought that to our success. But more than that, he is easy to get along with. He absolutely gets done what needs to get done. He needs a little prodding. Bob and I need a little prodding. So the three of us kind of stay on each other, kid each other a lot, but more than anything support each other to make this thing work.

Bob explained the synergy among the three:

We have been together eight years. I think we have a balance between our strengths and our weaknesses. There are some things Chris does extremely well that I don't do well. There are things that Tim puts into the formula that Chris and I could not do

as well as he does, and hopefully there are some things that I do well that they would need. I think just the three of us have synergies together that have really worked very positively for us. We kind of all feed off of each other. . . . Right now, each one of us has a different role in the company. I concentrate on operations, the people side of the business, the day-to-day going-on of the business. I think Chris has a little more of the strategic overview of the company, keeps us going in the direction we need to be going. He is very good at seeing things long-term. Tim is our food guy. Tim makes sure that we can all have a lot of fun. He has a lot of fun in his work. So we have a balance there. We all contribute and it all works.

Tim gave his perspective on how he fit in:

. . . My challenge: How do I fit in? . . . Partnerships of three are always hard but it has worked very well. I now understand my role and have been treated well. . . . [There is] nothing in life greater than having a great partnership. . . . We meet all the time. I never make a menu decision without them, Chris has eyes for the guest and Bob has eyes for the employee. . . . A lot of organizations bust up at the top, not bottom! I only want to work with Outback.

Competition—"We have all we need of the greatest kind of flattery"

A number of competitors in casual dining's steak dinner house subsegment had begun to make their presence felt. The most formidable competition was the Wichita, Kansas-based Lone Star Steakhouse & Saloon. However, there was also a growing set of players with a formula involving rustic buildings and beef value items that began operations in early 1990 and 1991. These in-cluded Sizzler International's Buffalo Ranch, Shoney's Barbwire, S&A Restaurant Corp.'s Montana Steak Co., and O'Charley Logan's Roadhouse. In addition, a number of chains had added or upgraded steak menu items in reaction to Outback.

Chris Sullivan explained his view of competition and what Outback had to do:

Our competitors—there are a lot . . . [We] can't run way from it—it's a fact. I think a lot of companies get in trouble because they start worrying about what the competitor is doing and they react to that. We really ask our people and we talk about—just go out and execute and do what you do best. The customers will decide . . . If we continue to do what we have been doing, we feel very, very confident that we will continue to be successful regardless of the number of competitors out there because with our situation, our setup, and the proprietors we have in our restaurants, I don't think there is anybody who can compete with us.

Outback's Future Outlook

The company as a whole was optimistic about its future. Wall Street analysts were skeptical, however. Citing the numerous entrants into the industry, they argued that casual dining operators such as Outback were close to saturation and questioned whether the firm could withstand the intense competitive pressures characteristic of the industry. However, Outback's management was unperturbed by Wall Street concerns or by the increasing competition. Joe Cofer summarized the management attitude:

I've heard so many times, "I love coming to your restaurant because your staff is so upbeat, they are so happy." They are always great people to have work for you. People just love the people here. . . . I see us as a McDonald's of the future, but a step up. I don't think anybody can come close to our efficiency because it is so simplistic and everyone is so laid back about it from the owners on down. And we are having such fun, making so much money. No one wants to go anywhere. I will never work for another company as long as I live. . . . You have that feeling mixed with the great food. I don't think anyone is a threat. . . . You have a very good investment with the stock. The stock has split three times in the last three years. . . . This is just going to split more and more and more. I'm just going to hold on to it forever. Hopefully, it will be my retirement.

The company intended to drive its future growth through a four-pronged strategy: (1) continuous expansion within the United States with an additional 300 to 350 Outback concept stores, (2) the rollout of Carrabbas Italian franchise as its second system of restaurants, (3) development of additional restaurant themes, and (4) international franchising. Chris Sullivan explained:

. . . We can do 500 to 600 restaurants, and possibly more over the next five years. . . . Our Italian concept, Carrabbas, that is in its infancy stage right now. . . . has the potential to have the same kind of growth pattern that we have had in Outback. . . . We will continue to focus on Outback and continue to build that because we have a lot of work left there. Develop Carrabbas and use that as our next growth vehicle and continue to look . . . for a third leg on that stool, and who knows what is going to be hot in a couple of years. . . . The world is becoming one big market, and we want to be in place so we don't miss that opportunity. There are some problems, some challenges with it, but at this point there have been some casual restaurants chains that *have gone [outside the United States] and their average unit sales are way, way above the sales level they enjoyed in the United States. So the potential is there. . . . We are real excited about the future internationally.*

In the face of the dire predictions from industry observers and analysts, Outback CEO Chris Sullivan put his organization's plans quite simply: "We want to be the major player in the casual dining segment."[19]

Endnotes

1. Jay Finegan, "Unconventional Wisdom," *Inc.*, December 1994, pp. 44–56.

2. Bill Carlino, "Top Dinner Houses Practice 3 R's for Growth," *Nation's Restaurant News*, August 1, 1994, pp. 110–14. In another 1993 survey of 2,500 diners Outback placed first overall jointly with General Mill's Olive Garden as the best restaurant chain in America. Categories of evaluation included food quality, menu variety, service, atmosphere, cleanliness, and convenience. (Rajan Chaudhry, "America Rates Its Favorite Chains," *Restaurants and Institutions*, February 1, 1994, pp. 48–69).

3. Short sellers target stocks they think are overvalued, putting downward pressure on their targets. Short sellers borrow from a broker and then sell them at current trading prices, betting the price will eventually decline. Shorts make money by later buying shares at the lower price to replace, or "cover," their borrowed shares.

4. Martin E. Dorf, *Restaurants That Work* (Whitney Press, 1992) pp. 12–13.

5. Ibid., pp. 16–25.

6. Ibid., p. 17.

7. With approximately 400,000 units and nine million workers, the industry is also the largest private U.S. employer (*Statistical Abstract of the United States*).

8. Carlino, "Top Dinner Houses Practice 3 R's for Growth."

9. Dorf, *Restaurants that Work*.

10. Ibid., p. 25.

11. Finegan, "Unconventional Wisdom."

12. "A Heaping Plate of Ventures for the Impresario of Chili's," *New York Times Biographical Service*, August 1992.

13. Dorf, *Restaurants that Work*.

14. "Restaurants," *Standards & Poor's Industry Surveys*, March 17, 1994, p. 48.

15. Press kit for the opening of Paducah, Kentucky, April 1995. Company documentation.

16. *Prospectus*, October 21, 1992, p. 17.

17. Press kit for the opening of Paducah, Kentucky, April 1995. Company documentation.

18. The following section draws heavily from the *Inc.* article that gave Outback the Entrepreneurs of the Year Award (December 1, 1994).

19. Rajan Chaudhry, "Outback's Bloomin' Success," *Restaurants and Institutions*, December 15, 1993, p. 51.

EXERCISES IN TEAMWORK

EXERCISE 1

My Best Manager

Preparation

Working alone, make a list of the *behavioral attributes* that describe the *best* manager you have ever worked for. This could be someone you worked for in a full-time or part-time job, summer job, volunteer job, student organization, or whatever. If you have trouble identifying an actual manager, make a list of behavioral attributes of the type of manager you would most like to work for in your next job.

Instructions

Form into groups as assigned by your instructor, or work with a nearby classmate. Share your list of attributes and listen to the lists of others. Be sure to ask questions and make comments on items of special interest. Work together to create a master list that combines the unique attributes of the "best" managers experienced by members of your group. Have a spokesperson share that list with the rest of the class.

Source: Adapted from John R. Schermerhorn, Jr., James G. Hunt, and Richard N. Osborn, *Managing Organizational Behavior*, 3rd ed. (New York: Wiley, 1988), pp. 32–33. Used by permission.

What Managers Do

Preparation

Think about the questions that follow. Record your answers in the spaces provided.

1. How much of a typical manager's time would you expect to be allocated to these relationships? (total should = 100%)

  ____% of time working with subordinates
  ____% of time working with boss
  ____% of time working with peers and outsiders

2. How many hours per week does the average manager work? ____ hours

3. What amount of a manager's time is typically spent in the following activities? (total should = 100%)

  ____% in scheduled meetings
  ____% in unscheduled meetings
  ____% doing desk work
  ____% talking on the telephone
  ____% walking around the organization/ work site

Instructions

Talk over your responses with a nearby classmate. Explore the similarities and differences in your answers. Be prepared to participate in class discussion led by your instructor.

Defining Quality

Preparation

Write your definition of the word *quality* here. QUALITY =

Instructions

Form groups as assigned by your instructor. (1) Have each group member present a definition of the word *quality*. After everyone has presented, come up with a consensus definition of *quality*. That is, determine and write down one definition of the word with which every member can agree. (2) Next, have the group assume the position of top manager in each of the following organizations. Use the group's *quality* definition to state for each a *quality objective* that can guide the behavior of members in producing high-"quality" goods and/or services for customers or clients. Elect a spokesperson to share group results with the class as a whole.

Organizations:

a. A college of business administration

b. A community hospital

c. A retail sporting goods store

d. A fast-food franchise restaurant

e. A United States post office

f. A full-service bank branch

g. A student-apartment rental company

h. A "tie-dye" T-shirt manufacturing company

i. A computer software manufacturing firm

Leading Through Participation

Preparation

Read each of the following vignettes. Write in the space to the left of each whether you think the leader should handle the situation with an individual decision (I), consultative decision (C), or group decision (G).

Vignette I

You are a general supervisor in charge of a large team laying an oil pipeline. It is now necessary to estimate your expected rate of progress in order to schedule material deliveries to the next field site. You know the nature of the terrain you will be traveling and have the historical data needed to compute the mean and variance in the rate of speed over that type of terrain. Given these two variables, it is a simple matter to calculate the earliest and latest times at which materials and support facilities will be needed at the next site. It is important that your estimate be reasonably accurate; underestimates result in idle supervisors and workers, and overestimates result in materials being tied up for a period of time before they are to be used. Progress has been good, and your 5 supervisors along with the other members of the gang stand to receive substantial bonuses if the project is completed ahead of schedule.

Vignette II

You are supervising the work of 12 engineers. Their formal training and work experience are very similar, permitting you to use them interchangeably on projects. Yesterday, your manager informed you that a request had been received from an overseas affiliate for 4 engineers to go abroad on extended loan for a period of 6 to 8 months. He argued and you agreed that for a number of reasons this request should be filled from your group. All your engineers are capable of handling this assignment, and from the standpoint of present and future projects there is no particular reason that any one should be retained over any other. The problem is complicated by the fact that the overseas assignment is in what is generally regarded in the company as an undesirable location.

Vignette III

You are the head of a staff unit reporting to the vice president of finance. He has asked you to provide a report on the firm's current portfolio including recommendations for changes in the *selection criteria* currently employed. Doubts have been raised about the efficiency of the existing system in the current market conditions, and there is considerable dissatisfaction with prevailing rates of return. You plan to write the report, but at the moment you are quite perplexed about the approach to take. Your own speciality is the bond market, and it is clear to you that a detailed knowledge of the equity market, which you lack, would greatly enhance the value of the report. Fortunately, 4 members of your staff are specialists in different segments of the equity market. Together, they possess a vast amount of knowledge about the intricacies of investment. However, they seldom agree on the best way to achieve anything when it comes to the stock market. Whereas they are obviously conscientious as well as knowledgeable, they have major differences when it comes to investment philosophy and strategy. The report is due in 6 weeks. You have already begun to familiarize yourself with the firm's current portfolio and have been provided by management with a specific set of constraints that any portfolio must satisfy. Your immediate problem is to come up with some alternatives to the firm's present practices and select the most promising ones for detailed analysis in your report.

Vignette IV

You are on the division manager's staff and work on a wide variety of problems of both an administrative and technical nature. You have been given the assignment of developing a universal method to be used in each of the 5 plants in the division for manually reading equipment registers, recording the readings, and transmitting the scoring to a centralized information system. All plants are located in a relatively small geographical region. Until now there has been a high error rate in the reading and/or transmittal of the data. Some locations have considerably higher error rates than others, and the methods used to record and transmit the data vary between plants. It is probable, therefore, that part of the error variance is a function of specific local conditions rather than anything else, and this will complicate the establishment of any system common to all plants. You have the information on error rates but no information on the local practices that generate these errors or on the local conditions that necessitate the different practices. Everyone would benefit from an improvement in the quality of the data because it is used in a number of important decisions. Your contacts with the plants are through the quality control supervisors responsible for collecting the data. They are a conscientious group committed to doing their jobs well but are highly sensitive to interference on the part of higher management in their own operations. Any solution that does not receive the active support of the various plant supervisors is unlikely to reduce the error rate significantly.

Instructions

Form groups as assigned by the instructor. Share your choices with other group members and try to achieve a consensus on how the leader should best handle each situation. Refer back to the discussion of the Vroom-Jago "leader-participation" theory presented in Chapter 13. Analyze each vignette according to their ideas. Do you come to any different conclusions? If so, why? Nominate a spokesperson to share your results in general class discussion.

Source: Victor H. Vroom and Arthur G. Jago, *The New Leadership* (Englewood Cliffs, NJ: Prentice Hall, 1988). Used by permission.

What Would the Classics Say?

Preparation

Consider this situation:

Six months after being hired, Bob, a laboratory worker, is performing just well enough to avoid being fired. He was carefully selected and had the abilities required to do the job really well. At first Bob was enthusiastic about his new job, but now he isn't performing up to this high potential. Fran, his supervisor, is concerned and wonders what can be done to improve this situation.

Instructions

Assume the identity of one of the following persons: Frederick Taylor, Henri Fayol, Max Weber, Abraham Maslow, Chris Argyris. Assume that *as*

this person you have been asked by Fran for advice on the management situation just described. Answer these questions as you think your assumed identity would respond. Be prepared to share your answers in class and to defend them based on the text's discussion of this person's views.

1. As (*your assumed identity*), what are your basic beliefs about good management and organizational practices?

2. As (*your assumed identity*), what do you perceive may be wrong in this situation that would account for Bob's low performance?

3. As (*your assumed identity*), what could be done to improve Bob's future job performance?

The Great Management History Debate

Preparation

Consider the question "What is the best thing a manager can do to improve productivity in her or his work unit?"

Instructions

The instructor will assign you, individually or in a group, to one of the following positions. Complete the missing information as if you were the man-

agement theorist referred to. Be prepared to argue and defend your position before the class.

- Position A: "Mary Parker Follett offers the best insight into the question. Her advice would be to . . . ". (advice to be filled in by you or the group).

- Position B: "Max Weber's ideal bureaucracy offers the best insight into the question. His advice would be to . . . ". (advice to be filled in by you or the group).

- **Position C:** "Henri Fayol offers the best insight into the question: His advice would be to . . . ". (advice to be filled in by you or the group).

- **Position D:** "The Hawthorne studies offer the best insight into the question. Elton Mayo's advice would be to . . . ". (advice to be filled in by you or the group).

EXERCISE 7

What Do You Value in Work?

Preparation

The following 9 items are from a survey conducted by Nicholas J. Beutell and O. C. Brenner ("Sex Differences in Work Values," *Journal of Vocational Behavior*, vol. 28, 1986, pp. 29–41). Rank order the 9 items in terms of how important (9 = most important) they would be to you in a job.

How important is it to you to have a job that:
____ Is respected by other people?
____ Encourages continued development of knowledge and skills?
____ Provides job security?
____ Provides a feeling of accomplishment?
____ Provides the opportunity to earn a high income?
____ Is intellectually stimulating?
____ Rewards good performance with recognition?
____ Provides comfortable working conditions?
____ Permits advancement to high administrative responsibility?

Instructions

Form into groups as designated by your instructor. Within each group, the *men in the group* will meet to develop a consensus ranking of the items as they think the *women* in the Beutell and Brenner survey ranked them. The reasons for the rankings should be shared and discussed so they are clear to everyone. The *women in the group* should not participate in this ranking task. They should listen to the discussion and be prepared to comment later in class discussion. A spokesperson for the men in the group should share the group's rankings with the class.

Optional Instructions

Form into groups as designated by your instructor but with each group consisting entirely of men or women. Each group should meet and decide which of the work values members of the *opposite* sex ranked first in the Beutell and Brenner survey. Do this again for the work value ranked last. The reasons should be discussed, along with the reasons why each of the other values probably was not ranked first . . . or last. A spokesperson for each group should share group results with the rest of the class.

Source: Adapted from Roy J. Lewicki, Donald D. Bowen, Douglas T. Hall, and Francine S. Hall, *Experiences in Management and Organizational Behavior*, 3rd ed. (New York: Wiley, 1988), pp. 23–26. Used by permission.

Confronting Ethical Dilemmas

Preparation

Read and indicate your response to each of the situations below.

a. Ron Jones, vice president of a large construction firm, receives in the mail a large envelope marked "personal." It contains a competitor's cost data for a project that both firms will be bidding on shortly. The data are accompanied by a note from one of Ron's subordinates saying: "This is the real thing!" Ron knows that the data could be a major advantage to his firm in preparing a bid that can win the contract. *What should he do?*

b. Kay Smith is one of your top-performing subordinates. She has shared with you her desire to apply for promotion to a new position just announced in a different division of the company. This will be tough on you since recent budget cuts mean you will be unable to replace anyone who leaves, at least for quite some time. Kay knows this and in all fairness has asked your permission before she submits an application. It is rumored that the son of a good friend of your boss is going to apply for the job. Although his credentials are less impressive than Kay's, the likelihood is that he will get the job if she doesn't apply. *What will you do?*

c. Marty Jose got caught in a bind. She was pleased to represent her firm as head of the local community development committee In fact, her supervisor's boss once held this position and told her in a hallway conversation, "Do your best and give them every support possible." Going along with this, Marty agreed to pick up the bill (several hundred dollars) for a dinner meeting with local civic and business leaders. Shortly thereafter, her supervisor informed everyone that the entertainment budget was being eliminated in a cost-saving effort. Marty, not wanting to renege on supporting the community development committee, was able to charge the dinner bill to an advertising budget. Eventually, an internal auditor discovered the mistake and reported it to you, the personnel director. Marty is scheduled to meet with you in a few minutes. *What will you do?*

Instructions

Working alone, make the requested decisions in each of these incidents. Think carefully about your justification for the decision. Meet in a group assigned by your instructor. Share your decisions and justifications in each case with other group members. Listen to theirs. Try to reach a group consensus on what to do in each situation and why. Be prepared to share the group decisions, and any dissenting views, in general class discussion.

Beating the Time Wasters

Preparation

1. Make a list of all the things you need to do tomorrow. Prioritize each item in terms of *how important it is to create outcomes that you can really value.* Use this classification scheme:
(a) Most important, top priority
(b) Important, not top priority
(c) Least important, low priority
Look again at all activities you have classified as B. Reclassify any that are really As or Cs. Look at your list of As. Reclassify any that are really Bs or Cs. Double-check to make sure you are comfortable with your list of Cs.

2. Make a list of all the "time wasters" that often interfere with your ability to accomplish everything you want to on any given day.

Instructions

Form into groups as assigned by the instructor. Have all group members share their lists and their priority classifications. Members should politely "challenge" each other's classifications to make sure that only truly "high-priority" items receive an A rating. They might also suggest that some C items are of such little consequence that they not be worth doing at all. After each member of the group revises his or her "to do" list based on this advice, go back and discuss the time wasters identified by group members. Develop a master list of time wasters and what to do about them. Have a group spokesperson be prepared to share discussion highlights and tips on beating common time wasters with the rest of the class.

Source: Developed from Roy J. Lewicki, Donald D. Bowen, Douglas T. Hall, and Francine S. Hall. *Experiences in Management and Organizational Behavior*, 3rd ed. (New York: John Wiley & Sons, 1988), pp. 314–16.

EXERCISE 10

Personal Career Planning

Preparation

Complete the following three activities, and bring the results to class. Your work should be in a written form suitable for your instructor's review.

Step 1: *Strengths and Weaknesses Inventory* Different occupations require special talents, abilities, and skills if people are to excel in their work. Each of us, you included, has a repertoire of existing strengths and weaknesses that are "raw materials" we presently offer a potential employer. Of course, actions can (and should!) be taken over time to further develop current strengths and to turn weaknesses into strengths. Make a list identifying your most important strengths and weaknesses at the moment in relation to the career direction you are most likely to pursue upon graduation. Place a * next to each item you consider most important to address in your courses and student activities *before* graduation.

Step 2: *Five-Year Career Objectives* Make a list of 3 to 5 career objectives that are appropriate given your list of personal strengths and weaknesses. Limit these objectives to ones that can be accomplished within 5 years of graduation.

Step 3: *Five-Year Career Action Plans* Write a specific action plan for accomplishing each of the 5 objectives. State exactly what you will do, and by when, in order to meet each objective. If you will need special support or assistance, identify it *and* state how you will obtain it. Remember, an outside observer should be able to read your action plan for each objective and end up feeling confident that (a) he or she knows exactly what you are going to do, and (b) why.

Instructions

Form into groups as assigned by the instructor. Share your career-planning analysis with the group; listen to those of others. Participate in a discussion that examines any common patterns and major differences among group members. Take advantage of any opportunities to gather feedback and advice from others. Have one group member be prepared to summarize the group discussion for the class as a whole. Await further class discussion led by the instructor.

Source: Developed in part from Roy J. Lewicki, Donald D. Bowen, Douglas T. Hall, and Francine S. Hall, *Experiences in Management and Organizational Behavior*. 3rd ed. (New York: John Wiley and Sons, 1988), pp. 261–67. Used by permission.

EXERCISE 11

Strategic Scenarios

Preparation

In today's turbulent environments, it is no longer safe to assume that an organization that was highly successful yesterday will continue to be so tomorrow—or that it will even be in existence. Changing times exact the best from strategic planners. Think about the situations currently facing the following well-known organizations; think, too, about the futures they may face.

McDonald's
Texaco
Xerox

Harvard University
United Nations
National Public Radio

Instructions

Form into groups as assigned by your instructor. Choose one or more organizations from the prior list (as assigned) and answer for that organization the following questions:

1. What in the future might seriously threaten the success, perhaps the very existence, of this organization? (As a group develop at least three such *future scenarios.*)

2. Estimate the probability (0 to 100 percent) of each future scenario occurring.

3. Develop a strategy for each scenario that will enable the organization to successfully deal with it.

Thoroughly discuss these questions within the group and arrive at your best possible consensus answers. Be prepared to share and defend your answers in general class discussion.

_____

Source: Suggested by an exercise in John F. Veiga and John N. Yanouzas. *The Dynamics of Organization Theory: Gaining a Macro Perspective* (St. Paul, MN: West, 1979), pp. 69–71.

EXERCISE 12

The MBO Contract

Listed below are performance objectives from an MBO contract for a plant manager.

1. To increase deliveries to 98% of all scheduled delivery dates

2. To reduce waste and spoilage to 3% of all raw materials used

3. To reduce lost time due to accidents to 100 work days/year

4. To reduce operating cost to 10% below budget

5. To install a quality-control system at a cost of less than $53,000

6. To improve production scheduling and increase machine utilization time to 95% capacity

7. To complete a management development program this year

8. To teach a community college course in human resource management

1. Study this MBO contract. In the margin write one of the following symbols to identify each objective as an improvement, maintenance, or personal development objective.

I = Improvement objective
M = Maintenance objective
P = Personal development objective

2. Assume that this MBO contract was actually developed and implemented under the following circumstances. After each statement, write "yes" if the statement reflects proper MBO procedures and write "no" if it reflects poor MBO procedures.
(a) The president drafted the 8 objectives and submitted them to Atkins for review.
(b) The president and Atkins thoroughly discussed the 8 objectives in proposal form before they were finalized.
(c) The president and Atkins scheduled a meeting in 6 months to review Atkins's progress on the objectives.
(d) The president didn't discuss the objectives with Atkins again until the scheduled meeting was held.
(e) The president told Atkins his annual raise would depend entirely on the extent to which these objectives were achieved.

3. Share and discuss your responses to parts 1 and 2 of the exercise with a nearby classmate. Reconcile any differences of opinion by referring back to the chapter discussion of MBO. Await further class discussion.

The Future Workplace

Instructions

Form groups as assigned by the instructor. Brainstorm to develop a master list of the major characteristics you expect to find in the future workplace in the year 2010. Use this list as background for completing the following tasks:

1. Write a one-paragraph description of what the typical "Workplace 2010 *manager's*" workday will be like.

2. Draw a "picture" representing what the "Workplace 2010 organization" will look like.

Choose a spokesperson to share your results with the class as a whole *and* explain their implications for the class members.

Dots and Squares Puzzle

1. Shown here is a collection of 16 dots. Study the figure to determine how many "squares" can be created by connecting the dots.

2. Draw as many squares as you can find in the figure while making sure a dot is at every corner of every square. Count the squares and write this number in the margin to the right of the figure.

3. Share your results with those of a classmate sitting nearby. Indicate the location of squares missed by either one of you.

4. Based on this discussion, redraw your figure to show the maximum number of possible squares.

Count them and write this number to the left of the figure.

5. Await further class discussion led by your instructor.

```
•    •    •    •

•    •    •    •

•    •    •    •

•    •    •    •
```

Interviewing Job Candidates

Preparation

Make a list of the "generic" questions you think any employment interviewer should ask any job candidate, regardless of the specific job or situation. Then, place an X next to those of the following items you think represent additional important questions to ask.

____ How old are you?
____ Where were you born?
____ Where are you from?
____ What religion are you?
____ Are you married, single, or divorced?
____ If not married, do you have a companion?
____ Do you have any dependent children or elderly parents?

Instructions

Form work groups as assigned by your instructor. Share your responses with other group members, and listen to theirs. Develop a group consensus on a list of "generic" interview questions you think any manager should be prepared to ask of job candidates. Also develop a group consensus on which of the items on the preceding list represent questions that an interviewer should ask. Elect a spokesperson to present the group's results to the class, along with the reasons for selecting these questions.

Work vs. Family—You Be the Judge

1. Read the following situation.

Joanna, a single parent, was hired to work 8:15 A.M. to 5:30 P.M. weekdays selling computers for a firm. Her employer extended her work day until 10 P.M. weekdays and from 8:15 A.M.– 5:30 P.M. on Saturdays. Joanna refused to work the extra hours, saying that she had a six-year old son and that so many work hours would lead to neglect. The employer said this was a special request during a difficult period and that all employees needed to share in helping out during the "crunch." Still refusing to work the extra hours, Joanna was fired. She sued the employer.

2. You be the judge in this case. Take an individual position on the following questions:

Should Joanna be allowed to work only the hours agreed to when she was hired? Or, is the employer correct in asking all employees, regardless of family status, to work the extra hours? Why?

3. Form into groups as assigned by the instructor. Share your responses to the questions and try to develop a group consensus. Be sure to have a rationale for the position the group adopts. Appoint a spokesperson who can share results with the class. Be prepared to participate in open class discussion.

Source: This case scenario is from Sue Shellenbarger, "Employees Challenge Policies on Family and Get Hard Lessons," *The Wall Street Journal* (December 17, 1997), p. B1.

Compensation and Benefits Debate

Preparation

Consider the following quotations.

On compensation: "A basic rule of thumb should be—pay at least as much, and perhaps a bit more, in base wage or salary than what competitors are offering."

On benefits: "When benefits are attractive or at least adequate, the organization is in a better position to employ highly qualified people."

Instructions

Form groups as assigned by the instructor. Each will be given *either* one of the preceding position statements *or* one of the following alternatives.

On compensation: Given the importance of controlling costs, organizations can benefit by paying as little as possible for labor.

On benefits: Given the rising cost of healthcare and other benefit programs and the increasing difficulty many organizations have staying in business, it is best to minimize paid benefits and let employees handle more of the cost on their own.

Each group should prepare to debate a counterpoint group on its assigned position. After time is allocated to prepare for the debate, each group will present its opening positions. Each will then be allowed one rebuttal period to respond to the other group. General class discussion on the role of compensation and benefits in the modern organization will follow.

Sources and Uses of Power

Preparation

Consider *the way you behaved* in each of the situations described below. They may be from a full-time or part-time job, student organization or class group, sports team, or whatever. If you do not have an experience of the type described, try to imagine yourself in one; think about how you would expect yourself to behave.

1. You needed to get a peer to do something you wanted that person to do but were worried he or she didn't want to do it.

2. You needed to get a subordinate to do something you wanted her or him to do but were worried the subordinate didn't want to do it.

3. You needed to get your boss to do something you wanted him or her to do but were worried the boss didn't want to do it.

Instructions

Form into groups as assigned by the instructor. Start with situation 1 and have all members of the group share their approaches. Determine what specific sources of power (see Chapter 13) were used. Note any patterns in group members responses. Discuss what is required to be successful in this situation. Do the same for situations 2 and 3. Note any special differences in how situations 1, 2, and 3 should be or could be handled. Choose a spokesperson to share results in general class discussion.

Empowering Others

Instructions

Think of times when you have been in charge of a group—this could be a full-time or part-time work situation, a student work group, or whatever. Complete the following questionnaire by recording how you feel about each statement according to this scale:

1 = Strongly disagree   2 = Disagree   3 = Neutral
4 = Agree   5 = Strongly agree
When in charge of a group I find

_____ 1. Most of the time other people are too inexperienced to do things, so I prefer to do them myself.

_____ 2. It often takes more time to explain things to others than to just do them myself.

_____ 3. Mistakes made by others are costly, so I don't assign much work to them.

_____ 4. Some things simply should not be delegated to others.

_____ 5. I often get quicker action by doing a job myself.

_____ 6. Many people are good only at very specific tasks and so can't be assigned additional responsibilities.

_____ 7. Many people are too busy to take on additional work.

_____ 8. Most people just aren't ready to handle additional responsibilities.

_____ 9. In my position, I should be entitled to make my own decisions.

Scoring

Total your responses: enter the score here [_____].

Interpretation

This instrument gives an impression of your *willingness to delegate*. Possible scores range from 9 to 45. The higher your score, the more willing you appear to be to delegate to others. Willingness to delegate is an important managerial characteristic: It is essential if you—as a manager—are to "empower" others and give them opportunities to assume responsibility and exercise self-control in their work. With the growing importance of empowerment in the new workplace, your willingness to delegate is worth thinking about seriously. Be prepared to share your results and participate in general class discussion.

Source: Questionnaire adapted from L. Steinmetz and R. Todd, *First Line Management*, 4th ed. (Homewood, IL: BPI/Irwin, 1986), pp. 64–67. Used by permission.

Gender Differences in Management

1. The question is "Do women or men make better managers?"

2. A research study by the Foundation for Future Leadership examined the management abilities of 645 men and 270 women in terms of supervisor, peer, and self-evaluations. Among the management skills studied were those listed below.

Skills	Women Higher	Men Higher	No Difference
Problem solving	_____	_____	_____
Planning	_____	_____	_____
Controlling	_____	_____	_____
Managing self	_____	_____	_____
Managing relationships	_____	_____	_____
Leading	_____	_____	_____
Communicating	_____	_____	_____

3. Indicate in the space provided whether you believe women scored higher on the average than men for each skill, men scored higher than women, or no difference in scores was found.

4. Meet in your discussion groups to share results and the rationale for your choices. Try to arrive at a group consensus regarding the likelihood of differences between women and men. Ask questions of one another:
- What is your experience with men as bosses?
- What is your experience with women as bosses?
- Why exactly do you think women/men would score better on each dimension?
- Is it useful to try and identify gender differences in management?
- Why is gender even relevant when it comes to questions about management skills?

5. Be prepared to summarize your results and participate in further class discussion led by the instructor.

Why Do We Work?

Preparation

Read the following "ancient story."

In days of old a wandering youth happened upon a group of men working in a quarry. Stopping by the first man he said, "What are you doing?" The worker grimaced and groaned as he replied, "I am trying to shape this stone, and it is backbreaking work." Moving to the next man he repeated the question. This man showed little emotion as he answered, "I am shaping a stone for a building." Moving to the third man, our traveler heard him singing as he worked. "What are you doing?" asked the youth. "I am helping to build a cathedral," the man proudly replied.

Instructions

In groups assigned by your instructor, discuss this short story. Ask and answer the question: "What are the lessons of this ancient story for (a) workers and (b) managers of today?" Ask members of the group to role-play each of the stonecutters, respectively, while they answer a second question asked by the youth: "Why are you working?" Have someone in the group be prepared to report and share the group's responses with the class as a whole.

_____

Source: Developed from Brian Dumaine, "Why Do We Work," *Fortune* (December 26, 1994), pp. 196–204.

EXERCISE 22

The Case of the Contingency Workforce

Preparation

Part-time and contingency work is a rising percentage of the total employment in the United States. Go to the library and read about the current use of part-time and contingency workers in business and industry. Ideally, go to the Internet, enter a government database, and locate some current statistics on the size of the contingent labor force, the proportion that is self-employed and part-time, and the proportion of part-timers who are voluntary and involuntary.

Instructions

In your assigned work group, pool the available information on the contingency workforce. Discuss the information. Discuss one another's viewpoints on the subject as well as its personal and social implications. Be prepared to participate in a classroom "dialog session" in which your group will be asked to role-play one of the following positions:

a. Vice president for human resources of a large discount retailer hiring contingency workers.

b. Owner of a local specialty music shop hiring contingency workers.

c. Recent graduate of your college or university working as a contingency employee at the discount retailer in (a).

d. Single parent with two children in elementary school, working as a contingency employee of the music shop in (b).

The question to be answered by the (a) and (b) groups is "What does the contingency workforce mean to me?" The question to be answered by the (c) and (d) groups is "What does being a contingency worker mean to me?"

EXERCISE 23

The "Best" Job Design

Preparation

Use the left-hand column to rank the following job characteristics in the order most important *to you* (1 = highest to 10 = lowest). Then use the right-hand column to rank them in the order in which you think they are most important *to others*.

____ Variety of tasks ____
____ Performance feedback ____
____ Autonomy/freedom in work ____
____ Working on a team ____
____ Having responsibility ____
____ Making friends on the job ____
____ Doing all of a job, not part ____
____ Importance of job to others ____
____ Having resources to do well ____
____ Flexible work schedule ____

Instructions

Form work groups as assigned by your instructor. Share your rankings with other group members. Discuss where you have different individual preferences and where your impressions differ from the preferences of others. Are there any major patterns in your group—for either the "personal" or the "other" rankings? Develop group consensus rankings for each column. Designate a spokesperson to share the group rankings and results of any discussion with the rest of the class.

Source: Developed from John M. Ivancevich and Michael T. Matteson, *Organizational Behavior and Management,* 2nd ed. (Homewood, IL: BPI/Irwin, 1990), p. 500. Used by permission.

EXERCISE 24

Upward Appraisal

Instructions

Form into work groups as assigned by the instructor. The instructor will then leave the room. As a group, complete the following tasks:

1. Within each group create a master list of comments, problems, issues, and concerns about the course experience to date that members would like to communicate with the instructor.

2. Select one person from the group to act as spokesperson and give your feedback to the instructor when he or she returns to the classroom.

3. The spokespersons from each group should meet to decide how the room should be physically arranged (placement of tables, chairs, etc.) for the feedback session. This should allow the spokespersons and instructor to communicate while they are being observed by other class members.

4. While the spokespersons are meeting, members remaining in the groups should discuss what they expect to observe during the feedback session.

5. The classroom should be rearranged. The instructor should be invited in.

6. Spokespersons should deliver feedback to the instructor while observers make notes.

7. After the feedback session is complete, the instructor will call on observers for comments, ask the spokespersons for their reactions, and engage the class in general discussion about the exercise and its implications.

Source: Developed from Eugene Owens, "Upward Appraisal An Exercise in Subordinate's Critique of Superior's Performance," *Exchange: The Organizational Behavior Teaching Journal,* vol. 3 (1978), pp. 41–42.

EXERCISE 25

Feedback and Assertiveness

Preparation

Indicate the degree of discomfort you would feel in each situation below by circling the appropriate number:

1, high discomfort; 2, some discomfort; 3, undecided; 4, very little discomfort; 5, no discomfort

1 2 3 4 5   **1.** Telling an employee who is also a friend that she or he must stop coming to work late.

1 2 3 4 5   **2.** Talking to an employee about his or her performance on the job.

1 2 3 4 5   **3.** Asking an employee if she or he has any comments about your rating of her or his performance.

1 2 3 4 5   **4.** Telling an employee who has problems in dealing with other employees that he or she should do something about it.

1 2 3 4 5   **5.** Responding to an employee who is upset over your rating of his or her performance.

1 2 3 4 5   **6.** An employee's becoming emotional and defensive when you tell her or him about mistakes on the job.

1 2 3 4 5   **7.** Giving a rating that indicates improvement is needed to an employee who has failed to meet minimum requirements of the job.

1 2 3 4 5   **8.** Letting a subordinate talk during an appraisal interview.

1 2 3 4 5   **9.** An employee's challenging you to justify your evaluation in the middle of an appraisal interview.

1 2 3 4 5 **10.** Recommending that an employee be discharged.

1 2 3 4 5 **11.** Telling an employee that you are uncomfortable with the role of having to judge his or her performance.

1 2 3 4 5 **12.** Telling an employee that her or his performance can be improved.

1 2 3 4 5 **13.** Telling an employee that you will not tolerate his or her taking extended coffee breaks.

1 2 3 4 5 **14.** Telling an employee that you will not tolerate her or his making personal telephone calls on company time.

Instructions

Form three-person teams as assigned by the instructor. Identify the 3 behaviors with which they indicate the most discomfort. Then each team member should practice performing these behaviors with another member, while the third member acts as an observer. Be direct, but try to perform the behavior in an appropriate way. Listen to feedback from the observer and try the behaviors again, perhaps with different members of the group. When finished, discuss the exercise overall. Be prepared to participate in further class discussion.

Source: Feedback questionnaire is from Judith R. Gordon, *A Diagnostic Approach to Organizational Behavior.* 3rd ed. (Boston: Allyn and Bacon, 1991), p. 298. Used by permission.

EXERCISE 26

How to Give, and Take, Criticism

Preparation

The "criticism session" may well be the toughest test of a manager's communication skills. Picture Setting I—you and a subordinate meeting to review a problem with the subordinate's performance. Now picture Setting 2—you and your boss, meeting to review a problem with *your* performance. Both situations require communication skills in giving and receiving feedback. Even the most experienced person can have difficulty, and the situations can end as futile gripe sessions that cause hard feelings. The question is "How can such 'criticism sessions' be handled in a positive manner that encourages improved performance . . . and good feelings?"

Instructions

Form into groups as assigned by the instructor. Focus on either Setting 1 or Setting 2, or both, as also assigned by the instructor. First, answer the question from the perspective assigned. Second, develop a series of action guidelines that could best be used to handle situations of this type. Third, prepare and present a mini-management training session to demonstrate the (a) unsuccessful and (b) successful use of these guidelines.

If time permits, outside of class prepare a more extensive management training session that includes a videotape demonstration of your assigned criticism setting being handled first poorly and then very well. Support the video-tape with additional written handouts and an oral presentation to help your classmates better understand the communication skills needed to successfully give and take criticism in work settings.

Work Team Dynamics

Preparation

Think about your course work group, a work group you are involved in for another course, or any other group suggested by the instructor. Indicate how often each of the following statements accurately reflects your experience in the group. Use this scale:

1 = Always   2 = Frequently   3 = Sometimes
4 = Never

_____ 1. My ideas get a fair hearing.
_____ 2. I am encouraged to give innovative ideas and take risks.
_____ 3. Diverse opinions within the group are encouraged.
_____ 4. I have all the responsibility I want.
_____ 5. There is a lot of favoritism shown in the group.
_____ 6. Members trust one another to do their assigned work.
_____ 7. The group sets high standards of performance excellence.

_____ 8. People share and change jobs a lot in the group.
_____ 9. You can make mistakes and learn from them in this group.
_____ 10. This group has good operating rules.

Instructions

Form groups as assigned by your instructor. Ideally, this will be the group you have just rated. Have all group members share their ratings, and make one master rating for the group as a whole. Circle the items over which there are the biggest differences of opinion. Discuss those items and try to find out why they exist. In general, the better a group scores on this instrument, the higher its creative potential. If everyone has rated the same group, make a list of the five most important things members can do to improve its operations in the future. Nominate a spokesperson to summarize the group discussion for the class as a whole.

Source: Adapted from William Dyer. _Team Building_, 2nd ed. (Reading, MA: Addison-Wesley, 1987), pp. 123–25.

Lost at Sea

Consider This Situation

You are adrift on a private yacht in the South Pacific when a fire of unknown origin destroys the yacht and most of its contents. You and a small group of survivors are now in a large raft with oars. Your location is unclear, but you estimate that you are about 1,000 miles south-southwest of the nearest land. One person has just found in her pockets 5 $1 bills and a packet of matches. Everyone else's pockets are empty. The following items are available to you on the raft.

	A	B	C
Sextant			
Shaving mirror			
5 gallons water			
Mosquito netting			
1 survival meal			
Maps of Pacific Ocean			
Flotable seat cushion			
2 gallons oil-gas mix			
Small transistor radio			
Shark repellent			
20 square feet black plastic			
1 quart 20-proof rum			
15 feet nylon rope			
24 chocolate bars			
Fishing kit			

Instructions

1. *Working alone*, rank in Column **A** the 15 items in order of their importance to your survival ("1" is most important and "15" is least important).

2. *Working in an assigned group*, arrive at a "team" ranking of the 15 items and record this ranking in Column **B**. Appoint one person as group spokesperson to report your group rankings to the class.

3. *Do not write in Column* **C** until further instructions are provided by your instructor.

Source: Adapted from "Lost at Sea: A Consensus-Seeking Task," in *The 1975 Handbook for Group Facilitators.* Used with permission of University Associates, Inc.

EXERCISE 29

Creative Solutions

Instructions

Complete these 5 tasks while working alone. Be prepared to present and explain your responses in class.

1. Divide the following shape into four pieces of exactly the same size.

2. Without lifting your pencil from the paper, draw no more than 4 lines that cross through all of the following dots.

3. Draw the design for a machine that will turn the pages of your textbook so you can eat a snack while studying.

4. Why would a wheelbarrow ever be designed this way?

5. Turn the following into words.
  (a) ____ program
  (b) r\e\a\d\i\n\g
  (c) ECNALG
  (d)   j
       u
     yousme
       t
  (e) stand
       i

Source: Ideas 2 and 5 found in Russell L. Ackoff, *The Art of Problem Solving* (New York: Wiley, 1978); ideas 1 and 4 found in Edward De Bono, *Lateral Thinking: Creativity Step by Step* (New York: Harper & Row, 1970); source for 5 is unknown.

Optional Instructions

After working alone, share your responses with a nearby classmate or with a group. See if you can develop different and/or better solutions based on this exchange of ideas.

EXERCISE 30

Force-Field Analysis

1. Form into your class discussion groups.

2. Review the concept of force-field analysis—the consideration of forces driving in support of a planned change and forces resisting the change.

3. Use this force-field analysis worksheet in the assignment:

  List of Driving Forces (those supporting the change)

  _____

  _____ . . . list as many as you can think of

  List of Resisting Forces (those working against the change)

  _____

  _____ . . . list as many as you can think of

3. Apply force-field analysis and make your lists of driving and resisting forces for one of the following situations:
(a) Due to rapid advances in Web-based computer technologies, the possibility exists that the course you are presently taking could be in part offered "online." This would mean a reduction in the number of required class sessions, but an increase in students' responsibility for completing learning activities and assignments through computer mediation.
(b) A new owner has just taken over a small walk-in-and-buy-by-the-slice pizza shop in a college town. There are presently 8 employees, 3 of whom are full-time and 5 of whom are part-timers. The shop is presently open 7 days a week from 10:30 A.M. to 10:30 P.M. each day. The new owner believes there is a market niche available for late-night pizza and would like to stay open each night until 2 A.M.
(c) A situation assigned by the instructor.

4. Choose the 3 driving forces that are most significant to the proposed change. For each force develop ideas on how it could be further increased or mobilized in support of the change.

5. Choose the 3 resisting forces that are most significant to the proposed change. For each force develop ideas on how it could be reduced or turned into a driving force.

6. Be prepared to participate in class discussion led by the instructor.

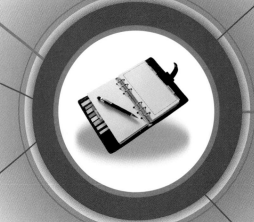

Management Skills Assessments

A 21st-Century Manager?

Instructions

Rate yourself on the following personal characteristics. Use this scale.

S = Strong, I am very confident with this one.
G = Good, but I still have room to grow.
W = Weak, I really need work on this one.
U = Unsure, I just don't know.

1. *Resistance to stress:* The ability to get work done even under stressful conditions.

2. *Tolerance for uncertainty:* The ability to get work done even under ambiguous and uncertain conditions.

3. *Social objectivity:* The ability to act free of racial, ethnic, gender, and other prejudices or biases.

4. *Inner work standards:* The ability to personally set and work to high performance standards.

5. *Stamina:* The ability to sustain long work hours.

6. *Adaptability:* The ability to be flexible and adapt to changes.

7. *Self-confidence:* The ability to be consistently decisive and display one's personal presence.

492

8. *Self-objectivity:* The ability to evaluate personal strengths and weaknesses and to understand one's motives and skills relative to a job.

9. *Introspection:* The ability to learn from experience, awareness, and self-study.

10. *Entrepreneurism:* The ability to address problems and take advantage of opportunities for constructive change.

Scoring

Give yourself 1 point for each S, and 1/2 point for each G. Do not give yourself points for W and U responses. Total your points and enter the result here [PMF = ____].

Interpretation

This assessment offers a self-described *profile of your management foundations (PMF)*. Are you a perfect 10, or is your PMF score something less than that? There shouldn't be too many 10s around. Ask someone who knows you to assess you on this instrument. You may be surprised at the differences between your PMF score as you described it and your PMF score as described by someone else. Most of us, realistically speaking, must work hard to grow and develop continually in these and related management foundations. This list is a good starting point as you consider where and how to further pursue the development of your managerial skills and competencies. The items on the list are recommended by the American Assembly of Collegiate Schools of Business (AACSB) as the skills and personal characteristics that should be nurtured in college and university students of business administration. Their success—and yours—as 21st-century managers may well rest on (1) an initial awareness of the importance of these basic management foundations and (2) a willingness to strive continually to strengthen them throughout the work career.

Source: See *Outcome Measurement Project*, Phase I and Phase II Reports (St. Louis: American Assembly of Collegiate Schools of Business, 1986 and 1987).

ASSESSMENT 2

Which Organizational Culture Fits You?

Instructions

Indicate which one of the following organizational cultures you feel most comfortable working in.

1. A culture that values talent, entrepreneurial activity, and performance over commitment; one that offers large financial rewards and individual recognition.

2. A culture that stresses loyalty, working for the good of the group, and getting to know the right people; one that believes in "generalists" and step-by-step career progress.

3. A culture that offers little job security; one that operates with a survival mentality, stresses that every individual can make a difference, and focuses attention on "turnaround" opportunities.

4. A culture that values long-term relationships; one that emphasizes systematic career development, regular training, and advancement based on gaining functional expertise.

Scoring

These labels identify the four different cultures: 1 = "the baseball team," 2 = "the club," 3 = "the fortress," and 4 = "the academy."

Interpretation

To some extent, your future career success may depend on working for an organization in which there is a good fit between you and the prevailing corporate culture. This assessment can help you learn how to recognize various cultures, evaluate how well they can serve your needs, and recognize how they may change with time. A risk taker, for example, may be out of place in a "club" but fit right in with a "baseball team." Someone who wants to seek opportunities wherever they may occur may be out of place in an "academy" but fit right in with a "fortress."

Source: Developed from Carol Hymowitz, "Which Corporate Culture Fits You?" *Wall Street Journal* (July 17, 1989), p. B1.

Decision-Making Biases

Instructions

How good are you at avoiding potential decision-making biases? Test yourself by answering the following questions:

1. Which is riskier:
(a) driving a car on a 400-mile trip?
(b) flying on a 400-mile commercial airline flight?

2. Are there more words in the English language:
(a) that begin with "r"?
(b) that have "r" as the third letter?

3. Mark is finishing his MBA at a prestigious university. He is very interested in the arts and at one time considered a career as a musician. Is Mark more likely to take a job:
(a) in the management of the arts?
(b) with a management consulting firm?

4. You are about to hire a new central-region sales director for the fifth time this year. You predict that the next director should work out reasonably well since the last four were "lemons" and the odds favor hiring at least one good sales director in five tries. Is this thinking
(a) correct?
(b) incorrect?

5. A newly hired engineer for a computer firm in the Boston metropolitan area has 4 years' experience and good all-around qualifications. When asked to estimate the starting salary for this employee, a chemist with very little knowledge about the profession or industry guessed an annual salary of $35,000. What is your estimate?
$_____ per year

Scoring

Your instructor will provide answers and explanations for the assessment questions.

Interpretation

Each of the preceding questions examines your tendency to use a different judgmental heuristic. In his book *Judgment in Managerial Decision Making*, 3rd ed. (New York: John Wiley & Sons, 1994), pp. 6–7, Max Bazerman calls these heuristics "simplifying strategies, or rules of thumb" used in making decisions. He states, "In general, heuristics are helpful, but their use can sometimes lead to severe errors. . . . If we can make managers aware of the potential adverse impacts of using heuristics, they can then decide when and where to use them." This assessment offers an initial insight into your use of such heuristics. An informed decision maker understands the heuristics, is able to recognize when they appear, and eliminates any that may inappropriately bias decision making.

Test yourself further. Before hearing from your instructor, go back and write next to each item the name of the judgmental heuristic (see Chapter 3 text discussion) that you think applies.

Then write down a situation that you have experienced and in which some decision-making bias may have occurred. Be prepared to share and discuss this incident with the class.

Source: Incidents from Max H. Bazerman, *Judgment in Managerial Decision Making*, 3rd ed. (New York: Wiley, 1994), pp. 13–14. Used by permission.

What Are Your Managerial Assumptions?

Instructions

Read the following statements. Use the space to the left to write "Yes" if you agree with the statement, or "No" if you disagree with it. Force yourself to take a "yes" or "no" position. Do this for every statement.

1. Are good pay and a secure job enough to satisfy most workers?

2. Should a manager help and coach subordinates in their work?

3. Do most people like real responsibility in their jobs?

4. Are most people afraid to learn new things in their jobs?

5. Should managers let subordinates control the quality of their work?

6. Do most people dislike work?

7. Are most people creative?

8. Should a manager closely supervise and direct the work of subordinates?

9. Do most people tend to resist change?

10. Do most people work only as hard as they have to?

11. Should workers be allowed to set their own job goals?

12. Are most people happiest off the job?

13. Do most workers really care about the organization they work for?

14. Should a manager help subordinates advance and grow in their jobs?

Scoring

Count the number of "yes" responses to items 1, 4, 6, 8, 9, 10, 12; write that number here as [X = ____]. Count the number of "yes" responses to items 2, 3, 5, 7, 11, 13, 14; write that score here [Y = ____].

Interpretation

This assessment sheds insight into your orientation toward Douglas McGregor's Theory X (your "X" score) and Theory Y (your "Y" score) assumptions. You should review the discussion of McGregor's thinking in Chapter 4 and consider further the ways in which you are likely to behave toward other people at work. Think, in particular, about the types of "self-fulfilling prophesies" you are likely to create.

ASSESSMENT 5

Cultural Attitudes Inventory

Instructions

Complete this inventory by circling the number that indicates the extent to which you agree or disagree with each of the following statements.

Strongly Disagree				Strongly Agree
1	2	3	4	5

1. Meetings are usually run more effectively when they are chaired by a man.

    1   2   3   4   5

2. It is more important for men to have a professional career than it is for women to have a professional career.

    1   2   3   4   5

3. Women do not value recognition and promotion in their work as much as men do.

    1   2   3   4   5

4. Women value working in a friendly atmosphere more than men do.

    1   2   3   4   5

5. Men usually solve problems with logical analysis; women usually solve problems with intuition.

    1   2   3   4   5

6. Solving organizational problems usually requires the active, forcible approach that is typical of men.

    1   2   3   4   5

7. It is preferable for a man to be in a high-level position rather than a woman.

1　2　3　4　5

8. There are some jobs in which a man can always do better than a woman.

1　2　3　4　5

9. Women are more concerned with the social aspects of their job than they are with getting ahead.

1　2　3　4　5

10. An individual should not pursue his or her own goals without considering the welfare of the group.

1　2　3　4　5

11. It is important for a manager to encourage loyalty and a sense of duty in the group.

1　2　3　4　5

12. Being accepted by the group is more important than working on your own.

1　2　3　4　5

13. Individual rewards are not as important as group welfare.

1　2　3　4　5

14. Group success is more important than individual success.

1　2　3　4　5

15. It is important to spell out job requirements and instructions in detail so that people always know what they are expected to do.

1　2　3　4　5

16. Managers expect workers to follow instructions and procedures closely.

1　2　3　4　5

17. Rules and regulations are important because they inform workers what the organization expects of them.

1　2　3　4　5

18. Standard operating procedures are helpful to workers on the job.

1　2　3　4　5

19. Operating instructions are important for workers on the job.

1　2　3　4　5

20. It is often necessary for a supervisor to emphasize his or her authority and power when dealing with subordinates.

1　2　3　4　5

21. Managers should be careful not to ask the opinions of subordinates too frequently.

1　2　3　4　5

22. A manager should avoid socializing with his or her subordinates off the job.

1　2　3　4　5

23. Subordinates should not disagree with their manager's decisions.

1　2　3　4　5

24. Managers should not delegate difficult and important tasks to their subordinates.

1　2　3　4　5

25. Managers should make most decisions without consulting subordinates.

1　2　3　4　5

Scoring

Add up your responses to items 1–9 and divide by 9; record the score here [MF = ____]. Add up your response to items 10–14 and divide by 5; record the score here [IC = ____]. Add up your responses to items 15–19 and divide by 5; record the score here [UA = ____]. Add up your responses to items 20–25 and divide by 6; record the score here [PD = ____].

Interpretation

Each of these scores corresponds to one of Hofstede's (see Chapter 5) dimensions of national culture: MF = masculinity-femininity; IC = individualism-collectivism; UA = uncertainty avoidance; PD = power distance. His research shows that various "national" cultures of the world score differently on these dimensions. Consider how closely *your* scores may represent *your* national culture. What are the implications of your score for your future work as a manager? Compare yourself to these scores from a sample of U.S. and

Mexican students; MF: U.S. = 2.78 and Mexico = 2.75; IC: U.S. = 2.19 and Mexico = 3.33; UA: U.S. = 3.41 and Mexico = 4.15; PD: U.S. = 1.86 and Mexico = 2.22. Are there any surprises in this comparison?

Source: Items are part of a larger instrument developed by Peter W. Dorfman and Jon P. Howell, New Mexico State University. Used by permission. The comparative data are from Stephen P. Robbins, *Management*, 3rd ed. (Englewood Cliffs, NJ: Prentice Hall, 1990). p. 670.

ASSESSMENT 6

Global Readiness Index

Instructions

Rate yourself on each of the following items to establish a baseline measurement of your readiness to participate in the global work environment.

Rating Scale:

1 = Very Poor
2 = Poor
3 = Acceptable
4 = Good
5 = Very Good

____ 1. I understand my own culture in terms of its expectations, values, and influence on communication and relationships.

____ 2. When someone presents me with a different point of view, I try to understand it rather than attack it.

____ 3. I am comfortable dealing with situations where the available information is incomplete and the outcomes unpredictable.

____ 4. I am open to new situations and am always looking for new information and learning opportunities.

____ 5. I have a good understanding of the attitudes and perceptions toward my culture as they are held by people from other cultures.

____ 6. I am always gathering information about other countries and cultures and trying to learn from them.

____ 7. I am well informed regarding the major differences in government, political, and economic systems around the world.

____ 8. I work hard to increase my understanding of people from other cultures.

____ 9. I am able to adjust my communication style to work effectively with people from different cultures.

____ 10. I can recognize when cultural differences are influencing working relationships and adjust my attitudes and behavior accordingly.

Interpretation

To be successful in the 21st-century work environment, you must be comfortable with the global economy and the cultural diversity that it holds. This requires a *global mind-set* that is receptive to and respectful of cultural differences, *global knowledge* that includes the continuing quest to know and learn more about other nations and cultures, and *global work skills* that allow you to work effectively across cultures.

Scoring

The goal is to score as close to a perfect "5" as possible on each of the three dimensions of global readiness. Develop your scores as follows.

Items (1 + 2 + 3 + 4)/4
= ____ Global Mind-set Score

Items (5 + 6 + 7)/3
= ____ Global Knowledge Score

Items ((8 + 9 + 10)/3
= ____ Global Work Skills Score

Source: Developed from "Is Your Company Really Global," *Business Week* (December 1, 1997).

Diversity Awareness

Instructions

Complete the following questionnaire.

Diversity Awareness Checklist

Consider where you work or go to school as the setting for the following questions. Indicate "O" for often, "S" for sometimes, and "N" for never in response to each of the following questions as they pertain to the setting.

____ 1. How often have you heard jokes or re-marks about other people that you consider offensive?

____ 2. How often do you hear men "talk down" to women in an attempt to keep them in an inferior status?

____ 3. How often have you felt personal discom-fort as the object of sexual harassment?

____ 4. How often do you work or study with African Americans or Hispanics?

____ 5. How often have you felt disadvantaged because members of ethnic groups other than yours were given special treatment?

____ 6. How often have you seen a woman put in an uncomfortable situation because of unwelcome advances by a man?

____ 7. How often does it seem that African Americans, Hispanics, Caucasians, women, men, and members of other mi-nority demographic groups seem to "stick together" during work breaks or other leisure situations?

____ 8. How often do you feel uncomfortable about something you did and/or said to someone of the opposite sex or a member of an ethnic or racial group other than yours?

____ 9. How often do you feel efforts are made in this setting to raise the level of cross-cultural understanding among people who work and/or study together?

____ 10. How often do you step in to communi-cate concerns to others when you feel ac-tions and/or words are used to the disad-vantage of minorities?

Scoring

There are no correct answers for the Diversity Awareness Checklist.

Interpretation

In the diversity checklist, the key issue is the extent to which you are "sensitive" to diversity issues in the workplace or university. Are you comfortable with your responses? How do you think others in your class responded? Why not share your re-sponses with others and examine different view-points on this important issue?

_____

Source: Items for the WV Cultural Awareness Quiz selected from a longer version by James P. Morgan Jr., and published by University Associates, 1987. Used by permission.

Your Intuitive Ability

Instructions

Complete this survey as quickly as you can. Be honest with yourself. For each question, select the response that most appeals to you.

1. When working on a project, do you prefer to

(a) be told what the problem is but be left free to decide how to solve it?

(b) get very clear instructions about how to go about solving the problem before you start?

2. When working on a project, do you prefer to work with colleagues who are

(a) realistic?
(b) imaginative?

3. Do you most admire people who are
(a) creative?
(b) careful?

4. Do the friends you choose tend to be
(a) serious and hard working?
(b) exciting and often emotional?

5. When you ask a colleague for advice on a problem you have, do you
(a) seldom or never get upset if he or she questions your basic assumptions?
(b) often get upset if he or she questions your basic assumptions?

6. When you start your day, do you
(a) seldom make or follow a specific plan?
(b) usually first make a plan to follow?

7. When working with numbers do you find that you
(a) seldom or never make factual errors?
(b) often make factual errors?

8. Do you find that you
(a) seldom daydream during the day and really don't enjoy doing so when you do it?
(b) frequently daydream during the day and enjoy doing so?

9. When working on a problem, do you
(a) prefer to follow the instructions or rules when they are given to you?
(b) often enjoy circumventing the instructions or rules when they are given to you?

10. When you are trying to put something together, do you prefer to have
(a) step-by-step written instructions on how to assemble the item?

(b) a picture of how the item is supposed to look once assembled?

11. Do you find that the person who irritates you *the most* is the one who appears to be
(a) disorganized?
(b) organized?

12. When an unexpected crisis comes up that you have to deal with, do you
(a) feel anxious about the situation?
(b) feel excited by the challenge of the situation?

Scoring

Total the number of "a" responses circled for questions 1, 3, 5, 6, 11; enter the score here [A = ____]. Total the number of "b" responses for questions 2, 4, 7, 8, 9, 10, 12; enter the score here [B = ____]. Add your "a" and "b" scores and enter the sum here [A + B = ____]. This is your *intuitive score.* The highest possible intuitive score is 12; the lowest is 0.

Interpretation

In his book *Intuition in Organizations* (Newbury Park, CA: Sage, 1989), pp. 10–11, Weston H. Agor states, "Traditional analytical techniques . . . are not as useful as they once were for guiding major decisions. . . . If you hope to be better prepared for tomorrow, then it only seems logical to pay some attention to the use and development of intuitive skills for decision making." Agor developed the preceding survey to help people assess their tendencies to use intuition in decision making. Your score offers a general impression of your strength in this area. It may also suggest a need to further develop your skill and comfort with more intuitive decision approaches.

Source: AIM Survey (El Paso, TX: ENFP Enterprises, 1989). Copyright © 1989 by Weston H. Agor. Used by permission.

ASSESSMENT 9

Time Management Profile

Instructions

Complete the following questionnaire by indicating "Y" (yes) or "N" (no) for each item. Force yourself to respond yes or no. Be frank and allow your responses to create an accurate picture of how you tend to respond to these kinds of situations.

____ **1.** When confronted with several items of similar urgency and importance, I tend to do the easiest one first.

____ 2. I do the most important things during that part of the day when I know I perform best.

____ 3. Most of the time I don't do things someone else can do; I delegate this type of work to others.

____ 4. Even though meetings without a clear and useful purpose upset me, I put up with them.

____ 5. I skim documents before reading them and don't complete any that offer a low return on my time investment.

____ 6. I don't worry much if I don't accomplish at least one significant task each day.

____ 7. I save the most trivial tasks for that time of day when my creative energy is lowest.

____ 8. My workspace is neat and organized.

____ 9. My office door is always "open"; I never work in complete privacy.

____ 10. I schedule my time completely from start to finish every workday.

____ 11. I don't like "to do" lists, preferring to respond to daily events as they occur.

____ 12. I "block" a certain amount of time each day or week that is dedicated to high-priority activities.

Scoring

Count the number of "Y" responses to items 2, 3, 5, 7, 8, 12. [Enter that score here ____.] Count the number of "N" responses to items 1, 4, 6, 9, 10, 11. [Enter that score here ____.] Add together the two scores.

Interpretation

The higher the total score, the closer your behavior matches recommended time management guidelines. Reread those items where your response did not match the desired one. Why don't they match? Do you have reasons why your behavior in this instance should be different from the recommended time management guideline? Think about what you can do (and how easily it can be done) to adjust your behavior to be more consistent with these guidelines. For further reading, see Alan Lakein, *How to Control Your Time and Your Life* (New York: David McKay, no date), and William Oncken. *Managing Management Time* (Englewood Cliffs, NJ: Prentice Hall, 1984).

_____

Source: Suggested by a discussion in Robert E. Quinn, Sue R. Faerman, Michael P. Thompson, and Michael R. McGrath, *Becoming a Master Manager: A Contemporary Framework* (New York: John Wiley & Sons, 1990), pp. 75–76.

ASSESSMENT 10

Entrepreneurship Orientation

Instructions

Answer the following questions.

1. What portion of your college expenses did you earn (or are you earning)?
(a) 50 percent or more
(b) less than 50 percent
(c) none

2. In college, your academic performance was/is
(a) above average.
(b) average.
(c) below average.

3. What is your basic reason for considering opening a business?
(a) I want to make money.
(b) I want to control my own destiny.

(c) I hate the frustration of working for someone else.

4. Which phrase best describes your attitude toward work?
(a) I can keep going as long as I need to; I don't mind working for something I want.
(b) I can work hard for a while, but when I've had enough, I quit.
(c) Hard work really doesn't get you anywhere.

5. How would you rate your organizing skills?
(a) superorganized
(b) above average
(c) average
(d) I do well to find half the things I look for.

6. You are primarily a(n)
(a) optimist.

(b) pessimist.
(c) neither.

7. You are faced with a challenging problem. As you work, you realize you are stuck. You will most likely
(a) give up.
(b) ask for help.
(c) keep plugging; you'll figure it out.

8. You are playing a game with a group of friends. You are most interested in
(a) winning.
(b) playing well.
(c) making sure that everyone has a good time.
(d) cheating as much as possible.

9. How would you describe your feelings toward failure?
(a) Fear of failure paralyzes me.
(b) Failure can be a good learning experience.
(c) Knowing that I might fail motivates me to work even harder.
(d) "Damn the torpedoes! Full speed ahead."

10. Which phrase best describes you?
(a) I need constant encouragement to get anything done.
(b) If someone gets me started, I can keep going.
(c) I am energetic and hard-working—a self-starter.

11. Which bet would you most likely accept?
(a) a wager on a dog race
(b) a wager on a racquetball game in which you play an opponent
(c) Neither. I never make wagers.

12. At the Kentucky Derby, you would bet on
(a) the 100-to-1 long shot.
(b) the odds-on favorite.
(c) the 3-to-1 shot.
(d) none of the above.

Scoring

Give yourself 10 points for each of the following answers: 1a, 2a, 3c, 4a, 5a, 6a, 7c, 8a, 9c, 10c, 11b, 12c; total the scores and enter the results here [I = ____]. Give yourself 8 points for each of the following answers: 3b, 8b, 9b; total the scores and enter the results here [II =____]. Give yourself 6 points for each of the following answers; 2b, 5b; total the scores and enter the results here [III = ____]. Give yourself 5 points for this answer: 1b; enter the result here [IV = ____]. Give yourself 4 points for this answer: 5c; enter the result here [V = ____]. Give yourself 2 points for each of the following answers: 2c, 3a, 4b, 6c, 9d, 10b, 11a, 12b; total the scores and enter the results here [VI = ____]. Any other scores are worth 0 points. Total your summary scores for I + II + III + IV + V + VI and enter the result here [EP = ____].

Interpretation

This assessment offers an impression of your *entrepreneurial profile*, or EP. It compares your characteristics with those of typical entrepreneurs. Your instructor can provide further information on each question as well as some additional insights into the backgrounds of entrepreneurs. You may locate your EP score on the following grid.

 100+ = Entrepreneur extraordinaire
80–99 = Entrepreneur
60–79 = Potential entrepreneur
 0–59 = Entrepreneur in the rough

Source: Instrument adapted from Norman M. Scarborough and Thomas W. Zimmerer, *Effective Small Business Management*, 3rd ed. (Columbus: Merrill, 1991), pp. 26–27. Used by permission.

ASSESSMENT 11

Internal/External Control

Instructions

Circle either "a" or "b" to indicate the item you most agree with in each pair of the following statements.

1. (a) Promotions are earned through hard work and persistence.
(b) Making a lot of money is largely a matter of breaks.

2. (a) Many times the reactions of teachers seem haphazard to me.
(b) In my experience I have noticed that there is usually a direct connection between how hard I study and the grades I get.

3. (a) The number of divorces indicates that more and more people are not trying to make their marriages work.
(b) Marriage is largely a gamble.

4. (a) It is silly to think that one can really change another person's basic attitudes.
(b) When I am right I can convince others.

5. (a) Getting promoted is really a matter of being a little luckier than the next guy.
(b) In our society an individual's future earning power is dependent upon his or her ability.

6. (a) If one knows how to deal with people, they are really quite easily led.
(b) I have little influence over the way other people behave.

7. (a) In my case the grades I make are the results of my own efforts; luck has little or nothing to do with it.
(b) Sometimes I feel that I have little to do with the grades I get.

8. (a) People like me can change the course of world affairs if we make ourselves heard.
(b) It is only wishful thinking to believe that one can really influence what happens in society at large.

9. (a) Much of what happens to me is probably a matter of chance.
(b) I am the master of my fate.

10. (a) Getting along with people is a skill that must be practiced.
(b) It is almost impossible to figure out how to please some people.

Scoring

Give 1 point for 1b, 2a, 3a, 4b, 5b, 6a, 7a, 8a, 9b, 10a.

8–10 = high *internal* locus of control
6–7 = moderate *internal* locus of control
5 = mixed locus of control
3–4 = moderate *external* locus of control

Interpretation

This instrument offers an impression of your tendency toward an *internal locus of control* or *external locus of control*. Persons with a high internal locus of control tend to believe they have control over their own destinies. They may be most responsive to opportunities for greater self-control in the workplace. Persons with a high external locus of control tend to believe that what happens to them is largely in the hands of external people or forces. They may be less comfortable with self-control and more responsive to external controls in the workplace.

Source: Instrument from Julian P. Rotter, "External Control and Internal Control," *Psychology Today* (June 1971), p. 42. Used by permission.

ASSESSMENT 12

Organizational Design Preference

Instructions

To the left of each item, write the number from the following scale that shows the extent to which the statement accurately describes your views.

5 = strongly agree
4 = agree somewhat
3 = undecided
2 = disagree somewhat
1 = strongly disagree

I prefer to work in an organization where

1. goals are defined by those in higher levels.

2. work methods and procedures are specified.

3. top management makes important decisions.

4. my loyalty counts as much as my ability to do the job.

5. clear lines of authority and responsibility are established.

6. top management is decisive and firm.

7. my career is pretty well planned out for me.

8. I can specialize.

9. my length of service is almost as important as my level of performance.

10. management is able to provide the information I need to do my job well.

11. a chain of command is well established.

12. rules and procedures are adhered to equally by everyone.

13. people accept the authority of a leader's position.

14. people are loyal to their boss.

15. people do as they have been instructed.

16. people clear things with their boss before going over his or her head.

Scoring

Total your scores for all questions. Enter the score here [____].

Interpretation

This assessment measures your preference for working in an organization designed along "organic" or "mechanistic" lines (see Chapter 11). The higher your score (above 64), the more comfortable you are with a mechanistic design; the lower your score (below 48), the more comfortable you are with an organic design. Scores between 48 and 64 can go either way. This organizational design preference represents an important issue in the new workplace. Indications are that today's organizations are taking on more and more organic characteristics. Presumably, those of us who work in them will need to be comfortable with such designs.

Source: John F. Veiga and John N. Yanouzas. *The Dynamics of Organization Theory: Gaining a Macro Perspective* (St. Paul, MN: West, 1979), pp. 158–60. Used by permission.

ASSESSMENT 13

Performance Appraisal Assumptions

Instructions

In each of the following pairs of statements, check off the statement that best reflects your assumptions about performance evaluation.

Performance evaluation is

1. (a) a formal process that is done annually.
(b) an informal process done continuously.

2. (a) a process that is planned for subordinates.
(b) a process that is planned with subordinates.

3. (a) a required organizational procedure.
(b) a process done regardless of requirements.

4. (a) a time to evaluate subordinates' performance.

(b) a time for subordinates to evaluate their manager.

5. (a) a time to clarify standards.
(b) a time to clarify the subordinate's career needs.

6. (a) a time to confront poor performance.
(b) a time to express appreciation.

7. (a) an opportunity to clarify issues and provide direction and control.
(b) an opportunity to increase enthusiasm and commitment.

8. (a) only as good as the organization's forms.
(b) only as good as the manager's coaching skills.

Scoring

There is no formal scoring for this assessment, but there may be a pattern to your responses. Check them again.

Interpretation

In general, the "a" responses represent a more traditional approach to performance appraisal that emphasizes its *evaluation* function. This role largely puts the supervisor in the role of documenting a subordinate's performance for control and administrative purposes. The "b" responses represent a more progressive approach that includes a strong emphasis on the *counseling* or *development* role. Here, the supervisor is concerned with helping the subordinate do better and with learning from the subordinate what he or she needs to be able to do better. There is more of an element of reciprocity in this role. It is quite consistent with new directions and values emerging in today's organizations.

_____

Source: Developed in part from Robert E. Quinn, Sue R. Faerman, Michael P. Thompson, and Michael R. McGrath, *Becoming a Master Manager: A Contemporary Framework* (New York: John Wiley & Sons, 1990), p. 187. Used by permission.

ASSESSMENT 14

"T-P" Leadership Questionnaire

Instructions

The following items describe aspects of leadership behavior. Respond to each item according to the way you would most likely act if you were the leader of a work group. Circle whether you would most likely behave in the described way: always (A), frequently (F), occasionally (O), seldom (S), or never (N).

A F O S N   **1.** I would most likely act as the spokesperson of the group.

A F O S N   **2.** I would encourage overtime work.

A F O S N   **3.** I would allow members complete freedom in their work.

A F O S N   **4.** I would encourage the use of uniform procedures.

A F O S N   **5.** I would permit the members to use their own judgment in solving problems.

A F O S N   **6.** I would stress being ahead of competing groups.

A F O S N   **7.** I would speak as a representative of the group.

A F O S N   **8.** I would push members for greater effort.

A F O S N   **9.** I would try out my ideas in the group.

A F O S N   **10.** I would let the members do their work the way they think best.

A F O S N   **11.** I would be working hard for a promotion.

A F O S N   **12.** I would tolerate postponement and uncertainty.

A F O S N   **13.** I would speak for the group if there were visitors present.

A F O S N   **14.** I would keep the work moving at a rapid pace.

A F O S N   **15.** I would turn the members loose on a job and let them go to it.

A F O S N   **16.** I would settle conflicts when they occur in the group.

A F O S N   **17.** I would get swamped by details.

A F O S N   **18.** I would represent the group at outside meetings.

A F O S N   **19.** I would be reluctant to allow the members any freedom of action.

A F O S N   **20.** I would decide what should be done and how it should be done.

A F O S N   **21.** I would push for increased performance.

A F O S N   **22.** I would let some members have authority which I could otherwise keep.

A F O S N   **23.** Things would usually turn out as I had predicted.

A F O S N   **24.** I would allow the group a high degree of initiative.

A F O S N   **25.** I would assign group members to particular tasks.

A F O S N   **26.** I would be willing to make changes.

A F O S N   **27.** I would ask the members to work harder.

A F O S N   **28.** I would trust the group members to exercise good judgment.

A F O S N   **29.** I would schedule the work to be done.

A F O S N   **30.** I would refuse to explain my actions.

A F O S N   **31.** I would persuade others that my ideas are to their advantage.

A F O S N   **32.** I would permit the group to set its own pace.

A F O S N   **33.** I would urge the group to beat its previous record.

A F O S N   **34.** I would act without consulting the group.

A F O S N   **35.** I would ask that group members follow standard rules and regulations.

Interpretation

Score the instrument as follows.

a. Write a "1" next to each of the following items if you scored them as S (seldom) or N (never).

8, 12, 17, 18, 19, 30, 34, 35

b. Write a "1" next to each of the following items if you scored them as A (always) or F (frequently).

1, 2, 3, 4, 5, 6, 7, 9, 10, 11, 13, 14, 15, 16, 20, 21, 22, 23, 24, 25, 26, 27, 28, 29, 31, 32, 33

c. Circle the "1" scores for the following items, and then add them up to get your TOTAL "P" SCORE = ___.

3, 5, 8, 10, 15, 18, 19, 22, 23, 26, 28, 30, 32, 34, 35

d. Circle the "1" scores for the following items, and then add them up to get your TOTAL "T" SCORE = ___.

1, 2, 4, 6, 7, 9, 11, 12, 13, 14, 16, 17, 20, 21, 23, 25, 27, 29, 31, 33

e. Record your scores on the following graph to develop an indication of your tendencies toward task-oriented leadership, people-oriented leadership, and shared leadership. Mark your T and P scores on the appropriate lines, then draw a line between these two points to determined your shared leadership score.

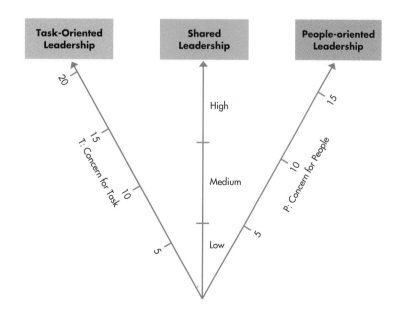

Source: Modified slightly from "T-P Leadership Questionnaire," University Associates, Inc., 1987. Used by permission.

"T-T" Leadership Style

Instructions

For each of the following 10 pairs of statements, divide 5 points between the two according to your beliefs or perceptions of yourself or according to which of the two statements characterizes you better. The 5 points may be divided between the a and b statements in any one of the following ways: 5 for a, 0 for b; 4 for a, 1 for b; 3 for a, 2 for b; 1 for a, 4 for b; 0 for a, 5 for b, but not equally (2-1/2) between the two. Weigh your choices between the two according to which one characterizes you or your beliefs better.

1. (a) As leader I have a primary mission of maintaining stability.
   (b) As leader I have a primary mission of change.

2. (a) As leader I must cause events.
   (b) As leader I must facilitate events.

3. (a) I am concerned that my followers are rewarded equitably for their work.
   (b) I am concerned about what my followers want in life.

4. (a) My preference is to think long range: What might be.
   (b) My preference is to think short range: What is realistic.

5. (a) As a leader I spend considerable energy in managing separate but related goals.
   (b) As a leader I spend considerable energy in arousing hopes, expectations, and aspirations among my followers.

6. (a) Although not in a formal classroom sense, I believe that a significant part of my leadership is that of teacher.
   (b) I believe that a significant part of my leadership is that of facilitator.

7. (a) As leader I must engage with followers on an equal level of morality.
   (b) As leader I must represent a higher morality.

8. (a) I enjoy stimulating followers to want to do more.
   (b) I enjoy rewarding followers for a job well done.

9. (a) Leadership should be practical.
   (b) Leadership should be inspirational.

10. (a) What power I have to influence others comes primarily from my ability to get people to identify with me and my ideas.
    (b) What power I have to influence others comes primarily from my status and position.

Scoring

Circle your points for items 1b, 2a, 3b, 4a, 5b, 6a, 7b, 8a, 9b, 10a and add up the total points you allocated to these items; enter the score here [T = ____]. Next, add up the total points given to the uncircled items 1a, 2b, 3a, 4b, 5a, 6b, 7a, 8b, 9a, 10b; enter the score here [T = ____].

Interpretation

This instrument gives an impression of your tendencies toward "transformational" leadership (your T score) and "transactional" leadership (your T score). You may want to refer to the discussion of these concepts in Chapter 13. Today, a lot of attention is being given to the transformational aspects of leadership—those personal qualities that inspire a sense of vision and the desire for extraordinary accomplishment in followers. The most successful leaders of the future will most likely be strong in both "T"s.

Source: Questionnaire by W. Warner Burke, Ph.D. Used by permission.

Least-Preferred Coworker Scale

Instructions

Think of all the different people with whom you have ever worked—in jobs, in social clubs, in student projects, or whatever. Next think of the *one person* with whom you could work *least* well—that is, the person with whom you had the most difficulty getting a job done. This is the one person—a peer, boss, or subordinate—with whom you would least want to work. Describe this person by circling numbers at the appropriate points on each of the following pairs of bipolar adjectives. Work rapidly. There are no right or wrong answers.

Pleasant	8 7 6 5 4 3 2 1	Unpleasant
Friendly	8 7 6 5 4 3 2 1	Unfriendly
Rejecting	1 2 3 4 5 6 7 8	Accepting
Tense	1 2 3 4 5 6 7 8	Relaxed
Distant	1 2 3 4 5 6 7 8	Close
Cold	1 2 3 4 5 6 7 8	Warm
Supportive	8 7 6 5 4 3 2 1	Hostile
Boring	1 2 3 4 5 6 7 8	Interesting
Quarrelsome	1 2 3 4 5 6 7 8	Harmonious
Gloomy	1 2 3 4 5 6 7 8	Cheerful
Open	8 7 6 5 4 3 2 1	Guarded
Backbiting	1 2 3 4 5 6 7 8	Loyal
Untrustworthy	1 2 3 4 5 6 7 8	Trustworthy
Considerate	8 7 6 5 4 3 2 1	Inconsiderate
Nasty	1 2 3 4 5 6 7 8	Nice
Agreeable	8 7 6 5 4 3 2 1	Disagreeable

Insincere	1 2 3 4 5 6 7 8	Sincere
Kind	8 7 6 5 4 3 2 1	Unkind

Scoring

This is called the "least-preferred coworker scale" (LPC). Compute your LPC score by totaling all the numbers you circled; enter that score here [LPC = ___].

Interpretation

The LPC scale is used by Fred Fiedler to identify a person's dominant leadership style (see Chapter 13). Fiedler believes that this style is a relatively fixed part of one's personality and is therefore difficult to change. This leads Fiedler to his contingency views, which suggest that the key to leadership success is finding (or creating) good "matches" between style and situation. If your score is 73 or above, Fiedler considers you a "relationship-motivated" leader; if your score is 64 and below, he considers you a "task-motivated" leader. If your score is between 65 and 72, Fiedler leaves it up to you to determine which leadership style is most like yours.

Source: Fred E. Fiedler and Martin M. Chemers. *Improving Leadership Effectiveness: The Leader Match Concept*, 2nd ed. (New York: John Wiley & Sons, 1984). Used by permission.

Two-Factor Profile

Instructions

On each of the following dimensions, distribute a total of "10" points between the two options. For example:

Summer weather (7) . . . . (3) Winter weather

1. Very responsible job (___) . . . . (___) Job security

2. Recognition for work accomplishments (___) . . . . (___) Good relations with coworkers

3. Advancement opportunities at work (___) . . . . (___) A boss who knows his/her job well

4. Opportunities to grow (___) . . . . (___) Good working
and learn on the job   conditions

5. A job that I can (___) . . . . (___) Supportive rules,
do well   policies of employer

6. A prestigious or (___) . . . . (___) A high base wage
high status job   or salary

Scoring

Summarize your total scores for all items in the *left-hand column* and write it here:
MF = ___.
Summarize your total scores for all items in the *right-hand column* and write it here: HF = ___.

Interpretation

The "MF" score indicates the relative importance that you place on motivating or satisfier factors in Herzberg's two-factor theory. This shows how important job content is to you.

The "HF" score indicates the relative importance that you place on hygiene or dissatisfier factors in Herzberg's two-factor theory. This shows how important job context is to you.

ASSESSMENT 18

Job Design Preference

Instructions

People differ in what they like and dislike about their jobs. Listed below are 12 pairs of jobs. For each pair, indicate which job you would prefer. Assume that everything else about the jobs is the same—pay attention only to the characteristics actually listed for each pair of jobs. If you would prefer the job in Column A, indicate how much you prefer it by putting a check mark in a blank to the left of the Neutral point. If you prefer the job in Column B, check one of the blanks to the right of Neutral. Check the Neutral blank only if you find the two jobs equally attractive or unattractive. Try to use the Neutral blank sparingly.

Column A		Column B

1. A job that offers little or no challenge.

| | | | | | | | | |
Strongly   Neutral   Strongly
prefer A   prefer B

A job that requires you to be completely isolated from coworkers.

2. A job that pays well.

| | | | | | | | | |
Strongly   Neutral   Strongly
prefer A   prefer B

A job that allows considerable opportunity to be creative and innovative.

3. A job that often requires you to make important decisions.

| | | | | | | | | |
Strongly   Neutral   Strongly
prefer A   prefer B

A job in which there are many pleasant people to work with.

4. A job with little security in a somewhat unstable organization.

Strongly prefer A · Neutral · Strongly prefer B

A job in which you have little or no opportunity to participate in decisions that affect your work.

5. A job in which greater responsibility is given to those who do the best work.

Strongly prefer A · Neutral · Strongly prefer B

A job in which greater responsibility is given to loyal employees who have the most *seniority*.

6. A job with a supervisor who sometimes is highly critical.

Strongly prefer A · Neutral · Strongly prefer B

A job that does not require you to use much of your talent.

7. A very routine job.

Strongly prefer A · Neutral · Strongly prefer B

A job in which your coworkers are not very friendly.

8. A job with a supervisor who respects you and treats you fairly.

Strongly prefer A · Neutral · Strongly prefer B

A job that provides constant opportunities for you to learn new and interesting things.

9. A job that gives you a real chance to develop yourself personally.

Strongly prefer A · Neutral · Strongly prefer B

A job with excellent vacation and fringe benefits.

10. A job in which there is a real chance you could be laid off.

Strongly prefer A · Neutral · Strongly prefer B

A job that offers very little chance to do challenging work.

11. A job that gives you little freedom and independence to do your work in the way you think best.

Strongly prefer A · Neutral · Strongly prefer B

A job with poor working conditions.

12. A job with very satisfying teamwork.

Strongly prefer A · Neutral · Strongly prefer B

A job that allows you to use your skills and abilities to the fullest extent.

Interpretation

People differ in their need for psychological growth at work. This instrument measures the degree to which you seek growth need satisfaction. Score your responses as follows:

For items 1, 2, 7, 8, 11, and 12 give yourself the following points for each item:

1	2	3	4	5	6	7

Strongly prefer A · Neutral · Strongly prefer B

For items 3, 4, 5, 6, 9, and 10 give yourself the following points for each item.

7	6	5	4	3	2	1

Strongly prefer A · Neutral · Strongly prefer B

Add up all of your scores and divide by 12 to find the average. If you score above 4.0 your desire for growth need satisfaction through work tends to be high and you are likely to prefer an enriched job. If you score below 4.0 your desire for growth need satisfaction through work tends to be low and you are likely to not be satisfied or motivated with an enriched job.

Source: Reprinted by permission from J. R. Hackman and G. R. Oldham, *The Job Diagnostic Survey: An Instrument for the Diagnosis of Jobs and the Evaluation of Job Redesign Projects, Technical Report 4* (New Haven, CT: Yale University, Department of Administrative Sciences, 1974).

Conflict Management Styles

Instructions

Think of how you behave in conflict situations in which your wishes differ from those of one or more other persons. In the space to the left of each of the following statements, write the number from the following scale that indicates how likely you are to respond that way in a conflict situation.

1 = very unlikely   2 = unlikely
3 = likely   4 = very likely

___ 1. I am usually firm in pursuing my goals.
___ 2. I try to win my position.
___ 3. I give up some points in exchange for others.
___ 4. I feel that differences are not always worth worrying about.
___ 5. I try to find a position that is intermediate between the other person's and mine.
___ 6. In approaching negotiations, I try to be considerate of the other person's wishes.
___ 7. I try to show the logic and benefits of my positions.
___ 8. I always lean toward a direct discussion of the problem.
___ 9. I try to find a fair combination of gains and losses for both of us.
___ 10. I attempt to work through our differences immediately.
___ 11. I try to avoid creating unpleasantness for myself.
___ 12. I try to soothe the other person's feelings and preserve our relationships.

___ 13. I attempt to get all concerns and issues immediately out in the open.
___ 14. I sometimes avoid taking positions that would create controversy.
___ 15. I try not to hurt others' feelings.

Scoring

Total your scores for items 1, 2, 7; enter that score here [*Competing* = ____]. Total your scores for items 8, 10, 13; enter that score here [*Collaborating* = ____]. Total your scores for items 3, 5, 9; enter that score here [*Compromising* = ____]. Total your scores for items 4, 11, 14; enter that score here [*Avoiding* = ____]. Total your scores for items 6, 12, 15; enter that score here [*Accommodating* = ____].

Interpretation

Each of the scores above corresponds to one of the conflict management styles discussed in Chapter 16. Research indicates that each style has a role to play in management but that the best overall conflict management approach is collaboration; only it can lead to problem solving and true conflict resolution. You should consider any patterns that may be evident in your scores and think about how to best handle the conflict situations in which you become involved.

Source: Adapted from Thomas-Kilmann, *Conflict Mode Instrument.* Copyright © 1974, Xicom, Inc., Tuxedo, NY 10987. Used by permission.

Facts and Inferences

Preparation

Read the following report:

Often, when we listen or speak, we don't distinguish between statements of fact and those of inference. Yet, *there are great differences between the two. We create barriers to clear thinking when we treat inferences (guesses, opinions) as if they are facts. You may wish at this point to test your ability to distinguish facts from inferences by taking the accompanying fact-inference test based on those by Haney (1973).*

Instructions

Carefully read the following report and the observations based on it. Indicate whether you think the observations are true, false, or doubtful on the basis of the information presented in the report. Write T if the observation is definitely true, F if the observation is definitely false, and ? if the observation may be either true or false. Judge each observation in order. Do not reread the observations after you have indicated your judgment, and do not change any of your answers.

A well-liked college instructor had just completed making up the final examinations and had turned off the lights in the office. Just then a tall, broad figure with dark glasses appeared and demanded the examination. The professor opened the drawer. Everything in the drawer was picked up and the individual ran down the corridor. The president was notified immediately.

_____ 1. The thief was tall, broad, and wore dark glasses.
_____ 2. The professor turned off the lights.
_____ 3. A tall figure demanded the examination.
_____ 4. The examination was picked up by someone.
_____ 5. The examination was picked up by the professor.
_____ 6. A tall, broad figure appeared after the professor turned off the lights in the office.
_____ 7. The man who opened the drawer was the professor.
_____ 8. The professor ran down the corridor.

_____ 9. The drawer was never actually opened.
_____ 10. Three persons are referred to in this report.

When told to do so by your instructor, join a small work group. Now, help the group complete the same task by making a consensus decision on each item. Be sure to keep a separate record of the group's responses and your original individual responses.

Scoring

Your instructor will read the correct answers. Score both your individual and group responses.

Interpretation

To begin, ask yourself if there was a difference between your answers and those of the group for each item. If so, why? Why do you think people, individually or in groups, may answer these questions incorrectly? Good planning depends on good decision making by the people doing the planning. Being able to distinguish "facts" and understand one's "inferences" are important steps toward improving the planning process. Involving others to help do the same can frequently assist in this process.

Source: Joseph A. Devito, *Messages: Building Interpersonal Communication Skills*, 3rd ed. (New York: HarperCollins, 1996), referencing William Haney, *Communicational Behavior: Text and Cases*, 3rd ed. (Homewood, II.: Irwin, 1973). Reprinted by permission.

ASSESSMENT 21

Stress Self-Test

Instructions

Complete the following questionnaire. Circle the number that best represents your tendency to behave on each bipolar dimension.

Am casual about appointments	1 2 3 4 5 6 7 8	Am never late
Am not competitive	1 2 3 4 5 6 7 8	Am very competitive
Never feel rushed	1 2 3 4 5 6 7 8	Always feel rushed
Take things one at a time	1 2 3 4 5 6 7 8	Try to do many things at once
Do things slowly	1 2 3 4 5 6 7 8	Do things fast
Express feelings	1 2 3 4 5 6 7 8	"Sit on" feelings
Have many interests	1 2 3 4 5 6 7 8	Have few interests but work

Scoring

Total the numbers circled for all items, and multiply this by 3; enter the result here [____].

Interpretation

This scale is designed to measure your personality tendency toward Type A or Type B behaviors. As described in Chapter 16, a Type A personality is associated with high stress. Persons who are Type A tend to bring stress on themselves even in situations where others are relatively stress-free. This is an important characteristic to be able to identify in yourself and in others.

Points	Personality
120+	A+
106–119	A
100–105	A−
90–99	B+
below 90	B

Source: Adapted from R. W. Bortner. "A Short Rating Scale as a Potential Measure of Type A Behavior." *Journal of Chronic Diseases*, vol. 22 (1966), pp. 87–91. Used by permission.

Research and Presentation Projects

PROJECT 1

Diversity Lessons—"What Have We Learned?"

There are many reports out there—*Workforce 2020*, *Workforce 2000*, and *Opportunity 2000*, among several others. Diversity in the workplace is clearly the subject of significant attention. Managers and employers are being urged to recognize and value diversity, and many are pursuing active programs to improve the environment for diversity in the workplace. Yet "glass ceilings" remain obstacles to career and personal accomplishment for too many females, African Americans, and other minorities.

QUESTION

What are the "facts" in terms of progress for minorities in the workplace? What lessons of diversity have been learned? What are the "best" employers doing?

Instructions

Use research sources at your disposal to complete a project report addressing the research question. Specific topics for consideration might include the following:

- Case studies of employers reported as having strong diversity programs. What do they have in common? What do they do differently? Is there a basic "model" that could be followed by managers in other settings?

- Investigation of diversity with specific reference to how well people of different racial, ethnic, gender, and generational groups work together. What do we know about this, if anything? What are the common problems, if any? What concerns do managers and workers have?
- Analysis of survey reports on how the "glass ceiling" may affect the careers of women and minorities in various occupational settings. Get specific data, analyze them, and develop the implications. Prepare a report that summarizes your research.
- A critical look at the substance of diversity training programs. What do these programs try to accomplish, and how? Are they working or not, and how do we know? Is there a good model for diversity training that may be used by others?
- Look at where we go from here. What diversity issues lie ahead to be successfully mastered by the *new* managers of tomorrow?

PROJECT 2

Corporate Culture—"Can It Be Changed?"

"Culture" is a popular topic in management circles. Conventional wisdom holds that strong cultures can bond employees to a common sense of mission and reinforce work habits needed to serve customers well and maintain productivity. The implication also is that cultures in organizations can and should be changed when necessary to improve performance. Skeptics, by contrast, seem to believe that it may be better to work with, or get the best out of, an existing culture rather than to try to change it.

QUESTION

What do you think? Can an organization's culture be changed? Should managers try to change the culture when an organization or work unit is not performing up to expectations?

Instructions

Use research sources at your disposal to complete a project report addressing this question. Specific topics for consideration might include the following:

- Look for the latest thinking of management scholars and consultants on the role of "corporate culture" in successful organizations. Many case examples and reports should be available on this topic. Look for success stories and try to interpret them in the context of the research question.
- Make a list, from your research, of things that can be done to change the culture of an organization or work unit. Critically evaluate each of these items in terms of these action criteria: (a) feasibility of dealing with the item, (b) length of time needed to achieve impact on the item, and (c) the follow-up or reinforcement needed to maintain this impact. Review your entire analysis and answer this question: "Can the recommended things really be accomplished by (a) a CEO, (b) a middle manager, and (c) a team leader?"

- Place the issue of corporate culture in the context of the growing number of international mergers, joint ventures, and strategic alliances found in the global economy. What is the importance of differences in "corporate cultures" as organizations of different "national cultures" try to work with one another? What do management consultants and scholars know or have to say about managing the problems of culture in this specific arena of business activity?

PROJECT 3

Foreign Investment in America— "What Are the Implications?"

Foreign investment in the United States is high and growing. For example, there are more than 1,500 Japanese manufacturing companies in the United States. The number of Americans employed in these firms is over 300,000 and growing. In smaller communities like Marysville, Ohio, and Smyrna, Tennessee, the presence of a Honda or Nissan plant has substantial implications for the local economy and for the local way of life in general. Indeed, some Americans view the growing Japanese investment in the United States as a cause for concern, not jubilation.

QUESTION

Which is it? Is foreign investment in the United States a cause for concern, or is it something to be welcomed?

Instructions

Use research sources at your disposal to complete a project report on this question. Specific topics for consideration might include the following:

- The status of current foreign investment in the United States. How much is there, how fast is it growing, in what major industries is it found, and where is it located?
- The primary benefits and costs of this investment for the local communities and regions in which foreign firms operate. What do the communities gain from their presence? What price do they pay?
- The nature of Japanese investment in particular. What are the effects of Japanese *keiretsu*. Do these linkages within business groups "spill over" to influence how Japanese firms operate in America? Do the *keiretsu* work to the disadvantage of non-Japanese firms wanting to do business with them in the United States?
- How do Americans feel about working for foreign employers. Do the Americans have opportunities for career advancement in the foreign firms? Do these opportunities vary for men and women? Are foreign companies considered to be "good" employers? Why or why not?

Corporate Social Responsibility—"What's the Status?"

The average fast-food restaurant generates enormous waste each day. Actions taken to reduce this waste are applauded. The U.S. Food and Drug Administration monitors food labeling to guard the public against inappropriate claims. Firms sanctioned by the FDA often pay a price in negative publicity. Waste management and product labeling are but two of a growing range of business activities that are being publicly scrutinized for their social responsibility implications.

QUESTION

Where do businesses stand today with respect to the criteria for evaluating social responsibility discussed in the textbook?

Instructions

Use research sources at your disposal to complete a project report on this question. Specific topics for consideration might include the following:

- Research and evaluate the "status" of McDonald's and Procter & Gamble on a variety of social responsibility performance matters. How well are they doing? Would you use them as "models" of social responsibility for others to follow, or not?
- Conduct research to identify current examples of the "best" and the "worst" organizations in terms of performance or social responsibility criteria. Pursue this investigation on an (a) international, (b) national, and/or (c) local scale.
- Choose an issue such as environmental protection or product labeling. Conduct research to identify the "best" and the "worst" organizations in terms of performance in these specific areas. Again, consider looking at this issue on an (a) international, (b) national, and/or (c) local scale.
- Create a "scale" that could be used to measure the social responsibility performance of an organization. Review the scholarly research in this area but use your own judgment. Test your scale by applying it to two or three local organizations.

Entrepeneurship—"Is It for You?"

Entrepreneurship offers unusual career opportunities in today's complex business environment. But entrepreneurship involves taking risk. There are rewards to be gained and potential costs to be borne.

QUESTION

Is entrepreneurship for you?

Instructions

Use the library and other research sources at your disposal to complete and submit a written report addressing this question. Specific topics for consideration might include the following:

- Start with *Fortune*, *Business Week*, and other business periodicals. Then hit the Internet. What are the opportunities for entrepreneurs today? Find some directions for further research and investigation.
- Find some success stories. Use them as examples to explain what can be done to encourage and sustain entrepreneurship—by yourself and others. Are there any patterns in evidence that can explain entrepreneurship success?
- Consider the "entrepreneurial personality." Is there such a thing? What is it? Do you have it? What are the implications of having or not having this personality?
- Interview one or more local entrepreneurs to inquire into their "stories"— where did they start, what did they do, what mistakes did they make, what did they learn, what would they recommend?
- Prepare a report that could be used for a formal briefing to a group of high school students on the topic—"Opportunities for career success through entrepreneurship."

PROJECT 6

Total Quality Management—"Is it Working?"

Business Week once went so far as to state, "Quality, in short, may be the biggest competitive issue of the late 20th and early 21st centuries." The textbook has introduced total quality management (TQM) as a general concept; now it's time to look further at what the "real world" is doing with it.

QUESTION

What are the "best of the best" doing with respect to total quality management, and where will they go from here? Is "TQM" working?

Instructions

Use research sources at your disposal to complete a project report addressing the research question. Specific topics for consideration might include the following:

- Every so often, business periodicals such as *Business Week* and *Fortune* publish special issues on quality. Examine some of these reports, as well as other sources. Choose examples that you feel meet the standards of "best" of the best. Cover both manufacturing and services, and business as well as nonprofits. Analyze the examples and identify common patterns as well as differences. Prepare a report entitled, "Total Quality Management: What It Takes to Succeed."
- Look again at your research to identify examples where technology makes a significant difference. Try to be specific about how managers can use technology to the best quality advantage. Be sensitive to potential differences in manufacturing and services, and businesses versus nonprofits. What patterns do you see, and what positive examples can you find?

- Look also at human resource issues and developments. What roles do people play in an organization's total quality movement? What are highly progressive organizations doing to ensure that they have a workforce that is both capable of and supportive of a total quality management approach? What lessons are we learning in this respect? What patterns do you see, and what positive examples can you find?
- Examine the research literature. What do the researchers say? Does total quality management really work? How do we know? What do we know? What don't we know?
- Prepare a "practitioner's" bibliography of recommended books and readings on total quality management. Annotate the bibliography to give management readers some insight into what is covered in a particular reference and to help them set priorities as to what to read first.
- Where does the total quality movement go from here? What new directions or steps are on the horizon? What should a truly informed manager be aware of in order to meet the leadership challenge of helping organizations achieve competitive advantage through quality products and services?

PROJECT 7

Reengineering—"Does It Work?"

Reports of reengineering are still in the news as many organizations try to improve performance through various forms of work and organizational restructuring. Reengineering offers the potential advantages of streamlined operations, but may also affect careers, jobs, and worker loyalties. The impression remains that since so many organizations are doing it, reengineering must work. Its benefits must be greater than its costs.

QUESTION

Do the benefits of reengineering outweigh its costs? What do we really know about the results of reengineering organizations?

Instructions

Use research sources at your disposal to complete a project report addressing this question. Specific topics for consideration might include the following:

- An examination of the issues from workers' perspectives. Look for reports on worker responses to reengineering programs. Try to find case examples that document how this type of organizational change affects people. Look, in particular, for both "success" and "failure" stories.
- An examination of organizational performance results. Try to find reports on how reengineering affects corporate profits, productivity, competitive advantage, and other success indicators. Look for case examples that document the impact of reengineering on performance—both positively and negatively.
- A review of the scholarly literature for empirical research on this and related topics. Summarize the findings. Identify questions for further study.

- Patterns from your analysis. Can you show when and under what conditions reengineering can succeed? Can you identify guidelines for managerial decision making and action that may increase the likelihood that it can be successful? Be diligent, persistent, frank, and inquisitive.

PROJECT 8

Affirmative Action—"Where Do We Go from Here?"

In a *Harvard Business Review* article ("From Affirmative Action to Affirming Diversity," March-April 1990), R. Roosevelt Thomas makes the following statement: "Sooner or later, affirmative action will die a natural death." He goes on to praise its accomplishments but then argues that it is time to "move beyond affirmative action" and learn how to "manage diversity." There are a lot of issues that may be raised in this context—issues of equal employment opportunity, hiring quotas, reverse discrimination, and others.

QUESTION

What about it? Where do we stand with affirmative action today and where are we going?

Instructions

Use research sources at your disposal to complete a project report addressing this question. Specific topics for consideration might include the following:

- Read the Thomas article. Make sure you are clear on the term *affirmative action* and its legal underpinnings. Research the topic, identify the relevant laws, and make a history line to chart its development over time.
- Examine current debates on "affirmative action" at the level of national policy. What are the issues? How are the "for" and "against" positions being argued?
- Consider "reverse discrimination." Is there any pattern to employment situations in which reverse discrimination emerges as a management concern? Identify cases where reverse discrimination has been charged. How have they been resolved and with what apparent human resource management implications?
- Examine current controversies over hiring "quotas." Is this what affirmative action is all about? What are the arguments, pro and con? What do the "experts" say about it? Where do we seem to be headed in this area?
- Look at organizational policies that deal with diversity matters. Find what you consider to be the "best" examples. Analyze them and identify the common ground. Prepare a summary that could be used as a policy development guideline for human resource directors who want to make sure their organizations truly support and value diversity in the workforce.
- Try to look at all of these issues and controversies from different perspectives. Talk to people of different "majority" and "minority" groups in your college or university. Find out how they view these things—and why. What are the implications for human resource management today?

Fringe Benefits—"Can They Be Managed?"

Good compensation and benefits systems help organizations attract and retain talented workers. But an increasingly diverse workforce is placing new and ever-greater demands on employers to provide benefits. Rising costs are making it ever more difficult for cost-conscious employers to maintain their benefits programs.

QUESTION

How can organizations best deal with the looming fringe benefits crisis? Can benefits programs fit the needs of both a diverse workforce and satisfy the cost control needs of employers?

Instructions

Use research sources at your disposal to complete a project report addressing this question. Specific topics for consideration might include the following:

- Look at the data on health-care costs. How are rising costs of health care affecting employers . . . and their employees? Examine the problems of those workers who may not be covered at all by employer-sponsored health insurance programs. Find some positive examples of organizations that are trying new and promising approaches to deal with rising costs of health-care-related fringe benefits while still treating their employees well in the process.
- Shift the focus to pension plans and related matters. Look at the growing complexity of financial planning alternatives and tax laws. How are progressive organizations coping? What are the implications for employees? Try to come up with a series of "pension-awareness guidelines" that could be offered to anyone entering the workforce today.
- Focus on the fringe benefits that best meet the needs of a diverse workforce. What special "needs" are appearing with greater frequency and sense of importance? Again, try to find examples of progressive employers who may be doing things that others could use as "benchmarks" for their own fringe benefit programs.
- Try to find surveys that report on workers' views of their fringe benefits. Look for similar reports on employer views. Examine the patterns and compare the perceptions. What are the implications for managers who want to establish the best support systems for employees in tomorrow's organizations?

PROJECT 10

CEO Pay—"Is It Too High?"

The high, sometimes extremely high, pay of CEOs in many American corporations has caught the public's eye. Many people aren't very happy with what they are discovering. One report states that CEOs take home, on average, 160 times the pay of their employees, and earn three to six times what their counterpart CEOs in Japanese and European companies earn. It is not only the magnitude of the pay that is bothersome. Controversial too is the belief that the pay of some CEOs goes up even when their firms' performance goes down.

QUESTION

What is happening in the area of executive compensation? Are CEOs paid too much? Are they paid for "performance," or are they paid for something else?

Instructions

Use research sources at your disposal to complete a project report addressing this question. Specific topics for consideration might include the following:

- Check the latest reports on CEO pay. Try to get the facts. Prepare a briefing report as if you were writing a short informative article for *Fortune* magazine. The title of your article should be "Status Report: Where We Stand Today on CEO Pay."
- Address the pay-for-performance issue. Do corporate CEOs get paid for performance or for something else? What do the researchers say? What do the business periodicals say? Find some examples to explain and defend your answers to these questions.
- Find some positive cases where you consider a CEO's pay to be justified. What criteria are you using to justify it?
- Take a position: Should a limit be set on CEO pay? If no, why not? If yes, what type of limit do we set? Should we deal with an absolute dollar limit, a multiple of what the lowest paid worker in a firm earns, or some other guideline? Why? Who, if anyone, should set these limits—Congress, company boards of directors, or someone else?
- Take a poll on campus. What do other students think about CEO pay? Do they think limits should be set? Take a poll in your local community. What does the public at large think? How does the public feel about limits to CEO pay? How about you—what is your conclusion? Is the "attack" on CEO pay justified?

PROJECT 11

Managing Your Boss—"Possible or Not?"

Today's workers must consider managing their relationships with "the boss" as part of their everyday job. It is no longer sufficient for a manager to be good only at dealing with subordinates. Increasingly, the network aspects of organizations require that managers do a good job of managing relationships with peers and bosses. But when it comes to the "bosses" in particular, one has to wonder about the guidelines.

QUESTION

What do we really know about the techniques of "managing one's boss?"

Instructions

Use research sources at your disposal to complete a project report addressing this question. Specific topics for consideration might include the following:

- Start with a classic *Harvard Business Review* article by John J. Gabarro and John P. Kotter entitled "How to Manage Your Boss" (January–February 1980, pp. 92–100). Analyze its main points and summarize them to create an initial set of guidelines. Check the literature further. Add to your list based on other useful insights that may be available.
- Examine the literature on power and influence. What do we know about how someone can use power to influence people at higher levels in organizations? Draft a set of guidelines that could be useful to a new college graduate who wants to be able to "manage" her new boss.
- Identify three or more conflict situations a manager may typically become involved in with his boss. Show how these situations might develop into "win-lose" or "lose-lose" outcomes. Show how "win-win" outcomes might be more likely *if* the manager takes appropriate action in each situation.
- Identify three or more negotiation situations a manager may typically become involved in with her boss. How do the Fisher and Ury ideas on "principled negotiation" apply in these situations? Read further on the subject of negotiation. What additional insights on handling these situations are available?
- Examine the literature on stress. What do researchers say and studies report on the role of "bosses" as sources of workplace stress for their subordinates? Is there anything that the subordinate can do to deal with a "high-stress" boss? What about the boss? What can he or she do to minimize the impact of his or her high-stress style on others?

PROJECT 12

Self-Managing Teams—"How Good Are They?"

In Geert Hofstede's framework for describing national cultures (see Chapter 5), the United States is described as the most "individualistic" country in his research sample. Americans, he suggests, are a people motivated by self-interests and opportunities for personal accomplishment and gain. This seems somewhat contrary to the growing emphasis on "teamwork" and the increasing use of self-managing teams and various types of employee involvement groups in organizations.

QUESTION

How well are self-managing teams working in the American workplace? What is the future of this approach?

Use research sources at your disposal to complete a project report addressing this question. Specific topics for consideration might include the following:

- Check the research on self-managing teams. Where have they been tried and with what success? Look for empirical data, not just theoretical arguments. Are there any patterns? What open questions remain to be answered?
- Look at the management guidelines for self-managing teams. What is the advice on how to ensure their success? What are the potential pitfalls in workplaces where one is changing *to* self-managing teams from other more traditional methods?
- Address the individualism issue. Can self-managing teams work with the highly individualistic American workers? What advice is available on how to deal with this individualism issue if, indeed, it is an issue at all?
- Address the organization structure issue. How must an organization's structure change in order to support the activities of self-managing teams best? What advice is available on handling these structural issues?
- Look more broadly at employee involvement groups in general. What do we know about the effectiveness of quality circles and other types of employee involvement groups? Are there any patterns that indicate when and under what conditions they tend to work best?
- Assume you have to give a formal briefing to a senior executive trying to decide if her organization should try self-managing teams and employee involvement groups. Based on your research, what will you say?

PROJECT 13

Virtual Teams—"Does Groupware Work?"

There are many reports on the growing use of "virtual teams" in organizations. These involve a range of technologies, with a growing emphasis on "groupware" that allows the computer mediation of relationships between group members. Clearly this is a pathway to the future. But skeptics remain.

QUESTION

What do we know about virtual teams? What is the current status of "groupware" alternatives and does the software really work? How far should we go in letting computers mediate relationships between work team members?

Instructions

Use research sources at your disposal to complete a project report addressing this question. Specific topics for consideration might include the following:

- An inventory of current groupware alternatives. What is available, from what sources, and at what costs? Are there any alternatives that seem to be more popular than others, and/or that represent the most likely alternatives to be found in your workplace of the future?

- Consider the argument about "depersonalizing" teamwork when you move it into the virtual environment. Start with the academic literature. What are the researchers saying? Look at the applied literature and news reports. What are they saying, and what do the workers themselves appear to be saying? Are there any patterns in these sources that shed light on the research question?
- Take a look at organizations operating in your area. Talk to managers and workers. Spend some time with those in charge of the organizations' information services function. Is virtual teamwork making its way into your community? If so, what is happening? What are the trends in the use of groupware? Do the people involved like it or not, and why?
- Prepare a report on the future of virtual teamwork. Include in this report your prediction regarding the "best" available groupware applications and specific guidelines for using virtual teams to best advantage in organizations. Be sure to address the potential limits of this technology as well as its advantages.

Self-Test Answers

Chapter 1

1. d
2. c
3. a
4. b
5. a
6. a
7. c
8. a
9. b
10. b
11. F
12. T
13. T
14. T
15. T
16. T
17. F
18. F
19. F
20. T
21. The manager is held accountable by his boss for performance results of the manager's work unit. The manager must answer back to the boss for unit performance. By the same token, the manager's subordinates must answer back to her or him for their individual performance. They are accountable to the manager.
22. If the glass ceiling effect operates in a given situation, it would act as a hidden barrier to advancement beyond a certain level. Top managers controlling promotions would not give them to African-American candidates, regardless of their capabilities.
23. Ohmae's term "borderless world" refers to the fact that more businesses are operating on a global scale and the countries are becoming very interdependent economically. Products are sold and resources purchased around the world, and business strategies increasingly target markets in more than one country.
24. Managers must respect subordinates as mature, responsible, adult human beings. The work setting should be organized and managed to protect individual privacy, provide freedom from sexual harassment, and offer safe and healthy job conditions. Failure to do so is socially irresponsible. It may also cause productivity losses.
25. One approach to this question is through the framework of essential management skills offered by Katz. At the first level of management, technical skills are important and I would feel capable in this respect. However, I would expect to learn and refine these skills through my work experiences. Human skills, the ability to work well with other people, will also be very important. Given the diversity anticipated for this team, I will need good human skills. I will also have a leadership responsibility to help others on the team develop and utilize these skills so that the team itself can function effectively. Finally, I would expect opportunities to develop my conceptual or analytical skills in anticipation of higher level appointments. In terms of personal development I should recognize that the conceptual skills will increase in importance relative to the technical skills as I move upward in management responsibility.

Chapter 2

1. a
2. d
3. b
4. d
5. b
6. d
7. c
8. c
9. a
10. b
11. F
12. T
13. F
14. F
15. T
16. F
17. T
18. T
19. T
20. F
21. Possible operating objectives reflecting a commitment to competitive advantage through customer service include: (a) providing high-quality goods and services, (b) providing low-cost goods and services, (c) providing short waiting times for goods and services, and (d) providing goods and services meeting unique customer needs.
22. External customers are the consumers or clients who buy the organization's goods or use its services. Internal customers are the individuals or groups within the organization who utilize goods and services produced by others also inside the organization.
23. The core culture of the organization consists of the values that shape and

direct the behavior of members. An example would be a "quality" value that encouraged everyone to always do the highest quality work. The observable culture is found in the everyday activities of the organization. It may exist in the form of stories, rituals, and heroes. For example, reward ceremonies to recognize high-performance accomplishments are a ritual; the repeated reminder at such ceremonies of a popular high performer of the past is an example of recognizing heroes.

24. Subcultures are important in organizations because of the diversity of the workforce. Although working in the same organization and sharing the same organizational culture, members may also differ in subculture affiliations based on such aspects as gender, age, and ethnic differences. It is important to understand how subculture differences may influence working relationships. For example, a 40-year-old supervisor of 20-year-old workers must understand that the values and behaviors of the younger workforce may not be totally consistent with what she or he believes in, and vice versa.

25. I disagree with this statement since a strong organizational or corporate culture can be a positive influence on any organization, large or small. The woman working for the large company is mistaken in thinking that the concept does not apply to her friend's small business. In fact, the friend as owner and perhaps founder of the business should be working hard to establish the values and other elements that will create a strong and continuing culture. Employees of any organization should have core organizational values to serve as reference points for their attitudes and behavior. The rites and rituals of everyday organizational life are also important to recognize positive accomplishments and add meaning to the employment relationships. It may even be that the friend's role as creator and sponsor of the corporate culture is more magnified in the small business setting. As the owner and manager, she is visible everyday to all employees. How she acts will have a great impact on any "culture" that is established in her store.

Chapter 3

1. c
2. a
3. c
4. b
5. c
6. a
7. c
8. b
9. a
10. b
11. F
12. F
13. T
14. T
15. F
16. F
17. F
18. F
19. T
20. T
21. An information system is intended to serve an organization and its decision makers by providing a convenient and accurate means of collecting, organizing, and distributing data in ways that make it meaningful as information.
22. The success of any information system depends on (1) the technical quality of the system, (2) management support for the system, and (3) the participation and involvement of users in the design and continuous improvement of the system. Managers should avoid the following common information system mistakes. (1) Assuming that more information is always better. (2) Assuming that new equipment and software is always better. (3) Assuming that once a computer system is in place nothing can go wrong with it. (4) Assuming that the computer can do everything. (5) Assuming that human judgement is no longer important.
23. Decision making is just one part of the broader problem-solving process. Problem solving involves: (1) finding and defining a problem, (2) generating alternative solutions, (3) evaluating alternatives and making a *decision* to pursue one of them, (4) implementing the chosen solution, and (5) evaluating results.
24. A systematic thinking manager is going to approach problem solving in a logical and rational fashion. The tendency will be to proceed in a lin-

ear step-by-step fashion, handling one issue at a time. A manager using intuitive thinking will be more spontaneous and open in problem solving. He or she may jump from one stage in the process to the other and deal with many different things at once.

25. This is what I would say: Continuing developments in information technology are changing the work setting for most employees. An important development for the traditional "white collar" worker falls in the area of office automation—the use of computers and related technologies to facilitate everyday office work. In the "electronic office" of today and tomorrow, you should be prepared to work with and take full advantage of the following: "Smart workstations" supported by desktop computers; "voice messaging" systems whereby computers take dictation, answer the telephone, and relay messages; "database" and "word-processing" software systems that allow storage, access, and manipulation of data as well as the preparation of reports; "electronic mail" systems that send mail and data computer to computer; "electronic bulletin boards" for posting messages; "computer conferencing" and "video conferencing" that allow people to work with one another every day over great distances. These are among the capabilities of the new workplace. To function effectively, you must be prepared not only to use these systems to full advantage but also to stay abreast of new developments as they become available.

Chapter 4

1. d
2. b
3. b
4. a
5. c
6. a
7. a
8. b
9. c
10. c
11. F
12. T
13. F
14. T

15. F
16. T
17. T
18. F
19. T
20. T
21. Theory Y assumes that people are capable of taking responsibility and exercising self-direction and control in their work. Under these assumptions they should positively respond to opportunities for greater participation and involvement.
22. According to the deficit principle, a satisfied need is not a motivator of behavior. The social need will only motivate if it is deprived or in deficit. According to the progression principle, people move step by step up Maslow's hierarchy as they strive to satisfy needs. For example, once the social need is satisfied the esteem need will be activated.
23. Contingency thinking takes an "if—then" approach to situations. It seeks to modify or adapt management approaches to fit the needs of each situation. An example would be to give more customer contact responsibility to workers who want to satisfy social needs at work, while giving more supervisory responsibilities to those who want to satisfy their esteem or ego needs.
24. The external environment is the source of the resources an organization needs to operate. In order to continue to obtain these resources the organization must be successful in selling its goods and services to customers. If customer feedback is negative, the organization must make adjustments or risk losing the support needed to obtain important resources.
25. A bureaucracy operates with a strict hierarchy of authority, promotion based on competency and performance, formal rules and procedures, and written documentation. Enrique can do all of these things in his store. However, he must be careful to meet the needs of the workers and not to make the mistake identified by Argyris of failing to treat them as mature adults. While remaining well organized, there is room for the store manager to help workers meet higher order esteem and self-fulfillment needs, as well as to exercise autonomy under Theory Y assumptions.

Chapter 5

1. d
2. b
3. b
4. c
5. b
6. a
7. a
8. c
9. a
10. c
11. F
12. T
13. F
14. F
15. T
16. F
17. F
18. T
19. T
20. T
21. The North American Free Trade Agreement, NAFTA, provides the framework for Mexico, the United States, and Canada, to free the flows of investments, products, and workers across their borders. This agreement creates a large consumer market and is an opportunity for businesses in all countries to take full advantage of all of North America as a resource and customer base.
22. MNC/host country relationships should be mutually beneficial. Sometimes host countries believe MNCs take unfair advantage of them. The complaints against MNCs include taking excessive profits, hiring the best local labor, not respecting local laws and customs, and dominating the local economy.
23. The power-distance dimension of national culture reflects the degree to which members of a society accept status and authority inequalities. Since management involves positions of superior and subordinate status, the nature of the relationship may vary from one culture to the next.
24. For each region of the world you should identify a major economic theme or issue or element. For example: Europe—the European Union should be discussed for its economic significance to member countries and to outsiders; Americas—NAFTA should be discussed for its current implications as well as potential significance once Chile and other nations join; Asia—the Asia-Pacific Economic Forum should be identified as a platform for growing regional economic cooperation among a very economically powerful group of countries, Africa—the new nonracial democracy in South Africa should be cited as a stimulus to broader outside investor interest in Africa.
25. Kim must recognize that the cultural differences between the United States and Japan may affect the success of quality circles and work teams. The United States was the most individualistic culture in Hofstede's study of national cultures; Japan is much more collectivist. Group practices such as the quality circle and teams are more consistent with the Japanese culture. When introduced into a more individualistic culture, these same practices may encounter difficulties. At the very least, Kim should proceed with caution, discuss the ideas with the workers before making any changes, and then monitor the changes closely so that adjustments can be made as the workers gain familiarity with them. The goal should be to improve operations with practices appropriate to the workers and culture.

Chapter 6

1. a
2. a
3. d
4. d
5. a
6. d
7. a
8. d
9. c
10. c
11. F
12. T
13. T
14. F
15. T
16. T
17. F
18. T
19. F
20. T
21. The individualism view is that ethical behavior is that which best serves long-term interests. The justice view is that ethical behavior is fair and

equitable in its treatment of people.

22. The rationalizations are believing that the behavior is not really illegal, the behavior is really in everyone's best interests, no one will find out, and the organization will protect you.

23. The socioeconomic view of corporate social responsibility argues that socially responsible behavior is in a firm's long-run best interests. It should be good for profits, it creates a positive public image, it helps avoid government regulation, it meets public expectations, and it is an ethical obligation.

24. Government agencies implement and enforce laws that are passed to regulate business activities. They act in the public's behalf to ensure compliance with laws on such matters as occupational safety and health, consumer protection, and environmental protection.

25. The manager could make a decision based on any one of the strategies. As an obstructionist, she may assume that Bangladesh needs the business and it is a local matter as to who will be employed to make the gloves. As a defensive strategy, the manager may decide to require the supplier to meet the minimum employment requirements under Bangladesh law. As an accommodation strategy, the manager may require that the supplier go beyond local laws and meet standards set by equivalent laws in the United States. A proaction strategy would involve the manager in trying to set an example by operating in Bangladesh only with suppliers who not only meet local standards, but who actively support the education of children in the communities in which they operate.

Chapter 7

1. d
2. d
3. d
4. d
5. b
6. b
7. a
8. d
9. b
10. c
11. T
12. T

13. F
14. F
15. F
16. T
17. F
18. T
19. F
20. F
21. (1) Define your objectives, (2) determine where you stand relative to objectives, (3) develop premises about future conditions, (4) identify and choose among action alternatives to accomplish objectives, (5) implement action plans and evaluate results.
22. A strategic plan sets long-term enterprise direction. For example, a strategic plan for a local bank might be to expand regionally to become the dominant bank in rural communities of fewer than 5000 population. An operational plan helps to implement a strategic plans. An operational plan for the bank may be to acquire three banks per year that serve communities of the target size and location.
23. Benchmarking is the use of external standards to help evaluate one's own situation and develop ideas and directions for improvement. The bookstore owner/manager might visit other bookstores in other towns which are known for their success. By observing and studying the operations of those stores and then comparing her store to them, the owner/manager can develop plans for future action.
24. Zero-based budgeting begins each new budget cycle from a "zero" base. This means the budget must be totally justified based on future needs. For example, a 6-month advertising budget for the sports department in a discount retailer would be negotiated based on projected campaigns and sales. It would not be done as a percentage increase or decrease to the budget that had been given in the prior 6 months.
25. I would begin the speech by describing MBO as an integrated planning and control approach. I would also clarify that the key elements in MBO are objectives and participation. Any objectives should be clear, measureable, and time defined. In addition, these objectives should be set with the full involvement and participation of the employees; they

should *not* be set by the manager and then told to the employees. Given this, I would describe how each business manager should jointly set objectives with each of his or her employees and jointly review progress toward their accomplishment. I would suggest that the employees should work on the required activities while staying in communication with their managers. The managers, in turn, should provide any needed support or assistance to their employees. This whole process could be formally recycled at least twice per year.

Chapter 8

1. a
2. b
3. c
4. c
5. d
6. b
7. c
8. a
9. b
10. c
11. T
12. F
13. T
14. F
15. F
16. T
17. T
18. F
19. F
20. F
21. A corporate strategy sets long-term direction for an enterprise as a whole. Functional strategies set directions so that business functions such as marketing and manufacturing support the overall corporate strategy.
22. A SWOT analysis is useful during strategic planning. It involves the analysis of organizational strengths and weaknesses, and of environmental opportunities and threats.
23. Entrepreneurship is individual risk taking to establish a new business venture. It is typically associated with smaller businesses and new business startups. Intrapreneurship is entrepreneurial behavior within a larger corporation. It may be accomplished by individuals or groups.
24. Strategic management is the process of leading the strategic planning

effort in a specific area of work responsibility. This leadership includes making sure that strategies are both well formulated and well implemented.

25. Porter's competitive strategy model involves the possible use of three alternative strategies: differentiation, cost leadership, and focus. In this situation, the larger department store seems better positioned to follow the cost leadership strategy. This means that Kim may want to consider the other two alternatives. A differentiation strategy would involve trying to distinguish Kim's products from those of the larger store. This might involve a "made in America" theme or an emphasis on leather or canvas or some other type of clothing material. A focus strategy might specifically target college students and try to respond to their tastes and needs rather than the larger community population. This might involve special orders and other types of individualized service for the college student market.

Chapter 9

1. a
2. b
3. d
4. b
5. c
6. c
7. d
8. c
9. b
10. c
11. T
12. F
13. F
14. T
15. T
16. T
17. T
18. F
19. T
20. T
21. Feedforward controls are done before the work begins and respond to the question. "What needs to be done before we begin?" They make sure that proper directions are set to guide work activities and that the right resources are available to accomplish them. By contrast, feedback controls take place after work is completed. They focus on end re-

sults and ask the question: "Now that we are finished, how well did we do?" Feedback controls provide information that can be used to better plan future activities.

22. McGregor's Theory Y views workers as responsible individuals who are willing both to work and to exercise self-control in their work activities. This perspective recognizes the potential for internal control to operate in the workplace. Such control must be based on a trusting relationship between the supervisor and subordinate, and it also depends on the presence of work objectives, ideally set by participation, that the worker understands and is committed to accomplishing.

23. A progressive discipline system clearly ties the severity of a reprimand to the frequency and significance of the violation committed by a worker. The goal is to achieve compliance with organizational expectations through the *least* extreme reprimand possible. This means that someone is punished more harshly for repeated inappropriate acts, such as a pattern of being late for work. It also means that someone is punished more harshly for acts that are more significantly negative. This means, for example, that being late for work would be treated less harshly than would employee theft or the use of alcohol during work hours.

24. Statistical quality control, an essential ingredient of any quality improvement program, is the process of statistically checking products or services to ensure that they meet predetermined quality standards. One example involves the use of control charts, which graphically plot the results of statistical samples against upper and lower control limits. Any points falling outside the limits represent quality problems.

25. Simply put, "just-in-time scheduling," or JIT, means arranging orders so that materials are available in the production process only as they are needed. The use of JIT attempts to reduce costs and improve workflows by scheduling materials to arrive at a work station or facility "just in time" to be used. This helps control and reduce inventory costs by minimizing carrying costs and maintaining almost no on-hand inventories. Ma-

terials are ordered and goods are produced only as needed or upon demand. This is an important concept since it helps to improve operating efficiencies in organizations. It avoids having resources tied up in nonproductive inventories and it also helps everyone involved to operate with maximum attention to inventory cost considerations.

Chapter 10

1. a
2. c
3. d
4. a
5. b
6. c
7. b
8. b
9. b
10. a
11. F
12. F
13. T
14. F
15. T
16. F
17. F
18. F
19. T
20. T
21. The product structure organizes work around a product, and the division or unit would be headed by a product manager or executive. The geographical structure organizes work by area or location. Different geographical regions would be headed by regional managers or executives.

22. The functional structure is prone to problems of internal coordination. One symptom may be that the different functional areas, such as marketing and manufacturing, are not working well together. This structure is also slow in responding to changing environmental trends and challenges. If the firm finds that its competitors are getting to market faster with new and better products, this is another potential indicator that the functional structure is not supporting operations properly.

23. A network structure often involves one organization "contracting out" aspects of its operations to other organizations who specialize in them. The example used in the text was of a company that contracted out its mail-

room services. Through the formation of networks of contracts, the organization is reduced to a core of essential employees whose expertise is concentrated in the primary business areas. The contracts are monitored and maintained in the network to allow the overall operations of the organization to continue even though they are not directly accomplished by full-time employees.

24. By reducing levels of management, the organization may benefit from lower overhead costs. It can also benefit as lower levels find they are in closer and more frequent contact with higher levels, and vice versa. Communication should flow more readily and quickly up and down the chain of command, as there are fewer levels to pass through. This should also mean that decisions are made more quickly.

25. Faisal must first have confidence in the two engineers—he must trust them and respect their capabilities. Second, he must have confidence in himself—trusting his own judgement to give up some work and allow these others to do it. Third, he should follow the rules of effective delegation. These include being very clear on what must be accomplished by each engineer. Their responsibilities should be clearly understood. He must also give them the authority to act in order to fulfill their responsibility, especially in relationship to the other engineers. And, he must not forget his own final accountability for the results. He should remain in control and, through communication, make sure that work proceeds as planned.

Chapter 11

1. b
2. d
3. b
4. a
5. c
6. b
7. d
8. b
9. c
10. a
11. T
12. F
13. T
14. F

15. T
16. F
17. F
18. T
19. T
20. F
21. The term contingency is used in management to indicate that management strategies and practices should be tailored to fit the unique needs of individual situations. There is no universal solution that fits all problems and circumstances. Thus, in organizational design, contingency thinking must be used to identify and implement organizational particular points in time. What works well at one point in time may not work well in another as the environment and other conditions change.

22. The environment is an important influence on organizational design. The more complex, variable, and uncertain are the elements in the general and specific environments, the more difficult it is for the organization to operate. In general, stable and more certain environments allow for mechanistic designs since operations can be more routine and predictable. This calls for more organic designs.

23. Differentiation and integration are somewhat conflicting in organizational design. As differentiation increases, that is as more differences are present in the complexity of the organization, the more integration is needed to ensure that everything functions together to the betterment of the whole organization. However, the greater the differentiation the harder it is to achieve integration. Thus, when differentiation is high organization design tends to shift toward the use of more complex horizontal approaches to integration and away from the vertical ones such as formal authority and rules or policies. In horizontal integration the focus is on such things cross functional teams and matrix structures.

24. The focus of process reengineering is on reducing costs and streamlining operations efficiency while improving customer service. This is accomplished by closely examining core business processes through the following sequence of activities: (1) identify the core processes,

(2) map them in a workflows diagram, (3) evaluate all tasks involved, (4) seek ways to eliminate unnecessary tasks, (5) seek ways to eliminate delays, errors, and misunderstandings in the workflows, and (6) seek efficiencies in how work is shared and transferred among people and departments.

25. This situation involves the basic contingency notion of organizational design. There is no one best way to design an organization and different designs serve organizations well under different circumstances. The first person is most likely working for an organization facing rather routine and known environmental demands. This allows for the organizational design to become more vertical and mechanistic, focusing as it does on predictable problems and outcomes. The individuals who remain in such a design are probably compatible with the internal climate of such an organization and thus find it a good "fit" resulting in reasonable levels of job satisfaction. By contrast the second person probably works for an organization facing uncertain challenges in a dynamic environment, with the result that it is by design a more adaptive or flexible structure emphasizing horizontal rather than vertical operations. In this case the design fits the demands of the environment and it is also most likely to satisfy those individuals who remain with it over time. Thus we have a good demonstration of two aspects of contingency factors in organizational design: the environment-structure-performance fit and the structure-individual fit.

Chapter 12

1. a
2. b
3. c
4. d
5. b
6. c
7. d
8. b
9. b
10. c
11. F
12. T
13. T
14. F
15. T

16. T
17. F
18. F
19. F
20. T

21. Internal recruitment deals with job candidates who already know the organization well. It is also a strong motivator because it communicates to everyone the opportunity to advance in the organization through hard work. External recruitment may allow the organization to obtain expertise not otherwise available internally. It also brings in employees with new and fresh viewpoints who are not biased by previous experience in the organization.

22. Orientation activities introduce a new employee to the organization and her or his work environment. This is a time when key attitudes may be set for the individual and during which performance expectations will also be established. Good orientation communicates positive attitudes and expectations and reinforces the desired organizational culture. It formally introduces the individual to important policies and procedures that everyone is expected to follow.

23. The graphic rating scale simply asks a supervisor to rate an employee on an established set of criteria, such as quantity of work or attitude toward work. This leaves a lot of room for subjectivity and debate. The behaviorally anchored rating scale asks the supervisor to rate the employee on specific job behaviors that have been identified as positively or negatively affecting performance in a given job. This is a more specific appraisal approach and leaves less room for debate and disagreement.

24. Mentoring is when a senior and experienced individual adopts a newcomer or more junior person with the goal of helping them develop into a successful worker. The mentor may or may not be the individual's immediate supervisor. The mentor meets with the individual and discusses problems, shares advice, and generally supports their attempts to grow and perform. Mentors are considered very useful for persons newly appointed to management positions.

25. As Sy's supervisor, you face a difficult but perhaps expected human resource management problem. Not only is Sy influential as an informal leader, he also has considerable experience on the job and in the company. Even though he is experiencing performance problems using the new computer system, there is no indication that he doesn't want to work hard and continue to perform for the company. Although retirement is an option, Sy may also be transferred, promoted, or simply fired. The latter response seems unjustified and may cause legal problems. Transferring Sy, with his agreement, to another position could be a positive move: promoting Sy to a supervisory position where his experience and networks would be useful is another possibility. The keys in this situation seem to be moving Sy out so that a computer-literate person can take over the job, while continuing to utilize Sy in a job that better fits his talents. Transfer and/or promotion should be actively considered both in his interests and in the company's.

Chapter 13

1. d
2. d
3. b
4. a
5. c
6. a
7. b
8. c
9. b
10. a
11. F
12. F
13. T
14. T
15. F
16. T
17. F
18. F
19. F
20. F

21. Position power is based on reward, coercion or punishment, and legitimacy or formal authority. Managers, however, need to have more power than that made available to them by the position alone. Thus, they have to develop personal power through expertise and reference. This personal power is essential in helping managers to get things done beyond the scope of their position power alone.

22. Leader-participation theory suggests that leadership effectiveness is determined in part by how well managers or leaders handle the many different problem or decision situations that they face every day. Decisions can be made through individual or authority, consultative, or group-consensus approaches. No one of these decision methods is always the best; each is a good fit for certain types of situations. A good manager or leader is able to use each of these approaches *and* knows when each is the best approach to use in various situations.

23. Position power—how much power the leader has in terms of rewards, punishments, and legitimacy. Leader-member relations—the quality of relationships between the leader and followers. Task structure—the degree to which the task is clear and well defined, or open ended and more ambiguous.

24. Drucker says that good leaders have more than the "charisma" or "personality" being popularized in the concept of transformational leadership. He reminds us that good leaders work hard to accomplish some basic things in their everyday activities. These include: (1) establishing a clear sense of mission, (2) accepting leadership as a responsibility and not a rank, and (3) earning and keeping the respect of others.

25. In his new position, Rod must understand that the transactional aspects of leadership are not sufficient to guarantee him long-term leadership effectiveness. He must move beyond the effective use of task-oriented and people-oriented behaviors and demonstrate through his personal qualities the capacity to inspire others. A charismatic leader develops a unique relationship with followers in which they become enthusiastic, highly loyal, and high achievers. Rod needs to work very hard to develop positive relationships with the team members and to emphasize in those relationships high aspirations for performance accomplishments, enthusiasm for the work and for one another, integrity and honesty in all dealings, and a clear vision of the future. By work-

ing hard with this agenda and by allowing his personality to positively express itself in the team setting. Rod should make continuous progress as an effective leader.

Chapter 14

1. c
2. d
3. d
4. b
5. b
6. d
7. c
8. b
9. d
10. a
11. F
12. F
13. T
14. F
15. F
16. F
17. T
18. F
19. F
20. F
21. People high in need for achievement will prefer work settings and jobs in which they have (1) challenging but achievable goals, (2) individual responsibility, and (3) performance feedback.
22. Participation is important to goal-setting theory because, in general, people tend to be more committed to the accomplishment of goals they have helped to set. When people participate in the setting of goals, they also understand them better. Participation in goal-setting improves goal acceptance and understanding.
23. Motivation is formally defined as the forces within an individual that account for the level, direction, and persistence of effort expended at work.
24. Herzberg suggests that job content factors are the satisfiers or motivators. Based in the job itself, they represent such things as responsibility, sense of achievement, and feelings of growth. Job context factors are considered sources of dissatisfaction. They are found in the job environment and include such things as base pay, technical quality of supervision, and working conditions. Whereas improvements in job con-

text make people less dissatisfied, improvements in job content are considered necessary to motivate them to high performance levels.

25. In answering question 21, it has already been pointed out that a high need achiever likes moderately challenging goals and performance feedback. Goal-setting with the participation of both manager and subordinate offers an opportunity to choose goals to which the need achievers will individually respond and which also serve the organization. Through goal-setting, furthermore, the manager and individual subordinates can identify performance standards or targets. Progress toward these targets can be positively reinforced by the manager. Such reinforcements can serve as indicators of progress to the high need achievers, thus responding to their desires for performance feedback. All in all, the existence of good goals gives the need achiever something to work toward; it gives the manager something against which to offer reinforcements in a positive manner.

Chapter 15

1. d
2. c
3. c
4. c
5. a
6. b
7. b
8. a
9. b
10. b
11. F
12. T
13. F
14. F
15. F
16. F
17. T
18. T
19. T
20. T
21. A psychological contract is the individual's view of the inducements he or she expects to receive from the organization in return for his or her work contributions. The contract is healthy when the individual perceives that the inducements and contributions are fair and in a state of balance.

22. Growth-need strength helps determine which individuals are good candidates for job enrichment. A person high in growth-need strength seeks higher order satisfaction of ego and self-fulfillment needs at work. These are needs to which job enrichment can positively respond. A person low in growth-need strength may not respond well to the demands and responsibilities of an enriched job.

23. The type A personality is characteristic of people who bring stress on themselves by virtue of personal characteristics. These tend to be compulsive individuals who are uncomfortable waiting for things to happen, who try to do many things at once, and who generally move fast and have difficulty slowing down. Type A personalities can be stressful for both the individuals and the people around them. Managers must be aware of type A personality tendencies in their own behavior and among others with whom they work. Ideally, this awareness will help the manager take precautionary steps to best manage the stress caused by this personality type.

24. The compressed workweek, or 4–40 schedule, offers employees the advantage of a 3-day weekend. However, it can cause problems for the employer in terms of ensuring that operations are covered adequately during the normal 5 work days of the week. Labor unions may resist, and the compressed workweek will entail more complicated work scheduling. In addition, some employees find that the schedule is tiring and can cause family adjustment problems.

25. The high performance equation states that: Performance = Ability × Support × Effort. The multiplication signs are important. They indicate that each of the performance factors must be high and positive in order for high performance to occur. That is, neither ability nor support nor effort can be neglected by Kurt or any of the managers/team leaders in his plant. Furthermore, the factors are straightforward in their managerial implications. Ability is an issue of proper selection, training and development of all employees. Support involves providing capable employees with such things as clear goals, appropriate technol-

ogy, helpful structures, and an absence of performance obstacles such as poor rules and procedures. Effort involves making sure that the environment is motivation and offers varied intrinsic as well as extrinsic rewards. Only by giving direct and serious attention to each of these factors can Kurt and his management team take full advantage of the insights of the high performance equation.

Chapter 16

1. b
2. a
3. c
4. b
5. c
6. b
7. b
8. d
9. c
10. a
11. F
12. T
13. T
14. F
15. T
16. T
17. F
18. F
19. T
20. T
21. The manager's goal in active listening is to help the subordinate say what she or he really means. To do this, the manager should carefully listen for the content of what someone is saying, paraphrase or reflect back what she or he appears to be saying, remain sensitive to nonverbal cues and feelings, and not be evaluative.
22. The halo effect occurs when a single attribute of a person, such as the way she or he dresses, is used to evaluate or form an overall impression of the person. Selective perception occurs when someone focuses in a situation on those aspects that reinforce or are most consistent with his or her existing values, beliefs, or experiences.
23. Win-lose outcomes are likely when conflict is managed through high assertiveness and low cooperativeness styles. In this situation of competition, the conflict is resolved by one person or group dominating an-

other. Lose-lose outcomes occur when conflict is managed through avoidance, where nothing is resolved, and possibly when it is managed through compromise, where each party gives up something to the other. Win-win outcomes are associated mainly with problem-solving and collaboration in conflict management, which is a result of high assertiveness and high cooperativeness.
24. In a negotiation, both substance and relationship goals are important. Substance goals relate to the content of the negotiation. A substance goal for example may relate to the final salary agreement between a job candidate and a prospective employer. Relationship goals relate to the quality of the interpersonal relationships among the negotiating parties. Relationship goals are important because the negotiating parties most likely have to work together in the future. For example, if relationships are poor after a labor—management negotiation, the likelihood is that future problems will occur.
25. Harold can do a number of things to establish and maintain a system of upward communication for his department store branch. To begin, he might set the tone for the department managers by using MBWA—"managing by wandering around." Once this pattern is established, trust will build between him and other store employees, and he should find that he learns a lot from interacting directly with them. Harold should also set up a formal communication structure, such as bimonthly store meetings, where he communicates store goals, results, and other issues to the staff, and in which he listens to them in return. An E-mail system whereby Harold and his staff could send messages to one another from their workstation computers would also be beneficial.

Chapter 17

1. d
2. b
3. c
4. d
5. b
6. d
7. b
8. c
9. a
10. b
11. F
12. T
13. T
14. F
15. F
16. F
17. F
18. T
19. T
20. T
21. Input factors can have a major impact on group effectiveness. In order to best prepare a group to perform effectively a manager should make sure that the right people are put on the group (maximize available talents and abilities), that these people are capable of working well together (membership characteristics should promote good relationships), that the tasks are clear, and that the group has the resources and environment needed to perform up to expectations.
22. A group's performance can be analyzed according to the interaction between cohesiveness and performance norms. In a highly cohesive group members tend to conform to group norms. Thus, when the performance norm is positive and cohesion is high, we can expect everyone to work hard to support the norm—high performance is likely. By the same token, high cohesion and a low performance norm will act the same—low performance is likely. With other combinations of norms and cohesion the performance results will be more mixed.
23. The textbook lists several symptoms of groupthink along with various strategies for avoiding groupthink (see notepad 17.2). For example, a group whose members censure themselves from contributing "contrary" or "different" opinions and/or whose members keep talking about outsiders as "weak" or the "enemy" may be suffering groupthink. This may be avoided or corrected, for example, by asking someone to be the "devil's advocate" for a meeting and by inviting in an outside observer to help gather different viewpoints.
24. In a traditional work group, the manager or supervisor directs the group. In a self-managing team, the members of the team provide for

self-direction. They plan, organize, and evaluate their work, share tasks, and help one another develop skills; they may even make hiring decisions. A true self-managing team does not need the traditional "boss" or supervisor since the team as a whole takes on the supervisory responsibilities.

25. Marcos is faced with a highly cohesive group whose members conform to a negative or low-performance norm. This is a difficult situation that is ideally resolved by changing the performance norm. In order to gain the group's commitment to a high-performance norm, Marcos should act as a positive role model for the norm. He must communicate the norm clearly and positively to the group. He should not assume that everyone knows what he expects of them. He may also talk to the informal leader and gain her or his commitment to the norm. He might carefully reward high performance behaviors within the group. He may introduce new members with high-performance records and commitments. And, he might hold group meetings in which performance standards and expectations were discussed with an emphasis on committing to new high-performance directions. If his attempts to introduce a high-performance norm fail, Marcos may have to take steps to reduce group cohesiveness so that individual members can pursue higher performance results without feeling bound by group pressures to restrict their performance.

Chapter 18

1. b
2. a
3. d
4. c
5. c
6. b
7. c
8. a
9. d
10. a
11. T
12. T
13. F
14. F
15. T
16. T
17. F
18. F
19. T
20. F

21. The possible internal targets for change include the following. The *tasks* being worked on including organizational mission, objectives, and strategy. The *people* doing the work, including their attitudes and skills. The *culture* or predominant value system of the organization. The *technology* being used and the integration of technology and people. The *structure* of the organization.

22. Lewin's three phases of planned change are: *Unfreezing*—preparing a system for change; *changing*—moving or creating change in a system; and *refreezing*—stabilizing and reinforcing change once it has occurred.

23. In general managers can expect that others will be more committed and loyal to changes that are brought about through shared power strate-

gies. Rational persuasion strategies can also create enduring effects if they are accepted. Force-coercion strategies tend to have temporary effects only.

24. The statement that "OD equals planned change *plus*" basically refers to the fact that OD tries *both* to create change in an organization *and* to make the organization members capable of creating such change for themselves in the future.

25. In any change situation, it is important to remember that successful planned change only occurs when all three phases of change—unfreezing, changing, and refreezing—have been taken care of. Thus, I would not rush into the changing phase. Rather, I would work with the people involved to develop a felt need for change based on their ideas and inputs as well as mine. Then I would proceed by supporting the changes and helping to stabilize them into everyday routines. I would also be sensitive to any resistance and respect that resistance as a signal that something important is being threatened. By listening to resistance I would be in a position to better modify the change to achieve a better fit with the people and the situation. Finally, I would want to take maximum advantage of the shared power strategy, supported by rational persuasion, and with limited use of force-coercion (if it is used at all). By doing all of this, I would like my staff to feel empowered and committed to constructive improvement through planned change.

Glossary

A

Accommodation or **smoothing** plays down differences and highlights similarities to reduce conflict.

An **accommodative strategy** accepts social responsibilities and tries to satisfy prevailing economic, legal, and ethical performance criteria.

Accountability is the requirement to show performance results to a supervisor.

Action research is a collaborative process of collecting data, using it for action planning, and evaluating the results.

Active listening involves taking action to help the source of a message say what he or she really means.

An **adaptive organization** operates with a minimum of bureaucratic features and encourages worker empowerment and teamwork.

The **administrative decision model** describes how managers act in situations of limited information and bounded rationality.

An **administrator** is a manager who works in a public or nonprofit organization.

An **affirmative action program** tries to increase employment opportunities for women and minorities.

An **analyzer strategy** seeks the stability of a core business while selectively responding to opportunities for innovation and change.

APEC, Asia-Pacific Economic Cooperation is a platform for regional economic alliances among Asian and Pacific Rim countries.

Applications software allows the user to perform a variety of information-based tasks without writing unique computer programs.

An **apprenticeship** is a special form of training that involves a formal assignment to serve as understudy or assistant to a person who already has the desired job skills.

Arbitration is the process by which parties to a dispute agree to abide by the decision of a neutral and independent third party, called an arbitrator.

In **arbitration** a neutral third party issues a binding decision to resolve a dispute.

The **Asian-Pacific Economic Forum (APEC)** is a platform for regional economic alliance among Asian and Pacific Rim countries.

An **assessment center** is a selection technique that engages job candidates in a series of experimental activities over a 1- or 2-day period.

Attribution error overestimates internal factors and underestimates external factors as influences on someone's behavior.

Authority is the right to assign tasks and direct the activities of subordinates in ways that support accomplishment of the organization's purpose.

An **authority decision** is a decision made by the leader and then communicated to the group.

Automation is the total mechanization of a job.

Avoidance involves pretending that a conflict doesn't really exists or hoping that a conflict will simply go away.

B

A **bargaining zone** is the area between one party's minimum reservation point and the other party's maximum reservation point.

Base compensation is a salary or hourly wage paid to an individual.

BATNA is the "best alternative to a negotiated agreement," or what can be done if an agreement cannot be reached.

The **BCG matrix** ties strategy formulation to an analysis of business opportunities according to market growth rate and market share.

A **behaviorally anchored rating scale (BARS)** is a performance appraisal method that uses specific descriptions of actual behaviors to rate various levels of performance.

Benchmarking is a process of comparing operations and performance with other organizations known for excellence.

A **bonus pay plan** provides cash bonuses to employees based on the achievement of specific performance targets.

Bottom-up planning begins with ideas developed at lower management levels, which are modified as they are passed up the hierarchy to top management.

Brainstorming is a group technique for generating a large quantity of ideas by free-wheeling contributions made without criticism.

A **budget** is a plan that commits resources to projects or programs; a formalized way of allocating resources to specific activities.

Bureaucracy is a rational and efficient form of organization founded on logic, order, and legitimate authority.

A **business plan** describes the direction for a new business and the financing needed to operate it.

A **business strategy** identifies the intentions of a division or strategic business unit to compete in its special product and/or service domain.

C

Career planning is the process of systematically matching career goals and individual capabilities with opportunities for their fulfillment.

A **career plateau** is a position from which someone is unlikely to move to a higher level of work responsibility.

A **career portfolio** documents academic and personal accomplishments for external review.

Centralization is the concentration of authority for most decisions at the top level of an organization.

In a **centralized communication network** communication flows only between individual members and a hub or center point.

A **certain environment** offers complete information on possible action alternatives and their consequences.

The **chain of command** links all persons with successively higher levels of authority.

A **change agent** is a person or group that takes leadership responsibility for changing the existing pattern of behavior of another person or social system.

Changing is the central phase in the planned-change process in which a planned change actually takes place.

A **charismatic leader** is a leader who develops special leader-follower relationships and inspires followers in extraordinary ways.

A **CIO** is a senior executive responsible for IT and its utilization throughout an organization.

The **classical decision model** describes how managers ideally make decisions using complete information.

Coaching is the communication of specific technical advice to an individual.

A **code of ethics** is a written document that states values and ethical standards intended to guide the behavior of employees.

Coercive power is the capacity to punish or withhold positive outcomes as a means of influencing other people.

Cohesiveness is the degree to which members are attracted to and motivated to remain part of a team.

Collaboration or **problem solving** involves working through conflict differences and solving problems so everyone wins.

Collective bargaining is the process of negotiating, administering, and interpreting a labor contract.

A **combination strategy** involves stability, growth, and retrenchment in one or more combinations.

A **committee** is a formal team designated to work on a special task on a continuing basis.

Communication is the process of sending and receiving symbols with meanings attached.

A **communication channel** is the medium through which a message is sent.

Comparative management is the study of how management practices differ systematically from one country and/or culture to the next.

Competition or **authoritative command** uses force, superior skill, or domination to "win" a conflict.

A **competitive advantage** is a special edge that allows an organization to deal with market and environmental forces better than its competitors.

A **compressed workweek** is any work schedule that allows a full-time job to be completed in less than the standard 5 days of 8-hour shifts.

Compromise occurs when each party to the conflict gives up something of value to the other.

A **conceptual skill** is the ability to think analytically and solve complex problems to the benefit of everyone involved.

A **concurrent control** or **steering control** is a control that acts in anticipation of problems and focuses primarily on what happens during the work process.

Conflict is a disagreement over issues of substance and/or an emotional antagonism.

Conflict resolution is the removal of the reasons—substantial and/or emtional—for a conflict.

Constructive stress acts in a positive way to increase effort, stimulate creativity, and encourage diligence in one's work.

A **consultative decision** is a decision made by a leader after receiving information, advice, or opinions from group members.

Contingency planning identifies alternative courses of action that can be taken if and when circumstances change with time.

Contingency thinking maintains that there is no one best way to manage; what is best depends on the situation.

Contingency workers are employed on a part-time and temporary basis to supplement a permanent workforce.

Continuous improvement involves always searching for new ways to improve operations quality and performance.

In **continuous-process production** raw production materials continuously move through an automated system.

A **control chart** is a method for quality control in which work results are displayed on a graph that clearly delineates upper control limits and lower control limits.

Controlling is the process of measuring performance and taking action to ensure desired results.

A **control process** is the process of establishing performance objectives and standards, measuring actual performance, comparing actual performance with objectives and standards, and taking necessary action.

A **core competency** is a special strength that gives an organization a competitive advantage.

Core values are underlying beliefs shared by members of the organization and that influence their behavior.

Corporate culture is the predominant value system for the organization as a whole.

Corporate governance is the system of control and performance monitoring of top management.

Corporate social responsibility is an obligation of an organization to act in ways that serve both its own interests and the interests of its many external publics.

A **corporate strategy** sets long-term direction for the total enterprise.

A **cost leadership strategy** is a corporate competitive strategy that seeks to achieve lower costs than competitors by improving efficiency of production, distribution, and other organizational systems.

Cost-benefit analysis involves comparing the costs and benefits of each potential course of action.

Creativity is ingenuity and imagination that results in a novel solution to a problem.

A **crisis problem** is an unexpected problem that can lead to disaster if not resolved quickly and appropriately.

A **critical incident technique** is a performance appraisal method that involves a running log of effective and ineffective job behaviors.

A **cross-functional team** is a team structure in which members from different functional departments work together as needed to solve problems and explore opportunities.

Cultural relativism suggests there is no one right way to behave; ethical behavior is determined by its cultural context.

Culture is a shared set of beliefs, values, and patterns of behavior common to a group of people.

Culture shock is the confusion and discomfort a person experiences when in an unfamiliar culture.

A **customer structure** is a divisional structure that groups together jobs and activities that serve the same customers or clients.

A **cybernetic control system** is a control system that is entirely self-contained in its performance monitoring and correction capabilities.

Cycle time is the elapsed time between the receipt of an order and the delivery of a finished good or service.

D

Decentralization is the dispersion of authority to make decisions throughout all levels of the organization.

A **decentralized communication network** allows all members to communicate directly with one another.

A **decision** is a choice among alternative courses of action for dealing with a "problem."

Decision making involves the identification of a problem and the choice of preferred problem-solving alternatives.

A **decision-support system** allows managers to interact with the computer to utilize information for solving structured and semistructured problems.

A **defender strategy** is a corporate competitive strategy that emphasizes existing products and current market share without seeking growth.

A **defensive strategy of social responsibility** seeks to protect the organization by doing the minimum legally required to satisfy social expectations.

Delegation is the process of distributing and entrusting work to other persons.

Departmentalization is the process of grouping together people and jobs under common supervisors to form various work units or departments.

Design for disassembly is the design of products with attention to how their component parts will be used when product life ends.

Design for manufacturing is creating a design that lowers production costs and improves quality in all stages of production.

Destructive stress impairs the performance of an individual.

Differentiation is the degree of differences that exists among people, departments, or other internal components of an organization.

A **differentiation strategy** is a corporate strategy that seeks competitive advantage through uniqueness, by developing goods and/or services that are clearly different from those offered by the competition.

Discipline is the act of influencing behavior through reprimand.

Discrimination is an active form of prejudice that disadvantages people by denying them full benefits of organizational membership.

A **distinctive competence** is a special strength that gives an organization a competitive advantage in its operating domain.

Distributive justice concerns the degree to which people are treated the same regardless of individual characteristics such as ethnicity, race, gender, or age.

Distributive negotiation focuses on "win-lose" claims made by each party for certain preferred outcomes.

A **divisional structure** groups together people who work on the same product, work with similar customers, or who work in the same area or processes.

A **dual-career couple** is one in which both adult partners are employed.

Dysfunctional conflict is destructive and hurts task performance.

E

The **economic order quantity (EOQ)** method orders a fixed number of items every time an inventory level falls to a predetermined point.

Effective communication occurs when the intended meaning of the source and the perceived meaning of the receiver are identical.

An **effective group** is a group that achieves and maintains high levels of both task performance and membership satisfaction over time.

Effective negotiation occurs when issues of substance and working relationships among the negotiating parties are maintained or even improved in the process.

An **effective team** achieves high levels of both task performance and membership satisfaction.

Efficient communication is communication that occurs at minimum cost in terms of resources expended.

Electronic commerce or *e-business* uses information technology to support online commercial transactions.

Emotional conflict results from feelings of anger, distrust, dislike, fear, and resentment as well as from personality clashes.

An **employee involvement team** meets on a regular basis to use its talents to help solve problems and achieve continuous improvement.

An **employee stock ownership plan** (ESOP) allows employees to share ownership of their employing organization through the purchase of stock.

Employment discrimination occurs when non-job relevant criteria are used for hiring and job placements.

An **enterprise-wide network** is a set of computer-communication links that connect a diverse set of activities throughout an organization.

An **entrepreneur** is willing to pursue opportunities in situations others view as problems or threats.

Entrepreneurial pay involves workers putting part of their compensation at risk in return for the right to pursue entrepreneurial ideas and share in any resulting profits.

Entrepreneurship is dynamic, risk taking, creative, and growth oriented behavior.

Environmentalism is the expression and demonstration of public concern for conditions of the natural or physical environment.

Equal employment opportunity (EEO) is the right to employment and advancement without regard to race, sex, religion, color, or national origin.

Escalating commitment is the tendency to continue to pursue a course of action, even though it is not working.

Ethical behavior is accepted as "right" or "good" in the context of a governing moral code.

An **ethical dilemma** is a situation with a potential course of action that, although offering potential benefit or gain, is also unethical.

The attempt to externally impose one's ethical standards on other cultures is criticized as a form of **ethical imperialism.**

Ethics form the code of morals that set standards as to what is good or bad, or right or wrong in one's conduct.

Ethics training seeks to help people better understand the ethical aspects of decision making and to incorporate high ethical standards into their daily behavior.

Ethnocentrism is the tendency to consider one's culture as superior to all others.

The **European Union (EU)** is a political and economic alliance of European countries that have agreed to support mutual economic growth and to lift barriers that previously limited cross-border trade and business development.

Eustress is stress that is constructive for an individual and helps her or him achieve a positive balance with the external environment.

An **executive information system** offers special support for top managers to access, process, and share information via computer to make a variety of operational and strategic decisions.

An **expatriate** lives and works in a foreign country.

Expectancy is a person's belief that working hard will result in high task performance.

Expert power is the capability to influence other people because of specialized knowledge.

An **expert system (EI)** is a computer program designed to analyze and solve problems at the level of the human expert.

Exporting is the process of producing products locally and selling them abroad in foreign markets.

External control is control that occurs through direct supervision or administrative systems, such as rules and procedures.

An **external customer** is the customer or client who buys or uses the organization's goods and/or services.

Extinction discourages a behavior by making the removal of a desirable consequence contingent on the occurrence of the behavior.

Extranets are computer networks that use the public Internet for communication between the organization and its environment.

An **extrinsic reward** is a reward given as a motivational stimulus to a person, usually by a superior.

F

Feedback is the process of telling someone else how you feel about something that person did or said or about the situation in general.

A **feedback control** or **postaction control** is a control that takes place after an action is completed.

A **feedforward control** or **preliminary control** ensures that proper directions are set and that the right resources are available to accomplish them before the work activity begins.

Filtering is the intentional distortion of information to make it appear most favorable to the recipient.

First-line managers oversee single units and pursue short-term performance objectives consistent with the plans of middle and top management levels.

A **flexible benefits program** allows employees to choose from a range of benefit options within certain dollar limits.

A **flexible budget** allows the allocation of resources to vary in proportion with various levels of activity.

Flexible manufacturing involves the ability to change manufacturing processes quickly and efficiently to produce different products or modifications of existing ones.

Flexible working hours are work schedules that give employees some choice in the pattern of daily work hours.

A **focus strategy** is a corporate competitive strategy that concentrates attention on a special market segment to serve its needs better than the competition.

A **force-coercion strategy** attempts to bring about change through formal authority and/or the use of rewards or punishments.

A **forecast** is an attempt to predict outcomes; it is a projection into the future based on historical data combined in some scientific manner.

A **formal group** is a group created by the formal authority within the organization.

Formal structure is the structure of the organization in its pure or ideal state.

A **formal team** is officially recognized and supported by the organization.

Franchising is a form of licensing in which the licensee buys the complete "package" of support needed to open a particular business.

Fringe benefits are additional nonmonetary forms of compensation (e.g., health plans, retirement plans) provided to an organization's workforce.

The **functional chimneys problem** is a lack of communication and coordination across functions.

Functional conflict is constructive and helps task performance.

A **functional group** is a formally designated work group consisting of a manager and subordinates.

Functional managers are responsible for one area of activity, such as finance, marketing, production, personnel, accounting, or sales.

A **functional strategy** guides activities within one specific area of operations.

A **functional structure** is an organizational structure that groups together people with similar skills who perform similar tasks.

A **functional team** is a formally designated work team with a manager or team leader.

G

A **gain-sharing plan** allows employees to share in any savings or "gains" realized through their efforts to reduce costs and increase productivity.

In the **General Agreement on Tariffs and Trade (GATT)** and **World Trade Organization (WTO)** member nations agree to ongoing negotiations and reducing tariffs and trade restrictions.

The **general environment** is comprised of the cultural, economic, legal–political, and educational conditions in the locality in which an organization operates.

General managers are responsible for complex organizational units that include many areas of functional activity.

A **geographical structure** is a divisional structure that groups together jobs and activities being performed in the same location or geographical region.

The **glass ceiling effect** is an invisible barrier that limits the advancement of women and minorities to higher level responsibilities in organizations.

The **global economy** is an economic perspective based on worldwide interdependence of resource supplies, product markets, and business competition.

A **global manager** works successfully across international boundaries.

Global sourcing is a process of purchasing materials or components in various parts of the world and then assembling them at home into a final product.

A **grapevine** is a common informal communication network.

A **graphic rating scale** is a performance appraisal method that uses a checklist of traits or characteristics thought to be related to high-performance outcomes in a given job.

A **group** is a collection of people who regularly interact with one another over time in respect to the pursuit of one or more common goals.

Group cohesiveness is the degree to which members are attracted to and motivated to remain part of a group.

A **group decision** is a decision made with the full participation of all group members.

A **group decision-support system** facilitates group efforts at solving complex problems while utilizing computerized information systems.

Group dynamics are forces operating in groups that affect task performance and membership satisfaction.

A **group norm** is a behavior, rule, or standard expected to be followed by group members.

Group process is the way team members work together to accomplish tasks.

Groupthink is a tendency for highly cohesive teams to lose their evaluative capabilities.

Groupware is a software system that allows people from different locations to work together in computer-mediated collaboration.

A **growth strategy** involves expansion of the organization's current operations.

Growth-need strength is an individual's desire to achieve a sense of psychological growth in her or his work.

H

A **halo effect** occurs when one attribute is used to develop an overall impression of a person or situation.

The **Hawthorne effect** is the tendency of persons singled out for special attention to perform as expected.

Heuristics are strategies for simplifying decision making.

Higher order needs, in Maslow's hierarchy, are esteem and self-actualization needs.

The **human relations movement** is based on the viewpoint that managers who use good human relations in the workplace will achieve productivity.

Human resource maintenance is a team's ability to maintain its social fabric so that members work well together.

Human resource management is the process of attracting, developing, and maintaining a talented and energetic workforce.

Human resource planning is the process of analyzing staffing needs and identifying actions to fill those needs over time.

Human resources are the people, individuals, and groups that help organizations produce goods or services.

A **human skill** is the ability to work well in cooperation with other people.

A **hygiene factor** is a factor in the work setting, such as working conditions, interpersonal relations, organizational policies, and administration, supervision, and salary.

I

Importing is the process of acquiring products abroad and selling them in domestic markets.

An **individual decision** is made when a manager chooses a preferred course of action without consulting others.

The **individualism view** is a view of ethical behavior based on the belief that one's primary commitment is to the advancement of long-term self-interests.

An **informal group** is not officially created and emerges based on relationships and shared interests among members.

Informal learning occurs as people interact informally throughout the work day.

Informal structure is the undocumented and officially unrecognized structure that coexists with the formal structure of an organization.

An **information system** collects, organizes, and distributes data regarding activities occurring inside and outside an organization.

Innovation is the process of taking a new idea and putting it into practice as part of the organization's normal operating routines.

An **input standard** is a standard that measures work efforts that go into a performance task.

Inside-out planning focuses planning on internal strengths and trying to do better than what one already does.

Instrumentality is a person's belief that various work-related outcomes will occur as a result of task performance.

Integration is the level of coordination achieved among subsystems in an organization.

Intellectual capital is the collective brainpower or shared knowledge of a workforce.

Intensive technology focuses the efforts and talents of many people with high interdependence to serve clients.

Internal control is self-control that occurs through self-discipline and the personal exercise of individual or group responsibility.

An **internal customer** is someone who uses or depends on the work of another person or group within the organization.

An **international business** conducts commercial transactions across national boundaries.

International management involves the conduct of business or other operations in foreign countries.

Interorganizational information systems facilitate information transfers among two or more organizations.

Intranets are computer networks that allow persons within an organization to share databases and communicate electronically.

Intrapreneurship is entrepreneurial behavior displayed by people or subunits within large organizations.

An **intrinsic** or **natural reward** is a reward that occurs naturally as a person performs a task or job.

Intuitive thinking occurs when someone approaches problems in a flexible and spontaneous fashion.

Inventory consists of materials or products kept in storage.

ISO 9000 certification is granted by the International Standards Organization to indicate that a business meets a rigorous set of quality standards.

J

A **job** is the collection of tasks a person performs in support of organizational objectives.

Job analysis is an orderly study of job requirements and facets that can influence performance results.

A **job description** is a written statement that details the duties and responsibilities of any person holding a particular job.

Job design is the allocation of specific work tasks to individuals and groups.

Job enlargement is a job-design strategy that increases task variety by combining into one job two or more tasks that were previously assigned to separate workers.

Job enrichment is a job-design strategy that increases job depth by adding to a job some of the planning and evaluating duties normally performed by the supervisor.

Job performance is the quantity and quality of task accomplishment by an individual or group.

Job rotation is a job-design strategy that increases task variety by periodically shifting workers among jobs involving different tasks.

Job satisfaction is the degree to which an individual feels positively or negatively about various aspects of the job, including assigned tasks, work setting, and relationships with coworkers.

Job scope is the number and combination of tasks an individual or group is asked to perform.

Job sharing is an arrangement that splits one job between two people.

Job simplification is a job-design strategy that involves standardizing work procedures and employing people in clearly defined and very specialized tasks.

A **job specification** is a list of the qualifications required of any job occupant.

A **joint venture** is a form of international business that establishes operations in a foreign country through joint ownership with local partners.

The **justice view** considers ethical behavior as that which treats people impartially and fairly according to guiding rules and standards.

Just-in-time scheduling (JIT) schedules materials to arrive at a work station or facility "just in time" to be used.

K

Keiretsu is a Japanese term describing alliances or business groups that link together manufacturers, suppliers, and finance companies with common interests.

Knowledge management is the processes utilizing organizational knowledge to achieve competitive advantage.

L

A **labor contract** is a formal agreement between a union and the employing organization that specifies the rights and obligations of each party with respect to wages, work hours, work rules, and other conditions of employment.

A **labor union** is an organization to which workers belong and that deals with employers on their collective behalf.

Thorndike's **law of effect** states that behavior followed by unpleasant consequences is likely to be repeated, whereas behavior followed by unpleasant consequences is not likely to be repeated.

Leadership is the process of inspiring others to work hard to accomplish important tasks.

Leadership style is the recurring pattern of behaviors exhibited by a leader.

Leading is the process of arousing enthusiasm and directing human-resource efforts toward organizational goals.

Lean production involves streamlining systems and implementing new technologies to allow work to be performed with fewer workers and smaller inventories.

Learning is any change in behavior that occurs as a result of experience.

A **learning organization** utilizes people, values, and systems to continuously change and improve its performance based on the lessons of experience.

Legitimate power is the capability to influence other people by virtue of formal authority or the rights of office.

A **licensing agreement** occurs when a firm pays a fee for the rights to make or sell another company's products.

Line managers have direct responsibility for activities making direct contributions to the production of the organization's basic goods or services.

In **long-linked technology** a client moves from point to point during service delivery.

In **lose-lose conflict** no one achieves his or her true desires and the underlying reasons for conflict remain unaffected.

Lower order needs, in Maslow's hierarchy, are physiological, safety, and social needs.

M

A **maintenance activity** is an action taken by a team member that supports the emotional life of the group.

Management is the process of planning, organizing, leading, and controlling the use of resources to accomplish performance goals.

Management by exception focuses managerial attention on substantial differences between actual and desired performance.

Management by objectives (MBO) is a process of joint objective setting between a superior and subordinate.

In **management by wandering around (MBWA)** workers at all levels talk with bosses about a variety of work-related matters.

Management development is training to improve knowledge and skills in the fundamentals of management.

A **management information system (MIS)** collects, organizes, and distributes data in such a way that the information meets managers' needs.

Management science or operations research is a scientific approach to management that uses mathematical techniques to analyze and solve problems.

A **manager** is a person in an organization who is responsible for the work performance of one or more other persons.

Managerial competency is a skill or personal characteristic that contributes to high performance in a management job.

Manufacturing resources planning (MRPII) is an operations planning and control system that extends MRP to include the control of all organizational resources.

Maquiladoras are foreign manufacturing plants that operate in Mexico with special privileges.

Mass customization involves manufacturing individualized products quickly and with the production efficiencies once only associated with mass production of uniform products.

Mass production is the production of a large number of one or a few products with an assembly-line type of system.

A **master budget** is a comprehensive short-term budget for an organization as a whole.

Materials requirements planning (MRP) is an operations planning and control system for ensuring that the right materials and parts are always available at each stage of production.

A **matrix structure** is an organizational form that combines functional and divisional departmentation to take best advantage of each.

A **mechanistic design** is highly bureaucratic, with centralized authority, many rules and procedures, a clearcut division of labor, narrow spans of controls, and formal coordination.

Mediating technology links together parties seeking a mutually beneficial exchange of values.

In **mediation** a neutral party engages in substantive discussions with conflicting parties in the hope that the dispute can be resolved.

Mentoring is the act of sharing experiences and insights between a seasoned and a junior manager.

Merit pay is a system of awarding pay increases in proportion to performance contributions.

Middle managers report to top-level management, oversee the work of several units, and implement plans consistent with higher level objectives.

The **mission** of an organization is its reason for existing as a supplier of goods and/or services to society.

A **mixed message** results when a person's words communicate one message while actions, body language, or appearance communicate something else.

Modeling demonstrates through personal behavior that which is expected of others.

In a **monochronic culture** people tend to do one thing at a time.

The **moral-rights view** is a view of ethical behavior that seeks to respect and protect the fundamental rights of people.

Motion study is the science of reducing a task to its basic physical motions.

Motivation is a term used in management theory to describe forces within the individual that account for the level, direction, and persistence of effort expended at work.

A **multicultural organization** is based on pluralism and operates with respect for diversity in the workplace.

Multiculturalism involves pluralism and respect for diversity in the workplace.

Multidimensional thinking is the capacity to view many problems at once, in relationship to one another, and across long and short time horizons.

A **multinational corporation (MNC)** is a business firm with extensive international operations in more than one foreign country.

A **multiperson comparison** is a performance appraisal method that involves comparing one person's performance with that of one or more persons.

N

NAFTA is the **North American Free Trade Agreement** linking Canada, the United States, and Mexico in a regional economic alliance.

A **narrative approach** to performance appraisal method uses a written essay description of a person's job performance.

A **need** is a physiological or psychological deficiency a person feels the compulsion to satisfy.

Need for Achievement (nAch) is the desire to do something better or more efficiently, to solve problems, or to master complex tasks.

Need for Affiliation (nAff) is the desire to establish and maintain good relations with people.

Need for Power (nPower) is the desire to control, influence, or be responsible for other people.

Negative reinforcement strengthens a behavior by making the avoidance of an undesirable consequence contingent on the occurrence of the behavior.

Negotiation is the process of making joint decisions when the parties involved have different preferences.

A **network** is a system of computers that are linked together to allow users to easily transfer and share information.

A **network structure** is an organizational structure that consists of a central core with "networks" of outside suppliers of essential business services.

Noise is anything that interferes with the effectiveness of the communication process.

The **nominal group technique** is a group technique for generating ideas by following a structured format of individual response, group sharing without criticism, and written balloting.

A **nonprogrammed decision** is unique and specifically tailored to a problem at hand.

Nonverbal communication is communication that takes place through channels such as body language and the use of interpersonal space.

A **norm** is a behavior, rule, or standard expected to be followed by team members.

O

Objectives are the specific results or desired end states that one wishes to achieve.

An **obstructionist strategy** avoids social responsibility and reflects mainly economic priorities.

An **OD intervention** is a structured activity initiated by consultants or managers that directly assists in a comprehensive organizational development program.

An **open system** interacts with its environment and transforms resource inputs into outputs.

Operant conditioning is the process of controlling behavior by manipulating its consequences.

An **operating budget** is a budget that assigns resources to a responsibility center on a short-term basis.

Operating objectives are specific results that organizations try to accomplish.

An **operational plan** is a plan of limited scope that addresses those activities and resources required to implement strategic plans.

Operations management is a branch of management theory that studies how organizations transform resource inputs into product and service outputs.

An **optimizing decision** results when a manager chooses an alternative that gives the absolute best solution to a problem.

An **organic design** is decentralized with fewer rules and procedures, more open divisions of labor, wide spans of control, and more personal coordination.

An **organization** is a collection of people working together in a division of labor to achieve a common purpose.

An **organization chart** is a diagram that describes the basic arrangement of work positions within an organization.

Organizational design is the process of creating structures that best organize resources to serve mission and objectives.

Organization development (OD) is the application of behavioral science knowledge in a long-range effort to improve an organization's ability to cope with change in its external environment and increase its internal problem-solving capabilities.

Organization structure is the system of tasks, reporting relationships, and communication that links people and groups together to accomplish tasks that serve the organizational purpose.

Organizational behavior is the study of individuals and groups in organizations.

Organizational behavior modification is the application of operant conditioning to influence human behavior at work.

Organizational communication is the process through which information is exchanged through interactions among people inside an organization.

Organizational culture is the system of shared beliefs and values that develops within an organization and guides the behavior of its members.

Organizational design is the process of creating structures that best organize resources to serve mission and objectives.

Organizational ecology is the study of how building design may influence communication and productivity.

The **organizational life cycle** is the evolution of an organization over time through different stages of growth.

Organizing is the process of arranging people and resources to work toward a common purpose.

Orientation consists of activities through which new employees are made familiar with their jobs, their co-workers, and the policies, rules, objectives, and services of the organization as a whole.

An **output standard** is a standard that measures performance results in terms of quantity, quality, cost, or time.

Outside-in planning uses analysis of the external environment and makes plans to take advantage of opportunities and avoid problems.

P

Participative planning is the inclusion in the planning process of as many people as possible from among those who will be affected by plans and/or asked to help implement them.

Part-time work is work done on a basis that classifies the employee as "temporary" and requires less than the standard 40-hour workweek.

Perception is the process through which people receive, organize, and interpret information from the environment.

Performance appraisal is a process of formally evaluating performance and providing feedback on which performance adjustments can be made.

Performance effectiveness is an output measure of a task or goal accomplishment.

Performance efficiency is a measure of the resource cost associated with goal accomplishment.

A **performance gap** is a discrepancy between the desired and actual state of affairs.

A **performance management system** sets standards, assesses results, and plans actions to improve future performance.

A **performance norm** identifies the level of work effort and performance expected of group members.

Personal staff are "assistant-to" positions that provide special administrative support to higher level positions.

Personal wellness is the pursuit of one's physical and mental potential through a personal-health promotion program.

A **plan** is a statement of intended means for accomplishing a desired result.

Planned change occurs as a result of specific efforts in its behalf by a change agent.

Planning is the process of setting objectives and determining what should be done to accomplish them.

A **policy** is a standing plan that communicates broad guidelines for making decisions and taking action.

Political risk is the possible loss of investment or control over a foreign asset because of political changes in the host country.

In a **polychronic culture** time is used to accomplish many different things at once.

A **portfolio planning** approach seeks the best mix of investments among alternative business opportunities.

Positive reinforcement strengthens a behavior by making a desirable consequence contingent on the occurrence of the behavior.

Power is the ability to get someone else to do something you want done or to make things happen the way you want.

Prejudice is the holding of negative, irrational attitudes toward individuals because of their group identity.

Principled/integrative negotiation uses a "win-win" orientation to reach solutions acceptable to each party.

Privatization is the selling of state-owned enterprises into private ownership.

A **proactive strategy** meets all the criteria of social responsibility, including discretionary performance.

A **problem** is a difference between an actual situation and a desired situation.

Problem solving is the process of identifying a discrepancy between an actual and desired state of affairs and then taking action to resolve it.

A **problem symptom** is a sign of the presence of a performance deficiency or opportunity that should trigger a manager to act.

Procedural justice concerns the degree to which policies and rules are fairly administered.

A **procedure** or **rule** is a standing plan that precisely describes what actions are to be taken in specific situations.

A **process** is a group of related tasks creating something of value to a customer.

Process reengineering systematically analyzes work processes to design new and better ones.

A **process structure** groups jobs and activities that are part of the same processes.

Process value analysis identifies and evaluates core processes for their performance contributions.

Product life cycle is the series of stages a product or service goes through in the "life" of its marketability.

A **product structure** is an organizational structure that groups together jobs and activities working on a single product or service.

Productivity is a summary measure of the quantity and quality of work performance with resource utilization considered.

A **profit-sharing plan** distributes a proportion of net profits to employees during a stated performance period.

The **program evaluation and review technique (PERT)** is a means for identifying and controlling the many separate events involved in the completion of projects.

A **programmed decision** applies a solution from past experience to the problem at hand.

Progressive discipline is the process of tying reprimands in the form of penalties or punishments to the severity of the employee's infractions.

Project management is the responsibility for making sure that all activities in a project are completed on time, in the order specified, and with high quality.

A **project schedule** is a single-use plan for accomplishing a specific set of tasks.

Projection is the assignment of personal attributes to other individuals.

A **prospector strategy** is a corporate competitive strategy that involves pursuing innovation and new opportunities in the face of risk and with the prospects of growth.

Proxemics is the use of interpersonal space, such as in the process of interpersonal communication.

A **psychological contract** is the shared set of expectations held by an individual and the organization, specifying what each expects to give and receive from the other in the course of their working relationship.

Punishment discourages a behavior by making an unpleasant consequence contingent on the occurrence of that behavior.

Q

Quality is a degree of excellence, often defined as the ability to meet customer needs 100 percent of the time.

A **quality circle** is a group of employees who meet periodically to discuss ways of improving the quality of their products or services.

Quality control involves checking processes, material, products, or services to ensure that they meet high standards.

Quality of work life (QWL) is the overall quality of human experiences in the workplace.

R

A **rational persuasion strategy** attempts to bring about change through persuasion backed by special knowledge, empirical data, and rational argument.

A **reactor strategy** is a corporate competitive strategy that involves simply responding to competitive pressures in order to survive.

Realistic job previews are attempts by the job interviewer to provide the job candidate with all pertinent information about a prospective job and the employing organization, without distortion and before a job offer is accepted.

A **reason strategy** of influence relies on personal power and persuasion based on data, needs, and/or values.

A **reciprocity strategy** of influence involves the mutual exchange of values and a search for shared positive outcomes.

Recruitment is a set of activities designed to attract a qualified pool of job applicants to an organization.

Referent power is the capability to influence other people because of their desires to identify personally and positively with the power source.

Refreezing is the final stage in the planned-change process during which the manager is concerned with stabilizing the change and creating the conditions for its long-term continuity.

Reliability refers to the ability of an employment test to yield the same result over time if taken by the same person.

Replacement is the management of promotions, transfers, terminations, layoffs, and retirements.

Responsibility is the obligation to perform that results from accepting assigned tasks.

A **responsibility center** is a work unit formally charged with budgetary responsibility for carrying out various activities.

A **retrenchment strategy** involves slowing down, cutting back, and seeking performance improvement through greater efficiencies in operations.

A **retribution strategy** of influence relies on position power and results in feelings of coercion or intimidation.

A **reward** is a work outcome of positive value to the individual.

Reward power is the capability to offer something of value—a positive outcome—as a means of influencing other people.

A **risk environment** is a problem environment in which information is lacking, but some sense of the "probabilities" associated with action alternatives and their consequences exists.

Robotics is the use of computer-controlled machines to completely automate work tasks previously performed by hand.

A **role** is a set of activities expected of a person in a particular job or position within the organization.

Role ambiguity occurs when a person in a role is uncertain about what others expect in terms of his or her behavior.

Role conflict occurs when the person in a role is unable to respond to the expectations held by one or more others.

Role overload occurs when too many role expectations are being communicated to a person at a given time.

Role underload occurs when a person is underutilized or asked to do too little and/or to do things that fail to challenge her or his talents and capabilities.

S

Satisficing involves choosing the first satisfactory alternative that comes to your attention.

A **satisfier factor** is a factor in job content, such as a sense of achievement, recognition, responsibility, advancement, or personal growth, experienced as a result of task performance.

Scenario planning identifies alternative future "scenarios" and makes plans to deal with each.

Scientific management involves developing a science for every job, including rules of motion and standardized work instruments, careful selection and training of workers, and proper supervisory support for workers.

Selection is the process of choosing from a pool of applicants the person or persons who best meet job specifications

Selective perception is the tendency to define problems from one's own point of view or to single out for attention things consistent with one's existing beliefs, values, or needs.

A **self-fulfilling prophecy** occurs when a person acts in ways in order to confirm another's expectations.

A **self-managing work team,** sometimes called an autonomous work group, is a group of workers whose jobs have been redesigned to create a high degree of task interdependence and who have been given authority to make decisions about how they go about the required work.

Self-serving bias explains personal success by internal causes and personal failures by external causes.

Semantic barriers are verbal and nonverbal symbols that are poorly chosen and expressed, creating barriers to successful communication.

Shaping is positive reinforcement of successive approximations to the desired behavior.

A **shared power strategy** is a participative change strategy that relies on involving others to examine values, needs, and goals in relationship to an issue at hand.

A **simultaneous structure** involves the co-existence of mechanistic and organic structures within an organization in the attempt to accomplish both production efficiency and innovation.

A **single-use plan** is used only once.

A **skill** is the ability to translate knowledge into action that results in the desired performance.

Skills-based pay is a system of paying workers according to the number of job-relevant skills they master.

Small-batch production is the production of a variety of custom products that are tailor-made, usually with considerable craftsmanship, to fit customer specifications.

A **small business** has fewer than 500 employees, is independently owned and operated, and does not dominate its industry.

A **social audit** is a systematic assessment and reporting of an organization's commitments and accomplishments in areas of social responsibility.

Social loafing is the tendency of some people to avoid responsibility by "free-riding" in groups.

Socialization is the process of systematically changing the expectations, behavior, and attitudes of a new employee in a manner considered desirable by the organization.

A **sociotechnical system** designs jobs so that technology and human resources are well integrated in high-performance systems with maximum opportunities for individual satisfaction.

Span of control is the number of subordinates reporting directly to a manager.

Specialized staff are positions that perform a technical service or provide special problem-solving expertise for other parts of the organization.

A **specific environment** is comprised of the actual organizations and persons with whom the focal organization must interact in order to survive and prosper.

A **stability strategy** maintains the present course of action.

Staff managers use special technical expertise to advise and support the efforts of line workers.

Stakeholders are the persons, groups, and institutions directly affected by an organization's performance.

A **standing plan** is used more than once.

Statistical quality control is the use of statistical techniques to assist in the quality control process.

A **stereotype** results when an individual is assigned to a group or category and then the attributes commonly associated with the group or category are assigned to the individual in question.

A **strategic business unit (SBU)** is a separate operating division that represents a major business area and operates with some autonomy vis-à-vis other similar units in the organization.

A **strategic constituencies analysis** is the review and analysis of the interests of external stakeholders of an organization.

Strategic human resource planning analyzes staffing needs and identifies actions to fill those needs.

Strategic management is the managerial responsibility for leading the process of formulating and implementing strategies that lead to longer term organizational success.

Strategic opportunism is the ability to remain focused on long-term objectives by being flexible in dealing with short-term problems and opportunity as they occur.

A **strategic plan** is comprehensive and addresses longer term needs and directions of the organization.

A **strategy** is a comprehensive plan or action orientation that sets critical direction and guides the allocation of resources for an organization to achieve long-term objectives.

Stress is a state of tension experienced by individuals facing extraordinary demands, constraints, or opportunities.

A **stressor** is anything that causes stress.

A **structured problem** is familiar, straightforward, and clear in its information requirements.

Subcultures within organizations are common to groups of people with similar values and beliefs based upon shared personal characteristics.

Substantive conflict is disagreement over such things as goals, the allocation of resources, distribution of rewards, policies, and procedures, and job assignments.

Substitutes for leadership are factors in the work setting that move work efforts toward organizational objectives without the direct involvement of a leader.

A **subsystem** is a work unit or smaller component within a larger organization.

Survivor syndrome is the stress experienced by people who fear for their jobs after having "survived" large layoffs and staff cutbacks in an organization.

A **SWOT analysis** sets the stage for strategy formulation by analyzing organizational strengths and weaknesses and environmental opportunities and threats.

A **symbolic manager** uses symbols to establish and maintain a desired organizational culture.

Synergy is the creation of a whole that is greater than the sum of its individual parts.

Systematic thinking occurs when someone approaches problems in a rational and analytical fashion.

T

A **task activity** is an action taken by a group member that contributes directly to the group's performance purpose.

A **task force** is a formal team convened for a specific purpose and expected to disband when that purpose is achieved.

Task goals are performance targets for individuals and/or groups.

A **team** is a collection of people who regularly interact to pursue common goals.

Team building is a sequence of collaborative activities to gather and analyze data on a team and make changes to increase its effectiveness.

Team leaders or supervisors report to middle managers and directly supervise non-managerial workers.

A **team structure** is an organizational structure through which permanent and temporary teams are created to improve lateral relations and solve problems throughout an organization.

Teamwork is the process of people working together in groups to accomplish common goals.

A **technical skill** is the ability to use a special proficiency or expertise in one's work.

Technology is the combination of equipment, knowledge, and work methods that allows an organization to transform inputs into outputs.

Telecommuting or **flexiplace** involves working at home or other places using computer links to the office.

Theory X is a set of managerial assumptions that people in general dislike work, lack ambition, are irresponsible and resistant to change, and prefer to be led than to lead.

Theory Y is a set of managerial assumptions that people in general are willing to work and accept responsibility and are capable of self-direction, self-control, and creativity.

Theory Z is a term that describes a management framework used by American firms following Japanese examples.

Top-down planning begins with broad objectives set by top management.

Top managers are the highest level managers and work to ensure that major plans and objectives are set and accomplished in accord with the organization's purpose.

Total quality management (TQM) is managing with an organization-wide commitment to continuous work improvement, product quality, and meeting customer needs completely.

Training involves a set of activities that provide learning opportunities through which people can acquire and improve job-related skills.

A **trait** is a relatively stable and enduring personal characteristic of an individual.

Transactional leadership is leadership that orchestrates and directs the efforts of others through tasks, rewards, and structures.

Transformational leadership is the ability of a leader to get people to do more than they originally expected to do in support of large-scale innovation and change.

A **transnational corporation** is an MNC that operates worldwide on a borderless basis.

A **type A personality** is a person oriented toward extreme achievement, impatience, and perfectionism and who may find stress in circumstances others find relatively stress-free.

360-degree feedback is an upward communication approach that involves upward appraisals done by a manager's subordinates, as well as additional feedback from peers, internal and external customers, and higher ups.

U

An **uncertain environment** is a problem environment in which information is so poor that it is difficult even to assign probabilities to the likely outcomes of known alternatives.

Unfreezing is the initial phase in the planned-change process during which the manager prepares a situation for change.

Unplanned change occurs spontaneously or at random and without a change agent's direction.

An **unstructured problem** involves ambiguities and information deficiencies.

The **utilitarian view** considers ethical behavior as that which delivers the greatest good to the greatest number of people.

V

Valence is the value a person assigns to work-related outcomes.

Validity refers to the ability of an employment test to measure exactly what it is intended to relative to the job specification.

Values are broad beliefs about what is or is not appropriate behavior.

A **virtual meeting** is a meeting conducted by a computer-mediated process of information sharing and decision making.

The **virtual office** enables workers to "commute" via computer networks, fax machines, and express mail delivery service.

A **virtual team** is a group of people who work together and solve problems through computer-based rather than face-to-face interactions.

Vision is a term used to describe a clear sense of the future.

W

A **whistleblower** exposes the misdeeds of others in organizations.

A **wholly owned subsidiary** is a local operation completely owned by a foreign firm.

A **win-lose conflict** occurs when one party achieves its desires at the expense and exclusion of the other party's desires.

A **win-win conflict** occurs when conflict is resolved to the mutual benefit of all concerned parties.

A **work process** is a related group of tasks that together create a value for the customer.

Work-at-home involves accomplishing a job while spending all or part of one's work time in the home.

Workflow is the movement of work from one point to another in a system.

Workforce diversity is a term used to describe demographic differences (age, gender, race and ethnicity, and able-bodiedness) among members of the workforce.

Work-life balance involves balancing career demands with personal and family needs.

Z

A **zero-based budget** allocates resources to a project or activity as if it were brand new.

Notes

Chapter 1 Notes

[1] Information from the *Fast Company* web site, <http://www.fastcompany.com/partners/mission.htm>

[2] For a research perspective see Denise M. Rousseau, "Organizational Behavior in the New Organizational Era," *Annual Review of Psychology*, Vol. 48 (1997), pp. 515–546; for a consultant's perspective see Tom Peters, *The Circle of Innovation* (New York: Alfred A. Knopf, 1997).

[3] *Fortune*, February 10, 1992, pp. 40–70. See also Johnson & Johnson home page at http://www.johnsonandjohnson.com/.

[4] Peter F. Drucker, *The Changing World of the Executive* (New York: T.T. Times Books, 1982), p. xi; see also, Peter Drucker, *Peter Drucker on the Profession of Management* (Cambridge, MA: Harvard Business School Press, 1997).

[5] Information from Thomas A. Stewart, "Brain Power," *Fortune* (March 17, 1997), p. 107; John A. Byrne, "Jack: A Close-Up Look at How America's #1 Manager Runs GE," *Business Week* (June 8, 1998), pp. 91–111.

[6] Max DePree, "It Begins with a Belief in People," *New York Times*, September 10, 1989, p. 2F; *Fortune*, February 10, 1992, pp. 40–70; and Herman Miller's home page at <http://www.hermanmiller.com/company/blueprint.html>.

[7] Ronald B. Lieber, "Why Employees Love These Companies," *Fortune*, January 12, 1998, pp. 72–74.

[8] Ibid.

[9] For a discussion of organizations as systems, see Lane Tracy, *The Living Organization* (New York: Quorum Books, 1994).

[10] Information on Daimler-Benz and Mercedes available at <http://www.mercedes-benz.com/e/about/default.htm>.

[11] Henry Mintzberg, "The Manager's Job: Folklore and Fact," *Harvard Business Review*, vol. 53 (July–August 1975): 61.

[12] Hal Lancaster, "Middle Managers Are Back—But Now They're 'High-Impact' Players," *Wall Street Journal*, April 14, 1998, p. B1.

[13] Ibid.

[14] For a perspective on the first-level manager's job, see Leonard A. Schlesinger and Janice A. Klein, "The First-Line Supervisor: Past, Present and Future," pp. 370–82, in Jay W. Lorsch (editor), *Handbook of Organizational Behavior* (Englewood Cliffs, N.J.: Prentice-Hall, 1987). Research reported in "Remember Us?" *Economist*, February 1, 1992, p. 71.

[15] R. Roosevelt Thomas Jr., "From Affirmative Action to Affirming Diversity," *Harvard Business Review* (March–April 1990), pp. 107–17; see also Mary Gentile (editor), *Differences That Work: Organizational Excellence through Diversity* (Boston: Harvard Business School Press, 1996) and Gary N. Powell, *Women and Men in Management* (Thousand Oaks, CA: Sage, 1993).

[16] Quotation from *Business Week*, August 8, 1990, p. 50, emphasis added.

[17] Taylor Cox Jr., "The Multicultural Organization," *Academy of Management Executives* vol. 5 (1991), pp. 34–47, and *Cultural Diversity in Organizations: Theory, Research and Practice* (San Francisco: Berrett-Koehler, 1993).

[18] Ann M. Morrison, Randall P. White, and Ellen Van Velso, *Breaking the Glass Ceiling* (Reading, MA: Addison-Wesley, 1987)

[19] See Anne Fisher, "Six Ways to Supercharge Your Career," *Fortune*, January 13, 1997, pp. 46–57.

[20] Thomas A. Mahoney, Thomas H. Jerdee, and Stephen J. Carroll, "The Job(s) of Management," *Industrial Relations*, vol. 4 (February 1965): 97–110.

[21] Information on this series of examples from "Accountants Have Lives, Too, You Know," *Business Week*, February 23, 1998, pp. 88–90.

[22] Henry Mintzberg, *The Nature of Managerial Work* (New York: Harper & Row, 1973), p. 30.

[23] John R. Veiga and Kathleen Dechant, "Wired World Woes: www.help," *Academy of Management Executive*, vol. 11 (August 1997): 73–79.

[24] Mintzberg, *Nature of Managerial Work*, p. 30.

[25] Ibid., p. 46.

[26] Morgan W. McCall Jr., Ann M. Morrison, and Robert L. Hannan, *Studies of Managerial Work: Results and Methods*. Technical Report #9 (Greensboro, NC: Center for Creative Leadership, 1978), pp. 7–9. See also John P. Kotter, "What Effective General Managers Really Do," *Harvard Business Review*, vol. 60 (November–December 1982): 156–57.

[27] Kotter, "What Effective General Managers Really Do," p. 164. See also his book, *The General Managers* (New York: The Free Press, 1982) and recent research by David Barry, Catherine Durnell Crampton, and Stephen J. Carroll, "Navigating the Garbage Can: How Agendas Help Managers Cope with Job Realities," *Academy of Management Executive*, vol. 11 (May 1997): 43–56.

[28] Robert L. Katz, "Skills of an Effective Administrator," *Harvard Business Review*, vol. 52 (September–October 1974), p. 94.

[29] Richard E. Boyatzis, *The Competent Manager: A Model for Effective Performance* (New York: Wiley, 1982). See also Edward A. Powers, "Enhancing Managerial Competence: The American Management Association Competency Program," *Journal of Management Development*, vol. 6 (1987): 7–18.

[30] Developed from the *Outcome Measurement Project of the Accreditation Research Committee, Phase II: An Interim* (St. Louis: American As-

sembly of Collegiate Schools of Business, 1984), pp. 15–18. See also the *Phase II Report*.

[31] Charles Handy, *The Age of Unreason* (Cambridge, MA: Harvard Business School Press, 1990) and *Beyond Certainty: The Changing Worlds of Organizations* (Cambridge, MA: Harvard Business School Press, 1997).

[32] Kenichi Ohmae, *The Borderless World: Power and Strategy in the Interlinked Economy* (New York: Harper, 1989) and *The End of the Nation State* (New York: The Free Press, 1996).

[33] Michael E. Porter, *The Competitive Advantage of Nations* (New York: The Free Press, 1994).

[34] Example from *Whirlpool 1990 Annual Report*.

[35] See, for example, Clarence Walton, *The Moral Manager* (New York: Harper Business, 1990).

[36] Credo selection from <http://johnsonandjohnson.com/who_is_jnj/cr_usa.htm/>. See also *Johnson & Johnson Annual Report 1997*.

[37] *Workforce 2000: Work and Workers for the 21st Century* (Indianapolis: Towers Perrin/Hudson Institute, 1987).

[38] Richard W. Judy and Carol D'Amico (editors), *Workforce 2020* (Indianapolis: Hudson Institute, 1997).

[39] Carol D'Amico, "Testimony of U.S. House of Representatives Committee on Education and the Workforce," June 5, 1997, provided at <http://www.al.com/hudson/wf2020/WF-HOUSE.HTM/>.

[40] Ibid.

[41] Information from "Diversity: Making the Business Case," *Business Week*, special advertising section, December 9, 1996.

[42] In addition to *Workforce 2020*, 1997, see *Opportunity 2000: Creative Affirmative Action Strategies for a Changing Workforce* (Indianapolis: Hudson Institute, 1988) and, *Workforce 2000: Competing in a Seller's Market: Is Corporate America Prepared?* (Indianapolis: Towers Perrin/Hudson Institute, 1990).

[43] Reported by Leon E. Wynter, "Business & Race," *Wall Street Journal*, December 3, 1997, p. B1.

[44] Information from "Perforations in the Glass Ceiling," *Business Week*, December 22, 1997, p. 44.

[45] "Diversity: Beyond the Numbers Game," *Business Week*, August 14, 1995, pp. 60–61; "Blacks in America: The Other Half," *Economist*, November 4, 1995, p. 35. See Roy S. Johnson, "The New Black Power," *Fortune*, August 4, 1997, p. 47; "Why Women Are So Invisible," *Business Week*, August 25, 1997, p. 136; "Minority Women Unhappy with Advancement," *Columbus Dispatch*, February 10, 1998, pp. 1E, 2E.

[46] Information from Andrew E. Serwer, "Lessons from America's Fastest Growing Companies," *Fortune*, August 8, 1994, pp. 42–60.

[47] Alvin Toffler and Heidi Toffler, *Powershift: Knowledge, Wealth, and Violence at the Edge of the 21st Century* (New York: Bantam, 1990).

[48] Alvin Toffler, "Toffler's Next Shock," *The World Monitor*, November 1990, p. 37.

[49] Handy, *The Age of Unreason*.

[50] Quotation from "Is Your Job Your Calling," *Fast Company*, no. 13, p. 108, taken from <http://www.fastcompany.com/13/hbrplus.htm>.

[51] This material is provided courtesy of Ronald Larimer and is used with his permission.

Chapter 2 Notes

[1] Information from Justin Martin, "Give 'Em *Exactly* What They Want," *Fortune*, November 10, 1997, pp. 283–84.

[2] *The New Blue: 1997 IBM Annual Report*, p. 8.

[3] See Michael E. Porter, *Competitive Strategy: Techniques for Analyzing Industries and Competitors* (New York: Free Press, 1980) and *Competitive Advantage: Creating and Sustaining Superior Performance* (New York: Free Press, 1986); also, Richard A. D'Aveni, *Hyper-Competition: Managing the Dynamics of Strategic Maneuvering* (New York: The Free Press, 1994).

[4] Information from *The Vermont Teddy Bear Company Gazette*, vol. 4 (summer 1993).

[5] Michael Porter, *The Competitive Advantage of Nations* (New York: Free Press, 1989).

[6] Joseph M. Juran, "Made in U.S.A.: A Renaissance in Quality," *Harvard Business Review*, July–August 1993, pp. 42–50.

[7] James D. Thompson, *Organizations in Action* (New York: McGraw-Hill, 1967), and Robert B. Duncan, "Characteristics of Organizational Environments and Perceived Environmental Uncertainty," *Administrative Science Quarterly*, vol. 17 (1972): 313–27. For discussion of the implications of uncertainty see Hugh Courtney, Jane Kirkland and Patrick Viguerie, "Strategy Under Uncertainty," *Harvard Business Review* (November–December, 1997), pp. 67–79.

[8] Quotation from Richard J. Shonberger and Edward M. Knod Jr., *Operations Management: Serving the Customer*, 3d ed. (Plano, TX: Business Publications, 1988), p. 4.

[9] *The Vermont Teddy Bear Company Gazette*, vol. 4 (summer 1993): 3.

[10] Shonberger and Knod, p. 5.

[11] Rosabeth Moss Kanter, "Transcending Business Boundaries: 12,000 World Managers View Change," *Harvard Business Review*, May–June 1991, pp. 151–64.

[12] Reported in Jennifer Steinhauer, "The Undercover Shoppers," *New York Times*, February 4, 1998, pp. C1, C2.

[13] *Business Week*, special issue, 1991, p. 14.

[14] For a classic discussion see Wickham Skinner, "Manufacturing—Missing Link in Corporate Strategy," *Harvard Business Review*, May–June 1969, pp. 136–45, and *Manufacturing in the Corporate Strategy* (New York: Wiley, 1978). For current thinking, see Richard J. Schonberger, *World Class Manufacturing—The Next Decade: Building Power, Strength, and Value* (New York: The Free Press, 1996) and Robert H. Hayes, Gary P. Pisano, and David M. Upton, *Strategic Operations: Competing through Capabilities* (New York: The Free Press, 1996).

[15] See Joseph M. Juran, *Quality Control Handbook*, 3d ed. (New York: McGraw-Hill, 1979) and "The Quality Trilogy: A Universal Approach to Managing for Quality," in H. Costin (editor), *Total Quality Management* (New York: Dryden, 1994); W. Edwards Deming, *Out of Crisis* (Cambridge, MA: MIT Press, 1986) and "Deming's Quality Manifesto," *Best of Business Quarterly*, vol. 12 (winter 1990–1991): 6–10. See also Howard S. Gitlow and Shelly J. Gitlow, *The Deming Guide to Quality and Competitive Position* (Englewood Cliffs, NJ: Prentice-Hall, 1987); Juran, "Made in U.S.A."

[16] "The Quality Imperative," special issue of Business Week, October 25, 1991, p. 58; "Does the Baldrige Award Really Work?" *Harvard Business Review*, January–February 1992, pp. 126–47.

[17] Christopher Knowlton, "What America Makes Best," *Fortune*, March 28, 1988, pp. 40–54; Roger L. Hale, Douglas R. Hoelscher, and Ronald E. Kowal, *Quest for Quality* (Minneapolis, MN: Tenant Company, 1989); and Roger L. Hale, Donald D. Carlton, Ronald E. Kowal, and Tim K. Sehnert, *Made in the USA: How One American Company Helps Satisfy Customer Needs through Strategic Supplier Quality Management* (Minneapolis, MN: Tenant Company, 1991).

[18] Philip B. Crosby, *Quality Is Free* (New York: McGraw-Hill, 1979); *The Eternally Successful Organization* (New York: McGraw-Hill, 1988).

[19] Rafael Aguay, *Dr. Deming: The American Who Taught the Japanese about Quality* (New York: The Free Press, 1997).

[20] Adapted from W. Edwards Deming, *Out of Crisis*.

[21] See Edward E. Lawler III, Susan Albers Mohrman, Gerald E. Ledford Jr., *Employee Involvement and Total Quality Management: Practices and Results in Fortune 1000 Companies*, (San Francisco: Jossey-Bass, 1992).

[22] Edward E. Lawler III and Susan Albers Mohrman, "Quality Circles after the Fad," *Harvard Business Review*, January–February 1985, pp. 65–71.

[23] Quotes from Arnold Kanarick, "The Far Side of Quality Circles," *Management Review*, vol. 70 (October 1981); 16–17.

[24] William M. Bulkeley, "Pushing the Pace:

The Latest Big Thing at Many Companies Is Speed, Speed, Speed," *Wall Street Journal*, December 23, 1994, pp. A1, A5.

[25] See B. Joseph Pine II, Bart Victor, and Andrew C. Boynton, "Making Mass Customization Work," *Harvard Business Review*, September–October 1993, pp. 108–19; and, "The Agile Factory: Custom-made, Direct from the Plant," *Business Week*, special report on "21st Century Capitalism," January 23, 1995, pp. 158–59.

[26] Examples are from *Business Week*, special issue, op. cit. (1991), p. 8; and Martin, op. cit., 1997, p. 283.

[27] Tom Peters, *The Circle of Innovation* (New York: Alfred A. Knopf, 1997), p. 429.

[28] Martin, op. cit., p. 284.

[29] Gene Bylinsky, "Manufacturing for Reuse," *Fortune*, February 6, 1995, pp. 102–12.

[30] Edgar H. Schein, "Organizational Culture," *American Psychologist*, vol. 45 (1990): 109–19. See also Schein's *Organizational Culture and Leadership*, 2d ed. (Reading, MA: Addison-Wesley, 1997).

[31] James Collins and Jerry Porras, *Built to Last* (New York: Harper Business, 1994).

[32] Schein, 1996; Terrence E. Deal and Alan A. Kennedy, *Corporate Cultures: The Rites and Rituals of Corporate Life* (Reading, MA: Addison-Wesley, 1982); Ralph Kilmann, *Beyond the Quick Fix* (San Francisco: Jossey-Bass, 1984).

[33] In their book *Corporate Culture and Performance* (New York: MacMillan, 1992), John P. Kotter and James L. Heskett make the point that strong cultures have the desired effects over the long term only if they encourage adaptation to a changing environment. See also Collins and Porras, *Built to Last* 1994.

[34] This is a simplified model developed from Schein, *Organizational Culture*.

[35] Deal and Kennedy *Corporate Cultures*.

[36] James C. Collins and Jerry I. Porras, "Building Your Company's Vision," *Harvard Business Review*, September–October 1996, pp. 65–77.

[37] Information provided by Bell Atlantic media services, memorandum, December 5, 1997.

[38] Ralph H. Kilmann, Mary J. Saxton, and Roy Serpa, "Issues in Understanding and Changing Culture," *California Management Review*, vol. 28 (1986): 87–94.

[39] Wendy Zellner, "Mary Kay Is Singing I Feel Pretty," *Business Week* (December 2, 1991), p. 102; Barbara James, "From Rouges to Riches," *The Columbus Dispatch* (June 4, 1998), p. B1.

[40] Information from Nina Munk, "The New Organization Man," *Fortune*, March 16, 1998, pp. 62–74.

[41] Roosevelt Thomas, "From 'Affirmative Action' to 'Affirming Diversity,'" *Harvard Business Review*, November–December 1990, pp. 107–17; Taylor Cox Jr., *Cultural Diversity in Organizations* (San Francisco: Berrett-Koehler Publishers, Inc., 1994).

[42] Joseph A. Raelin, *Clash of Cultures* (Cambridge, MA: Harvard Business School Press, 1986).

[43] Geert Hofstede, *Culture's Consequences* (Beverly Hills: Sage, 1982).

[44] For examples of role model approaches see Anthony Robbins and Joseph McClendon III, *Unlimited Power: A Black Choice* (New York: The Free Press, 1997) and Augusto Failde and William Doyle, *Latino Success: Insights from America's Most Powerful Latino Executives* (New York: The Free Press, 1996).

[45] See Suneel Ratan, "Generational Tension in the Office: Why Buster's Hate Boomers," *Fortune*, October 4, 1993, pp. 56–70.

[46] Barbara Benedict Bunker, "Appreciating Diversity and Modifying Organizational Cultures: Men and Women at Work," chapter 5 in Suresh Srivastva, David L. Cooperrider, ?? *Appreciative Management and Leadership* (San Francisco: Jossey-Bass, 1990).

[47] See Gary N. Powell, *Women & Men in Management* (Thousand Oaks, CA: Sage Publications, 1993) and Cliff Cheng (editor), *Masculinities in Organizations* (Thousand Oaks, CA: Sage Publications, 1996). For added background, see also Sally Helgesen, *Everyday Revolutionaries: Working Women and the Transformation of American Life* (New York: Doubleday, 1998).

[48] John B. Cullen, Bart Victor, and Carroll Stephens, "An Ethical Weather Report: Assessing the Organization's Ethical Climate," *Organizational Dynamics*, winter 1990, pp. 50–63.

Chapter 3 Notes

[1] "Virtual Campuses Offer Compelling Reasons for Business Schools to Improve their Distance Vision," *AACSB Newsline*, spring, 1998, pp. 2–10.

[2] Thomas A. Stewart, *Intellectual Capital: The Wealth of Organizations* (New York: Doubleday, 1997).

[3] Peter F. Drucker, "Looking Ahead: Implications of the Present," *Harvard Business Review*, September–October 1997, pp. 18–32.

[4] Paul Roberts, "Humane Technology—PeopleSoft," *Fast Company*, no. 14, p. 122.

[5] Alvin Toffler, "Toffler's Next Shock," *World Monitor*, November 1990, pp. 34–44. See also Toffler's book *Powershift* (New York: Bantam Books, 1990).

[6] For a description of the technical elements of electronic commerce see Turban, McClean, and Wetherbe, *Information Technology for Management*, 2d ed. (New York: John Wiley & Sons, 1998).

[7] Information from "What Is an E-Business? And Why Should You Be One?" *Far Eastern Economic Review*, May 14, 1998, p. 43.

[8] Information from "Amazon.com: Earth's Biggest Bookstore," corporate advertisement, 1998; "The 'Click Here' Economy," *Business Week* (June 22, 1998), pp. 122–129.

[9] "Building Business around Information," *Business Week*, special advertising section, July 14, 1997.

[10] Drucker, "Looking Ahead," 1997, p. 22.

[11] Information from "Making Service Personal at Fidelity" in special supplement "Quality '93," *Fortune* (September 20, 1993); and *Business Week*, op. cit., 1997; "Fidelity Takes on the World," Business Week (June 22, 1998), p. 184.

[12] "Building Business around Information," *Business Week*, July 14, 1997, special advertising section.

[13] Jacyln Fierman, "Winning Ideas from Maverick Managers," *Fortune*, February 6, 1995, pp. 66–80.

[14] The article by Dorothy Leonard-Barton and John J. Sviokla, "Putting Expert Systems to Work," *Harvard Business Review*, vol. 66 (March–April 1988): 91–98, provides a practical overview of expert systems and their management applications. See also Barbara Garson, *The Electronic Sweatshop* (New York: Viking Penguin, 1989).

[15] Mary J. Cronin, "Ford's Intranet Success," *Fortune*, March 30, 1998, p. 158; and Steven V. Brull, "Networks That do New Tricks," *Business Week*, April 6, 1998, p. 100.

[16] Turban, McClean, and Wetherbe, Information Technology, 1998.

[17] Ibid.

[18] Jonathan Clements, "While Brokers Suffer, a Mutual Fund Firm Thrives in Stock Surge," *Wall Street Journal*, July 16, 1990, pp. A1, A5.

[19] For scholarly reviews, see Dean Tjosvold, "Effects of Crisis Orientation on Managers' Approach to Controversy in Decision Making," *Academy of Management Journal*, vol. 27 (1984): 130–38; Ian I. Mitroff, Paul Shrivastava, and Firdaus E. Udwadia, "Effective Crisis Management," *Academy of Management Executive*, vol. 1 (1987): 283–92.

[20] John Huey, "In Search of Roberto's Secret Formula," *Fortune*, December 29, 1997, 230–34.

[21] See Hugh Courtney, Jane Kirkland, and Patrick Viguerie, "Strategy Under Uncertainty," *Harvard Business Review*, November–December 1997, pp. 67–79.

[22] For a good discussion, see Weston H. Agor, *Intuition in Organizations: Leading and Managing Productively* (Newbury Park, CA: Sage, 1989); Herbert A Simon, "Making Management Decisions: The Role of Intuition and Emotion," *Academy of Management Executive*, vol. 1 (1987): 57–64; Orlando Behling and Norman L. Eckel, "Making Sense Out of Intuition," *Academy of Management Executive*, vol. 5 (1991): 46–54.

[23] Agor, *Intuition in Organizations*, 1989, p. 11.

[24] Daniel J. Isenberg, "How Senior Managers Think," *Harvard Business Review*, vol. 62 (November–December, 1984): 81–90.

[25] Daniel J. Isenberg, "The Tactics of Strategic Opportunism," *Harvard Business Review*, vol. 65 (March–April 1987): 92–97.

[26] See George P. Huber, *Managerial Decision Making* (Glenview, IL: Scott, Foresman 1975). For a comparison, see the steps in Xerox's problem-solving process as described in "David A. Garvin, "Building a Learning Organization," *Harvard Business Review*, July–August 1993, pp. 78–91.

[27] Peter F. Drucker, *Innovation and Entrepreneurship: Practice and Principles* (New York: Harper & Row, 1985).

[28] Peter F. Drucker, "Marketing for a Fast-Changing Decade," *Wall Street Journal* November 20, 1990, p. A20.

[29] For a sample of Simon's work, see Herbert A. Simon, *Administrative Behavior* (New York: Free Press, 1947); James G. March and Herbert A. Simon, *Organizations* (New York: Wiley, 1958); Herbert A. Simon, *The New Science of Management Decision* (New York: Harper, 1960); Simon, ("Making Management Decisions,") 1987.

[30] This presentation is based on the work of R. H. Hogarth, D. Kahneman, A. Tversky, and others, as discussed in Max H. Bazerman, *Judgment in Managerial Decision Making*, 3d ed. (New York: Wiley, 1994).

[31] Barry M. Staw, "The Escalation of Commitment to a Course of Action," *Academy of Management Review*, vol. 6 (1981): 577–87; Barry M. Staw and Jerry Ross, "Knowing When to Pull the Plug," *Harvard Business Review*, vol. 65 (March–April 1987): 68–74.

[32] Incident reported in "Behind the UPS Mystique: Puritanism and Productivity," *Business Week*, June 6, 1983, p. 66.

[33] Peter F. Drucker, "The Future That has Already Happened," *Harvard Business Review*, vol. 75 (September–October 1997): 20–24.

[34] Peter F. Drucker, Esther Dyson, Charles Handy, Paul Daffo, and Peter M. Senge, "Looking Ahead: Implications of the Present," *Harvard Business Review*, vol. 75 (September–October, 19).

[35] Steven E. Prokesch, "Unleashing the Power of Learning," *Harvard Business Review* September–October 1997, pp. 147–68.

[36] Peter Senge, *The Fifth Discipline* (New York: Harper, 1990).

[37] Ibid.

[38] Prokesch, "Unleashing," 1997.

[39] Richard Waters, "Own Words: Jack Welch, General Electric," *Financial Times*, October 1, 1997.

[40] Thomas A. Stewart, "Gray Flannel Suit?" *Fortune*, March 16, 1998, pp. 76–82.

[41] See, for example, Thomas H. Davenport and Laurence Prusak, *Working Knowledge: How Organizations Manage What They Know* (Cambridge, MA: Harvard Business School Press, 1997).

[42] Hal Lancaster, "Contributors to Pools of Company Know-How Are Valued Employees," *The Wall Street Journal* (December 9, 1997), p. B1; Thomas A. Stewart, "Is This Job Really Necessary?" *Fortune* (January 12, 1998), pp. 154–155.

[43] "In Terms of Business, 'Knowledge Management' Gaining Ground," *AACSB Newsline* (Fall 1997).

[44] Waters, op. cit., 1997.

Chapter 4 Notes

[1] Pauline Graham, *Mary Parker Follett—Prophet of Management: A Celebration of Writings from the 1920's* (Boston: Harvard Business School Press, 1995). See also Dana Wechsler Linden, "The Mother of Them All," *Forbes*, January 16, 1995, pp. 75–76.

[2] For a time line of twentieth-century management ideas see "75 Years of Management Ideas and Practices: 1922–1997," *Harvard Business Review*, supplement, September–October 1997.

[3] A thorough review and critique of the history of management thought, including management in ancient civilizations, is provided by Daniel A. Wren, *The Evolution of Management Thought*, 4th ed. (New York: Wiley, 1993); see also Daniel A. Wren and John A. Pearce II (eds.), *Papers Dedicated to the Development of Modern Management: Celebrating 100 Years of Modern Management* (Mississippi State, Academy of Management, 1986).

[4] For a sample of this work see Henry L. Gantt, *Industrial Leadership* (Easton, MD: Hive, 1921; Hive edition published in 1974); Henry C. Metcalfe and Lyndall Urwick (eds.), *Dynamic Administration: The Collected Papers of Mary Parker Follett* (New York: Harper & Brothers, 1940); James D. Mooney, *The Principles of Administration*, rev. ed. (New York: Harper & Brothers, 1947); Lyndall Urwick, *The Elements of Administration* (New York: Harper & Brothers, 1943) and *The Golden Book of Management* (London: N. Neame, 1956).

[5] References on Taylor's work are from Frederick W. Taylor, *The Principles of Scientific Management* (New York: W. W. Norton, 1967), originally published by Harper & Brothers in 1911. See Charles W. Wrege and Amedeo G. Perroni, "Taylor's Pig-Tale: A Historical Analysis of Frederick W. Taylor's Pig-Iron Experiments," *Academy of Management Journal*, vol. 17 (March 1974): 6–27, for a criticism; see Edwin A. Lock, "The Ideas of Frederick W. Taylor: An Evaluation," *Academy of Management Review*, vol. 7 (1982): p. 14, for an examination of the contemporary significance of Taylor's work. See also the recent biography, Robert Kanigel, *The One Best Way* (New York: Viking, 1997).

[6] Kanigel, *One Best Way*.

[7] Information from *Fortune*, October 22, 1990, p. 124.

[8] See Frank B. Gilbreth, *Motion Study* (New York: Van Nostrand, 1911).

[9] Information from *Fortune*, January 18, 1989.

[10] Available in the English language as Henri Fayol, *General and Industrial Administration* (London: Pitman, 1949); subsequent discussion is based on M. B. Brodie, *Fayol on Administration* (London: Pitman, 1949).

[11] M. P. Follett, *Freedom and Coordination* (London: Management Publications Trust, 1949). Discussion developed in part from Judith Garwood, "A Review of Dynamic Administration: The Collected Papers of Mary Parker Follett," New Management, vol. 2 (1984): 61–62; eulogy from Richard C. Cabot, *Encyclopedia of Social Work*, vol. 15, s.v., "Follett, Mary Parker," p. 351.

[12] Garwood, op. cit. *New Management*.

[13] A. M. Henderson and Talcott Parsons (eds. and trans.), *Max Weber: The Theory of Social Economic Organization* (New York: The Free Press, 1947).

[14] Ibid., p. 337.

[15] The Hawthorne studies are described in detail in F. J. Roethlisberger and William J. Dickson, *Management and the Worker* (Cambridge: Harvard University Press, 1966) and G. Homans, *Fatigue of Workers* (New York: Reinhold, 1941). For an interview with three of the participants in the relay-assembly testroom studies, see R. G. Greenwood, A. A. Bolton, and R. A. Greenwood, "Hawthorne a Half Century Later: "Relay Assembly Participants Remember," *Journal of Management*, vol. 9 (1983): 217–31.

[16] The criticisms of the Hawthorne studies are detailed in Alex Carey, "The Hawthorne Studies: A Radical Criticism," *American Sociological Review*, vol. 32 (1967): 403–16; H. M. Parsons, "What Happened at Hawthorne?" *Science*, vol. 183 (1974): 922–32; B. Rice, "The Hawthorne Defect: Persistence of a Flawed Theory," *Psychology Today*, vol. 16 (1982): 70–74. See also Wren, *Evolution*.

[17] This discussion of Maslow's theory is based on Abraham H. Maslow, *Eupsychian Management* (Homewood, IL: Richard D. Irwin, 1965), and Abraham H. Maslow, *Motivation and Personality*, 2d ed. (New York: Harper & Row, 1970).

[18] Information from *Training*, June 1991, pp. 21–26.

[19] Douglas McGregor, *The Human Side of Enterprise* (New York: McGraw-Hill, 1960).

[20] Information from R. Roosevelt Thomas Jr., "From Affirmative Action to Affirming Diversity," *Harvard Business Review*, March–April 1990, pp. 107–17, and corporate communication, 1998.

[21] Chris Argyris, *Personality and Organization* (New York: Harper & Row, 1957).

22 The ideas of Ludwig von Bertalanffy contributed to the emergence of this systems perspective on organizations. See his article, "The History and Status of General Systems Theory," *Academy of Management Journal*, vol. 15 (1972): 407–26. This viewpoint is further developed by Daniel Katz and Robert L. Kahn in their classic book, *The Social Psychology of Organizations* (New York: Wiley, 1978). For an integrated systems view, see Lane Tracy, *The Living Organization* (New York: Quorum Books, 1994). For an overview, see W. Richard Scott, *Organizations: Rational, Natural, and Open Systems*, 4th ed. (Upper Saddle River, NJ: Prentice-Hall, 1998).

23 Peter F. Drucker, "The Future That has Already Happened," *Harvard Business Review*, vol. 75 (September–October 1997): 20–24.

24 For an overview see Scott, *Organizations*.

25 Jay R. Galbraith, *Organizational Design* (Reading, MA: Addison-Wesley, 1977).

26 See W. Edwards Deming, *Quality, Productivity, and Competitive Position* (Cambridge, MA: MIT Press, 1982); Joseph M. Juran, *Quality Control Handbook*, 3d ed. (New York: McGraw-Hill 1979).

27 Thomas J. Peters and Robert H. Waterman Jr., *In Search of Excellence: Lessons from America's Best-run Companies* (New York: Harper & Row, 1982).

28 Information from Justin Martin, "Mercedes: Made in Alabama," *Fortune* (July 7, 1997), pp. 150–58; "A Plant Grows in Alabama," *Mercedes Momentum* (Spring, 1998), pp. 56–61.

29 William Ouchi, *Theory Z: How American Businesses Can Meet the Japanese Challenge* (Reading, MA: Addison-Wesley, 1981) and Richard Tanner Pascale and Anthony G. Athos, *The Art of Japanese Management: Applications for American Executives* (New York: Simon & Schuster, 1981).

30 Ouchi, op cit., 1981; see also the review by J. Bernard Keys, Luther Tray Denton, and Thomas R. Miller, "The Japanese Management Theory Jungle-Revisited," *Journal of Management*, Vol. 20 (1994), pp. 373–402.

31 John Gardner, *No Easy Victories* (New York: Harper & Row, 1968).

32 "The 21st Century Executive," *U.S. News & World Report* (May 7, 1988), pp. 48–56.

33 Peter F. Drucker, "Looking Ahead: Implications of the Present," *Harvard Business Review* (September–October, 1997), pp. 18–32.

34 Ralph Z. Sorenson, "A Lifetime of Learning to Manage Effectively," *Wall Street Journal* (February 28, 1983), p. 18.

Chapter 5 Notes

1 See, for example, Hal Lancaster, "Learning to Manage in a Global Marketplace," *The Wall Street Journal* (June 2, 1998), p. B1.

2 See Kenichi Ohmae, *The Evolving Global Economy* (Cambridge, Mass.: Harvard Business School Press, 1995).

3 Rosabeth Moss Kanter, *World Class: Thinking Locally in the Global Economy* (New York: Simon & Schuster, 1995), preface.

4 For an overview see "Europe's Mid-Life Crisis," *The Economist: A Survey of the European Union* (May 31, 1997).

5 "Special Report: The Euro," *Business Week* (April 27, 1998), pp. 90–94.

6 Information from Dana Milbank, "New Competitor: East Europe Industry Is Raising Its Quality and Taking on West," *Wall Street Journal*, September 21, 1994, pp. 1, A4.

7 Michael L. Wheeler, "Global Diversity: Reality, Opportunity, and Challenge," *Business Week*, special report, December 1, 1997.

8 A monthly publication that covers the *maquiladora* industries is the *Twin Plant News* (El Paso, Texas).

9 Joel Millman, "High-Tech Jobs Transfer to Mexico with Surprising Speed," *Wall Street Journal*, April 9, 1998, p. A18.

10 Scott Shuster, "The Business Future of the Americas," *Business Week*, April 27, 1998, special advertising section.

11 See "Latin America: A Region in Transition," *Global Business White Papers No. 6*, The Conference Board (October 1992); and Sarita Kendall and Nancy Dunne, "Business Spurs All-America Free Trade Accord," *Financial Times*, March 22, 1996, p. 3.

12 Scott Shuster, "The Business Future of the Americas," *Business Week*, April 27, 1998, special advertising section; and Kerry Capell, "What a 'Euro' Could Do for the Latins," *Business Week*, April 13, 1998, p. 100.

13 "Special Report: The Growing Power of Asia," *Fortune*, October 7, 1991, pp. 118–60; "Special Report: Asia—The Next Era of Growth," *Business Week*, November 11, 1991, pp. 56–68. See also Jim Rohwer, *Asia Rising: Why America Will Prosper as Asia's Economies Boom*, (New York: Simon & Schuster, 1995); and John Frankenstein, special report, "The Business of Business: Values and Outlook," *Far Eastern Economic Review*, August 7, 1997.

14 "Asian Crisis Offers Unexpected Opportunities," *Wall Street Journal*, April 23, 1998, p. B17.

15 See "The China Syndrome," *The Economist* (June 21, 1997), p. 63; "Time for Plain Talk," *Business Week* (June 22, 1998), pp. 54–56.

16 Mike Pramik, "Salient's Dealings in China Illustrate Need to Prepare for Differing Practices," *Columbus Dispatch*, May 4, 1998, p. 3.

17 See George B. N. Ayittey, "African Thugs Kept their Continent Poor," *Wall Street Journal*, January 2, 1998, p. 8. Paul Magnusson and Dean Foust, "Don't Waste a Huge Opportunity on Africa," *Business Week*, April 6, 1998, p. 37.

18 Michael M. Phillips, "Into Africa," *Wall Street Journal*, September 18, 1997, pp. R6, R20.

19 See Helene Cooper, "Sub-Saharan Africa Is Seen as Big Loser in GATT New World Trade Accord," *Wall Street Journal*, August 15, 1994, p. A7.

20 Information from Mort Rosenblum, "Turnaround: Once a Basket Case, Mozambique now a Free-Market Example," *The Columbus Dispatch* (December 14, 1997), p. 4c.

21 James A. Austin and John G. McLean, "Pathways to Business Success in Sub-Saharan Africa," *Journal of African Finance and Economic Development*, Vol. 2 (1996), pp. 57–76.

22 Information from "International Business: Consider Africa," *Harvard Business Review*, Vol. 76 (January–February 1998), pp. 16–18.

23 Udayan Gupta, "African-American Firms Gain Foothold in South Africa," *The Wall Street Journal* (October 6, 1994), p. B2; Ken Wells, "U.S. Investment in South Africa Quickens," *The Wall Street Journal* (October 6, 1994), p. A14.

24 Information from Magnusson and Foust, op cit., 1998.

25 *Business Week*, February 29, 1988, pp. 63–66.

26 "Best Practices for Global Competitiveness," *Fortune*, March 30, 1998, pp. S1–S3, special advertising section.

27 Anthony J. F. O'Reilly, "Establishing Successful Joint Ventures in Developing Nations: A CEO's Perspective," *Columbia Journal of World Business*, spring 1988, pp. 65–71; and "Best Practices for Global Competitiveness," *Fortune*, March 30, 1998, pp. S1–S3, special advertising section.

28 See, for example, "The Global Giants," *Wall Street Journal*, September 19, 1997, pp. R24–R27; "1997 Global 500," *Fortune*, August 4, 1997, pp. 119–25; and Anne Fisher, "The World's Most Admired Companies," *Fortune*, October 27, 1997, pp. 220–40. Such reports are published annually by these and other business periodicals.

29 Carl Quintanilla, "Profit of 3M to Disappoint," *Wall Street Journal*, December 18, 1997, p. A3.

30 This framework is introduced in David P. Rutenberg, *Multinational Management*, Boston: Little, Brown, 1982.

31 Peter F. Drucker, "The Global Economy and the Nation-State," *Foreign Affairs*, vol. 76 (September–October 1997): 159–71.

32 Information from "Borderless Management: Companies Strive to Become Truly Stateless," *Business Week*, May 23, 1994, pp. 24–26; Oscar Suris, "Behind the Wheel," *Wall Street Journal*, November 18, 1996, pp. R14, R17.

33 Quoted from "Own Words: Percy Barnevik, ABB and Investor," *Financial Times Limited*, 1998, <http://www.ft.com/reports/vdef46.htm>.

[34] For an example of problems with state-owned enterprises in transitionary economies, see Richard Tomlin, "A Chinese Giant Forges a Capitalist Soul," *Fortune*, September 29, 1997, pp. 184–92.

[35] See "Slow Healing at Mitsubishi," *Business Week*, September 22, 1997, pp. 74–75; Ben Rand, "When Cultures Clash," *Rockland Journal-News*, October 26, 1997, p. E1.

[36] Sylvia Ann Hewlett, "The Boundaries of Business: The Human Resource Deficit," *Harvard Business Review*, July–August 1991, pp. 131–33. See also William B. Johnston, "Global Workforce 2000: The New World Labor Market," *Harvard Business Review*, March–April 1991, pp. 115–27.

[37] Data reported in "Multinational Firms Tighten Control over World Economy," *New Straits Times*, August 31, 1993, p. 16.

[38] Adapted from R. Hall Mason, "Conflicts between Host Countries and Multinational Enterprise," *California Management Review*, vol. 17 (1974): 6, 7.

[39] For a good overview, see Randall E. Stross, *Bulls in the China Shop and Other Sino-American Business Encounters* (New York: Pantheon, 1991).

[40] For a recent discussion see Craig Smith, "Foreign Investors Break Free From Chinese Partners," *The Wall Street Journal* (June 11, 1998), p. A17.

[41] *New York Times* "An Industry Monitors Child Labor," October 16, 1997, B1, B9.

[42] Examples reported in Neil Chesanow, *The World-Class Executive* (New York: Rawson Associates, 1985).

[43] Based on Barbara Benedict Bunker, "Appreciating Diversity and Modifying Organizational Cultures: Men and Women at Work," in Suresh Srivastva, David L. Cooperrider, *Appreciative Management and Leadership: The Power of Positive Thought and Action in Organizations* (San Francisco: Jossey-Bass, 1990), pp. 127–49.

[44] For a good overview of the practical issues, see Philip R. Harris and Robert T. Moran, *Managing Cultural Differences*, 2d ed. (Houston: Gulf Publishing, 1987); and Martin J. Gannon, *Understanding Global Cultures* (Thousand Oaks, CA: Sage, 1994).

[45] Information from Ronald B. Lieber, "Flying High, Going Global," *Fortune*, July 7, 1997, pp. 195–97.

[46] Edward T. Hall, *Hidden Differences* (New York: Doubleday, 1990).

[47] Geert Hofstede's research is summarized in the article, "Motivation, Leadership, and Organization: Do American Theories Apply Abroad?" *Organizational Dynamics*, vol. 9 (summer 1980): p. 43. It is presented in detail in his book *Culture's Consequences* (Beverly Hills: Sage, 1984). Hofstede and Michael H. Bond further explore Eastern and Western perspectives on national culture in their article "The Confucius Connection: From Cultural Roots to Economic Growth," *Organizational Dynamics*, vol. 16 (1988): pp. 4–21, which presents comparative data from Bond's "Chinese Values Survey."

[48] For reports on the new fifth dimension, see Hofstede and Bond, "The Confucious Connection."

[49] See John E. Rehfeld, *Alchemy of a Leader* (New York: John Wiley & Sons, 1994).

[50] Fons Trompenaars, *Riding the Waves of Culture: Understanding Cultural Diversity in Business* (London: Nicholas Brealey Publishing, 1993).

[51] See Robert B. Reich, "Who Is Them?" *Harvard Business Review*, March–April 1991, pp. 77–88.

[52] "Going International: Willett Systems Limited," *Fortune*, February 16, 1998, p. S6, special advertising section.

[53] Information from "Digital's 'Borderless Asean,'" *Business Asia*, May 19, 1997, p. 2.

[54] "Borderless Management," *Business Week*, May 23, 1994, pp. 24–26.

[55] For a perspective on the role of women in expatriate managerial assignments, see Mariann Jelinek and Nancy J. Adler, "Women: World-Class Managers for Global Competition," *Academy of Management Executive* (February 1988), pp. 11–19; for a discussion of the globalization of management careers see Lancaster, op cit., 1998.

[56] Geert Hofstede, "Motivation, Leadership, and Organization," p. 43. See also Hofstede's "Cultural Constraints in Management Theories," *Academy of Management Review*, vol. 7 (1993): 81–94.

[57] For a good discussion, see Chapters 4 and 5 in Miriam Erez and P. Christopher Early, *Culture, Self-Identity, and Work* (New York: Oxford University Press, 1993).

[58] J. Bernard Keys, Luther Tray Denton, and Thomas R. Miller, "The Japanese Management Theory Jungle—Revisited," *Journal of Management*, vol. 20 (1994): 373–402.

[59] Carla Rapoport, "Why Japan Keeps on Winning," *Fortune*, July 15, 1991, pp. 76–85.

[60] Quote from Kenichi Ohmae, "Japan's Admiration for U.S. Methods Is an Open Book," *Wall Street Journal*, October 10, 1983, p. 21. See also his book *The Borderless World: Power and Strategy in the Interlinked Economy* (New York: Harper, 1989).

[61] Geert Hofstede, "A Reply to Goodstein and Hunt," *Organizational Dynamics*, vol. 10 (summer 1981): 68.

Chapter 6 Notes

[1] See Joel Makower, *Beyond the Bottom Line: Putting Social Responsibility to Work for your Business and the World* (New York: Simon & Schuster, 1994).

[2] "Quad/Graphics's Environmental Philosophy," corporate document, Pewaukee, WI: Quad/Graphics, 1998.

[3] Larry Reynolds, "A New Job Title Is Popping Up on Executive Doors Today: Vice President of the Environment," *Business Ethics*, vol. 5 (March–April 1991): 22–24; "When Green Begets Green," *Business Week*, November 10, 1997, pp. 98–99.

[4] Reported in Adam Smith, "Wall Street's Outrageous Fortunes," *Esquire*, April 1987, p. 73.

[5] Desmond Tutu, "Do More Than Win," *Fortune*, December 30, 1991, p. 59.

[6] For an overview, see Francis Joseph Aguilar, *Managing Corporate Ethics: Learning from America's Ethical Companies How to Supercharge Business Performance* (New York: Oxford, 1994); and Linda K. Trevino and Katherine A. Nelson, *Managing Business Ethics* (New York: John Wiley & Sons, 1995).

[7] *Columbus Dispatch*, December 26, 1991, p. 6D.

[8] Tom Chappell, *The Soul of a Business: Managing for Profit and for the Common Good* (New York: Bantam Books, 1993), and Makower, *Beyond the Bottom Line*.

[9] Gerald F. Cavanagh, Dennis J. Moberg, and Manuel Velasquez, "The Ethics of Organizational Politics," *Academy of Management Review*, vol. 6 (1981): 363–74; Justin G. Longnecker, Joseph A. McKinney, and Carlos W. Moore, "Egoism and Independence: Entrepreneurial Ethics," *Organizational Dynamics* (winter 1988): 64–72; Justin G. Locknecker, Joseph A. McKinney, and Carlos W. Moore, "The Generation Gap in Business Ethics," *Business Horizons*, September–October 1989, pp. 9–14.

[10] Raymond L. Hilgert, "What Ever Happened to Ethics in Business and in Business Schools," *The Diary of Alpha Kappa Psi*, April 1989, pp. 4–8.

[11] Robert D. Haas, "Ethics—A Global Business Challenge," *Vital Speeches of the Day*, June 1, 1996, pp. 506–9.

[12] Thomas Donaldson, "Values in Tension: Ethics Away from Home," *Harvard Business Review*, vol. 74 (September–October 1996): 48–62.

[13] Thomas Donaldson and Thomas W. Dunfee, "Towards a Unified Conception of Business Ethics: Integrative Social Contracts Theory," *Academy of Management Review*, vol. 19 (1994): 252–85.

[14] Reported in Barbara Ley Toffler, "Tough Choices: Managers Talk Ethics," *New Management*, vol. 4 (1987): 34–39. See also Barbara Ley Toffler, *Tough Choices: Managers Talk Ethics* (New York: Wiley, 1986).

[15] The case and subsequent discussion are developed from Steven N. Brenner and Earl A. Mollander, "Is the Ethics of Business Changing?" *Harvard Business Review*, vol. 55 (January–February 1977): 57.

[16] Saul W. Gellerman, "Why 'Good' Managers Make Bad Ethical Choices," *Harvard Business Review*, vol. 64 (July–August, 1986): 85–90.

[17] Information from Thomas Teal, "Not a Fool, Not a Saint," *Fortune*, November 11, 1996, pp. 201–4.

[18] The Body Shop has come under recent scrutiny over the degree to which its business practices actually live up to this charter and the company's self-promoted green image. See, for example, John Entine, "Shattered Image," *Business Ethics*, September–October 1994, pp. 23–28.

[19] Information on this case from William M. Carley, "Antitrust Chief Says CEOs Should Tape all Phone Calls to Each Other," *Wall Street Journal*, February 15, 1983, p. 23; "American Air, Chief End Antitrust Suit, Agree Not to Discuss Fares with Rivals," *Wall Street Journal* (July 15, 1985), p. 4; "American Airlines Loses Its Pilot," *Economist*, April 18, 1998, p. 58.

[20] Alan L. Otten, "Ethics on the Job: Companies Alert Employees to Potential Dilemmas," *Wall Street Journal*, July 14, 1986, p. 17; and "The Business Ethics Debate," *Newsweek*, May 25, 1987, p. 36.

[21] Developed from Otten, "Ethics on the Job," and "The Business Ethics Debate," Newsweek.

[22] Timothy L. O'Brien, "Rabid Infighting Brings Dog Days to ASPCA," *Wall Street Journal*, August 3, 1994, pp. B1, B8. See also "Whistle-Blowers on Trial," *Business Week*, March 24, 1997, pp. 172–78; "NLRB Judge Rules for Massachusetts Nurses in Whistle-Blowing Case," *American Nurse*, January–February 1998, p. 7.

[23] For a good review of whistleblowing, see Marcia P. Micelli and Janet P. Near, *Blowing the Whistle* (Lexington, MA: Lexington Books, 1992); see also Micelli and Near, "Whistleblowing: Reaping the Benefits," *Academy of Management Executive*, vol. 8 (August 1994): 65–72.

[24] See "Blowing the Whistle without Paying the Piper," *Business Week*, June 3, 1991, pp. 138–40; Daniel Wesman, *Whistleblowing: The Law of Retaliatory Discharge* (New York: BNA Books); and see "Blowing the Whistle without Paying the Piper"; Daniel Wesman, *Whistleblowing*.

[25] Information from James A. Waters, "Catch 20.5: Mortality as an Organizational Phenomenon," *Organizational Dynamics*, vol. 6 (spring 1978): 3–15.

[26] "Robert D. Gilbreath, "The Hollow Executive," *New Management*, vol. 4 (1987): 24–28.

[27] Developed from recommendations of the Government Accountability Project reported in "Blowing the Whistle without Paying the Piper."

[28] All reported in Charles D. Pringle and Justin G. Longnecker, "The Ethics of MBO," *Academy of Management Review*, vol. 7 (April 1982); 309. See also Barry Z. Posner and Warren H. Schmidt, "Values and the American Manager: An Update," *California Management Review*, vol. 26 (spring 1984): 202–16.

[29] See Rick Wartzman, "Nature or Nurture? Study Blames Ethical Lapses on Corporate Goals," *Wall Street Journal*, October 9, 1987, p. 21; Amanda Bennett, "Ethics Codes Spread Despite Criticism," *Wall Street Journal*, July 15, 1988, p. 13.

[30] "The Walt Disney Company Code of Conduct for Manufacturers," corporate document, <http://www.disney.com/Business_Info/codes_manufacturers.htm>.

[31] Developed from a discussion in Makower, *Beyond the Bottom Line*, pp. 17–18.

[32] The historical framework of this discussion is developed from Keith Davis, "The Case for and against Business Assumption of Social Responsibility," *Academy of Management Journal*, June 1973, pp. 312–22; Keith Davis and William Frederick, *Business and Society: Management: Public Policy, Ethics*, 5th ed. (New York: McGraw-Hill, 1984). The debate is also discussed by Makower, *Beyond the Bottom Line* pp. 28–33. See also, "Civics 101," *Economist*, May 11, 1996, p. 61.

[33] The Friedman quotation is from Milton Friedman, *Capitalism and Freedom* (Chicago: University of Chicago Press, 1962); the Samuelson quotation is from Paul A. Samuelson, "Love That Corporation," *Mountain Bell Magazine*, spring 1971. Both are cited in Davis, "The Case for and against."

[34] Davis and Frederick, *Business and Society*.

[35] "Tom's of Maine: Company Overview," Kennebunk, Maine: Tom's of Maine, 1998.

[36] See Makower, op cit., 1994, pp. 71–75; and Sandra A. Waddock and Samuel B. Graves, "The Corporate Social Performance-Financial Performance Link," *Strategic Management Journal* (1997), pp. 303–319.

[37] Davis, op cit.

[38] Archie B. Carroll, "A Three-Dimensional Model of Corporate Performance," *Academy of Management Review*, vol. 4 (1979): 497–505.

[39] Information from G. Pascal Zachary, "Exporting Rights: Levi Tries to Make Sure Contract Plants in Asia Treat Workers Well," *Wall Street Journal*, July 28, 1994, pp. A1, A6; and "Managing by Values," *Business Week*, August 1, 1994, pp. 46–52. See also Jane Palley Katz, *Levi Strauss & Co.: Global Sourcing (A)* (Boston, MA.: Harvard Business School Publishing, 1996).

[40] Elizabeth Gatewood and Archie B. Carroll, "The Anatomy of Corporate Social Response," *Business Horizons*, vol. 24 (September–October 1981): 9–16.

[41] Information on Quad/Graphics from Makower, pp. 85, 121–22; and, "Quad/Graphics's Environmental Philosophy," corporate document, Pewaukee, WI: Quad/Graphics, 1998.

[42] For the other side of this issue and the support available through government sources for small businesses, see "When Bureaucrats Are a Boon," *Business Week*, Enterprise issue, September 1, 1997, pp. ENT4–6.

Chapter 7 Notes

[1] Information from T. J. Rodgers, with William Taylor and Rick Foreman, "No Excuses Management," *World Executive's Digest*, May 1994, pp. 26–30.

[2] From the *1985 Eaton Corporation Annual Report*.

[3] See U.S. Healthcare, *Annual Report 1990*, pp. 9–10; John George, "HMO Opens New Center with Service in Mind," *Philadelphia Business Journal* (October 22–28, 1990; Marcy Abramson, "Quality: Crucial to Success of the Health Care Industry," *Quality* (February 1991); Gilbert M. Gaul, "U.S. Healthcare Has Found a Prescription for Profits," *Philadelphia Inquirer* (May 14, 1991); C. Begole, "How to Get the Productivity Edge," *Working Woman* (May 1991), pp. 47–60.

[4] Henry Mintzberg, "The Manager's Job: Folklore and Fact," *Harvard Business Review*, vol. 53 (July–August 1975): 54–67; Henry Mintzberg, "Planning on the Left Side and Managing on the Right," *Harvard Business Review*, vol. 54 (July–August 1976): 46–55. U.S. Healthcare, *Annual Report 1990*, pp. 9–10; John George, "HMO Opens New Center with Service in Mind," *Philadelphia Business Journal* (October 22–28, 1990); Marcy Abramson, "Quality: Crucial to Success of the Health Care Industry," *Quality*, February 1991; Gilbert M. Gaul, "U.S. Healthcare Has Found a Prescription for Profits," *Philadelphia Inquirer*, May 14, 1991; C. Begole, "How to Get the Productivity Edge," *Working Woman*, May 1991, pp. 47–60.

[5] See Ronald Henkoff, "How to Plan for 1995," *Fortune*, December 31, 1990, pp. 70–77.

[6] Stephen Covey and Roger Merrill, "New Ways to Get Organized at Work," *USA Weekend*, February 6–8, 1998, p. 18.

[7] For a classic study, see Stanley Thune and Robert House, "Where Long-Range Planning Pays Off," *Business Horizons*, vol. 13 (1970): 81–87. For a critical review of the literature, see Milton Leontiades and Ahmet Teel, "Planning Perceptions and Planning Results," *Strategic Management Journal*, vol. 1 (1980): 65–75; J. Scott Armstrong, "The Value of Formal Planning for Strategic Decisions," *Strategic Management Journal*, vol. 3 (1982): 197–211. For special attention to the small business setting, see Richard B. Robinson Jr., John A. Pearce II, George S. Vozikis, and Timothy S. Mescon, "The Relationship between Stage of Development and Small Firm Planning and Performance," *Journal of Small Business Management*, vol. 22 (1984): 45–52; Christopher Orphen, "The Effects of Long-Range Planning on Small Business Performance: A Further Examination," *Journal of*

Small Business Management, vol. 23 (1985): 16–23. For a recent empirical study of large corporations, see Vasudevan Ramanujam and N. Venkatraman, "Planning and Performance: A New Look at an Old Question," *Business Horizons*, vol. 30 (1987): 19–25.

[8] Information from *Business Week*, August 8, 1994, pp. 78–86.

[9] R. Alex MacKenzie, *The Time Trap* (New York: AMACOMA, American Management Associations, 1972).

[10] William Oncken Jr. and Donald L. Wass, "Management Time: Who's Got the Monkey?" *Harvard Business Review*, vol. 52 (September–October, 1974): 75–80, and featured in an *HBR* retrospect, *Harvard Business Review*, vol. 65 (March–April 1987).

[11] Shelly Branch, "So Much Work, So Little Time," *Fortune*, February 3, 1997, pp. 115–17.

[12] Covey and Merrill, "New Ways to Get Organized," p. 18.

[13] See Elliot Jaques, *The Form of Time* (New York: Russak & Co., 1982). For a report on this research, see Walter Kiechel III, "How Executives Think," *Fortune*, December 21, 1987, pp. 139–44.

[14] See Henry Mintzberg, "Rounding Out the Manager's Job," *Sloan Management Review*, fall 1994, pp. 1–25.

[15] See Romuald A. Stone, "AIDS in the Workplace: An Executive Update," *Academy of Management Executive*, vol. 8 (August 1994): 52–64.

[16] "Avoiding a Time Bomb: Sexual Harassment," *Business Week*, Enterprise issue, October 13, 1997, pp. ENT20–21.

[17] "Avoiding a Time Bomb: Sexual Harassment," *Business Week*, Enterprise issue, October 13, 1997, pp. Ent20–22.

[18] Kevin Hopkins, "A Level Playing Field," *Business Week*, October 28, 1991, pp. 30–32; Gary McWilliams with Patrick Oster, "DEC Tries to Learn New Tricks in the Old World," *Business Week*, November 25, 1991, p. 38.

[19] Marcia H. Pounds, "Business Plan Sets Course for Growth," *Columbus Dispatch*, March 16, 1998, p. 9.

[20] Paul Reynolds, "The Truth about Start-Ups," *Inc.*, February 1995, p. 23.

[21] Information in Pounds, "Business Plan," as provided by the Florida Atlantic University Small Business Development Center.

[22] Dick Levin, *The Executive's Illustrated Primer of Long-Range Planning* (Englewood Cliffs, NJ: Prentice-Hall, 1981), p. 81. Reprinted by permission of Prentice-Hall, Englewood Cliffs, NJ.

[23] Christopher Farrell and Edith Updike, "So You Think the World Is Your Oyster," *Business Week*, Enterprise issue, June 9, 1997, pp. ENT4–9.

[24] Levin, *Executive's Illustrated Primer*, pp. 93–94. Reprinted by permission of Prentice-Hall, Inc., Englewood Cliffs, NJ.

[25] Russell L. Ackoff, *Management in Small Doses* (New York: Wiley, 1986).

[26] For a thorough review of forecasting, see J. Scott Armstrong, *Long-Range Forecasting*, 2d ed. (New York: Wiley, 1985).

[27] Information from Linda Grant, "GE's 'Smart Bomb' Strategy," *Fortune*, July 21, 1997, pp. 109–10.

[28] The scenario-planning approach is described in Peter Schwartz, *The Art of the Long View* (New York: Doubleday/Currency, 1991); and Arie de Geus, *The Living Company: Habits for Survival in a Turbulent Business Environment* (Boston, MA: Harvard Business School Press, 1997).

[29] Information from Schwartz, *The Art of the Long View*, and de Geus, *The Living Company*.

[30] "How Classy Can 7-Eleven Get?" *Business Week*, September 1, 1997, pp. 74–75.

[31] *Fortune*, December 31, 1990, pp. 70–78; Jack Welch, "Create a Company of Ideas," *Fortune*, December 30, 1991, p. 25.

[32] See Dale D. McConkey, *How to Manage by Results*, 3d ed. (New York: AMACOM, 1976); Stephen J. Carroll Jr. and Henry J. Tosi Jr., *Management by Objectives: Applications and Research* (New York: Macmillan, 1973); and Anthony P. Raia, *Managing by Objectives* (Glenview, IL: Scott, Foresman, 1974).

[33] Douglas McGregor, *The Human Side of Enterprise* (New York: McGraw-Hill, 1960).

[34] The work on goal setting and motivation is summarized in Edwin A. Locke and Gary P. Latham, *Goal Setting: A Motivational Technique That Works!* (Englewood Cliffs, NJ: Prentice-Hall, 1984).

[35] For a discussion of research, see Carroll and Tosi, *Management by Objectives*; Raia, *Managing by Objectives*; 1974; Steven Kerr, "Overcoming the Dysfunctions of MBO," *Management by Objectives* 5, no. 1 (1976).

[36] Quotes from Levin, *Executive's Illustrated Primer*, p. 14.

Chapter 8 Notes

[1] Bill Saporito, "Is Wal-Mart Unstoppable?" *Fortune*, May 6, 1991, pp. 50–59; Janice Castro, "Mr. Sam Stuns Goliath," *Time*, February 25, 1991, pp. 62–63; Bob Ortega, Dillard, "Wal-Mart and Cifra in Venture to Open Department Stores in Mexico," *Wall Street Journal*, October 17, 1994, p. B5; Louise Lee and Cacilie Rohwedder, "Wal-Mart to Acquire German Retailer, Moving into Europe for the First Time, *Wall Street Journal*, December 19, 1997, pp. A2, A10.

[2] Gary Hamel and C. K. Prahalad, "Strategic Intent," *Harvard Business Review*, May–June, 1989, pp. 63–76.

[3] See Michael E. Porter, *Competitive Strategy: Techniques for Analyzing Industries and Competitors* (New York: The Free Press, 1980), and *Competitive Advantage: Creating and Sus-taining Superior Performance* (New York: The Free Press, 1986); and Richard A. D'Aveni, *Hyper-Competition: Managing the Dynamics of Strategic Maneuvering* (New York: The Free Press, 1994).

[4] Hugh Courtney, Jane Kirkland, and Patrick Viguerie, "Strategy under Uncertainty," *Harvard Business Review*, November–December 1997, pp. 97–79.

[5] D'Aveni, *Hyper-Competition* p. 28.

[6] "Memorable Memo: McDonald's Sends Operators to War on Fries," *Wall Street Journal*, December 18, 1997, p. B1.

[7] Robert M. Grant, *Contemporary Strategy Analysis: Concepts, Techniques, Applications* (Cambridge, MA: Blackwell Publishers, 1995), pp. 8–10, 26.

[8] Peter F. Drucker, "Five Questions," *Executive Excellence*, November 6, 1994, pp. 6–7.

[9] Peter F. Drucker, *Management: Tasks, Responsibilities, Practices* (New York: Harper & Row, 1973), p. 122.

[10] Ibid.

[11] See Laura Nash, "Mission Statements—Mirrors and Windows," *Harvard Business Review*, (March–April 1988), pp. 155–56. Russell L. Ackoff, *Management in Small Doses* (New York: Wiley, 1986), pp. 38–42, offers additional thoughts on the purposes served by corporate mission statements. See also James C. Collins and Jerry I. Porras, "Building Your Company's Vision," *Harvard Business Review*, September–October, 1996, pp. 65–77.

[12] Collins and Porras, "Building Your Company's Vision," p. 69.

[13] *Baxter International Annual Report*, 1993.

[14] Terrence E. Deal and Allen A. Kennedy, *Corporate Cultures: The Rites and Rituals of Corporate Life* (Reading, MA: Addison-Wesley, 1982), p. 22. For a good additional review of corporate culture, see also Ralph H. Killmann, M. J. Saxon, and R. Serpa (eds.), *Managing Corporate Cultures* (San Francisco: Jossey-Bass, 1985).

[15] Collins and Porras, "Building Your Company's Vision," p. 68.

[16] Peter F. Drucker's views on organizational objectives are expressed in his classic books, *The Practice of Management* (New York: Harper & Row, 1954); and *Management: Tasks, Responsibilities, Practices* (New York: Harper & Row, 1973). For a more recent commentary, see his article, "Management: The Problems of Success," *Academy of Management Executive*, vol. 1 (1987): 13–19.

[17] C. K. Prahalad and Gary Hamel, "The Core Competencies of the Corporation," *Harvard Business Review*, May–June 1990, pp. 79–91.

[18] Information on Starbucks from "Starbucks: Making Values Pay," *Fortune*, September 29, 1997, pp. 261–72; Howard Schultz and Dori Jones Yang, *Pour Your Heart Into It* (San Francisco: Hyperion, 1997); and, Starbucks Com-

pany Fact Sheet, Seattle, WA: Starbucks, 1998.

19 For a good discussion, see Grant, *Contemporary Strategy Analysis*, pp. 41–43.

20 Julian Baum, "Riding High," *Far Eastern Economic Review*, May 7, 1998, pp. 58–59.

21 The four grand strategies were originally described by William F. Glueck, *Business Policy: Strategy Formulation and Management Action*, 2d ed. (New York: McGraw-Hill, 1976). For a discussion of strategy alternatives, see Peter Wright, Mark J. Kroll, and John Parnell, *Strategic Management Concepts* (Upper Saddle River, NJ: Prentice-Hall, 1998).

22 Neil King Jr., "A Soviet Defense Giant Saw the Inevitable and Decided to Diversify," *Wall Street Journal*, January 2, 1998, pp. 1, 4.

23 D'Aveni, *Hyper-Competition*, pp. 13–16, 21–24.

24 D' Aveni, *Hyper-Competition*.

25 Richard G. Hammermesh, "Making Planning Strategic," *Harvard Business Review*, vol. 64 (July–August 1986): 115–120.

26 See Gerald B. Allan, "A Note on the Boston Consulting Group Concept of Competitive Analysis and Corporate Strategy," Harvard Business School, Intercollegiate Case Clearing House, ICCH9-175-175 (Boston: Harvard Business School, June 1976).

27 For a discussion of Michael Porter's approach to strategic planning, see his books *Competitive Strategy, and Competitive Advantage*; and his *Harvard Business Review* article,.

28 Information from Suzanne Steel, "Quality in Bloom," *Business Today*, August 22, 1994, pp. 1–2.

29 The adaptive model is described in Raymond E. Miles and Charles C. Snow's book, *Organizational Strategy, Structure, and Process* (New York: McGraw-Hill, 1978); and their articles, "Designing Strategic Human Resources Systems," *Organizational Dynamics*, vol. 13 (summer 1984): 36–52, and "Fit, Failure, and the Hall of Fame," *California Management Review*, vol. 26 (spring 1984): 10–28.

30 See George V. Potts, "Exploit Your Product's Life Cycle," *Harvard Business Review*, September–October 1988, pp. 32–36.

31 James Brian Quinn, "Strategic Change: Logical Incrementalism," *Sloan Management Review*, vol. 20 (fall 1978): 7–21.

32 Henry Mintzberg, *The Nature of Managerial Work* (New York: Harper & Row, 1973); John R. P. Kotter, *The General Managers* (New York: The Free Press, 1982).

33 Henry Mintzberg, "Planning on the Left Side and Managing on the Right," *Harvard Business Review*, vol. 54 (July–August 1976): 46–55; Henry Mintzberg and James A. Waters, "Of Strategies, Deliberate and Emergent," *Strategic Management Journal*, vol. 6 (1985): 257–72; Henry Mintzberg, "Crafting Strategy," *Harvard Business Review*, vol. 65 (July–August 1987): 66–75.

34 For research support, see Daniel H. Gray, "Uses and Misuses of Strategic Planning," *Harvard Business Review*, vol. 64 (January–February 1986): 89–97.

35 Developed from Levin, *Executive's Illustrated Primer*, pp. 98–100; David A. Aaker, "How to Select a Business Strategy," *California Management Review*, vol. 26 (spring 1984): 167–75.

36 Wright, Kroll, and Parnell, 239.

37 Jon R. Katzenbach, "The Myth of the Top Management Team," *Harvard Business Review*, November–December 1997, pp. 82–91.

38 For a discussion of corporate governance issues, see Hugh Sherman and Rajeswararao Chaganti, *Corporate Governance and the Timeliness of Change* (Westport, CT: Quorum Books, 1998).

39 See, for example, Donald F. Kuratko and Richard M. Hodgetts, *Entrepreneurship: A Contemporary Approach* (Chicago: The Dryden Press, 1989).

40 Based on Charles R. Kuehl and Peggy A. Lambing, *Small Business: Planning and Management*, 2d ed. (Chicago: The Dryden Press, 1990), p. 39. See also Matthew C. Sonfield and Robert N. Lussier, "The Entrepreneurial Strategy Matrix," *Business Horizons*, May–June, 1997, pp. 73–77.

41 See *The State of Small Business: A Report of the President* (Washington, D.C.: U.S. Government Printing Office, 1988); and *The Small Business Forum* (Winter 1991).

42 See, for example, William A. Sahlman, "How to Write a Good Business Plan," *Harvard Business Review* (July–August 1997), pp. 98–108.

43 Christopher Farrell, "When Bureaucrats Are a Boon," *Business Week*, Enterprise issue (September 1, 1997), pp. ENT4–6.

44 Ibid.

45 Gifford Pinchot III, *Intrapreneuring, or Why You Don't Have to Leave the Corporation to Become an Entrepreneur* (New York: Harper & Row, 1985).

Chapter 9 Notes

1 Information from Thomas Petzinger Jr., "How a Ski Maker on a Slippery Slope Regained Control," *Wall Street Journal*, October 3, 1997, p. 3.

2 "The Renewal Factor: Friendly Fact, Congenial Controls," *Business Week*, September 14, 1987, p. 105.

3 Information from Raju Narisetti, "For IBM, a Groundbreaking Sales Chief," *Wall Street Journal*, January 19, 1998, pp. B1, B5.

4 See, for example, Robert C. Camp, *Business Process Benchmarking* (Milwaukee: ASQ Quality Press 1994); Michael J. Spendolini, *The Benchmarking Book* (New York: AMACOM, 1992); and Christopher E. Bogan and Michael J. English, *Benchmarking for Best Practices; Winning through Innovative Adaptation* (New York: McGraw-Hill, 1994).

5 Toddi Gutner, "Better Your Business: Benchmark It," *Business Week*, Enterprise issue (April 27, 1998), pp. ENT4–6.

6 Information from Leon E. Wynter, "Allstate Rates Managers on Handling Diversity," *Wall Street Journal*, October 1, 1997, p. B1.

7 Information from Raymond W. Smith, "Business as War Game: A Report from the Battlefront," *Fortune* (September 30, 1996), pp. 190–191.

8 Example from Cortlandt Cammann and David A. Nadler, "Fit Control Systems to Your Management Style," *Harvard Business Review*, vol. 54 (January–February, 1976), pp. 65–72.

9 Adapted from Harold Koontz and Cyril O'Donnell, *Essentials of Management* (New York: McGraw-Hill, 1974), pp. 362–365.

10 See William Newman, *Constructive Control: Design and Use of Control Systems* (Englewood Cliffs, NJ: Prentice-Hall, 1975).

11 See John F. Love, *McDonald's: Behind the Arches* (New York: Bantam Books, 1986; and William McGurn, "Burger Boom," *Far Eastern Economic Review*, November 20, 1997, pp. 66–69.

12 Ibid.

13 Ibid.

14 Information from Louis Lee, "I'm Proud of What I've Made Myself Into—What I've Created," *Wall Street Journal*, August 27, 1997, pp. B1, B5.

15 Douglas McGregor, *The Human Side of Enterprise* (New York: McGraw-Hill, 1960).

16 Cited in Peter F. Drucker, *Management: Tasks, Responsibilities, and Practices* (New York: Harper & Row, 1973), p. 797.

17 See Jeremy Main, "The Battle over Benefits," *Fortune*, December 16, 1991, pp. 91–96.

18 Eric L. Harvey, "Discipline vs. Punishment," *Management Review*, vol. 76 (March 1987): 25–29.

19 The "hot stove rules" are developed from R. Bruch McAfee and William Poffenberger, *Productivity Strategies: Enhancing Employee Job Performance* (Englewood Cliffs, NJ: Prentice-Hall, 1982), pp. 54–55. They are originally attributed to Douglas McGregor, "Hot Stove Rules of Discipline," in *Personnel: The Human Problems of Management*, G. Strauss and L. Sayles, eds. (Englewood Cliffs, NJ: Prentice-Hall, 1967).

20 Shawn Tully, "Purchasing's New Muscle," *Fortune*, February 20, 1995, p. 75.

21 Claudia H. Deutsch, "Taking Penny-Pinching to the Next Level," *New York Times* (November 6, 1996), p. C1.

22 Information from Myron Magnet, "The New Golden Rule of Business," *Fortune*, February 21, 1994, pp. 60–64.

[23] Richard J. Schonberger, "A Revolutionary Way to Streamline the Factory," *Wall Street Journal*, November 15, 1982, p. 24; see also, Richard J. Schonberger, *World Class Manufacturing: The Next Decade* (New York: The Free Press, 1996).

[24] Information from "ISO 9000 Update," *Fortune*, September 30, 1996, p. 134.

[25] See General Electric annual report for 1997.

Chapter 10 Notes

[1] Information from Richard Teitelbaum, "The Wal-Mart of Wall Street," *Fortune*, October 13, 1997, pp. 128–30.

[2] See James O'Toole, *Vanguard Organizations* (New York: Doubleday, 1985); and Robert W. Kerdel, "Rethinking Organizational Design," *Academy of Management Executive*, vol. 8 (1994): 12–29.

[3] The classic work is Alfred D. Chandler, *Strategy and Structure* (Cambridge, MA: MIT Press, 1962).

[4] See Alfred D. Chandler Jr., "Origins of the Organization Chart," *Harvard Business Review*, March–April 1988, pp. 156–57.

[5] For a good discussion see David Krackhardt and Jeffrey R. Hanson, "Informal Networks: The Company behind the Chart," *Harvard Business Review*, July–August 1993, pp. 104–11.

[6] Maggie Jackson, "Work's Lessons Occurring in Unexpected Places," *Rockland Journal-News*, January 7, 1998, pp. 4A, 4E.

[7] See Kenneth Noble, "A Clash of Styles: Japanese Companies in the U.S," *New York Times*, January 25, 1988, p. 7.

[8] For a discussion of departmentalization, see H. I. Ansoff and R. G. Bradenburg, "A Language for Organization Design," *Management Science*, vol. 17 (August 1971): B705–B731; Mariann Jelinek, "Organization Structure: The Basic Conformations," in *Organizations by Design: Theory and Practice*, Mariann Jelinek, Joseph A. Litterer, and Raymond E. Miles, eds. (Plano, TX: Business Publications, 1981), pp. 293–302; Henry Mintzberg, "The Structuring of Organizations," in *The Strategy Process: Concepts, Contexts, and Cases*, James Brian Quinn, Henry Mintzberg, and Robert M. James, eds. (Englewood Cliffs, NJ: Prentice-Hall, 1988), pp. 276–304.

[9] Robert L. Simison, "Jaguar Slowly Sheds Outmoded Habits," *Wall Street Journal*, July 26, 1991, p. A6; and Richard Stevenson, "Ford Helps Jaguar Get Back Old Sheen," *International Herald Tribune*, December 14, 1994, p. 11.

[10] These alternatives are well described by Mintzberg, "The Structuring of Organizations."

[11] Information from "*Worthington Industries*' Philosophy," corporate document, 1998.

[12] Michael Hammer, *Beyond Reengineering* (New York: Harper Business, 1996).

[13] Excellent reviews of matrix concepts are found in Stanley M. Davis and Paul R. Lawrence, *Matrix* (Reading, MA: Addison-Wesley, 1977); Paul R. Lawrence, Harvey F. Kolodny, and Stanley M. Davis, "The Human Side of the Matrix," *Organizational Dynamics*, vol. 6 (1977): 43–61; Harvey F. Kolodny, "Evolution to a Matrix Organization," *Academy of Management Review*, vol. 4 (1979): 543–53.

[14] Davis and Lawrence, *Matrix*.

[15] Ibid.

[16] Susan Albers Mohrman, Susan G. Cohen, and Allan M. Mohrman Jr., *Designing Team-Based Organizations* (San Francisco: Jossey-Bass, 1996).

[17] See Glenn M. Parker, *Cross-Functional Teams* (San Francisco: Jossey-Bass, 1995).

[18] See Rahul Jacob, "The Struggle to Create an Organization for the 21st Century," *Fortune*, April 3, 1995, pp. 90–100.

[19] Jon R. Katzenbach and Douglas K. Smith, "The Discipline of Teams," *Harvard Business Review*, March–April 1993, pp. 111–20.

[20] Information from William Bridges, "The End of the Job," *Fortune*, September 19, 1994, pp. 62–74; Alan Deutschman, "The Managing Wisdom of High-Tech Superstars," *Fortune*, October 17, 1994, pp. 197–206.

[21] See Ron Ashkenas, Dave Ulrich, Todd Jick, Steve Kerr, *The Boundaryless Organization: Breaking the Chains of Organizational Structure* (San Francisco: Jossey-Bass, 1996); Rupert F. Chisholm, *Developing Network Organizations: Learning from Practice and Theory* (Reading, MA: Addison Wesley, 1998).

[22] Information from Thomas Petzinger Jr., "June Holley Brings a Touch of Italy to Appalachian Effort," *The Wall Street Journal* (October 24, 1997), p. B1.

[23] See, for example, "Outsourcing: The New Midas Touch," Special Supplement, *Business Week* (December 15, 1997).

[24] See "The Odd Couple of Steel," *Business Week* (November 7, 1994), pp. 106–108; and "Go-Go Goliaths," *Business Week* (February 13, 1995), pp. 64–70.

[25] David Van Fleet, "Span of Management Research and Issues," *Academy of Management Journal*, vol. 26 (1983): 546–52.

[26] Developed from Roger Fritz, *Rate Your Executive Potential* (New York: Wiley, 1988), pp. 185–86; Roy J. Lewicki, Donald D. Bowen, Douglas T. Hall, and Francine S. Hall, *Experiences in Management and Organizational Behavior*, 3d ed. (New York: Wiley, 1988), p. 144.

[27] See George P. Huber, "A Theory of Effects of Advanced Information Technologies on Organizational Design, Intelligence, and Decision Making," *Academy of Management Review*, vol. 15 (1990): 67–71.

[28] Information from John Rau, "Nothing Succeeds Like Training for Success," *Wall Street Journal*, September 12, 1994, p. A14.

[29] See, for example, Dean Takahashi, "In Computerese, Technical Assistant Means Big Wheel, *The Wall Street Journal* (August 6, 1998), p. B1.

Chapter 11 Notes

[1] Carla Rapoport, "Nestle's Brand Building Machine," *Fortune*, September 19, 1994, pp. 147–56.

[2] Jessica Lipnack and Jeffrey Stamps, *The Age of the Network: Organizing Principles for the 21st Century* (Essex Junction, VT: Omneo, 1994).

[3] For a discussion of organization theory and design, see W. Richard Scott, *Organizations: Rational, Natural, and Open Systems*, 4th ed. (Upper Saddle River, NJ: Prentice-Hall, 1998).

[4] See Jay R. Galbraith, *Organizational Design* (Reading, MA: Addison Wesley, 1977).

[5] See Gareth Morgan, *Images of Organizations*, 2d ed. (Thousand Oaks, CA: Sage Publications, 1997).

[6] Andrew Ross Sorkin, "Gospel According to St. Luke's," *New York Times* (February 12, 1998), pp. C1, C7.

[7] Max Weber, *The Theory of Social and Economic Organization*, A. M. Henderson trans. and H. T. Parsons (New York: The Free Press, 1947).

[8] For classic treatments of bureaucracy, see Alvin Gouldner, *Patterns of Industrial Bureaucracy* (New York: The Free Press, 1954); Robert K. Merton, *Social Theory and Social Structure* (New York: The Free Press, 1957).

[9] Tom Burns and George M. Stalker, *The Management of Innovation* (London: Tavistock, 1961, republished by Oxford University Press, London, 1994.

[10] See Henry Mintzberg, *Structure in Fives: Designing Effective Organizations* (Englewood Cliffs, NJ: Prentice-Hall, 1983). This discussion is based on Henry Mintzberg, "The Structuring of Organizations," in *The Strategy Process: Concepts, Contexts, and Cases*, James Brian Quinn, Henry Mintzberg, and Robert M. James, eds. (Englewood Cliffs, NJ: Prentice-Hall, 1988), pp. 276–304.

[11] Thomas J. Peters and Robert H. Waterman Jr., *In Search of Excellence* (New York: Harper & Row, 1982).

[12] See Rosabeth Moss Kanter, *The Changing Masters* (New York: Simon & Schuster, 1983). Quotation from Rosabeth Moss Kanter and John D. Buck, "Reorganizing Part of Honeywell: From Strategy to Structure," *Organizational Dynamics*, vol. 13 (winter 1985): 6.

[13] Information from Thomas Petzinger Jr., "Self-Organization Will Free Employees to Act Like Bosses," *Wall Street Journal*, January 3, 1997, p. B1.

14 Brian Dumaine, "The Bureaucracy Busters," *Fortune*, June 17, 1991, pp. 35–50. The article includes observations by such organizational scholars as Paul Lawrence, Raymond Miles, and Michael Beer.

15 See Jay R. Galbraith, Edward E. Lawler III, and Associates, *Organizing for the Future* (San Francisco: Jossey-Bass Publishers, 1993).

16 A classic treatment of environment and organizational design is found in James D. Thompson, *Organizations in Action* (New York: McGraw-Hill, 1967). See also Scott, *Organizations*, pp. 264–69.

17 Alfred D. Chandler Jr., *Strategy and Structure: Chapter in the History of American Industrial Enterprise* (Cambridge, MA: MIT Press, 1962).

18 See, for example, Danny Miller, "Configurations of Strategy and Structure: Towards a Synthesis," *Strategic Management Journal*, vol. 7 (1986): 233–49.

19 Joan Woodward, *Industrial Organization: Theory and Practice* (London: Oxford University Press, 1965, republished by Oxford, University Press, 1994.

20 This classification is from Thompson, *Organizations in Action*.

21 See Peter M. Blau and Richard A. Schoennerr, *The Structure of Organizations* (New York: Basic Books, 1971); and Scott, *Organizations*, pp. 259–63.

22 D. E. Gumpert, "The Joys of Keeping the Company Small," *Harvard Business Review*, vol. 64 (July–August 1986): 6–8, 12–14.

23 John R. Kimberly, Robert H. Miles, *The Organizational Life Cycle* (San Francisco: Jossey-Bass, 1980).

24 Kim Cameron, Sarah J. Freeman, and Naneil K. Mishra, "Best Practices in White-Collar Downsizing: Managing Contradictions," *Academy of Management Executive*, vol. 5 (August 1991): 57–73.

25 See Gifford Pinchot III, *Intrapreneuring: Or Why You Don't Have to Leave the Corporation to Become an Entrepreneur* (New York: Harper & Row, 1985).

26 Dumaine, op cit.

27 See Jay Lorsch and John Morse, *Organizations and Their Members: A Contingency Approach* (New York: Harper & Row, 1974); and, Scott, *Organizations*, pp. 263–64.

28 "The Rebirth of IBM," *The Economist* (June 6, 1998), pp. 65–68.

29 Paul R. Lawrence and Jay W. Lorsch, *Organizations and Environment* (Boston: The Division of Research, Graduate School of Business Administration, Harvard University, 1967).

30 See Jay R. Galbraith, *Organizational Design* (Reading, MA: Addison-Wesley, 1977); and, Susan Albers Mohrman, "Integrating Roles and Structure in the Lateral Organization," chapter 5 in Galbraith, Lawler, and *Organizing for the Future*,

31 For a good discussion of coordination and integration approaches, see Scott, *Organizations*, pp. 231–39.

32 Michael Hammer and James Champy, *Reengineering the Corporation: A Manifesto for Business Revolution* (New York: Harper Business, 1993).

33 Michael Hammer, *Beyond Reengineering* (New York: Harper Business, 1997).

34 Brian Dumaine, "Earn More by Moving Faster," *Fortune*, October 7, 1991, pp. 89–94.

35 Hammer, *Beyond Reengineering*, p. 5.

36 Thomas M. Koulopoulos, *The Workflow Imperative* (New York: Van Nostrand Reinhold, 1995); Hammer, *Beyond Reengineering*.

37 Paul Roberts, "Humane Technology—PeopleSoft," *Fast Company*, vol. 14 (1998): 122.

38 Ronni T. Marshak, "Workflow Business Process Reengineering," special advertising section, *Fortune*, 1997.

39 A similar example is found in Hammer, *Beyond Reengineering*, pp. 9, 10.

40 Ibid, pp. 28–30.

41 Ibid, p. 29.

42 Ibid, p. 27.

43 Information from Thomas Petzinger Jr., "A Plant Manager Keeps Reinventing His Production Line," *The Wall Street Journal* (September 19, 1997), p. B1.

44 Gene Bylinsky, "The Virtual Factory," *Fortune* (November 14, 1994), pp. 92–110.

45 Gail Edmondson and Stephen Baker, "Silicon Valley on the Rhine," *Business Week* (November 3, 1997), pp. 162–166.

46 Ibid.

Chapter 12 Notes

1 Information from "Coopers & Lybrand: Weaving Diversity into the Fabric of Business," *Fortune*, June 23, 1997, special advertising section.

2 See, for example, "Rethinking Work," special report, *Business Week*, October 17, 1994, pp. 74–87.

3 Nancy J. Perry, "The Workers of the Future," *Fortune*, "The New American Century" (special issue) (spring–summer 1991), pp. 68–72.

4 Boris Yavitz, "Human Resources in Strategic Planning," in *Executive Talent: Developing and Keeping the Best People*, Eli Ginzberg (ed.) (New York: Wiley, 1988), p. 34.

5 Quote from William Bridges, "The End of the Job," *Fortune*, September 19, 1994, p. 68.

6 Information from *Wall Street Journal*, August 10, 1994, p. A10.

7 Information from "America's Largest Untapped Market," *Fortune*, March 2, 1998, special advertising section.

8 See Boris Yavitz, "Human Resources in

Strategic Planning," in *Executive Talent: Developing and Keeping the Best People*, Eli Ginzberg (ed.)(New York: Wiley, 1988), p. 34.

9 Information from Thomas A. Stewart, "In Search of Elusive Tech Workers," *Fortune*, February 16, 1998, pp. 171–72.

10 See Ernest McCormick, "Job and Task Analysis," in *Handbook of Industrial and Organizational Psychology* Marvin Dunnette (ed.) (Chicago: Rand McNally, 1976), pp. 651–96.

11 "Key to Success: People, People, People," *Fortune*, October 27, 1997, p. 232.

12 "The Big Picture: Job Turnover Tab," *Business Week*, April 20, 1998, p. 8.

13 See John P. Wanous, *Organizational Entry: Recruitment, Selection, and Socialization of Newcomers* (Reading, MA: Addison-Wesley, 1980), pp. 34–44.

14 "Key to Success," *Fortune*.

15 See Dale Yoder and Herbert G. Heneman (eds.) *ASPA Handbook of Personnel and Industrial Relations*, vol. 1 (Washington: Bureau of National Affairs, 1974), pp. 152–54; Walter Kiechel III, "How to Pick Talent," *Fortune*, December 8, 1986, pp. 201–3. *HRM Magazine*, April 1991, pp. 42–43.

16 Information from Justin Martin, "Mercedes: Made in Alabama," *Fortune*, July 7, 1997, pp. 150–58.

17 "Would You Hire This Person Again?" *Business Week*, Enterprise issue, June 9, 1997, pp. ENT32.

18 Information from William M. Bulkeley, "Replaced by Technology: Job Interviews," *Wall Street Journal*, August 22, 1994, pp. B1, B4.

19 For a scholarly review, see John Van Maanen and Edgar H. Schein, "Toward a Theory of Socialization," in *Research in Organizational Behavior*, vol. 1, Barry M. Staw, ed. (Greenwich, CT: JAI Press, 1979), pp. 209–64; for a practitioner's view, see Richard Pascale, "Fitting New Employees into the Company Culture," *Fortune*, May 28, 1984, pp. 28–42.

20 This involves the social information processing concept as discussed in Gerald R. Salancik and Jeffrey Pfeffer, "A Social Information Processing Approach to Job Attitudes and Task Design," *Administrative Science Quarterly*, vol. 23 (June 1978): 224–53.

21 Information from Ronald Henkoff, "Finding, Training, and Keeping the Best Service Workers," *Fortune*, October 3, 1994, pp. 110–22.

22 Occasional reports on this issue appear in the business press. See, for example, "Education: The Wall Street Journal Reports," *Wall Street Journal*, February 9, 1990; "A Shortage of Basic Skills," *Business Week*, January 13, 1991, p. 39. See also the report by Richard W. Judy and Carol D'Amico (eds.), *Workforce 2020* (Indianapolis: Hudson Institute, 1997).

23 "Key to Success."

[24] Peter Petre, "Games That Teach You to Manage," *Fortune*, October 29, 1984, pp. 65–72.

[25] Developed in part from Larry L. Cummings and Donald P. Schwab, *Performance in Organizations: Determinants and Appraisal* (Glenview, IL: Scott, Foresman, 1973).

[26] S. Gellerman and W. G. Hodgson, "Cyanamid's New Take on Performance Appraisal," *Harvard Business Review*, vol. 66 (May–June 1988), pp. 36–41.

[27] Patricia Smith, "Behaviors, Results, and Organizational Effectiveness," in *Handbook of Industrial and Organizational Psychology*, Marvin Dunnette, ed. (Chicago: Rand McNally, 1976), pp. 745–75.

[28] Charles Handy, *The Age of Unreason* (Cambridge, MA.: Harvard Business School Press, 1990), p. 55.

[29] See Thomas P. Ference, James A. F. Stoner, and E. Kirby Warren, "Managing the Career Plateau," *Academy of Management Review*, vol. 2 (October 1977): 602–12; and Julie Connelly "Have You Gone as Far as You Can Go? *Fortune*, December 26, 1994, p. 231–32.

[30] Information from David Coburn, "Balancing Home, Work Still Big Concern," *Columbus Dispatch*, February 16, 1998, pp. 8, 9.

[31] See Betty Friedan, *Beyond Gender: The New Politics of Work and the Family* (Washington, DC: Woodrow Wilson Center Press, 1997) and James A. Levine, *Working Fathers: New Strategies for Balancing Work and Family* (Reading, MA: Addison-Wesley, 1997).

[32] "Work and Family," *Business Week*, September 15, 1997, pp. 96–104.

[33] Sue Shellenbarger, "Businesses Compete to Make the Grade as Good Workplaces," *Wall Street Journal*, August 27, 1997, p. B1.

[34] "Work and Family," *Business Week*, September 15, 1997, pp. 96–104.

[35] For a good review, see Richard B. Freeman and James L. Medoff, *What Do Unions Do?* (New York: Basic Books, 1984); and Charles C. Heckscher, *The New Unionism* (New York: Basic Books, 1988).

[36] "Trade Union Membership," *Economist*, December 6, 1997, p. 114.

[37] See "Reinventing Labor: An Interview with Union President Lynn Williams," *Harvard Business Review*, July–August 1993, pp. 115–25.

[38] "Look Who's Pushing Productivity," *Business Week*, April 7, 1997, pp. 72–73.

Chapter 13 Notes

[1] Max DePree, "An Old Pro's Wisdom: It Begins with a Belief in People," *New York Times*, September 10, 1989, p. F2; Max DePree, *Leadership Is an Art* (New York: Doubleday, 1989); David Woodruff, "Herman Miller: How Green Is My Factory," *Business Week*, September 16, 1991, pp. 54–56; Max De-Pree, *Leadership Jazz* (New York: Doubleday, 1992).

[2] Abraham Zaleznick, "Leaders and Managers: Are They Different?" *Harvard Business Review*, May–June, 1977, pp. 67–78.

[3] For additional thoughts, see Warren Bennis, *Why Leaders Can't Lead* (San Francisco: Jossey-Bass, 1996).

[4] Quotations from Marshall Loeb, "Where Leaders Come From," *Fortune*, September 19, 1994, pp. 241–42; Genevieve Capowski, "Anatomy of a Leader: Where Are the Leaders of Tomorrow?" *Management Review*, March 1994, pp. 10–17.

[5] Two periodicals that follow current leadership topics in a variety of organizational settings are *Non-Profit Management and Leadership* and *Leader to Leader*, both published by Jossey-Bass.

[6] James M. Kouzes and Barry Z. Posner, "The Leadership Challenge," *Success*, April 1988, p. 68. See also their book, *The Leadership Challenge: How to Get Extraordinary Things Done in Organizations* (San Francisco: Jossey-Bass, 1987), and James M. Kouzes and Barry Z. Posner, *Credibility: How Leaders Gain and Lose It; Why People Demand It* (San Francisco: Jossey-Bass, 1996).

[7] Quotation from General Electric Company annual report 1997, p. 5.

[8] See Kouzes and Posner, "The Leadership Challenge," *The Leadership Challenge: How to Get Extraordinary Things Done in Organizations.* See also James C. Collins and Jerry I. Porras, "Building Your Company's Vision," *Harvard Business Review*, September–October 1996, pp. 65–77.

[9] Rosabeth Moss Kanter, "Power Failure in Management Circuits," *Harvard Business Review*, vol. 47 (July–August 1979): 65–75.

[10] For a good managerial discussion of power, see David C. McClelland and David H. Burnham, "Power Is the Great Motivator," *Harvard Business Review*, vol. 54 (March–April 1976): 100–110.

[11] See John R. P. French Jr. and Bertram Raven, "The Bases of Social Power," in *Group Dynamics: Research and Theory* Darwin Cartwright, ed. (Evanston, IL: Row, Peterson, 1962), pp. 607–13. For managerial applications of this basic framework, see Gary Yukl and Tom Taber, "The Effective Use of Managerial Power," *Personnel*, vol. 60 (1983): 37–49; Robert C. Benfari, Harry E. Wilkinson, and Charles D. Orth, "The Effective Use of Power," *Business Horizons*, vol. 29 (1986): pp. 12–16.

[12] Gary A. Yukl, *Leadership in Organizations*, 4th ed. (Englewood Cliffs, NJ: Prentice-Hall, 1998), includes "information" as a separate, but related, power source.

[13] Based on David A. Whetten and Kim S. Cameron, *Developing Management Skills*, 2d ed. (New York: HarperCollins, 1991), pp. 281–97.

[14] Ibid., p. 282.

[15] Chester A. Barnard, *Functions of the Executive* (Cambridge, MA: Harvard University Press, 1938).

[16] Jay A. Conger, "Leadership: The Art of Empowering Others," *Academy of Management Executive*, vol. 3 (1989): 17–24.

[17] Esther Wachs Book, "Leadership for the Millennium," *Working Woman*, March 1998, pp. 29–34.

[18] DePree, "An Old Pro's Wisdom," op cit.

[19] The early work on leader traits is well represented in Ralph M. Stogdill, "Personal Factors Associated with Leadership: A Survey of the Literature," *Journal of Psychology*, vol. 25 (1948): 35–71. See also Edwin E. Ghiselli, *Explorations in Management Talent* (Santa Monica, CA: Goodyear, 1971), and Shirley A. Kirkpatrick and Edwin A. Locke, "Leadership: Do Traits Really Matter?" *Academy of Management Executive* (1991): 48–60.

[20] See also John W. Gardner's article, "The Context and Attributes of Leadership," *New Management*, vol. 5 (1988): 18–22; John P. Kotter, *The Leadership Factor* (New York: The Free Press, 1988); and Bernard M. Bass, *Stogdill's Handbook of Leadership* (New York: The Free Press, 1990).

[21] Kirkpatrick and Locke, "Leadership," 1991.

[22] Joseph Weber, "Meet DuPont's In-house Conscience," *Business Week*, June 24, 1991, pp. 62–65; Sue Shellenbarger, "Executives Reflect on Past Choices Made for Family and Jobs," *Wall Street Journal*, December 31, 1997, p. B1.

[23] See, for example, Jan P. Muczyk and Bernie C. Reimann, "The Case for Directive Leadership," *Academy of Management Review*, vol. 12 (1987): 637–47.

[24] See Bass, *Stogdill's Handbook of Leadership.*

[25] Robert R. Blake and Jane Srygley Mouton, *The New Managerial Grid III* (Houston: Gulf Publishing, 1985).

[26] For a good discussion of this theory, see Fred E. Fiedler, Martin M. Chemers, and Linda Mahar, *The Leadership Match Concept* (New York: Wiley, 1978); Fiedler's current contingency research with the cognitive resource theory is summarized in Fred E. Fiedler and Joseph E. Garcia, *New Approaches to Effective Leadership* (New York: Wiley, 1987).

[27] Paul Hersey and Kenneth H. Blanchard, *Management and Organizational Behavior* (Englewood Cliffs, NJ: Prentice-Hall, 1988). For an interview with Paul Hersey on the origins of the model, see John R. Schermerhorn Jr., "Situational Leadership: Conversations with Paul Hersey," *Mid-American Journal of Business*, fall 1997, pp. 5–12.

[28] See Claude L. Graeff, "The Situational Leadership Theory: A Critical View," *Academy of Management Review*, vol. 8 (1983): 285–91.

[29] See, for example, Robert J. House, "A Path-Goal Theory of Leader Effectiveness," *Administrative Sciences Quarterly*, vol. 16 (1971): 321–38; Robert J. House and Terrence R. Mitchell, "Path-Goal Theory of Leadership," *Journal of Contemporary Business*, autumn 1974, pp. 81–97; the path-goal theory is reviewed by Bernard M. Bass in *Stogdill's Handbook of Leadership*, and Yukl in *Leadership in Organizations*. A supportive review of research is offered in Julie Indvik, "Path-Goal Theory of Leadership; A Meta-Analysis," in *Academy of Management Best Paper Proceedings 1986*, John A. Pearce II and Richard B. Robinson Jr., eds. pp. 189–92.

[30] See Steven Kerr and John Jermier, "Substitutes for Leadership: Their Meaning and Measurement," *Organizational Behavior and Human Performance*, vol. 22 (1978): 375–403; Jon P. Howell and Peter W. Dorfman, "Leadership and Substitutes for Leadership among Professional and Nonprofessional Workers," *Journal of Applied Behavioral Science*, vol. 22 (1986): 29–46.

[31] Information from John Huey, "The New Post-Heroic Leaders," *Fortune* (February 21, 1994), pp. 42–50. W. L. Gore & Associates, corporate communication, 1998.

[32] Victor H. Vroom and Arthur G. Jago, *The New Leadership: Managing Participation in Organizations* (Englewood Cliffs, NJ: Prentice-Hall, 1988); Victor H. Vroom, "A New Look in Managerial Decision-Making," *Organizational Dynamics* (spring 1973), pp. 66–80; Victor H. Vroom and Phillip Yetton, *Leadership and Decision-Making* (Pittsburgh: University of Pittsburgh Press, 1973).

[33] For a good discussion see Edgar H. Schein, *Process Consultation: Volume I Its Role in Organization, Development* 2nd ed. (Reading, MA: Addison-Wesley, 1988).

[34] For a review see Yukl, *Leadership in Organizations*, 1998.

[35] Among the popular books addressing this point of view are Warren Bennis and Burt Nanus, *Leaders* (New York: Harper & Row, 1985); Max DePree, *Leadership Is an Art* (Lansing: Michigan State University Press, 1987); Kotter, *The Leadership Factor*; The Leadership Challenge Kouzes and Posner, op. cit. A number of the issues are well summarized in James O'Toole, ed., "Special Section on Leadership," *New Management: The Magazine for Innovative Managers*, vol. 5 (1988): 2–31.

[36] See, for example, Jay A. Conger, "Inspiring Others: The Language of Leadership," *Academy of Management Executive*, vol. 5 (1991): 31–45.

[37] The distinction was originally made by James McGregor Burns, *Leadership* (New York: Harper & Row, 1978) and was further developed by Bernard Bass, *Leadership and Performance beyond Expectations* (New York: The Free Press, 1985) and Bernard M. Bass,

"Leadership: Good, Better, Best," *Organizational Dynamics*, vol. 13 (winter 1985): 26–40.

[38] Information from Alan Farnham, "Mary Kay's Lessons in Leadership," *Fortune* (September 20, 1993), pp. 68–77.

[38] This list is based on Kouzes and Posner, op. cit.; Gardner, op. cit.

[40] Information from "Women and Men, Work and Power," *Fast Company*, Issue 13 (1998), p. 71.

[41] Research on gender issues in leadership is reported in Sally Helgesen, *The Female Advantage: Women's Ways of Leadership* (New York: Doubleday, 1990); Judith B. Rosener, "Ways Women Lead," *Harvard Business Review* (November–December 1990), pp. 150–60; and Alice H. Eagly, Steven J. Karau, and Blair T. Johnson, "Gender and Leadership Style among School Principals: A Meta Analysis," *Administrative Science Quarterly*, vol. 27 (1992): 76–102. See also Harriet Rubin, *Machiavelli for Women* (New York: Doubleday, 1997).

[42] For debate on whether some transformational leadership qualities tend to be associated more with female than male leaders, see Judy B. Rosener, "Ways Women Lead," *Harvard Business Review*, November–December 1990, pp. 119–25; "Debate: Ways Women and Men Lead," *Harvard Business Review*, January–February 1991, pp. 150–60.

[43] Peter F. Drucker, "Leadership: More Doing than Dash," *Wall Street Journal*, January 6, 1988, p. 16. For a compendium of writings on leadership sponsored by the Drucker Foundation, see Frances Hesselbein, Marshall Goldsmith, and Richard Beckhard, *Leader of the Future* (San Francisco: Jossey-Bass, 1997).

[44] General Electric Company annual report 1997, p. 5.

[45] Gardner, "The Context and Attributes of Leadership," 1988.

[46] For a view of the "spiritual" aspects of leadership, see Lee G. Bolman and Terrence E. Deal, *Leading With Soul* (San Francisco: Jossey-Bass, 1995). See also Steven R. Covey, *Principle-Centered Leadership* (New York: The Free Press, 1992).

[47] De Pree, "An Old Pro's Wisdom."

Chapter 14 Notes

[1] Thomas J. Peters and Robert H. Waterman Jr., *In Search of Excellence* (New York: Warner books, 1982); "Global Business Sets Its Goals," *Fortune*, August 4, 1997, p. S5.

[2] Example taken from Kevin Kelley, "I'm the Boss, That's Why," *Business Week*, Enterprise issue, June 9, 1997, p. ENT 32.

[3] For a comprehensive treatment of extrinsic rewards, see Bob Nelson, *1001 Ways to Re-*

ward Employees (New York: Workman Publishing, 1994).

[4] For a research perspective, see Edward Deci, *Intrinsic Motivation* (New York: Plenum, 1975); Edward E. Lawler III, "The Design of Effective Reward Systems," in *Handbook of Organizational Behavior* Jay W. Lorsch, ed. (Englewood Cliffs, NJ: Prentice-Hall, 1987), pp. 255–71.

[5] Michael Maccoby's book, *Why Work: Leading the New Generation* (New York: Simon & Schuster, 1988), deals extensively with this point of view.

[6] Ellen Graham, "Work May Be a Rat Race, But It's Not a Daily Grind," *Wall Street Journal*, September 19, 1997, pp. R1, R4.

[7] "Starbuck's Secret Weapon," *Fortune*, September 29, 1997, p. 268.

[8] See Abraham H. Maslow, *Eupsychian Management* (Homewood, IL: Richard D. Irwin, 1965); Abraham H. Maslow, *Motivation and Personality*, 2d ed. (New York: Harper & Row, 1970). For a research perspective, see Mahmoud A. Wahba and Lawrence G. Bridwell, "Maslow Reconsidered: A Review of Research on the Need Hierarchy," *Organizational Behavior and Human Performance*, vol. 16 (1976): 212–40.

[9] See Clayton P. Alderfer, *Existence, Relatedness, and Growth* (New York: The Free Press, 1972).

[10] The complete two-factor theory is in Frederick Herzberg, Bernard Mausner, and Barbara Block Snyderman, *The Motivation to Work*, 2d ed. (New York: Wiley, 1967); Frederick Herzberg, "One More Time: How Do You Motivate Employees?" *Harvard Business Review*, vol. 47 (January–February 1968): 53–62, and reprinted as an *HBR* classic in vol. 65, September–October 1987, pp. 109–20.

[11] Critical reviews are provided by Robert J. House and Lawrence A. Wigdor, "Herzberg's Dual-Factor Theory of Job Satisfaction and Motivation: A Review of the Evidence and a Criticism," *Personnel Psychology*, vol. 20 (winter 1967): 369–89; Steven Kerr, Anne Harlan, and Ralph Stogdill, "Preference for Motivator and Hygiene Factors in a Hypothetical Interview Situation," *Personnel Psychology*, vol. 27 (winter 1974): 109–24.

[12] Frederick Herzberg, "Workers' Needs: The Same around the World," *Industry Week*, September 21, 1987, pp. 29–32.

[13] For a collection of McClelland's work, see David C. McClelland, *The Achieving Society* (New York: Van Nostrand, 1961); "Business Drive and National Achievement," *Harvard Business Review*, vol. 40 (July–August 1962): 99–112; David C. McClelland and David H. Burnham, "Power Is the Great Motivator," *Harvard Business Review*, vol. 54 (March–April 1976): 100–10; David C. McClelland, *Human Motivation* (Glenview, IL: Scott, Foresman, 1985); David C. McClelland and Richard E.

Boyatsis, "The Leadership Motive Pattern and Long-Term Success in Management," *Journal of Applied Psychology*, vol. 67 (1982): 737–43.

[14] Developed from a discussion in Edward E. Lawler III, *Motivation in Work Organizations* (Monterey, CA: Brooks/Cole Publishing, 1973), pp. 30–36.

[15] See, for example, J. Stacy Adams, "Toward an Understanding of Inequity," *Journal of Abnormal and Social Psychology*, vol. 67 (1963): 422–36; J. Stacy Adams, "Inequity in Social Exchange," in *Advances in Experimental Social Psychology*, vol. 2, L. Berkowitz, ed. (New York: Academic Press, 1965), pp. 267–300.

[16] Victor H. Vroom, *Work and Motivation* (New York: Wiley, 1964, republished by Jossey-Bass, 1994).

[17] The work on goal-setting theory is well summarized in Edwin A. Locke and Gary P. Latham, *Goal Setting: A Motivational Technique That Works!* (Englewood Cliffs, NJ: Prentice-Hall, 1984). See also Edwin A. Locke, Kenneth N. Shaw, Lisa A. Saari, and Gary P. Latham, "Goal Setting and Task Performance 1969–1980," *Psychological Bulletin*, vol. 90 (1981): 125–52; Mark E. Tubbs, "Goal Setting: A Meta-Analytic Examination of the Empirical Evidence," *Journal of Applied Psychology*, vol. 71 (1986): 474–83.

[18] Gary P. Latham and Edwin A. Locke, "Self-Regulation through Goal Setting," *Organizational Behavior and Human Decision Processes*, vol. 50 (1991): 212–47.

[19] Portions of this presentation of reinforcement theory originally adapted from John R. Schermerhorn Jr., James G. Hunt, and Richard N. Osborn, *Managing Organizational Behavior* (New York: Wiley, 1982), pp. 138–56. Used by permission.

[20] E. L. Thorndike, *Animal Intelligence* (New York: Macmillan, 1911), p. 244.

[21] See B. F. Skinner, *Walden Two* (New York: Macmillan, 1948); *Science and Human Behavior* (New York: Macmillan, 1953); *Contingencies of Reinforcement* (New York: Appleton-Century-Crofts, 1969).

[22] OB mod is clearly explained in Fred Luthans and Robert Kreitner, *Organizational Behavior Modification* (Glenview, IL: Scott, Foresman, 1975); Luthans and Kreitner, op. cit., 1985.

[23] "Mary Kay's Off-Road Bonus," *Business Week*, April 6, 1998, p. 8.

[24] For a good review, see Lee W. Frederickson (ed.), *Handbook of Organizational Behavior Management* (New York: Wiley-Interscience, 1982); Luthans and Kreitner, 1985.

[25] Edwin A. Locke, "The Myths of Behavior Mod in Organizations," *Academy of Management Review*, vol. 2 (October 1977): 543–53.

[26] For a discussion of compensation and performance, see Rosabeth Moss Katner, "The Attack on Pay," *Harvard Business Review*, vol. 65 (March–April 1987): 60–67; Edward E. Lawler III, *Strategic Pay* (San Francisco: Jossey-Bass, Inc., 1990).

[27] *Restoring Competitive Luster to American Industry: An Agenda for Success* (Cleveland, OH: Lincoln Electric Company), unpaged; Jeanne Johnson, "Incentive . . . The Key to Quality," August 1983, pp. 14–15; Gene Epstein, "Inspire Your Team," *Success*, October 1989; and Barnaby J. Feder, "Carrots, Sticks, and Growing Pains," *International Herald Tribune*, September 8, 1994, pp. 9, 10.

[28] Joann S. Lublin, "Executive Pay: Pay for Performance," *Wall Street Journal Reports*, April 9, 1998, and, Thomas A. Stewart, "Can Even Heroes Get Paid Too Much?" *Fortune*, June 8, 1998, p. 289.

[29] Information from Jaclyn Fierman, "The Perilous New World of Fair Pay," *Fortune*, June 13, 1994, pp. 57–61.

[30] Tove Helland Hammer, "New Developments in Profit Sharing, Gain Sharing, and Employee Ownership," chapter 12 in John P. Campbell, Richard J. Campbell, *Productivity in Organizations: New Perspectives from Industrial and Organizational Psychology* (San Francisco: Jossey-Bass, 1988).

[31] Jaclyn Fierman, "The Perilous New World of Fair Pay," *Fortune*, June 13, 1994, pp. 57–61.

[32] Amanda Bennett, "Paying Workers to Meet Goals Spreads, but Gauging Performance Proves Tough," *Wall Street Journal*, September 10, 1991, p. B1.

[33] "Key to Success: People, People, People," *Fortune*, October 27, 1997, p. 232.

Chapter 15 Notes

[1] Information from Diane E. Lewis, "Ernst & Young Eases Fears among Workers Using 'Flex' Programs," *Columbus Dispatch*, January 5, 1998, p. 11; Sue Shellenbarger, "Accounting Firms Battle to be Known as Best Workplaces," *Wall Street Journal*, January 21, 1998, p. B1.

[2] For a discussion of trends in the organization of work, see William Bridges, "The End of the Job," *Fortune*, September 14, 1994, pp. 62–74; and "Rethinking Work," special report, *Business Week*, October 17, 1994, pp. 76–87.

[3] Lyrics from "9 to 5" by Dolly Parton. Published by Velvet Apple/Fox Fanfare Music, Inc. © 1980 Velvet Apple Music & Warner-Tamerlane Publishing Corp. All rights reserved. Used by permission.

[4] This example is reported in *Esquire*, December 1986, p. 243. Emphasis is added to the quotation. Note: Nussbaum became director of the Labor Department's Women's Bureau during the Clinton administration.

[5] John P. Kotter, "The Psychological Contract: Managing the Joining Up Process," *California Management Review*, vol. 15 (spring 1973): 91–99; and Denise Rousseau, "Corporate Culture Isn't Easy to Change," *Wall Street Journal*, August 12, 1996, p. A12. See also Denise Rousseau, "Changing the Deal while Keeping the People," *Academy of Management. Executive*, vol. 10 (1996): 50–59.

[6] Linda Grant, "Unhappy in Japan," *Fortune*, January 13, 1997, p. 142.

[7] For a thought-provoking discussion of this issue, see Ben Hamper, *Rivethead: Tales from the Assembly Line* (New York: Warner, 1991).

[8] Studs Terkel, *Working* (New York: Avon Books, 1975).

[9] Sue Shellenbarger, "In Real Life, Hard Choices Upset any Balancing Act," *Wall Street Journal*, April 19, 1995, p. B1.

[10] For an overview, see Paul E. Spector, *Job Satisfaction* (Thousand Oaks, CA: Sage, 1997).

[11] "Nine to Five: How Workers Feel," *Wall Street Journal*, September 19, 1997, p. R4.

[12] Information from Sue Shellenbarger, "Employers Are Finding It Doesn't Cost Much to Make a Staff Happy," *The Wall Street Journal* (November 19, 1997), p. B1.

[13] Linda Grant, "Happy Workers, High Returns," *Fortune*, January 12, 1998, p. 81.

[14] Linda Grant, "Happy Workers, High Returns," *Fortune* (January 12, 1998), p. 81.

[15] See Melvin Blumberg and Charles D. Pringle, "The Missing Opportunity in Organizational Research: Some Implications for a Theory of Work Motivation," *Academy of Management Review*, vol. 7 (1982): 560–69.

[16] Developed from an example in Edward E. Lawler III, *Motivation in Work Organizations* (Monterey, CA: Brooks-Cole, 1973), pp. 154–55.

[17] Neil Gross, "Now Software Isn't Safe from Japan," *Business Week*, February 11, 1991, p. 84.

[18] The complete two-factor theory is in Frederick Herzberg, Bernard Mausner, and Barbara Block Snyderman, *The Motivation to Work*, 2d ed. (New York: Wiley, 1967). The quotation is from Frederick Herzberg, "One More Time: How Do You Motivate Employees?" *Harvard Business Review*, vol. 47, January–February 1968, pp. 53–62, and reprinted as an *HBR* classic in vol. 65, September–October 1987, pp. 109–20.

[19] For a complete description of the job characteristics model, see J. Richard Hackman and Greg R. Oldham, *Work Redesign* (Reading, MA: Addison-Wesley, 1980); additional descriptions of directions in job design research and practice are available in Ramon J. Aldag and Arthur P. Brief, *Task Design and Employee Motivation* (Glenview, IL: Scott, Foresman, 1979); and Ricky W. Griffin, *Task Design: An Integrative Approach* (Glenview, IL: Scott, Foresman, 1982).

[20] See Richard E. Walton, *Up and Running: Integrating Information Technology and the Organization* (Boston, MA: Harvard Business School Press, 1989).

[21] Richard Walton, "From Control to Commitment in the Workplace," *Harvard Business Review*, vol. 64 (March–April 1985): 77–94; and William A. Pasmore, *Designing Effective Organizations; A Sociotechnical Systems Perspective* (New York: Wiley, 1988).

[22] See, for example, "When GM's Robots Ran Amok, *Economist*," August 10, 1991 pp. 64–65; and Richard B. Lafferty, "Humans Shown to Outwork Robots on Many Jobs," *Columbus Dispatch*, April 14, 1991, p. 6F.

[23] Quotation from *Business Week*, October 28, 1991, pp. 120–23.

[24] Paul J. Champagne and Curt Tausky, "When Job Enrichment Doesn't Pay," *Personnel*, vol. 3 (January–February 1978): 30–40.

[25] William W. Winipsinger, "Job Enrichment: A Union View," in *Organizational Design, Development, and Behavior: A Situational View*, Karl O. Magnusen, ed. (Glenview, IL: Scott, Foresman, 1977), p. 22.

[26] Barney Olmsted and Suzanne Smith, *Creating a Flexible Workplace: How to Select and Manage Alternative Work Options* (New York: American Management Association, 1989). See also, "Family-Friendly Work Policies," *Work & Family*, November–December 1993, pp. 50–51.

[27] Information from "Aetna's Family-Friendly Executive," *Business Week*, June 28, 1993, p. 83.

[28] See Allen R. Cohen and Herman Gadon, *Alternative Work Schedules: Integrating Individual and Organizational Needs* (Reading, MA: Addison-Wesley, 1978), p. 125; Simcha Ronen and Sophia B. Primps, "The Compressed Work Week as Organizational Change: Behavioral and Attitudinal Outcomes," *Academy of Management Review*, vol. 6 (1981): 61–74.

[29] Information from Lesli Hicks, "Workers, Employers Praise Their Four-Day Workweek," *Columbus Dispatch*, August 22, 1994, p. 6.

[30] Deutschman, op. cit.; Cathy Trost, "To Cut Costs and Keep the Best of People, More Concerns Offer Flexible Work Plans," *Wall Street Journal*, February 18, 1992, pp. B1, B6.

[31] "Networked Workers," *Business Week*, October 6, 1997, p. 8; and Diane E. Lewis, "Flexible Work Arrangements as Important as Salary to Some," *Columbus Dispatch*, May 25, 1998, p. 8.

[32] This survey is reported in *Wall Street Journal*, January 20, 1988, p. 31.

[33] See Sue Shellenbarger, "Overwork, Low Morale Vex the Mobile Office," *Wall Street Journal*, August 17, 1994, pp B1, B7.

[34] Timothy Aeppel, "Full Time, Part Time, Temp—All See the Job in a Different Light," *Wall Street Journal*, March 18, 1997, p. 1, 10.

[35] Statistics on the part-time and contingency workforces are reported in Janet Novack, "Is Lean, Mean?" *Forbes*, August 15, 1994, pp. 88–89; and a survey by the Economic Policy Institute of Washington is reported in Laura Newpoff and Lornet Turnbull, "Temporary Workers Find Permanent Niche," *Columbus Dispatch*, September 8, 1997, p. 10.

[36] Steven Greenhouse, "Equal Work, Less Equal Perks," *New York Times*, March 30, 1998, p. C1.

[37] Adapted from Arthur P. Brief, Randall S. Schuler, and Mary Van Sell, *Managing Job Stress* (Boston: Little, Brown, 1981), pp. 7, 8.

[38] Sue Shellenbarger, "Do We Work More or Not? Either Way, We Feel Frazzled," *Wall Street Journal*, July 30, 1997, p. B1.

[39] Michael Weldholz, "Stress Increasingly Seen as Problem with Executives More Vulnerable," *Wall Street Journal*, September 28, 1982, p. 31.

[40] Alan Farnham, "Who Beats Stress Best—and How," *Fortune*, October 7, 1991, pp. 71–86.

[41] Worries at Work," *Wall Street Journal*, April 7, 1988, p. 31. See also Diane E. Lewis, "Workers Enjoy Their Jobs But Feel Unrewarded, Survey Shows," *Columbus Dispatch*, November 3, 1997, p. 9.

[42] Meyer Friedman and Ray Roseman, *Type A Behavior and Your Heart* (New York: Knopf, 1974). See also Jerry E. Bishop, "Prognosis for the 'Type A' Personality Improves in a New Heart Disease Study," *Wall Street Journal*, January 14, 1988, p. 29.

[43] See John M. Ivancevich and Michael T. Matteson, "Optimizing Human Resources: A Case for Preventive Health and Stress Management," *Organizational Dynamics*, vol. 9 (autumn 1980): 6–8. See also John M. Ivancevich, Michael T. Matteson, and Edward P. Richards Ill, "Who's Liable for Stress on the Job?" *Harvard Business Review*, vol. 64 (March–April 1985): 60–71.

[44] See Robert Kreitner, "Personal Wellness: It's Just Good Business," *Business Horizons*, vol. 25 (May–June 1982): 28–35.

[45] Developed from Kreitner, "Personal Wellness," and, "Plain Talk about Stress," National Institute of Mental Health Publication (Rockville, MD: U.S. Department of Health and Human Services).

Chapter 16 Notes

[1] These case examples are reported in *Business Week*, July 8, 1991, pp. 60–61. For more information on the Center for Creative Leadership, Greensboro, North Carolina, see:<http:>

[2] For a description of the centrality of communication to managerial roles see Henry Mintzberg, *The Nature of Managerial Work* (New York: Harper & Row, 1973).

[3] *Business Week*, February 10, 1992, pp. 102–8.

[4] See also Eric Matson, "Now That We Have Your Complete Attention," *Fast Company*, February–March, 1997, pp. 124–32.

[5] See Robert H. Lengel and Richard L. Daft, "The Selection of Communication Media as an Executive Skill," *Academy of Management Executive*, vol. 2 (August 1988): 225–32.

[6] Quotations from John Huey, "America's Most Successful Merchant," *Fortune*, September 23, 1991, pp. 46–59.

[7] David McNeill, *Hand and Mind: What Gestures Reveal about Thought* (Chicago: University of Chicago Press, 1992).

[8] Adapted from Richard V. Farace, Peter R. Monge, and Hamish M. Russell, *Communicating and Organizing* (Reading, MA: Addison-Wesley, 1977), pp. 97–98.

[9] Tom Peters and Nancy Austin, *A Passion for Excellence* (New York: Random House, 1985).

[10] This discussion is based on Carl R. Rogers and Richard E. Farson, "Active Listening" (Chicago: Industrial Relations Center of the University of Chicago), n.d.

[11] A useful source of guidelines is John J. Gabarro and Linda A. Hill, "Managing Performance," Note 9-96-022, Harvard Business School Publishing, Boston, MA.

[12] Developed from John Anderson, "Giving and Receiving Feedback," in Paul R. Lawrence, Louis B. Barnes, and Jay W. Lorsch, *Organizational Behavior and Administration*, 3d ed. (Homewood, IL: Richard D. Irwin, 1976), p. 109.

[13] Information from Esther Wachs Book, "Leadership for the Millennium," *Working Woman*, March 1998, pp. 29–34.

[14] Information from "How'm I Doing" No, Really, *Business Week*, Enterprise Issue, September 1, 1997, pp. ENT10–12.

[15] Information from Hilary Stout, "Self-Evaluation Brings Change to a Family's Ad Agency," *Wall Street Journal*, January 6, 1998, p. B2.

[16] Brian O'Reilly, "360 Feedback Can Change Your Life," *Fortune*, October 17, 1994, pp. 93–100.

[17] A classic work on proxemics is Edward T. Hall's book *The Hidden Dimension* (Garden City, NY: Doubleday, 1986).

[18] Mirand Wewll, "Alternative Spaces Spawning Desk-Free Zones," *Columbus Dispatch*, May 18, 1998, pp. 10–11.

[19] Alan Deutschman, "The Managing Wisdom of High-Tech Superstars," *Fortune*, October 17, 1994, pp. 197–206; and "Man of the Year: Intel's Andrew Grove," *Time*, December 29, 1997, pp. 48–72.

[20] Brian Williams, "Companies Use Varied Means to Keep Employees Informed," *Columbus Dispatch*, January 12, 1998, pp. 8–9.

[21] See Edward T. Hall, *The Silent Language* (New York: Doubleday, 1973).

[22] Information from "Corporate Community Service: Seeking America's Leaders," *Fortune*, October 17, 1994, special insert.

[23] See H. R. Schiffman, *Sensation and Perception: An Integrated Approach*, 3d ed. (New York: John Wiley, 1990).

[24] A good review is E. L. Jones, (eds.), *Attribution: Perceiving the Causes of Behavior* (Morristown, NJ: General Learning Press, 1972). See also John H. Harvey and Gifford Weary, "Current Issues in Attribution Theory and Research," *Annual Review of Psychology*, vol. 35 (1984): 427–59.

[25] See Ann M. Morrison, Randall P. White, and Ellen Van Velsor, *Breaking the Glass Ceiling* (Reading, MA: Addison-Wesley, 1987).

[26] See Roy S. Johnson, "The New Black Power," *Fortune*, August 4, 1997, pp. 46–82; Stephan Thernstrom and Abigail Thernstrom, *America in Black and White* (New York: Simon & Schuster, 1997); and David A. Thomas and Suzy Wetlaufer, "A Questions of Color: A Debate on Race in the U.S. Workplace," *Harvard Business Review*, September–October 1997, pp. 118–32.

[27] These examples are from Natasha Josefowitz, *Paths to Power* (Reading, MA: Addison-Wesley, 1980), p. 60.

[28] The classic work is Dewitt C. Dearborn and Herbert A. Simon, "Selective Perception: A Note on the Departmental Identification of Executives," *Sociometry*, vol. 21 (1958): 140–44. See also, J. P. Walsh, "Selectivity and Selective Perception: Belief Structures and Information Processing," *Academy of Management Journal* vol. 24 (1988): 453–70.

[29] Quotations from Dana Milbank, "Managers Are Sent to 'Charm Schools' to Discover How to Polish Up Their Acts," *Wall Street Journal*, December 14, 1990, pp. B1, B3.

[30] Richard E. Walton, *Interpersonal Peacemaking: Confrontations and Third-Party Consultation* (Reading, MA: Addison-Wesley, 1969), p. 2.

[31] Elizabeth Kpelman and Andrea Kupfer Schneider, *Beyond Machiavelli: Tools for Coping with Conflict* (Cambridge, MA: Harvard University Press, 1994).

[32] See Kenneth W. Thomas, "Conflict and Conflict Management," in *Handbook of Industrial and Organizational Behavior*, M. D. Dunnett, ed. (Chicago: Rand McNally, 1976), pp. 889–935.

[33] Information from E. S. Browning, "Chip Project Brings Rivals Together, but Cultures Clash," *The Asian Wall Street Journal* (May 5, 1994), pp. 1, 7.

[34] See Robert R. Blake and Jane Strygley Mouton, "The Fifth Achievement," *Journal of Applied Behavioral Science*, vol. 6 (1970), pp. 413–427; Alan C. Filley, *Interpersonal Conflict Resolution* (Glenview, IL: Scott Foresman, 1975).

[35] This discussion is based on Filley, op. cit.; and, Vincent L. Ferraro and Sheila A. Adams, "Interdepartmental Conflict: Practical Ways to Prevent and Reduce It," *Personnel*, vol. 61 (1984), pp. 12–23.

[36] Portions of this treatment of negotiation are adapted from John R. Schermerhorn Jr., James G. Hunt, and Richard N. Osborn, *Managing Organizational Behavior*, 4th ed. (New York: Wiley, 1991), pp. 382–87. Used by permission.

[37] Roger Fisher and William Ury, *Getting to Yes: Negotiating Agreement without Giving in* (New York: Penguin, 1983); and William L. Ury, Jeanne M. Brett, and Stephen B. Goldberg, *Getting Disputes Resolved* (San Francisco: Jossey-Bass, 1997).

[38] Fisher and Ury, *Getting to Yes;* see also James A. Wall Jr., *Negotiation: Theory and Practice* (Glenview, Il: Scott Foresman, 1985).

[39] Fisher and Ury, *Getting to Yes.*

[40] Ibid.

[41] Developed from Max H. Bazerman, *Judgment in Managerial Decision Making*, 3d ed. (New York: Wiley, 1994), chap. 7.

[42] Ibid; and Fisher and Ury, *Getting to Yes*, pp. 10–14.

[43] Roy J. Lewicki and Joseph A. Litterer, *Negotiation* (Homewood, IL: Irwin, 1985).

Chapter 17 Notes

[1] Information from Jennifer Scott, "Working Better Together Is the Challenge," *Columbus Dispatch*, November 3, 1997, pp. 10–11.

[2] See, for example, Edward E. Lawler III, Susan Albers Mohrman, and Gerald E. Ledford Jr., *Employee Involvement and Total Quality Management: Practices and Results in Fortune 1000 Companies* (San Francisco: Jossey-Bass, 1992). Thomas A. Stewart, "The Great Conundrum: You vs. the Team," *Fortune*, November 25, 1996, pp. 165–66.

[3] Jon R. Katzenbach and Douglas K. Smith, *The Wisdom of Teams: Creating the High Performance Organization* (Boston: Harvard Business School Press, 1993).

[4] See Marvin E. Shaw, *Group Dynamics: The Psychology of Small Group Behavior*, 2d ed. (New York: McGraw-Hill, 1976); Harold J. Leavitt, "Suppose We Took Groups More Seriously," in *Man and Work in Society* Eugene L. Cass and Frederick G. Zimmer, eds. (New York: Van Nostrand Reinhold, 1975), pp. 67–77.

[5] See W. Jack Duncan, "Why Some People Loaf in Groups While Others Loaf Alone," *Academy of Management Review*, vol. 8 (1004): 79–80.

[6] For insights on how to run an effective meeting see Mary A. De Vries, *How to Run a Meeting* (New York: Penguin, 1994).

[7] The "linking pin" concept is introduced in Rensis Likert, *New Patterns of Management* (New York: McGraw-Hill, 1962).

[8] See Susan D. Van Raalte, "Preparing the Task Force to Get Good Results," *S.A.M. Advanced Management Journal*, vol. 47 (winter 1982): 11–16; Walter Kiechel III, "The Art of the Corporate Task Force," *Fortune*, January 28, 1991, pp. 104–6.

[9] Ron Carter, "Team Concept Puts Workers and Bosses in Same Boat," *Columbus Dispatch*, October 27, 1997, pp. 8, 9.

[10] Information from "Diversity: America's Strength," special advertising section, *Fortune*, June 23, 1997; corporate communication, 1998.

[11] For a good discussion of quality circles, see Edward E. Lawler III and Susan A. Mohrman, "Quality Circles after the Fad," *Harvard Business Review*, vol. 63 (January–February 1985): 65–71; Gerald E. Ledford Jr., Edward E. Lawler III, and Susan A. Mohrman, "The Quality Circle and Its Variations," chapter 10 in John R. Campbell, Richard J. Campbell and *Productivity in Organizations* (San Francisco: Jossey-Bass, 1988); and Lawler, Mohrman, and Ledford, 1992, *Employee Involvement.*

[12] Information from "Ford Team Find Ways to Recycle Car Parts," special from *Chicago Tribune*, as reported in *Columbus Dispatch*, December 20, 1997, p. G1.

[13] Wanda J. Orlikowski and J. Debra Hofman, "An Improvisational Model for Change Management: The Case of Groupware Technologies," *Sloan Management Review*, fall 1993, pp. 27–36.

[14] R. Brent Gallupe and William H. Cooper, "Brainstorming Electronically," *Sloan Management Review*, winter 1997, pp. 11–21.

[15] William M. Bulkeley, "Computerizing Dull Meetings Is Touted as an Antidote to the Mouth That Bored," *Wall Street Journal*, January 28, 1992, pp. B1, B2.

[16] See, for example, Paul S. Goodman, Rukmini Devadas, and Terri L. Griffith Hughson, "Groups and Productivity: Analyzing the Effectiveness of Self-Managing Teams," chapter 11 in John R. Campbell, Richard J. Campbell, *Productivity in Organizations* (San Francisco: Jossey-Bass, 1988); Jack Orsbrun, Linda Moran, Ed Musslewhite, and John H. Zenger, with Craig Perrin, *Self-Directed Work Teams: The New American Challenge* (Homewood, IL: Business One Irwin, 1990); Dale E. Yeatts and Cloyd Hyten, *High Performing Self-Managed Work Teams* (Thousand Oaks, CA: Sage, 1997).

[17] Bradley L. Kirkman and Debra L. Shapiro, "The Impact of Cultural Values on Employee Resistance to Teams: Toward of Model of Globalized Self-Managing Work Team Effectiveness," *Academy of Management Review*, vol. 22 (1997): 730–57.

[18] For a review of research on group effectiveness, see J. Richard Hackman, "The Design of Work Teams," in *Handbook of Organizational Behavior* Jay W. Lorsch, ed. (Englewood Cliffs, NJ: Prentice-Hall, 1987), pp. 315–42.

[19] Ibid.

[20] See Patricia Doyle Corner and Angelo J. Kinicki, "A Proposed Mediator between Top

Team Demography and Financial Performance," *Academy of Management Proceedings '97*, pp. 7–11.

[21] See Stephen H. Rhinesmith, *A Manager's Guide to Globalization: Six Keys to Success in a Changing World* (Alexandria, VA: American Society for Training and Development, 1993).

[22] See Warren Watson, "Cultural Diversity's Impact on Interaction Process and Performance," *Academy of Management Journal*, vol. 16 (1993).

[23] Bruce W. Tuckman, "Developmental Sequence in Small Groups," *Psychological Bulletin*, vol. 63 (1965): 384–99; Bruce W. Tuckman and Mary Ann C. Jensen, "Stages of Small-Group Development Revisited," *Group & Organization Studies*, vol. 2 (1977): 419–27. For a slightly different model, see also J. Steven Heinen and Eugene Jacobson, "A Model of Task Group Development in Complex Organizations and a Strategy of Implementation," *Academy of Management Review*, vol. 1 (1976): 98–111.

[24] For a good discussion, see Robert F. Allen and Saul Pilnick, "Confronting the Shadow Organization: How to Detect and Defeat Negative Norms," *Organizational Dynamics*, spring 1973, pp. 13–17.

[25] Information from "Importing Enthusiasm," *Business Week*, special section on "21st Century Capitalism," November 7, 1994.

[26] See Schein, 1988, pp. 76–79.

[27] A classic work in this area is the 1948 article in the *Journal of Social Issues*, vol. 2: 42–47, by K. Benne and P. Sheets. See also Rensis Likert, *New Patterns of Management*, pp. 166–69; Schein, pp. 49–56.

[28] Portions adapted from John R. Schermerhorn Jr., James G. Hunt, and Richard N. Osborn, *Organizational Behavior*, 6th ed. (New York: John Wiley & Sons, 1997), pp. 351–52. Used by permission.

[29] Research on communication networks is found in Alex Bavelas, "Communication Patterns in Task-Oriented Groups," *Journal of the Accoustical Society of America*, vol. 22 (1950): 725–30; see also Marvin E. Shaw, *Group Dynamics: The Psychology of Small Group Behavior* (New York: McGraw-Hill, 1976).

[30] Schein, op cit. pp. 69–75.

[31] See Kathleen M. Eisenhardt, Jean L. Kahwajy, and L. J. Bourgeois III, "How Management Teams Can Have a Good Fight," *Harvard Business Review*, July–August 1997, pp. 77–85.

[32] Victor H. Vroom and Arthur G. Jago, *The New Leadership: Managing Participation in Organizations* (Englewood Cliffs, NJ: Prentice-Hall, 1988); Victor H. Vroom, "A New Look in Managerial Decision-Making," *Organizational Dynamics*, spring 1973, pp. 66–80; Victor H. Vroom and Phillip Yetton, *Leadership and Decision-Making* (Pittsburgh: University of Pittsburgh Press, 1973).

[33] Norman F. Maier, "Assets and Liabilities in Group Problem Solving," *Psychological Review*, vol. 74 (1967): 239–49.

[34] Ibid.

[35] See Irving L. Janis, "Groupthink," *Psychology Today*, November 1971, pp. 43–46; *Victims of Groupthink*, 2d ed. (Boston: Houghton Mifflin, 1982).

[36] These techniques are well described in Andre L. Delbecq, Andrew H. Van de Ven, and David H. Gustafson, *Group Techniques for Program Planning* (Glenview, IL: Scott, Foresman, 1975).

[37] See William D. Dyer, *Team-Building* (Reading, MA: Addison-Wesley, 1977).

[38] Dennis Berman, "Zap! Pow! Splat!" *Business Week*, Enterprise issue (February 9, 1998), p. ENT22.

[39] Katzenbach & Smith, 1993.

[40] Developed from Carl E. Larson and Frank M. J. LaFasto, *Team Work: What Must Go Right/What Can Go Wrong* (Newbury Park, CA: Sage, 1990).

[41] See Jon R. Katzenbach, "The Myth of the Top Management Team," *Harvard Business Review*, vol. 75 (November–December 1997): 83–91.

Chapter 18 Notes

[1] Information from "On the Road to Innovation," in special advertising section, "Charting the Course: Global Business Sets Its Goals," *Fortune*, August 4, 1997.

[2] Peter Senge, *The Fifth Discipline* (New York: Harper, 1990).

[3] Tom Peters, *The Circle of Innovation* (New York: Alfred A. Knopf, 1997).

[4] George Melloan, "Herman Miller's Secrets of Creativity," *Wall Street Journal*, May 3, 1988, p. 23.

[5] Senge, *The Fifth Discipline*, see also Brian Dumaine, "Mr. Learning Organization," *Fortune*, October 17, 1994, pp. 147–57.

[6] See, for example, Roger von Oech, *A Whack on the Side of the Head* (New York: Warner Books, 1983) and *A Kick in the Seat of the Pants* (New York: Harper & Row, 1986).

[7] Cited in Peter F. Drucker, *Management: Tasks, Responsibilities, and Practices* (New York: Harper & Row, 1973), p. 797.

[8] This discussion is based on the thorough review of the concept of innovation provided by Edward B. Roberts, "Managing Invention and Innovation," *Research Technology Management* (January–February 1988): 1–19.

[9] Information from "How to Grow a New Product Every Day," *Fortune*, November 14, 1994, pp. 269–70; corporate communication, 1998.

[10] Roberts, "Managing Invention and Innovation."

[11] See, for example, *Breakthroughs!* (New York: Rawson Associates, 1986); and "The Drought Is Over at 3M," *Business Week*, November 7, 1994, pp. 140–41; "Global Insights 98," *Fortune*, March 30, 1998, p. S3.

[12] This discussion is stimulated by James Brian Quinn, "Managing Innovation Controlled Chaos," *Harvard Business Review*, vol. 63 (May–June 1985). Selected quotations and examples from Kenneth Labich, "The Innovators," *Fortune*, June 6, 1988, pp. 49–64.

[13] Ibid.

[14] Peter F. Drucker, "Best R&D Is Business Driven," *Wall Street Journal*, February 10, 1988, p. 11.

[15] See Roberts, "Managing Invention and Innovation."

[16] *Wall Street Journal*, May 3, 1988, p. 23.

[17] Developed in part from Quinn, "Managing Innovation Controlled Chaos."

[18] Carol Hymowitz, "Task of Managing Changes in Workplace Takes a Careful Hand," *The Wall Street Journal* (July 1, 1997), p. B1.

[19] G. Christian Hill and Mike Tharp, "Stumbling Giant Big Quarterly Deficit Stuns BankAmerica, Adds Pressure on Chief," *Wall Street Journal*, July 18, 1985, pp. 1, 16.

[20] Robert Rose, "Kentucky Plant Workers Are Cranking Out Good Ideas," *Wall Street Journal*, August 13, 1996, p. B1.

[21] See Edward E. Lawler III, "Strategic Choices for Changing Organizations," chapter 12 in Allan M. Mohrman Jr., Susan Albers Mohrman, Gerald E. Ledford Jr., Thomas G. Cummings, Edward E. Lawler III, and associates, *Large Scale Organizational Change* (San Francisco: Jossey-Bass, 1989).

[22] The classic description of organizations on these terms is by Harold J. Leavitt, "Applied Organizational Change in Industry: Structural, Technological and Humanistic Approaches," in *Handbook of Organizations* James G. March, ed. (Chicago: Rand McNally, 1965), pp. 1144–70. Another timely approach is described by Ralph H. Kilmann in *Beyond the Quick Fix* (San Francisco: Jossey-Bass, 1984).

[23] Information from "Changing the Face of Management," *Working Woman*, November 1994, pp. 21–22.

[24] Kurt Lewin, "Group Decision and Social Change," in *Readings in Social Psychology*, G. E. Swanson, T. M. Newcomb and E. L. Hartley, eds. (New York: Holt Rinehart, 1952), pp. 459–73.

[25] This discussion is based on Robert Chin and Kenneth D. Benne, "General Strategies for Effecting Changes in Human Systems," in eds. *The Planning of Change*, 3d ed., Warren G. Bennis, Kenneth D. Benne, Robert Chin, and Kenneth E. Corey, (New York: Holt, Rinehart, 1969), pp. 22–45; Patrick E. Connor, "Strategies for Managing Technological Change," *Harvard International Review*, vol. 10 (1988): 10–13.

[26] The change strategy examples in this section are developed from an exercise reported in J. William Pfeiffer and John E. Jones, *A Handbook of Structured Experiences for Human Relations Training*, vol. 2 (La Jolla, CA: University Associates, 1973).

[27] Sue Shellenbarger, "Some Employers Find Way to Ease Burden of Changing Shifts," *Wall Street Journal*, March 25, 1998, p. B1.

[28] Ibid.

[29] John P. Kotter and Leonard A. Schlesinger, "Choosing Strategies for Change," *Harvard Business Review*, vol. 57 (March–April 1979): 109–12.

[30] Wanda J. Orlikowski and J. Debra Hofman, "An Improvisational Model for Change Management: The Case of Groupware Technologies," *Sloan Management Review*, winter 1997, pp. 11–21.

[31] Ibid.

[32] Overviews of organization development are provided by W. Warner Burke, *Organization Development: A Normative View* (Reading, MA: Addison-Wesley, 1987); and Wendell L. French and Cecil H. Bell Jr., *Organization Development*, 5th ed. (Englewood Cliffs, NJ: Prentice-Hall, 1995).

[33] See, for example, Dan Chiampa, *Total Quality* (Reading, MA.: Addison-Wesley, 1992); and Edward E. Lawler III, Susan Albers Mohrman, and Gerald E. Ledford Jr., *Employee Involvement and Total Quality Management* (San Francisco: Jossey-Bass, 1992).

[34] Tom Peters, "The Brand Called You," *Fast Company*, August-September 1997).

[35] Ibid.

[36] Stephen Covey, "How to Succeed in Today's Workplace," *USA Weekend*, August 29–31, 1997, pp. 4–5.

Chapter 1 Margin Photo Essay Notes

Whole Foods Market information from Ronald B. Lieber, "Why Employees Love These Companies," *Fortune*, January 12, 1998, pp. 72–74.

Solectron Corporation information from Michael S. Malone, "Translating Diversity into High-Tech Gains," *New York Times*, July 18, 1993.

Hudson Institute, <http://www.al.com/hudson/wf2020/>.

Reebok information from "Perforations in the Glass Ceiling," *Business Week*, December 22, 1997, p. 44.

Ritz-Carlton Hotels information from Steven Covey, "How to Succeed in Today's Workplace," *USA Weekend*, August 29–31, 1997, pp. 4–5.

Chapter 2 Margin Photo Essay Notes

Hewlett-Packard, information from *Success*, April 1988, p. 16, and *Business Week*, October 25, 1991, p. 16.

Jaguar PLC information from "Jaguar Starts to Claw Its Way Back," *Business Week*, February 2, 1998, p. 56.

Nordstrom information from James C. Collins and Jerry I. Porras, "Building Your Company's Vision," *Harvard Business Review*, September–October 1996, pp. 65–77.

Stride Rite information from Jane Easter Bahls, "Meeting the Child-Care Challenge," *Entrepreneurial Woman*, April, 1991, pp. 56–60, and "Corporate Citizenship at Stride Rite," corporate document, July 28, 1997.

Service Performance Corporation information from "Great Performances," special advertising section, *Fortune*, February 16, 1998, p. S1.

Chapter 3 Margin Photo Essay Notes

D'Artagan information from *The Worker* Magazine, July 4, 1996, pp. 12–14.

Pentagon Entertainment information from Robert La Franco, "Freedom of Information and We Mean Free," *Forbes*, December 15, 1997, pp. 41–44.

Motorola information from Mary J. Cronin, "Intranets Reach the Factory Floor," *Fortune*, August 18, 1997, p. 208.

Ernst & Young information from Thomas Stewart, "Is This Job Really Necessary?" *Fortune*, January 12, 1998, pp. 154–55.

Chapter 4 Margin Photo Essay Notes

Four Seasons Hotels information from E. Larry Armstrong with William C. Symonds, "Beyond 'May I Help You?'" *Business Week*, October 25, 1991, pp. 100–101.

Xerox information from Jeremy Main, "How to Win the Baldrige Award," *Fortune*, April 23, 1990, pp. 101–16.

Chapter 5 Margin Photo Essay Notes

Quicksilver Enterprises information from Mark Robichaux, "Three Small Businesses Profit by Taking on the World," *Wall Street Journal*, November 8, 1990, p. B2.

SBC Communications information from Mort Rosenblum, "The Other Africa," *Columbus Dispatch*, December 14, 1997, p. C1.

Shelby, North Carolina, information from Michael M. Phillips, "Globalization Comes to a Southern Town," *Wall Street Journal*, February 12, 1998, p. A2.

Nike, "Nike Gets Its Feet Burnt," *New York Times*, June 25, 1997, p. 16.

Honda information from "Can Honda Build a World Car?" *Business Week*, September 8, 1997, pp. 100–108.

Chapter 6 Margin Photo Essay Notes

Council on Economic Priorities information from "Sweatshop Police," *Business Week*,

October 20, 1997, p. 39; information available directly from Council on Economic Priorities, New York, or at <http://www.accesspt.com/CEP>.

Florist Directory Assistance information from Rodney Ho, "Don't Like Your Boss's Tactics? Become a Competitor," *Wall Street Journal*, December 16, 1997, p. B2.

GE Plastics, corporate communication, 1998.

The Gap Inc. information from Aaron Berstein, "A Potent Weapon in the War Against Sweatshops," *Business Week*, December 1, 1997, p. 40.

City of San Francisco information from "Going Beyond City Limits?" *Business Week*, July 7, 1997, pp. 98–99.

Chapter 7 Margin Photo Essay Notes

Lucent Technologies information from "Avoiding a Time Bomb: Sexual Harassment," *Business Week*, Enterprise supplement, October 13, 1997, pp. ENT20–22.

McDonald's information from Richard Ghison, "Burger Wars Sizzle as McDonald's Clones the Whopper," *Wall Street Journal*, September 17, 1997, p. B1.

Xerox information from John Seely Brown, "Research that Reinvents the Corporation," *Harvard Business Review*, January–February 1991, pp. 102–11.

Chapter 8 Margin Photo Essay Notes

America West Airlines information from America West Airlines corporate home page, <http://www.americawest.com>.

Worthington Industries information from Worthington Industries 1997 corporate report. See also Justin Martin, "So, You Want to Work for the Best," *Fortune*, January 12, 1998, pp. 77–78.

McDonald's information from "Memorable Memo: McDonald's Sends Operators to War on Fries," *Wall Street Journal*, December 18, 1997, p. B1.

Cape Cod Potato Chips information from "A Passion for Chips," *Fortune*, August 18, 1997, p. 228.

Chapter 9 Margin Photo Essay Notes

General Electric information from William M. Carley, "To Keep GE's Profits Rising, Welch Pushes Quality-Control Plan," *Wall Street Journal*, January 13, 1997, p. 1.

Society for Human Resource Management information from "Would You Hire this Person Again?" *Business Week*, enterprise supplement, June 9, 1997, pp. ENT32.

U.S. Army information from "New Ideas from the Army (Really)," *Fortune*, September 19, 1994, pp. 203–12.

C & S Mystery Shoppers information from

Jennifer Steinhauer, "The Undercover Shoppers," *New York Times*, February 4, 1998, p. C1.

Chapter 10 Margin Photo Essay Notes

KPMG Peat Marwick information from "Empowering People with Technology," *Business Week*, September 20, 1993, special advertising supplement.

Intel information from William Bridges, "The End of the Job," *Fortune*, September 19, 1994, pp. 62–74; Alan Deutschman, "The Managing Wisdom of High-Tech Superstars," *Fortune*, October 17, 1994, pp. 197–206.

Heinz information from Rekha Balu, "Heinz's Johnson to Divest Operations, Scrap Management of Firm by Regions," *Wall Street Journal*, November 8, 1997, p. B22.

Delta Airlines information from "A Break in the Clouds for Delta," *Business Week*, December 22, 1997, pp. 93–94.

Chapter 11 Margin Photo Essay Notes

Rickard Group, Inc., corporate communication, November 21, 1997.

3M information from Gail Edmondson and Stephen Baker, "Silicon Valley on the Rhine," *Business Week*, November 3, 1997, pp. 162–66.

Patricia Seybold Group information from Ronni T. Marschak, "Workflow Business Process Reengineering," *Fortune*, special advertising supplement, 1998.

Chapter 12 Margin Photo Essay Notes

Johnson & Johnson home page, <http://www.johnsonandjohnson.com/who_is _jnj/cr_usa.htm/>.

Coca-Cola information from *Fortune*, August 4, 1997, p. 34; John Huey, "In Search of Roberto's Secret Formula," *Fortune*, December 29, 1997, pp. 230–34.

Southwest Airlines information from Justin Martin, "So, You Want to Work for the Best . . ." *Fortune*, January 12, 1998, pp. 77–78.

Chapter 13 Margin Photo Essay Notes

Harley-Davidson information from company annual reports.

WorldCom information from "The Best Managers," *Business Week*, January 12, 1998, p. 56.

Banana Republic information from "The Best Managers," *Business Week*, January 12, 1998, p. 58.

Chapter 14 Margin Photo Essay Notes

Roppe Corporation information from "Productivity: No More Clock Watchers," *Inc.*, February 1994, p. 83.

Silicon Graphics information from G. Pascal Zachary, "The New Search for Meaning in 'Meaningless' Work," *Wall Street Journal*, January 9, 1997, pp. B1, B7.

Rocky Shoes & Boots, "The Last Steps of Production," *Columbus Dispatch*, July 21, 1997, pp. 8–9.

Pratt & Whitney information from Joseph B. White, "How a Creaky Factory Got Off the Hit List, Won Respect at Last," *Wall Street Journal*, December 26, 1996, pp. 1–2.

Chapter 15 Margin Photo Essay Notes

Mariott Hotels information from Ronald Henkoff, "Finding, Training, and Keeping the Best Service Workers," *Fortune*, October 3, 1994, pp. 110–22.

International Survey Research information from Linda Grant, "Unhappy in Japan," *Fortune*, January 13, 1997, p. 142.

Pulaski Furniture Corporation reported in *Business Week*, October 17, 1994, p. 80.

Lotus Development Corp. information from C. Pascal Zachary, "The Search for New Meaning in 'Meaningless' Work," *Wall Street Journal*, January 9, 1997, p. B1.

Catalyst information from the Associated Press, "Working Couples Want Flexibility, Survey Finds," *Columbus Dispatch*, January 21, 1998, p. F1.

Chapter 16 Margin Photo Essay Notes

BankBoston information from Carol Hymowitz, "New Top Managers Often Find They Miss Close Peers, Counsel," *Wall Street Journal*, November 25, 1997, p. B1.

Scott's Co. information from Brian Williams, "Companies Use Varied Means to Keep Employees Informed," *Columbus Dispatch*, January 12, 1998, p. 8.

Alcoa information from Raju Narisetti, "Executive Suites' Walls Come Tumbling Down," *Wall Street Journal*, June 29, 1994, pp. B1, B12.

Coopers & Lybrand information from "The Big Picture, All Isn't Forgiven," *Business Week*, January 19, 1998, p. 6.

Chapter 17 Margin Photo Essay Notes

Rockport, Co. information from Carol Hymowitz, "Task of Managing Changes in Workplace Takes a Careful Hand," *Wall Street Journal*, July 1, 1997, p. B1.

TeleSpan Publishing Corporation information from "Conferencing and Collaboration: Using the Network to Work Together," special advertisement, *Fortune*, February 16, 1998, p. S2.

Goodyear information from "The Drive for Safer Tires," *Columbus Dispatch*, December 13, 1997, p. F1.

Worthington Industries information from Justin Martin, "So, You Want to Work for the Best," *Fortune*, January 12, 1998, pp. 77–78.

Chapter 18 Margin Photo Essay Notes

Olympus Optical Co. information from "The Sound of Tomorrow," special advertising section on "Global Business Sets Its Goals," *Fortune*, August 4, 1997.

Toro information from *Fortune*, December 1991, pp. 56–62.

Hyatt Hotels information from James S. Hirsh, "Tracking Travel," *Asian Wall Street Journal*, March 10, 1993, p. 20.

Motorola information from "Changing the Face of Management," *Working Woman*, November, 1994, pp. 21–22.

Clorox Co. information from John A. Byrne, "Management Theory—Or Fad of the Month?" *Business Week*, June 23, 1997, p. 47.

Case 1 Notes

[1] Hey, John. "The World's Best Brand," *Fortune*, May 31, 1993, 46.

[2] McCarthy, Michael. "Soft-Drink Firms Search for Answers as Volumes Drop," *Wall Street Journal*, July 27, 1992.

[3] Mallory, Maria. "Behemoth on a Tear," *Business Week*, October 3, 1994, 54.

[4] Lesley, Elizabeth. "Does Snapple Have the Juice to Go National?" *Business Week*, January 18, 1993, 52–53.

[5] Mallory, op cit., p. 55.

[6] Mallory, Maria. "At Coke, Marketing Is It," *Business Week*, February 21, 1994, 39.

[7] Mallory, Maria. "The Cola Wars Go to College," *Business Week*, September 19, 1994, 42.

[8] Saporito, Bill. "How U.S. Soccer Hopes to Score," *Fortune*, June 27, 1994, 127.

[9] Barnathan, Joyce. "Destination, Vietnam," *Business Week*, February 14, 1994, 26–27.

[10] Templeton, John. "Nestle: A Giant in a Hurry," *Business Week*, March 22, 1993, 50.

[11] Deogun, Nikhil. "Investor Sees Rise in Sales, Opportunity for Coke in Asia's Turmoil," *Wall Street Journal*, December 11, 1997, A4.

[12] Deogun, Nikhil. "Coca-Cola May Purchase Orangina," *Wall Street Journal*, December 22, 1997, B1, B8.

Case 2 Notes

[1] Eiskmeyer, Charles. 1998. The Saturn Enthusiast's Page. http://www.saturnalbuquerque.com/saturnalia/index.html.

[2] Child, Charles, and Peter Brown. "Possibilities for Saturn include SUB, hybrid, light truck," *Automotive News*, February 9, 1998, 6.

[3] "Saturn Cuts Output; Will Not Resort to Incentives," *Ward's Automotive News*, October 1997, 35.

[4] Bohl, Don. "Saturn Corporation," *American Management Association Compensation and Benefits Review*, November 21, 1997, 51.

[5] Ibid.

[6] Ibid.

[7] Meredith, Robyn. "Saturn Union Votes to Retain Its Cooperative Company Pact," *New York Times*, March 12, 1998.

[8] Child, Op cit.

[9] Bohl, Op cit.

[10] Ibid.

[11] Ibid.

Case 3 Notes

[1] Hof, Robert D. "Netspeed at Netscape," *Business Week*, February 10, 1997, 78–86.

[2] Ibid., p. 78.

[3] "Why Netscape Isn't Dead," *Economist*, July 5, 1997.

[4] Kirkpatrick, David. "Can Netscape Compete?" *Fortune*, June 9, 1997, 135.

[5] Kirkpatrick, David. "The Saga of How the Web Was Won," *Fortune*, July 7, 1997.

[6] Hof, Op cit., p. 80.

[7] Markoff, John. "Microsoft vs. Netscape: The Border War Heats Up," *New York Times*, September 29, 1997, D4.

[8] Rynecki, David. "Internet Upstarts Need Strategy to Defend Their Territory," *USA Today*, January 7, 1998, 2B.

[9] Kirkpatrick, June, Op. cit., p. 35.

[10] Grant, Lorrie. "Struggling Netscape Refocuses," *USA Today*, January 7, 1998, 2B.

[11] "Netscape Gets Webbier?" *cnnfn.com*, March 13, 1998. http://www.cnnfm.com.

[12] Ibid.

[13] Hof, Op cit., p. 80.

[14] Kirkpatrick, Op cit., p. 135.

Case 4 Notes

[1] Boyd, Malia. "Harley-Davidson Motor Company," *Incentive*, September 1993, 26–27.

[2] Shrader, Charles, Susanah Chance, Stuart Hinrichs, and Alan Hoffman. "Harley-Davidson, Inc.—1991," in Fred R. David, *Strategic Management*, 4th ed. (New York: Macmillan Publishing Company, 1993), 655.

[3] Ibid.

[4] Peak, Martha H. "Harley-Davidson: Going Whole Hog to Provide Stakeholder Satisfaction," *Management Review* 82 (June 1993): 53.

[5] Harley-Davidson, 1992 Form 10-K, 33.

[6] Peak, Op. cit., p. 53.

[7] Kelly, Kevin, and Karen Lowrey Miller. "The Rumble Heard Round the World: Harleys," *Business Week*, May 24, 1993, 60.

[8] Ibid.

[9] Shrader, Op. cit., p. 655.

[10] Kelly, Op. cit., p. 60.

[11] Potok, Mark, and Rae Tyson. "100,000 Converge to Pay Homage," *USA Today*, June 10, 1993, 1–2.

[12] Kelly, Op cit., p. 60.

[13] Peak, Op cit., p. 53.

[14] Harley-Davidson, 1922 Annual Report. 14; 19.

[15] Harley-Davidson and Porsche Set Up Joint Venture.

[16] Bleustein Appointed Chief Executive Officer of Harley-Davidson, Inc.

[17] Dallas, Sandra, and Emily Thorton. "Japan's Bikers: The Tame Ones," *Business Week*, October 6, 1997, 30D.

[18] Ibid.

[19] Stevens, Karen, and Dale Kurschner "That Vroom! You Hear May Not Be a Harley," *Business Week*, October 20, 1997, 159.

[20] Ibid.

[21] Ibid.

Case 5 Notes

[1] Maremont, Mark. "Kodak: Shoot the Works," *Business Week*, November 15, 1993, 31.

[2] Nulty, Peter. "Kodak Grabs for Growth Again," *Fortune*, May 16, 1994, 77.

[3] Maremont, Mark. "Kodak's New Focus," *Fortune*, January 30, 1995, 65.

[4] Austin, Nancy K. "Motivating Employees without Pay or Promotions," *Working Woman*, October 1994, 18.

[5] *Hoover's Handbook of American Business*. Austin, Texas: Hoover's Business Press; 1997.

[6] Ibid.

[7] Ibid.

[8] Smith, Geoffrey. "Can George Fisher Fix Kodak?" *Business Week*, October 20, 1997.

[9] "Kodak's Imperfect Picture," *The Columbus Dispatch*, November 12, 1997: G1–G2.

[10] Smith, Op. cit.

[11] Holstein, William. "Not a Pretty Picture in Rochester," *US News and World Report*, November 14, 1997.

Case 6 Notes

[1] Zinn, Laura, "Tom Chappell: Sweet Success from Unsweetened Toothpaste," *Business Week*, September 2, 1991, 52.

[2] Bamford, Janet, "Changing Business as Usual," *Working Women* 18 (November 1993): 106.

[3] Cox, Craig, "Interview: Tom Chappell, Minister of Commerce," *Business Ethics* 8 (January 1994): 42.

[4] Quinn, Judy, "Tom's of Maine," *Incentive*, December 1993, A4.

[5] Ibid.

[6] Martin, Mary, "Toothpaste and Theology," *Boston Sunday Globe*, October 10, 1993, A4.

[7] Cox, Op. cit., p. 42.

[8] Martin, Mary, "A 'Nuisance' to Rivals," *Boston Sunday Globe*, October 10, 1993, A4.

[9] Cox, Op. cit., p. 42.

[10] Ibid.

[11] Martin, Op. cit., p. A4.

[12] Quinn, Op. cit., p. A4.

[13] Martin, Op. cit., p. A4.

[14] E.E.S., "Paying Employees to Work Elsewhere," *Inc.*, February 1993, 29.

[15] Quinn, Op. cit., p. A4.

[16] Ibid.

[17] M.E., "Profiles in Marketing: Katie Shisler," *Sales and Marketing Management*, March 1993, 12.

[18] Quinn, Op. cit., p. A4.

[19] Cox, Op. cit., p. 42.

[20] Ibid.

[21] Ibid.

[22] Barasch, Douglas, "God and Toothpaste," *New York Times*, December 22, 1996, 27.

[23] Tode, Chantal, "Natural Brands Find New Home: Mass Market," *Capital Cities Media*, 33, 174: 8.

[24] Barasch, Op. cit., p. 27

[25] Gardner, Christine. "Hippie Toothpaste Brushing against Giants," *Chicago Tribune*, September 12, 1994, Business 8.

Case 7 Notes

[1] Schwartz, Nelson. "Why Wall Street's Buying Wal-Mart Again," *Fortune*, February 16, 1998.

[2] Saporito, Bill. "Is Wal-Mart Unstoppable?" *Fortune*, May 6, 1991, 50–52.

[3] "Wal-Mart Picks up the PACE," *Business Week*, November 15, 1993, 45.

[4] Ibid.

[5] Zellner, Wendy. "Warehouse Clubs Butt Heads—and Reach for the Ice Pack," *Business Week*, April 19, 1993, 68.

[6] Marsh, Barbara. "Merchants Mobilize to Battle Wal-Mart in a Small Community," *Wall Street Journal*, June 5, 1991, A1.

Ortega, Bob. "Ban the Bargains: Aging Activists Turn Attention to Wal-Mart Protests," *Wall Street Journal*, October 11, 1994, A8.

[7] Saporito, Bill. "David Glass Won't Crack under Fire," *Fortune*, February 8, 1993, 75, 78.

[8] Symonds, William C. "Invasion of the Retail Snatchers," *Business Week*, May 9, 1994, 72–73.

[9] Bryd, Veronica. "The Avon Lady of the Amazon," *Business Week*, October 24, 1994, 96.

[10] Annual Report, 1977.

[11] Ibid.

[12] Zellner, Wendy. "A Grand Reopening for Wal-Mart," *Business Week*, February 9, 1998.

[13] Ibid.

[14] Ibid.

[15] 1997 Annual Report, Op. cit.

Case 8 Notes

[1] Ansberry, Clare. "Nucor Steel's Sheen Is Marred by Deaths of Workers in Plants," *Wall Street Journal*, May 10, 1991, A1.

[2] "How Nucor Works." *New Steel*, November 1997.

[3] Ibid.

Case 9 Notes

[1] United Parcel Service home page, http://www.ups.com.

[2] Kamuf, Rachael. "UPS Upping Employment as well as Technology," *Business First*, March 9, 1998.

[3] Grant, Linda. "Why Fedex is Flying High," *Fortune*, November 10, 1997.

[4] UPS Homepage, Op. cit.

[5] Walker, Karen. "Brown Is Beautiful," *Airline Business*, November 1997.

[6] Ibid.

[7] Kamuf, Op. cit.

[8] Walker, Op. cit.

[9] Grant, Op. cit.

Case 10 Notes

[1] Picker, Ida. "Will AT&T Bobble Its Triple Play?" *Institutional Investor*, June 1996, 99. AT&T home page, http://www.att.com

[2] "AT&T," *Hoover's Handbook of American Business*, (Austin, TX: Hoover's Business Press, 1997).

[3] Ibid.

[4] Ibid.

[5] Picker, Op. cit., p. 99.

[6] Ibid.

[7] Ibid.

[8] Arnst, Catherine. "Divide and Conquer?" *Business Week*, October 2, 1998, 56.

[9] Goldblatt, Henry. "AT&T Finally Has an Operator," *Fortune*, February 16, 1998.

[10] Elstrom, Peter. "New Boss, New Plan," *Business Week*.

[11] Grant, Lorrie. "SBC Could Add Convolution to AT&T Stock Evolution," *USA Today*, June 16, 1998, 3B.

Case 11 Notes

[1] Abelson, Reed. "Two of the Big Six in Accounting Plan to Form New No. 1," *New York Times*, September 19, 1997, A1. Price Waterhouse home page, http://www.pw.com.

[2] Caldmanis, Thor. "Price Waterhouse, Coopers to Merge," *USA Today*, September 19, 1997, 1B.

[3] Ibid.

[4] Wolf, Barnet. "Merger of Accountants to Shrink Big Six by One," *Columbus Dispatch*, September 19, 1997, 1F.

[5] Abelson, Op. cit., A1.

[6] "Accounting: The Big Five?" *Economist*, September 20, 1991.

[7] "Professional Business Services," *U.S. Industry and Trade Outlook*, 1998 (New York: McGraw-Hill, 1997), 49-1–49-9.

[8] Ibid.

[9] Accounting . . . , Op. cit.

[10] Ibid.

[11] Abelson, Op. cit., A1.

[12] Rehfeld, Barry. "The Big Six, Five, Four . . . ," *Mergers and Acquisitions*, January 1998.

Case 12 Notes

[1] Hammonds, Keith. "Commentary: A Portfolio with a Heart Still Needs a Brain," *Business Week* web site, at http://www.business-week.com/1998/04/b3562128.htm.

[2] Laabs, Jennifer. "Ben and Jerry's Caring Capitalism," *Personnel Journal*, November 1992, 54.

[3] Ibid.

[4] Sonenclar, Robert J. "Ben and Jerry's: Management with a Human Flavor," *Hemisphere*, March 1993, 26.

[5] Ibid.

[6] Laabs, Jennifer. "Ben and Jerry's Caring Capitalism," *Personnel Journal*, November 1992, 54.

[7] Hammonds, Keith. "Commentary: A Portfolio with a Heart Still Needs a Brain," *Business Week* web site, at http://www.business-week.com/1998/04/b3562128.htm.

Case 13 Notes

[1] *Current Biography*, January 1997, vol. 58 (1): 28–31.

[2] Ibid.

[3] Ibid.

[4] Ibid.

[5] Ibid.

[6] Ibid.

[7] Ibid.

[8] Ibid.

[9] Ibid.

[10] Ibid.

[11] Reilly, Rick. "That's Shoe Business," *Sports Illustrated*, April 26, 1993.

[12] Crothers, Tim. "Duke Takes a Dive: The Absence of Mike Krzyzewski Has Hastened the Blue Devils' Fall," *Sports Illustrated*, January 30, 1995.

[13] "Coach K," the official Web site of coach Mike Krzyzewski, at http://www.CoachK.com/career.html.

[14] Wolff, Alexander. "Blue Angel," *Sports Illustrated*, April 16, 1992.

[15] Ibid.

Case 14 Notes

[1] Zagorin, Adam. "BET's Too Hot a Property: A Founder Wants to Buy Back His Firm; The Shareholders Want More Money," *Time*, October 20, 1997, 80.

[2] Perl, Peter. "His Way," *Washington Post*, December 14, 1997, magazine section, W08.

[3] Ibid.

[4] Ibid.

[5] Ibid.

[6] Ibid.

[7] Ibid.

[8] Ibid.

[9] Ibid.

[10] Ibid.

[11] Zagorin, Op. cit., p. 80.

[12] Perl, Op. cit., p. W08.

[13] Zagorin, Op. cit., p. 80.

[14] "Black Entertainment Television," Hoover's company capsule, Hoover's Inc., http://www.pathfinder.com/money/hoovers/corpdirectoryplus/b/btv.html.

[15] Zagorin, Op. cit., p. 80.

[16] Perl, Op. cit., p. W08.

[17] "Special Independent Committee of BET Holdings, Inc., Board of Directors Has Determined That $48.00 Offer for Outstanding Shares Is Not Adequate," PR Newswire, at http://biz.yahoo.com/prnews/980123/dc_bet_hol_1.html.

Case 15 Notes

[1] Boeing," *Hoover's Handbook of American Business*, (Austin, TX: Hoover's Business Press, 1997). Boeing home page, http://www.boeing.com.

[2] Ibid.

[3] "A Fierce Downdraft at Boeing," *Business Week*, January 26, 1998.

[4] "Partners of Boeing Nemesis Airbus Plan Formal Merger," *Columbus Dispatch*, March 28, 1998, 2C.

[5] Ibid.

[6] Proctor, Paul. "Boeing Explores New Development Strategy," *Aviation Week and Space Technology*, February 2, 1998, p. 34–35.

[7] *Wall Street Journal*, February 18, 1998.

[8] Proctor, Op. cit., p. 34–35.

[9] Henkoff, Ronald. "Boeing's Big Problem," *Fortune*, January 12, 1998.

[10] Ibid.

[11] Ibid.

[12] Proctor, Op. cit., p. 34–35.

[13] Henkoff, Op. cit.

[14] Ibid.

[15] Cook, William. "Surfeit in Seattle: As Orders Pour in, Boeing Stumbles," *U.S. News Online*, November 17, 1997.

[16] Henkoff, Op. cit.

[17] Ibid.

[18] Ibid.

[19] Ibid.

Case 16 Notes

[1] Lablich, Kenneth. "Is Herb Kelleher America's Best CEO?" *Fortune*, May 2, 1994, 45.

[2] Feldman, Joan M. "Seriously Successful," *Air Transport World*, January 1994, 67.

[3] Quick, Jame Campbell. "Crafting an Organizational Culture: Herb's Hand at Southwest Airlines," *Organizational Dynamics*, vol. 21, August 1992, 47.

[4] Teitelbaum, Richard S. "Where Service Flies Right," *Fortune*, August 24, 1992, 115.

[5] Barrett, Colleen. "Pampering Customers on a Budget," *Working Woman*, April 1993, 19, 22.

[6] Martin, Justin. "So, You Want to Work for the Best . . . ," *Fortune*, January 12, 1998, 77.

[7] O'Brian, Bridget. "Southwest Agrees to Pilots Pact Offering No Wage Boost in First Five of 10 Years," *Wall Street Journal*, November 18, 1994, A2.

[8] "Did We Say Cheap?" *Inc.*, October 1997, p. 60.

[9] Teitelbaum, Op. cit., p. 116.

Case 17 Notes

[1] Steinway and Sons home page, http://www.steinway.com.

[2] Ibid.

[3] Cox, Meg. "Steinway Faces Yamaha Push in Piano Market," *Wall Street Journal*, January 19, 1988.

[4] Boston Piano home page, http://www.steinway.com/html/boston/boston.html.

[5] 1996 Steinway Musical Instruments annual report, New York, NY: Steinway Musical Instruments, 1997.

Case 18 Notes

[1] "Disney," *Hoover's Handbook of American Business* (Austin, TX: Hoover's Business Press, 1997).

[2] Ibid.

[3] Michael Eisner's biography, http://www.achievement.org/autodoc/page/eis0bio-1.

[4] Oneal, Michael. "Disney's Kingdom," *Business Week*, August 14, 1995, 30–34.

[5] "Disney," *Value Line Investment Survey*, 1998.

[6] Gunther, Marc. "What's Wrong with This Picture?" *Fortune*, January 12, 1998.

[7] Ibid.

[8] Ibid.

[9] Oneal, Op. cit., p. 30–34.

Photo Credits

Chapter 1

Page 3: Courtesy Fast Company. Reproduced with permission. **Page 4:** Rob Kearney/Photonica. **Page 5:** Courtesy Herman Miller, Inc. **Page 7:** Courtesy Daimler-Benz AG. **Page 14:** Courtesy Solectron Corporation. **Page 17:** Courtesy Whirlpool Corp. **Page 18:** Courtesy Workforce 2020: Work and Workers in the 21st Century, by Hudson Institute, April 1997. **Page 19:** Adri Berger/Tony Stone Images/New York, Inc. **Page 20 (top):** Courtesy Ritz-Carlton Buckhead. **Page 20 (bottom):** Courtesy Ronald Larimer.

Chapter 2

Page 27: Doug Armand/Tony Stone Images/New York, Inc. **Page 29:** Courtesy The Vermont Teddy Bear Company. **Page 31:** John Lund/Tony Stone Images/New York, Inc. **Page 32:** Courtesy Hewlett Packard. **Page 35:** Courtesy Tennant Company. **Page 37:** Courtesy Jaguar Cars. **Page 39:** Courtesy Nordstrom. **Page 40:** Courtesy Bell Atlantic of Washington. **Page 41:** Photo by Rick Ridgeway, courtesy Patagonia. **Page 42:** Charles Thatcher/Tony Stone Images/New York, Inc. **Page 43:** Courtesy Service Performance Corporation.

Chapter 3

Page 49: David Joel/Tony Stone Images/New York, Inc. **Page 51:** Amazon.com is a registered trademark in the U.S. and other countries. ©1998 Amazon.com. All rights reserved. **Page 53:** Ed Honowitz/Tony Stone Images/New York, Inc. **Page 60:** Courtesy D'Artagnan. **Page 63:** JW Burkey/Tony Stone Images/New York, Inc. **Page 64:** Lonnie Duka/Tony Stone Images/New York, Inc. **Page 66:** Bruce Ayres/Tony Stone Images/New York, Inc.

Chapter 4

Page 71: Reprinted with permission of Harvard Business School Press. Copyright 1995 by President and Fellows of Harvard College. All rights reserved. **Page 74:** Courtesy of United Parcel Service. **Page 75:** Painting by Otto Neumann, 1920/Corbis-Bettmann. **Page 77:** Courtesy Four Seasons Hotels, Inc. **Page 79:** Courtesy Digital Equipment Corp. **Page 81:** Courtesy Xerox Corporation. **Page 84:** Courtesy Mercedes-Benz of North America.

Chapter 5

Page 91: Marvin E. Newman/The Image Bank. **Page 93:** Tim Macpherson/Tony Stone Images/New York, Inc. **Page 94:** Courtesy Air Tech. **Page 96:** Brian Seed/Tony Stone Images/New York, Inc. **Page 99:** Courtesy Ford Motor Company. **Page 100:** Mark Peters/Gamma Liaison. **Page 101:** T. Anderson/The Image Bank. **Page 103:** Courtesy British Airways. **Page 105:** Robert Bossi/Tony Stone Images/New York, Inc. **Page 107:** Robin Smith/Tony Stone Images/New York, Inc. **Page 109:** Courtesy Honda of America.

Chapter 6

Page 115: Carlos Navajas/The Image Bank. **Page 117:** Courtesy Tom's of Maine. **Page 120:** Courtesy Council on Economic Priorities. **Page 121:** Photo by Nicholas Wheeler, courtesy of Malden Mills Industries, Inc., Lawrence, MA. **Page 122:** Rene Sheret/Tony Stone Images/New York, Inc. **Page 125:** Courtesy GE Plastics. **Page 127:** ©William Waldron. **Page 128:** Courtesy Levi Strauss & Company. **Page 129:** Courtesy Quad/Graphics. **Page 130:** Bruce Hands/Tony Stone Images/New York, Inc.

Chapter 7

Page 135: Courtesy Cypress Semiconductor. **Page 136:** Photo by Lonnie Duka, courtesy Aetna/US Healthcare. **Page 138:** Courtesy Lucent Technologies' Microelectronics Group. **Page 145:** Courtesy Meter-Man. **Page 146:** Bartee/Stock Imagery. **Page 148:** Photo by Vince Streano, courtesy Shell Oil Company. **Page 149:** Courtesy Xerox Corporation.

Chapter 8

Page 157: Courtesy Wal-Mart Stores, Inc. **Page 158:** Etienne De Malglaive/Tony Stone Images/New York, Inc. **Page 163:** Nick Gunderson/Tony Stone Images/New York, Inc. **Page 165:** David Sutherland/Tony Stone Images/New York, Inc. **Page 168:** Courtesy Worthington Industries. **Page 169:** John Lamb/Tony Stone Images/New York, Inc. **Page 171:** Photo by Laurence Dutton. Used with permission from McDonald's Corporation. **Page 174:** ©George Simian Photography.

Chapter 9

Page 181: Courtesy Volant Ski Company. **Page 184:** Photo courtesy of General Electric. **Page 185:** Courtesy Bell Atlantic North. **Page 187:** Courtesy Wal-Mart Stores, Inc. **Page 188:** Peter Poulides/Tony Stone Images/New York, Inc. **Page 189 (top):** Courtesy United States Army. **Page 189 (bottom):** Courtesy Steelcase, Inc. **Page 190:** Courtesy C & S Mystery Shoppers. **Page 194:** ©George Simian Photography.

Chapter 10

Page 201: Courtesy Edward Jones. **Page 204:** Courtesy Siemens Corporation. **Page 206:** Courtesy Jaguar Cars. **Page 210 (top):** Bruce Ayres/Tony Stone Images/New York, Inc. **Page 210 (bottom):** Courtesy ACEnet. **Page 211:** Courtesy Intel Corporation. **Page 212:** Courtesy Nucor Corp. **Page 214:** Courtesy Heinz USA, Inc. **Page 216:** Courtesy Delta Air Lines, Inc.

Chapter 11

Page 221: Courtesy Nestle Corporation. **Page 222:** Courtesy Rickard Group, Inc. **Page 224:** Shaun Egan/Tony Stone Images/New York, Inc. **Page 227:** Courtesy 3M Corporation. **Page 230:** Courtesy Coleman Co., Inc. **Page 233 (top):** Courtesy Dana Corporation. **Page 233 (bottom):** Patricia Seybold Group.

Chapter 12

Page 239: Courtesy Coopers & Lybrand. **Page 241:** Courtesy Johnson & Johnson. **Page 244:** Rob Nelson/Black Star/Picture Network International, Ltd. **Page 246:** Courtesy Southwest Airlines Co. **Page 247:** Courtesy Mercedes-Benz of North America. **Page 248:** ©Tony Stone Images/New York, Inc. **Page 254:** Courtesy Autodesk, Inc. **Page 256:** Courtesy Xerox Corporation.

Chapter 13

Page 261: Courtesy Herman Miller, Inc. **Page 265 (top):** Artwork courtesy Harley-Davidson Motor Company, Inc. **Page 265 (bottom):** Courtesy PC Connection, Inc. **Page 267:** Courtesy DuPont. **Page 268:** Gary Hunter/Tony Stone Images/New York, Inc. **Page 273:** Photo by Walt Ennis, courtesy W. L. Gore & Associates, Inc. **Page 275:** Courtesy Mary Kay Cosmetics, Inc. **Page 276:** ©William Waldron.

Chapter 14

Page 283: Courtesy Dana Corporation. **Page 287:** Courtesy Roppe Corporation. **Page 290:** Courtesy Silicon Graphics. **Page 295:** Courtesy Rocky Shoes & Boots, Inc. **Page 296:** Courtesy Lincoln Electric Company. **Page 297:** Courtesy Pratt & Whitney.

Chapter 15

Page 305: Courtesy Ernst & Young. **Page 307:** Courtesy Marriott Hotels. **Page 308:** David Crosier/Tony Stone Images/New York, Inc. **Page 309:** Frank Herholdt/Tony Stone Images/New York, Inc. **Page 310:** Courtesy Lotus Corporation. **Page 315:** Courtesy Boeing Corporation. **Page 316:** Billy Hustace/Tony Stone Images/New York, Inc. **Page 318:** Chip Henderson/Tony Stone Images/New York, Inc.

Chapter 16

Page 327: Courtesy Center For Creative Leadership. **Page 329:** Courtesy Wal-Mart. **Page 331:** Courtesy Bank-Boston. **Page 334:** Courtesy Scotts Company. **Page 335:** Toby Seger/Gamma Liaison. **Page 336:** Courtesy Hyatt Hotels. **Page 340:** Walter Hodges/Tony Stone Images/New York, Inc. **Page 341:** Courtesy of International Business Machines Corporation.

Chapter 17

Page 351: Courtesy American Electric Power Corporation. **Page 355:** Courtesy American Express Company. **Page 356:** Courtesy Ford Motor Company. **Page 360:** Courtesy Rockport Company. **Page 362:** Courtesy Motorola, Penang, Malaysia. **Page 366:** Dan Bosler/Tony Stone Images/New York, Inc. **Page 368:** Michael Banks/Tony Stone Images/New York, Inc. **Page 370:** Courtesy Worthington Industries.

Chapter 18

Page 377: Courtesy Mitsubishi. **Page 380:** Courtesy Rubbermaid, Inc. **Page 381:** Courtesy Olympus Optical Co., Ltd. **Page 383:** Courtesy Toro Company. **Page 385:** Courtesy Mellon Bank Corporation. **Page 388:** Courtesy Hyatt Hotels. **Page 389:** Courtesy Motorola. **Page 390:** Courtesy Clorox Company.

The Career Readiness Workbook

Cell phone: Steve Horrell/Photo Researchers, Inc. **Globe:** ©PhotoDisc. **Palm III Palm Pilot:** Courtesy 3Com. **Laptop:** ©PhotoDisc. **Compact disk:** Mchau Kulyk/Photo Researchers, Inc. **Screen shot of world wide web:** David Parker/Photo Researchers, Inc. **Newspaper composite:** Andy Whale/Tony Stone Images/New York, Inc. **Day planner:** ©PhotoDisc.

Company Index

Name Index

Subject Index